Beginning Programming

ALL-IN-ONE

2nd Edition

by Wallace Wang

Beginning Programming All-in-One For Dummies®, 2nd Edition

Published by: **John Wiley & Sons, Inc.,** 111 River Street, Hoboken, NJ 07030-5774, www.wiley.com

Copyright © 2022 by John Wiley & Sons, Inc., Hoboken, New Jersey

Published simultaneously in Canada

For general information on our other products and services, please contact our Customer Care Department within the U.S. at 877-762-2974, outside the U.S. at 317-572-3993, or fax 317-572-4002. For technical support, please visit https://hub.wiley.com/community/support/dummies.

Wiley publishes in a variety of print and electronic formats and by print-on-demand. Some material included with standard print versions of this book may not be included in e-books or in print-on-demand. If this book refers to media such as a CD or DVD that is not included in the version you purchased, you may download this material at http://booksupport.wiley.com. For more information about Wiley products, visit www.wiley.com.

Library of Congress Control Number: 2022936302

ISBN 978-1-119-88440-8 (pbk); ISBN 978-1-119-88441-5 (ebk); ISBN 978-1-119-88442-2 (ebk)

SKY10034371_050522

Contents at a Glance

Table of Contents

Introduction

I f you enjoy using a computer, you may have even more fun learning to control a computer by writing your own programs. To learn how to program a computer, you need to:

>> **Understand that computer programming is nothing more than problem solving.** Before you even think about writing a program, you need to know what problem you want your program to solve and how it will solve it.

>> **Learn the basic ideas behind computer programming that work with all programming languages on any computer.** Although programming a Windows computer is different from programming a Mac, a smartphone, a smart watch, or a super computer, the general principles remain the same. By learning what these common programming principles are and why they exist, you can learn different ways to tell a computer what to do, step-by-step.

>> **Learn a specific programming language.** A programming language represents just one way to express your ideas in a language that the computer can understand. By combining your knowledge of a programming language with programming principles and the type of problem you want the computer to solve, you can create your own computer programs for fun or profit.

About This Book

If you have any interest in programming but don't know where to start, this book can give you a nudge in the right direction. You won't learn how to write programs in a specific programming language, but you'll learn the basics of computer programming so you'll have no trouble learning more on your own.

If you already know something about programming, this book can still help you learn more by introducing you to the variety of programming languages available and make it easy for you to pick up different programming languages quickly. The more you understand the advantages and disadvantages of different programming languages, the better you'll be able to choose the language that's best suited for a particular task.

Whether you're a novice or an intermediate programmer, you'll find this book can work as a tutorial to teach you more and as a reference to help refresh your memory on programming topics you may not normally use every day. This book won't turn you into an expert overnight, but it will open the doors to more information about programming than you may have ever known even existed.

This book is a reference — you don't need to read the chapters in order from front cover to back and you don't have to commit anything you read here to memory. Also, *sidebars* (text in gray boxes) and anything marked with the Technical Stuff icon are skippable.

Finally, within this book, you may note that some web addresses break across two lines of text. If you're reading this book in print and want to visit one of these web pages, simply key in the web address exactly as it's noted in the text, pretending as though the line break doesn't exist. If you're reading this as an e-book, you've got it easy — just click the web address to be taken directly to the web page.

Foolish Assumptions

When writing this book, I made two assumptions about you, the reader:

>> You may have no experience in computer programming or a limited amount of experience, but you're eager to learn.

>> You have a computer (whether it's the latest model on the market or simply an older model that still works). Ideally, your computer can connect to the Internet.

That's it! As long as you have a computer and the desire to learn, you have everything you need to learn computer programming.

Icons Used in This Book

Icons highlight important or useful information that you may want to know about. Here's a guide to the icons:

The Tip icon highlights information that can save you time or make it easier for you to do something.

REMEMBER

The Remember icon emphasizes information that's so important you should commit it to memory.

WARNING

Look out! The Warning icon highlights something dangerous that you need to avoid before making an irreversible mistake that could make you curse your computer forever.

TECHNICAL STUFF

The Technical Stuff icon highlights interesting technical information that you can safely ignore, but which may provide additional background about programming a computer.

Beyond the Book

In addition to what you're reading right now, this product also comes with a free access-anywhere Cheat Sheet that summarizes different types of programming principles, common ways to store and organize data, and lists of suggested software to use. To get this Cheat Sheet, simply go to www.dummies.com and type **Beginning Programming All-in-One For Dummies Cheat Sheet** in the Search box.

Where to Go from Here

You can use this book as a tutorial or a reference. Although you can just flip through this book to find the information you need, programming novices should start with Book 1 before tackling any other books. After you understand the basics of programming from Book 1, you can freely jump around to read only the information that interests you.

Programming is more than learning a particular programming language or even knowing how to program a particular type of computer. Basically, programming is about tackling difficult problems and breaking them down into smaller problems until you ultimately solve one much bigger problem. If you like the idea of solving problems, this may be the perfect book to introduce you to the wonderful world of computer programming!

1
Getting Started with Programming

Contents at a Glance

Chapter **1**

Getting Started Programming a Computer

B elieve it or not, if you can write a recipe on an index card, you can program a computer! At the simplest level, computer programming is nothing more than writing instructions for a computer to follow, step-by-step. The most important part of programming isn't knowing how to write a program or how to use a particular programming language, but knowing what to create in the first place.

Some of the most popular and useful computer programs were created by people who didn't have any formal training in math or computer science. Dan Bricklin invented the spreadsheet while studying for his MBA at Harvard. Scott Cook, who worked in marketing and product development at Procter & Gamble, created the popular money-management program Quicken after hearing his wife complain about the tedium of paying bills. Nineteen-year-old Shawn Fanning created Napster, the first peer-to-peer file-sharing network, after hearing a friend complain about the difficulty of finding his favorite songs on the Internet. Game developer Dona Bailey wanted to create a video game that would appeal to both men and women; as the only woman working at Atari's coin-op division, she created the video game Centipede, which became Atari's second best-selling coin-op game.

The point is that anyone can figure out how to program a computer. What's more important than knowing how to program a computer is knowing what to do with your programming skills. As Albert Einstein said, "Imagination is more important than knowledge." After you have an idea for a program, you can use programming to turn your idea into reality.

How Computer Programming Works

Computer programming is nothing more than problem solving. Every program is designed to solve a specific problem. The more universal the problem (calculating formulas in a spreadsheet, managing your money, searching for music files over the Internet, or keeping people amused playing a game creating virtual buildings), the more useful and popular the program will be.

Identifying the problem

Before you even touch a computer, identify the specific problem you want the computer to solve. For example, spreadsheets eliminate the tedium of writing and calculating formulas manually. Word processors make editing and formatting text fast and easy. Even video games solve the problem of challenging people with puzzles, obstacles, and battles.

Although the most popular programs solve universal problems, literally thousands of programs are designed to solve specific problems in niche markets, such as hotel reservation software, construction billing and invoice management programs, and dental office management programs. If you can identify a problem that a computer can solve or simplify, you have an idea for a computer program.

REMEMBER

You must know exactly what you want your program to do before you start designing and writing it. One of the most common reasons programs fail is because the program doesn't solve the right problem that people really need.

THE FBI'S $170 MILLION FLOP

The Federal Bureau of Investigation (FBI) had a problem. It had so much information, stored on paper, scattered among so many agents around the country that finding and using this information was nearly impossible. One agent might have vital information that could help a second agent crack a case, but unless those two agents knew what each other had, that information might as well never have existed in the first place.

So, the FBI had a bright idea: Create a computer program that would allow agents to store and share information through the computer. Several years and $170 million later, the FBI had its program, dubbed Virtual Case File, which consisted of more than 700,000 lines of error-prone commands that never even worked. Rather than try to salvage the project, the FBI decided it was easier just to cancel the whole thing and basically flush 170 million taxpayer dollars down the drain.

What went wrong? Although many factors contributed to the project's failure, one reason stands out in particular: According to an audit of the program conducted by the U.S. Department of Justice, a prime cause for failure was "poorly defined and slowly evolving design requirements." In other words, the FBI never knew exactly what it wanted the program to do.

How can you aim at a target if you don't know what it is? You can't. Or you can try, just as long as you spend $170 million to discover that if you don't know what you want, you're probably never going to get it.

Defining the steps

After you know what you want your program to do, you need to define all the steps that tell the computer how to solve that particular problem. The exact steps that define how the program should work is called an *algorithm.* An algorithm simply defines one of many possible ways to solve a problem.

REMEMBER

There's no single "best" algorithm for writing a program. The same program can be written in a million different ways so the "best" way to write a program is any way that creates a useful, working, and reliable program as quickly as possible. Anything else is irrelevant.

Knowing what you want the computer to do is the first step. The second step is telling the computer how to do it, which is what makes programming so difficult. The more you want the computer to do, the more instructions you need to give the computer.

Think of a computer program as a recipe. It's easy to write a recipe for making spaghetti. Just boil water, throw in the noodles until they're soft, drain, and serve. Now consider a recipe for making butternut squash and potato pie with tomato, mint, and sheep's milk cheese from Crete. Not as simple as boiling water to make spaghetti, is it?

The same principle holds true for computer programming. The simpler the task, the simpler the program. The harder the task, the bigger and more complicated the program. If you just want a program that displays today's date on the screen, you won't need to write many instructions. If you want to write a program that simulates flying a space shuttle in orbit around the Earth, you'll need to write a lot more instructions.

The more instructions you need to write, the longer it takes and the more likely you'll make a mistake somewhere along the way.

REMEMBER

Ultimately, programming boils down to two tasks:

>> Identifying exactly what you want the computer to do

>> Writing step-by-step instructions that tell the computer how to do what you want

The History of Computer Programming

Although computer programming may seem like a recent invention, the idea behind writing instructions for a machine to follow has been around for over a century. One of the earliest designs for a programmable machine (in other words, a computer) came from a man named Charles Babbage way back in 1834.

That was the year Charles Babbage proposed building a mechanical, steam-driven machine dubbed the Analytical Engine. Unlike the simple calculating machines of that time that could perform only a single function, Charles Babbage's Analytical Engine could perform a variety of tasks, depending on the instructions fed into the machine through a series of punched cards. By changing the number and type of instructions (punch cards) fed into the machine, anyone could reprogram the Analytical Engine to make it solve different problems.

The idea of a programmable machine caught the attention of Ada Lovelace, a mathematician and daughter of the poet Lord Byron. Sensing the potential of a programmable machine, Ada wrote a program to make the Analytical Engine calculate and print a sequence of numbers known as the *Bernoulli numbers*.

**TECHNICAL
STUFF**

Because of her work with the Analytical Engine, Ada Lovelace is considered to be the world's first computer programmer. In her honor, the Department of Defense named the Ada programming language after Ada Lovelace. Nvidia named a family of graphics cards after Ada Lovelace as well.

Although Charles Babbage never finished building his Analytical Engine, his steam-driven mechanical machine bears a striking similarity to today's computers. To make the Analytical Engine solve a different problem, you just had to feed it different instructions. To make a modern computer solve a different problem, you just have to run a different program.

Over a century later, the first true computer appeared in 1943 when the U.S. Army funded a computer to calculate artillery trajectories. This computer, dubbed ENIAC (short for Electronic Numerical Integrator and Computer), consisted of vacuum tubes, switches, and cables. To give ENIAC instructions, you had to physically flip its different switches and rearrange its cables.

**TECHNICAL
STUFF**

The first ENIAC programmers were all women.

Physically rearranging cables and switches to reprogram a computer worked, but it was tedious and clumsy. Instead of having to physically rearrange the computer's wiring, computer scientists decided it would be easier if they could leave the computer physically the same but just rearrange the type of instructions given to it. By giving the computer different instructions, they could make the computer behave in different ways.

In the old days, computers filled entire rooms and cost millions of dollars. Today, computers have shrunk so far in size that they're essentially nothing more than a little silicon wafer, about the size of a coin.

A *processor* is essentially an entire computer. To tell the processor what to do, you have to give it instructions written in *machine language* (a language that the processor can understand).

**TECHNICAL
STUFF**

To make faster computers, engineers combine multiple processors (called *cores*) together and make them work as a team. So, instead of having a single processor in your computer, the latest computers have multiple processors or cores working together.

Talking to a processor in machine language

To understand how machine language works, you have to understand how processors work. Basically, a processor consists of nothing more than millions of tiny switches that can turn on or off. By turning certain switches on or off, you can make the processor do something useful.

Instead of physically turning switches on or off, machine language lets you turn a processor's switches on or off by using two numbers: 1 (one) and 0 (zero), where the number 1 means "turn a switch on" and the number 0 means "turn a switch off." So a typical machine language instruction might look like this:

```
1011 0000 0110 0001
```

If the preceding instruction doesn't make any sense, don't worry. The point is that machine language is just a way to tell a processor what to do.

TECHNICAL STUFF

Using 1s and 0s is *binary arithmetic.* Because binary arithmetic can be so hard to read, programmers also represent binary numbers in hexadecimal. Where binary arithmetic uses only 2 numbers, *hexadecimal* uses 16 numbers and letters (0–9 and A–F). So, the binary number 1011 0000 0110 0001 could be represented as the hexadecimal number B061.

Machine language is considered the *native* language of CPUs, but almost no one writes a program in machine language because it's so tedious and confusing. Mistype a single 1 or 0, and you can accidentally give the wrong instruction to the CPU. Because writing instructions in machine language can be so difficult and error-prone, computer scientists have created a somewhat simpler language: *assembly language.*

Using assembly language as a shortcut to machine language

The whole purpose of assembly language is to make programming easier than machine language. Basically, one assembly language command can replace a dozen or more machine language commands. So, instead of requiring you to write ten machine language commands (and risk making a mistake in all ten of those commands), assembly language lets you write one command that does the work of ten (or more) machine language commands.

Not only does this reduce the chance of mistakes, but it also makes writing a program in assembly language much faster and easier. Best of all, assembly language commands represent simple mnemonics such as MOV (move) or JMP (jump). These mnemonic commands make assembly language much easier to understand than a string of binary commands (1s and 0s).

REMEMBER

The goal of every programming language is to make programming simpler and easier. Unfortunately, because no one can define exactly what *simpler* and *easier* really mean, computer scientists keep creating new and improved programming languages that promise to make programming simpler and easier, at least until someone else invents another new and improved programming language.

To understand how assembly language works, you must first understand how processors store and manipulate data. The *processor* is the "brain" of the computer that does all the work. By itself, the processor is fairly useless.

Think of Einstein's brain floating in a jar of formaldehyde. It may be one of the smartest brains in the world, but if it can't communicate with the outside world, it's completely useless as anything other than a very unusual paperweight. Like Einstein's brain in a jar, your computer's processor is useful only if it can communicate with the outside world. The processor communicates with the other parts of the computer through a series of wires called a *bus*.

When a processor needs to work with data, it retrieves it from another part of the computer (such as the hard disk or memory) and temporarily stores that data in a storage area called a *register*, as shown in Figure 1-1.

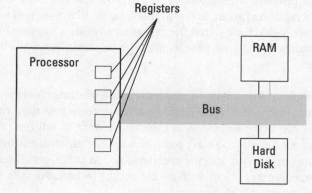

FIGURE 1-1: A processor uses its registers to temporarily store data.

The processor then edits the data in its registers and sends the changed data back to another part of the computer, such as the memory or hard disk.

So, computer programming progressed from physically rearranging wires and switches (with ENIAC), to flipping switches using 1s and 0s (with machine language), to telling the computer which data to store in which registers and how to manipulate that data (with assembly language).

A typical assembly language command might look like this:

```
mov al, 061h
```

This command tells the processor to move (mov) the hexadecimal number 061h into the specific register named al. Other assembly language commands might tell the processor to add (add) or subtract (sub) a value from the number stored in a specific register.

When you use assembly language, you have to tell the processor what data to store in which registers, how to manipulate the data in the registers, and when to remove data out of the registers.

Sound tedious? It is. Although assembly language is far easier to understand and write than machine language, it's still too complicated to use for creating really big computer programs, like word processors or video games.

TECHNICAL
STUFF

In the old days, most programs were written in assembly language, but as programs grew larger and more complicated, assembly language proved too cumbersome to write, edit, and modify.

The biggest problem with assembly language is that you need to manipulate the processor's registers just to do the simplest tasks. If you wanted to add two numbers together, you'd have to tell the processor to store a number in a register, add a second number to the number in the register, and then yank the result out of the register.

Forcing people to know how to manipulate the processor's registers before they can program a computer is like forcing people to know how their carburetor works before they can drive a car. Ideally, you don't want to tell the processor how to manipulate data in its registers; you just want the processor to add two numbers without worrying about specific registers. So, to make computer programming even easier, computer scientists have hidden the technical details of manipulating registers by creating *high-level languages.*

TECHNICAL
STUFF

Every processor understands only its own particular assembly language. So an Intel processor won't understand the assembly language of an Advanced RISC Machine (ARM) processor and vice versa. However, some companies make processors that work identically to other processors. For example, a company called Advanced Micro Devices (AMD) makes processors that work just like Intel processors, so an assembly language program written for an Intel processor also works on an AMD processor.

Hiding the details of a computer with a high-level language

The whole purpose of high-level languages is to make programming more intuitive. So, rather than tell the computer to store the number 2 in register a1, add the number 3 to the number stored in register a1, and then yank out the result from register a1, high-level languages let you tell the computer what to do and not worry about how the computer does it. So, a typical high-level language command might look like this:

```
Total = 2 + 3
```

As you can see, high-level languages are much easier to read and understand, even if you know nothing about programming. Where assembly language forces you to tell the processor what to do and how to do it, high-level languages just let you tell the processor what to do.

TECHNICAL STUFF

Early popular high-level languages include Fortran (formerly FORTRAN, short for FORmula TRANslator), BASIC (short for Beginner's All-purpose Symbolic Instruction Code), COBOL (short for COmmon Business Oriented Language), and Pascal (named after the French philosopher Blaise Pascal).

Besides making programming more intuitive, high-level languages also make programming easier because a single high-level language command can do the work of a dozen (or more) assembly language commands.

A thousand lines of assembly language commands might do nothing more than multiply two numbers together. A thousand lines of high-level language commands might create a video game, a music player, or a stock market analysis program. By using high-level languages, programmers can spend more time being productive and less time worrying about the technical details of the computer.

Combining the best of both worlds with the C programming language

High-level languages isolate you from the technical details of programming, but by isolating you from these details, high-level languages also limit what you can do. So, as a compromise between assembly language (which can manipulate the processor) and high-level languages (which isolate you from the details of manipulating the processor), computer scientists created an intermediate language dubbed C.

The idea behind the C programming language is to give programmers the ability to manipulate the processor directly like assembly language, but also give them the chance to ignore these technical details, if they want, like a high-level language.

As a result, a C program doesn't look as cryptic as assembly language, but it also isn't as easy to read as a high-level language, as the following C program demonstrates:

```
#include <stdio.h>
int main(void)
{
  printf("Hello World!\n");
  exit(0);
}
```

REMEMBER

Just by looking at this C program, you can probably figure out that it prints Hello World! on the screen. However, you may see a bunch of cryptic curly brackets, back slashes, and other odd symbols and characters that may make no sense whatsoever. Don't worry. Just notice how confusing C programs can look while at the same time being somewhat understandable.

TECHNICAL
STUFF

Because C lets you directly control the processor like assembly language does, but still write programs that look somewhat understandable and easy to read and write, many operating systems — such as Linux, macOS, and Microsoft Windows — are written all or partially in C.

Weighing the pros and cons of programming languages

The whole purpose of machine language, assembly language, high-level language, and the C language is to give you different ways to give instructions to the processor (computer). Ultimately, it doesn't matter which type of programming language you use because it's possible to write the exact same program in machine language, assembly language, a high-level language (like BASIC or Fortran), and C.

The only difference is that writing a program in machine language takes a really long time and is very difficult to write, fix, and understand. A similar program written in assembly language is smaller and simpler than an equivalent machine language program.

Writing the same program in the C language makes the program even smaller and much easier to write and understand. If you use a high-level language, the program would most likely require writing less code and be easiest to understand out of them all.

So, given these advantages of C or high-level languages, why would anyone ever use machine language or assembly language? The answer is simple: speed and efficiency.

If you want to write the fastest program possible that uses the least amount of memory, use machine language because machine language is the native language of all computers. Unfortunately, machine language is so hard to understand, write, and modify that writing anything but small programs in machine language is nearly impossible.

Instead of using machine language, most programmers use assembly language when they need speed and efficiency. Assembly language creates small and fast programs, but they'll never be as small or fast as machine language programs. That's because processors understand only machine language, so when you write an assembly language program, you have to translate that assembly language program into machine language.

Translating assembly language into machine language by hand would be slow and error-prone, so computer scientists have created special programs that can do this automatically. These programs are *assemblers*.

An assembler takes an assembly language program and converts it into machine language, but this conversion process isn't perfect. That's why assembly language tends to create bigger and slower programs than equivalent handcrafted machine language programs. However, assembly language programs are much easier to write and modify later than machine language programs are, so assembly language is used much more often than machine language.

High-level languages are much easier to write and understand than machine language or assembly language. The problem is that processors don't understand high-level languages either, so you have to translate a high-level language program into equivalent machine language commands.

Doing this by hand is nearly impossible, so computer scientists have created special programs — *compilers* — to do this for them. A compiler takes a program written in a high-level language and translates it into equivalent commands written in machine language.

This translation process isn't perfect, which is why programs written in high-level languages tend to be much bigger and slower than equivalent programs written in machine language or assembly language. So, when programmers want to create large, complicated programs that still run fast and take up as little space as possible, they tend to rely on the C programming language. That's why so many programs are written in C — C creates programs *nearly* as small and fast as assembly language programs, while also being *nearly* as easy to write and understand as high-level languages. (Note the emphasis on the word *nearly.*)

As a general rule, if you want to make programming easy where speed and efficiency aren't that crucial, use a high-level programming language. If you want to make a small and fast program and don't care how inconvenient it may be to write it, use machine language or assembly language.

What if you want to write a big and fast program (like an operating system or word processor) and also make it convenient for you to write? You'd use the C programming language.

TECHNICAL STUFF

Although C is a fast and powerful language, it's not the safest. C lets you access all parts of a computer, which means if you're not careful, your programs can corrupt the computer's memory (known as *memory leaks*) and cause all types of unintended havoc. For that reason, computer scientists have used C as a reference to create "safer" versions of the language. Many of today's popular programming languages (such as C#, Java, Objective-C, Python, and Swift) have been directly or indirectly inspired by C. Because C uses curly brackets to define the beginning and end of code blocks, C-based languages are often called *curly-bracket languages.*

REMEMBER

Ultimately, no one cares what language you use as long as your program works. A program that works is far better than a small, fast, and efficient program that doesn't work. Think of a programming language as a tool. A good programmer can use any tool well, but a bad programmer can screw up using the best tool in the world. The programmer's skill always determines the quality of any program; the type of programming language used is always secondary. So the goal isn't to become a "C programmer" or a "Fortran programmer." The goal is to become a *good* programmer, regardless of the language you ultimately use.

Figuring Out Programming

After you understand that programming is nothing more than telling a computer how to solve a problem, you may wonder how you can get started figuring out programming on your own. If you want to figure out how to program a computer, this is what you need:

- » Desire

- » A computer

- » An editor

- » An assembler or compiler

- » A lot of time on your hands

TIP

Find out more about programming tools, like an editor and a compiler, in Book 1, Chapter 4.

Desire beats technical training every time

Desire is probably the biggest factor in studying how to program a computer. Many people think that you need a college degree or a mathematical background to know computer programming. Although a college degree and a mathematical background can definitely help, they aren't necessary. Saying you need to know math before figuring out computer programming is like saying you need a college degree in biology before you can reproduce.

Some of the most influential and popular programs in the world were created by people who had no formal training in computer programming or computer science. (Conversely, some of the most intelligent PhD candidates in computer science have done nothing to make this world a better place using their programming skills.)

So, if you have an idea for a program, you can create it. After you have the desire to understand computer programming, you have (almost) everything you need to program a computer.

Picking a computer and an operating system

If you want to know how to program a computer, you need a computer to practice on. You can actually discover programming on any computer, from a top-of-the-line machine to an obsolete relic (that was once a top-of-the-line machine) to a simple handheld computer. As long as you have a computer, you can figure out how to program it.

Although it's possible to figure out programming by using an ancient Commodore 64 or an antique Radio Shack TRS-80, it's probably best to figure out programming on a computer that's going to be around in the future. That way you can directly apply your programming skills to a computer used in the real world, which boils down to a computer that runs one of the following operating systems: Linux, macOS, or Windows.

Some websites let you practice writing and running code completely within a browser. This spares you the trouble of installing a compiler directly on your computer and lets anyone learn to program as long as they have a browser and access to the Internet.

An *operating system* is a special program that makes all the hardware of your computer work together. The operating system tells the processor how to work with the hard disk, read keystrokes typed on a keyboard, and display information on the monitor. Without an operating system, your computer is nothing more than separate chunks of hardware that do absolutely nothing.

One of the most popular operating systems in the world is Unix, commonly run on big, expensive computers. Linux is based on Unix, so if you understand how to program a Linux computer, you can also program a Unix computer and vice versa.

It's still possible to write programs for obsolete computers like the Atari ST, PDP-11, or Commodore Amiga, but most people choose to write programs for one of the following operating systems:

>> **Linux:** Linux is a free operating system for almost every computer (including PCs). Linux is becoming more popular with big companies (as opposed to individual users), so there's a growing market for talented Linux programmers.

>> **macOS:** macOS is the operating system that runs the Apple Mac computer. Although Macs aren't as popular as Windows computers, macOS is still a large and lucrative market.

>> **Windows:** Windows is the operating system that runs on most personal computers (PCs). Because so many people use Windows PCs at work and at home, the software market for Windows is huge and lucrative.

If you want to prepare yourself for the future, it's probably best to begin programming on any computer that runs Linux, macOS, or Windows.

With virtualization software such as VirtualBox (`www.virtualbox.org`), you can run different operating systems at the same time, such as running both Linux and Windows on a PC or running both Linux and macOS on a Mac. That way you can practice writing programs for different operating systems on a single computer.

Most programmers use a desktop computer running Linux, macOS, or Windows to write software. With the growing popularity of mobile devices, wearable computers, and browser-based apps, there's a huge market for writing apps for these devices as well:

>> **Android:** Android is Google's free operating system that runs on the majority of smartphones and some tablets.

>> **iOS and iPadOS:** iOS and iPadOS are the operating systems that run on the iPhone and iPad, respectively. The iPhone is the most popular smartphone in the world, and the iPad is the dominant tablet in the world.

>> **watchOS:** watchOS is the operating system that runs on the Apple Watch. The Apple Watch is one of the most popular wearable devices in the world.

>> **Wear OS:** Wear OS is Google's free operating system for smart watches. It's a version of Android that runs on smart watches to compete against the Apple Watch.

To write apps for mobile and wearable operating systems, you normally need to use a computer that runs Linux, macOS, or Windows. However, you can use some of the more powerful tablets to write apps for smartphones and tablets, too.

Writing programs with an editor

After you have a computer that runs Linux, macOS, or Windows (or a powerful tablet), the next step is to get an editor. An *editor* acts like a simple word processor that lets you type, change, and save program commands in a file.

REMEMBER

In the world of computer programming, a single program command is a *line of code*. Most programs consist of thousands of lines of code, although a large program (like Microsoft Windows) consists of millions of lines of code. When you write a program, you don't tell people, "I'm writing a program." You say, "I'm writing code." It sounds cooler — at least to other programmers.

In the old days, you had to buy a programming editor. Today, you can often get a powerful, professional editor for free. Some editors are bundled with an integrated development environment (IDE), which combines the features of an editor with a *compiler* (to convert your code to assembly language or machine language) and a *debugger* (to find and fix problems in your code).

Some popular editors include the following:

>> **GNU Emacs** (www.gnu.org/software/emacs): Editor only for Linux, macOS, and Windows

>> **Playgrounds** (www.apple.com/swift/playgrounds): iPadOS and macOS

>> **Visual Studio** (https://visualstudio.microsoft.com): macOS and Windows, with a limited version available for Linux

>> **Xcode** (https://developer.apple.com/xcode): macOS only

Unlike a word processor, which offers commands for formatting text to make it look pretty or appear in different colors, text editors are just designed for typing commands in a particular programming language, such as C++, Java, or Swift:

>> The simplest editor just lets you type commands in a file.

>> More sophisticated editors can help you write a program by

● Color-coding program commands (to help you identify them easily)

● Indenting your code automatically (to make it easier to read)

● Typing in commonly used commands for you

Figure 1-2 shows a simple editor used to write a Swift program that creates a hypotrochoid art figure.

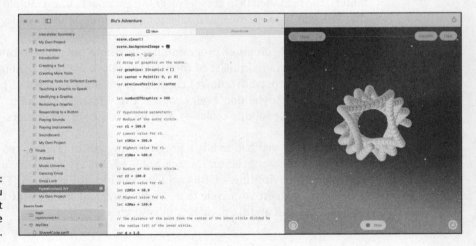

FIGURE 1-2:
An editor lets you write and edit the source code of a program.

Without an editor, you can't write a program. With an editor, you can write a program. And with a really good editor, you can write a program quickly and easily.

Professional programmers often get passionate (to the point of fanaticism) about their favorite editors. The quickest way to get into an argument with programmers is to either insult their favorite programming language or insult their favorite editor. If you insult a programmer's mother, the programmer will probably just shrug and not care one bit.

Program commands stored in one or more files are called the program's *source code.* Think of a program's source code as the recipe that makes the program work. If someone can steal or copy your source code, they've effectively stolen your program. That's why companies like Microsoft jealously guard the source code to all their programs, such as Windows or Excel.

Converting source code with an assembler or compiler

An editor lets you type and save program commands (or *source code*) in a file. Unless you've written a program completely in machine language, your source code may as well have been written in Swahili because processors don't understand any language other than machine language.

So, to convert your source code into machine language commands, you have to use an assembler (if you wrote your program commands in assembly language) or a compiler (if you wrote your program commands in the C language or a high-level language like Java).

After converting your source code into equivalent machine language commands, an assembler or compiler saves these machine language commands in a separate file, often called an *executable file* (or just an *EXE file*). When you buy a program, such as a video game or an antivirus program, you're really buying an executable file. Without an assembler or a compiler, you can't create your program.

Compilers translate source code into *machine language,* which is the native language of a specific processor. But what if you want your program to run on different processors? To do this, you have to compile your program into machine language for each different processor. You wind up with one executable file for each processor, such as an executable file for an Intel processor and a separate executable file for an ARM processor.

Many Mac programs advertise themselves as a *universal binary* — which means the program actually consists of two executable files smashed into a single file:

>> One executable file contains machine language code for the *M-series processor* (used in newer Mac computers)

>> The second executable file contains machine language code for the *Intel processor* (used in old Mac computers)

Most compilers work only on one specific operating system and processor. So, a Windows compiler may only create programs that run under the Windows operating system. Likewise, a Linux compiler may only create programs that run under the Linux operating system.

If you write a program that runs under Windows, you can recompile it to run under Linux. Unfortunately, you may have to modify your program slightly (or a lot) to make it run under Linux.

Big companies, like Adobe and Microsoft, can afford to pay programmers to write and modify programs to run under different operating systems, such as macOS and Windows. Most smaller companies and individuals don't have the time to rewrite a program to run under multiple operating systems. That's why most small companies write programs for Windows — because it's the largest market. If the program proves popular, they can later justify the time and expense to rewrite that program and compile it to run under macOS.

Choose your compiler carefully. If you use a compiler that can create only Windows programs, you may never be able to recompile that program to run on a different operating system, such as Linux or macOS. One reason Microsoft gives away its compilers for free is to trap people into writing programs that can run only under Windows. For example, if you write a program in C#, you may not be able to run that program on Linux or macOS without major modifications, which most people will probably never do.

To make it easy to create programs for multiple operating systems, you can use a cross-platform compiler. This means you can write a program once and then choose to compile it for two or more operating systems such as macOS and Windows or Android and iOS. Cross-platform tools make it easy to write the same program for multiple operating systems, but you may need to write additional code to take advantage of the unique features of each operating system.

Translating source code with an interpreter

In the old days, compilers were notoriously slow. You could feed source code to a compiler and literally come back the next morning to see if the compiler was done. If you made a single mistake in your program, you had to correct it and recompile your program all over again — with another overnight wait to see if it even worked.

Trying to write a program with such slow compilers proved maddening, so computer scientists created something faster called an *interpreter.* A computer interpreter is just like a foreign language interpreter who listens to each sentence you speak and then translates that sentence into another language. Type a program command into an interpreter, and the interpreter immediately translates that command into its equivalent machine language command. Type in another command, and the interpreter translates that second command right away.

The problem with interpreters is that they only store the equivalent machine language commands in memory instead of in a separate file like a compiler does. If you want to sell or distribute your program, you have to give people your source code, along with an interpreter that can convert your source code into machine language commands. Because giving away your source code essentially means giving away your program, everyone who wants to sell their programs uses a compiler instead of an interpreter.

**TECHNICAL
STUFF**

The original reason why computer scientists developed interpreters was because compilers were so slow. But after computer scientists started creating faster compilers, most people stopped using interpreters and just used compilers. Nowadays, computer scientists use interpreters for running certain types of programming languages known as *scripting languages.* (Find out more about scripting languages in Book 1, Chapter 3.)

Combining a compiler with an interpreter to create p-code

Creating separate executable files for each processor can get clumsy, and giving away your source code with an interpreter may be unreasonable. A third approach is to compile your program into an intermediate format called *bytecode* or *pseudocode* (often abbreviated as *p-code*). Unlike compiling source code directly into machine language, you compile your program into a p-code file instead.

You can take this p-code file and copy it on any computer. To run a p-code file, you need a special p-code interpreter, or a *virtual machine.* The virtual machine acts like an interpreter and runs the instructions compiled into the p-code file.

The advantage of p-code is that you can distribute a single p-code version of your program, which can run on multiple computers. But P-code has a couple disadvantages:

>> P-code programs don't run as fast as programs compiled into machine language.

>> If a computer doesn't have the right virtual machine installed, it can't run your program.

The most popular programming language that uses p-code is Java. After you write a Java program, you can compile it into a p-code file, which can run on any computer that has a copy of the Java virtual machine, such as Android, Linux, macOS, and Windows. Microsoft's .NET framework is similar to p-code that (theoretically) lets you run a program on any computer that can run the complete .NET framework.

WARNING

The theory behind p-code is that you write a program once, and you can run it anywhere. The reality is that every operating system has its quirks, so it's more common to write a program and be forced to test it on multiple operating systems. More often than not, a p-code program runs perfectly fine on one operating system (like Windows) but suffers mysterious problems when running on another operating system (such as Linux). Languages, such as Java, are getting better at letting you run the same program on multiple operating systems without major modifications, but be careful because p-code doesn't always work as well as you may think.

Taking the time to understand

Programming is a skill that anyone can acquire. Like any skill, the best way to understand is to take the time to experiment, make mistakes, and learn from your failures. Some programmers prefer to spend their time mastering a single programming language. Others prefer to master the intricacies of writing programs for a specific operating system, such as Windows. Still others spend their time discovering a variety of programming languages and writing programs for different operating systems.

There is no right or wrong way to figure out programming. The only "right" way is the way that works for you. That's why self-taught programmers can often write programs that are just as good as (or even better than) programs written by PhD computer scientists.

Like any skill, the more time you spend programming a computer, the better you get. This book is designed to help you get started, but ultimately, it's up to you to take what you know and start programming your own computer.

Believe it or not, programming a computer is actually fairly straightforward. The hard part is trying to write a program that actually works.

KNOWING HOW TO PROGRAM VERSUS KNOWING A PROGRAMMING LANGUAGE

There's a big difference between knowing how to program and knowing a specific programming language. This book describes how programming works, which means you'll understand the principles behind programming no matter what programming language you decide to use.

When you understand a specific programming language, you'll figure out how to write a program using that language. Don't confuse knowing how to program with knowing a programming language!

When people learn to speak their native language, they often think their particular spoken language is the only way to talk. So, when they learn a foreign language, they try to speak the foreign language just like they speak their native language, but using different words. That's why literal translations of foreign languages can sound so funny and awkward to a native speaker.

That's exactly the same problem with understanding programming. To understand programming, you have to use a specific programming language, but each programming language works a certain way. So, if you know how to write programs in the C programming language, you may mistakenly think that the way the C language works is the way computer programming also works, but that's not true.

Like human languages, programming languages differ wildly. Someone who knows how to write programs in the C language thinks differently about programming than someone who knows how to write programs in assembly language.

To describe how programming works, this book uses a variety of examples from different programming languages. You don't have to understand how each program example in this book works. Just understand that programming languages can look and solve identical problems in very different ways.

(continued)

(continued)

First, try to understand general programming principles without worrying about the way a particular programming language works. Then try to understand how a particular programming language works. As long as you know how to keep these two topics separate, you can figure out how to program a computer without the distraction of knowing a particular programming language.

Besides, programming languages rise and fall in popularity all the time, so if you know only one programming language, your skills may become obsolete within a few years.

At one time, most programmers used assembly language. For programmers who wanted a simpler language, they used BASIC or Pascal. When BASIC and Pascal fell out of favor, programmers gravitated toward C. Because C was so dangerous to use, many people started using C++ and Java. Microsoft created its own version of C++ called C#. Apple initially adopted a language similar to C++ called Objective-C, but then it created its own language called Swift. After running into legal problems using Java, Google adopted Kotlin as the official language for writing Android apps.

When learning any programming language, the only certainty is that new programming languages will appear all the time, so you should master the popular programming languages and keep learning the newer ones as well.

Remember: Focus on understanding programming, and *then* worry about understanding a particular programming language. After you understand how programming works, you can adapt to the next popular programming language of tomorrow, whatever that may be.

IN THIS CHAPTER

» Spaghetti programming without a plan

» Planning ahead with structured programming

» Making user interfaces with event-driven programming

» Organizing a program with object-oriented programming

» Using protocol-oriented programming

» Using design patterns

Chapter **2**

Different Methods for Writing Programs

The goal of computer science is to find the best ways to write a program. The reality of computer science is that nobody really knows what they're doing, so they're making up stuff as they go along and pretending there's a scientific basis for everything they do. The fact that multimillion-dollar programming projects routinely fall behind schedule and sometimes never work at all pretty much shows that computer programming is still less a science than an art.

Despite these problems, computer scientists are always searching for ways to make programming easier, faster, and more reliable by constantly developing

» Better tools

» Better programming languages

» Better techniques for writing programs

Just as a carpenter doesn't build a house with rusty saws and a broken hammer, computer scientists are always developing better tools to help them write, fix, and create programs. One of the first improvements computer scientists made was in developing faster compilers. Instead of waiting overnight to see if a program worked, programmers could use a fast compiler that could show them the results in seconds. Other tool improvements included editors that would show programmers the specific line where an error occurred and special programs (known as *debuggers*) for making sure that every part of a program worked correctly.

Another way to improve programmer efficiency involves creating better programming languages. Assembly language was easier to write and modify than machine language, and high-level languages are easier to write and modify than assembly language.

Computer scientists are constantly inventing new programming languages or improving existing ones. These improvements or new languages typically offer some feature that existing languages don't offer or solve certain types of problems that existing languages do poorly. For example, the C++ language improves upon the C language, whereas the Java language improves upon the C++ language.

Perhaps two of the biggest problems with programming involve writing a program from scratch and modifying an existing program. When you write a program from scratch, you want to write a working program quickly with as few problems as possible.

That's why programming languages include so many built-in commands. The idea is that the more built-in commands available, the fewer commands you'll need to use to write a program and the shorter and easier your program will be to write in the first place.

In addition, many programming languages include built-in error-checking features to keep you from writing a program that doesn't work. With some languages, it's possible to write commands that work perfectly but can also crash the computer if you give those commands the wrong type of data.

TIP

In Book 1, Chapter 3, you find out more about the features of different programming languages.

More than half the battle of programming is writing a program that works. The second half is modifying that program later. When you need to modify an existing program, you must first understand how that existing program works and then you need to modify it without messing up the existing program commands.

To help you understand how a program works, many programming languages let you divide a large program into separate parts. The theory is that if one part of a program isn't working or needs to be modified, you can yank out part of the program, rewrite it, and then plug it back into the existing program, much like snapping LEGO building blocks together.

Finally, the best tools and the latest programming languages won't help you unless you know how to use them correctly. That's why computer scientists are constantly developing new programming techniques that work no matter what tools or language you use.

TIP

In Book 1, Chapter 4, you find out more about the different programming tools computer scientists have created to make programming easier, faster, and more reliable.

This chapter discusses programming techniques based on problems encountered by programmers working in the real world. Basically, computer scientists keep developing and refining programming techniques after they see what really works and what doesn't.

Spaghetti Programming

In the early days of programming, most programs were fairly short and simple. A typical program may just calculate a mathematical equation, which to a computer, is just a little more challenging than adding two numbers together.

To write such small, single-task programs, programmers would typically start typing commands in their favorite programming language with little planning, just to write a program quickly.

Unfortunately, many programs aren't just written once and then used forever. If a program isn't working exactly right, or if the program needs to do something new that the original programmer didn't include, you must take an existing program and modify it.

Modifying an existing program sounds simple, but it's not. First, you have to understand how the program works so you'll know exactly how to modify that program. If you try modifying a program without understanding how it works, there's a good chance you could wreck the program and keep it from working, much like ripping out cables from your car engine without knowing what you're really doing.

After you understand how a program works, the second step involves writing new commands into the existing program. Now, here's where the problem occurs. Take an existing program and modify it once. Now take that same program and modify it again. Now take that same program and modify it 20 more times, and what do you get? Most likely, you'll have a mishmash collection of code that works but isn't organized logically, as shown in Figure 2-1.

FIGURE 2-1: Constantly modifying a program eventually creates an unorganized mess.

Original Program

Original Program
Modification #1
Modification #2

Original Program
Modification #5
Modification #1
Modification #3
Modification #2
Modification #4

Modifying a program several times by yourself may not be so bad because you probably remember what you changed and why. But what happens if seven other programmers modify the same program seven different times and then none of them is around to help you understand what changes they made? Yep, you'd wind up with a bigger mess than before.

With constant modifications, a small, simple program can grow into a convoluted monstrosity that may work, but nobody quite understands how or why. Because the program consists of so many changes scattered throughout the code, trying to figure out how the program even works can get harder with each new modification.

With a simple program, the computer follows each command from start to finish, so it's easy to see how the program works. After a program gets modified multiple times, trying to follow the order of commands the computer follows can be like untangling spaghetti (hence, the term *spaghetti programming*).

As programs kept getting bigger and more complicated, computer scientists realized that just letting programmers rush out to write or modify a program wasn't going to work anymore. That's when computer scientists created the first programming techniques to help programmers write programs that would be easy to understand and modify later.

SPAGHETTI PROGRAMMING WITH THE GOTO COMMAND

Although you can write spaghetti programs in any language, the BASIC programming language is most closely associated with spaghetti programming. Early versions of BASIC used a GOTO command, which essentially told the computer to "go to" another part of the program.

The problem with the GOTO command was that it could tell the computer to "go to" any part of the program. If you had a large program that consisted of several hundred (or several thousand) lines of code, the GOTO command could tell the computer to jump from one part of the program to another in any order, as the following BASIC program shows:

```
10 GOTO 50
20 PRINT "This line prints second"
30 END
40 GOTO 20
50 PRINT "This line prints first"
60 GOTO 40
```

Line 10 (the first line) tells the computer to "go to" line 50.

Line 50 tells the computer to print This line prints first onscreen. After the computer follows this command, it automatically runs the next command below it, which is line 60.

Line 60 tells the computer to "go to" line 40.

Line 40 tells the computer to "go to" line 20.

Line 20 tells the computer to print This line prints second onscreen. After the computer follows this command, it automatically follows the command on the next line, which is line 30.

Line 30 tells the computer this is the end of the program.

Even though this program consists of six lines, you can already see how the GOTO command makes the computer jump around, so it's hard to understand how this program works. Now imagine this program multiplied by over several hundred lines of code, and you can see how spaghetti programming can make reading, understanding, and modifying even the simplest program much harder.

Structured Programming

The problem with creating programs without any planning is that it inevitably leads to a mess. So, the first step involves keeping a program organized right from the start.

The three parts of structured programming

To keep programs organized, structured programming teaches programmers that any program can be divided into three distinct parts:

>> **Sequences:** *Sequences* are simply groups of commands that the computer follows, one after another. Most simple programs consist of a list of commands that the computer follows from start to finish, as shown in Figure 2-2.

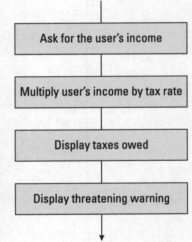

FIGURE 2-2: Sequences consist of groups of commands that the computer follows, one after another.

>> **Branches:** *Branches* consist of two or more groups of commands. At any given time, the computer may choose to follow one group of commands or another. Branches allow a program to make a decision based on a certain condition.

For example, at the end of most video games, the program asks you, "Do you want to play again (Yes or No)?" If you choose Yes, the program lets you play the video game again. If you choose No, the program stops running, as shown in Figure 2-3.

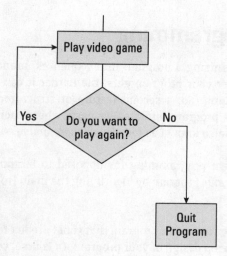

FIGURE 2-3: Branches let the computer choose which group of commands to run at any given time.

A branch starts with a command that evaluates a condition (such as determining whether the user chose Yes or No). Then, based on this answer, whether it's true or false, the branch chooses which group of commands to follow next.

>> **Loops:** Sometimes you may want the computer to run the same commands over and over again. For example, a program may ask the user for a password. If the user types an invalid password, the program displays an error message and asks the user to type the password again.

If you wanted your program to ask the user for a password three times, you could write the same group of commands to ask for the password three times, but that would be wasteful. Not only would this force you to type the same commands multiple times, but if you wanted to modify these commands, you'd have to modify them in three different locations as well. *Loops* are basically a shortcut to writing one or more commands multiple times.

A loop consists of two parts:

- The group of commands that the loop repeats

- A command that defines how many times the loop should run

By combining sequences, branches, and loops, you can design any program and understand how the program works at each step.

Dividing a program into sequences, branches, and loops can help you isolate and organize groups of related commands into discrete "chunks" of code. That way, you can yank out a chunk of code, modify it, and plug it back in without affecting the rest of the program.

Top-down programming

For small programs, organizing a program into sequences, branches, and loops works well. But the larger your program gets, the harder it can be to view and understand the whole thing. So, a second feature of structured programming involves breaking a large program into smaller parts where each part performs one specific task. This is also known as *top-down programming*.

The idea behind top-down programming (as opposed to bottom-up programming) is that you design your program by identifying the main (top) task that you want your program to solve.

For example, if you wanted to write a program that could predict the next winning lottery numbers, that is a top design of your program. Of course, you can't just tell a computer, "Pick the next winning lottery numbers." You must divide this single (top) task into two or more smaller tasks.

One of these smaller tasks may be, "Identify the lottery numbers that tend to appear often." A second task may be, "Pick the six numbers that have appeared most often and display those as the potential future winning numbers."

The idea is that writing a large program may be tough, but writing a small program is easy. So, if you keep dividing the tasks of your program into smaller and smaller parts, eventually you can write a small, simple program that can solve that task. Then you can paste these small programs together like building blocks, and you'll have a well-organized big program — theoretically.

Now if you need to modify part of the large program, just find the small program that needs changing, modify it, and plug it back into the larger program, and you've just updated the larger program.

Ideally, each small program should be small enough to fit on a single sheet of paper or a single screen. This makes each small program easy to read, understand, and modify. When you divide a large program into smaller programs, each small program is a *subprogram*.

If you divide a program into multiple subprograms, you have two options for where to store your subprograms:

WARNING

TIP

» **Store all your subprograms in a single file.**

This option is fine for small programs, but after you start dividing a program into multiple subprograms, trying to cram all your subprograms into a single file is like trying to cram your entire wardrobe into your sock drawer. It's possible, but it makes finding anything later that much more difficult.

» **Store subprograms in separate files, as shown in Figure 2-4.**

Storing subprograms in separate files offers three huge advantages:

● The fewer subprograms crammed into a single file, the easier it is to find and modify any of them.

● If you store subprograms in a separate file, you can copy that file (and any subprograms stored in that file) and then plug it into another program. In that way, you can create a library of useful subprograms and reuse them later.

● By reusing subprograms that you've tested already to make sure they work properly, you can write more complicated programs in less time, simply because you're reusing subprograms and not writing everything from scratch.

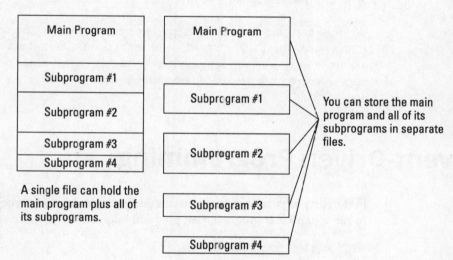

FIGURE 2-4: You can store subprograms in one big file or in separate files.

A single file can hold the main program plus all of its subprograms.

You can store the main program and all of its subprograms in separate files.

STRUCTURED PROGRAMMING AND PASCAL

You can use structured programming techniques with any programming language, including machine language or assembly language (see Book 1, Chapter 1). However, the one language most closely associated with structured programming is Pascal.

Unlike other languages that later adopted structured programming, Pascal was designed to encourage (force) programmers to use structured programming from the start. A typical Pascal program may look like this:

```
Program Print2Lines;
Begin
  Writeln ('This line prints first');
  Writeln ('This line prints second');
End.
```

Without knowing anything about the Pascal language, you can immediately make sense out of what it does.

- First, it prints the line, This line prints first.

- Next, it prints the second line, This line prints second.

Unlike the BASIC example that allows spaghetti programming (see "Spaghetti programming with the GOTO command," earlier in this chapter), Pascal forces programmers to structure programs using sequences, branches, and loops. As a result, Pascal helps programmers create well-organized programs that are much easier to read and understand.

Event-Driven Programming

In the early days, using a program was fairly simple. After you typed the command to run a particular program, that program might ask a question such as

```
What is your name?
```

At this point, you had no choice but to type a name, such as **Charlie Smith**. After you typed in your name, the program might respond with

```
Hello, Charlie Smith. What month were you born?
```

The moment you typed in a month, such as **April**, the program might respond:

```
What day were you born?
```

And so on. If you wanted to type your day of birth before your month of birth, you couldn't because the program controlled your options.

Not surprisingly, using a computer like this was frustrating to most people, so computer scientists soon invented something called a *graphical user interface* (GUI). A GUI displays multiple options to the user in the form of drop-down lists, windows, buttons, and check boxes. Suddenly, instead of the computer dictating what the user could do at any given time, the user could tell the computer what to do at any given time, just by choosing one of many available commands.

Forcing each program to display menus and windows had two advantages for users:

>> **It made using a computer much easier.** Instead of having to type in commands, users could just click the command they wanted to use.

>> **It's fairly easy to figure out how to use different types of programs.** After you understand that you can choose the Print command from the File menu, you know how to print in any program — whether it's a word processor, a database, or an image-editing program.

Unfortunately, although drop-down lists made programs easy for users, they made writing programs much harder for programmers:

>> Programmers had to write extra commands just to display all these fancy drop-down lists and windows. (Even worse, programmers had to make sure all those extra commands used to create drop-down lists and windows actually worked correctly.)

>> Programmers now had to write programs that could react to whatever command the user chose. Instead of presenting the user with options in a specific, predictable order, programs had to handle the unpredictable choices of the user.

To solve this dual problem of creating drop-down lists and knowing how to handle the different commands the user may choose at any given time, computer scientists developed *event-driven programming*.

In event-driven programming, an *event* is something that the user does or that the computer must respond to. The user might click a drop-down list or click a button displayed in a window. The computer might need to respond to an incoming email or a file being added to a directory. Event-driven programming simply focuses on displaying different commands onscreen and then handling these different events when they occur.

Event-driven programming divides programming into three distinct parts:

>> **The user interface (UI):** The commands the user sees onscreen

>> **The event handler:** The part of the program that reacts to the commands the user chooses from the UI

>> **The actual program:** The part of the program that actually does something useful, such as drawing pictures or predicting the winners of horse races

In the old days, creating a UI essentially tripled a programmer's work. You had to:

1. Write your program.
2. Write commands to create a UI.
3. Write commands to make your UI actually work.

Instead of forcing you to write commands to display drop-down lists and windows onscreen, a tool called a rapid application development (RAD) program lets you visually design your UI, such as the number, placement, and size of buttons.

After you've designed your UI (without having to write a single command to do it), you can write short programs that respond to everything the user could possibly do, which is called an *event*. If the user clicks a drop-down list, that's an event. If the user clicks a button in a window, that's a different event. When you write a small program to handle an event, the program is called an *event handler*.

Without event-driven programming, you'd be forced to write commands to create a UI and more commands to make the UI work. With event-driven programming, you just have to write commands to make your UI work. The fewer commands you have to write, the faster you can create a program and the easier the program will be to read, understand, and modify later.

The most popular language that defined event-driven programming is Visual Basic although other languages have adopted event-driven programming as well.

Event-driven programming doesn't replace structured programming; it supplements it. Structured programming techniques are useful for helping you write your program. Event-driven programming is useful for helping you design a UI for your program.

TECHNICAL STUFF

REMEMBER

Basically, event-driven programming divides programming into three distinct steps: designing the UI, writing event handlers to make the UI work, and writing the actual program.

Designing a user interface

The main advantage of event-driven programming is how quickly it allows you to design a UI without writing a single command whatsoever. Instead of writing commands, you create a UI using a two-step process:

1. **Visually draw your UI on a window by choosing which UI parts you want, such as buttons, check boxes, or menus, as shown in Figure 2-5.**

   After you've drawn your UI, you wind up with a *generic* UI.

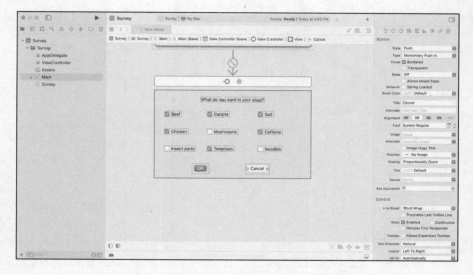

FIGURE 2-5:
Designing a UI involves drawing what you want to appear on your program's UI.

2. **Customize each part of your UI by defining its appearance and behavior.**

   To customize part of a UI, you must modify that UI's properties. Each part of your UI contains properties that define its appearance and behavior. For example, if you wanted to change the size of a check box, you'd modify that check box's Width or Height property, as shown in Figure 2-6.

With event-driven programming, designing a UI involves drawing your UI and then customizing it by changing its properties. After you've designed your UI, it will appear to work, but it won't actually do anything until you write an event handler.

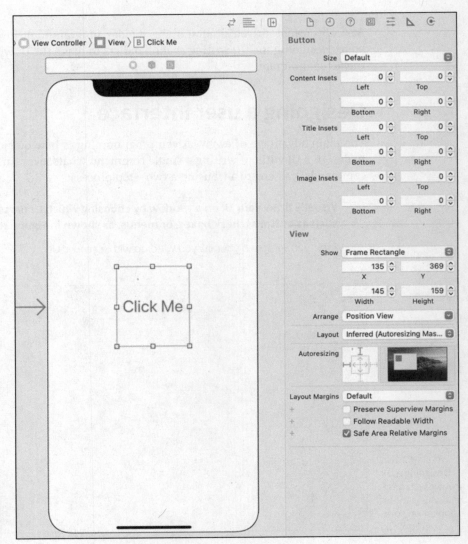

FIGURE 2-6:
Properties define how each part of a UI looks and behaves.

Writing event handlers

The whole purpose of an event handler is to work as a middleman between your actual program and your program's UI. To create an event handler, you need to identify the following:

>> **A UI item,** such as a button or a check box

>> **The event to respond to,** such as a click of the mouse

An event handler responds to a certain event triggered by a specific UI item, as shown in Figure 2-7. A UI item can have one or more event handlers so it can respond to different types of events, such as the user clicking a mouse button or pressing a key. A single event handler can respond to the same event coming from different UI items such as three different buttons.

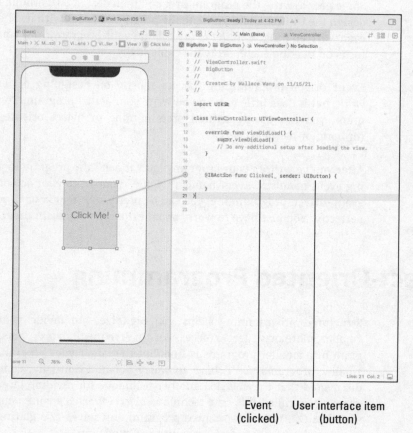

FIGURE 2-7:
An event handler
tells the UI how
to behave when
the user does
something,
such as click
the mouse over
a button.

Event   User interface item
(clicked)   (button)

The user can do dozens of different possible events, but some common events are clicking the mouse or pressing a key. Event handlers typically do one of three things:

» **Identify what the user did,** such as click a button

» **Retrieve information from the UI,** such as when the user types something in a text box

» **Display information to the user,** such as an error message

After you've written one or more event handlers for your UI, you have a complete working UI. Now you just have to attach this UI to a working program.

Writing your program

Some people write the program first and then design a UI around it. Other people design the UI first and then write the program to work with it. The whole point of event-driven programming is to separate your program from your UI so you can focus on making each part work individually.

Event-driven programming focuses mostly on designing a UI and making it work, but it does little to help you write your actual program. To write your program, you can use structured programming or object-oriented programming (or both, or neither).

After you've written your program, you "attach" the program to your UI by writing event handlers. Event handlers "glue" your UI to your actual program. With event-driven programming, you can be pretty sure that your UI will always work perfectly. You just have to worry about errors in your main program.

Object-Oriented Programming

Structured programming helps you organize and divide your program into smaller, more manageable pieces. For small to medium programs, dividing a program into smaller programs is fine, but the larger your program gets, the more smaller programs you'll have to worry about. Eventually, computer scientists discovered that they needed another technique for dividing large programs into parts. They called this new technique *object-oriented programming* (often abbreviated as OOP). Object-oriented programming solves two glaring problems with structured programming: reusability and modeling.

Reusability means that you can collect smaller programs that work together, store them in a larger group called an *object,* and then plug those objects into different programs like LEGO building blocks. Where structured programming encourages reusability by letting you reuse subprograms, object-oriented programming encourages reusability on a larger scale by letting you reuse objects (which contain multiple smaller programs). Reusing individual subprograms is like using bricks to build a house. Reusing objects is more like using premanufactured walls to build a house.

Modeling means making the parts of a program more intuitive. One of the reasons why assembly language is so hard to understand is because manipulating data in the processor's registers has nothing to do with solving problems like adding two numbers together. Likewise, dividing a large program into smaller tasks, using structured programming, does nothing to help you understand the actual problem the program is trying to solve.

With modeling, you divide a problem into real-life objects. If you were writing a program to control a car, one object might be the steering mechanism, another object might be the braking mechanism, and a third object might be the electrical system. By making each part of a program (each object) model a real-life object, it can be far easier to understand the purposes of the different parts of a program and how they work together.

For example, suppose you had to write a program to land a rocket on the Moon. This is how you might write this program using structured programming:

```
Land a rocket on the Moon
    Launch rocket
    Guide rocket through space
    Find a landing area on the Moon
    Put rocket down on landing area
```

So far, structured programming seems logical, but what happens when you keep dividing tasks into smaller tasks? Just focusing on the `Guide rocket through space` task, you might wind up with the following:

```
Guide rocket through space
    Get current coordinates
            Compare current coordinates with Moon coordinates
    Adjust direction
```

Dividing the `Adjust direction` task into smaller tasks, you might get this:

```
Adjust direction
    Identify current speed and direction
    Determine angle needed to steer toward the Moon
    Fire thrusters to change the angle of the rocket
```

Notice that the deeper you keep dividing tasks, the more removed you get from knowing what the main purpose of the program may be. Just by looking at the task `Identify current speed and direction`, you have no idea whether this task involves flying a rocket to the Moon, driving a car down a road, or controlling a walking robot to an electric outlet to recharge its batteries.

The more you divide a larger task into smaller tasks, the harder it can be to understand what problem you're even trying to solve. This gets even worse when you start writing actual program commands.

The two parts of most programs are the commands that tell the computer what to do and the data that the program manipulates. So, if you wrote a program to identify the current speed and direction of a rocket, the commands would tell the computer how to retrieve this information, and the speed and direction would be the actual data the program uses.

Essentially, program commands are separate from the data they manipulate. If one part of a program manipulates data incorrectly, the rest of the program winds up using that contaminated data and you, as the programmer, won't know which part of the program screwed up the data. This is like sitting in a baseball game, ordering a hot dog from a vendor, and having six people pass your hot dog down to you. When you see fingerprints all over your hot dog, can you tell which person touched your food?

Isolating data

Object-oriented programming avoids the problem of not knowing the purpose of code by combining data and the commands that manipulate them into a single entity called (surprise!) an *object*. With a well-designed object-oriented program, each object models part of the real-life problem so it's easier to understand the purpose of the code inside that object.

So, if you were designing a program to launch a rocket to the Moon, object-oriented programming would let you divide the program into objects. One object might be the rocket, a second object might be the Moon, and a third object might be the Earth.

You can also divide a large object into smaller ones. So the rocket object might be divided into an engine object and a guidance object. The engine object could be further divided into a fuel pump object, a nozzle object, and a fuel tank object.

Suppose you wrote a program to calculate a rocket's trajectory to the Moon, and the engineers suddenly designed the rocket with a more powerful engine? With object-oriented programming, you could just yank the engine object out of your program, rewrite or replace it, and plug it back into the program again.

In structured programming, modifying the program to reflect a new rocket engine would mean finding the program commands that manipulate the data that represents the engine's thrust, and then making sure that new data gets fed into the program at the proper location and still works with any other program commands that also handle that same data. (If the explanation in this paragraph sounded confusing and convoluted to you, that just shows you the less-than-intuitive problem of modifying a structured program versus an object-oriented program.)

Simplifying modifications

Besides organizing a large program into logical pieces, objects have another purpose: code reusability. In school, it was always easier to copy someone else's homework than it was to do it yourself. Similarly, programmers find that it's easier to copy and reuse somebody else's program rather than write their own program from scratch.

In structured programming, you could divide a large program into subprograms and then store those subprograms in a separate file. Now you could copy that file to reuse those subprograms in another program.

Copying subprograms makes programming easier, but here are two problems:

» **What if you copy a subprogram and then later find an error in that subprogram?** Now you have to fix that subprogram in every copy. If you made 17 copies of a subprogram, you'd have to fix the same error 17 times in 17 different copies of the same subprogram.

» **What if you wanted to modify and improve a subprogram?** Suppose you find a subprogram that asks the user to type in a password of no more than 10 characters, but you want your program to allow users to type in passwords up to 25 characters. At this point, you could either

- **Write your own password-verifying subprogram from scratch (which would take time).**

- **Copy the existing subprogram and modify it (which would take much less time).** It's easier to make a copy of an existing subprogram and then modify the copy. Now you have two copies of (almost) the same subprogram, but uh-oh, suddenly you discover an error in the original subprogram. Once again, you have to correct this error in the original subprogram and also in the modified subprogram. If you made 20 different modifications to a subprogram, you would have the problem of not only correcting the error in every copy of the original subprogram, but also fixing that same error in all your modified versions of that original subprogram.

But after you modify a subprogram, will you remember which subprogram you copied and modified originally? Even worse, you could copy a subprogram and modify it, and then copy your modified subprogram and modify that copy. Do this several times and you'll wind up with several slightly different versions of the same subprogram, but now you may not have any idea which subprogram you copied originally.

So, now if you find an error in the original subprogram, how can you find and fix that same error in any modified copies of that subprogram? Most likely, you can't because you won't know for sure which modified versions of the subprogram you (or another programmer) might have created.

Because programmers are always going to copy an existing program that works, object-oriented programming helps manage the copying process by using *inheritance*. The whole idea behind inheritance is that instead of making physical copies of code, you have only one copy of code (called a *class*) at all times.

Instead of physically copying all the code stored in a class, objects *inherit* all the code in a class by essentially pointing to the subprogram that they want to copy. This saves physical space by eliminating the need to make multiple copies of the same code.

Now instead of copying code (and risking creating duplicate copies), you can reuse existing code and add your own code. Now you can build more complicated programs by reusing existing objects like building blocks. If you modify code in one class, that modification automatically appears in any classes that inherit from that original class, as shown in Figure 2-8.

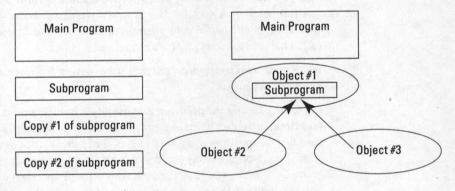

FIGURE 2-8: Object-oriented programming never physically copies code but "points to" or "inherits" code.

Copying a subprogram creates multiple copies of that subprogram.

Instead of making copies of a subprogram, objects "inherit" a subprogram. This leaves a single copy of a subprogram that can be used in multiple objects.

Object-oriented programming makes programs easier to write (by dividing a large program into parts), easier to understand (by organizing code into classes that mimic the actual problem the program is trying to solve), and easier to modify (by automatically updating any copies of code). All these advantages allow you, as the programmer, to focus more on solving problems and less on keeping track of trivial details.

TIP

Discover more about the details of object-oriented programming in Book 2, Chapter 7. For now, it's just important that you understand why programmers use object-oriented programming. Then you can worry about figuring out how to use object-oriented programming.

Using Protocol-Oriented Programming

As computer scientists started using object-oriented programming techniques, they noticed the same limitations. Object-oriented programming encapsulates variables (properties) and functions (methods) that manipulate that data to model real-life objects like an engine. Object-oriented programming made it easy to copy and reuse code, but it also added complexity by creating objects that inherited more and more code that often wasn't needed.

To help minimize the needless copying of code that would ultimately be ignored or modified, computer scientists created protocol-oriented programming. The main difference is that when you use object-oriented programming, you must define the method names and code to make that method work. With protocol-oriented programming, you can simply define the method name without writing any code within that method at all.

The purpose of simply defining the method name without writing any actual code is to create uniform method names that can be reused by your code just like objects. However, the advantage is that each class can adopt or conform to a protocol but write its own code for a particular method. Where object-oriented programming forces you to copy method names and the code that you may not need, protocol-oriented programming lets you just copy method names and customize the code to make it work the way you want. This reduces complexity and increases flexibility.

Protocol-oriented programming isn't meant to replace object-oriented programming; it's meant to work with it. Sometimes you may want to use object-oriented programming, and sometimes you may want to use protocol-oriented programming. Protocol-oriented programming is simply a way to reduce the complexity inherent in object-oriented programming.

Design Patterns

Although every program is different, all programs tend to require similar types of solutions. Rather than force programmers to reinvent solutions, computer scientists have identified common solutions to specific types of problems. These common solutions are called *design patterns*.

The main idea behind a design pattern is to show the best way to solve a specific type of problem. By following these best practices defined by a design pattern, you can spend less time thinking about the optimal way to solve a problem and simply use a design pattern to guide you into solving that particular problem using any programming language.

Design patterns focus on solving three types of common programming problems:

>> **Creational:** Defines the best way to create classes for different purposes

>> **Structural:** Defines the best way to design classes

>> **Behavioral:** Defines the best way for classes to share data and communicate with each other

Think of design patterns as cookie cutters to help you structure your code without telling you specifically how to write that code. By using design patterns, you can (hopefully) spend less time designing the structure of your program and more time writing reliable code faster than before.

DESIGNING PROGRAMS WITH TODAY'S METHODOLOGY

Each step — from spaghetti programming, to structured programming, to event-driven programming, to object-oriented programming, to protocol-oriented programming, to design patterns — is meant to guide programmers into writing better-organized programs that can be modified quickly and easily. Today, object-oriented programming, protocol-oriented programming, and design patterns are popular, but tomorrow, another programming methodology will likely arrive to deal with the shortcomings of object-oriented programming, protocol-oriented programming, and design patterns.

You want to avoid spaghetti programming, but structured programming, event-driven programming, object-oriented programming, and protocol-oriented programming are often used in the same program. You may use object-oriented programming and protocol-oriented programming to divide a program into objects, and then use structured programming to organize the commands you write and store inside each object. Finally, you may use event-driven programming to design a fancy UI so people know how to use your program.

By using each programming methodology's strengths, you can create a well-designed program, on time, that actually works. Given the track record of government agencies and Fortune 500 corporations, creating working software on time is the closest thing to a miracle that most people will ever experience in a lifetime!

IN THIS CHAPTER

» Deciding on your first language

» Understanding curly-bracket languages

» Determining artificial intelligence languages

» Figuring out scripting languages

» Understanding database programming languages

» Weighing up different programming languages

Chapter **3**

Types of Programming Languages

After you understand how to plan, organize, and create a program through one or more methodologies (such as structured programming, event-driven programming, object-oriented programming, or protocol-oriented programming), you're ready to start learning a particular programming language.

Just as your native spoken language can shape the way you think and speak, so can your first computer programming language influence the way you think, design, and write a computer program.

You can choose from literally thousands of different programming languages with obscure names, like Algol 60, APL, Forth, Icon, and Scheme. Although you can understand programming by using any programming language, it's probably best to start with one of the more popular programming languages for the operating system you want to target.

In the world of Windows, one popular language is C#, which is Microsoft's version of Java and C++. In the world of Apple products (Mac, iPhone, iPad, Apple Watch, and Apple TV), the most popular language is Swift, which replaces Apple's former official language of Objective-C.

If you want to write apps for Android, learn Kotlin, which has Google's official support to replace Java. Google also has another unique language called Flutter, based on the Dart programming language, which can be used to create Android and iOS apps at the same time.

If you want to write programs that run on servers to create interactive websites, look at Java, JavaScript, or Python. If you want to get involved in low-level programming, look at C and assembly language.

TIP

Because most popular programming languages are derived from C, learning C and its object-oriented version, C++, will always provide you with a strong foundation for learning practically any other programming language in the future.

Knowing a popular programming language simply gives you more opportunities. Just as knowing Arabic, Chinese, English, or Spanish allows you to travel and speak with more people around the world (compared to knowing Eskimo, Mayan, or Swahili), so can knowing one or more popular programming languages give you more opportunities to work and write programs anywhere you go.

TECHNICAL STUFF

Sometimes there's a good reason to know an obscure programming language. One of the oldest programming languages, COBOL, was heavily used by businesses back when computers filled entire rooms and millions of dollars. Because many COBOL programs are still running today, COBOL programmers can actually make a nice living because so few programmers know COBOL. Knowing an obscure language may limit your opportunities, but at the same time, if someone needs a programmer who knows that language, you could be the only one they could hire (and have to pay big bucks as a result).

Your First Language

So, should you start studying C as your first programming language? Yes and no. C may be the foundation for nearly all popular programming languages, but it's not the easiest language to learn, especially for beginners. As a novice, learning C can be difficult because it forces you to learn both the fundamentals of programming and the confusing syntax of the C programming language at the same time.

As a result, many beginners get frustrated with C as their first programming language and wind up more confused than ever. Imagine how many people would want to drive a car if it meant knowing how to refine their own gasoline and build their own engine. Understanding C isn't quite as difficult as refining gasoline or building an engine, but it can seem that way, especially when you're programming for the first time and you start with the C language.

If you'd rather learn the fundamentals of programming without getting bogged down in the complexities of the C language, consider learning an alternative programming language first, like one of the languages in the following sections.

BASICally disrespected

One of the first programming languages designed specifically to teach beginners is BASIC (short for Beginner's All-purpose Symbolic Instruction Code). Although BASIC is one of the oldest programming languages around, it isn't used often in commercial applications. Currently the most popular version of BASIC is Microsoft's Visual Basic, which made designing user interfaces (UIs) easy.

However, Visual Basic has fallen out of favor despite its initial popularity. Even worse from a financial point of view, BASIC programmers usually earn less than C programmers, even if they're doing the exact same job. Part of the reason is that BASIC suffers from the perception that it's a *toy language* — unsuitable for commercial use. Although that was true at one time, the BASIC language has evolved to the point where it can do almost anything C or other languages can do.

Microsoft created both Visual Basic and C# as nearly equivalent programming languages, so when you learn Visual Basic, you'll find it's easy to learn C#.

Although you can use BASIC to create anything from satellite navigation systems to Wall Street financial trading programs, BASIC programmers will probably always get paid less, so you'll need to know another language like C anyway, just to get paid more and have more opportunities. Because BASIC programmers tend to get paid less than other programmers, many programmers feel that they may as well skip BASIC and just figure out C instead.

However, if you want a much simpler introduction to programming, learning BASIC through Visual Basic or another version of BASIC will be far easier than learning C. When you understand the principles of programming through BASIC, learning another programming language will be much easier.

Visual programming with Scratch

To encourage children to learn programming, many organizations have created programming languages designed to be easy to learn, yet powerful enough to teach people the principles of programming. One popular language designed for kids is called Scratch (`https://scratch.mit.edu`).

Instead of requiring you to type text like most programming languages do, Scratch lets you design programs by connecting building blocks together like LEGO blocks, as shown in Figure 3-1. This visual way of learning programming can make programming easier to learn, more understandable, and more enjoyable because you avoid the problem of typing (and mistyping) program commands.

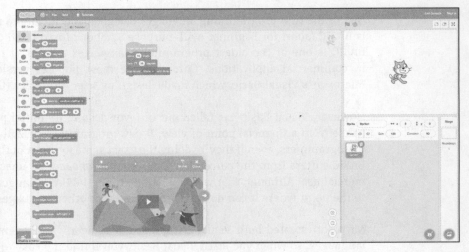

FIGURE 3-1:
Programming in Scratch means connecting visual building blocks together.

Just keep in mind that Scratch is meant to teach programming principles, but it doesn't let you create commercial applications. When you learn C or any C-derived language like C#, Python, or Swift, you're forced to learn programming principles and language syntax at the same time. When you learn Scratch, you can just focus on learning programming principles so you're learning one thing at a time.

When you feel ready, you can take your knowledge of programming principles and then tackle the second problem of learning a particular language syntax. So, learning programming through Scratch is a two-step process, while learning programming through a language like C is a massive, and possibly overwhelming, single-step process.

Programming robots with LEGO Mindstorms

Kids love building things with LEGO building blocks, so to encourage kids to build actual working robots, LEGO released a LEGO robot-building kit called Mindstorms. Not only can you build a working robot with LEGO building blocks, but you can also program the robot using the Mindstorms programming language.

To write a program, you don't have to type a thing. Instead, you arrange icons that represent different types of actions your robot can do, such as move forward or respond to a light, as shown in Figure 3-2. After writing the program on your computer, you load that program into your LEGO robot and watch it go.

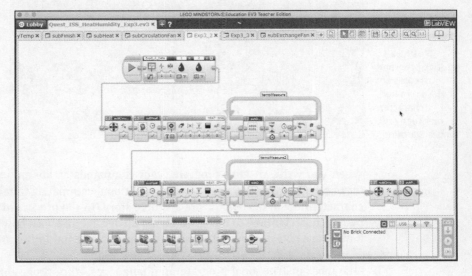

FIGURE 3-2: LEGO Mindstorms programming connects visual building blocks together to control a working robot.

By using LEGO Mindstorms, anyone can figure out both programming skills and robot-making skills. Unlike other programming languages, LEGO Mindstorms lets you see your working program in action as a walking, rolling, or crawling LEGO robot.

Learning object-oriented programming with Alice

Nearly all modern programming languages support object-oriented programming. Unfortunately, figuring out object-oriented programming can be difficult, especially for beginners who already have enough trouble just figuring out how to program a computer.

To help beginners understand object-oriented programming, Carnegie Mellon University created a free programming language dubbed Alice (www.alice.org). To make programming fun and teach object-oriented principles at the same time, Alice lets beginners write simple programs to animate characters onscreen, as shown in Figure 3-3.

FIGURE 3-3: An Alice program creates an animated character onscreen and moves it around.

When you write an Alice program, your commands create an animated character onscreen. Then you need to write additional commands to tell that animated character how to move to create a simple story. In the process of telling the animated character how to move, you wind up discovering both how to program and how to use object-oriented principles, while having fun in the process.

Like most instructional programming languages, Alice programming uses plain English commands, like move forward or play sound. By using simple commands, Alice lets you focus on understanding the principles of object-oriented programming without getting bogged down in understanding the peculiar syntax of a specific programming language.

Programming a killer robot

Studying how to program by controlling a LEGO robot can be fun (see "Programming robots with LEGO Mindstorms," earlier in this chapter), but to combine the thrill of controlling a robot with the joy of playing a video game, computer scientists have also created games that let you write a simple program for controlling a battling robot, as shown in Figure 3-4.

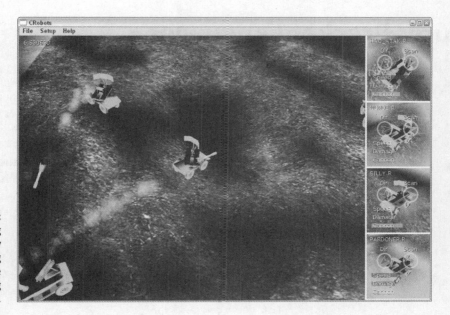

FIGURE 3-4:
Using a battling
robot to study
programming
can make
programming
more exciting.

Instead of writing a program just to control a robot, these games force you to write a program to move a robot onscreen, search for other robots nearby, and then attack those other robots with a cannon.

After you finish your program, you can see the results by watching your robot battle another robot in a gladiator-style battle. Write a "good" program, and your robot can defeat another robot. Write a "bad" program, and your robot gets blasted into chunks of (virtual) charred metal.

To program a "battling robot," use a simplified version of a popular programming language, such as C, C++, or Java. That way, not only do you figure out the basics of a popular programming language, but you also can start writing "real" programs that actually do something interesting right from the start. Table 3-1 lists some popular "battling robot" programming games.

TABLE 3-1

Popular "Battling Robot" Programming Games

Program	Language Used	Where to Find It
C++ Robots	C++	www.gamerz.net/c++robots
Crobots	C	https://crobots.deepthought.it
Robocode	Java	https://robocode.sourceforge.io

Curly-Bracket Languages

Whether you learn about programming using a simpler language or jump right in and start with C, you'll eventually need to learn one of the more popular programming languages based on C. This family of related languages is known as the curly-bracket language family.

The curly-bracket language family gets its name because all the languages use curly brackets to define the start and end of a block of commands, like this:

```
#include <stdio.h>

void main()
{
    printf("Notice how the curly brackets\n");
    printf("identify the beginning and end\n");
    printf("of your commands?\n");
}
```

TECHNICAL STUFF

Rather than use curly brackets, programming languages like Ada or Pascal use descriptive words, like Begin or End, to identify the start and end of a block of code. Descriptive words look clearer but can be more cumbersome to type. To eliminate curly brackets or descriptive words like Begin or End, Python uses indentation to define the beginning and end of a block of code.

Learning programming with C

The most popular curly-bracket language is C. The C language is popular for several reasons:

>> Power

>> Efficiency

>> Portability

The power of C

The C language is a curious combination of assembly language and high-level languages, like BASIC. Like assembly language, C provides commands for directly manipulating every part of the computer, including memory, hard disks, and printers. Like a high-level language, C lets you focus on the logic of your program without worrying about the technical details of the computer, so you get the best of both assembly language and high-level languages.

Because C programs are *nearly* (note the emphasis on the word *nearly*) as easy to write and understand as higher-level languages but still give you the power of accessing the computer's hardware like assembly language, C is often used for creating large, complicated programs (such as operating systems and word processors) along with more exotic programs (like antivirus utilities or disk diagnostic programs).

With great power comes great responsibility, and C is no exception. Because C programs can access every part of the computer's hardware, C programs can fail dramatically by crashing other programs, including the entire operating system.

The efficiency of C

A C compiler tends to create smaller, faster, more efficient programs than compilers for other programming languages. The reason is that the C language is much simpler and, thus, easier to translate into equivalent machine language commands.

What makes the C language simpler is its small number of commands or keywords. *Keywords* are special commands used in every programming language. The more keywords a programming language uses, the fewer commands you need to make the computer do something. The fewer keywords a programming language offers, the more commands you need to make the computer do something.

Think of keywords like words in a human language. The fewer words you know, the more limited your communication is. If a little kid only knows the word *hot*, they can only express themselves in a limited manner, such as describing something as "very hot," "a little hot," or "not so hot." However, if the kid knows a lot of different words, they can express themselves much better. Rather than use two or more words to describe something as "very hot," "a little hot," or "not so hot," a kid with a richer vocabulary could describe the same items as "scalding," "warm," or "cool."

A programming language with a lot of keywords allows you to write a program with fewer commands. That's great from the programmer's point of view but inefficient from the computer's point of view.

The more keywords used in a language, the more work the compiler needs to do to translate all these keywords into machine language. As a result, programs written in languages that use a lot of keywords tend to run much slower than programs written in C.

A C program compiles to smaller, more efficient machine language commands because instead of offering a large number of keywords, the C language offers just a handful of keywords. This makes it easy for a compiler to translate the limited number of keywords into machine language.

However, as a programmer, you need to use C's limited number of keywords to create subprograms that mimic the built-in commands of other programming languages. Because this can be impractical, the C language often includes libraries of subprograms that mimic the built-in commands of other programming languages.

The bottom line is that C programs tend to run faster and more efficiently than equivalent programs written in other programming languages. So, if you need speed, efficiency, and access to the computer hardware, the C language is the most popular choice.

The portability of C

By using much fewer commands than most programming languages, the C language makes it easy to create compilers that can translate a C program into machine language. Because it's so much easier to create C compilers than it is to create compilers for other programming languages, you can find a C compiler for nearly every computer and operating system.

Theoretically, this means it's possible to take a C program, written on Windows, copy it to another computer and operating system, and run that program on a different operating system, like Linux or macOS, with little or no modifications. When you can copy and run a program on multiple computers and operating systems, the program and the language it's written in are portable.

So, not only does C create small, fast, and efficient programs, but C also allows you to copy and run your program on different operating systems and computers. Given all these advantages, the C language remains popular despite its age (it was created in 1972).

Adding object-oriented programming with C++

Although the C programming language is popular, it's not perfect. When object-oriented programming became popular for designing and maintaining large programs, computer scientists created an object-oriented version of C called C++.

Because more people are writing and organizing large programs with object-oriented programming, more programs are being written in C++. Some people study C so they can understand the peculiarities of the C language. When they feel comfortable with C, they start studying C++ and object-oriented programming.

Other people just skip C and start studying C++ right away. The theory is that as a professional programmer, you'll probably wind up writing and modifying C++ programs anyway, so you may as well study C++ from the start. After you know C++, you pretty much know enough to teach yourself how to write and modify C programs, too.

TECHNICAL STUFF

A far less popular object-oriented version of C is Objective-C, which used to be Apple's official programming language until Apple switched to Swift.

Gaining true portability with Java

Although C and C++ programs are supposed to be *portable* — you can copy and run them on other computers — they're not really. Sometimes you have to make minor changes to get a C/C++ program to run on another computer, but more often, you have to make major changes.

That's why Sun Microsystems created the Java programming language. Like C++, Java is also based on the C language, but it includes several features to make Java programs safer than C or C++ programs. Specifically, Java isolates the programmer from directly accessing the computer's memory. This reduces the power of Java somewhat but translates into safer programs that (hopefully) won't crash as often as C/C++ programs do.

Perhaps the most important feature of Java is its portability. Rather than try to compile a Java program into machine language for different types of processors, Java compiles Java programs into an intermediate file format called *bytecode* or *pseudocode* (also called *p-code*).

To run a Java program that's compiled into bytecode, you need a free Java virtual machine (VM). As long as a computer has a Java VM, it can run a Java compiled bytecode program.

TECHNICAL STUFF

Like most promises made by computer scientists, Java programs aren't always portable. You can write a Java program correctly, compile it to bytecode format, and make the program run perfectly on a specific computer and operating system. But copy that same bytecode program to another computer, and suddenly, the Java program doesn't run correctly. The problem can occur when the Java VM, on either computer, has errors in it. So, although Java programs are more portable than C/C++ programs, they still aren't 100 percent portable.

Besides creating full-fledged programs, like word processors or spreadsheets, Java can also create *applets* (smaller programs), which can be used to create interactive web pages.

TIP

If you're looking for a programming language that makes programming safer and more portable, consider Java. Java programmers are in demand almost as much as C/C++ programmers, and the similarities between Java and C/C++ make it relatively easy to understand after you know C. (Or you can study Java first and then study C/C++ later.)

Programming more safely with C#

Microsoft took one look at C/C++ and decided it could create an improved language, which it dubbed C# (pronounced *C-sharp*).

C# advantages

C# has a couple advantages over languages such as C, C++, and even Java.

IT'S OBJECT-ORIENTED

One main advantage of C# over C++ is that C# is a true object-oriented programming language, so you have to use object-oriented programming to write a program in C#.

Being forced to use only object-oriented programming techniques may seem like a drawback until you realize that C++ is a hybrid language that lets you choose whether to use object-oriented programming. Although C++ gives you, the programmer, more flexibility, C++ programs can also be a mishmash of structured programming mingled in with object-oriented programming.

Trying to decipher such a mix of programming techniques can be confusing. By forcing all programmers to use object-oriented programming (and isolate their structured programming techniques only inside objects), C# programs can be much easier to understand and modify.

IT'S TYPE-SAFE

A second advantage of C# is that it's a type-safe language. Basically, if a C# program stores data, such as a whole number (such as 3 or 49, but not 5.48), the C# compiler checks to make sure no other part of the program accidentally changes that whole number into a decimal.

With languages that aren't type-safe, the compiler lets a program change data types, such as storing a decimal or negative number where the program expects a whole number. Obviously, if your program is expecting a whole number but instead receives a decimal number, the program may get confused and crash.

THE PROS AND CONS OF TYPE-SAFE LANGUAGES

So, why isn't every programming language type-safe? Good question. Here are two reasons:

- **Creating a type-safe language means more work** to create a compiler that can examine an entire program and check to make sure data types (such as numbers and text) aren't getting changed around unexpectedly. This translates into a slower and more complicated compiler, which is more work for the programmers who have to create the compiler in the first place.

- **Type-safe languages can be restrictive,** like trying to ride a motorcycle in a padded suit. The padded suit may protect you, but it also restricts your movement. Similarly, by not checking that data types remain consistent throughout a program, other languages give the programmer more freedom.

  Use this freedom wisely and you can create programs without the nuisance of type-safe checking, which can feel like having your parents staring over your shoulder every time you browse the Internet. Use this freedom poorly, and you'll wind up writing a program that crashes the computer.

Although non-type-safe languages are popular, the growing trend is to use type-safe languages that protect the programmer from writing programs that can mess up its data and crash the entire computer. C#, Java, and other languages, such as Swift, are considered type-safe languages.

.NET compatibility

Because Microsoft invented C#, it also invented a special program — the .NET framework. The idea behind the .NET framework is that instead of compiling a C# program into machine language, you compile a C# program into *p-code* or Common Intermediate Language (CIL), which is similar to the bytecode intermediate file format of Java.

The .NET framework allows you to both

» Run C# programs on any computer with the .NET framework.

» Write programs in multiple languages that all link together through the .NET framework, as shown in Figure 3-5.

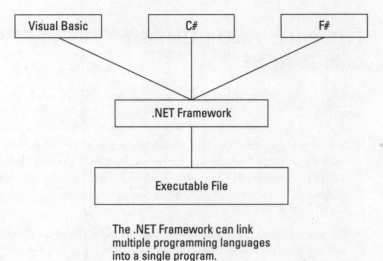

FIGURE 3-5:
The .NET
framework can tie
programs, written
in multiple
languages, into a
single program.

The .NET Framework can link
multiple programming languages
into a single program.

By letting you write a program with different languages, the .NET framework lets you use each language's strengths without forcing you to put up with the language's weaknesses.

TECHNICAL STUFF

The only programming languages you can use with the .NET framework are languages specifically designed to work with the .NET framework. So, if you want to write a program using a combination of C# and BASIC, you have to find a BASIC compiler that works with the .NET framework, such as Microsoft's own Visual Basic language.

A final advantage of the .NET framework is that it lets you use event-driven programming to create your UI and then write event handlers in any .NET language, such as C#.

Because C# is similar to C, C++, and Java, you can study C# first and then study the other languages (or vice versa).

For that reason, many programmers prefer to first understand C or C++, and then understand C#.

Choosing a curly-bracket language

If you plan to write programs professionally, you'll probably need to know a curly-bracket language. If you know C, C++, Java, or C#, you can pick up any of the other curly-bracket languages fairly easily:

>> **Knowing C can be great because it's the basis for all the other languages.** Plus, while figuring out C, you can get used to its cryptic syntax without having to worry about understanding object-oriented programming at the same time.

>> **Begin with C++ if you want to get started using object-oriented programming based on your knowledge of C.** While figuring out C++, you can ignore its object-oriented features. After you feel comfortable with writing C++ programs, you can gradually start developing object-oriented programming techniques as well.

>> **If you want to write programs that can run on different computers, use Java.** Java forces you to know object-oriented programming right from the start (like C#), so knowing Java means you can figure out object-oriented programming at the same time. Because Java isn't as confusing as C or C++, understanding Java first is likely much easier than understanding C or C++.

>> **If you want to learn a safer version of C, consider trying C# or Python.** The C# language is quickly becoming the standard language for writing Windows programs, while Python is popular for being easier to learn than C and being nearly as versatile as C.

REMEMBER

As long as you know at least one curly-bracket language, you know one of the most popular programming languages in the world.

Artificial Intelligence Languages

Programming languages, such as C, are often considered procedural or functional languages because they divide a large program into separate procedures or functions that tell the computer how to solve a problem step-by-step.

Although telling the computer what to do step-by-step might seem like the most logical way to program a computer, another way to program a computer is by using a declarative language. Instead of describing how to solve a problem, declarative programming languages describe

>> **Facts:** Information about the problem

>> **Rules:** Relationships between this information

By using facts and rules, programs written in declarative languages can literally figure out an answer on their own without being told explicitly how to do it.

REMEMBER

Ultimately, every program, including those written in declarative languages, must get translated into machine language. That means every program must eventually tell the computer how to solve a problem step-by-step. Declarative languages simply free you from having to describe these steps to the computer.

The most popular declarative programming language is *Prolog* (short for *Programming in Logic*). A typical Prolog fact might look like this:

```
father("Sally", "Jesse").
```

The preceding fact tells the computer that Jesse is the father of Sally. Now if you want to know who the father of Sally might be, you could ask the following:

```
?- father("Sally", X).
```

Using the fact that earlier stated that the father of Sally was Jesse, the preceding Prolog command would simply return:

```
X = "Jesse".
```

At this point, Prolog simply uses a predefined fact to come up with an answer. Notice that even in this simple example, no instructions told the Prolog program how to use the fact that Jesse is the father of Sally.

A list of facts by themselves can be made more useful by including rules that define relationships between facts. Consider the following Prolog program that defines two facts and one rule:

```
father("Jesse", "Frank").
father("Sally", "Jesse").

grandFather(Person, GrandFather) :-
    father(Person, Father),
    father(Father, GrandFather).
```

The two facts tell the computer that Frank is the father of Jesse, and Jesse is the father of Sally. The grandfather rule tells the computer that someone is a grandfather if they're the father of someone's father.

Suppose you typed the following Prolog command:

```
?- grandFather("Sally", Y).
```

The Prolog program tells the computer to use its known facts and rules to deduce an answer, which is:

```
Y = "Frank".
```

In other words, Frank is the grandfather of Sally. (Frank is the father of Jesse, and Jesse is the father of Sally.)

Just from this simple example, you can see how different a Prolog program works compared to a program written in C or Java. Instead of telling the computer how to solve a problem, declarative programming languages let you state the facts and the rules for manipulating those facts so the computer can figure out how to solve the problem.

TECHNICAL STUFF

A Prolog program can actually create additional facts (and delete old facts) while it's running, so it can appear to think. That's why Prolog is commonly used in the field of artificial intelligence (AI). The whole idea behind AI is to make computers smarter and literally think for themselves. (That's because computer scientists have pretty much given up hope that people will ever get smarter or begin to think for themselves.)

REMEMBER

Just as knowing two or more human languages can help you better understand how people communicate, so can knowing two or more drastically different programming languages help you better understand how programming can work. The key is to figure out two different programming languages, like C++ and Prolog. Knowing two similar programming languages, like C++ and C#, won't show you much of a difference.

One of the most popular programming languages favored by the AI community is LISP (which stands for *LISt Processing*). The basic idea behind LISP is that everything is a list that can be manipulated by the computer. For example, a typical LISP command might look like this:

```
(print "Hello world")
```

This LISP command is a list that displays the following onscreen:

```
"Hello world"
```

The enclosing parentheses define the start and end of a list. A different way to print "Hello world" onscreen would be to use this LISP command:

```
(list "Hello world")
```

The preceding command would print the following:

```
("Hello world")
```

In this case, the list command tells the computer to treat "Hello world" as a list, so it encloses it in parentheses. Now consider what happens if you insert a command (list) inside another command (list):

```
(list (print "Hello world"))
```

This is how the preceding LISP command works:

1. The innermost command (list) runs first, which is the (print "Hello world") list.

This displays the following onscreen:

```
"Hello world"
```

From the computer's point of view, the original LISP command now looks like this:

```
(list "Hello world")
```

2. This command now displays the following onscreen:

```
("Hello world")
```

So, the command

```
(list (print "Hello world"))
```

prints the following:

```
"Hello world"
("Hello world")
```

In the previous example, LISP treats the (print "Hello world") list first as a command (to print "Hello world" onscreen) and then as data to feed into the list command to display the list ("Hello world") onscreen.

With traditional programming languages, like C or Java, commands and data are separate where data may change but commands never change. With LISP, a list can be both a command and data. That makes it possible for a program to change its lists (treated either as data or as a command), essentially allowing a program to modify itself while running, which can mimic the learning and thinking process of a human being.

As you can see, both LISP and Prolog offer radically different ways to program a computer compared to C or Java. Just as languages, like C and Java, free you from the tedium of manipulating registers and memory addresses to program a computer, so do LISP and Prolog free you from the tedium of writing explicit step-by-step instructions to program a computer.

Although the idea that a LISP program can modify its own commands might seem like science fiction, LISP is actually the second-oldest programming language still in use today. (Fortran is the oldest programming language still in popular use.) LISP was invented in 1958, and although it's been used primarily as a research tool, people have created commercial programs using LISP.

Scripting Languages

Languages, such as C and C++, are often dubbed *system programming languages* because they can create programs that access and manipulate the hardware of a computer, such as an operating system (for example, Linux or Windows) or a utility program (for example, an antivirus or anti-spyware program). However, using system programming languages, like C++, for everything can get clumsy. Instead of writing an entirely new program from scratch using a system programming language, more people are likely to use an existing program and customize it in some way. Programming languages that customize existing programs are typically called *scripting languages.*

Scripting languages work with one or more existing programs and act as "glue" that connects different parts of an existing program together. For example, Microsoft Office consists of several programs including a word processor (Microsoft Word), a spreadsheet (Microsoft Excel), and a database (Microsoft Access). By using the scripting language that comes with Microsoft Office, you can write a program that can automatically yank information from an Access database, create a chart from that information in an Excel spreadsheet, and then copy both the data and its accompanying chart into a Word document for printing.

Trying to yank information from a database, create a chart with it, and print the data and chart using a system programming language, like C++ or Java, would mean creating everything from scratch including a database, a spreadsheet, and a word processor. By using a scripting language, you use existing components and simply "glue" them together. The existing components do all the work, while the scripting language just passes the data from one component to another.

Because scripting languages work with existing programs, they differ from traditional programming languages (like C++ or Java) in two important ways:

- **Because scripting languages work with one or more existing programs, scripting languages are usually interpreted rather than compiled.** Therefore, if someone else wants to run your program, written in a scripting language, they need the source code to your program along with all the programs your scripting program needs, such as Microsoft Word and Microsoft Access. As a result, scripting languages are used less to create commercial applications and more to create custom solutions.

- **To make scripting languages easy to understand and use, even for nonprogrammers, most scripting languages are *typeless* languages.** System programming languages, like C++ and Swift, are *strongly typed* or *type-safe* languages. Strongly-typed languages force you to define the type of data your program can use at any given time. So, if your program asks the user to type a name, a strongly typed language makes sure that the user doesn't type in a number by mistake. This protects a program from accidentally trying to manipulate the wrong type of data, which could crash the program as a result.

  In comparison, typeless languages don't care what type of data the program stores at any given time. This makes writing programs much easier because your program assumes if it's going to yank data from a particular program, such as Microsoft Excel, the data is probably going to be the right "type" anyway, so type-checking would just be restrictive and tedious.

Scripting languages are typically used in four different ways:

- To automate repetitive tasks

- To customize the behavior of one or more programs

- To transfer data between two or more programs

- To create stand-alone programs

Automating a program

At the simplest level, scripting languages (also called *macro languages)* can automate repetitive tasks that essentially record your keystrokes so you can play them back at a later time. For example, if you regularly type the term *Campylobacteriosis* (a disease caused by the *Campylobacter* bacteria), you have two choices:

- Type the term manually, and hope that you spell it correctly each time.

- Type the term just once (the easier solution), record your keystrokes, and use those captured keystrokes to create a scripting language program that you can save and run in the future.

Figure 3-6 shows a scripting language, Visual Basic for Applications (VBA), that has captured keystrokes and saved them in a VBA scripting language program.

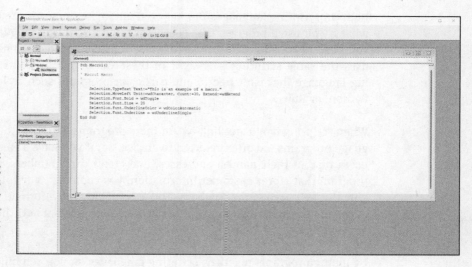

FIGURE 3-6: Recording keystrokes automatically creates the equivalent VBA code in Microsoft Word.

Customizing a program

Besides letting you automate a program, scripting languages also let you customize a program, which can make the program easier to use. For example, you may have a spreadsheet that calculates your company's invoices. However, to use this spreadsheet, you need to know the specific place in the spreadsheet to type new invoice information. Type this information in the wrong place, and the spreadsheet doesn't work right.

To avoid this problem, you can write a program in a scripting language that can display a window with boxes to type in new invoice information. Then the scripting language program automatically plugs that new information in the correct place in the spreadsheet every time.

For even more power, a scripting language can combine automation with customization to make programs perform tasks on their own. By using VBA in Microsoft Office, you could write a VBA program that tells your computer to copy data from an Excel spreadsheet, paste it into a Word document at a specific time each day, and then save your document.

Transferring data among multiple programs

Built-in scripting languages can help you automate or customize a program, but what if you use a program that doesn't include a scripting language? Or what if you need to transfer data between two or more programs, but neither program uses the same scripting language? In these cases, you'll need to use a scripting language that isn't tied to any particular program, such as JavaScript, Perl, Python, or Ruby.

When scripting languages link two or more programs together, the scripting language programs are often referred to as *glue.* So, if you have a web page that lets users type in their names, addresses, and credit card numbers, and a database program that stores customer information, you could use a scripting program to glue the web page to the database. The user would type information into the web page, and the scripting language would then yank this data off the web page and shove it into the database.

By gluing programs together, scripting languages let you combine existing programs to create custom applications. Because scripting languages are interpreted rather than compiled, they can run on any computer with the proper language interpreter. So, whether you use Linux, macOS, or Windows, you can still use the same scripting language (and programs) on different computers.

Creating stand-alone programs

If you wanted to create your own program, you could write everything from scratch. So, if you wanted to include features of a spreadsheet and a database, you would have to create your own spreadsheet and database.

Obviously this would be difficult to do, so by using scripting languages within existing programs, you can create custom programs that rely on the features of an existing program like Microsoft Excel.

Now instead of writing a spreadsheet from scratch, you can use the features of the Excel spreadsheet and create a custom program based on Excel. This lets you reuse proven features of an existing program while letting you focus solely on writing the features you need.

Stand-alone programs, based on existing programs, can simply make that existing program much easier to use. For example, Microsoft Excel is a powerful spreadsheet that many people don't know how to use. By creating a stand-alone program based on Excel, your stand-alone program can gently guide users into solving problems without forcing them to learn Excel.

Database Programming Languages

Programming languages, such as C++, are general-purpose languages because they can literally be used to create any type of program from operating systems and word processors to antivirus utilities and video games. However, in the business world, the most common type of custom programs needed are those that store and retrieve data, such as invoices, inventory, customer information, and so on.

Although it's possible to write a database program in C++, that essentially doubles the amount of work you need to do. You have to write your program's UI and commands for manipulating data *and* write commands to store and retrieve data, essentially creating a database program from scratch.

Instead of rewriting (and testing) your own database program, it's much easier just to customize an existing database program. Many database programs include their own programming language. By using a database programming language, you just have to customize the appearance of the database program by designing a UI along with commands for manipulating data. The database program does all the work of storing, retrieving, and rearranging the actual data so you can focus on what your program should *do* with data and not with the technical details for how it should *store* data.

One of the most popular Windows database programs, Microsoft Access, offers the VBA scripting language. Of course, Microsoft Access runs only on the Windows operating system, so if you need to create database applications that run on both Windows and macOS, you can choose Claris FileMaker (www.claris.com/filemaker).

Like Microsoft Access, FileMaker offers a scripting language: ScriptMaker. Best of all, you can create stand-alone versions of your FileMaker databases and sell them to anyone who uses macOS or Windows.

TECHNICAL STUFF

Many specialized database programs, such as medical office management programs or multilevel marketing programs, have been created using FileMaker.

Comparing Programming Languages

With so many different programming languages available, the question isn't "Which programming language should I study and use?" Instead, the real question is "How can I become a better programmer and choose the best language for solving a particular problem?"

Programming languages just offer different ways to express your ideas, and depending on what you need to accomplish, sometimes a language like C++ is best and sometimes another language like LISP may be better. The goal is to choose the best language for the job.

Unfortunately, it's impossible to know and master every programming language, so it's usually best to focus on mastering two or three languages instead. The more you know about using a particular language, the faster and more efficient you can write programs in that language.

REMEMBER

A mediocre programmer using a programming language designed for a specific job is likely more efficient than an expert programmer using an inappropriate language for that same job. Assembly language might create the fastest and most efficient programs, but if you need to write a program quickly and you don't care about efficiency, a scripting language like JavaScript may be much easier, faster, and less buggy. Sometimes, a program that gets the job done now is preferable to a program that works ten times as fast but takes a million times longer to write.

IN THIS CHAPTER

» **Choosing a compiler and interpreter**

» **Using a virtual machine**

» **Working with editors, debuggers, toolkits, and profilers**

» **Getting a handle on source code**

» **Creating help files**

» **Using installers and disassemblers**

Chapter **4**

Programming Tools

The two most important tools a programmer needs are an editor and a compiler. An *editor* lets you type and save language commands (called the *source code*) in a plaintext file. (Unlike a word processor file, a plaintext file doesn't contain any formatting, like italics or fonts.) A *compiler* converts your source code into machine code and stores those machine code commands in a separate file (often called an *executable file*). After you store your program in an executable file, you can sell and distribute that executable file to other people.

An editor and a compiler are absolutely necessary to write and distribute programs. However, most programmers also use a variety of other tools to make programming easier. To help them track down *bugs* (problems) in a program, programmers use a special tool called a *debugger.* To help them identify which parts of a program may be making the entire program run too slow, programmers can use another tool, called a *profiler.*

For distributing programs, programmers often use a help file creator and an installer program. The *help file creator* makes it easy for the programmer to create, organize, and display help that the user can read while using the program. The *installer program* makes it easy for users to copy all the necessary files on to their computer so the program runs correctly.

Finally, programmers may also use a special tool called a *disassembler*, which can pry open another program to reveal how it works. Disassemblers are often used by security professionals to analyze how viruses, worms, and spyware programs work. For less honorable uses, programmers can also use a disassembler to dissect a rival program and study how it works.

In many cases, programmers use an integrated development environment (IDE) that combines the features of an editor with a compiler and a debugger. That way, they can just use a single program to write, debug, and compile a program, instead of relying on two or more separate programs.

REMEMBER

Programmers often get so attached to their favorite programming tools that they argue the merits of their favorite editor or compiler with all the passion of a religious fanatic. Just as there is no single programming language that's the best language to use at all times, there is no single programming tool that's the best tool to use all the time.

Choosing a Compiler

No two compilers work exactly the same, even compilers designed for the same language, such as two competing C++ compilers. It's perfectly possible (and quite common) to write a program that works perfectly with one compiler but doesn't run at all under another compiler without minor (or massive) changes.

When Microsoft wrote the Mac version of its Microsoft Office suite, it used CodeWarrior, which is a C++ compiler. Unfortunately, the CodeWarrior compiler ran only on the PowerPC processors, which were used in older Mac computers. When Apple switched to Intel processors, Microsoft had to dump the CodeWarrior compiler and use a different compiler called Xcode.

Because CodeWarrior and Xcode are both C++ compilers, Microsoft could theoretically compile the same C++ program under both CodeWarrior and Xcode with no problems. Realistically, Microsoft had to rewrite major portions of their C++ programs just to get them to run under the Xcode compiler. The moral of the story is that switching compilers is rarely an easy decision, so it's important to choose the "right" compiler from the start.

REMEMBER

At one time, the CodeWarrior compiler was considered the "right" compiler to use for creating Mac programs. What made CodeWarrior suddenly turn into the "wrong" compiler was when Apple switched from PowerPC processors to Intel processors. Everyone who had used the CodeWarrior compiler had to switch to the Xcode compiler. Bottom line: What may seem like the "right" compiler today could later turn out to be the "wrong" compiler through no fault of your own or the compiler company.

When choosing a compiler, you have to consider your needs, the compiler company's reputation, and the compiler's technical features.

Defining your needs for a compiler

The most important choice for a compiler centers solely on what you need. Follow these steps:

1. **Decide which programming language you want to use.**

   If you want to write C++ programs, you need a C++ compiler. If you want to write C# programs, you need a C# compiler.

   Many compilers can work with multiple languages, such as C and C++.

REMEMBER

2. **Decide which operating system you want to use.**

   If you want to write C++ programs for macOS, your choices immediately narrow to the small list of C++ compilers that run under macOS.

3. **Choose a compiler that has the best chance of being around years from now.**

   - Most companies prefer using compilers from brand-name companies, like Apple or Microsoft.

REMEMBER

     Even compilers from big-name companies are no guarantee against obsolescence. Microsoft has stopped supporting its compilers over the years, such as Microsoft Pascal and Visual Basic 6. If you used either of these compilers to write a program, you had to change compilers when Microsoft stopped developing them.

   - Many people are choosing open-source compilers. *Open source* simply means that the source code to the compiler is available freely to anyone. Not only does this mean that open-source compilers are free (compared to the hundreds of dollars you can pay for a brand-name compiler), but it also guarantees that the compiler can't become obsolete due to lack of support.

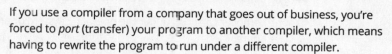

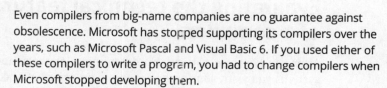
WARNING

     If you use a compiler from a company that goes out of business, you're forced to *port* (transfer) your program to another compiler, which means having to rewrite the program to run under a different compiler.

Because anyone can examine and modify the source code to an open-source compiler, anyone can make changes to the compiler to improve it. One of the most popular open-source compilers is GCC (`https://gcc.gnu.org`), which stands for *GNU Compiler Collection*.

Programming Tools

Xcode, the free compiler that Apple distributes with every Mac computer, is actually the GCC compiler.

Originally, GCC only compiled C source code, but later versions of GCC compile several different languages, including Ada, C, C++, Java, and Objective-C, with more programming languages being supported every year. Even better, the GCC compiler also runs on a variety of operating systems, such as Linux and Windows, so if you write a program using the GCC compiler, you can recompile your program to run under another operating system with minimal changes (ideally).

The GCC compiler actually consists of two parts:

>> The **front end** of the compiler translates source code into an intermediate format:

- To write C++ programs, you must use the C++ front end of the GCC compiler.

- To write Ada programs, use the Ada front end of the GCC compiler.

- By creating front ends for different languages, programmers can make the GCC compiler compile more programming languages.

>> The **back end** of the compiler finishes translating the intermediate code into actual machine code.

Evaluating the technical features of a compiler

After you choose a particular programming language and pick which operating systems you want your programs to run on, your list of compiler choices is likely narrowed to one or two choices. Given two compilers that both meet your needs, you can pick the "best" compiler by examining their technical features.

The technical features of a compiler are meaningless if

>> The compiler stops being developed and supported.

>> The compiler can't run under the operating system or processor you need in the future.

>> A particular technical feature is something you don't need or care about.

Supported language standards

No two compilers are alike, even those that compile the same programming language, such as C++. The problem is that every programming language has an official "standard," but the standard for most programming languages is usually far behind what people in the real world are actually using. (By the time an official standards committee agrees on the features of a given programming language, programmers have already created new features that eventually become standards in future versions of that language.)

As a result, most compilers support a given language standard plus additional features that programmers have developed. Therefore, every compiler actually works with a different dialect of a programming language. So, C++ programs that run under the Microsoft Visual Studio compiler may or may not run the same when compiled under the GCC compiler, even though both compilers claim to support the "standard" C++ programming language.

REMEMBER

Language standards are nice but generally useless when comparing compilers. What's more important is whether a particular compiler offers the specific features you need or want, regardless of whatever particular standard it may follow.

Code generation and optimization

Every compiler converts source code into machine language, but some compilers can translate source code into more efficient machine language commands than other compilers. As a result, it's possible to compile the same C++ program under two different C++ compilers and create identically working programs that consist of different machine language instructions.

The goal of every compiler is to create a program that takes up as little memory and disk space as possible while running as fast as possible. Usually, compilers make a trade-off. To make a program run faster, the executable file may take up a large amount of disk space or require a lot of memory. If the compiler can reduce the size of your program and the amount of memory it needs to run, it may create a slow program.

To help you tweak your program for the best balance of speed, size, and memory requirements, many compilers offer optimization settings. By fiddling with these optimization settings, you can tell the compiler how to speed up or shrink your program, as shown in Figure 4-1.

Programming Tools

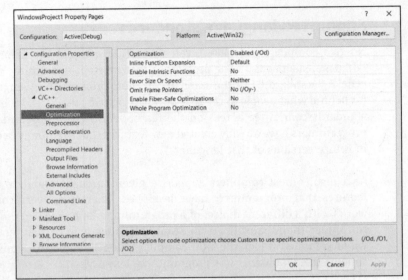

FIGURE 4-1:
Compiler optimization settings let you make your program as small and as fast as possible.

One major feature of a compiler's code generation capabilities involves speed, which can measure two different features:

» **How quickly the compiler works in translating your source code to machine code:** In the old days, compilers could take hours or days to compile a simple program. Nowadays, compilers often work in minutes or even seconds. Shove in a program that consists of 800,000 lines of code, and in less than a minute, the compiler can create an executable file for you. The faster the compiler works, the less time you waste waiting to run and test your program.

» **The performance of the machine language code that the compiler creates:** Given the same program, one compiler may create a program that runs quickly, whereas a second compiler may create that same program that runs much slower.

REMEMBER

Ideally, you want a compiler that both *compiles* fast and creates programs that *run* fast.

Target platforms

Most compilers can compile programs only for a specific operating system, such as Linux or Windows. However, what happens if you need to write a program that runs on two or more operating systems?

You could write the program twice with two different compilers — one for each operating system. So, if you wanted to write a C++ program that runs under macOS and Windows, you could compile that program by using Microsoft Visual Studio (for Windows) and then write a similar program to compile by using Xcode (for macOS).

Of course, writing the same program two times for two different compilers on separate operating systems is a tremendous waste of time. As an alternative, some compilers are known as *cross-compilers* — they can create programs that work on multiple operating systems, such as Linux, macOS, and Windows. Figure 4-2 shows the Xojo cross-compiler, which lets you choose whether to compile a program for Linux, macOS, or Windows.

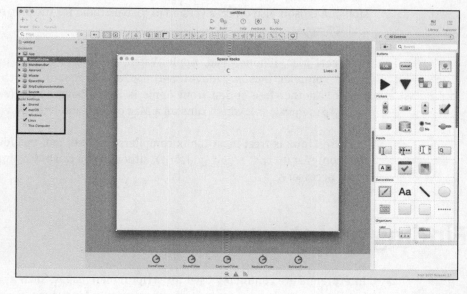

FIGURE 4-2:
A cross-compiler lets you write a program and compile it for multiple operating systems at the click of a mouse.

With a cross-compiler, you can write a program once and compile it to run on multiple operating systems, effectively doubling or tripling your potential market. *Without* a cross-compiler, you may need to write a program for each compiler, under a different operating system, essentially doubling or tripling your work.

REMEMBER

Although the idea of writing a program once and having it run on multiple operating systems may seem appealing, cross-compilers aren't perfect. Chances are, you'll have to tweak your program to run under each operating system, but those minor tweaks will be much easier than rewriting huge chunks of your program if you had to use two separate compilers.

Programming Tools

Cost

Paying for a compiler doesn't necessarily mean you're getting a better compiler. The GCC compiler is free and one of the best compilers available.

TIP

Generally, you should only pay for a compiler if it offers a unique feature or programming language that you need or want to use. For learning purposes, you can find plenty of free compilers so you can study different programming languages without spending any money at all.

Windows users will most likely want to consider Microsoft Visual Studio (https://visualstudio.microsoft.com), which comes in both free and commercial versions. Microsoft also offers a version of Visual Studio for the Mac to create macOS and iOS apps.

To create Mac, iPhone, iPad, Apple Watch, or Apple TV apps, use Apple's free Xcode compiler (https://developer.apple.com/xcode), which only runs on a Mac. Another free option from Apple is Swift Playgrounds (www.apple.com/swift/playgrounds), which runs on a Mac or iPad and lets you write Swift code.

Because Linux is free, most Linux compilers are free, too, including the popular GCC compiler (https://gcc.gnu.org), although you can buy commercial compilers if necessary.

Finding an Interpreter

Interpreters are commonly used for scripting languages, such as Perl or Python, but they're rarely used for system programming languages, such as C++. That's because if you write a program and use an interpreter, you must distribute a copy of your source code with the interpreter. Giving away your source code essentially gives away your program, so most commercial programs use a compiler instead.

However, interpreters can be useful for learning a programming language. By using an interpreter, you can focus solely on learning a programming language without the distraction of creating a complete program.

One popular type of interpreter is the online interpreter, which lets you use any browser to practice typing specific language commands. JDoodle (www.jdoodle.com) lets you select from dozens of popular and obscure programming languages such as C++ and Swift, along with less common languages like Forth and Smalltalk.

If you're interested in Flutter, Google's cross-platform tool for creating Windows, Android, macOS, iOS, and Fuchsia apps, you can practice writing Dart code on the Flutter website (https://flutter.dev), as shown in Figure 4-3.

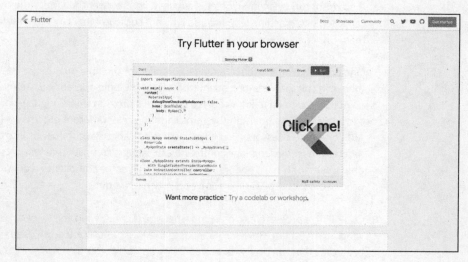

FIGURE 4-3: The Flutter website lets you type and run code using any browser.

Nearly every web browser comes with a JavaScript interpreter. Web designers use JavaScript for creating interactive web pages, verifying information typed on a web page (such as a username and password), or opening pop-up windows that display advertisements.

Although JavaScript interpreters can be found in any web browser, you may have to download and install interpreters for other programming languages. Some popular programming languages for running programs on *web servers* (those computers responsible for displaying and retrieving information from web pages, such as shopping data) include

>> Perl (www.perl.com)

>> PHP (www.php.net)

>> Python (www.python.org)

>> Ruby (www.ruby-lang.org)

Not only do the preceding four languages have free interpreters that you can copy, but their interpreters also run on different operating systems. That means a Perl or Ruby program written on a Windows computer should run identically if it's copied and run on a Linux or Mac computer.

THE ADVANTAGES OF INTERPRETED LANGUAGES

A program run by an interpreter is almost always slower than the same program compiled into machine language, so why not compile every language rather than run them under an interpreter?

One of the reasons is that creating a compiler for multiple operating systems is much more difficult than creating an interpreter for multiple operating systems. To create a compiler, you need to know how to translate a programming language into machine code, but because operating systems can run under different processors (such as the ARM or Intel processors), you have to translate language commands into completely different machine language commands. Creating a compiler that works correctly for one processor is hard enough, but creating that same compiler to work under multiple processors identically and error-free is much more difficult.

Compiling a program into machine language is great when you want to distribute a program to others. However, languages like Perl or Ruby are often used to create short programs that run on a web server. Using an interpreter may run a program more slowly, but you can write a program and run it right away without compiling it first. Also, by running the source code directly, interpreters let you see the source code of each program that's running, so you can edit that source code and see how your changes affect the program. You can still do this with a compiler, but having to compile a program and then store a separate executable version of that program is a minor annoyance that you can avoid completely just by using an interpreter.

Compilers are great for distributing programs. Interpreters are much better for writing and running shorter programs when you don't care whether anyone can see or copy the source code.

Compiling to a Virtual Machine

The problem with compilers is that they're difficult to make for multiple operating systems and processors. The problem with interpreters is that they need the source code of a program to run, making interpreters unsuitable for distributing software. To solve both these problems, computer scientists created a third alternative — a virtual machine (VM).

TECHNICAL STUFF

To speed up programs, computer scientists have developed just-in-time (JIT) compilers. These types of compilers translate code into native code on the fly, making programs run faster than ordinary interpreted programs running on a virtual machine.

To protect the source code of a program, a VM lets you compile your program into an intermediate file called *bytecode* or *pseudocode* (also known as *p-code*). To make a program run on multiple operating systems, you need a VM that runs on each operating system, as shown in Figure 4-4.

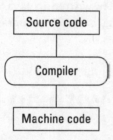

Source code → Compiler → Machine code

A compiler normally converts source code directly into machine code for a specific type of processor.

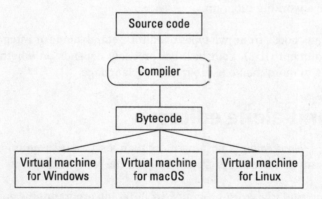

Source code → Compiler → Bytecode → Virtual machine for Windows / Virtual machine for macOS / Virtual machine for Linux

When compiled to bytecode, a program can run on any operating system that has the bytecode virtual machine installed.

FIGURE 4-4:
A virtual machine acts like a combination of an interpreter and a compiler.

TECHNICAL STUFF

When you compile a program into bytecode, it's still possible to *disassemble* (reverse-engineer) that bytecode file and view the original source code.

The most popular programming language that uses a VM is Java (www.oracle.com/java/technologies), which was created by Sun Microsystems and is now owned by Oracle. The idea behind Java is to let you write a single program in Java,

Programming Tools

compile it into a bytecode file, and then distribute that bytecode file to any computer that has a Java VM installed.

Theoretically, you can write a program once and make it run on Linux, macOS, and Windows with no modifications whatsoever. Realistically, you may still need to tweak the program a bit to get it to run flawlessly on different operating systems, but that's still much easier than writing a program from scratch for another operating system.

Despite these drawbacks, Java has grown in popularity. Many companies write and sell programs entirely written in Java. As computers get faster and Oracle improves the performance of its VM, programs written in Java probably will run fast enough for most uses.

Writing a Program with an Editor

To write programs, you need an editor, which acts like a special word processor just for helping you write commands in your favorite programming language. After you type your program commands in an editor, you can save this file (known as the *source code*). Then, you can feed this source code file into a compiler to turn it into a working program.

You can choose from two types of editors: stand-alone or integrated development environment (IDE). Your best bet probably depends on whether you write programs in more than one programming language.

Stand-alone editors

A *stand-alone editor* is nothing more than a separate program that you run when you want to edit your program. You run the compiler separately.

TIP

If you regularly write programs in different programming languages, you may want to use a stand-alone editor. That way you can get familiar with all the features of a single editor.

You can buy stand-alone editors, but here are two popular free ones; both of these editors run on multiple operating systems (such as Linux, macOS, and Windows):

>> GNU Emacs (www.gnu.org/software/emacs/emacs.html)

>> VIM (www.vim.org)

TIP

The nearby sidebar, "Common editor features," lists features you find in most editors, including stand-alone editors.

COMMON EDITOR FEATURES

Whether you prefer a stand-alone editor or an integrated development environment, most editors offer the following features:

- **Multiple undo/redo commands** let you experiment with making changes to your source code. If they don't work out, you can undo your changes. Typically, editors let you undo a large number of changes you made, such as the last 100 changes.

- **Multiple file editing** comes in handy so you can view different files in separate windows and copy code from one window to another, or just study how one part of your program will interact with another part of that same program.

- **Syntax completion and highlighting** is when the editor recognizes certain programming languages, such as C++ and Java. The moment you type a valid language command, the editor can finish typing that command for you at the touch of a button, thereby saving you time. So, if you type a typical if-then statement, the editor automatically types in a generic if-then statement (complete with necessary parentheses), so you just type in the actual data to use.

- **Syntax highlighting** occurs after you write a program; the editor highlights valid language commands to help you separate language commands from any data and commands you create. Without syntax highlighting, source code can look like a mass of text. With syntax highlighting, source code can be easier to read and understand.

- **Automatic indentation and parentheses matching** where indentation can align your code to make it follow a standard indentation format while parentheses matching helps you identify where an opening parenthesis, square bracket, or curly bracket begins and ends.

- **Macros** let you customize the editor and essentially program the editor to repeat commonly needed tasks, such as always displaying program commands in uppercase letters. If the editor doesn't offer a feature you want or need, its macro language lets you add that feature. Without a macro language, an editor won't give you the flexibility to work the way you want.

- **Project management** helps you keep your source code files organized. Most programs no longer consist of a single file but of multiple files. Trying to keep track of which files belong to which project can be confusing, so an editor can help you store and organize your files so you won't lose track of them.

Integrated development environments

An IDE combines an editor with a compiler in a single program so you can easily edit a program and compile it right away. It gives you access to these features within a consistent user interface (UI), as shown in Figure 4-5.

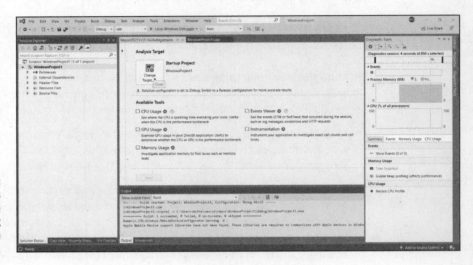

FIGURE 4-5:
An IDE provides access to multiple programming tools within a single UI.

TIP

If you mostly write programs in a single programming language, using an IDE can be more convenient than a stand-alone editor.

Features

In addition to a compiler and all the usual features of stand-alone editors (see the "Common editor features" sidebar), many IDEs include other features in a convenient UI:

>> A **debugger** helps identify problems in your program.

>> **File management** helps organize the source code for your various projects.

>> A **profiler** helps identify which parts of your program may be slowing down the performance of your entire program.

>> A **graphical user interface (GUI) designer** helps you design the appearance of your program's windows, drop-down lists, and buttons.

Free software

Many compilers come with their own IDE, but you can always use another IDE or a stand-alone editor instead. These IDEs are popular (and free):

>> **Apache NetBeans** (https://netbeans.apache.org): Designed for writing Java programs, it can be used for writing C and C++ programs as well. NetBeans is available for multiple operating systems.

>> **Atom** (https://atom.io): Atom is an open-source editor for Linux, macOS, and Windows.

>> **Eclipse** (www.eclipse.org): Designed for writing Java programs, it can also be used for writing C, C++, PHP, and even COBOL programs. Eclipse is available for multiple operating systems.

Fixing a Program with a Debugger

Eventually, everyone makes a mistake writing a program. That mistake could be as simple as incorrectly typing a command or forgetting a closing parenthesis, or it could be as complicated as an algorithm that works perfectly except when receiving certain data. Because writing error-free programs is nearly impossible, most programmers use a special tool called a *debugger.*

REMEMBER

Program errors are called *bugs*, so a debugger helps you find and eliminate bugs in your program.

Two common debugger features include

>> Stepping or tracing

>> Variable watching

TECHNICAL STUFF

Not all bugs are created equal:

>> Some bugs are just annoying, such as the wrong color on a drop-down list.

>> Some bugs are critical, such as a bug that adds two numbers wrong in an accounting program.

>> Any bug that keeps a program from running correctly is a showstopper.

Stepping line-by-line

Stepping or *tracing* lets you run your program line-by-line, so you can see exactly what the program is doing at any given time. The second you see your program doing something wrong, you also see the exact command in your program that caused that problem. Then you can fix the problem, as shown in Figure 4-6.

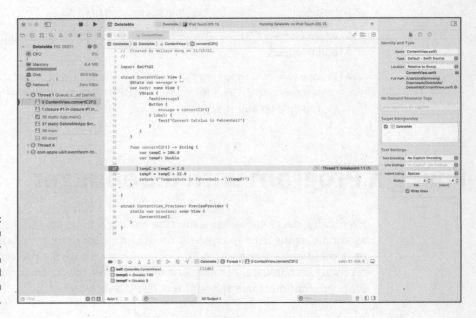

FIGURE 4-6:
Stepping through a program, line-by-line, can help you find errors or bugs in your program.

REMEMBER

Sometimes when programmers find one error and fix it, their fix accidentally creates another error in the program.

Here are the two types of debuggers:

TECHNICAL STUFF

» **Source level:** Lets you examine your source code line-by-line. So if you write a program in C++, a source-level debugger shows you each line of your entire C++ program.

» **Machine language:** Lets you examine the machine language code, line-by-line, that your compiler created from your source code. Programmers often use machine-language debuggers to examine programs when they don't have access to the source code, such as a computer virus or a rival's program.

Stepping line-by-line through a small program may be feasible, but in a large program that consists of a million lines of code, stepping line-by-line would take far too long. So, to make stepping easier, most debuggers include breakpoints and stepping over/stepping out commands.

Breakpoints

A *breakpoint* lets you skip over the parts of your program that you already know work. So, if you have a program that's 10,000 lines long and you know the problem is somewhere in the last 1,000 lines of code, there's no point in stepping through those first 9,000 lines of code.

A breakpoint lets you tell the computer, "Skip from the beginning of the program to the breakpoint, and then step through the rest of the program line-by-line." Figure 4-7 shows how you can highlight a line with a breakpoint. That way your program runs from the beginning to the first breakpoint. After your program stops at a breakpoint, you can step through the rest of your program line-by-line.

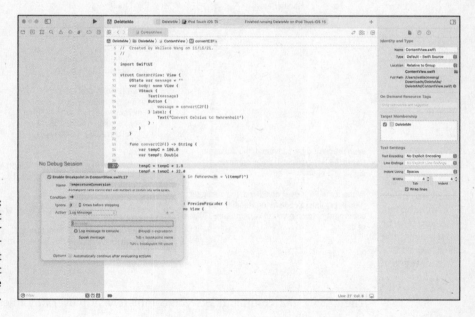

FIGURE 4-7: Breakpoints let you skip over parts of your program that you don't want to examine line-by-line.

Over and out

The stepping over and stepping out commands are used to debug a large program that consists of multiple subprograms. Normally, stepping would force you to examine every subprogram, line-by-line. However, what if you know the problem isn't in a specific subprogram?

By using the step over and step out commands, you can avoid stepping through lines of code stored in a subprogram.

STEP OVER

To avoid stepping through every subprogram, debuggers let you use the step over command. This command tells the computer, "See that entire subprogram? Treat it as a single command, and don't bother stepping through it line-by-line." Figure 4-8 shows how the step over command works.

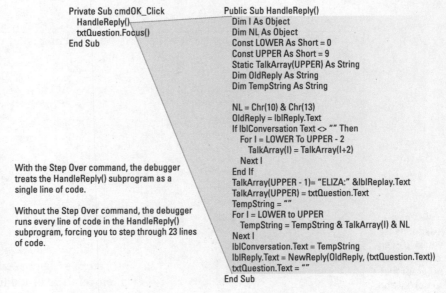

FIGURE 4-8:
The step over command lets you skip, or "step over," the lines stored in a subprogram.

The step over command lets you completely skip over any lines of code stored inside of a subprogram.

STEP OUT

Suppose you start examining a subprogram line-by-line and suddenly want to stop. As an alternative to stepping through the rest of the subprogram, you can use the step out command, which tells the computer, "Stop stepping through the subprogram line-by-line right now!"

Watching variables

When you step or trace through a program, line-by-line, you can see how the program works. For more insight into your program's behavior, you can *watch your variables.*

TIP

You can read more about variables in Book 2, Chapter 2. For now, just think of a *variable* as a temporary place to store data, such as a number or a word.

Watching a variable lets you see what data your program is storing and using at any given time. That way, if your program is supposed to print a name but actually prints that person's phone number, you can step through your program line-by-line and watch to see which line stores the wrong data for the program to print.

Not only can you "watch" how your program stores data, but a debugger lets you change data while your program is running. By changing data, you can see how your program responds.

For example, suppose a program converts temperatures between Celsius and Fahrenheit. If you store a valid temperature, such as 15, you can see how your program handles the number 15. But what happens if the user types in an invalid number, such as 500000 or -170000?

To find out how and why your program seems to randomly change the temperature, you can step through your program and watch the number stored as the age. By changing your variable while the program is running, you can type in different temperature values to see how your program responds.

TIP

When testing different values, always start off with values for which you already know how your program should respond. For example, a temperature of 0 in Celsius should be 32 in Fahrenheit. Likewise, a temperature of 100 in Celsius should be 212 in Fahrenheit.

Without the ability to change the value of variables while the program is running, debugging a program is much slower and more tedious. By changing the value of variables while the program is running, you can test different values without having to trace through the program multiple times using different values. Just run the program once, and change the value of the variable as many times as you want, as shown in Figure 4-9.

Programming Tools

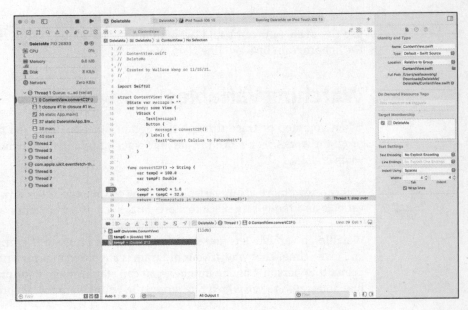

FIGURE 4-9: Watching and changing variables can show you how a program reacts to different data.

Saving Time with Third-Party Components

Programmers are naturally lazy and often look for the simplest way to solve any problem. When faced with creating a program, programmers prefer to cheat by using *third-party components*, which are programs that somebody else has created already (and, hopefully, tested).

Third-party components usually offer commonly needed features, such as a word processor, a spreadsheet, or a database, that you can plug into your own program. So, instead of having to write your own word processor, you can buy a word processor component and plug it into your own program — now your program has word-processing capabilities with little additional programming on your part.

WARNING

Third-party components can give your program instant features, but they can also give you instant problems, too. If the third-party component doesn't work right, your program won't work right either, and you can't fix the problem until the company that sells the third-party component fixes the problem. Basically, third-party components put you at the mercy of another company. If that other company stops updating and improving their component, you're stuck with an outdated and possibly buggy component.

Depending on the features, third-party components can range in cost from a few hundred dollars to a few thousand dollars or more. Most third-party components aren't cheap, but because they can save you a lot of time, they may be worth the price.

Optimizing a Program with a Profiler

Not all parts of a program are equal. Some parts of a program may run only once or twice, whereas other parts of a program may run hundreds or even thousands of times. For example, suppose you have a program that stores names and addresses. To use this program, you must first type in your name and password before you can sort and search through the program's list of names and addresses.

In this example, the part of the program that asks for a username and password runs only once, but the part of the program that searches and sorts through your list of names and addresses may run multiple times. So, which part of your program determines its speed? The part that runs once (asking for a username and password) or the part that runs multiple times (searching and sorting names and addresses)?

Obviously, if you wanted to speed up your program, you'd focus on the part that runs most often, and that's what a profiler does. A *profiler* examines your program and identifies the most frequently used parts of that program. After you know which parts of your program run most often, you can work on making that part of the program run faster, a process known as *optimizing*.

Profilers typically use two methods for examining a program:

» **Sampling:** Sampling examines your entire program at fixed time intervals. Through sampling, a profiler can get a rough estimate on which parts of your program (often referred to as *hot spots*) are being run most often.

» **Instrumentation mode:** After you use sampling to identify hot spots, you can use this mode to examine the program in more detail to determine exactly what each program line does and how much time it takes.

By identifying the hot spots, you can speed up your entire program by rewriting or optimizing those frequently run parts of the program.

By optimizing a small part of your program, such as 10 percent of it, you can often improve the entire program's performance dramatically.

TIP

Managing Source Code

In the old days, programs were often created by an individual or small teams of people who worked in the same room. If they needed to talk to each other or share code, they could simply copy files from one computer to another.

However, as programs have gotten much larger and more complicated, it has become common for multiple teams to work on a single program. Even worse, these separate teams may be located in completely different parts of the world and in different time zones. How can multiple teams work on the same program simultaneously? The answer is through version control or source management.

The problem is that at any given time, only one person can work on a program. Because most large programs are divided into multiple files, all files get stored in a central repository so there's only one copy of a program.

When someone needs to edit the program, they can check out the file they need. When they check out the file, the repository stops anyone else from checking out that same file. That way two or more people don't try to modify separate copies of the same file and then wind up not knowing which version of the file to use in the future.

When someone gets done editing a file, they can return it back to the repository for someone else to check out. Although there's only one copy of a file that others can check out, the repository will often save the previous versions of each file. That way, if a modified version of a file causes catastrophic errors, it's easy to revert back to the previous version of that same file.

Sometimes two or more programmers will be allowed to check out the same file, and when they're done, the version control software can merge the two different file versions into a single, new version. However, merging changes made in separate copies of a file can cause problems if the changes in one file interfere with the changes in another file.

For example, suppose one programmer deletes a function in a file because it causes problems, but a second programmer writes new code that relies on that function. Merging the two changed files will then be tricky because if the deleted function is added or kept out of the file, it risks causing problems either way.

Whether a program is small or massive, it can benefit from version control management. Version control makes sure you always work with the latest approved versions of a file and that you'll always have backup copies to fall back on in case you make a mistake.

If you work alone, version control management can keep you from losing crucial data. If you work in teams, version control management can improve everyone's efficiency by making it easy to work on multiple files simultaneously.

Creating a Help File

Hardly anyone reads software manuals, so when people need help, they typically turn to the program's help file for answers. This help file is essentially the software manual organized as miniature web pages that you can view and click to see similar (linked) information.

Almost every program has a help file but creating a help file can be tedious and time-consuming. So, to simplify this process, many programmers use special help file creation programs.

Just as a word processor makes it easy to write, edit, and format text, help file creators make it easy to write, edit, organize, and link text together to create a help file.

Installing a Program

Before anyone can use your program, they need to install it. Some programs are simple enough that the user can simply copy it where they want to store it. However, most programs consist of multiple files that may require creating new folders to store data or allow access to the Internet.

Installation programs simply automate the process of storing a program on a computer to make the process as simple and easy as possible. This may include adding shortcuts or icons to the computer for faster access to running the program.

Even if a program is simple enough to be copied as a single file, it's usually best to use an installation program to install that program instead. That way you can be certain all files are copied in the correct location.

Dissecting Programs with a Disassembler

A disassembler acts like a reverse compiler. A compiler converts your program (written in any programming language, such as C++ or Swift) into machine language; a disassembler takes an executable file (which contains machine-language code) and converts it into assembly language.

TECHNICAL STUFF

Disassemblers can't convert machine language back into its original source code language (such as C++) because disassemblers can't tell which programming language was originally used. An executable file created from a C++ program looks no different from an executable file created from a Kotlin or Swift program. Therefore, disassemblers can only convert machine language into assembly language.

Disassemblers have both honorable and shady uses. On the honorable side, antivirus companies use disassemblers to dissect how the latest viruses, worms, and Trojan horses work. After they know how these nasty programs work, they can figure out how to detect, stop, and remove them.

On the shady side, many companies use disassemblers to tear apart their rivals' products and see how they work. After you know how a competitor's program works, you can copy those features and use them in your own program.

Programming languages, such as C#, Java, and Visual Basic .NET, get compiled into bytecode format; therefore, a disassembler can reverse-compile a bytecode file into its original source code. So, if you compile a Java program into bytecode format, a Java disassembler can convert the bytecode file into Java source code. Likewise, if you compile a C# or Visual Basic .NET program, you can disassemble that bytecode file into its original C# or Visual Basic .NET source code.

To protect their bytecode files from disassemblers, programmers use another program called an *obfuscator.* An obfuscator essentially scrambles a bytecode file. The bytecode file can still run, but if other people try to disassemble an obfuscated bytecode file, they can't retrieve the original source code.

TIP

If you use a programming language that compiles into bytecode (such as C#, Java, or Visual Basic .NET), consider using an obfuscator to protect your source code from prying eyes.

At the bare minimum, all you need is an editor (to write programs) and a compiler (to convert your programs into executable files). However, most programmers use a debugger, version control software, and an installer. Although most programmers are happy when they can get their programs to work, some programmers use a profiler to help them speed up and optimize their program.

Finally, some programmers use disassemblers to peek inside the inner workings of other programs, such as viruses or rival software. Disassemblers are never necessary for creating a program, but they can prove useful for legal and not-so-legal purposes.

The tools of a programmer are highly subjective. Some programmers swear by certain tools, such as their favorite editor or compiler, whereas others are happy with whatever tool is available. Just remember that programmer tools can help you write faster and more reliable programs, but the best tool in the world can never substitute for decent programming skills in the first place.

Programming Basics

2

Contents at a Glance

Chapter **1**

How Programs Work

Programming is nothing more than problem-solving. Every program is designed to solve a specific problem, such as taking the trouble out of editing text (a word processor), calculating rows and columns of numbers (spreadsheets), or searching and sorting information (a database). Even a video game solves the problem of keeping players entertained for hours at a time.

Before you write any program, you must first know what problem you want the computer to solve. Computers are best at solving repetitive tasks, such as calculating rows and columns of numbers in a spreadsheet. Anyone can do similar calculations by hand, but computers make the task much faster and more accurate.

After you know what problem to solve, the next step is figuring out how to solve that problem. Many problems may have multiple solutions. For example, how can someone get from the airport to your house? One way may be to take the highway, which may be the simplest route although not necessarily the fastest. Another way may take you through winding roads that can be harder to navigate.

In general, every problem has multiple solutions, and each solution has pros and cons. Should you tell someone to take the shortest way to your house (which may be harder to follow) or the easiest way to your house (which may take longer)?

Computer programs face this same dilemma in choosing the "best" solution. One solution may be slow but require less memory to run. Another solution may be fast but require gobs of memory. When deciding on a solution, you always have to consider additional factors, such as what type of computer the program runs on, what type of environment the program is used in, and what type of people are using it.

After you choose a solution, the next step involves dissecting how your chosen solution works so you can translate those steps into instructions for the computer to follow.

Every program consists of step-by-step instructions. Just as you can write the same instructions for a person in English, French, Spanish, Arabic, or Japanese, so can you write the same program for a computer in different programming languages.

You can literally write a program with thousands of possible programming languages. Every programming language is designed to solve some problems exceptionally well but may solve other types of problems poorly.

For example, the BASIC programming language is meant to teach programming, but it's not very good for controlling the hardware of a computer, such as for writing an operating system or antivirus program. On the other hand, the C programming language is meant to give you absolute control over every part of the computer, which is why most operating systems and antivirus programs are written in C. However, the C language can be much more frustrating and confusing for novices to understand than BASIC is.

Ideally, you want to pick the programming language best suited for solving your particular problem. Realistically, you probably know only a handful of programming languages, so out of all the languages you know, pick the one that's best suited for solving your problem.

REMEMBER

You can write any program in any programming language. The only difference is that some programming languages can make writing certain programs easier than others. The "best" programming language to use is always the language that makes writing a program easy for you.

THE TROLLEY PROBLEM

There's a philosophical thought exercise called the trolley problem, which highlights the fact that some problems may have no good solutions at all. The idea behind the trolley problem is that a runaway trolley is hurtling down the tracks, but you happen to be standing near a switch that can redirect the trolley down a different track.

The dilemma is that if you do nothing, the trolley will hit and kill five people walking on the tracks. However, if you pull the lever to switch the trolley to a different track, the trolley will hit and kill just one person walking along those different tracks.

So, the choice is: Do you let five people die by doing nothing or do you save those five people and deliberately let one other person die? This is essentially the same problem that self-driving car algorithms will face. If a self-driving car drives down a street and a child dashes in front, should the self-driving car hit and kill the child, or should it swerve off the road to save the child, but risk killing the passengers and any pedestrians by the side of the road?

Problems can't always be solved through more processing power. The trolley problem highlights the difficulties programmers face when creating programs that have to make split-second decisions, based on incomplete information.

Some problems have one right answer, but most problems have either multiple answers that are all equally good or multiple answers that are all equally bad.

Using Keywords as Building Blocks

Every program consists of one or more *commands* (instructions), and each command typically represents a single line of code. The more lines of code, the more complicated the program.

REMEMBER

The goal of programming is to write the fewest lines of code that do the maximum amount of work.

Each command tells the computer to do one thing. Put enough commands together, and you can create a simple program, as shown in Figure 1-1.

Every programming language provides a list of commands dubbed *keywords* or *reserved words*. By typing keywords one after another, you can tell the computer what to do.

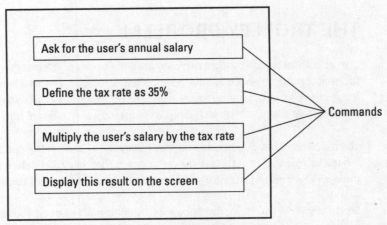

FIGURE 1-1:
If you put enough commands together, you can create any type of program.

A "program" for calculating the amount of taxes you owe based on your salary.

A programming language's keywords act like the letters of the alphabet. Type letters in different combinations, and you can create different words. Type keywords in different combinations, and you can create different commands, as shown in Figure 1-2.

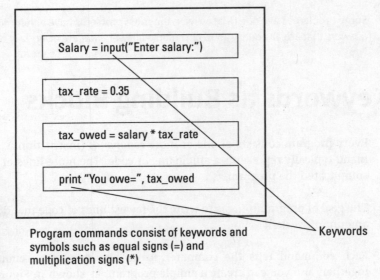

FIGURE 1-2:
Multiple keywords, along with various symbol characters, can create a single command.

Program commands consist of keywords and symbols such as equal signs (=) and multiplication signs (*).

MORE VERSUS FEWER KEYWORDS

Computer scientists are divided on whether it's better for a programming language to offer a lot of keywords. By offering a lot of keywords, a programming language can let programmers write fewer keywords that do more work. By offering *fewer* keywords, a programming language makes programmers write a lot of simple keywords just to do something that another language may be able to do with one keyword.

Given these choices, having a lot of keywords in a programming language seems to make more sense. The problem is that the more keywords that are used, the harder it is to write a compiler for that programming language. And the harder it is to write a compiler, the less efficient that compiler is in converting source code into machine language, just as it's much harder to translate a Russian scientific paper into English than it is to translate a Russian children's story into English.

That's one problem with the Ada programming language. Ada uses lots of keywords, which makes programming easier but creating compilers for Ada much harder. This is one of the reasons why Ada compilers are much less widespread than compilers for the C programming language.

Unlike Ada, C offers a bare minimum of keywords. This makes programming in C harder because you need to write a lot of keywords to do something as seemingly simple as storing a text string. However, C's handful of keywords makes it much easier to write a C compiler.

To compensate for the lack of keywords, most C compilers include libraries of commonly used subprograms that can make C programming easier and more useful.

As a result, you can find C compilers for practically every computer because it's much easier to write a C compiler than it is to write an Ada compiler. The more C compilers available, the easier it is to *port* (transfer) a C program to another computer. The C programming language is popular partly because you can run C programs on almost every computer.

With a lot of keywords, Ada makes programming easier for humans but harder for computers. In contrast, the smaller number of keywords in C makes programming harder for humans but much easier for computers. Given a choice between Ada and C, more people choose C, so having a programming language with fewer keywords seems to be more efficient (at least for the computer).

This creates a dilemma. On the one hand, some programming languages are easier for people to read and understand but harder for computers to compile to create efficient, portable programs. On the other hand, some programming languages are easier for computers to compile but harder for people to read and understand. Programming languages often fall into one category or another, which is partially why some programmers favor one language over another.

Organizing a Program

Every program consists of one or more commands, but there are different types of commands. Some commands tell the computer how to manipulate data, such as adding two numbers together. Other commands may tell the computer how to print data, display it onscreen, or save it on a disc.

Although you could jumble all your commands together and still have a working program (see Book 1, Chapter 2 for more on programs), you can make your program easier to read and modify by organizing similar commands in different parts of your program.

So, if your program isn't printing correctly, you don't have to search through the entire program to find the faulty commands. Instead, you can just look at the part of the program where you grouped all your printing commands, as shown in Figure 1-3.

Printing commands	Math commands
Math commands	Math commands
Saving commands	Saving commands
Math commands	Saving commands
Printing commands	Printing commands
Saving commands	Printing commands
Printing commands	Printing commands

FIGURE 1-3: Dividing a large program into parts can make it easier to find specific commands in your program.

Storing commands with no organization makes the program harder to read and understand.

By just organizing related commands together, you can make a program easier to read and understand.

When you write a simple program that consists of a handful of commands, organizing related commands in groups isn't too important, but when you start writing bigger programs that consist of hundreds or thousands of commands, organizing commands can mean the difference between writing a program that nobody can understand and writing a program that's easy for anyone to understand and modify.

When you save your program, you can save it as a single file on the computer. However, the more commands you write, the bigger your program gets and the bigger the file you need to store the whole program.

No matter how carefully you organize your commands, eventually your program will get too big and cumbersome as a single massive file to read and modify easily. That's when you need to break your program into smaller parts.

Dividing a Program into Subprograms

The smaller the program, the easier it is to write, read, and modify later. So rather than create a massive program, with related commands organized into groups, you can divide a large program into smaller pieces, called *subprograms*.

TECHNICAL STUFF

Every programming language has its own term for dividing a program into smaller pieces. In BASIC, mini-programs are called subprograms, but in C and languages inspired by C, mini-programs are called *functions*. Some other synonyms for mini-programs include *procedures, subroutines,* and *methods.*

Subprograms essentially break up a large program into multiple miniature programs with each miniature program acting like a building block to create a much larger program, as shown in Figure 1-4. So, rather than build a large program entirely out of keywords, you can build a program out of keywords and subprograms (which are themselves made up of keywords).

REMEMBER

Think of subprograms as a way to create keywords that aren't built into the programming language. For example, the C programming language doesn't have any keywords for working with text strings, so programmers have used C's existing keywords to create subprograms that can work with text strings. By using these existing subprograms, other C programmers can manipulate text strings without writing their own commands.

Using keywords alone to create a program is like trying to build a skyscraper out of bricks. It's possible, but it takes a long time to layer enough bricks to reach the height of a typical 50-story skyscraper.

Using subprograms to create a larger program is like using I beams to build a skyscraper. Essentially, I beams act like bigger bricks the same way that subprograms act like bigger building blocks than keywords by themselves.

Math subprogram
Saving subprogram
Printing subprogram

Math commands
Math commands
Saving commands
Saving commands
Printing commands
Printing commands
Printing commands

FIGURE 1-4: Subprograms create reusable building blocks that you can use to make writing programs even easier.

Subprograms act like bigger building blocks that make a large program easier to read and understand.

The program on the left, divided into subprograms, is equivalent to this program with every command visible.

You can store subprograms in two ways:

>> **In one file:** Storing subprograms in the same file is no different from grouping related commands together in one file. It's like storing your socks, underwear, and T-shirts in the same drawer but pushing them into separate corners. The drawer may be organized, but such an arrangement is suitable only if you don't have many clothes to worry about. When you get more clothes, you need a bigger drawer to hold it all. The same holds true with storing subprograms in a single file. Eventually, if you group enough commands into subprograms, a single file crammed full of subprograms can still be cumbersome to read and modify.

>> **In separate files:** To keep files down to a reasonable size, programmers store subprograms in separate files, as shown in Figure 1-5. Not only does this avoid cramming everything into a single file, but separate files also give you the option of creating reusable libraries of subprograms that you can copy and reuse in another program.

TIP

Libraries of subprograms, stored as separate files, make it easy to reuse code in multiple projects. When you create a subprogram that works reliably, you can share this subprogram with others so they don't have to write their own subprogram and test it.

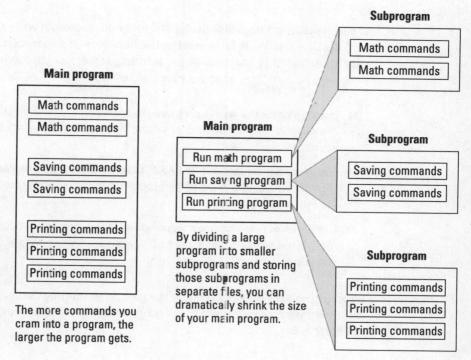

FIGURE 1-5: Storing subprograms in separate files can make it easier to read and modify one part of a large program without having to see any other part of that same program.

The more commands you cram into a program, the larger the program gets.

By dividing a large program into smaller subprograms and storing those subprograms in separate files, you can dramatically shrink the size of your main program.

Programmers often sell their libraries of subprograms to others, although each library of subprograms is usually designed to work only with a specific programming language and operating system, such as C++ running on Windows. Many Windows libraries of subprograms are stored as dynamic link libraries (DLLs) although you may see some libraries sold as something called *.NET components*.

The name simply tells you what type of programming languages and computers you can use the programming library on. So, if you're using a programming language that can use .NET components, you can use subprogram libraries stored as .NET components.

TECHNICAL STUFF

When you get a library of subprograms (for free or for a fee), you may also get the source code to those subprograms. With the source code, you can modify the subprograms. However, most subprogram libraries don't include the source code, so you have to pay for an updated version of the subprogram library in the future.

By storing subprograms in separate files, you can write a program in multiple programming languages. That way, you can write your main program in C++ and then write subprograms in C or Java. By doing this, you don't have to limit yourself to the strengths and weaknesses of a single programming language. Instead, you can take advantage of the strengths of each programming language.

If you're writing a hard disk diagnostic program, you could write the whole thing in C because C is great for accessing the hardware of a computer. However, you may find that C is too clumsy for printing reports or displaying information onscreen. In that case, what are your choices? You can

>> **Use C to write the whole program.** This option is great for accessing computer hardware but hard for writing the rest of the program, like the user interface (UI).

>> **Use an easier language, like BASIC, to write the whole program.** This is great for writing every part of the program except the part needed to access the computer hardware.

>> **Use a mix of two or more programming languages.** Use BASIC to write most of the program and then use C to write a subprogram to access the computer hardware.

By giving you the option to choose the best programming language for a specific task, subprograms help make it easier for you to write larger programs, as shown in Figure 1-6.

Written in the C
programming language

Written in the BASIC
programming language

Written in the C
programming language

| User Interface |
| Examine hard disk |
| Displaying report |
| Printing |
| Save report |

| User Interface |
| Displaying report |
| Printing |
| Save report |

| Examine hard disk |

FIGURE 1-6: Subprograms give you the option of using different programming languages to write different parts of a larger program.

A large program may consist of several subprograms all written in the same programming language.

Storing subprograms in separate files gives you the option of writing subprograms in a different programming language.

Dividing a Program into Objects

The more complicated programs get, the larger they get. If programs get too big, they get harder to write, understand, and modify. This is why dividing a large program into multiple smaller subprograms can make programming much easier. Just write a bunch of little programs and then paste them together to create a bigger program.

Unfortunately, dividing a large program into subprograms isn't without its problems. In theory, if you want to update a program, you can modify a subprogram and plug that modified subprogram back into the main program to create an updated version.

In reality, that almost never works. The problem comes from the fact that subprograms aren't always independent entities that you can yank out and replace without affecting the rest of the program. Sometimes one subprogram relies on data manipulated by a second subprogram. Change that first subprogram, and those changes could affect the first subprogram in a domino-like effect, as shown in Figure 1-7.

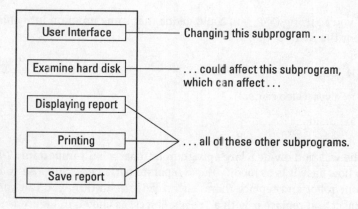

FIGURE 1-7:
Changing one part of a program can affect other parts of that same program.

TECHNICAL STUFF

When subprograms are highly dependent on each other, they're *high, strong,* or *tight coupling.* When subprograms aren't dependent on each other, they're *low, weak,* or *loose coupling.* You want your subprograms to have low, weak, or loose coupling. That way, changing one part of your program doesn't accidentally affect another part of your program.

To enforce weak coupling, computer scientists have created *object-oriented programming* (OOP). The main idea behind OOP is to divide a large program into objects.

Objects act like "super" subprograms. Whereas subprograms give programmers the choice of making a tightly or loosely coupled subprogram, objects encourage programmers to create loosely coupled subprograms.

By encouraging programmers to create loosely coupled subprograms, objects make it easy to modify a program without worrying about any unintended side effects. OOP lets you yank out an object, modify it, and plug it back in without worrying if your changes may affect the rest of the program.

Objects offer another advantage over subprograms. Whereas subprograms typically represent a specific action, objects represent specific physical items in the real world.

For example, if you're writing a program to control a robot, you could divide the program into the following subprograms that make the robot:

>> Move

>> Sense obstacles (through sight and touch) in its way

>> Navigate

If you're using OOP, you could divide that same program into objects that represent the robot's

>> Legs

>> Eyes (video camera)

>> Brain

The way you divide a large program into parts isn't important. What's important is how easy it is to modify those separate parts later. Suppose you rip the legs off your robot and replace them with treads. In an OOP, you can yank out the Legs object and replace it with a Treads object, as shown in Figure 1-8.

Although the robot now uses treads instead of legs to move, the Brain object can still give the same type of commands to make the robot move, such as Move Forward, Move Backward, and Stop.

How do you change the equivalent program divided into subprograms? First, you have to change the Move subprogram to reflect the change in movement from legs to treads. Then you may need to change the Navigate subprogram so it knows how to navigate in different directions with treads instead of legs. Finally, you need to make sure the changes you make in the Navigate and Move subprograms don't accidentally affect the Sense subprogram.

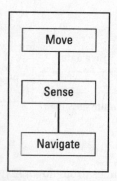

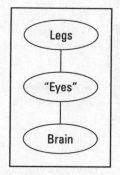

FIGURE 1-8: Object-oriented programming divides your program into logical parts that correspond to the real world.

Subprograms are often tightly coupled with each other, so making changes in one subprogram can affect other subprograms.

Objects divide a program into logical, real world components that are loosely coupled to each other.

Sounds like a lot of work just to make a simple change, doesn't it? That's why loose coupling between subprograms is so important. Programmers can't always be trusted to make sure their subprograms are loosely coupling, so OOP makes it easier to do, which can make it easier to modify a program later.

Creating a User Interface

The three actions of most programs are:

1. Get data.

2. Manipulate that data.

3. Display a result.

A football-picking program takes in data about both teams, uses a formula to predict a winner, and prints or displays its answer onscreen. A hotel reservation program gets a request for a room from the user (hotel clerk), scans its list of rooms for one that's available and that matches the user's criteria (no smoking, two beds, and so on), and displays that result onscreen.

Basically, every program takes in data, calculates a result, and displays that result. To accept data from the user and display a result back to the user again, every program needs a UI, as shown in Figure 1-9.

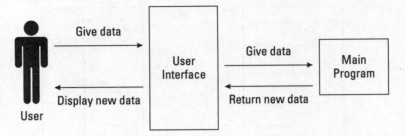

FIGURE 1-9:
The UI accepts
data and displays
the results of
its calculations
back to the user.

REMEMBER

The UI of most computer programs includes drop-down lists, buttons, and dialog boxes. If a program doesn't get data from a person, its UI may be just a physical cable connection because its user could be another computer feeding it information like stock quotes.

To create a program, you have to create both your program and your UI. The UI acts like a middleman between the user and the program. Here are some common ways to create a UI:

>> Create it from scratch by writing code.

>> Use a subprogram library.

>> Use a rapid application development (RAD) tool.

Creating your own UI takes time to write and even more time to test. Although there's nothing wrong with creating your own UI, the time you spend creating a UI could be better spent writing your actual program. For that reason, few programmers create their own UIs unless they have special needs, such as designing a UI for scuba divers to use underwater.

Because creating a UI can be so troublesome and most UIs look alike anyway, some programmers create libraries of subprograms that do nothing but create a UI. That way you can create your program, slap on the UI by adding the library of subprograms, and have a finished program.

Such UI libraries can be particularly handy for creating a UI quickly. For example, many financial applications use charts to display data. If you wanted to create and display bar, pie, line, spider, radar, or stock charts, you could either write code to create these charts yourself (time-consuming) or buy a library of subprograms that can already do this. That way, you could save time by just combining this library with your own program.

Because nearly every program needs a UI and most UIs look the same anyway (at least on the same operating systems, such as Windows, Android, macOS, or iOS), programmers have created RAD tools that simplify creating UIs, as shown in Figure 1-10.

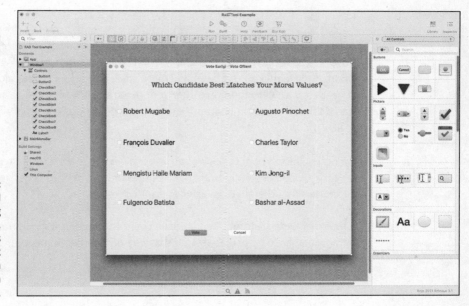

FIGURE 1-10:
Creating a UI involves picking common items, such as buttons and check boxes, and then drawing them on a window.

A RAD tool lets you drag and drop items to create a UI without writing any code at all. The only time you need to write code is to make your program respond to that UI.

PROGRAMMING IS ABOUT MAINTAINING EXISTING PROGRAMS

Creating a new program can be fun and exciting. In the real world, it's also extremely rare. That's because there's less of a need to create new programs and a far more pressing need to maintain existing programs.

Maintenance involves fixing bugs, adding new features, or optimizing code. No matter how stable or useful a program might be, programs often need to be modified over time. Adding new features is a great marketing tactic to convince more people to buy that particular program.

Fixing bugs is necessary but far less glamorous compared to adding new features. Operating systems constantly need updates to patch bugs and security flaws, but other programs often need patching to make them more reliable.

Adding new features can increase the power of a program, while fixing bugs can make a program more reliable. Both of these tasks translate into greater profitability.

(continued)

(continued)

That's why companies often ignore the third maintenance task of optimizing or refactoring code because optimizing code simply means going through an existing program and rewriting code to make it run faster and more efficiently or yanking out old code that isn't needed at all. Refactoring can often reduce the size of a program and make it run faster at the same time, but because it's such an arduous process, it's often done rarely, if at all.

If a program (mostly) works, people see less of a need to make it run faster and take up less space. Customers always want new features or want to have bugs fixed. Customers may not care if a program runs faster or takes up less space.

Because maintenance forms the bulk of software engineering, it's important to write programs that are easy to understand. That way, other programmers can easily add new features, fix bugs, and optimize your code.

Chapter **2**

Variables, Data Types, and Constants

E very program consists of a list of instructions that tell the computer what to do. The simplest program consists of a single instruction, such as one that tells the computer to display the words Hello, world! onscreen.

Of course, any program that does the same thing over and over again isn't very useful or interesting. What makes a program useful is when it can accept information from the outside world and then respond to that information.

So, instead of just displaying Hello, world! onscreen, a more useful program might ask for the user to type a name in so the program could display Hello, Bob!

Programs don't always have to get information from a person. Sometimes, programs can retrieve data that's stored somewhere else, such as a list of employees stored on another computer.

That program could access a database over a network and determine which person has been assigned to which computer in the building. Then the program can retrieve each person's name so when they turn on the computer, the program displays their name on the screen.

An even more sophisticated program could work with a webcam hooked up to the computer along with a database that includes employee names and their photographs. So every time any computer's webcam spots someone sitting at the computer, the program could examine the person's image through the webcam, compare that image to the photographs of all employees stored in the database, and then find the name that matches the person. Then the program could display that person's name onscreen.

To be useful, every program needs to retrieve and respond to data from an outside source whether it comes from a person, a device such as a webcam, or even another computer program. Where the data comes from is less important than what the program does with the data after the program receives it.

Declaring Variables

If somebody handed you a $20 bill, you could put it in your pocket. When someone hands a program some data, the program also needs a place to put that data. Programs don't have pockets to store stuff, so they store stuff in a computer's memory.

However, keeping track of specific memory locations in a computer can be tedious (that's partly why assembly language is so complicated and confusing). Instead of forcing programmers to manipulate specific memory locations (called *registers*), programming languages let you store data in abstract locations called *variables.*

Just as your pockets can hold money, rocks, or dead frogs, so can a variable hold different types of data, such as numbers or words. The contents of a variable can vary, which is why they're called *variables.*

REMEMBER

The whole purpose of variables is to make a program more flexible. Instead of behaving the same way using identical data, programs can retrieve, store, and respond to data from the outside world.

You can't shove anything in your pockets until you have a pocket. Likewise, you can't shove any data in a variable until you first create that variable. To create a variable, you must first *declare* the variable.

Declaring a variable tells the computer, "I need a pocket to store data." When you declare a variable, the computer carves up a chunk of its memory for your program to use for storing data. You don't need to know exactly where in memory the computer is going to store your data. You just need to know that you can retrieve that data later.

Of course, you can't just dump data in a variable without knowing how to find it again. In the real world, you can find something by remembering whether you stored it in the left or right pocket. In a program, you can remember where you stored data by giving a variable a unique name. When you create a variable, you declare that variable's name at the same time as the following Swift code demonstrates:

```
var x = 9
```

This Swift code tells the computer the following:

1. Create a variable (using a keyword called var).

2. Give that variable an arbitrary name such as x.

3. Store the number 9 in the variable named x.

Variable naming conventions

Variable names are for your convenience only; the computer doesn't care what names you choose for your variables. Computers are perfectly happy using generic variable names, like X or Y, but the more descriptive the name, the easier it will be for you (or another programmer) to understand what type of data the variable holds.

For example, looking at the earlier Swift code of var x = 9, can you tell what the x or the 9 represents? Now look at the same code, but using a descriptive variable name:

```
var baseballPlayers = 9
```

By just changing the variable x to a more descriptive baseballPlayers name, you can guess that the number 9 refers to the number of players on a baseball team.

Variable names can be as simple as a single word, such as Age, Name, or Salary. However, a single word may not adequately describe the contents of some variables, so programmers often use two or more words for their variable names.

This is where different programmers use different styles. Some programmers like to cram multiple words into one long variable name like this:

```
salestax
```

For two words, this can be acceptable, but when you're creating variable names out of three or more words, this can start getting messy:

```
salestaxfor2008
```

To help identify the separate words that make up a long variable name, some programmers use the underscore character (_):

```
sales_tax_for_2008
```

Other programmers prefer to use uppercase letters at the beginning of each new word:

```
SalesTaxFor2008
```

You can always mix and match both conventions if you want:

```
SalesTaxFor_2008
```

No matter which naming style you prefer, it's best to stick with one style to prevent your program from looking too confusing with lots of different variable naming styles all over the place.

REMEMBER

Every variable needs a unique name. If you try to give two variables identical names, the computer gets confused and refuses to run your program. In some languages, the new variable will overwrite the earlier, identically named variable, which probably isn't what you want.

WARNING

In some languages, such as the curly-bracket family, which includes C, C++, C#, Java, and Swift, variable names are case-sensitive. So, the `salestax` variable is completely different from the `SalesTax` variable.

Creating variables in a command

The simplest way to create a variable is when you need it in a command. Suppose you have a program that asks the user for his annual salary, such as the following command (written in the Python programming language):

```
salary = input("What is your annual salary?")
```

This command displays, `What is your annual salary?` onscreen and waits for the user to type in a number.

CAMEL-CASE NAMING

One common way to create consistent, descriptive variable names is called *camel case,* which gets its name because the way capital letters are used resemble the humps of a camel. The idea behind camel case is that the first letter of every variable is lowercase, but the first letter of each additional word is uppercase, like this:

```
thisIsAnExampleOfCamelCase
```

Camel case is just one way to standardize the appearance and naming of variables. Feel free to develop your own naming style, but keep in mind that using a naming convention that's common within a specific programming language can make it easier for other programmers to understand your code. When you're familiar with using camel case (or any other naming convention), you'll have a much easier time understanding other people's code as well.

As soon as the user types in a number, such as **20000**, the program needs a variable to store this number. In this example, the program creates a `salary` variable and stores the number `20000` in that variable.

Creating variables whenever you need them in a command is simple and convenient — and potentially troublesome if you aren't careful. The biggest problem is that when you create a variable within a command, that variable can store any type of data.

Two types of common data that variables can hold include

>> **Numbers:** Typically used to represent quantities or measurements

>> **Text:** Sometimes called *strings,* as in "text strings"; used to represent non-numeric data, such as names or mailing addresses

You can always perform mathematical calculations on numbers, but never on text. So, if a program expects to store a number in a variable, it gets confused if it receives text instead. The following Python program works perfectly just as long as the user types in a number.

```python
salary = float(input("What is your annual salary?"))
taxrate = 0.30
print ("This is how much you owe in taxes = ", salary * taxrate)
```

This program works as follows:

>> **Line 1:** The program displays, "What is your annual salary?" and then waits for the user to type in a number. If the user types in **20000**, the program stores the string 20000 in the salary variable but then converts it to a float (decimal) number.

>> **Line 2:** Store the number 0.30 in the taxrate variable.

>> **Line 3:** Multiply the number in the salary variable by the number in the taxrate variable and print out the result. If the salary variable holds the number 20000, the program prints, "This is how much you owe in taxes = 6000.0".

Instead of typing the number **20000**, what if the user types **20,000**? Because the program doesn't recognize 20,000 as a valid number (because of the comma), the program treats 20,000 as text that's no different than **twenty thousand**. Trying to multiply the number 0.30 by the text twenty thousand doesn't make sense, so the program stops running, as shown in Figure 2-1.

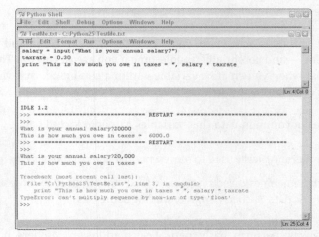

FIGURE 2-1:
If a program tries to store the wrong type of data in a variable, the program stops running.

Declaring the data type of a variable

You can never stop users from typing in the wrong type of data, such as typing in the words **twenty thousand** instead of the number 20000. However, you can protect yourself from trying to do something wrong, like multiplying a number by text. In the Python programming language, the following program actually runs:

```
salary = input("What is your annual salary?")
taxrate = "Thirty percent"
print ("This is how much you owe in taxes = ", salary * taxrate)
```

In this program, the third line tries to multiple the `salary` variable by the `taxrate` variable. If the program asks the user, "What is your annual salary?", and the user types **20000**, the third line of the program tries to multiply the number 20000 (stored in the `salary` variable) by the text `Thirty percent`. Obviously, you can't multiply a number by a word, so this program would appear to work but prints only:

```
This is how much you owe in taxes =
```

The problem occurs because the program multiplies the `salary` variable by the text `Thirty percent`. This causes the program to crash.

If you're writing a small program, you could examine your program, line-by-line, to see where the problem might be, but in a large program that consists of thousands of lines, trying to track down this simple problem could be time-consuming and frustrating.

To avoid this problem, many programming languages force you to *declare* (define) your variable names and the type of data they can hold. By doing this, you can have the compiler check your program to make sure you aren't mixing data types accidentally, such as trying to multiply a number by text.

If your program does try to mix data types by multiplying a number by text, the compiler refuses to run your program, displays an error message, and highlights the problem so you can fix it right away, as shown in Figure 2-2.

FIGURE 2-2:
You can't compile your program until the compiler is certain that you aren't mixing different data types.

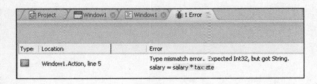

Variables, Data Types, and Constants

DECLARING VARIABLES

Every programming language has its own way of declaring variables and defining a data type:

- In the C programming language, you declare the data type followed by the variable name:

  ```
  int salary;
  ```

- In the Swift programming language, you first define a variable declaration heading (var) and then declare the variable name followed by the data type:

  ```
  var salary : Int
  ```

- In the Visual Basic programming language, you declare the variable name by using a Dim keyword, followed by the variable name, the As keyword, and then the data type of that variable:

  ```
  Dim salary As Integer.
  ```

All three programming language examples create the same salary variable and define that variable to hold only integer data types, which are any whole number, such as 45, 1093, or –39.

In programming languages considered *type-safe,* you must always declare a variable before you can use it (otherwise, the computer doesn't know what type of data you want to store in that variable). Most of the time, you declare your variables at the top of a program. This makes it easy for anyone to see not only how many variables the program uses, but also all their names and data types at a glance.

Some programmers prefer to declare all their variables in one place; other programmers prefer to declare a variable only when they need to use it. Whatever method you use, it's best to be consistent so other programmers will be able to understand and modify your code easily.

Using Different Data Types

Defining a specific data type makes it easy to

>> Know the type of data a variable can hold (either numbers or text).

>> Restrict the range of data the variable can hold.

Figure 2-3 shows common categories of data types.

Common Programming Data Types

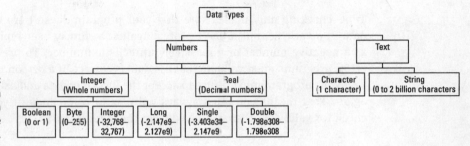

FIGURE 2-3:
Different data
types that can
hold a range
of values.

TECHNICAL
STUFF

Every programming language stores different ranges of data, so be sure you understand the range of values different data types can hold in the programming language you're using.

Defining the range of data can prevent a variable from storing incorrect data. For example, if your program asks the user to type in their age, invalid data would include strings (such as "Fifty-six").

TECHNICAL
STUFF

The range of numbers listed for Long (long integer), Single (single-precision floating-point number), and Double (double-precision floating-point number) data types are listed as exponential numbers (that's the lowercase e). So, the Long data type can store a number as large as 2.147 with the decimal place moved nine places to the right, or approximately 2,147,000,000.

REMEMBER

Every programming language offers different data types, so use Figure 2-3 as a guideline rather than a strict reference.

For example, if you want to store a person's age in a variable, you probably want to store it as a whole number (such as 45) rather than a real number (such as 45.029).

Next, you want to choose a data type that contains the range of values a person's age might be. From Figure 2-3, you can see that a Boolean data type can hold only a 0 or a 1. An Integer data type can hold negative numbers as small as −32,768 or positive numbers as large as 32,767. However, the range of an Integer data type is much larger for a person's age. Nobody has a negative age and nobody has an age anywhere close to 32,767.

The best data type to choose for storing a person's age is the Byte data type, which can store numbers from 0 to 255. If your program tries to store a number less than 0 or greater than 255 as a person's age, the Byte data type screams in protest and refuses to do it, a process known as *type-checking*.

REMEMBER

Type-checking only makes sure that your program doesn't try to store invalid data in a variable, but it can't protect against a clumsy user typing in their age as a negative number or a massively unrealistic number. To prevent user input error, programs must validate that the data is correct. If a person types 0 for their age, your program must refuse to accept the incorrect data and ask the user to try again. That means you must always write extra commands in your program to check for valid data that's received from the outside world.

Another reason to use different data types is to reduce the amount of memory your program needs. You can declare an Age variable as either a Byte or Integer data type, as shown in the following Visual Basic code:

```
Dim Age As Byte
```

Or

```
Dim Age As Integer
```

Although both Age variables can store whole numbers, such as 39, the Byte data type uses less memory (1 byte) than the Integer data type (4 bytes). However, saving a small amount of memory may not be worth the hassle of using different data types, so you need to decide what's best for your particular project.

TECHNICAL STUFF

A *byte* is just a measurement unit where 1 byte represents the space needed to store a single character (such as B or 8). In comparison, a typical sentence requires 100 bytes of storage, a page in a book might require 10,000 bytes, and a novel might require 1 million bytes.

Bytes measure both storage space and memory so a Byte data type (storing the number 48) needs only 1 byte of space whereas an Integer data type (storing the same number 48) would need four times as much space. If you choose the wrong data type, your program will still work, but it'll use up more hard disk space or memory than necessary. Table 2-1 lists common storage requirements for different data types. Notice that the more data you have to store, the larger the storage requirements.

TABLE 2-1

Typical Storage Requirements for Different Data Types

Data Type	Storage Size
Byte	1 byte
Boolean	2 bytes
Character	2 bytes
Integer	4 bytes
Single	4 bytes
Long	8 bytes
Double	8 bytes
String	10 bytes + (2 × string length)
	(If you had a string consisting of three letters, that string would take up 10 bytes of storage space + (2 × 3), which is 16 bytes.)

So, when declaring variables as specific data types, you want to choose the data type that can

>> Hold a range of valid values.

>> Use the least amount of space possible.

TYPE INFERENCE

To make programming easier, some languages use something called *type inference*. That's where you can declare a variable and assign it a value without declaring its data type at all. Then the compiler infers the data type based on the value assigned to that variable.

- In the Swift programming language, you can declare a variable and assign it a value like this:

```
var salary = 8
```

(continued)

(continued)

Because 8 is an integer, the compiler infers that the data type of salary can only store integer (Int) data types. So the preceding is equal to this:

```
var salary: Int = 8
```

Although type inference lets you omit an explicit data type declaration, it can be confusing. In the following Swift variable declarations, what is the data type?

```
var salary = 8.0
```

Because 8.0 is a decimal value, Swift infers that the data type must be Double. When working with decimal numbers, it's often better to clarify exactly the data type you want the variable to hold. That's because decimal numbers can be of different data types such as:

```
var salary: Double = 8.0
var newSalary: Float = 8.0
```

The salary variable can hold Double data types, but the newSalary variable can hold only Float data types, even though they both store the exact same decimal number.

When using type inference, it's a good idea to explicitly declare data types, especially with decimal numbers, to make it clear exactly what data type a variable can hold.

Storing Data in a Variable

After you declare a variable, store data in that variable as the following C program demonstrates:

```
int age;
age = 15;
```

The first line declares the age variable as an integer (int) data type. The second line stuffs the number 15 into the age variable.

You can assign a fixed value (like 15) to a variable or any equation that creates a value, such as

```
taxes_owed = salary * 0.30;
```

If the value of the `salary` variable is 1000, this command multiplies 1000 (the `salary` variable's value) by 0.30, which is 300. The number 300 then gets stored in the `taxes_owed` variable.

When storing data in variables, make sure the variable either is empty or contains data you can afford to lose. Variables can hold only one item at a time, so storing a new value in a variable wipes out the old value, as shown in Figure 2-4 and in the following BASIC code:

```
Salary = 25000
Salary = 17000 + 500
PRINT "This is the value of the Salary variable = ", Salary
```

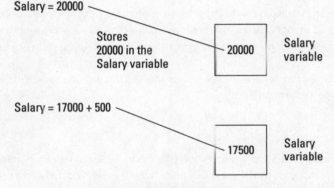

Salary = 20000

Stores 20000 in the Salary variable → 20000 Salary variable

Salary = 17000 + 500 → 17500 Salary variable

Adds 17000 + 500 (17500), erases the old value in the Salary variable (20000), and stores 17500 in the Salary variable

FIGURE 2-4: Assigning a new value to a variable wipes out the old value.

PRINT "This is the value of the Salary variable = ", Salary

This is the value of the Salary variable = 17500

If you store a value in a variable and then immediately store a second value in that same value, you wipe out the first value in that variable. Obviously, there's no point in storing data in a variable only to wipe it out later, so when you store a value in a variable, you'll eventually want to use that value again. (Otherwise, there's no point in storing that data in the first place.)

OPTIONAL VARIABLES

Suppose you declare a variable but don't assign a value to it like this:

```
var x: Int
```

The above declaration defines a variable called x that can hold integer (Int) data types, but doesn't actually store anything in that variable. If you try to use that variable before it gets assigned any data, your program will crash. One clumsy solution is to give every variable a default value. However, you run the risk that your program will accidentally use this default value instead of any actual data. The default value will keep your program from crashing but could return an unexpected result such as your program claiming someone's age is –1.

To avoid this problem, some programming languages let you declare optional variables. By default, an optional variable holds a nil value. This nil value prevents your program from crashing if it tries to use the optional variable before you store any data in it.

In Swift, you can declare an optional variable like this with a question mark after the data type declaration like this:

```
var x: Int?
```

The question mark just lets you know that this variable can contain nothing (nil). Optional variables can be especially useful when retrieving data from a user interface (UI) where the user might skip over an option — for example, leaving a text field empty rather than typing in a value (their middle name).

Retrieving Data from a Variable

After you store data in a variable, you can treat that variable exactly like a fixed value. In this first Python language example, the print command just prints, "This is when I plan on retiring = 65".

```
print ("This is when I plan on retiring = ", 65)
```

Replacing the fixed value (65) with a variable and assigning the value of 65 to that variable creates the following:

```
age = 65
print ("This is when I plan on retiring = ", age)
```

The first line stores the value 65 into the age variable. The second line prints, "This is when I plan on retiring = ", takes the last value stored in the age variable (which is 65), and prints that value out so the entire message that appears on the screen is:

```
This is when I plan on retiring = 65
```

In addition to using variables as if they're a fixed value, you can also assign the value of one variable to another, such as

```
first_number = 39
second_number = first_number + 6
```

Here, the first line stores the number 39 in the first_number variable. The second line adds the number 6 to the value in the first_number variable (39) and assigns this sum (45) into the second_number variable.

You can also modify a variable by itself, as shown in this example:

```
people = 5
people = people + 12
```

The first line stores the value of 5 into the people variable. The second line tells the computer to do the following:

1. Find the value stored in the people variable (5) and add it to the number 12 for a total of 17.

2. Store the value of 17 into the people variable, wiping out the last value stored there (which was 5).

Essentially, variables are nothing more than values that can change while the program runs. In the preceding example, one moment the value of the people variable was 5, and the next moment the value of that same people variable was 17.

Using Constant Values

As a general rule, never use fixed values directly in your program. The reason for this is simple: Suppose you need to calculate the sales tax in three different places in your program. Near the top of your program, you might have a command like this:

```
Material_cost = Item_cost + (Item_Cost * 0.075)
```

Buried in the middle of your program, you might have another command like this:

```
Product_cost = Part_cost + (Part_Cost * 0.075)
```

Near the bottom of your program, you might have a third command like this:

```
Project_cost = Material_cost + Product_cost + (Material_cost +
    Product_cost) * 0.075
```

In all three commands, the number 0.075 represents the current sales tax (7.5 percent). What happens if the sales tax suddenly jumps to 8 percent? Now you have to go through your entire program, find the number 0.075, and replace it with the number 0.080.

Searching and replacing one value with another can be tedious, especially in a large program. As an alternative to using fixed values directly in your commands, you can use constants instead.

As the name implies, constants are like variables that hold only a single value that never changes. So, you could define the value of your sales tax just once, as the following Visual Basic code shows:

```
Const sales_tax As Single = 0.075
```

This command tells the computer:

>> Use the Const keyword to create a sales_tax constant.

>> Define the sales_tax variable as a Single data type.

>> Store the value 0.075 into the sales_tax variable.

By using constants, you can eliminate fixed values in your commands and replace them with a constant instead, which no part of your program can ever change by mistake, such as

```
Const sales_tax As Single = 0.075
Material_cost = Item_cost + (Item_Cost * sales_tax)
Product_cost = Part_cost + (Part_Cost * sales_tax)
Project_cost = Material_cost + Product_cost + (Material_cost +
    Product_cost) * sales_tax
```

Now if the sales tax changes from 7.5 percent to 8 percent, you just need to change this value in one constant declaration, such as

```
Const sales_tax As Single = 0.080
```

This one change effectively plugs in the value of 0.080 everywhere your program uses the sales_tax constant. So, constants offer two advantages:

>> They let you replace fixed values with descriptive constant names.

>> They let you change the value of a constant once and have those changes occur automatically in the rest of your program.

So, use constants to replace fixed values and use variables to store different types of data retrieved from the outside world. Every program needs to use variables, but not every program needs to use constants.

After you understand how to store data temporarily in variables, your program can start manipulating that data to do something useful.

Defining the Scope of a Variable

The scope of a variable defines which part of your program can store and retrieve data in a variable. Because variables store data that your program needs to work correctly, your program must make sure that no other part of the program accidentally modifies that data.

If your program stores a person's credit card number in a variable, you don't want another part of your program to accidentally retrieve that data and change the numbers around or send a hundred copies of each credit card number to customers outside the company.

So, when creating variables, limit the variables' scope. The *scope* simply defines which parts of your program can access a variable. When you declare a variable, you also define one of three possible scope levels for that variable:

>> Global

>> Module

>> Subprogram

Handling global variables with care

In a global variable, any part of your program can access that variable, including storing new data in that variable (and wiping out any existing data already stored in that variable), changing the data in a variable, or wiping out the data in a variable altogether, as shown in Figure 2-5.

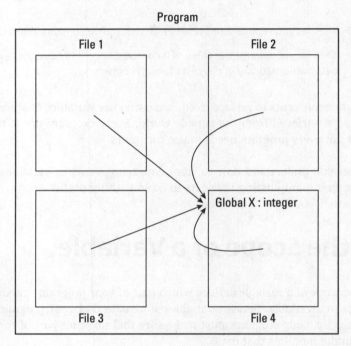

WARNING

Use global variables sparingly. If you create a global variable and some part of your program keeps modifying that variable's data by mistake, you have to search through your entire program to find which command is messing up that variable. If you have a million-line program, guess what? You have to examine a million lines of code to find the one line that's changing that variable by mistake. If that's your idea of fun, go ahead and use global variables.

In the old days, all programming languages let you create global variables, and it was up to the programmer to make sure no commands accidentally modified that variable in unintended ways. When working on small programs, programmers can do this easily, but when working on massive programs created by teams of programmers, the odds of abusing global variables increases dramatically.

Think of a shelf where you can store your books, wallet, and laptop computer. If you're the only person who has access to that shelf, you can be sure anything you put on that shelf is there when you look for it again.

Now imagine putting your shelf of personal belongings (books, wallet, and laptop computer) on a shelf located in Grand Central Station where thousands of people can grab anything they want off that shelf or put something else on the shelf instead. Would you feel safe leaving your wallet and laptop on such a shelf? If not, you probably wouldn't feel safe putting your data in a global variable either.

Because global variables can be so dangerous, most programming languages don't let you create a global variable unless you specifically tell the computer to create one. To create a global variable, you often have to use a special keyword, such as `global` or `public`, like this:

```
Global X : Integer
```

The preceding command tells the computer to create a global variable, called X, that can hold an integer data type. You type a global variable declaration in any file that contains your main program or a library of subprograms.

Restricting scope to a module

A *module* is another term for a separate file. If you divide a large program into subprograms and store those subprograms in separate files, each file is a module. A *module variable* lets you create a variable that can be accessed only by code stored in that particular module, as shown in Figure 2-6.

The advantage of module variables is that they give you the convenience of a global variable but without the danger of letting every part of a program access that variable. Instead, module scope limits access only to code in that file.

Although they're an improvement over global variables, module variables also have some of the disadvantages of global variables. If a file contains a lot of subprograms, trying to find which line of code is messing up your module variable can still be troublesome.

To create a module variable, you generally just declare a variable at the top of any file except you don't use the `Global` or `Public` keyword. In some programming languages, you declare a module variable with the `Private` keyword, such as

```
Private X : Integer;
```

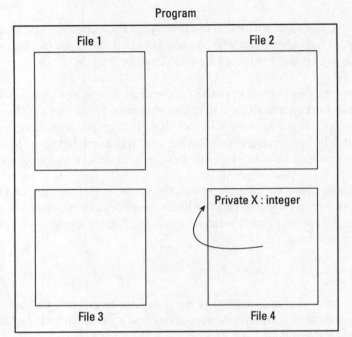

Program

File 1

File 2

Private X : integer

FIGURE 2-6:
Module variables
restrict access to
code stored in a
particular file.

File 3

File 4

The preceding code would declare a module variable called X, which can hold an integer data type.

Isolating variables in a subprogram

Because global and module variables can be dangerous to use because any part of a program can change them, most programmers use global and module variables sparingly. Most of the time, programmers declare variables within a subprogram. Therefore, the only code that can access that variable is inside the subprogram itself, as shown in Figure 2-7.

To create a variable with subprogram scope, you have to declare your variable at the top of that particular subprogram. The subprogram effectively isolates that variable from any other part of your program.

**TECHNICAL
STUFF**

One main feature of object-oriented programming is that not only can you isolate variables within an object, but you also can isolate any code that manipulates those variables inside that same object as well. With both variables and the code that manipulates those variables stored in the same object, you can easily find the code that may be modifying a variable wrong.

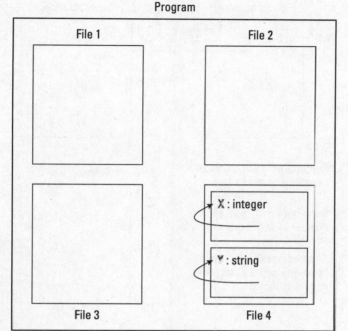

FIGURE 2-7:
Subprogram
variables restrict
access only to
code stored in
that particular
subprogram.

Passing data among subprograms

If one subprogram needs to use data stored in another subprogram, what's the solution? The easiest (and most dangerous) solution is to let multiple subprograms access that variable as a global or module variable.

The better solution is to isolate that variable as a subprogram variable and then *pass* (share) that data to another subprogram. This means you have to declare two subprogram variables, one in each subprogram. Although cumbersome (now you know why programs create global or module variables instead), passing data from one variable to another, called *parameter passing*, helps keeps the data isolated in the subprograms that actually need to use that data, as shown in Figure 2-8.

As a general rule, restrict the scope of your variables as small as possible. This makes sure that the least lines of code can access that variable and potentially mess up your program.

TIP

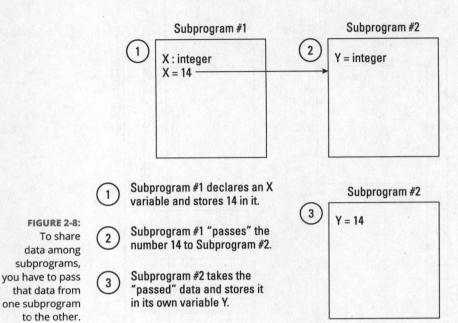

FIGURE 2-8:
To share
data among
subprograms,
you have to pass
that data from
one subprogram
to the other.

Subprogram #1

① X : integer
X = 14

Subprogram #2

② Y = integer

① Subprogram #1 declares an X
variable and stores 14 in it.

② Subprogram #1 "passes" the
number 14 to Subprogram #2.

③ Subprogram #2 takes the
"passed" data and stores it
in its own variable Y.

Subprogram #2

③ Y = 14

Chapter **3**

Manipulating Data

E very program accepts data from the outside world, manipulates that data in some way, and then calculates a useful result. Data can be

» Numbers

» Text

» Input from a keyboard, mouse, controller, or joystick (for a video game)

To manipulate numbers, computers can perform a variety of mathematical operations, which is just a fancy way of saying a computer can add, subtract, multiply, and divide. To manipulate *strings* (as in *text strings*), computers can perform a variety of string manipulation operations, which can chop out a letter of a word or rearrange the letters that make up a word.

Every programming language provides *operators* (built-in commands) for manipulating numbers and strings, but some programming languages are better at manipulating numbers (or *strings*) than others.

For example, Fortran is specifically designed to make scientific calculations easy, so Fortran has more operators for mathematical operations than a language such as SNOBOL, which was designed primarily for manipulating text strings. You can still manipulate strings in Fortran or calculate mathematical equations in SNOBOL; however, you need to write a lot more commands to do so.

Programming languages typically provide two types of data manipulation commands:

» **Operators:** Usually symbols that represent simple calculations, such as addition (+) or multiplication (*)

» **Functions:** Commands that perform more sophisticated calculations, such as calculating the square root of a number. Unlike operators, which are usually symbols, functions are usually short commands, such as SQRT (square root).

By combining both operators and functions, you can create your own commands for manipulating data in different ways.

Storing Data with the Assignment Operator

The simplest operator that almost every programming language has is the *assignment operator*, which is nothing more than the equal sign (=), such as

```
VariableName = Value
```

The assignment operator simply *assigns* (stores) a value to a variable. That value can be a fixed number, a specific string, or a mathematical equation that calculates a single value. Some examples of the assignment operator are shown in Table 3-1.

TABLE 3-1   ## Examples of Using the Assignment (=) Operator

Example	What It Does
Age = 35	Stores the number 35 into the Age variable
Name = "Cat"	Stores the string "Cat" into the Name variable
A = B + 64.26	Adds the value stored in the B variable to the number 64.26 and stores the sum in the A variable
Answer = true	Stores the Boolean value "true" in the Answer variable

Using Math to Manipulate Numbers

Because manipulating numbers (or *number crunching*) is such a common task for computers, every programming language provides commands for addition, subtraction, multiplication, and division. Table 3-2 lists common mathematical operations and the symbols to use.

TABLE 3-2 ## Common Mathematical Operators

Operation	Symbol	Example	Result
Addition	+	3 + 10.27	13.27
Subtraction	−	89.4 − 9.2	80.2
Multiplication	*	5 * 9	45
Division	/	120 / 5	24
Integer division	\	6 \ 4	1
Modulo	% or mod	6 % 4 or 6 mod 4	2
Exponentiation	^ or **	2^4 or 2**4	16

REMEMBER

Integer division always calculates a whole number, which represents how many times one number can divide into another one. In Table 3-2, the 6 \ 4 operation asks the computer, "How many times can you divide 6 by 4?" You can only do it once, so 6 \ 4 = 1. Here are some other examples of integer division:

```
23 \ 5 = 4
39 \ 7 = 5
13 \ 3 = 4
```

The modulo operator divides two numbers and returns the remainder. Most of the curly-bracket languages, such as C++, use the percentage sign (%) as the modulo operator whereas other languages, such as BASIC, use the mod command. Here are some examples of modulo calculation:

```
23 % 5 = 3
39 % 7 = 4
13 % 3 = 1
```

The exponentiation operator multiplies one number by itself a fixed number of times. So, the 2^4 command tells the computer to multiply 2 by itself four times or 2 * 2 * 2 * 2 = 16. Here are some other examples of exponentiation:

```
2^3 = (2 * 2 * 2) = 8
4^2 = (4 * 4) = 16
9^1 = (9 * 1) = 9
```

Organizing equations with operator precedence

To do multiple calculations, you can type one mathematical calculation after another, such as

```
X = 34 + 7
X = X * 89
```

Although this works, it can get clumsy, especially if you need to write more than a handful of equations. As a simple solution, you can cram multiple equations into a single, big equation, such as

```
X = 34 + 7 * 89
```

The problem is, how does the computer calculate this equation? Does it first add 34 + 7 and then multiply this result (41) by 89? Or does it first multiply 7 * 89 and then add this result (623) to 34? Depending on the order it calculates its mathematical operators, the result is either 3649 or 657, two obviously different answers.

To calculate any equation with multiple mathematical operators, computers follow rules that define which mathematical operators get calculated first (known as *operator precedence*). Table 3-3 lists common operator precedence for most programming languages where the operator listed first in the table has the highest precedence, and the operator listed last in the table has the lowest precedence.

Multiplication and division have equal precedence with each other. Similarly, addition and subtraction have equal precedence with each other.

If an equation contains operators that have equal precedence, the computer calculates the result from left to right, such as

```
X = 8 - 3 + 7
```

TABLE 3-3

Operator Precedence

Operator	Symbol
Exponentiation	^ or **
Multiplication	*
Division	/
Integer division	\
Modulo	% or mod
Addition	+
Subtraction	−

First, the computer calculates 8 − 3, which is 5. Then it calculates 5 + 7, which is 12.

If an equation contains operators with different precedence, the computer calculates the highest-precedence operator first. Looking at this equation, you can see that the multiplication (*) operator has higher precedence than the addition (+) operator.

```
Y = 34 + 7 * 89
```

So, the computer first calculates 7 * 89, which is 623; then it adds 623 + 34 to get 657.

What if you really wanted the computer to first calculate 34 + 7 and then multiply this result (41) by 89? To do this, you have to enclose that part of the equation in parentheses, such as

```
Y = (34 + 7) * 89
```

The parentheses tell the computer to calculate that result first. So, this is how the computer calculates the preceding equation:

```
Y = (34 + 7) * 89
Y = 41 * 89
Y = 3649
```

TIP

You should always use parentheses to make sure the computer calculates your equation exactly the way you want in case there could be multiple ways to calculate the equation.

Using built-in math functions

Using basic mathematical operators, you can create any type of complicated formulas, such as calculating a quadratic equation or generating random numbers. However, writing equations to calculate something as common (to scientists and mathematicians, anyway) as logarithms may seem troublesome. Not only do you have to waste time writing such an equation, but you have to spend even more time testing to make sure it works correctly as well.

So, to prevent people from rewriting commonly needed equations, most programming languages include built-in math functions that are either

>> Part of the language itself (such as in many versions of BASIC)

>> Available as separate libraries (such as math libraries included with most C compilers)

The advantage of using built-in math functions is that you can use them without having to write any extra command that you may not want to do or may not know how to do. For example, how do you calculate the square root of a number?

Most likely, you won't have any idea, but you don't have to because you can calculate the square root of a number just by using that language's built-in square-root math function. So, if you wanted to know the square root of 34 and store it in an Answer variable, you could just use the sqrt math function, such as

```
Answer = sqrt(34)
```

REMEMBER

In some languages, such as BASIC, it doesn't matter if you type a math function in either uppercase or lowercase. In other languages, such as C, commands like SQRT and sqrt are considered two completely different functions, so you have to know whether your language requires you to type a math function in all uppercase, all lowercase, or mixed case (such as Sqrt).

Table 3-4 lists some common built-in math functions found in many programming languages.

By using math operators and math functions, you can create complex equations, such as

```
x = 67 * cos (5) + sqrt (7)
```

TABLE 3-4

Common Built-In Math Functions

Math Function	What It Does	Example
abs (x)	Finds the absolute value of x	abs (−45) = 45
cos (x)	Finds the cosine of x	cos (2) = − 0.41614684
exp (x)	Returns a number raised to the power of x	exp (3) = 20.0855369
log (x)	Finds the logarithm of x	log (4) = 1.38629436
sqrt (x)	Finds the square root of x	sqrt (5) = 2.23606798

Instead of plugging fixed values into a math function, it's more flexible just to plug in variables instead, such as

```
Angle = 5
Height = 7
X = 67 * cos (Angle) + sqrt (Height)
```

Manipulating Strings

Just as math operators can manipulate numbers, so can string operators manipulate strings. The simplest and most common string operator is the *concatenation operator*, which smashes two strings together to make a single string.

Most programming languages use either the plus sign (+) or the ampersand (&) symbol as the concatenation operator, such as

```
Name = "Joe " + "Smith"
```

or

```
Name = "Joe " & "Smith"
```

TECHNICAL STUFF

In the Perl language, the concatenation symbol is the dot (.) character:

```
$Name = "Joe " . "Smith";
```

In the preceding examples, the concatenation operator takes the string "Joe " and combines it with the second string "Smith" to create a single string that contains "Joe Smith".

REMEMBER

When concatenating strings, you may need to insert a space between the two strings. Otherwise, the concatenation operator smashes both strings together like "JoeSmith", which you may not want.

For more flexibility in manipulating strings, many programming languages include built-in string functions. These functions can help you manipulate strings in different ways, such as counting the number of characters in a string or removing characters from a string. Table 3-5 lists some common built-in string functions found in many programming languages.

TABLE 3-5

Common Built-In String Functions

String Function	What It Does	Example
length (x)	Counts the number of characters in a string (x), including spaces	length ("Hi there!") = 9
trim (x)	Removes spaces from the beginning and end of a string	trim (" Mary ") = "Mary"
index (x, y)	Returns the position of a string within another string	index ("korat", "ra") = 3
compare (x, y)	Compares two strings to see if they're identical	compare ("A", "a") = False
replace (x, y, z)	Replaces one string from within another	replace ("Batter", "att", "ik") = Biker

REMEMBER

Not all programming languages include these string functions, and if they do, they'll likely use different names for the same functions. For example, Visual Basic has a Substring function for removing characters from a string, but Perl uses a substr function that performs the same task.

Finding Strings with Regular Expressions

Before you can manipulate a substring within a larger string, you first must *find* it. Although some programming languages include string searching functions, most of them are fairly limited to finding exact matches of strings.

To remedy this problem, many programming languages (such as Perl and Tcl) use regular expressions. (A *regular expression* is just a series of symbols that tell the computer how to find a specific pattern in a string.)

If a programming language doesn't offer built-in support for regular expressions, many programmers have written subprogram libraries that let you add regular expressions to your program. By using regular expressions, your programs can perform more sophisticated text searching than any built-in string functions could ever do.

REMEMBER

There are slightly different variations of regular expressions, so be aware of this when using regular expressions in your favorite programming language.

Pattern-matching with the single character (.) wildcard

The simplest way to search for a pattern is to look for a single character. For example, you may want to know if a certain substring begins with the letter *b*, ends with the letter *t*, and contains exactly one character between. Although you could repetitively check every three-character string that begins with *b* and ends with *t*, like bat or but, it's much easier to use a single-character wildcard instead, which is a period (.).

So if you want to find every three-letter substring that begins with a *b* and ends with a *t*, you'd use this regular expression:

```
b.t
```

To search for multiple characters, use the single-character (.) wildcard multiple times to match multiple characters. So, the pattern b..t matches the strings boot and boat with the two-character wildcard (..) representing the two characters between the *b* and the *t*.

Of course, the b..t pattern doesn't match bat because bat has only one character between the *b* and the *t*. Nor does it match boost because boost has more than two characters between the *b* and the *t*.

REMEMBER

When using this wildcard, you must know the exact number of characters to match.

Pattern-matching for specific characters

The single-character wildcard (.) can find any character, whether it's a letter, number, or symbol. Instead of searching for any character, you can search for a list of specific characters by using square brackets ([ ]).

Enclose the characters you want to find inside the square brackets. So, if you want to find all strings that begin with *b*, end with *t*, and have an *a*, *o*, or *u* between, you could use this regular expression:

```
b[aou]t
```

The preceding example finds strings like bat or bot but doesn't find boat or boot because the regular expression looks only for a single character sandwiched between the *b* and the *t* characters.

As an alternative to listing the specific characters you want to find, you can also use the not character (^) to tell the computer which characters you *don't* want to find, such as

```
b[^ao]t
```

This tells the computer to find any string that doesn't have an *a* or an *o* between the *b* and the *t*, such as but. If you have the string bat, the b[^ao]t regular expression ignores it.

Pattern-matching with the multiple-character (*) and plus (+) wildcards

Sometimes you may want to find a string that has a specific character, but you don't care how many copies of that character you find. That's when you can use the multiple-character wildcard (*) to search for zero or more specific characters in a string.

So, if you want to find a string that begins with *bu* and contains zero or more *z* characters at the end, you could use this regular expression:

```
buz*
```

This finds strings like bu, buz, buzz, and buzzzzzz. Because you want to find zero or more copies of the *z* character, you place the multiple-character wildcard after the *z* character.

The multiple-character wildcard finds zero or more characters, but what if you want to find at least *one* character? That's when you use the plus wildcard (+) instead. To search for a character, you place the plus wildcard after that character, such as

```
buz+
```

This finds buz and buzzzz but not bu because the plus wildcard needs to find at least one *z* character.

Pattern-matching with ranges

Wildcards can match zero or more characters, but sometimes you may want to know whether a particular character falls within a range of characters. To do this, you can use ranges. For example, if you want to know whether a character is any lowercase letter, you could use the pattern [a-z] as follows:

```
bu[a-z]
```

This finds strings, such as but, bug or bus, but not bu (not a three-character string). Of course, you don't need to search for letters from *a* to *z*. You can just as easily search for the following:

```
bu[d-s]
```

This regular expression finds bud and bus but not but (because the *t* lies outside the range of letters from *d* to *s*).

You can also use ranges to check whether a character falls within a numeric range, such as

```
21[0-9]
```

This finds the strings 212 and 210. If you only wanted to find strings with numbers between 4 and 7, you'd use this regular expression:

```
21[4-7]
```

This finds the string 215 but not the strings 210 or 218 because both 0 and 8 lie outside the defined range of 4 through 7. Table 3-6 shows examples of different regular expressions and the strings that they find.

TECHNICAL STUFF

This section shows a handful of regular-expression wildcards you can use to search for string patterns. A lot more regular expressions can perform all sorts of weird and wonderful pattern searching. You can always find out more about these other options by going to www.regular-expressions.info.

By stringing multiple regular-expression wildcards together, you can search for a variety of different string patterns, as shown in Table 3-6.

TABLE 3-6

Examples of Pattern-Matching with Different Regular Expressions

Pattern	Matches These Strings
t..k	talk tusk
f[aeiou]t	fat fit fet
d[^ou]g	dig dmg
zo*	zo zoo z
zo+	zo zoo
sp[a–f]	spa spe spf
key[0–9]	key4
p[aei].[0–9]	pey8 pit6 pa21

You can always combine regular expressions to create complicated search patterns, such as the last regular expression in Table 3-6:

```
p[aei].[0–9]
```

This regular expression may look like a mess, but you can dissect it one part at a time. First, it searches for this four-character pattern:

» The first character must start with *p*.

» The second character must only be an *a, e,* or *i:* [aei].

» The third character uses the single-character wildcard (.), so it can be anything from a letter, number, or symbol.

» The fourth character must be a number within 0 through 9: [0–9].

As you can see, regular expressions give you a powerful and simple way to search for various string patterns. After you find a particular string, you can manipulate it with the built-in string manipulation functions and operators in a specific programming language.

Using Comparison Operators

Unlike math and string operators that can change data, comparison operators compare two chunks of data to determine which one is bigger than the other. Table 3-7 lists common comparison operators. When comparison operators compare two items, the comparison operator returns one of two values: True or False.

TABLE 3-7 ## Common Comparison Operators

Comparison Operator	What It Means	Example	Result
= or ==	Equal to	45 = 37 "A" = "A"	False True
<	Less than	563 < 904 "a"< "A"	True False
<=	Less than or equal to	23 <= − 58 "b" <= − "B"	True False
>	Greater than	51 > 4 "A" > "a"	True False
>=	Greater than or equal to	76 >= 76 "z" >= − "a"	True True
<> or !=	Not equal to	46 <> 9 "a" <> "g"	True True

TECHNICAL STUFF

A single comparison operation is also called a *conditional expression*.

The values True and False are known as Boolean values. (The mathematician who invented Boolean arithmetic was named George Boole.) Computers are essentially built on Boolean values because you program them by flipping switches either on (True) or off (False). All programming ultimately boils down to a series of on/off commands, which is why machine language consists of nothing but 0s and 1s.

TECHNICAL STUFF

Many curly-bracket languages, such as C, use != as their not-equal comparison operator instead of <>.

WARNING

Curly-bracket languages, such as C and C++, use the double equal sign (==) as the equal comparison operator, whereas other languages just use the single equal sign (=). If you use a single equal sign in C or C++, you'll assign a value rather than compare two values. In other words, your C or C++ program will work, but it won't work correctly.

REMEMBER

Knowing whether two values are equal, greater than, less than, or not equal to one another is useful for making your program make decisions (see Chapter 4 of this minibook).

Comparing two numbers is straightforward, such as

    5 > 2

Comparing two numbers always calculates the same result. In this case, 5 > 2 always returns a True value. What gives comparison operators more flexibility is when they compare variables, such as

    Age > 2

Depending on what the value of the Age variable may be, the value of this comparison can be either True or False.

Comparing numbers may be straightforward, but comparing strings can be more confusing. *Remember:* Computers only understand numbers, so they use numbers to represent characters, such as symbols and letters.

Computers use the number 65 to represent *A*, the number 66 to represent *B*, all the way to the number 90 to represent *Z*. To represent lowercase letters, computers use the number 97 to represent *a*, 98 to represent *b*, all the way up to 122 to represent *z*.

TECHNICAL STUFF

The specific numbers used to represent every character on the keyboard can be found on the ASCII table, which you can view at www.asciitable.com.

That's why, in Table 3-7, the comparison between A > a is False because the computer replaces each character with its equivalent code. So, the comparison of characters

    "A" > "a"

actually looks like this to the computer:

    65 > 97

The number 65 isn't greater than 97, so this comparison returns a False value.

Comparing a string of characters works the same way as comparing single characters. The computer examines each string, character by character, and translates them into their numeric equivalent. So, if you had the comparison

```
"aA" > "aa"
```

The computer converts all the characters into their equivalent values, such as

```
97 65 > 97 97
```

The computer examines the first character of each string. If they're equal, it continues with a second character, a third character, and so on.

In the preceding example, the computer sees that the numbers 97 (which represent the character *a*) are equal, so it checks the second character. The number 65 (which represents the character *A*) isn't greater than the number 97 (which represents the character *a*), so this comparison returns a False value.

What happens if you compare unequal strings, such as

```
"aA" > "a"
```

The computer compares each character as numbers, as follows:

```
97 65 > 97
```

The first numbers of each string (97) are equal, so the computer checks the second number. Because the second string (a) doesn't have a second character, its value is 0. Because 65 > 0, the preceding comparison returns a True value.

Now look at this comparison:

```
"Aa" > "a"
```

The computer translates these characters into their equivalent numbers, as follows:

```
65 97 > 97
```

Comparing the first numbers (or *characters*), the computer sees that 65 > 97, so this comparison returns a False value. Notice that as soon as the computer can decide whether one character is greater than another, it doesn't bother checking the second character in the first string.

Using Boolean Operators

Comparison operators always return a `True` or `False` value, which are Boolean values. Just as you can manipulate numbers (addition, subtraction, and so on) and strings (trimming or searching for characters), so can you also manipulate Boolean values.

When you manipulate a Boolean value, you get another Boolean value. Because there are only two Boolean values (`True` or `False`), every Boolean operator returns a value of either `True` or `False`.

Most programming languages offer four Boolean operators:

» Not

» And

» Or

» Xor

REMEMBER

Like comparison operators, Boolean operators are most useful for making a program evaluate external data and react to that data. For example, every time you play a video game and get a score, the video game uses a comparison operator to compare your current score with the highest score. If your current score is greater than the highest score, your score now becomes the highest score. If your score isn't higher than the highest score, your score isn't displayed as the highest score.

Using the Not operator

The `Not` operator, depicted with an exclamation point (`!`) in C and other curly-bracket languages, takes a Boolean value and converts it to its opposite. So, if you have a `True` value, the `Not` operator converts it to `False`, and vice versa. At the simplest example, you can use the `Not` operator like this:

```
Not(True) = False
```

Like using fixed values in comparison operators (5 > 2), using fixed values with Boolean operators is rather pointless. Instead, you can use variables and comparison operators with Boolean operators, such as

```
Not(Age > 2)
```

If the value of the Age variable is 3, this Boolean operation evaluates to

```
Not(Age > 2)
Not(3 > 2)
Not(True)
False
```

Using the And operator

The And operator depicted with double ampersands (&&) in C and many other curly-bracket languages, takes two Boolean values and converts them into a single Boolean value. If both Boolean values are True, the And operator returns a True value; otherwise, the And operator always returns a False value, as shown in Table 3-8, or the *truth table*.

TABLE 3-8

The And Truth Table

First Value	Second Value	Result
True	True	True
True	False	False
False	True	False
False	False	False

So, if the value of the Age variable is 3, this is how the following And operator evaluates an answer:

```
(Age > 2) AND (Age >= 18)
(3 > 2) AND (3 >= 18)
True AND False
False
```

If the value of the Age variable is 25, this is how the And operator evaluates an answer:

```
(Age > 2) AND (Age >= 18)
(25 > 2) AND (25 >= 18)
True AND True
True
```

The And operator only returns a True value if both values are True.

Using the Or operator

Like the And operator, the Or operator, depicted with double vertical lines (||) in C and many other curly-bracket languages, takes two Boolean values and converts them into a single Boolean value. If both Boolean values are False, the Or operator returns a False value; otherwise, the Or operator always returns a True value, as shown in Table 3-9.

TABLE 3-9

The Or Truth Table

First Value	Second Value	Result
True	True	True
True	False	True
False	True	True
False	False	False

So, if the value of the Age variable is 3, this is how the following Or operator evaluates an answer:

```
(Age > 2) OR (Age >= 18)
(3 > 2) OR (3 >= 18)
True OR False
True
```

If the value of the Age variable is 1, this is how the Or operator evaluates an answer:

```
(Age > 2) OR (Age >= 18)
(1 > 2) OR (1 >= 18)
False OR False
False
```

The Or operator only returns a False value if both values are False.

Using the Xor operator

The Xor operator, depicted with the caret symbol (^) in C and other curly-bracket languages, is an exclusive Or. The Xor operator takes two Boolean values and converts them into a single Boolean value. If both Boolean values are True or both Boolean values are False, the Xor operator returns a False value; if one Boolean value is True and the other Boolean value is False, the Xor operator returns a True value, as shown in Table 3-10.

TABLE 3-10

The Xor Truth Table

First Value	Second Value	Result
True	True	False
True	False	True
False	True	True
False	False	False

So, if the value of the Age variable is 3, this is how the following Xor operator evaluates an answer:

```
(Age > 2) XOR (Age >= 18)
(3 > 2) XOR (3 >= 18)
True XOR False
True
```

If the value of the Age variable is 1, this is how the Xor operator evaluates an answer:

```
(Age > 2) XOR (Age >= 18)
(1 > 2) XOR (1 >= 18)
False XOR False
False
```

REMEMBER

The Xor operator returns a False value if both values are False or if both values are True.

Boolean operators are used most often to make decisions in a program, such as a video game asking, "Do you want to play again?" When you choose either Yes or No, the program uses a comparison operator, such as

```
Answer = "Yes"
```

The result depends on your answer:

>> If your answer is Yes, the preceding comparison operation returns a True value. If this comparison operation is True, the video game plays again.

>> If your answer is No, the preceding comparison operation returns a False value. If this comparison operation is False, the video game doesn't play again.

Converting Data Types

Programming languages are often divided into two categories, depending on their variables:

>> A **strongly typed language** forces you to declare your variables, and their data types, before you can use them. (See Chapter 2 in this minibook for more information about declaring variables types.)

>> A **weakly typed language** lets you store any type of data in a variable.

One moment, a weakly typed language variable can hold a string, another moment it can hold an integer, and then another moment it may hold a decimal number.

Both options have their pros and cons, but one issue with strongly typed languages is that they prevent you from mixing data types. For example, suppose you need to store someone's age in a variable. You may declare your Age variable as a Byte data type, like this in Visual Basic:

```
Dim Age As Byte
```

As a Byte data type, the Age variable can hold only numbers from 0 to 255, which is exactly what you want. However, what if you declare an AverageAge variable as a Single (decimal) data type, and a People variable as an Integer data type, such as

```
Dim People As Integer
Dim AverageAge As Single
```

At this point, you have three different data types: Byte, Integer, and Single. Now what would happen if you try mixing these data types in a command, such as

```
AverageAge = Age / People
```

The AverageAge variable is a Single data type, the Age variable is a Byte data type, and the People variable is an Integer data type. Strongly typed languages, such as Swift, would scream and refuse to compile and run this program simply because you're mixing data types together.

To get around this problem, you must use special data conversion functions that are built into the programming language. Data conversion functions simply convert one data type into another so that all variables use the same data type.

REMEMBER

Most programming languages have built-in data conversion functions, although their exact names vary from one language to another.

In the preceding example, the AverageAge variable is a Single data type, so you must make sure every variable is a Single data type before you can store its contents into the AverageAge variable, such as

```
Dim People As Integer = 10
Dim AverageAge As Single = 45
Dim Age As Byte = 38
AverageAge = CSng(Age) / CSng(People)
```

The CSng function converts the Age variable from a Byte to a Single data type. Then the second CSng function converts the People variable from an Integer to a Single data type. Only after all values have been converted to a Single data type can you store the value into the AverageAge variable, which can hold only a Single data type.

WARNING

When you convert data types, you may lose some precision in your numbers. For example, converting an Integer data type (such as 67) to a Single data type means converting the number 67 to 67.0. But what if you convert a Single data type (such as 3.74) to an Integer data type? Then the computer may either round the value to the nearest whole number, so the number 3.74 gets converted into 4, or it may just drop the decimal values altogether so 3.74 gets converted into 3. So, when converting between data types, make sure you can afford to lose any precision in your numbers, or else your program may wind up using inexact values, which could wreck the accuracy of your calculations.

No matter what type of data you have, every programming language allows multiple ways to manipulate that data. The way you combine operators and functions determines what your program actually does.

Chapter **4**

Making Decisions by Branching

The simplest program lists commands one after another in a sequence, much like following the steps of a recipe. Follow a recipe step-by-step, and you always create the same dish. If a program lists commands step-by-step, the computer always produces the same result.

In some cases, you may want a program to do the exact same thing over and over again, such as a simple program to display traffic signals. However, for most programs, you want the computer to react to outside data. To make a computer respond in different ways, a program needs to offer two or more choices for the computer to follow.

When you quit a program, the program may ask, "Do you really want to exit?" At this point, the program is giving the computer a choice of two possible actions to take based on your answer.

If you answer Yes, the computer quits the program. If you answer No, the computer keeps running the program.

When a program gives the computer a choice of two or more commands to follow, that's called a *branching* or *decision* statement.

All branching statements work the same way:

>> A comparison operator (or a *conditional expression*) compares an expression (such as A > 45) to determine a True or False value.

>> The branching statement offers at least two groups of commands for the computer to follow based on whether its comparison is True or False.

Picking One Choice with the IF-THEN Statement

The simplest branching statement is an IF-THEN statement, which looks like this:

```
IF (Something is True or False) THEN Command
```

The IF-THEN checks whether something is True or False:

>> If something is True, the IF-THEN command tells the computer to run exactly one command.

>> If something is False, the computer doesn't run this command.

An example of a simple IF-THEN statement might occur while playing a video game:

```
IF (Player hits the Pause button) THEN Pause game
```

If the player hits the pause button (True), you want the computer to pause the game. If the player doesn't hit the pause button (False), you don't want to pause the game, as shown in Figure 4-1.

The simple IF-THEN statement runs only one command if a certain condition is True. What if you want to run two or more commands? In that case, you must define a list of commands to run. A group of commands is sometimes called a *block of commands* or just a *block*.

So, if you want to run more than one command in an IF-THEN statement, you must define a block of commands. In the curly-bracket language family, such as C, you use curly brackets to define the beginning and end of a block of commands:

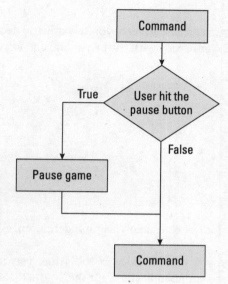

FIGURE 4-1: A simple IF–THEN statement runs one extra command if something is True.

```
if (True or False)
{
   command #1
   command #2
   .
   .
   command #3
}
```

REMEMBER

In C/C++, there is no "then" keyword used to create the IF statement.

The curly brackets tell the IF–THEN statement to run the entire block of commands enclosed within the curly brackets.

In other languages, the IF–THEN statement itself defines the start of a block, and then you use an END IF command to define the end of a block, such as this BASIC language example:

```
IF (True or False) THEN
   Command #1
   Command #2
   .
   .
   Command #3
END IF
```

Finally, some languages, such as Pascal, force you to explicitly declare the beginning and end of a block of commands with the begin and end keywords, such as:

```
If (True or False) then
  Begin
    Command #1
    Command #2
    .
    .
    Command #3
  End;
```

In Python, you specify a block of code solely using indentation.

No matter what language you use, the idea is the same; you must define the beginning and end of all the commands you want the IF–THEN statement to run.

Picking Two Choices with the IF-THEN-ELSE Statement

The simple IF–THEN statement either runs a command (or block of commands) or it doesn't. But what if you want the computer to take one action if something is True and a completely different action if something is False? In that case, you must use a variation: an IF–THEN–ELSE statement.

The IF–THEN–ELSE statement gives the computer a choice of two mutually exclusive choices, as shown in Figure 4-2.

Like the simple IF–THEN statement, the IF–THEN–ELSE statement can run a single command or a block of commands, such as:

```
if (True or False) then
{
  command #1
  command #2
  .
  .
  command #3
}
else
{
```

```
    command #1
    command #2
    .
    .
    command #3
}
```

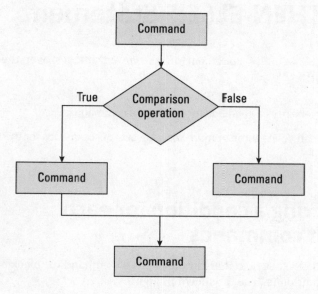

FIGURE 4-2:
An IF–THEN–
ELSE statement
offers two
different sets
of commands
to follow.

The IF–THEN–ELSE statement tells the computer, "Check whether something is True. If so, follow this set of commands. Otherwise, follow this second set of commands."

One problem with the IF–THEN–ELSE statement is that it only checks a single condition. If that single condition is False, it always runs its second set of commands, such as:

```
IF (Salary > 100000) THEN
  TaxRate = 0.45
ELSE
  TaxRate = 0.30
END IF
```

In this BASIC language example, if the value of the Salary variable is greater than 100000, the TaxRate variable is always set to 0.45.

However, if the Salary variable *isn't* greater than 100000 (it's less than or equal to 100000), the ELSE portion of the IF–THEN–ELSE statement always sets the TaxRate variable to 0.30.

Making Decisions
by Branching

The IF-THEN-ELSE always gives the computer a choice of exactly two, mutually exclusive choices. What if you want to give the computer three or more possible choices? Then you must use the IF-THEN-ELSEIF statement.

Picking Three or More Choices with the IF-THEN-ELSEIF Statement

The IF-THEN-ELSEIF statement offers two advantages over the IF-THEN-ELSE statement:

>> You can check a condition for each set of commands.

>> You can define three or more separate sets of commands for the computer to follow.

Checking a condition for each set of commands

The IF-THEN-ELSEIF statement only runs a command (or block of commands) if some condition is True, as shown in Figure 4-3.

If every conditional expression is False, the IF-THEN-ELSEIF statement doesn't run any commands. Only if one of its conditional expressions is True does the IF-THEN-ELSEIF statement run exactly one set of commands, such as:

```
IF (Salary > 100000) THEN
   TaxRate = 0.45
ELSEIF (Salary > 50000) THEN
   TaxRate = 0.30
END IF
```

In this example, the computer has three possible choices:

>> If Salary > 100000, set TaxRate = 0.45.

>> If Salary > 50000 (but less than or equal to 100000), set TaxRate = 0.30.

>> If Salary <= 50000, do nothing.

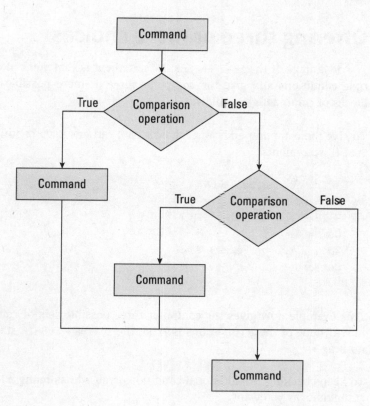

FIGURE 4-3:
An IF–THEN–
ELSEIF
statement offers
two different sets
of commands
to follow.

The first choice checks whether the value of the Salary variable is greater than 100000, such as 250000. If so, it tells the computer to set the TaxRate variable to 0.45 and immediately exit out of the entire IF–THEN–ELSEIF statement.

The second choice only checks whether the value of the Salary variable is greater than 50000. What happens if the Salary value is 150000? In that case, the first choice runs (Salary > 100000), so this second choice would've never been checked at all.

So, although the second choice might seem to run if the Salary variable is greater than 50000, it really won't run unless Salary > 50000 and the first choice did not run, which means that the Salary variable must be less than or equal to 100000.

If the value of the Salary variable is less than or equal to 50000, the third choice is to not run any additional commands at all. Unlike the IF–THEN–ELSE statement, which always runs at least one set of commands, it's possible for an IF–THEN–ELSEIF statement to run no commands.

Offering three or more choices

The advantage of the `IF–THEN–ELSEIF` statement is that you can check for multiple conditions and give the computer three or more possible commands (or blocks of commands) to follow.

To give the computer additional choices, you can just keep tacking on additional `ELSEIF` statements:

```
IF (True or False) THEN
   Command
ELSEIF (True or False) THEN
   Command
ELSEIF (True or False) THEN
   Command
END IF
```

This example now gives the computer three possible sets of commands to follow. If none of these conditions is True, the `IF–THEN–ELSEIF` statement may do nothing.

To keep checking for additional conditions, you add as many additional `ELSEIF` statements as you want.

REMEMBER

The `IF–THEN–ELSEIF` statement makes the computer run exactly zero or one command (or block of commands), no matter how many additional `ELSEIF` statements you add on.

If you want to make sure the `IF–THEN–ELSEIF` statement always runs one command (or block of commands), you can tack on the `ELSE` statement at the very end:

```
IF (True or False) THEN
   Command
ELSEIF (True or False) THEN
   Command
ELSEIF (True or False) THEN
   Command
ELSEIF (True or False) THEN
   Command
ELSE
   Command
END IF
```

The ELSE statement at the end ensures that the entire IF–THEN–ELSEIF statement always runs at least one command. Notice that the ELSE statement doesn't check a condition because it runs only if all preceding conditions are False, such as in the following example:

```
IF (Age > 65) THEN
   Status = Retired
ELSEIF (Age > 20) THEN
   Status = Working
ELSE
   Status = Bum
END IF
```

In this example, the IF–THEN–ELSEIF statement gives the computer three possible choices:

>> Set Status = Retired only if Age > 65.

>> Set Status = Working only if Age > 20 (and less than or equal to 65).

>> Set Status = Bum only if Age is less than or equal to 20 (which means the other two conditions are False).

Playing with Multiple Boolean Operators

To make a decision in an IF–THEN statement, the computer must use a conditional expression that's either True or False. Simple conditional expressions might be

```
Age = 55
Salary <= 55000
Name <> "John Smith"
```

You can also use Boolean operators (AND, OR, NOT, and XOR) to calculate multiple conditions. Suppose you want to check whether a variable falls within a range of values, such as being greater than 20 but less than or equal to 65:

```
(Age > 20) AND (Age <= 65)
```

REMEMBER

Depending on the programming language, you may be able to type a Boolean operator in lowercase (and), uppercase (AND), or a mix of both uppercase and lowercase (And). Whichever style you like best, use it consistently throughout your program.

REMEMBER

Chapter 3 of this minibook contains more information about how Boolean operators work.

Table 4-1 shows how different values for the Age variable determine the value of the preceding Boolean expression.

TABLE 4-1

Multiple Boolean Expressions Ultimately Evaluate to a Single True or False Value

Value of the Age Variable	Value of (Age > 20) Expression	Value of (Age <= 65) Expression	Value of Complete Boolean Expression
15	False	True	False
35	True	True	True
78	True	False	False

Because multiple Boolean expressions ultimately evaluate to a single True or False value, you can use multiple Boolean expressions in any IF–THEN statements:

```
IF (Age > 20) AND (Age <= 65) THEN
  Status = Working
ELSE
  Status = Bum
END IF
```

There's no limit to the number of Boolean expressions you can combine with Boolean operators. The following is a perfectly valid Boolean expression that ultimately evaluates to a single True or False value:

```
(Age > 20) AND (Age <= 65) OR (Age = 72) OR (Name = "John")
```

TIP

The more Boolean expressions you string together with Boolean operators, the more confusing everything gets, so it's generally best not to use multiple Boolean expressions and Boolean operators (AND, OR, NOT, or XOR) at a time.

It's possible for a SELECT CASE statement to run no commands if the CASE statement can't match a variable to any specific value:

```
SELECT CASE Age
CASE 65
  Status = Retired
```

```
CASE 21
   Status = Adult
END SELECT
```

The preceding SELECT CASE statement doesn't do anything if the Age variable is 13, 25, or 81. To make sure the SELECT CASE statement always runs at least one command, you must add the ELSE statement:

```
SELECT CASE Age
CASE 65
   Status = Retired
CASE 21
   Status = Adult
ELSE
   Status = Child
END SELECT
```

In this example, if the value of the Age variable is 24 or 5, it doesn't match any of the specific values, so the command under the ELSE statement runs instead (Status = Child).

Instead of using the ELSE statement, the curly-bracket languages use a default statement:

```
switch (age)
  {
  case 65: status = retired;
           break;
  case 21: status = adult;
           break;
  default: status = child;
  }
```

Both the ELSE and default statements force the SELECT CASE (or switch) statement to always do something.

As a general rule, use the IF–THEN statements for making the computer choose one or two commands (or blocks of commands). If you need the computer to choose from three or more commands (or blocks of commands), the SELECT CASE (switch) statement may be easier to read and write instead.

Making Multiple Choices with the SELECT CASE Statement

The IF-THEN-ELSEIF statement can check multiple conditions and offer two or more choices for the computer to follow. However, the more choices available, the harder the IF-THEN-ELSEIF statement can be to understand, as shown in the following example:

```
IF (Age = 65) THEN
   Status = Retired
ELSEIF (Age = 21) THEN
   Status = Adult
ELSE
   Status = Child
END IF
```

For two or three choices, the IF-THEN-ELSE statement may be easy to understand, but after you need to offer four or more choices, the IF-THEN-ELSEIF statement can start getting clumsy. As an alternative, most programming languages offer a SELECT CASE statement:

```
SELECT CASE Variable
      CASE X
         Command #1
      CASE Y
         Command #2
END SELECT
```

The SELECT CASE statement examines a variable, and if it's equal to a specific value, the computer follows a command (or block of commands). The preceding SELECT CASE statement is equivalent to the following IF-THEN-ELSEIF statement:

```
If Variable = X THEN
   Command #1
ELSEIF Variable = Y THEN
   Command #2
END IF
```

The basic idea behind the SELECT CASE statement is to make it easier to list multiple choices. Both an IF-THEN-ELSEIF statement and a SELECT CASE (also called a switch statement) perform the same function; it's just that the SELECT CASE statement is easier to read and understand.

Consider the following IF-THEN-ELSEIF statement:

```
IF (Age = 65) THEN
   Status = Retired
ELSEIF (Age = 21) THEN
   Status = Adult
ELSE
   Status = Child
END IF
```

Rewriting this as a SELECT CASE statement might look like this:

```
SELECT CASE Age
    CASE 65
       Status = Retired
    CASE 21
       Status = Adult
    ELSE
       Status = Child
END SELECT
```

As you can see, the SELECT CASE statement is much less cluttered and easier to read and understand than the IF-THEN-ELSEIF statement.

USING THE SWITCH STATEMENT IN C AND SIMILAR LANGUAGES

Instead of using a SELECT CASE statement, curly-bracket languages, like C, use a switch statement. The equivalent SELECT CASE statement written as a switch statement in C looks like this:

```
switch (Variable)
   {
   case X: Command #1;
          break;
   case Y: Command #2;
   }
```

(continued)

(continued)

A SELECT CASE statement in BASIC might look like this:

```
SELECT CASE Age
CASE 65
   Status = Retired
CASE 21
   Status = Working
ELSE
   Status = Child
END SELECT
```

The equivalent switch statement in C might look like this:

```
switch (age)
   {
   case 65: status = retired;
            break;
   case 21: status = adult;
            break;
   default: status = child;
   }
```

The most crucial difference between the SELECT CASE statement in other languages and the switch statement in the curly-bracket languages is the use of the break command. If you omit the break command, the switch statement doesn't know when to stop running commands.

In the preceding example, the break command stops the computer from running the other commands stored in the rest of the switch statement. So, if the value of the age variable is 65, the preceding C program does the following:

1. Sets the status variable to retired

2. Stops running the switch statement

Suppose you didn't include the break command, as follows:

```
switch (age)
   {
   case 65: status = retired;
   case 21: status = adult;
   default: status = child;
   }
```

If the value of the age variable is 65, this is how this C program works:

1. Sets the status variable to retired

2. Sets the status variable to working

3. Sets the status variable to student

Without the break command, many curly-bracket languages, like C, simply run every command all the way through the switch statement until it reaches the bottom, which probably isn't what you want.

Remember: When using the switch statement in C (and many other curly-bracket languages), always use the break command unless you specifically don't need it, as I explain in the following section.

Matching multiple values in a SELECT CASE statement

The simplest SELECT CASE statement checks whether a variable matches a single value, such as:

```
SELECT CASE Age
CASE 65
   Status = Retired
CASE 21
   Status = Adult
ELSE
   Status = Child
END SELECT
```

This SELECT CASE statement doesn't do anything unless the value of the Age variable is exactly 65, 21, or 15. If the value of the Age variable is 66, 23, or 17, the SELECT CASE statement does nothing.

Matching exact values may be useful, but sometimes you may want to run the same command (or block of commands) if a variable matches one or more values. For example, rather than match the number 65 exactly, you may want the SELECT CASE statement to match 65, 66, or 67. In that case, you can write the SELECT CASE statement like this:

```
SELECT CASE Age
  CASE 65, 66, 67
```

```
    Status = Retired
CASE 21
   Status = Adult
ELSE
   Status = Child
END SELECT
```

With a `switch` statement in a curly-bracket language, like C, you can do the following:

```
switch (age)
{
  case 67:
  case 66:
  case 65: status = retired;
           break;
  case 21: status = adult;
           break;
  default: status = child;
}
```

By not using the `break` command if the value of the `age` variable is 67 or 66, the computer just continues down, line-by-line, until it runs the command if the `age` variable was 65. Then it hits the `break` command directly under the `status =` `retired` command and stops.

TIP

The `switch` command can be easier to read because all the matching values (67, 66, 65, 21, and 15) appear in a vertical column. The equivalent `SELECT CASE` statement can be slightly harder to read because all the values don't line up in a single vertical column.

Checking a range of values

Matching values exactly can be cumbersome, as in the following, which sets Status = Retired if the Age variable is between 65 and 75:

```
SELECT CASE Age
CASE 65, 67, 68, 69, 70, 71, 72, 73, 74, 75
   Status = Retired
CASE 21
   Status = Adult
ELSE
   Status = Child
END SELECT
```

To avoid this problem, many languages let you check for a range of values. So, if you want to check whether a variable is greater than or equal to 65 and less than or equal to 75, you could define the range of 65 TO 75 like this:

```
SELECT CASE Age
CASE 65 TO 75
   Status = Retired
CASE 21
   Status = Adult
ELSE
   Status = Child
END SELECT
```

Comparing values

Listing a range of values can be useful, but what if there's no upper (or lower) limit? For example, anyone over the age of 65 might be considered retired, so you need to use a comparison operator to check a variable with a value, such as Age >= 65.

To use a comparison operator in a SELECT CASE statement, languages such as BASIC use the following syntax:

```
SELECT CASE Age
CASE IS >= 65
   Status = Retired
CASE 21 TO 64
   Status = Adult
ELSE
   Status = Child
END SELECT
```

In this example, the first part of the SELECT CASE statement tells the computer to check whether the value in the Age variable is (note the IS keyword) >= 65.

The second part of the SELECT CASE statement checks whether the Age variable falls within the range of 21 to 64.

The third part of the SELECT CASE statement runs if the value of the Age variable is not within 21 through 64 or greater than 65.

As you can see, each part of a SELECT CASE statement can check a value by checking a range of values or using a comparison operator.

Branching simply gives the computer multiple options to use when running. By accepting outside information and comparing its value, a branching statement can help the computer choose an appropriate response out of many possible responses.

Chapter 5

Repeating Commands by Looping

To write any program, you must specify what the computer needs to do at any given time. Sometimes, you may need to write the same command multiple times. For example, suppose you want to print your name five times. You could just write the same command five times like this:

```
PRINT "John Smith"
PRINT "John Smith"
PRINT "John Smith"
PRINT "John Smith"
PRINT "John Smith"
```

Writing the same five commands is cumbersome. Even worse, what if you suddenly decide you want to print your name not just 5 times, but 5,000 times? Do you really want to write the same command 5,000 times?

Probably not, which is why computer scientists invented loops. A *loop* is just a shortcut for making the computer run one or more commands without writing those commands multiple times. So, rather than type the same command five times as in the preceding example, you could use a loop like this:

```
FOR I = 1 TO 5
   PRINT "John Smith"
NEXT I
```

This tells the computer to run the PRINT "John Smith" command five times. If you want to print John Smith 5,000 times, you just have to change the number of times you want the loop to run by replacing the 5 with 5000, such as:

```
FOR I = 1 TO 5000
   PRINT "John Smith"
NEXT I
```

Loops basically make one or more commands run more than once, as shown in Figure 5-1.

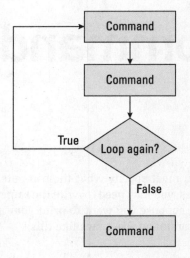

FIGURE 5-1:
A loop can run
one or more
commands over
and over.

Looping a Fixed Number of Times with the FOR-NEXT Loop

The simplest loop runs one or more commands a fixed number of times, such as five or ten times. Such loops that run a fixed number of times are FOR-NEXT loops, and they look like this:

```
FOR Variable = InitialValue TO EndValue
   Command
NEXT Variable
```

The first line serves two purposes: The first time the FOR-NEXT loop runs, this line sets the value of the variable to an initial value, such as 1. The second and all additional times the FOR-NEXT loop runs, it checks whether its variable is still within a range of values, such as between 1 and 10. If so, the FOR-NEXT loop runs again.

The second line consists of one or more commands that you want to run multiple times.

The third line tells the FOR-NEXT loop to increase the value of its variable by 1 and run the FOR-NEXT loop again.

The FOR-NEXT loop defines four items:

>> A variable

>> The initial value of the variable (often 0 or 1)

>> The ending value of the variable

>> One or more commands that run multiple times

Using a FOR-NEXT loop variable

Like all variables, the name of a FOR-NEXT loop variable can be anything, although it's best to use a descriptive name if possible. So, if you want to print the names of all the employees of a company by using a FOR-NEXT loop, you could use EmployeeID as a descriptive variable name, such as:

```
FOR EmployeeID = 1 TO 150
   PRINT EmployeeName(EmployeeID)
NEXT EmployeeID
```

This example would print out each name (EmployeeName) starting with the employee who has the EmployeeID of 1 and continuing until it prints the employee with the EmployeeID of 150.

If your FOR-NEXT loop variable is meant only for counting and doesn't represent anything, like employee numbers, you can just use a generic variable name, such as I or J, such as:

```
FOR I = 1 TO 15
   PRINT "John Smith"
NEXT I
```

This FOR-NEXT loop just prints the name "John Smith" onscreen 15 times.

Never change the value of a FOR-NEXT loop's variable within the loop or else you risk creating an *endless loop* — the computer keeps running the same commands over and over again without stopping. This makes your program appear to *freeze* or *hang*, essentially stopping your program from working altogether. The following example creates an endless loop:

```
FOR I = 1 TO 5
  PRINT "John Smith"
  I = 3
NEXT I
```

This FOR-NEXT loop should run five times. The first time the FOR-NEXT loop runs, the value of the I variable is set to 1. But within the FOR-NEXT loop, the value of the I variable is then set to 3. So each time the FOR-NEXT loop runs again, it checks to see whether the I variable's value is between 1 and 5.

Because the FOR-NEXT loop always resets the value of the I variable to 3, the I variable never falls outside the range of 1 to 5, so this FOR-NEXT loop runs indefinitely.

The curly-bracket language family creates a FOR-NEXT loop that looks slightly different from the way other languages do. For example, this is how BASIC creates a FOR-NEXT loop:

```
FOR I = 1 TO 15
  PRINT "John Smith"
NEXT I
```

This is the equivalent FOR-NEXT loop in C:

```
for (i = 1; i <= 15; i++)
{
  printf("John Smith");
}
```

The first line consists of three parts:

>> i = 1: Sets the value of the i variable to 1

>> i <= 15: Makes the FOR-NEXT loop keep repeating as long as the value of the i variable is less than or equal to 15

>> i++: Increases the value of the i variable by 1

**TECHNICAL
STUFF**

In any programming language, you can add 1 to any variable by doing this:

```
I = I + 1
```

The curly-bracket language family gives you a shortcut for adding 1 to any variable, which is known as the *increment operator*, such as:

```
i++
```

This is equivalent to:

```
i = i + 1
```

The increment operator is used more often than writing out the entire i = i + 1 command because it's shorter. There's also a similar decrement operator that looks like this:

```
i--
```

This is equivalent to:

```
i = i - 1
```

Counting by a different range

Normally, the FOR–NEXT loop counts from 1 to another number, such as 15. However, you can also count from any number range, such as 23 to 41, 102 to 105, or 2 to 8. The main reason to use a different range of numbers is if those numbers represent something in your program.

For example, suppose employees are assigned an employee number starting with 120 and there are four employees, as shown in Table 5-1.

TABLE 5-1 **A Database of Employee Names Assigned
with Specific Employee ID Numbers**

Employee Name	Employee ID Number
John Smith	120
Maggie Jones	121
Susan Wilson	122
Emir Kelly	123

You could use a FOR-NEXT loop like this:

```
FOR EmployeeID = 120 TO 123
  PRINT EmployeeName (EmployeeID)
NEXT EmployeeID
```

Each time this FOR-NEXT loop runs, it prints the employee name associated with a particular employee number, so it prints out the following:

```
John Smith
Maggie Jones
Susan Wilson
Emir Kelly
```

TIP

Counting by different number ranges is useful only if those numbers mean something to your program. If you just need to count a fixed number of times, it's much clearer to count from 1 to a specific value instead. The following FOR-NEXT loop actually runs four times (120, 121, 122, and 123):

```
FOR EmployeeID = 120 TO 123
  PRINT EmployeeName
NEXT EmployeeID
```

Notice that counting from 120 to 123 doesn't make it clear exactly how many times the FOR-NEXT loop runs. At first glance, it appears that the FOR-NEXT loop may repeat only three times.

To clarify exactly how many times the FOR-NEXT loop runs, it's always much clearer to count from 1, such as:

```
FOR EmployeeID = 1 TO 4
  PRINT EmployeeName(EmployeeID)
NEXT EmployeeID
```

Counting by different increments

Normally, the FOR-NEXT loop counts by 1. So consider the following FOR-NEXT loop:

```
FOR I = 1 TO 4
  PRINT "The value of I = ",I
NEXT I
```

This FOR-NEXT loop would print the following:

```
The value of I = 1
The value of I = 2
The value of I = 3
The value of I = 4
```

If you want to count by a number other than 1, you must define an increment. So, if you want to count by 2, you'd have to define an increment of 2, such as:

```
FOR I = 1 TO 4 STEP 2
  PRINT "The value of I = ",I
NEXT I
```

This modified FOR-NEXT loop would only print the following:

```
The value of I = 1
The value of I = 3
```

Although many languages, such as BASIC, assume the FOR-NEXT loop always increments by 1 unless you specifically tell it otherwise, the curly-bracket languages always force you to define an increment value. To define a FOR-NEXT loop in C to increment by 2, you can define i = i + 2, as follows:

```
for (i = 1; i <= 4; i = i + 2)
  {
  printf("The value of i = %d", i);
  }
```

Counting backward

Rather than count forward from 1 to 4, you can also make a FOR-NEXT loop count backward, like this:

```
FOR I = 4 DOWNTO 1
  PRINT "The value of I = ",I
NEXT I
```

REMEMBER

Much like using different number ranges, such as 34 to 87, counting backward makes sense only if those numbers have a specific meaning to your program, such as:

```
FOR I = 10 DOWNTO 1
```

```
  PRINT I
NEXT I
PRINT "BLASTOFF!"
```

This example would print the following:

```
10
9
8
7
6
5
4
3
2
1
BLASTOFF!
```

Although languages, such as BASIC, use a specific keyword (DOWNTO) to make a FOR–NEXT loop count backward, curly-bracket languages let you count backward by changing both the initial and ending value of the for–next variable and then defining an increment that subtracts instead of adds, such as:

```
for (i = 10; i >= 1; i = i - 1)
{
  printf("%d\n", i);
}
printf("Blastoff!");
```

Counting over arrays and other items

A for loop often specifies exactly how many times to loop. However, many programming languages let for loops count over arrays and other data structures that contain multiple items. By doing this, you don't need to specify how many times the for loop runs because the number of items defines how many times the for loop runs.

In Python, you can retrieve each item in an array like this:

```
for x in ["Mustang", "VW", "Ferrari", "Humvee", "Jeep"]:
  print(x)
```

This array contains five items, so the for loop runs exactly five times and prints out each item in the array like this:

```
"Mustang"
"VW"
"Ferrari"
"Humvee"
"Jeep"
```

In Swift, you can also define how many times a for loop runs by the number of characters in a string like this:

```
for x in "Hello" {
    print (x)
}
```

This tells the for loop to keep running once for each character in the string "Hello", which contains five characters. Thus, the for loop runs exactly five times and prints:

```
"H"
"e"
"l"
"l"
"o"
```

By using a for loop with an array or list, you don't need to define exactly how many times the for loop should run. Instead, the for loop simply counts the total number of items in the array or list and then runs once for each item in the array or list.

Looping Zero or More Times with the WHILE Loop

The FOR–NEXT loop is great when you know exactly how many times you want to run one or more commands. However, what if the number of times you want to run a loop can vary?

For example, you might have a loop that asks the user for a password, as shown in Figure 5-2. How many times should this loop run?

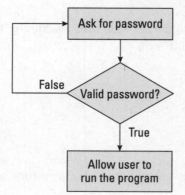

FIGURE 5-2:
The WHILE loop keeps running as long as a certain condition remains true.

The answer is that the loop should keep running until the user types in a valid password. Because you don't know how many times the loop needs to run, you need to use a WHILE loop to check a True or False (Boolean) expression. In this case, the Boolean expression is, "Did the user type in a valid password?" If the answer is Yes (True), the user can run the program. If the answer is No (False), the loop asks the user to try typing in a password again.

The WHILE loop typically looks like this:

```
WHILE (True or False Boolean expression)
   Command
   Command to change Boolean expression
WEND
```

With the curly-bracket languages, the WHILE loop looks like this:

```
while (True or False Boolean expression)
{
   command
   command to change Boolean expression
}
```

The WHILE loop consists of four parts:

» The beginning of the WHILE loop, which checks a Boolean expression for a True or False value

» One or more commands to run

» One or more commands that can change the Boolean expression in the beginning of the WHILE loop

» The end of the WHILE loop

Before the WHILE loop runs even once, it checks a Boolean expression for a True or False value. If this value is True, the WHILE loop runs. If this value is False, the WHILE loop doesn't run.

Within the WHILE loop, there must be one or more commands that can change the Boolean expression of the WHILE loop to False.

WARNING

If a WHILE loop doesn't include at least one command that can change its Boolean expression, the WHILE loop runs indefinitely, creating an endless loop that hangs or freezes your program.

The following WHILE loop keeps asking for a password until the user types **SECRET**:

```
DIM Answer as String
PROMPT "Enter password: ", Answer
WHILE (Answer <> "SECRET")
  PRINT "Invalid password!"
  PROMPT "Enter password: ", Answer
WEND
```

REMEMBER

Right before most WHILE loops is usually a line that sets an initial value to a variable used in the loop's Boolean expression. In the preceding example, the value of the Answer variable is *initialized* (set) to whatever the user types in response to the Enter password: prompt. Then the WHILE loop checks whether the value of the Answer variable is SECRET.

The first line defines the Answer variable as a string data type. The second line asks the user for a password and stores that answer in the Answer variable.

The WHILE loop first checks whether the Answer variable is SECRET. If not, the loop runs the two commands that print Invalid password and then displays Enter password: onscreen once more.

Whatever reply the user types gets stored in the Answer variable. Then the WHILE loop checks this Answer variable again before running.

TECHNICAL STUFF

You can make a WHILE loop count like a FOR-NEXT loop. Suppose you had the following FOR-NEXT loop:

```
FOR I = 10 DOWNTO 1
  PRINT I
NEXT I
PRINT "BLASTOFF!"
```

The equivalent WHILE loop might look like this:

```
I = 10
WHILE (I >= 1)
  PRINT I
  I = I - 1
WEND
PRINT "BLASTOFF!"
```

Although the WHILE loop can count, notice that it takes more lines of code to do so, and the WHILE loop isn't as easy to understand as the FOR–NEXT loop. If you need a loop to run a fixed number of times, use the FOR–NEXT loop. If you aren't sure how many times you need a loop to run, use the WHILE loop.

Looping at Least Once with the DO Loop

Before a WHILE loop runs, it checks a Boolean expression to see whether it's True or False. If this Boolean expression is False, the WHILE loop never runs at all. What if you want to ensure that the loop runs at least once? In that case, you must use a DO loop.

A DO loop acts like an upside-down WHILE loop. First, the DO loop runs once; then it checks a Boolean expression. A typical DO loop looks like this:

```
DO
  Command
  Command to change the Boolean expression
LOOP WHILE (True or False Boolean expression)
```

This DO loop keeps repeating while a Boolean expression remains True. As long as this Boolean expression stays True, the DO loop keeps running.

You could use a DO loop to ask the user to type in a password like this:

```
DIM Password as String
DO
  PROMPT "Enter password: ", Password
LOOP WHILE (Password <> "SECRET")
```

This DO loop always prints Enter your password: at least once before check-ing its Boolean expression Password <> "SECRET". If this Boolean expression is False, the DO loop stops running. If the Boolean expression is True, the DO loop repeats again.

REMEMBER

Like the WHILE loop, you often need to initialize a variable, which is part of the loop's Boolean expression to determine when the loop can stop running.

In the curly-bracket language family, the DO loop looks like this:

```
do
  {
  command
  command to change Boolean expression
  }
while (True or False Boolean expression);
```

This DO loop keeps repeating while a Boolean expression is True. When this Bool-ean expression becomes False, the DO loop stops running.

Playing with Nested Loops

Every loop (FOR–NEXT, WHILE, and DO) can run one or more commands multiple times. Therefore, it's possible for a loop to run another loop (which, in turn, can run a third loop, and so on).

REMEMBER

When loops appear inside one another, they're *nested loops.*

The following shows a FOR–NEXT loop nested inside another FOR–NEXT loop, as shown in Figure 5-3:

```
FOR I = 1 TO 4
  PRINT "Outer loop run #"; I
  FOR J = 1 TO 3
    PRINT "   Nested loop run #"; J
  NEXT J
NEXT I
```

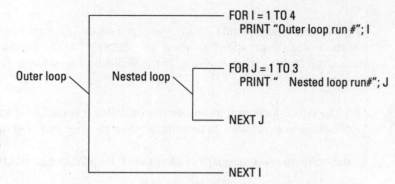

```
                                    ┌── FOR I = 1 TO 4
                                    │     PRINT "Outer loop run #"; I
                                    │
                                    │
                        ┌─── Nested loop ──┌── FOR J = 1 TO 3
    Outer loop ┐        │                  │     PRINT "   Nested loop run#"; J
               │        │                  │
               │        │                  └── NEXT J
               │        │
               │        │
               │        │
               └────────┴───────────────────── NEXT I
```

FIGURE 5-3:
A nested loop appears inside another loop.

When one loop is nested inside another loop, the *nested* (inner) loop completely finishes first. Then the outer loop runs once. Then the outer loop repeats running the nested loop again.

REMEMBER

The statements inside the nested loop run more often than those in the outer loop.

In the preceding example, the outer loop runs 4 times and the nested loop runs 3 times every time the outer loop runs, so the nested loop ultimately runs 12 times (3×4), as shown here:

```
Outer loop run #1
   Nested loop run #1
   Nested loop run #2
   Nested loop run #3
Outer loop run #2
   Nested loop run #1
   Nested loop run #2
   Nested loop run #3
Outer loop run #3
   Nested loop run #1
   Nested loop run #2
   Nested loop run #3
Outer loop run #4
   Nested loop run #1
   Nested loop run #2
   Nested loop run #3
```

TIP

The more nested loops you have, the harder it can be to tell exactly what your program actually does. As a general rule, it's best to nest only one loop inside another.

Prematurely Exiting from a Loop

Loops normally run a fixed number of times (with a FOR–NEXT loop) or until a Boolean expression changes (with a WHILE or DO loop). However, it's possible to exit prematurely out of a loop by using a special EXIT command.

Prematurely exiting a loop means not waiting for the loop to stop on its own, such as:

```
DO
  Play video game
  IF Player wants to quit THEN EXIT
LOOP WHILE (Game over <> true)
```

In this case, the loop ends in one of two ways: when the game ends or when the user specifically quits the game.

To prematurely exit a loop, you always need to check whether another Boolean expression is True or False. Generally, it's not a good idea to prematurely exit out of a loop because it can make your program harder to understand.

TECHNICAL STUFF

The curly-bracket languages don't have an EXIT command; instead, they have a break command, which works the same way, like this:

```
do
  {
  Play video game;
  if (Player wants to quit) break;
  }
while (Game over <> true);
```

Checking Your Loops

Although loops eliminate the need to write the same command multiple times, loops also introduce the risk of making your program harder to understand as a result (and also harder to fix and update). So, when using loops, keep these points in mind:

>> To loop a fixed number of times, use a FOR–NEXT loop.

>> To loop zero or more times, use a WHILE loop.

» To loop at least once, use a DO loop.

» Both WHILE and DO loops usually need a variable or a Boolean expression to determine when the loop ends.

» A WHILE or DO loop always needs a command that changes its Boolean expression that determines when the loop will eventually stop.

» A loop that never stops running is an *endless loop*.

» Some programming languages let you use an EXIT (or break command) to stop a loop prematurely. Use this with caution because it can make your program harder to understand.

When using a loop, always make sure you know how that loop will eventually stop.

Almost every program needs to use loops, so make sure you understand the differences between all the different loop variations you can use. Ultimately, loops let you run multiple commands without explicitly writing them all out, so think of loops as a programming shortcut.

Chapter 6

Breaking a Large Program into Subprograms

The bigger the program, the harder that program is to read, fix, and modify. Just as it's easier to spot a spelling mistake in a recipe printed on a single page than it is to find that same spelling mistake buried inside a 350-page cookbook, it's easier to fix problems in a small program than it is in a big one.

Because small programs can perform only simple tasks, the idea behind programming is to write a lot of little programs and paste them together, like building blocks, creating one massive program. Because each little program is part of a much bigger program, those little programs are *subprograms*, as shown in Figure 6-1.

WARNING

The biggest problem with dividing a large program into multiple subprograms is to make each subprogram as independent, or *loosely coupled*, as possible. That means if one subprogram fails, it doesn't wreck the entire program along with it, like yanking out a single playing card from a house of cards.

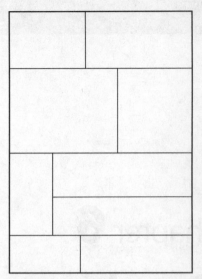

FIGURE 6-1:
Every large
program is made
up of smaller
subprograms
that act as
building blocks.

A program can consist of one
massive chunk of code.

Subprograms divide a large program
into smaller pieces to make the
large program easier to create and
modify.

One major advantage of subprograms is that you can isolate common program features in a subprogram that you can copy and reuse in another program. For example, suppose you wrote a word processor. Although you could write it as one massive, interconnected tangle of code, a better approach might be dividing the program functions into separate parts. By doing this, you could create a separate subprogram for

>> Displaying drop-down lists

>> Editing text

>> Spell-checking

>> Printing a file

If you wanted to write a horse-race prediction program, you wouldn't have to write the whole thing from scratch. You could copy the subprograms from another program and reuse them in your new project, as shown in Figure 6-2.

By reusing subprograms, you can create more complicated programs faster than before. After programmers create enough useful subprograms, they can store these subprograms in a "library" that they and other programmers can use in the future.

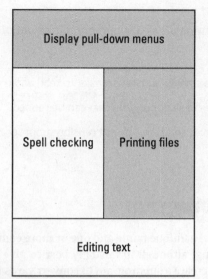

Display pull-down menus

Spell checking | Printing files

Editing text

Display pull-down menus

Calculate the winning race horse | Printing files

Analyze race horse statistics

FIGURE 6-2: Reusing subprograms can make writing new programs easier and faster.

A word processor can consist of four separate subprograms that work together.

A completely different program, such as a horse race prediction program, can reuse subprograms to make programming faster and easier.

Creating and Using Subprograms

A subprogram essentially yanks out one or more commands from your main program and stores them in another part of your main program or in a separate file, as shown in Figure 6-3.

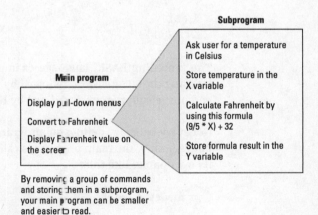

Main program

Display pull-down menus

Ask user for a temperature in Celsius

Store temperature in the X variable

Calculate Fahrenheit by using this formula
(9/5 C * X) + 32

Store formula result in the Y variable

Display Fahrenheit value on the screen

Without subprograms, you must list every step, which can make your main program bigger and harder to read.

Main program

Display pull-down menus

Convert to Fahrenheit

Display Fahrenheit value on the screen

By removing a group of commands and storing them in a subprogram, your main program can be smaller and easier to read.

Subprogram

Ask user for a temperature in Celsius

Store temperature in the X variable

Calculate Fahrenheit by using this formula
(9/5 * X) + 32

Store formula result in the Y variable

FIGURE 6-3: Subprograms let you remove and isolate commands out of your main program.

The reasons for isolating commands in a subprogram (and out of your main program) are to

» Keep your main program smaller and, thus, easier to read and modify.

» Isolate related commands in a subprogram that can be reused.

» Make programming simpler and faster by just reusing subprograms from other projects.

Creating a subprogram

Every subprogram consists of a unique name and one or more commands. You can name a subprogram anything, although it's usually best to give a subprogram a descriptive name. So, if you create a subprogram to convert yards into meters, you might name your subprogram Yards2Meters or MetricConverter.

TIP

A descriptive name for a subprogram can help you identify the purpose of that subprogram.

After you define a name for your subprogram, you can fill it up with one or more commands that tell that subprogram what to do. So, if you wanted to write a subprogram that prints your name onscreen, your main subprogram might look like this:

```
SUB PrintMyName
  FOR I = 1 TO 5
    PRINT "John Smith"
  NEXT I
END SUB
```

The preceding BASIC language example defines the beginning of a subprogram by using the SUB keyword followed by the subprogram's name, PrintMyName. The end of the subprogram is defined by the END SUB keywords.

Not every language defines subprograms with keywords. In the curly-bracket language family, the main program is called main and every subprogram is just given its own name, like this:

```
print_my_name ()
{
  for (i = 1; i < 5; i++)
  {
```

```
    printf ("John Smith");
  }
}
```

Instead of using the term *subprogram*, the curly-bracket languages use the term *function*.

You can store subprograms in the same file as the main program or in a separate file. If you store a subprogram in the same file as the main program, you can place the subprogram at the beginning or end of the file, as shown in Figure 6-4.

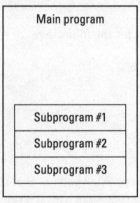

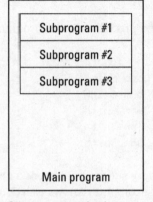

FIGURE 6-4:
Subprograms
usually appear at
the beginning or
end of a file.

Some programming languages make you store subprograms at the end of a file, after the main program.

Other programming languages make you store subprograms at the beginning of a file, before the main program.

REMEMBER

Programmers often put subprograms at the beginning or end of a file to make them easy to find.

"Calling" a subprogram

After you isolate commands inside a subprogram, your program can't run those commands until it "calls" the subprogram. Calling a subprogram basically tells the computer, "See those commands stored in that subprogram over there? Run those commands now!"

To call a subprogram, you must use the subprogram's name as a command. So, if you had the following subprogram:

```
SUB PrintMyName
  FOR I = 1 TO 5
    PRINT "John Smith"
  NEXT I
END SUB
```

To run this subprogram, you would use its name as a command in any part of your program, like this:

```
PRINT "The subprogram is going to run now."
PrintMyName
END
```

The preceding BASIC program would print the following:

```
The subprogram is going to run now.
John Smith
John Smith
John Smith
John Smith
John Smith
```

REMEMBER

Every subprogram needs a unique name so when you call that subprogram to run, the computer knows exactly which subprogram to use. You can call a subprogram from any part of a program, even from within another subprogram.

In the curly-bracket language family, calling a *function* (subprogram) is the same. Use the subprogram's name as a command. So, if you had the following subprogram:

```
print_my_name ()
{
  for (i = 1; i < 5; i++)
  {
    printf ("John Smith");
  }
}
```

You could call that subprogram as follows:

```
main ()
{
  print_my_name ();
}
```

If you've stored a subprogram in a separate file, you may need to go through two steps to call a subprogram. First, you need to specify the filename that contains the subprogram you want to use. Second, you need to call the subprogram you want by name.

In the curly-bracket languages, like C you specify a filename where your subprogram is stored, like this:

```
#include <filename>
main()
{
   subprogram name ();
}
```

In this C example, the `#include<filename>` command tells the computer that if it can't find a subprogram in the main program file, it should look in the file dubbed *filename.*

TECHNICAL STUFF

The `#include` command tells the computer to pretend that every subprogram stored in a separate file is actually *included* in the main program file.

Passing Parameters

Every time you call a subprogram, that subprogram runs its commands. So, if you had a subprogram like this:

```
SUB PrintJohnSmith
   FOR I = 1 TO 5
      PRINT "John Smith"
   NEXT I
END SUB
```

Calling that subprogram from another part of your program would always print the name *John Smith* exactly five times. If you wanted a subprogram that could print the name *Mary Jones* 16 times, you'd have to write another similar subprogram, like this:

```
SUB PrintMaryJones
   FOR I = 1 TO 16
      PRINT "Mary Jones"
   NEXT I
END SUB
```

Obviously, writing similar subprograms that do nearly identical tasks is wasteful and time-consuming. So, instead, you can write a generic subprogram that accepts additional data, called *parameters.*

These parameters let you change the way a subprogram works. So, instead of writing one subprogram to print the name *John Smith* 5 times and a second subprogram to print the name *Mary Jones* 16 times, you could write a single subprogram that accepts two parameters that define

>> The name to print

>> The number of times to print that name

Here's what that would look like:

```
SUB PrintMyName (PrintTimes As Integer, Name As String)
  FOR I = 1 TO PrintTimes
    PRINT Name
  NEXT I
END SUB
```

REMEMBER

The list of parameters, enclosed in parentheses, is a *parameter list.*

This BASIC language example defines a subprogram named `PrintMyName`, which accepts two parameters. The first parameter is an integer variable — `PrintTimes` — which defines how many times to print a name. The second parameter is a string variable — `Name` — which defines the name to print multiple times.

TECHNICAL STUFF

Every programming language offers slightly different ways of creating a subprogram. Here's what an equivalent Python subprogram might look like:

```
def print_my_name(print_times, name):
    for I in range(print_times):
        print (name)
```

By writing a generic subprogram that accepts parameters, you can create a single subprogram that can behave differently, depending on the parameters it receives.

To give or *pass* parameters to a subprogram, you need to call the subprogram by name along with the parameters you want to give that subprogram. So, if a subprogram accepted two parameters (an integer and a string), you could call that subprogram by doing the following:

```
PrintMyName (5, "John Smith")
PrintMyName (16, "Mary Jones")
```

The first command tells the PrintMyName subprogram to use the number 5 and the string John Smith as its parameters. Because the number defines how many times to print and the string defines what to print, this first command tells the PrintMyName subprogram to print *John Smith* five times, as shown in Figure 6-5.

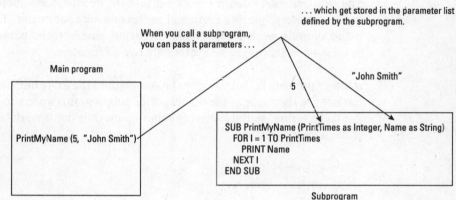

FIGURE 6-5:
When you call a subprogram, you may also need to pass parameters to that subprogram.

The second command tells the PrintMyName subprogram to use the number 16 and the string Mary Jones as its parameters, which prints *Mary Jones* 16 times.

Calling a subprogram works the same way in other programming languages. So, if you want to call the following Python subprogram:

```
def print_my_name(print_times, name):
    for I in range(print_times):
        print (name)
```

You could print the name *John Smith* four times with this command:

```
print_my_name(4, "John Smith")
```

WARNING

When you call a subprogram, you must give it the exact number and type of parameters it expects to receive. So, the PrintMyName subprogram accepts two parameters whereas the first parameter must be an integer and the second parameter must be a string, such as the following:

```
PrintMyName (4, "Hal Berton")
PrintMyName (53, "Billie Buttons")
```

If you don't give a subprogram the right number of parameters, your program doesn't work. So, if a subprogram is expecting two parameters, the following statements don't work because they don't give the subprogram exactly two parameters:

```
PrintMyName (4)
PrintMyName (4, 90, "Roberta Clarence")
```

The first command doesn't work because the PrintMyName subprogram expects two parameters, but this command passes only one parameter. The second command doesn't work because this command passes three parameters, but the PrintMyName subprogram expects only two parameters.

Another problem is that you give the subprogram the exact number of parameters, but not the right *type* of parameters. This subprogram expects to receive an integer and a string, so the following subprogram calls don't work because they give it the wrong data:

```
PrintMyName (98, 23)
PrintMyName ("Victor Harris", 7)
```

The first command doesn't work because the PrintMyName subprogram expects an integer and a string, but this command tries to give it two numbers. The second command doesn't work because the PrintMyName subprogram expects an integer first and a string second, but this command gives it the data in the wrong order.

REMEMBER

If a subprogram doesn't need any parameters, you can just call that subprogram by using its name, like this:

```
PrintMyName
```

If you aren't passing any parameters in some programming languages, you must leave the *parameter list* (the stuff between the parentheses) blank, like this:

```
PrintMyName ();
```

Passing parameters by reference

When a program calls and passes parameters to a subprogram, the computer makes duplicate copies of those parameters. One copy of those parameters stays with the main program, and the second copy gets passed to the subprogram.

Now if the subprogram changes those parameters, the values of those parameters stay trapped within the subprogram, as shown in Figure 6-6.

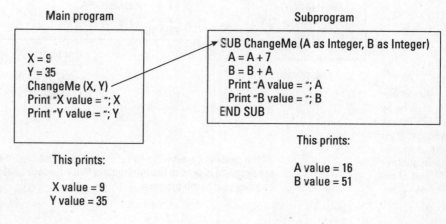

Main program

```
X = 9
Y = 35
ChangeMe (X, Y)
Print "X value = "; X
Print "Y value = "; Y
```

This prints:

X value = 9
Y value = 35

Subprogram

```
SUB ChangeMe (A as Integer, B as Integer)
    A = A + 7
    B = B + A
    Print "A value = "; A
    Print "B value = "; B
END SUB
```

This prints:

A value = 16
B value = 51

FIGURE 6-6: Normally when you pass parameters to a subprogram, the computer makes a second copy for the subprogram to use.

When passing parameters by value, any changes the subprogram makes to the parameters won't be sent back to any other part of the program.

TECHNICAL STUFF

When you pass parameters to a subprogram and make duplicate copies of those parameters, that's called *passing by value*.

Most of the time when you call a subprogram and pass it parameters, you don't want that subprogram to change the value of its parameters; you just want the subprogram to modify its behavior based on the parameters it receives, such as the subprogram that prints a name a specific number of times.

Instead of giving a subprogram parameters that modify its behavior, you can also give a subprogram parameters that the subprogram can modify and send back to the rest of the program.

To make a subprogram modify its parameters, you must use a technique called *pass by reference*. Essentially, instead of letting a subprogram use a copy of data, passing by reference gives the subprogram the actual data to manipulate, as shown in Figure 6-7.

Suppose you have a subprogram that converts temperatures from Celsius to Fahrenheit with this formula:

```
Tf = ((9 / 5) * Tc) + 32
```

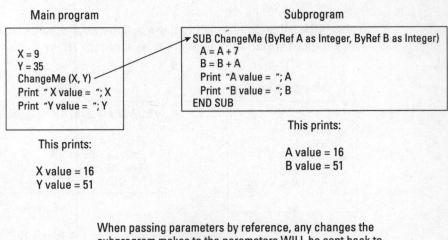

Main program

```
X = 9
Y = 35
ChangeMe (X, Y)
Print " X value =  "; X
Print "Y value =  "; Y
```

This prints:

X value = 16
Y value = 51

Subprogram

```
SUB ChangeMe (ByRef A as Integer, ByRef B as Integer)
    A = A + 7
    B = B + A
    Print "A value =  "; A
    Print "B value =  "; B
END SUB
```

This prints:

A value = 16
B value = 51

FIGURE 6-7:
Passing by
reference means
the subprogram
can manipulate
data that another
part of the
program will use.

When passing parameters by reference, any changes the subprogram makes to the parameters WILL be sent back to another part of the program.

Your subprogram could look like this:

```
SUB ConvertC2F (ByRef Temperature as Single)
    Temperature = ((9 / 5) * Temperature) + 32
END SUB
```

This is how the preceding subprogram works:

» The first line defines the subprogram name — ConvertC2F — and its parameter list as accepting one Single variable called Temperature. To specify that this parameter will be passed by reference, this BASIC language example uses the ByRef keyword.

» The second line plugs the value of the Temperature variable into the conversion equation and stores the result back in the Temperature variable, erasing the preceding value that was stored there.

» The third line ends the subprogram. At this point, the modified value of the Temperature variable is sent back to the main program to use.

TECHNICAL STUFF

Every programming language uses different ways to identify when a parameter will be passed by reference. The BASIC language uses the ByRef keyword, whereas the C language uses the ampersand symbol (&) to identify parameters passed by reference. In the following C example, the a parameter is passed by value but the x parameter is passed by reference:

```
subprogram_example (int a, float &x);
```

If you had the following BASIC subprogram:

```
SUB ConvertC2F (ByRef Temperature as Single)
  Temperature = ((9 / 5) * Temperature) + 32
END SUB
```

You could call that subprogram like this:

```
DIM Temp AS SINGLE
Temp = 12
PRINT "This is the temperature in Celsius = "; Temp
ConvertC2F (Temp)
PRINT "This is the temperature in Fahrenheit = "; Temp
END
```

Running this program would produce the following:

```
This is the temperature in Celsius = 12
This is the temperature in Fahrenheit = 53.6
```

Notice that right before calling the ConvertC2F subprogram, the value of the Temp variable is 12, but the ConvertC2F subprogram changes that value because the subprogram was passed the Temp value by reference. What happens if you run the same program except change the subprogram to accept parameters passed by value instead, such as the following?

```
DIM Temp AS SINGLE
Temp = 12
PRINT "This is the temperature in Celsius = "; Temp
ConvertC2F (Temp)
PRINT "This is the temperature in Fahrenheit = "; Temp
END
SUB ConvertC2F (Temperature as Single)
  Temperature = ((9 / 5) * Temperature) + 32
END SUB
```

This program would print the following:

```
This is the temperature in Celsius = 12
This is the temperature in Fahrenheit = 12
```

Although the ConvertC2F subprogram changed the value of the Temperature parameter, it never passes the changed value back to the main program. So, the main program blissfully uses the current value of the Temp variable, which is always 12.

Passing data by reference means that the subprogram can change any data used by another part of a program. This can increase the chance of problems because the more ways data can be changed, the harder it can be to track down errors.

Storing values in a subprogram name

One problem with passing parameters by reference is that you may not always know when a subprogram will change its parameter values. To make it clear when a subprogram returns modified data, you can create a special type of subprogram called a *function*.

A function is nothing more than a subprogram with the subprogram name representing a value. So a typical function might look like this:

```
FUNCTION Name (parameter list) As DataType
   Commands
   RETURN value
END FUNCTION
```

In BASIC, you identify a function with the FUNCTION keyword to define a subprogram as a function. After listing a parameter list, the first line also defines the data type that the function name can hold, such as an integer, a string, or a single (decimal) number.

Defining a function in the C language to return a value looks like this:

```
datatype function_name (parameter list)
   {
   commands
   return value;
   }
```

Defining a function in the Swift language to return a value looks like this:

```
func_function_name (parameter list) -> DataType
   {
   commands
   return value;
   }
```

In this Swift example, you specify the data type to return such as an Int or String. Then you use the return keyword to define the value to return, such as 78 or "Greetings".

Inside the function, one or more commands must calculate a new result. Then you use the RETURN (or return) keyword to define what value to store in the function name. Whatever value this is, it must be the same data type that you defined for the function name in the first line. So, if you defined a function as a String data type, you can't return an integer value from that function.

A typical function in BASIC might look like this:

```
FUNCTION ConvertC2F (Temperature As Single) As Single
    Temperature = ((9 / 5) * Temperature) + 32
    RETURN Temperature
END FUNCTION
```

The function name ConvertC2F can hold a Single data type.

Unlike a subprogram that may or may not return a modified value, functions always return a value. To call a function, you must assign the function name to a variable or use the function name itself as a variable, such as

```
PRINT "Temperature in Fahrenheit = "; ConvertC2F (12)
```

REMEMBER

Because functions always return a value, they (almost always) have a parameter list. So, you can identify functions in a program by looking for the parameter list in parentheses.

```
DIM Temp As Single
Temp = 12
PRINT "Temperature in Celsius = "; Temp
PRINT "Temperature in Fahrenheit = "; ConvertC2F (Temp)
END

FUNCTION ConvertC2F (Temperature AS SINGLE) AS SINGLE
    Temperature = ((9 / 5) * Temperature) + 32
    RETURN Temperature
END FUNCTION
```

Unlike a subprogram that you can call just by typing its name on a line by itself, you can call a function only by using that function name as if it's a variable.

This same function as seen in the Python language might look like this:

```
def convertc2f(temperature):
    new = ((9.0 / 5.0) * temperature) + 32
    return new
```

To run this function, you could use the following program:

```
temp = 12
print ("Temperature in Celsius = ", temp)
print ("Temperature in Fahrenheit = ", convertc2f(temp))
```

Repeating a Subprogram with Recursion

In Chapter 5 of this minibook, you can read about loops that can repeat one or more commands multiple times. If you want to repeat the commands stored in a subprogram, you can just call that subprogram from within a loop, such as

```
FOR I = 1 TO 4
   Subprogram name
NEXT I
```

This example would run all the commands in a subprogram four times. However, here's another way to run a subprogram multiple times: *recursion.* The idea behind recursion is that instead of defining how many times to run a subprogram, you let the subprogram call itself multiple times, like this:

```
SUB MySubprogram
   MySubprogram
END SUB
```

When this subprogram runs, it calls itself, essentially making a second copy of itself, which then makes a third copy of itself, and so on. A common problem used to demonstrate recursion is calculating a *factorial* (which multiplies a number by a gradually decreasing series of numbers).

REMEMBER

Not every programming language supports recursion, including some versions of BASIC.

A factorial is often written like this:

```
4!
```

To calculate a factorial, you multiply a number (4, in this case) by a number that's one less (3) and keep repeating this until you get the value of 1, such as

```
4! = 4 * 3 * 2 * 1
   = 24
```

To calculate a factorial, you could use a BASIC program like this:

```
FUNCTION Factorial (N as INTEGER) As REAL
  IF N > 1 THEN
    Factorial = N * Factorial (N - 1)
  ELSE
    Factorial = 1
  END IF
END FUNCTION
```

This function uses recursion to run another copy of itself, as shown in Figure 6-8.

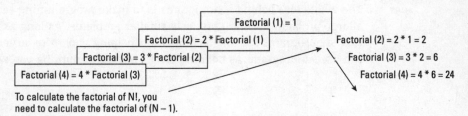

Factorial (1) = 1

Factorial (2) = 2 * Factorial (1)

Factorial (3) = 3 * Factorial (2)

Factorial (4) = 4 * Factorial (3)

Factorial (2) = 2 * 1 = 2

Factorial (3) = 3 * 2 = 6

Factorial (4) = 4 * 6 = 24

To calculate the factorial of N!, you need to calculate the factorial of (N – 1).

Eventually a recursive subprogram must calculate a single value, which then gets used in previous recursive subprograms until they calculate a single value.

FIGURE 6-8: Recursion makes multiple copies of the same subprogram.

Ultimately, every subprogram that calls itself needs to end. (Otherwise, it can get trapped in an endless series of function calls that never end, which hangs or freezes your computer.) When a subprogram finally ends, it returns a value to the preceding subprogram, which returns its value to the preceding subprogram, and so on until a value is finally calculated by the first copy of the subprogram that initially ran.

The advantage of recursion is that it's much simpler to write. If you didn't use recursion, this is how you could calculate factorials using an ordinary FOR–NEXT loop:

```
FUNCTION Factorial (N as INTEGER) as REAL
  DIM Total as REAL
  DIM M as INTEGER
  Total = 1
  FOR M = N DOWNTO 1
    Total = Total * M
    Factorial = Total
  NEXT M
END FUNCTION
```

This subprogram calculates the exact same results as the recursion version.

Naturally, recursion has its disadvantages:

» **Recursion can gobble up lots of memory.** It runs the same subprogram multiple times, so it makes additional copies of itself.

» **Recursion can crash your computer if it doesn't end.** Your subprogram can keep making endless copies of itself until it runs out of memory.

If you couldn't isolate commands in a subprogram, you could never have recursion.

The whole idea behind subprograms is to make programming easier by breaking a large problem into progressively smaller problems. As long as you understand that subprograms are one technique for helping you write larger programs, you can use subprograms as building blocks to create anything you want.

IN THIS CHAPTER

» **Understanding object-oriented programming**

» **Clarifying encapsulation, inheritance, and polymorphism**

» **Explaining design patterns**

» **Using object-oriented languages**

» **Providing real-life programming examples**

Chapter **7**

Breaking a Large Program into Objects

Breaking a large program into multiple subprograms makes programming easier. Instead of trying to write a single, monolithic chunk of code, you just have to write small subprograms that work as building blocks that you can stack together to create a much larger program.

Unfortunately, computer scientists found that just dividing a large program into multiple subprograms didn't magically solve all the problems of creating software. Some of the most prominent problems of subprograms include

» **Interconnectedness:** Instead of acting as independent entities, subprograms are often allowed to interfere with other parts of a program. Not only does this cause problems in tracking down *bugs* (problems), but it also prevents subprograms from being reused easily in other projects. Instead of easily sliding a subprogram out of a program like a building block, it's more like ripping a plant out of the ground by its roots.

» **Task orientation:** Subprograms focus on solving one specific task. Unfortunately, trying to understand how this one task fits into the overall design of a large program can be confusing, much like trying to understand how a car works by studying a single gear. As a result, subprograms make large programs hard to understand and modify. Not only do you not know how a subprogram works with the rest of the program, but you also don't know how changing a subprogram might inadvertently affect other parts of the program.

>> **Reusability:** Theoretically, you can yank out a subprogram and reuse it in another program. However, if you copy and later modify a subprogram, you now have two nearly identical copies of the same subprogram. If you find a problem in the original subprogram, you now have to find and fix that same problem in any copies you made of that subprogram — provided you can find them all in the first place.

To overcome the limitations of subprograms, computer scientists invented object-oriented programming (OOP). Like structured programming, which encourages you to break a large program into subprograms, OOP encourages you to break a large program into smaller parts, called *objects.*

TECHNICAL STUFF

OOP has actually been around since 1962 when two Norwegian computer scientists Ole-Johan Dahl and Kristen Nygaard developed a language called SIMULA, which was designed to help simulate real-world events. It took nearly 40 more years for OOP to finally be accepted as a practical tool, so just because an idea is proven to work, doesn't mean people will accept it if they can continue being comfortable (and getting paid) to keep doing something that doesn't work.

How Object-Oriented Programming Works

Like subprograms, objects divide a large program into smaller, interchangeable parts. The main difference is that subprograms divide a program into separate tasks, whereas objects divide a program into real-world items.

For example, consider a hotel reservation program used by the front desk when a guest checks in. Dividing this problem into tasks might create the following:

>> **Subprogram #1:** RoomAvailable (checks if a hotel room is available)

>> **Subprogram #2:** RoomBeds (checks if the room has one or two beds)

>> **Subprogram #3:** RoomType (checks if it's a smoking or a nonsmoking room)

>> **Subprogram #4:** RoomPrice (checks the price)

Dividing this problem into objects, you could create the following:

- **Object #1:** Guest

- **Object #2:** Front desk clerk

- **Object #3:** Hotel room

Figure 7-1 shows how a task-oriented solution might break a program into multiple subprograms. The main program works by running each subprogram, one at a time, with each subprogram performing a specific task (such as determining whether a room is smoking or nonsmoking).

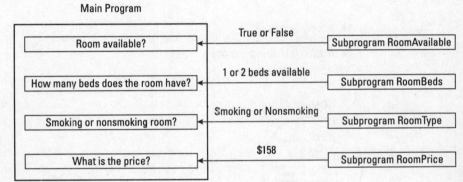

FIGURE 7-1:
Dividing a program into tasks can obscure the actual purpose of a program.

Figure 7-2 shows an equivalent object-oriented solution to the same program where each object represents a real-world item. Instead of having a single main program controlling multiple subprograms (like one boss controlling a dozen subordinates), OOP divides a program into multiple objects that pass messages to one another (like having a bunch of workers cooperating with one another as equals).

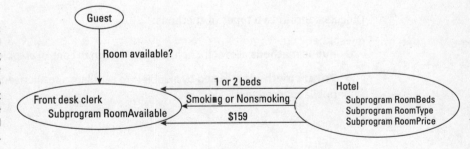

FIGURE 7-2:
Object-oriented programming divides a large program into objects that behave like their real-world counterparts.

Although both subprograms and objects solve the same problem, they use different solutions. OOP is basically a different way of thinking about how to solve problems.

REMEMBER

Objects aren't an alternative to subprograms. Subprograms solve a single task. Objects just organize related subprograms together.

REMEMBER

There's no single "right" way to divide a large program into objects. Two programmers tackling the same problem will likely divide the same program into different objects. The way you define your objects reflects how you view a particular problem.

Every object consists of two parts, as shown in Figure 7-3:

>> *Properties* (data)

>> *Methods* (subprograms)

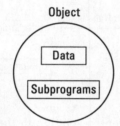

FIGURE 7-3:
The parts of a typical object.

Objects contain two types of properties:

>> **Public properties** are accessible by other parts of the program.

>> **Private properties** within the object are hidden from the rest of the program.

Objects contain two types of methods:

>> **Public methods** allow other parts of a program to control an object.

>> **Private methods** are used by an object to calculate a result needed by its public subprograms.

The difference between public and private is accessibility:

>> **Public** properties and methods are what the rest of a program can "see" and use in an object:

- Public properties typically describe the object in some way. For example, a video-game program might create an object that represents a monster. This object may need data, representing x- and y-coordinates, to define the monster's location onscreen.

- Public methods allow other parts of a program to manipulate an object. For example, an object representing a monster might include a Move method that can change the value of the object's x- and y-coordinates (to determine where to display the cartoon monster onscreen).

>> **Private** properties and methods are what an object uses to do something useful, so the object doesn't need to allow other parts of the program to access this information.

The Monster object might contain a private method that calculates exactly how the Monster object moves. Because other parts of the program don't need to know exactly how the Monster object calculates its movement, this type of information would be private and hidden from the rest of the program.

Ultimately, OOP is another way to make programming easier. Just as high-level languages (like BASIC) simplify programming by using real-life commands (such as PRINT), OOP simplifies organizing programs by modeling real-life items. The three advantages that objects have over ordinary subprograms are encapsulation, inheritance, and polymorphism (all of which I cover in the following sections).

OOP provides tools for making programming easier, but it's still possible to write horrible software with OOP. Think of OOP like lines painted on the highway. If you follow the lines, you'll probably arrive safely at your destination, but if you ignore the lines and do whatever you want, you'll probably crash your car. Like traffic lines painted on the road, OOP guides you into writing software that can be created and modified easily, but you can still mess things up if you're not careful.

Encapsulation Isolates Data and Subprograms

Subprograms have two problems. First, subprograms can work with data from any part of a program. That's what makes subprograms useful, but that's also what makes subprograms harder to modify and fix. If you don't know what data a subprogram might manipulate and when, any changes you make to that subprogram could affect a program in unpredictable ways.

For example, suppose someone writes a weather forecasting program that has a subprogram for predicting tomorrow's temperature measured in Fahrenheit. What happens if another programmer modifies this subprogram to forecast temperatures in Celsius?

Figure 7-4 shows two phases of a program:

» The first phase (on the left) shows the main program sending the current temperature (32°F) to the forecasting subprogram, which then returns its prediction (as 30°F).

» The second phase (on the right) shows the same program except now the forecasting subprogram has been modified to return Celsius temperatures. So now when the main program sends the current temperature (in Fahrenheit) to the forecasting subprogram, this subprogram returns its forecast in Celsius. The main program now uses this faulty value.

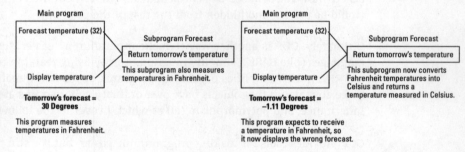

FIGURE 7-4:
Changing a subprogram can wreck a perfectly working program.

This problem occurs because the forecasting subprogram has no idea how its data is being used by another part of the program. OOP can partially solve this problem by organizing data, and all the subprograms that manipulate that data, into a single location, or an *object.* By grouping properties and all the methods that manipulate that data in one place, it's much easier to understand how that data is being used.

The whole idea behind an object is to isolate and "hide" properties and methods by using *encapsulation.* Encapsulation acts like a wall, as shown in Figure 7-5, that wraps around properties and methods to

» Keep other parts of a program from manipulating properties inside an object.

» Keep methods inside that object from manipulating data outside that object.

» Keep programmers from modifying code stored in another object.

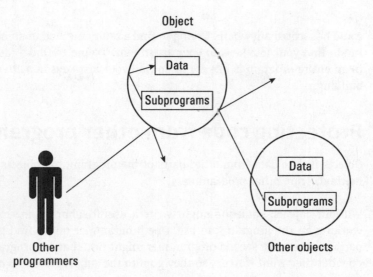

FIGURE 7-5:
Encapsulation isolates a chunk of code as an independent object.

Shielding data inside an object

Think of data as a wallet full of cash. The more people who handle your wallet before giving it back to you, the greater the chance that someone takes money out of that wallet (manipulating the properties). Ideally, you want as few people to handle your wallet as possible and if people absolutely must handle your wallet, you want them close enough so you can keep an eye on them.

That's the same idea behind encapsulating properties inside an object. In a program divided into multiple subprograms, data gets passed around like a hot potato. The more subprograms capable of changing a chunk of data, the more likely one of those subprograms can accidentally change that data incorrectly.

By encapsulating properties inside of an object, you prevent anything outside that object from manipulating the properties.

Grouping methods inside of an object

After you isolate properties inside an object, you also need to isolate all the methods that manipulate that data inside that same object. By storing all methods that manipulate the same properties, objects make it easy to isolate any problems.

If a property inside an object gets messed up, the faulty method can be located only inside that same object. This makes troubleshooting easier. In comparison, if data gets messed up in a non-object-oriented program, the faulty subprogram could be located anywhere. Trying to find a faulty method in an object is like trying to find your lost keys in your apartment. Trying to find a faulty subprogram in an entire program is like trying to find your lost keys in a 20-story apartment building.

Protecting code from other programmers

Objects isolate data from other parts of the program, but objects can also isolate methods from other programmers.

Without objects, someone might write a useful subprogram that everyone else working on the program can use. One programmer might find that subprogram perfect, whereas a second programmer might find that subprogram doesn't quite do what they want it to do, so they go into the subprogram and change the code.

These changes wreck the subprogram for the first programmer, who now has to go back and fix the changes made by the second programmer. These changes make the subprogram work well for the first programmer, but now wreck the subprogram for the second programmer, and so on in an endless cycle.

The problem is that the more people you have working on the same program, the more likely someone might accidentally modify one part of a program without notifying the other programmers. Even one change in a program can affect another part of that same program, so OOP defines distinct boundaries that keep programmers from modifying code stored in objects created by someone else.

When creating an object-oriented program, every programmer is given control of certain objects and no one is supposed to modify the code in any objects but their own.

To define an object, you must first create a class. You can create a class in a separate file or store several classes in the same file. At this point, a class is no different from storing a group of related subprograms in a separate file and keeping other programmers from modifying that separate file. However, the difference becomes more apparent when you want to reuse code.

REMEMBER

Encapsulation serves two purposes:

>> It protects properties from being changed by other parts of a program.

>> It isolates methods to minimize the chances they'll be changed by other programmers.

Sharing Code with Inheritance

After programmers write some useful subprograms, they often store those subprograms in separate files for other programmers to use. However, no one is supposed to modify these subprograms.

So, what happens if someone creates a subprogram that almost does what you need, but not quite? You can't modify the subprogram without the risk of wrecking it for other parts of the program, but you can copy that subprogram and then modify that copy. Now you'll have two separate and nearly identical copies of the same subprograms, as shown in Figure 7-6.

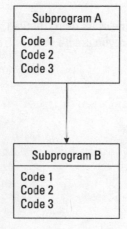

FIGURE 7-6:
If you modify a subprogram, you need to create a separate copy of that subprogram and modify that copy.

What happens if the original subprogram (that you copied) gets modified to make it even more awesome and useful? Now you're stuck with two equally unappealing choices with your modified version of that same subprogram:

» Dump your modified subprogram, copy the new modified subprogram, and re-modify this new version.

» Modify your subprograms yourself to incorporate the changes made to the subprogram you originally copied.

Neither solution will be easy because with the first option, you must modify the revised original subprogram all over again. If you made extensive modifications to that subprogram, you'll have to make those same extensive modifications once more. Each time the original subprogram gets modified, you'll have to repeat this step over and over again.

The second option is just as difficult because now you have to study the changes made in the original subprogram and add those changes to your modified subprogram. If you do this incorrectly, your modified version won't work right. Each time the original subprogram gets modified, you'll have to keep up with those changes so you can add them to your modified version of that same subprogram.

Sound like a lot of trouble? It is, which is what makes inheritance so attractive. With *inheritance,* you don't make multiple, physical copies of subprograms. Instead, you first store the subprogram in a class file.

Next, you *inherit* that class. Inheritance tells the computer to copy a class (along with all the methods stored inside that class) and store all the properties and methods from that first class into the second class.

Physically, this second class contains no code of its own. Instead, the second class *points* to the code of the original class. Then you create objects from both classes, as shown in Figure 7-7.

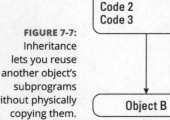

FIGURE 7-7:
Inheritance lets you reuse another object's subprograms without physically copying them.

When you run methods in this second object, the second object tells the computer, "Hey, those methods are really stored in this other object that I inherited them from."

Inheritance offers two advantages:

>> Because it doesn't make multiple copies of the same methods, inheritance saves space.

>> Because only one copy of a method physically exists, inheritance makes it easy to update a method.

Make a change to the original method, and those changes instantly appear in any object that inherited that method. The reason for this instant update is because all those other objects always point to the same method in the first place.

Inheritance lets you reuse code from another object without physically copying that code. Now you can add methods to your new object and your new object contains only your new methods, as shown in Figure 7-8.

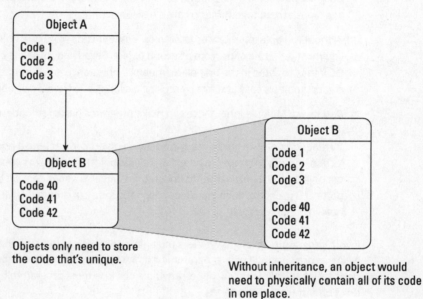

FIGURE 7-8:
Objects contain code that's unique to only that object.

Objects only need to store the code that's unique.

Without inheritance, an object would need to physically contain all of its code in one place.

By keeping the amount of code stored inside each object to a minimum, OOP makes it easy to understand how each object works. Through inheritance, OOP makes it easy to update one method that's reused in other objects.

As a result, inheritance makes reusing objects (and their methods) practical and modifying those objects' methods fast, simple, and easy.

REMEMBER

Inheritance offers the convenience of reusing code without the inconvenience of updating duplicate code stored in multiple locations.

SINGLE VERSUS MULTIPLE INHERITANCE

When one object inherits everything from another object, that's *single inheritance*. Some programming languages, such as C++, also can allow objects to inherit from two or more objects, which is *multiple inheritance*. Here's the good news and the bad news when it comes to multiple inheritance:

- **Good news:** Multiple inheritance can use the best parts from two or more objects and smash them together to create a new object.

  Without multiple inheritance, you can only inherit code from one object and then you must duplicate code from a second object. Because duplicating code is what OOP tries to avoid in the first place, multiple inheritance is yet another way to make creating objects easy and fast by reusing existing code from other objects.

- **Bad news:** Multiple inheritance can make programs harder to understand.

  By inheriting parts from so many objects, an object can become a hodgepodge collection of parts from everywhere. So, a single object that inherits code from multiple objects is not only harder to understand, but also dependent on too many other parts of a program. Such interdependency of code is a problem OOP tries to eliminate in the first place.

If your programming language offers multiple inheritance, try it to see if its benefits outweigh its drawbacks. If your programming language doesn't offer multiple inheritance, don't feel that you're missing out on anything because most programming languages don't offer multiple inheritance.

Polymorphism: Modifying Code without Changing Its Name

Besides reusing existing methods (without modifying them) and adding new methods to an object, you can also modify an inherited method through *polymorphism*.

Polymorphism allows something called *method overloading*, which lets you inherit a subprogram from another object and then replace the code in that subprogram with brand-new code. So, essentially, all you're really reusing is the original method's name, as shown in Figure 7-9.

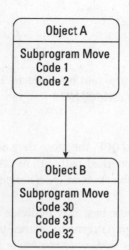

FIGURE 7-9:
Polymorphism lets you reuse a method name in another object.

```
Object A
Subprogram Move
  Code 1
  Code 2
```

```
Object B
Subprogram Move
  Code 30
  Code 31
  Code 32
```

The purpose of method overloading is to let multiple objects use the same descriptive method name. Normally, two subprograms can't share the same name. Otherwise, when you call a subprogram by name, the computer doesn't know which subprogram you actually want to use.

However, when you call a method inside an object, you must specify both the object and the method name stored inside that object. So, if you wanted to run the `Move` subprogram inside an `Airplane` object, you could call that method by using this command:

```
Airplane.Move
```

This `Airplane.Move` command might tell the computer to move a cartoon airplane in a video game. Now what if this video game needs to display a spaceship onscreen? You could write a new `Spaceship` object from scratch (which takes time) or you could just inherit all the code stored in the `Airplane` object to create a `Spaceship` object.

Of course, a spaceship moves differently from an airplane, so you could inherit the `Move` method from the `Airplane` object and modify that subprogram's code, and you've instantly created a new `Spaceship` object in very little time. Now you can use the same method name (`Move`) to change the position of two different objects, like this:

```
Airplane.Move
Spaceship.Move
```

REMEMBER

Encapsulation protects properties and methods from being changed. Method overloading reuses and modifies code without affecting the original method name. Inheritance reuses code without physically copying it.

Design Patterns

There's no single "right" way to divide a program into objects. When faced with the same problem, two programmers may divide up the program into completely different objects.

However, the more that programmers used OOP, the more they noticed that some ways of dividing a program into objects worked better than other ways. These specific ways of dividing a program into objects is called a *design pattern*.

A design pattern provides a blueprint for the best way to divide specific types of problems into objects. Because these design patterns have been proven already to work, you can use a design pattern to help solve your particular problem.

Without design patterns, you're forced to design objects by yourself and risk choosing a faulty design that you wouldn't know about until you might have already created most of your program.

Three examples of different design patterns (and their unusual names) include

>> **Interface pattern:** Defines an object that simplifies access to something else. For example, suppose someone has written a library of useful subprograms. Rather than let other programmers access these subprograms directly, an interface pattern defines an object to provide access to these subprograms instead. By doing this, an interface pattern keeps your program focused on using object-oriented features.

This library might contain subprograms for displaying graphics and calculating mathematical equations. You could use the interface pattern to define one object for accessing the graphics subprograms and a second object for accessing the mathematical equations subprograms, as shown in Figure 7-10.

>> **Flyweight pattern:** A *flyweight pattern* is used to create multiple objects. For example, you could create a word processor with every character defined as an object that contains formatting information, such as font, font size, underlining, and so on. However, a typical word processor document would contain thousands of objects, and because each object gobbles up memory, creating so many objects would likely swamp the computer's memory.

The flyweight pattern solves this problem by removing repetitive information from multiple objects (such as formatting information) and replacing it with a pointer to another object that contains this information, as shown in Figure 7-11.

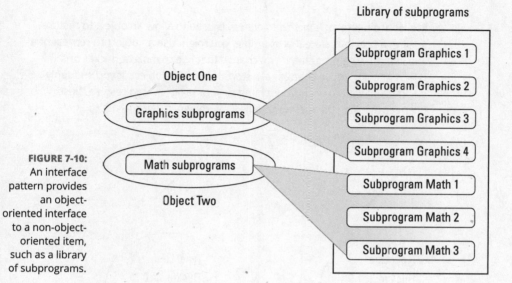

FIGURE 7-10: An interface pattern provides an object-oriented interface to a non-object-oriented item, such as a library of subprograms.

Library of subprograms

Object One

Graphics subprograms

Math subprograms

Object Two

Subprogram Graphics 1

Subprogram Graphics 2

Subprogram Graphics 3

Subprogram Graphics 4

Subprogram Math 1

Subprogram Math 2

Subprogram Math 3

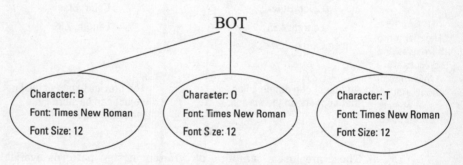

BOT

Character: B
Font: Times New Roman
Font Size: 12

Character: O
Font: Times New Roman
Font Size: 12

Character: T
Font: Times New Roman
Font Size: 12

Representing each character as an object stores
redundant information, such as Font and Font Size.

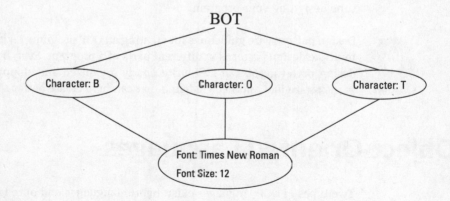

BOT

Character: B

Character: O

Character: T

Font: Times New Roman
Font Size: 12

FIGURE 7-11: The flyweight pattern simplifies objects that contain repetitive information.

The flyweight pattern uses a reference object that contains
repetitive data that multiple, smaller objects share.

>> **Memento pattern:** A *memento pattern* is used to allow an object to restore itself to a previous state. For example, you might use an object to represent a line in a drawing program. If you change that line to make it thicker or a different color, those changes are stored in the line object. If you suddenly decide you want to undo your changes, your program can restore those changes by using the memento object, as shown in Figure 7-12.

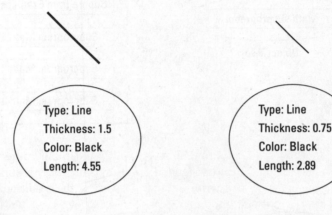

FIGURE 7-12:
The memento pattern uses one object to store information about another object's previous state.

Type: Line
Thickness: 1.5
Color: Black
Length: 4.55

An object can define a line that appears on the screen.

Type: Line
Thickness: 0.75
Color: Black
Length: 2.89

The previous state of the line object can be stored in a memento object.

These are just a sampling of different design patterns available and how they solve specific problems that occur when using OOP. Before rushing out to create a program using OOP, take some time to learn about design patterns. That way, you can pick a design pattern that solves your program's specific needs, and you save time designing your program.

REMEMBER

Design patterns are guidelines for creating an OOP program, so it's possible to use multiple design patterns in different parts of a program. Even if you use the right design pattern, you can still write poorly organized and sloppy code, so design patterns are just another guideline that can help create better software.

Object-Oriented Languages

Two types of OOP languages exist: hybrid languages and pure languages.

Hybrid languages

A *hybrid language* is simply a language originally designed without object-oriented features, but with object-oriented features added on. Here are some popular examples of hybrid languages:

Original Language	Hybrid, Object-Oriented Version
Ada	ObjectAda
BASIC	Visual Basic, Xojo
C	C++, C#, Objective-C
COBOL	Object-Oriented COBOL
Pascal	Delphi

Because hybrid languages are based on popular languages, they make it easy for current programmers to understand and use. Unlike "pure" object-oriented languages that force you to design a program completely around objects, hybrid languages often let you write programs by using the traditional task-oriented, subprogram approach and only add object-oriented features sparingly until you get comfortable using and designing programs with OOP.

Because hybrid languages are based on languages that have been around for decades, a hybrid language lets you take an existing program and add object-oriented features to it. COBOL programs have been around since the 1960s, so companies are reluctant to rewrite working programs in another language just to gain object-oriented features. Rather than rewrite a perfectly working COBOL program in C++, programmers can just use Object-Oriented COBOL instead, which effectively extends the life of ancient COBOL programs.

WARNING

Hybrid languages do have one major drawback. Because programs written in hybrid languages tend to be a mishmash of traditional and object-oriented programming, they can be hard to understand and even harder to modify.

Pure languages

Although programmers can quickly adapt to the object-oriented language based on a language they already know, most programmers tend to stick with writing programs the way they've always done it, which often means not using OOP techniques at all or using the object-oriented features poorly.

To get around this problem, computer scientists have developed pure object-oriented languages, which forces programmers to use object-oriented techniques, whether they like it or not. Some popular pure OOP languages include

>> Java

>> Perl

>> JavaScript

>> Smalltalk

>> Swift

By forcing you to use OOP techniques, pure object-oriented languages make sure that every program written in that particular language can be easily understood in terms of objects. A program written in a hybrid language can be as sloppy as a native Arabic speaker writing a letter in both Arabic and English. A program written in a pure object-oriented language may be sloppy and poorly written, but it's like forcing a native Arabic speaker to write a letter completely in English, so at least it's easier for English speakers to understand.

So, which type of language should you learn and use? If you need to update programs written in older programming languages, like C, BASIC, or Pascal, you may have no choice but to update those programs by using a hybrid language.

Ultimately, it's probably best to force yourself to know at least one pure object-oriented language so you fully understand the benefits of OOP and put those benefits into practical use. After you completely understand how to design and use object-oriented techniques, you're more likely to use OOP features in a hybrid language.

REMEMBER

The programming language you use is less important than designing a program correctly from the start. Languages are tools to help you achieve a goal, so don't get caught up in the "religious" wars arguing whether one programming language is "better" than another. The "best" programming language is the one that makes you most efficient.

Disadvantages of object-oriented programming

Despite its clear-cut advantages, OOP isn't perfect and suffers its share of drawbacks:

>> **OOP is best suited for organizing large programs.** If you need to write a small program to make a printer work with an operating system, organizing your program into objects won't likely give you any benefits and may take more time to write.

>> **OOP requires more memory to run than non-OOP programs.** So, if you're writing a small program that needs to be fast and use as little memory as possible, OOP actually makes your program slower to run.

Like all programming techniques, such as structured programming, OOP isn't a magical solution for writing large programs flawlessly. Instead, OOP is more of a guideline for steering you into using proven techniques for organizing programs and making them easier to modify and update.

REMEMBER

The ultimate goal of any programmer is to write software that works, is easy to fix and modify, and gets completed on time. If you can achieve these three goals on a consistent basis, you'll always have plenty of people wanting to hire you.

Real-Life Programming Examples

To fully understand OOP, you need to see how to use OOP in a real programming language. Basically, the steps to using OOP involve

>> Defining an object with a class file

>> Creating an object based on a class

>> Using methods in an object

>> Inheriting an object

>> Using polymorphism to rewrite an inherited method

REMEMBER

Although the following examples use Swift, don't worry about the particular syntax of the programming language examples. Every programming language uses different syntax and commands, so focus on understanding the principles behind creating and using objects.

Defining an object with a class

To create an object, you must first create a class, stored in a separate file that defines

>> The properties the object contains

>> The methods the object uses to manipulate its data

At the simplest level, a Swift class consists of the class keyword along with a descriptive name for your class, such as

```
class ClassName
{
}
```

So, if you wanted to name your class Animal, your class would now look like this:

```
class Animal
{
}
```

Next, you need to define the public properties and methods by optionally using the public keyword. Then you must define the private properties and methods by using the private keyword, like this:

```
class Animal
{
    public var variableName1: dataType

    private var variableName2: dataType

}
```

If you omit the public keyword in Swift, Swift assumes the property or method is public.

If you wanted to define an x_coordinate and y_coordinate variable as public and an X variable as private, you'd do this:

```
class Animal
{
    public var  x_coordinate: Int = 0
    public var y_coordinate: Int = 0

    private var x: Int = 0

}
```

Not all objects have both public and private properties and methods. Some objects may just have public properties and methods.

The preceding code creates three integer variables — x_coordinate, y_coordinate, and x and assigns an initial value of zero (0) to each variable. After you define the properties your object will use, the next step is to define the methods it will use, such as an initial_position and a move method:

```
class Animal {
    public var x_coordinate: Int = 0
    public var y_coordinate: Int = 0
    private var x: Int = 0
    func initial_position (init_x: Int, init_y: Int) {
        x_coordinate = init_x
        y_coordinate = init_y
    }
    func move (new_x: Int, new_y: Int) {
        x = 5
        x_coordinate = x_coordinate + new_x + x
        y_coordinate = y_coordinate + new_y
    }
}
```

The preceding code defines two methods — initial_position and move. The initial_position and move methods both accept two integers in their parameter list. Inside each method is the actual Swift code to make each method work.

The initial_position method defines an initial value for the two public variables x_coordinate and y_coordinate.

The move method adds a new value to the current x_coordinate and y_coordinate values. This method also uses the private variable (x), sets its value to 5, and uses that value to modify the value of the x_coordinate variable.

At this point, you've defined a class. The next step is to use this class in an actual program.

Every class defines exactly one object. If a program needs a dozen different objects, you need to create a dozen different classes.

When you define an object from a class, that's often called *instantiating* an object. Classes are like cookie cutters that define the details. Objects are like the cookies created by the class.

Creating an object from a class

Before you can use a class in your program, you need to

>> Declare a name for your object.

>> Define your object based on a class.

If you wanted to create an object based on the Animal class, you could do the following in Swift:

```
var cat = Animal()
```

Right away, this cat object would contain three properties, all set to an initial value of zero (0) because this value of 0 is what is defined inside the Animal class:

>> x_coordinate

>> y_coordinate

>> x

Running methods stored in an object

After you define an object in your main program, you can run a method stored in that object. So, if you wanted to run the initial_position method, stored in the cat object, you'd identify the object name followed by the object's method to run, like this:

```
var cat = Animal()
cat.initial_position(init_x: 5, init_y: 7)
```

The preceding code creates a cat object based on the Animal class. Next, it runs the initial_position method, which accepts two integer parameters named init_x and init_y. The init_x parameter gets assigned the value of 5 and the init_y parameter gets assigned the value of 7.

If you wanted to run the move method, you'd define the object name (cat) followed by the method name (move) and wind up with a command like this:

```
cat.move(new_x: 10, new_y: 10)
```

The move method accepts two parameters named new_x and new_y. Both the new_x parameter and the new_y parameter get assigned a value of 10.

Running the whole program together might look like this:

```swift
class Animal {
    public var x_coordinate: Int = 0
    public var y_coordinate: Int = 0
    private var x: Int = 0
    func initial_position (init_x: Int, init_y: Int) {
        x_coordinate = init_x
        y_coordinate = init_y
    }
    func move (new_x: Int, new_y: Int) {
        x = 5
        x_coordinate = x_coordinate + new_x + x
        y_coordinate = y_coordinate + new_y
    }
}
var cat = Animal()
cat.initial_position(init_x: 5, init_y: 7)
print (cat.x_coordinate)
print (cat.y_coordinate)
cat.move(new_x: 10, new_y: 10)
print (cat.x_coordinate)
print (cat.y_coordinate)
```

If you ran this Swift program, the following would appear onscreen:

```
5
7
20
17
```

The print (cat.x_coordinate) command prints 5.

The print (cat.y_coordinate) command prints 7.

The move method adds x (5) to the value of new_x (10) and the value of x_coordinate (5) so the new x_coordinate value is now 20.

The move method adds the value of new_y (10) and the value of y_coordinate (7) so the new x_coordinate value is now 17.

Inheriting an object

To inherit an object, you must first create another class file. So, if you wanted to create a Human class and have it inherit from the Animal class, you'd do this:

```
class Human : Animal {

}
```

Although the Human class behaves identically to the Animal class, the Human class is actually empty because it inherits all its code from the Animal class. Now any code you add to the Human class is unique just to that Human class, like this:

```
class Human: Animal {
    public var iq: Int = 0
    func getSmart(iq_boost: Int) {
        iq = iq + iq_boost
    }
}
```

Because this inherits all the code from the Animal class, the Human class is actually equivalent to the following, where the highlighted code highlights the code unique to the Human class:

```
class Human: Animal {
    public var x_coordinate: Int = 0
    public var y_coordinate: Int = 0
    private var x: Int = 0
    func initial_position (init_x: Int, init_y: Int) {
        x_coordinate = init_x
        y_coordinate = init_y
    }
    func move (new_x: Int, new_y: Int) {
        x = 5
        x_coordinate = x_coordinate + new_x + x
        y_coordinate = y_coordinate + new_y
    }

    public var iq: Int = 0
    func getSmart(iq_boost: Int) {
        iq = iq + iq_boost
    }
}
```

As you can see, without inheritance, the code stored inside an object can soon grow out of control, but by using inheritance, each object contains only unique code.

An object that inherits code is treated no differently from an object created entirely from scratch. The following program shows how to use the Human class:

```
class Animal {
    public var x_coordinate: Int = 0
    public var y_coordinate: Int = 0
    private var x: Int = 0
    func initial_position (init_x: Int, init_y: Int) {
        x_coordinate = init_x
        y_coordinate = init_y
    }
    func move (new_x: Int, new_y: Int) {
        x = 5
        x_coordinate = x_coordinate + new_x + x
        y_coordinate = y_coordinate + new_y
    }
}
class Human: Animal {
    public var iq: Int = 0
    func getSmart(iq_boost: Int) {
        iq = iq + iq_boost
    }
}
var timmy = Human()
timmy.getSmart(iq_boost: 125)
print (timmy.iq)
```

Running this program displays the following onscreen:

```
125
```

The iq property is initially set to 0. When the getSmart method runs, it passes in a value of 125 to the iq_boost parameter, which gets added to the current value of iq (0). Thus, printing timmy.iq displays 125.

Using method overloading to rewrite an inherited subprogram

After you inherit code from another object, you can use method overloading to rewrite the code inside of a method. To overload a method, you may need to define which methods in an object can be changed.

In Swift, you define a method to be overloaded by using the override keyword. So, if you wanted to overload the move method in the Human class, you'd have to rewrite the move method inside the Human class like this:

```
class Human: Animal {
    public var iq: Int = 0
    func getSmart(iq_boost: Int) {
        iq = iq + iq_boost
    }
    override func move(new_x: Int, new_y: Int) {
        x_coordinate = x_coordinate + new_x
        y_coordinate = (y_coordinate + new_y) * 2
    }
}
```

The override keyword lets you reuse the move method name and parameter list, but change the code inside.

REMEMBER

Not every object-oriented language requires you to identify polymorphic methods. Some languages let you inherit and modify methods without identifying them first.

Suppose you write an entire Swift program like this:

```
class Animal {
    public var x_coordinate: Int = 0
    public var y_coordinate: Int = 0
    private var x: Int = 0

    func initial_position (init_x: Int, init_y: Int) {
        x_coordinate = init_x
        y_coordinate = init_y
    }

    func move (new_x: Int, new_y: Int) {
        x = 5
        x_coordinate = x_coordinate + new_x + x
        y_coordinate = y_coordinate + new_y
    }
}
```

```
class Human: Animal {
    public var iq: Int = 0

    func getSmart(iq_boost: Int) {
        iq = iq + iq_boost
    }

    override func move(new_x: Int, new_y: Int) {
        x_coordinate = x_coordinate + new_x
        y_coordinate = (y_coordinate + new_y) * 2
    }
}

var timmy = Human()
print (timmy.x_coordinate)
print (timmy.y_coordinate)
timmy.move(new_x: 5, new_y: 3)
print (timmy.x_coordinate)
print (timmy.y_coordinate)
```

Running the main program would now print the following onscreen:

```
0
0
5
6
```

Notice that the program prints 0 (x_coordinate) and 0 (y_coordinate). Then it uses the move method stored in the Human class, which adds a new value to the x_coordinate but adds a new value to the y_coordinate before multiplying it by 2. So the timmy.move (new_x: 5, new_y: 3) command sets the human's x_coordinate to 5 (0 + 5) and the y_coordinate to 6 ((0 + 3) × 2).

Although these examples use Swift, the basic steps to using objects remain the same:

1. **Create a class that defines properties and methods.**

   These can be a mixture of public and private.

2. **Create one or more additional classes that inherit code from another class.**

3. Use method overloading to rewrite code inherited from another object.

4. Declare an object as a specific class type.

5. Use an object's methods to manipulate that object's properties.

REMEMBER

OOP can help you design large programs faster, but ultimately, your own skill as a programmer determines the quality of your programs.

Chapter **8**

Reading and Saving Files

Almost every program needs to save data. Spreadsheets need to save numbers and formulas, word processors need to store text, databases need to store names and addresses, and even video games need to store the top ten highest scores.

To save data, programs store information in a file. After a program stores data in a file, it eventually needs to open that file and retrieve that data again. To save data in files, programs generally use one of four methods:

» Text files

» Random-access files

» Untyped files

» Database files

Storing Data in Text Files

A *text file*, sometimes called a *plaintext file*, contains nothing but characters, such as letters, numbers, and symbols.

Text files only store actual data, such as names and addresses, but they don't contain any formatting information, such as fonts or underlining. Because text files contain only data, they represent a universal file format that any computer — from an ancient Commodore 64 to a Cray supercomputer — can read and use.

Text files typically store data as one long string of data like this:

```
Joe Smith 123 Main Street New York NY 10012
```

However, to identify data that should logically be lumped together, programs such as databases and spreadsheets offer the option of saving text files as either

>> A **comma-delimited text file** (also known as a *comma separated value,* or CSV, file) simply divides text into logical chunks, such as

```
Joe Smith, 123 Main Street, New York, NY, 10012
```

>> A **tab-delimited text file** divides text by tabs, like this:

```
Joe Smith    123 Main Street    New York    NY    10012
```

REMEMBER

A comma- or tab-delimited text file makes it easy for database and spreadsheet programs to read data from a text file and know which data to store in separate *fields* (for databases) or *cells* (for spreadsheets).

THE "OTHER" UNIVERSAL FILE FORMAT

The biggest drawback with text files is that they can't contain any formatting information. So, if you need to transfer a word processor document from an ancient Atari ST computer to a modern iPad, you lose all formatting in that document.

To prevent this problem, computer scientists have created multiple universal file formats that can retain both data and formatting. One popular universal file format, *XML* (short for *Extensible Markup Language*), contains both data and instructions for how to display the data. For example, the sentence "This is the text you would actually see" looks like this in an XML file:

```
<para>This is the text you would actually see</para>
```

An XML file is a text file that contains formatting instructions or *tags* that define the appearance of data. Because XML files are text files, any computer can read them. To fully read an XML file, a computer needs a special program — called an *XML parser* — which not only reads the data but also translates the XML formatting tags that tell the computer how to display that data.

To create a universal file format for word processor documents, spreadsheets, databases, and presentation files, computer scientists have created a new file format, based on XML — the OpenDocument standard. The main idea behind the OpenDocument standard is to define a universal file format that retains both data and formatting commonly found in word processors, spreadsheets, databases, and presentation program files. Unlike proprietary file formats, which a single company can control, the OpenDocument standard is freely available to anyone.

The OpenDocument file format has even gained the support of many governments, which want to ensure that people can still read and edit their files no matter what computer or software they may be using in the future. If you store important files in a proprietary file format, such as Microsoft Word or Microsoft Access, there's a chance that programs in the future won't know how to open those files, which means your data could potentially be lost forever. By using the OpenDocument standard, your data can remain accessible forever (or at least until computer scientists create another "universal" file format).

Back in 1987, Microsoft tried to define another universal, cross-platform, file format that could retain both data and formatting instructions. This file format, Rich Text Format (RTF), creates *tags* that define the appearance of text. Consider the following text:

>> This is **bold**.

>> This is *italicized.*

The RTF file of the preceding text looks like this:

>> This is \b bold\b0 .\par

>> This is \i italicized\i0 .\par

So, if you ever want to transfer text from one computer or program to another, your safest bet if you want to retain all the formatting is to save the file as an RTF file.

Creating a text file

A text file stores data as lines of text. So, if you want to store three names in a text file, you could store those names on a single line like this:

```
Joe Smith Mary Evans Donna Dickens
```

Of course, the more names you want to store, the longer this single line of text gets. That's why most text files store data on separate lines, where each line of text contains a single chunk of data, such as

```
Joe Smith
Mary Evans
Donna Dickens
```

TECHNICAL
STUFF

The end of each line in a text file actually contains invisible codes that define the end of a line:

» **Carriage return** (CR): The CR code tells the computer to move to the front of the line.

» **Line feed** (LF): The LF code tells the computer to move down to the next line.

TECHNICAL
STUFF

Unix systems only use the line feed character to define the end of a line, while Windows systems use both a carriage return and a line feed character.

So, the preceding example of a text file actually looks like this:

```
Joe Smith <CR><LF>
Mary Evans <CR><LF>
Donna Dickens <CR><LF>
```

Creating a text file typically requires three steps:

1. **Name the text file.**

2. **Assign a variable to that text file.**

3. **Store one or more lines of text in the text file.**

The following Python language example creates a text file named `mytext.txt` and stores the names `Joe Smith`, `Mary Evans`, and `Donna Dickens` in that file:

```
names = """Joe Smith
Mary Evans
Donna Dickens"""
```

```
myfile = open("mytext.txt", "w")
myfile.write(names)
myfile.close()
```

The Python program follows these steps:

1. The Python program stores the names Joe Smith, Mary Evans, and Donna Dickens in a names variable.

   In Python and some other programming languages, triple quotation marks let you define multiple lines of text.

2. The program *opens* (creates) a text file named mytext.txt and assigns this file to a myfile variable.

   The "w" symbol tells the program to open the mytext.txt file so that you can write or add data to that text file.

   TECHNICAL STUFF

   The "w" symbol tells the computer to erase any existing text inside the mytext.txt text file. If you want to add new data to a text file without erasing its entire contents, replace the "w" symbol with the "a" (append) symbol instead, like this:

   ```
   scraps = open("mytext.txt", "a")
   scraps.write("\nSal Lankins")
   scraps.close()
   ```

   The preceding three lines of code would open the mytext.txt file, add a new line (the \n characters), and tack the name Sal Lankins at the end of the text file.

3. The myfile.write(names) command tells the computer to take the data stored in the names variable and *write* (save) it in the text file assigned to the myfile variable.

4. The myfile.close() command tells the computer to shut or close the file.

Reading a text file

After you store data in a text file, you eventually need to retrieve it again by "reading" the text file. *Reading* a text file means retrieving data, starting from the beginning of a text file, line-by-line, until the computer reaches the end of the file. So, if the name Donna Dickens was stored as the third line in a text file, the computer couldn't retrieve Donna Dickens until it first scanned the first and second lines of the text file.

A computer can only retrieve data from a text file starting at the beginning and reading the entire file until it reaches the end. That's why text files are sometimes called *sequential* files because they act like an audio tape that doesn't let you hear the fifth song until you fast-forward past the first four songs. Likewise, computers can't retrieve the fifth line in a text file until it scans past the first four lines in that text file.

Reading a text file typically requires three steps:

1. **Identify the name of a text file.**

2. **Assign the name of the text file to a variable name.**

3. **Read all the lines of data stored in the text file until the end of the text file is reached.**

So, if you had a text file named mytext.txt, you could retrieve data out of that file by using the following Python language example:

```
fu = open("mytext.txt", "r")
while True:
    line = fu.readline()
    if not line:
        break
    print (line)
fu.close()
```

First, this program identifies the text file to use (mytext.txt) and assigns the text file to the fu variable. (The "r" symbol tells the computer to read the data from the mytext.txt file.)

Next, a while loop reads the text file, identified by the fu variable, line-by-line, and prints each line. As soon as this loop reaches the end of the file, the while loop stops running.

The fu.close() command closes the text file.

Text files are useful for transferring data between different programs or computers and for storing small amounts of data. If you need to store and retrieve large amounts of data, or if you need to preserve formatting information, you have to use another type of a file besides a text file.

Many websites can store information on your computer in a *cookie* (a text file that stores your website settings, such as your username). That way if you visit that website again, the website retrieves the cookie off your computer and uses that information to customize the web page that you see.

For programmers, the most common text file is the source code to any program no matter which programming language is used, such as C++, Perl, Prolog, or Tcl.

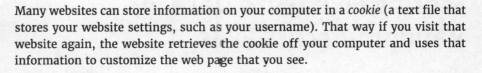

THE PORTABLE DOCUMENT FORMAT (PDF)

Although you can share plaintext files among different computers, you always lose the formatting of that data. To avoid this problem, Adobe developed its own "universal" file format — the Portable Document Format (PDF). The idea behind PDF files is to allow people to create and distribute files that display data exactly the same no matter what computer they may use. So, if you create a flyer or a newsletter, the appearance of your flyer or newsletter looks the same on a Mac as it does on a computer running a completely different operating system, such as Linux or Windows.

PDF files have two drawbacks:

- **You can't edit them without special software.** For this reason, PDF files are meant more for displaying information than for letting you actually change that information. That's why many governments distribute documents and forms as PDF files so people can see the information, such as tax forms, but they can't change it.

- You can't view the contents of a PDF file unless you have a special PDF viewing or reader program, which Adobe gives away for free. Most browsers can open and display PDF files, and nearly every operating system includes a program capable of opening and displaying PDF files.

Despite these drawbacks, PDF files are popular for sharing information among different computers and operating systems while retaining the original appearance of a file, such as a word processor document. If you just want to share information, PDF files are currently the most popular way to do so.

Storing Fixed-Size Data in Random-Access Files

One of the biggest problems with text files is that retrieving data requires reading the entire text file from beginning to end. In a large text file, this makes retrieving data clumsy and slow.

Whereas text files act more like old audiocassette tapes, random-access files are more like compact discs (CDs) that allow you to skip right to the data you want to retrieve (which is why they're *random-access* files).

A random-access file organizes data in equally sized chunks called *records* or *structures.* A record defines what type of data to store, such as a first and last name, age, and phone number, as shown in Figure 8-1.

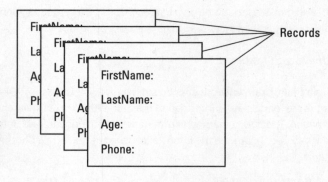

FIGURE 8-1: A record organizes related data together.

Not only do records define what type of data to store, but they also define how much space to allocate for each chunk of data. So, if you want to allocate 20 characters for a person's first and last name and 12 characters for a person's phone number, you could define a record in BASIC, as follows:

```
Type PeopleRecord
    LastName as String * 20
    FirstName as String * 20
    Age as Integer
    Phone as String * 12
End Type
```

The preceding code defines the LastName and FirstName variables to hold a maximum of 20 characters. The Age variable is an integer. The Phone variable can hold a maximum of ten characters. The combination of all these variables represents a single chunk of data.

TECHNICAL STUFF

A record is a user-defined data type because the user (you) defines the type of information the record can hold. Just as you can't store data directly into other data types (integers, strings, and so on), you can't store data in a record until you first declare a variable to represent your record.

Dividing a random-access file into fixed chunks of space makes it easy to find data later. If you store 26 records in a file and want to retrieve the first record, the computer knows that each record takes up a fixed amount of space. By knowing exactly where each record begins and ends, the computer knows how to find each record quickly, as shown in Figure 8-2.

FIGURE 8-2:
The fixed size of each record makes it easy to identify the physical location of each record in a file.

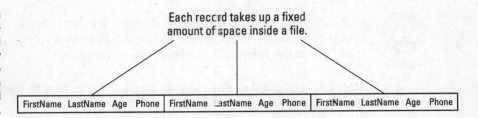

Each record takes up a fixed amount of space inside a file.

| FirstName | LastName | Age | Phone | FirstName | LastName | Age | Phone | FirstName | LastName | Age | Phone |

Writing data

To write data to a random-access file, define a variable that represents your records like this:

```
Type PeopleRecord
    LastName as String * 20
    FirstName as String * 20
    Age as Integer
    Phone as String * 12
End Type

Dim Contact as PeopleRecord
```

After you define a variable to represent your record, store data in the Contact variable, like this:

```
Contact.LastName = "Smith"
Contact.FirstName = "Joey"
Contact.Age = 28
Contact.Phone = "310-123-1234"
```

The next step is to create a random-access file by defining a filename like this:

```
Open "MyFile.dat" for Random as #1 Len = Len(Contact)
```

This code opens a random-access file named Myfile.dat, identified by the number 1 (#1) and divided into chunks defined by the size or length (Len) of the Contact record.

You can choose any number to represent the random-access file. Using a number, such as #1 or #8, is much easier than typing out the entire filename every time you need to identify which file to use again.

When you open a random-access file to store data, you must correctly define the size of the records. If you define the record size too small, you may lose data. If you define the record size too large, you waste space.

After you create and open a random-access file, you have to store data into that file like this:

```
Put #1, 1, Contact
```

The Put command tells the computer to use the file identified as #1 and store the Contact data as the first (1) record. To add more data to the random-access file, you'd have to store different data into the Contact variable and use additional Put commands, such as the following, to store data as the second record in the random-access file:

```
Put #1, 2, Contact
```

When you're done adding records to a random-access file, close the file, like this:

```
Close #1
```

This command tells the computer that you're done working with that file.

Reading data

After you store one or more records in a random-access file, you can read data from that random-access file by identifying the file to use, assigning a number to that file, and defining the size of each record in that file, like this:

```
Open "MyFile.dat" For Random As #1 Len = Len(Contact)
```

WARNING

When you open a random-access file to read data, you must correctly define the size of the records stored in that file. If you incorrectly define the size of the records, the computer can't retrieve the data correctly.

After you open an existing random-access file, you can retrieve data by using the Get command like this:

```
Get #1, 2, Contact
```

This command tells the computer to get information out of the file identified as the #1 file, retrieve the second record, and store it back into the Contact variable. At this point, you could store the data from the Contact variable into another variable and then retrieve another record from the random-access file. When you're done using the random-access file, you have to close it like this:

```
Close #1
```

REMEMBER

Random-access files make it easy to store and retrieve data. Because you retrieve only the data you want, random-access files don't waste time reading the entire file.

Storing Varying-Size Data in Untyped Files

Random-access files are great for storing chunks of data of equal size. However, what if you want to store data that may vary in size? You could define a record as the largest size data you need to store, but that means you wind up wasting space. As a more efficient alternative, you can store data in untyped files. *Untyped* files still organize data in records, but each record can vary in size, as shown in Figure 8-3.

Records can be any size in an untyped file.

FIGURE 8-3: Untyped files contain records that can vary in size.

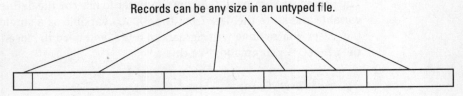

Writing data

To store data in an untyped file, you must first name and create an untyped file. In the Delphi programming language, you can create an untyped file by declaring a variable as a File type, such as

```
var
   myFile : File;
```

After you create a variable name, you need to assign that variable name to an actual filename, such as

```
AssignFile(myFile, 'MyData.dat');
```

REMEMBER

In some languages, such as BASIC, you assign a number to an actual filename. In Delphi and other languages, you assign a name to an actual file. The purpose of assigning a number or a name is so that you can refer to a file without typing the complete filename.

Before you can add any data to an untyped file, use the ReWrite command, which defines the filename to use and the number of blocks to add to the file. (Each *block* of data typically corresponds to one byte of data.) So, if you wanted to define a 5-byte block of data, you'd use the following:

```
ReWrite(myFile, 5);
```

After you define the filename (through the myFile variable name) and the block size, you can start adding actual data by using the BlockWrite command, which specifies the filename to use, the actual data to add, and the number of records to add, like this:

```
BlockWrite(myFile, MyData, 1);
```

The preceding command tells the computer to use the file defined by the myFile variable and store the data from the MyData variable as a single record into the file. After you're done writing data to a file, you need to close the file by using the CloseFile command, like this:

```
CloseFile(myFile);
```

Reading data

After you store data in an untyped file, you can retrieve it again by first using the Reset command that defines the filename to use and the size of the records you want to retrieve.

If you want to retrieve data from an untyped MyData.dat file, you could assign the variable name myFile to the MyData.dat file, like this:

```
AssignFile(myFile, 'MyData.dat');
```

Then you could use the Reset command to tell the computer to open the file defined by the myFile variable, like this:

```
Reset(myFile, 5);
```

The Reset command also defines the size of each block of data to retrieve, typically measured in bytes. The preceding command defines a block of 5 bytes.

Because untyped files contain records of varying sizes, there are two ways to read an untyped file:

>> **Scanning the file from beginning to end, like a text file:** To do that in Delphi, you can use a while loop. Inside the while loop, you can put a BlockRead command that defines which file to read data from, a variable to store the data, and how many bytes to retrieve at a time like this:

```
while not Eof(myFile) do
  begin
    BlockRead(myFile, Storage, 1);
    ShowMessage(IntToStr(Storage));
  end;
```

The while loop tells the computer to keep looping as long as the computer hasn't reached the end of the file (Eof) identified by the myFile variable. Inside the while loop is the BlockRead command, which tells the computer to read one (1) block of data at a time (when each block of data is defined in size by the Reset command), as shown in Figure 8-4.

After the BlockRead command retrieves data from the file identified by the myFile variable, it stores this data in a Storage variable. The ShowMessage command displays the value of the Storage variable onscreen.

>> **Using a pointer:** Reading an untyped file from start to finish can be as slow and cumbersome as reading an entire text file from start to finish. So, as a second way to retrieve data from an untyped file, you can use a pointer to "point" to different data blocks.

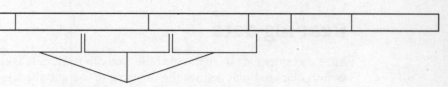

FIGURE 8-4:
The computer
can retrieve data
from an untyped
file in blocks
or chunks.

To retrieve data from an untyped file, the computer
retrieves a fixed chunk of data at a time.

For example, suppose you use the Reset command to define a block of
5 bytes:

```
Reset(myFile, 5);
```

This command divides an untyped file into 5-byte blocks.

To access an untyped file, like a random-access file, you can use the Seek
command, which defines which untyped file to use and which data chunk to
retrieve, like this:

```
Seek(myFile, 3);
```

This command tells the computer to use the untyped file identified by the
myFile variable and retrieve all the data in the third block of data, as shown
in Figure 8-5.

FIGURE 8-5:
By defining which
chunk of data you
want to retrieve,
you can retrieve
data from an
untyped file
without scanning
the entire file
from start
to finish.

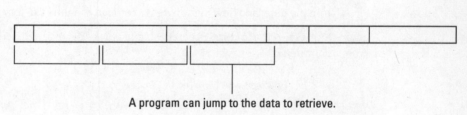

A program can jump to the data to retrieve.

After the computer finishes retrieving data from the file, it needs to close the file
by using the CloseFile command:

```
CloseFile(myFile);
```

REMEMBER

The main idea behind untyped files is that they can hold records of varying sizes.
When you retrieve data from an untyped file, you have to read the data in chunks
that you define.

In many programming languages, such as C++, an untyped file is considered to be a *stream* of data.

Using Database Files

One problem with random-access and untyped files is that two programs can use untyped files but the structure of one untyped file can differ wildly from the structure of a second untyped file. As a result, transferring or sharing data from one program to another can be difficult.

Proprietary file formats are nothing more than random-access or untyped files that store data in a specific way that only a single company truly understands.

To solve this problem, many programs simply store data in popular file formats used by other programs. Because many programs need to store large amounts of data, they often store data in file formats used by popular database programs to make it easy to share this data.

The most popular databases are Structured Query Language (SQL) databases. Some popular programs used to create and manipulate SQL databases are MySQL and PostgreSQL.

At one time, dBASE was the most popular database file format, so you still see many programs that can create, store, and save data in a dBASE file. Because many companies made dBASE-compatible programs, the dBASE file format is also known by the generic term *xBASE*.

Looking at the structure of a database

To understand how programs can store information in a database file, you need to understand the basic structure of a database. A database file (which is what you physically store and save on a disk) typically consists of one or more tables, with each table organizing related data. For example, you might have a database file containing customer information. Then you might divide that database file into three tables, with one table containing current customers, a second table containing potential customers, and a third table containing inactive customers, as shown in Figure 8-6.

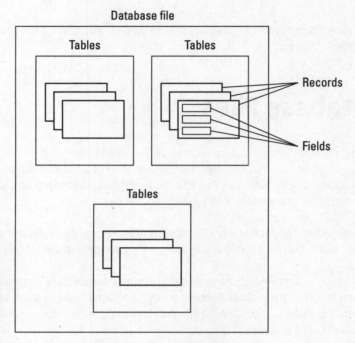

FIGURE 8-6:
Database files are divided into tables, and each table is further divided into records and fields.

Each table is further divided into records, with each record containing information about a single item, such as a customer. Each record is further divided into fields, with each field storing a single chunk of data, such as a name, a telephone number, or an email address.

Most database files are *relational* databases because information, stored in separate tables, can be linked or related to one another. For example, one table might contain a list of customers, and a second table might contain a list of orders that each customer placed. Even though each table is separate, the information each one contains is related.

Relational databases make it easy to group data logically but keep them separated physically. Without a relational database, you would have to cram all data together, and that would likely be clumsy and cumbersome to manage.

A prospect table might physically contain the customer information, whereas the customer table might only contain unique information, such as the type of product the customer bought and the total sales amount. To retrieve the customer's name and address, the customer table simply points to that information stored in the prospect table, as shown in Figure 8-7.

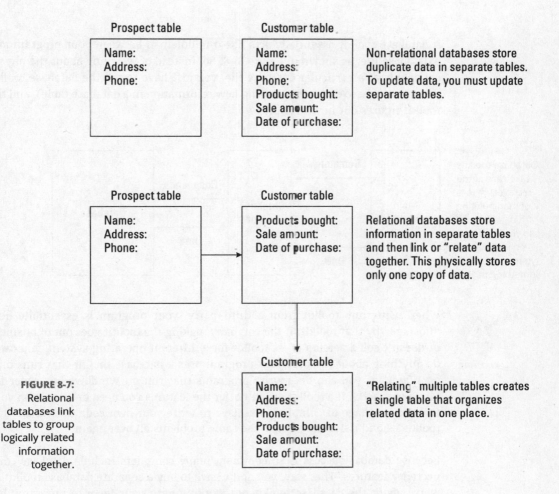

Prospect table

Name:
Address:
Phone:

Customer table

Name:
Address:
Phone:
Products bought:
Sale amount:
Date of purchase:

Non-relational databases store duplicate data in separate tables. To update data, you must update separate tables.

Prospect table

Name:
Address:
Phone:

Customer table

Products bought:
Sale amount:
Date of purchase:

Relational databases store information in separate tables and then link or "relate" data together. This physically stores only one copy of data.

Customer table

Name:
Address:
Phone:
Products bought:
Sale amount:
Date of purchase:

"Relating" multiple tables creates a single table that organizes related data in one place.

FIGURE 8-7:
Relational databases link tables to group logically related information together.

Connecting to a database

To save information to a database file, a program needs to identify

>> The database file to use

>> The table to use

>> The record to use

>> The specific field to view, edit, or store data

Although you can write your own subprograms to access a database file; retrieve information from a specific table, record, and field; and then save those changes again, this usually takes way too long to write and test. As a faster alternative, most programmers either buy a third-party database toolkit or (if they're lucky) use the built-in database controls that come with their language compiler.

A database toolkit essentially acts like a middleman between your program and a database file, as shown in Figure 8-8. So, instead of worrying about the physical details of a particular database file, you just have to tell the database toolkit what you want to do (such as saving new information in a database table), and the toolkit figures out how to do it.

FIGURE 8-8:
Database toolkits take care of the technical details of manipulating a database file so you can focus on just making your program do something useful.

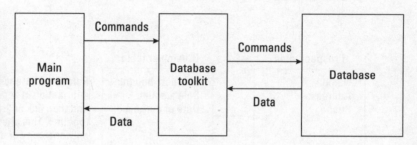

WARNING

When using any toolkit from a third-party, your program is essentially held "hostage" by that toolkit. If the company making the toolkit goes out of business or doesn't sell a version of its toolkit for a different operating system, you can't do anything about it. So, if your program uses a database toolkit that runs only on Windows, you can only write programs that run on Windows but never for Linux or macOS. If a toolkit doesn't offer the features you need or work with your favorite language or compiler, you have to write your own code or find another toolkit — and risk running into the same problems all over again.

Because database access is so common, many compilers include database connectivity features. That way, you don't have to buy a separate database toolkit or worry about the database toolkit not working with your favorite programming language.

To add database connectivity, you use database controls, which let you define the database file, table, and field to use. After you define what parts of a database file to use, you can then use database viewing controls to display and edit data stored in specific fields.

Database connectivity may let you write commands in a database language, such as SQL, and link it to your program. By linking database commands to whatever programming language you're using, you don't have to write commands to manipulate data in a programming language like C or Java, as shown in Figure 8-9.

REMEMBER

Database controls take care of the details of how to connect to a database so you can just focus on using a database file.

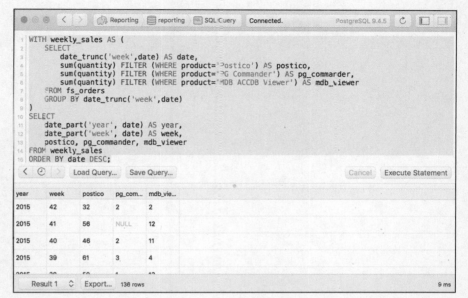

FIGURE 8-9:
A database toolkit
can manipulate
data using a
familiar database
language like
SQL so you don't
have to use a
programming
language that
isn't designed for
managing data.

When a program connects to a database file, that program often acts as a front end to that database. A *front end* basically wraps a friendly user interface (UI) around the database file. So, instead of forcing users to figure out arcane commands to retrieve, print, edit, search, or sort through a database file, a front end provides a simplified interface for manipulating data, as shown in Figure 8-10.

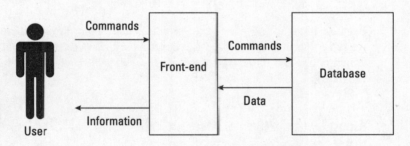

FIGURE 8-10:
Programs often
act as a front end
to a database file.

Database files are best for storing large amounts of information that you can share with other people and programs. If sharing data with other programs isn't important, use a random-access or untyped file. The drawback is that both of these files force you to write additional commands to store and retrieve data. For storing small amounts of data, use a text file.

Storing information in a file is a crucial part of most programs, so determine what type of data you need to save and then choose the file format that makes the most sense for your program.

Chapter **9**

Documenting Your Program

There are two big problems with writing programs. First, you have to worry about getting the program to work. Second, you'll probably need to fix and modify it later. To solve both types of problems, you have to understand how the program works in the first place. To understand how a program works, programmers have to explain

» What problem the program is trying to solve

» How the program is designed

» How each part of the program works

In the early days when programs were small, programmers could figure out all the preceding questions by studying the source code of the program. When programs got bigger and tackled more complicated problems, programmers could no longer understand how a program worked by examining the source code. That's when programmers were forced to start writing additional explanations, or *documentation*. By studying this documentation, other people could understand how a program works without trying to decipher the actual source code of a program.

Adding Comments to Source Code

One of the first attempts at explaining how a program worked was by making the source code more understandable by using high-level languages, like BASIC or Pascal, to create *self-documenting code*. So, rather than try to decipher cryptic code like this:

```
SECTION .data
  msg db "It's alive!!",0xa;
  len equ $ - msg

SECTION .text
  global main
main:
  mov eax,4;
  write system call
  mov ebx,1
  mov ecx,msg
  mov edx,len
  int 0x80
  mov eax,1 system call
  mov ebx,0
  int 0x80
```

You could replace the preceding assembly language commands with a shorter, more descriptive, high-level language command like this:

```
PRINT "It's alive!"
```

Such self-documenting code helps explain what a single line of code does, but it doesn't necessarily tell you how the entire program works as a whole or what problem the program even solves.

Instead of relying on "self-explanatory" language commands, programmers started adding explanations directly into the source code itself by using comments.

A *comment* is nothing more than text embedded in the source code. To keep the compiler from thinking a comment is an actual command, every comment needs a special symbol in front of the comment, like this:

```
REM This is a comment in BASIC.
' This is another comment in BASIC.
// This is a comment in C++ and Java.
# This is a comment in Perl and Python.
; This is a comment in LISP and assembly language.
```

Comments allow you to write short explanations, directly in the source code, that describe what the source code does. Looking at the following code, can you understand what it does?

```
C = SQRT(A * A + B * B)
```

Deciphering this code is straightforward. This command multiplies two variables by themselves, A and B; adds the results together; and finds the square root of the sum, which gets stored in the C variable. However, knowing how the command works doesn't tell you what this code is doing or why it's doing this. By adding comments to the source code, you can explain this, as follows:

```
' Calculates the hypotenuse of a triangle (C) using the
' Pythagorean theorem: C = Square root (A * A + B * B)
C = SQRT(A * A + B * B)
```

Even if you don't know (or care) about the Pythagorean theorem, the comments help you understand what the command is calculating.

WARNING

Some programmers use comments to insert jokes, profanity, or remarks about their coworkers directly in their source code. Just be aware that other people besides you may need to look at your source code. So, if you've laced your program with profanity-ridden tirades against your coworkers, don't be surprised if one of your coworkers finds and reads the comments you made about them, which could be humorous or embarrassing.

You can put comments anywhere in a program because the compiler ignores them anyway. Don't be afraid to add comments because they won't increase the program size or slow it down in any way.

Identifying the two types of comments

The two types of comments are *line comments* and *block comments*.

Line comments

Line comments appear directly on a line that already contains a command like this:

```
C = SQRT(A * A + B * B)   ' Calculates Pythagorean theorem
```

The problem with line comments is that they can make source code somewhat harder to read. That's why some programmers prefer putting comments on separate lines like this:

```
' Calculates Pythagorean theorem
C = SQRT(A * A + B * B)
```

REMEMBER

Comments exist purely for other people to read, so it doesn't matter whether you put them on a line with a command or on a separate line.

TIP

To make comments easier to read, use plenty of blank lines and spaces. The following example looks crowded:

```
' Calculates the hypotenuse of a triangle (C)
C = SQRT(A * A + B * B) ' Calculates Pythagorean theorem
```

By adding blank lines and extra spaces, you can make each comment easier to find and read:

```
' Calculates the hypotenuse of a triangle (C)

C = SQRT(A * A + B * B)         ' Calculates Pythagorean theorem
```

Block comments

If you need to write several lines of comments, typing the comment character in front of each line can get annoying. As a simpler alternative, many programming languages let you create block comments.

A block comment lets you identify the beginning and end of a comment. So, if you wanted to write a comment on two separate lines in C++, you'd have to type the // symbols in front of each line, such as

```
// Calculates the hypotenuse of a triangle (C) using the
// Pythagorean theorem: C = square root (A * A + B * B)
```

If you created this as a block comment, you could use the /* and */ symbols to mark the start and end of a comment like this:

```
/* Calculates the hypotenuse of a triangle (C) using the
   Pythagorean theorem: C = square root (A * A + B * B)
*/
```

No matter how many comments you add, you only need to use the /* and */ comment symbols once, like this:

```
/* Calculates the hypotenuse of a triangle (C) using the
   Pythagorean theorem C = square root (A * A + B * B).
   The length of the hypotenuse is then used to move a
   cartoon figure on the screen.
*/
```

REMEMBER

Block comments just make it easier to add multiple lines of comments. Programmers often use both line and block comments in a single program like this:

```
/* Calculates the hypotenuse of a triangle (C) using the
   Pythagorean theorem: C = square root (A * A + B * B).
   The length of the hypotenuse is then used to move a
   cartoon figure on the screen.
*/

c = sqrt(a * a + b * b) // Pythagorean theorem
```

WARNING

The comment symbol in one language may have a completely different meaning in another language, so make sure you don't mix them up.

>> In the curly-bracket languages (such as C++ and Java), the curly brackets are used to define a block of commands like this:

```
int main()
{
    cout << "Hello, world!\n";
}
```

>> In Pascal, the curly brackets are used to create block comments like this:

```
{ Calculates the hypotenuse of a triangle (C) using the
  Pythagorean theorem: C = square root (A * A + B * B).
  The length of the hypotenuse is then used to move a
  cartoon figure on the screen.
}
```

TIP

To make important block comments stand out, many programmers surround comments with additional symbols. So, instead of writing a simple block comment like this:

```
/* This code calculates how many megatons will
   be needed to blow up at least 75 percent of
```

```
        the Earth and throw huge chunks of the
        planet into orbit around the moon.
*/
```

Many programmers emphasize the block comments by inserting extra symbols, such as asterisks, as follows:

```
/*********************************************\
 * This code calculates how many megatons will *
 * be needed to blow up at least 75 percent of *
 * the Earth and throw huge chunks of the       *
 * planet into orbit around the moon.           *
\*********************************************/
```

The compiler ignores all these extra symbols and just focuses on the /* symbols to identify the beginning of the comments and the */ symbols to identify the end of the comments.

Instead of surrounding comments with extra symbols, some programmers use extra symbols in the left margin, like this:

```
/*
** This code calculates how many megatons will
** be needed to blow up at least 75 percent of
** the Earth and throw huge chunks of the
** planet into orbit around the moon.
*/
```

TIP

Every programmer eventually develops a preferred style for writing comments. As long as you're consistent, other programmers will have no trouble finding and reading your comments.

Describing code and algorithms

Comments are typically used to explain what one or more lines of code do or how they work. For example, suppose you had the following code:

```
F = P / (1 + (B * exp(-c * t)))
```

Looking at this code, you can tell how the computer calculates a result, but you have no idea what result this code is calculating. So, you could add a comment that explains what this code does, like this:

```
' This formula calculates the spread of
' a flu epidemic as a function of time.

F = P / (1 + (B * exp(-c * t)))
```

Now that you've identified what the code does, you can use additional comments to explain how it works:

```
' This formula uses the epidemic model to calculate the
' spread of a flu epidemic as a function of time.

' F = Function of time
' P = Current population of a city
' t = Time measured in weeks
' c = Number of people in contact with an infected person
' B = A constant value that can be determined by the initial
'      parameters of the flu epidemic

F = P / (1 + (B * exp(-c * t)))
```

Although you may still not understand what the preceding code does, the comments can help you understand what the code does (calculating a flu epidemic) and how it works. Without these comments, the code itself tells you little about what it does.

You may also want to add links or references to books to make it easy for anyone to get further information to understand your code.

REMEMBER

Sometimes you may write code, put it aside, and then look at it three weeks later — and find nothing seems to make sense anymore. So, write comments to help other programmers (and also to help yourself) in the future.

TECHNICAL
STUFF

There are two schools of thought regarding comments. One says to use comments liberally to explain both what code does and how it works. The other believes that if you have to add comments to explain what and how your code works, your code is probably too complicated in the first place. This second school of thought believes that, instead of writing comments, programmers should focus on writing self-explanatory code. Most programmers try to write self-explanatory code and use comments whenever necessary.

Another use for comments is to explain the logic behind your code. For example, if you declared a variable as a Byte data type instead of an Integer data type, you might include a comment explaining why you chose one data type or another like this:

```
' Declared the "Age" variable as a Byte data type because
' Byte data types only accept values from 0 to 255.

Dim Age As Byte
```

Use comments sparingly only when the purpose of the code isn't obvious. Redundant comments help no one, as the following example shows:

```
' Calculates interest payments by multiplying the
' principal by the interest rate and the time.

Payments = Principal * Rate * Time
```

If a comment repeats information that anyone could read from the source code, take the comment out. You don't want to clutter your source code with useless comments. You want to add comments that can help someone (even you) easily understand the code as quickly as possible. When in doubt, add clarifying comments wherever there's even the remote possibility that there could be confusion on what the code is doing and why.

Documentation

Comments can explain the purpose of one or more lines of code, but many programmers also use comments to document entire subprograms, such as the following:

>> Describing what the subprogram does

>> Listing the original programmer (along with contact information, such as an email address)

>> Defining the original creation date and last date of modification

The following code shows how to use a block comment to document a subprogram:

```
/********************************************\
* Description:                              *
*                                           *
* This subprogram calculates the angle needed *
* to track and aim a laser for shooting down *
* anti-aircraft missiles fired at airplanes  *
```

```
 * as they land or take off.             *
 *                                         *
 * Author: John Smith (Jsmith@dodwaste.com)  *
 *                                         *
 * Creation date: January 21, 2026         *
 *                                         *
 * Last modified: September 5, 2027         *
 \*****************************************/
```

When you place such a descriptive comment at the beginning of every sub-program, you ensure that other people can understand what the subprogram does and who to contact (blame) without having to examine the source code line-by-line.

Debugging

Comments can temporarily *ignore* lines of code for testing. For example, suppose your program included the following:

```
Y = log(Y) - (500 + sin(Angle))
X = Rate * exp(X) / Y
PRINT "The value of x = ", X
```

If you wanted to see how your program would work if you eliminated the first line of code and replaced it with a new line of code, you could delete the top line and type a new line, like this:

```
Y = cos(Angle) * Y
X = Rate * exp(X) / Y
PRINT "The value of x = ", X
```

Now if you wanted to replace the top line with the previously erased line, you'd have to delete the top line and retype the preceding line all over again. A simpler method would be to comment out the top line and type in a new line, like this:

```
' Y = log(Y) - (500 + sin(Angle))
Y = cos(Angle) * Y
X = Rate * exp(X) / Y
PRINT "The value of x = ", X
```

This causes the compiler to ignore the top line (treating it as a comment). Now if you want to "insert" the top line back into the program, you can comment out the second line and remove the comment symbol from the first line:

```
Y = log(Y) - (500 + sin(Angle))
' Y = cos(Angle) * Y
X = Rate * exp(X) / Y
PRINT "The value of x = ", X
```

The preceding code is equivalent to the following:

```
Y = log(Y) - (500 + sin(Angle))
X = Rate * exp(X) / Y
PRINT "The value of x = ", X
```

REMEMBER

By commenting out code, you can temporarily *ignore* code without *deleting* it. Then you can add the code back into your program by removing the comment symbol rather than retyping the entire line again.

TECHNICAL STUFF

In some editors, such as Xcode, you can use comments to define the beginning of a chunk of code. Then you can browse through a list of comments so you can jump to the beginning of the code chunk you want to view.

Writing Software Documentation

Most source code makes no sense to nonprogrammers. Even worse, most source code often makes no sense even to the original programmers after they stop working on it.

Many programmers work on a program and understand all the idiosyncrasies and quirks of that program. Then they work on another program and forget how the first program worked. When they return to the first program, the source code can look as alien as someone else's handwriting. For that reason, software documentation is crucial.

Documentation types

Documentation typically consists of text that's physically separate from the source code. The three types of documentation are

>> Design specifications

>> Technical designs

>> User manuals

REMEMBER

Although software documentation is often treated as an afterthought, it can be a crucial step in completing any program. The key to software documentation is to make it easy to create while still being useful. If you can do that, your software documentation will be a success no matter how much (or how little) time you spend putting it together.

Design specifications

Design specifications list the program requirements so the programmers can understand what problem they need to solve. Unfortunately, projects tend to change over time, so it's common to specify one type of program and then halfway through the project, someone suddenly decides to add an entirely new feature.

Trying to design everything beforehand is like trying to describe the perfect apple pie without even knowing what an apple pie looks or tastes like. Design specifications can help give a project focus, but their ultimate goal is to help programmers create a useful, working program.

Technical design

Programmers use a technical design document to organize how to write the program. This means specifying how the program will work, what programming language and compiler to use, and how to divide the program into parts, as well as assigning teams of programmers to work on each part.

WARNING

Technical design documents usually start off being fairly complete and accurate, but trying to design a program is much different than actually writing that same program. Therefore, the design of a program can change as programmers run into obstacles that they didn't foresee ahead of time.

When this happens, the programmers often focus on solving the problem and forget about updating the technical design documents, so the technical design documents eventually become inaccurate and obsolete. Programmers rarely want to update technical design documents because the program may likely change again later anyway.

VIDEO TUTORIALS

Because most people don't read user manuals, many companies are resorting to video tutorials that show movies of the program in action. That way users can see exactly how to use the program without having to search for that information buried somewhere inside a thick manual.

Unfortunately, video tutorials are limited. They take time to create, so they usually cover only the more common features of a program. If you need help with a specific command, you need to find the video file that contains the answer and then skim through the video until you find the information you need.

As a result, video tutorials act more as supplements to the user manual than as replacements for it. Video tutorials work best when they're kept short and focused on common tasks that every user needs to know. After users get familiar with a program with the help of video tutorials, they'll feel more confident using the help files and reading the user manual.

User manuals

User manuals are meant to teach people how to use the program. Ideally, a program should be so intuitive that users don't need a user manual. Because that rarely happens, most programs include a user manual that explains how to use every feature in a program.

Documentation tools

Unfortunately, most user manuals are notoriously inaccurate, confusing, and incomplete. If the programmers write the user manual, they tend to write instructions geared more toward other programmers. If other people write the user manual, they often don't fully understand how the program actually works.

The problem with all forms of documentation stems from the dual nature of a software project:

>> Writing a program is completely different from writing documentation.

>> Writing the best documentation in the world is useless if the program never gets done or works incorrectly.

Programmers can use a couple of techniques for writing better documentation.

Agile documentation

Many programmers prefer using agile documentation methods. Just as agile programming means being able to adapt to changing conditions, *agile documentation* means updating the documentation just enough to be accurate but without wasting time trying to make it perfect.

Automation

Computer scientists have developed special documentation generators that can examine source code and create simple explanations for how different parts of a large program work.

By using such automated tools, keeping documentation updated is much faster and easier than forcing a reluctant programmer to write and update documentation manually. After documentation has been partially completed with an automated tool, the programmers can edit the documentation to keep it up to date.

Help files

Partially to avoid writing and printing manuals that few people bother to read anyway, programmers are writing help files instead. Help files essentially condense the user manual into short explanations that give users three options for finding help by

>> Browsing through a table of contents of logically organized topics

>> Searching an index for specific commands or topics organized alphabetically

>> Searching for specific terms or phrases

Help files can be read like a book, browsed through like a dictionary, or searched like a search engine that returns pages of related information. Like ordinary user manuals, help files often require the aid of programmers to explain and verify that the explanations in the help files are accurate and complete.

To make creating help files easier, many programmers use special help file creation programs, which can turn an ordinary user manual into a help file. By using such tools, programmers don't have to create user manuals and help files separately; they can just create a user manual and then turn that user manual into a help file.

REMEMBER

Ultimately, any form of documentation is meant to help explain what a program does and how it works. When writing documentation for your program, make it easy on yourself and write as little as possible while trying to be as complete as possible. It's not an easy task, but it's a necessary one.

Chapter **10**

Principles of User Interface Design

You can divide every program into two parts: a user interface (UI) and the part of the program that actually does something useful, such as predicting winning lottery numbers or editing video images.

The whole purpose of a UI is to give a program a way to

>> Accept commands from the user

>> Accept data from the user.

>> Display information back to the user.

The UI basically lets you give information to a program and receive useful information back again, as shown in Figure 10-1. Without a UI, you can't control a program or retrieve any useful information from the program. The best UI is the one that makes it easy for someone to use the program regardless of how ugly the UI may look to others.

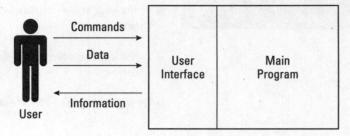

The Evolution of User Interfaces

To better understand UIs, you need to know how they've evolved and how current UI designs are meant to solve the problems of the past.

Command-line interface

In the old days, programmers focused on writing the useful part of their program. Then, as an afterthought, they created a simple UI for controlling that program. Because the programmers already knew how to control their own programs, they often created a bare-bones UI that looked as confusing as this:

```
A:\>
```

At this point, the user is supposed to know not only all possible valid commands to use, but also how to spell and use each command. Such bare-bones UIs are called *command-line interfaces* because they force users to type in commands one line at a time.

The problem with command-line interfaces is that they're too hard to use:

>> **You have to know all valid commands you can use.**

>> **You have to know what each command does so you know which one to pick.**

>> **You have to type each command in correctly.** Spell a command wrong or leave out a space, and the program rejects that command and makes you type it all over again.

Menus

Command-line interfaces made using programs too difficult for the average person, so UIs soon evolved from primitive command-line interfaces to simple menus that listed options for the user to choose from, as shown in Figure 10-2.

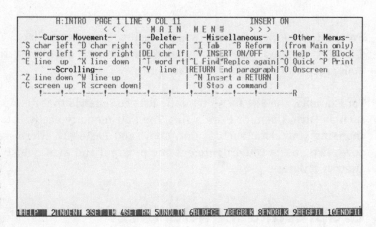

FIGURE 10-2:
Early user interfaces were simple menus of keystroke combinations.

To choose a command listed in a menu, you had to either press a function key (such as F3) or a unique keystroke combination (such as Ctrl+K+X). The problem with these simple menus was that they gobbled up space onscreen. The more commands a program offered, the bigger the menus got.

The solution to this problem was to organize commands in different menus that would appear only when the user needed them. Such menus typically appeared at the top of the screen and would appear when the user clicked or *pulled down* the menu, like pulling down a window shade, as shown in Figure 10-3.

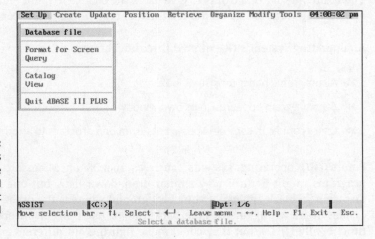

FIGURE 10-3:
Drop-down lists help organize commands and tuck them out of sight until needed.

The main advantages of drop-down lists are that they hide program commands until you need them, and you can choose a command from a drop-down list by clicking it with the mouse as opposed to typing a cryptic keystroke command.

Eventually, more programs started using drop-down lists. To make using different programs even easier, programs started organizing their commands under identical drop-down list categories.

For example, the File menu typically lists commands that manipulate your data, such as Save, Open, or Print a file. The Edit menu typically lists commands for changing your data, such as Cut, Copy, and Paste. By offering standard drop-down lists, users could figure out one program and then quickly adapt to using another program.

Graphical user interface

The next great leap forward in user interface design occurred with operating systems. In the early days of computers, most operating systems offered only command-line interfaces, so programmers had to create their own drop-down list UIs themselves. Therefore, every program tended to look slightly different even if it used nearly identical drop-down lists.

To create a consistent appearance for all programs and give users the ability to run two or more programs at the same time, operating systems soon abandoned their clunky command-line interfaces and adapted a graphical user interface (GUI).

REMEMBER

The main purpose of a GUI is to give users the chance to point and click the commands they want rather than force them to type in the actual command name.

An operating system's GUI offered three advantages:

>> All programs had a consistent look.

>> Each program appeared in its own window.

>> Users could cut, copy, and paste data from one program to another.

Before GUI operating systems, such as macOS or Microsoft Windows, two programs might both display similar drop-down lists, but one program might display it in black against a white background whereas the other program might display it in red against a blue background. Such visual differences might be functionally trivial, but they could make figuring out different programs harder for many people.

By forcing all programs to look similar, GUI operating systems made figuring out programs much easier. After you knew how one program worked, you could easily switch to another program.

REMEMBER

The only purpose of a UI is to make it easy for people to use a program. The best user interface is *transparent* to the user — someone can use the program just by looking at it, instead of being forced to read 300-page manuals first.

Elements of a User Interface

To create a UI, you have two choices:

>> **Write it from scratch.** Writing a UI from scratch basically means writing and testing your program and then writing and testing a UI, essentially doubling your work. Because the code that creates a UI can be separate from the code that actually makes your program do something useful, many programmers use UI frameworks that contain libraries of subprograms for creating the standard elements of a UI, such as drop-down lists and windows.

>> **Use a rapid application development (RAD) tool.** As an even simpler alternative, programmers also use RAD tools that let you visually design your UI. After you design your UI, you write code that attaches this UI to the rest of your program.

No matter which method you use to create a UI, every UI needs to offer ways to do the following:

>> Let the user control (give commands) to the program.

>> Let the user give data to the program.

>> Display information for the user to see.

REMEMBER

The UI has to make sense only to the people who want to use the program. If you design a UI that looks great to you but confuses the people who use the program, the UI fails no matter how pretty it may look.

Displaying commands to a user interface

Unlike command-line interfaces that force users to memorize and type commands, GUIs always display commands onscreen so the user can point and click with the mouse to choose a command.

The simplest way to display a command to the user is through a button. Because buttons can take up so much space onscreen, buttons are most useful for displaying a limited number of common commands to the user, such as two or three possible choices, as shown in Figure 10-4.

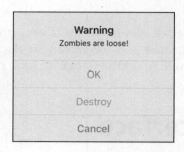

FIGURE 10-4:
Buttons can
display the entire
command name
for the user
to see.

The problem with buttons is that they take up screen space, so using more than a handful of buttons can crowd the screen and confuse the user. Instead of bombarding users with screens full of buttons, programs generally use buttons to offer choices that users need to make frequently.

For example, when quitting a program, the program may ask the user if they want to save the file before quitting. The limited number of choices are Don't Save, Save, and Cancel.

REMEMBER

Buttons are useful for limiting the user's choices to a handful of options. However, buttons are impractical for displaying a large number of commands.

The most popular way for displaying multiple commands to the user is through drop-down lists. drop-down lists organize commands into categories, such as File, Edit, Window, and Help.

Unfortunately, drop-down lists aren't easy to use when a program has hundreds of possible commands. As a result, commands often get buried within multiple drop-down lists.

To solve this problem, many programs group related commands within submenus, but now you have the problem of trying to find a command buried within a submenu, which is buried in a drop-down list, as shown in Figure 10-5.

Because drop-down lists can get overloaded with so many commands, UI designers started displaying commands as icons and grouping icons together in toolbars that usually appear directly underneath drop-down lists, as shown in Figure 10-6.

The advantage of icons is that they take up much less space than buttons with command names written inside them. The disadvantage of icons is that users have no idea which icons represent which commands.

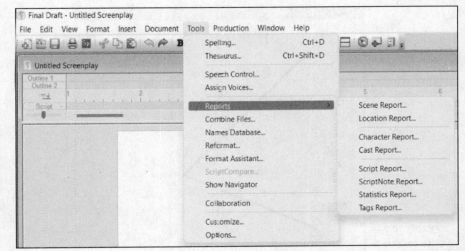

FIGURE 10-5:
Submenus
reduce the
number of
commands in
a drop-down
list but make
it harder to
find a specific
command.

FIGURE 10-6:
Icons, organized
in toolbars, allow
one-click access
to multiple
commands.

As a result, most programs display short descriptions of each icon's purpose if you move the mouse pointer over that icon. So, if you move the mouse pointer over a disk icon, the program might display the word *Save* underneath in a little window to let you know that clicking the disk icon represents the Save command.

TECHNICAL STUFF

Microsoft groups related icons together under tabs, which is called the Ribbon. When you click a tab, you can find related commands represented as icons. The trouble is finding the command you want if you don't know which tab it's stored under. Because Microsoft developed the Ribbon, many Windows programs have adopted the Ribbon as well.

Another way to organize icons is in a *toolbox* on the side of the screen, which is popular for accessing groups of commonly used commands, as shown in Figure 10-7.

REMEMBER

Icons provide one-click access to commonly used commands. However, users should still be able to choose the same command from a drop-down list if they want.

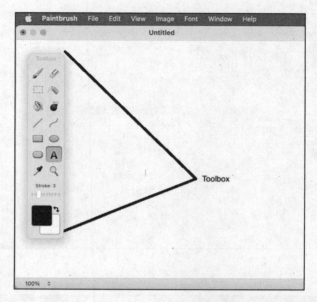

FIGURE 10-7:
Toolboxes provide another way to group icons for easy access.

Giving data to the user interface

Besides giving a program commands, users also need to give a program data to use for calculating a useful result. At the simplest level, users can just type in data they want to give the program. To accept typed-in data, UIs need to display a *text box* (a box for the user to click and type something in). Text boxes are commonly used when the program needs data that can't be predicted in advance, such as asking for someone's name, as shown in Figure 10-8.

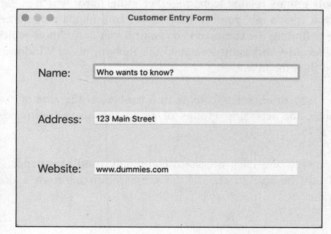

FIGURE 10-8:
Users can type any information inside a text box, including invalid data.

Text boxes are great for accepting textual data, such as names, passwords, or search phrases, but text boxes also allow users to type in invalid data such as typing "twelve" instead of "12." To weed out invalid data, write extra code to verify that any information typed into a text box is actually valid.

If the type of data the user can give to the program is limited to a fixed range of choices, it's better to use one of the following UI elements instead:

>> Radio buttons

>> Check boxes

>> List boxes

>> Combo boxes

>> Sliders

Restricting choices to one option with radio buttons

Radio buttons (also called *option buttons*) get their name from old car radios that let you assign a favorite radio station to a button. Instead of having to tune in your favorite radio station manually, you pressed a radio button, and the radio would jump to a preset station. Just as you can only listen to one radio station at a time, you can only choose one option at a time with radio/option buttons on a UI.

UI radio buttons work the same way. Each radio button represents one possible choice, and the user can pick only one of them, as shown in Figure 10-9.

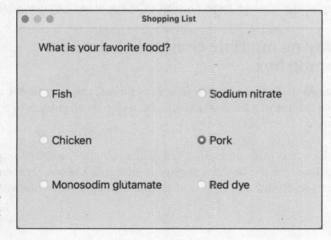

FIGURE 10-9:
Radio buttons can display multiple choices, but they only let you pick one option.

The main advantage of radio buttons is that they show the user all possible choices, so instead of typing in the data (and risk spelling it wrong), users can just click the radio button that represents the one choice they want to give a program.

Restricting choices with check boxes

Radio buttons are useful for restricting the type of data the user can give to a program. However, if you want to display all possible choices but allow the user to choose two or more of those choices, you can use check boxes instead, as shown in Figure 10-10.

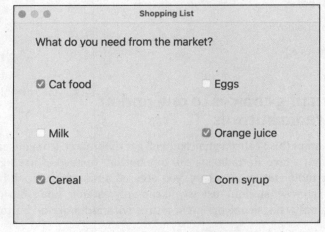

FIGURE 10-10:
Check boxes can display multiple choices and allow users to pick more than one option.

The drawback of both radio buttons and check boxes is that they take up space onscreen. Displaying 4 or 5 radio buttons or check boxes onscreen is reasonable, but displaying 20 or 30 radio buttons or check boxes can get cumbersome.

Displaying multiple choices in a list box or combo box

If you need to display a large number of choices, you may find it easier to display all those choices in a list box. A list box can display all choices or a limited number of choices.

If the list box is large enough, it can display all choices. If the number of options is more than the list box can display at once, the list box displays a scroll bar so users can scroll through the list of all available options, as shown in Figure 10-11.

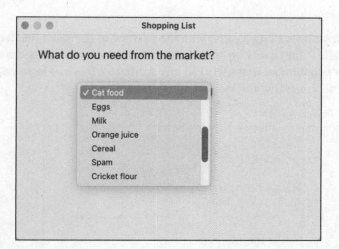

FIGURE 10-11:
List boxes display
a list of options.

Similar to list boxes are *combo boxes* (also called *drop-down boxes*), which combine the features of a text box with a list box. Like a text box, a combo box lets users type data directly into the program. Like a list box, a combo box also displays a list of options that the user can choose, as shown in Figure 10-12.

FIGURE 10-12:
Combo boxes let
you either make
a choice or type
data directly.

REMEMBER

Unlike list boxes, combo boxes always hide all choices until the user clicks the combo box.

Restricting numeric choices with a slider

If users need to give numeric data to a program, they can type the numeric values in a text box. However, if you want to restrict the range of valid numbers that the user can type in, you can use a slider.

A *slider* moves along a ruler, with the position of the slider determining a specific numeric value or setting, as shown in Figure 10-13. Not only can sliders limit the range of a number that users can give a program (such as from 0 to 100), but sliders can also define the increments of numeric data.

FIGURE 10-13:
A slider lets users
visually choose
a numeric value
or setting by
dragging a slider
along a ruler.

If a slider restricted values from 0 to 100 with increments of 0.5, that means the user could give the program numbers such as 0, 0.5, 1, 1.5, 2, 2.5, and so on.

Showing information back to the user

UIs can show information to the user in a variety of ways, such as through text, graphics, or even sound. Typically, a UI displays data in a window where users can manipulate that data and see their changes directly, as shown in Figure 10-14.

Using any program is like talking to the computer. You tell the computer what you want to do (start writing a letter), the computer obeys (loads your word processor) and waits for you to do something else, you give another command to the computer (to format text you just typed), the computer obeys and waits until you decide what to do next, and so on.

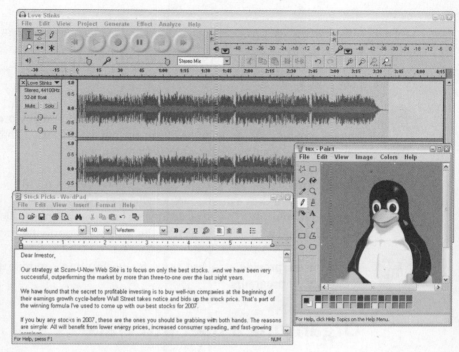

FIGURE 10-14:
A user interface displays data in a window that users can manipulate, whether that data represents text, numbers, pictures, or sound.

Normally, when you give a command to a program, the program responds right away. However, sometimes the program asks the user for more information. For example, if you give the command to print a document, the program may want to know how many pages to print. Whenever a program needs more information to carry out a command, it displays a dialog box, as shown in Figure 10-15.

FIGURE 10-15:
Dialog boxes ask the user for more data before carrying out a command.

| Print | × |

Selection	Options
● All pages	☑ Include title page
○ Pages:	☐ Black and white
○ Scenes:	☑ Include highlighting
○ Character:	☑ Include tags
○ Revisions: White	☐ Element highlighting Configure...
	Revisions as: Text colors

OK   Cancel

A dialog box is the computer's way of saying, "I'm trying to obey your instructions, but I'm not quite sure exactly what you want." Some common dialog boxes are used to

>> Open a file.

>> Save a file.

>> Print a file.

REMEMBER

Because dialog boxes are so common in every program, many programming languages provide built-in features for displaying dialog boxes. That way, you don't have to create your own dialog boxes from scratch.

The Open dialog box lets you click a filename that you want to open. The Save dialog box lets you click a drive or folder where you want to store a file and then type a name for your file. The Print dialog box lets a program ask the user how many pages and copies to print, as well as the page size or orientation.

REMEMBER

Dialog boxes provide standard ways for performing common tasks needed by almost every program.

Organizing a user interface

One problem with designing a UI is fitting everything in a single window. To help organize a UI, many programs use either boxes or tabs.

Boxes draw lines around items on the UI, such as multiple radio buttons, and visually separate items, as shown in Figure 10-16.

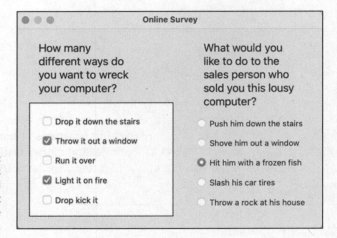

FIGURE 10-16:
Boxes draw lines to separate and organize different user interface items.

Another way to organize a UI is to use tabs. Each tab can display entirely different UI items (buttons, text labels, check boxes, and so on). When you click a different tab, the tab shows you different UI items, as shown in Figure 10-17.

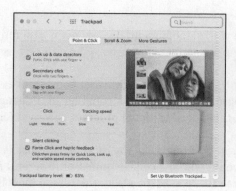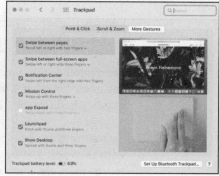

FIGURE 10-17:
Tabs let you
organize and
display different
user interface
items in the same
window.

REMEMBER

The goal of boxes and tabs is to organize your UI. As far as users are concerned, the UI is the only part of your program that they can see, so if you design a cluttered or confusing UI, people think of your program as cluttered and confusing.

Designing a User Interface

There's a big difference between knowing the elements of a UI and knowing how to put together an effective UI. That's like the difference between knowing how to write every letter of the alphabet and knowing how to write a best-selling novel.

That's why designing a UI is part art and part science. After you design enough UIs and use the UIs of different programs, you can see what you like and don't like. Then you can apply your own ideas to designing your idea of a perfect UI.

Although it's difficult to teach the *art* of designing a UI, it's much easier to teach the *science* behind designing a UI. By following certain UI principles, you can increase the chances that your UI will at least be competent and usable.

TIP

To see drastic differences between UIs, compare the UIs of commercial programs from Adobe, Apple, or Microsoft, and then look at the UIs on open-source or niche commercial programs (such as astrology charting programs or horse race prediction programs). Big companies spend a lot of time and money testing their UIs. In comparison, many individual programmers just slap together a UI and start selling their program — and you can see the difference.

Know the user

Most people find computers hard to use because the UIs of most programs are too confusing. Usually the problem lies with the fact that the programmers know how their program works, so they automatically assume that everyone else must also know how the program works, too. Essentially, too many programs are written by programmers for other programmers and ignore the ordinary user.

Before you design your UI, you have to know what your users expect. A program designed for other programmers (such as a compiler or a debugger) can have a drastically different UI than an educational program designed for 6-year-olds.

No matter who the typical user might be, the UI's sole purpose is to communicate with the user. Just as you'd talk to a college professor differently than you'd talk to a 6-year-old child, so must you adapt a UI to the person most likely to use your program. After you know who the user is, you'll know the best ways your UI can "talk" to that person.

Hide/disable unusable options

At any given time, the users should know what they can do. Unfortunately, poor UIs either

>> Expect the user to know what to do next.

>> Bombard the user with so much information that the user still doesn't know what to do next.

The command-line prompt is an example of a poor UI that expects that the user already knows all valid commands and how to spell them. If you don't know which commands may be valid, the UI won't help you.

Even worse than sparse UIs are UIs that show too much information, such as the drop-down lists in Figure 10-18. The program in this figure displays an Attribute submenu within the Text menu title.

However, every option on the Attribute submenu appears dimmed, which makes the Attribute submenu useless. This can frustrate users if they never know how they can access that particular command.

To avoid this problem, many UIs simply hide commands if they aren't available at the moment. Although this strategy can simplify the UI, it can also confuse users if certain commands seem to appear and disappear for no reason and they have no idea how to make a command appear again that was once visible.

A well-designed UI should always show all possible choices and not overwhelm the users with choices they can't pick anyway. It's up to you as the programmer to choose whether it's best to show all commands (and disable the ones users can't choose at the moment) or hide commands that can't be selected at the moment.

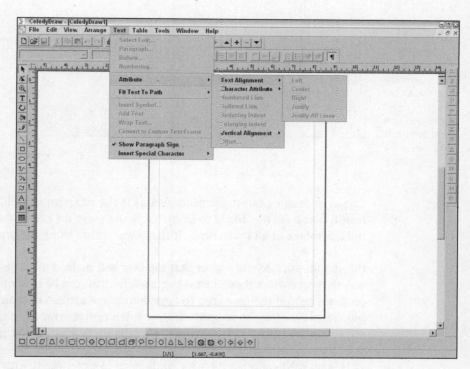

FIGURE 10-18:
This program's drop-down list lets you view a bunch of submenus that you can't access.

Tolerate mistakes

UIs are meant for people to use, and it's no surprise that people make mistakes. Sometimes they type in the wrong data and sometimes they give a command that they didn't really want to give.

If users make a mistake, they should be able to

» Undo or take back that mistake.

» Give the right command or data.

Unfortunately, too many UIs don't let users undo their mistakes, which can make users anxious and timid because they're afraid that if they do something wrong, they can't reverse that mistake. As a result, anxious and timid users tend not to trust a program or use it to its maximum capabilities.

Even worse is when UIs provide cryptic feedback if the user does something wrong. Examining the error message in Figure 10-19, can you tell what you might have done wrong and what you can do in the future to make sure this error message doesn't appear again?

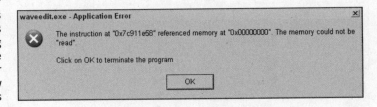

Cryptic messages can make users feel as if the program is scolding them. As a result, users are less likely to enjoy using the program and probably won't take full advantage of all its features, if they even bother using the program at all.

UIs should tolerate and expect that the user will make a mistake and then find a way to recover from these mistakes gracefully. This can be as simple as having the program beep if the user tries to type their name instead of their Social Security number, or having the program display a descriptive error message that not only tells users what they did wrong but also tells them what to do right.

This way, a UI can give the user confidence to experiment with a program and learn its features without reading a 300-page manual. Instead, the user can gradually figure out how to use a program with the program guiding them every step of the way.

Be consistent

One reason chain restaurants are so popular is because people know what to expect when they eat there. UIs also need to make a great first impression on users and then remain consistent so users generally know what to expect from a program at any given time.

For example, suppose a program displays a toolbox of icons on the left side of the screen. Now what happens if the user chooses a command and suddenly the toolbox of icons either disappears or appears on another part of the screen for no apparent reason at all?

Having the UI suddenly change its appearance or behavior while the program is running is certain to confuse and annoy users. By staying consistent in appearance and behavior, a UI can be predictable so the user feels more comfortable using it (just as long as the UI was designed properly in the first place).

Give the user freedom to customize the user interface

Many UIs can overwhelm the user with so many options that it's hard to see what to do first. That's why many programs give the user options to hide certain parts of the UI or modify what appears on the UI, as shown in Figure 10-20.

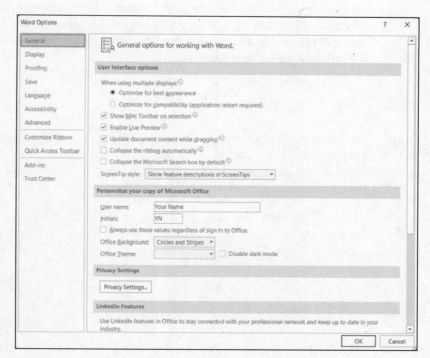

FIGURE 10-20:
Customization options let a user change the user interface to suit their preferences.

Such customization options can make even the most intimidating program feel easier to use. However, give the user a simple way to return to the default appearance of the UI. That way if the user makes a mistake customizing the UI, they can go back to the beginning and start all over again.

Make navigation easy

After users start working with a program, they need to switch back and forth between viewing their data in different ways. For example, a web browser lets users view web pages (data) and new or previous web pages easily by either typing in a new website address, clicking a hyperlink, or clicking the Back and Forward buttons. By making it easy for the user to do what they want, the UI aids the user without drawing attention to itself.

At any given time, users should always be able to view their data in a previous state (such as seeing the preceding web page) or view their data in a new way (such as seeing a new web page or changing the size of text on the current web page). By making it easy and predictable for users to manipulate data, a good UI can make even the most complicated program simple to understand and eventually master.

There's no "perfect" UI because every UI must cater to different types of users and programs. However, by following UI design guidelines, you can make sure your program not only looks good but also helps the user get some work done, which is the ultimate goal of any program.

Chapter **11**

Debugging and Testing

W riting a program isn't easy. Not only do you have to write a program that solves a big problem, but you must also solve a bunch of little problems along the way. Some of those problems might be mini-steps on the way to solving the big problem (such as how to predict whether a given sports team will win this week) while other problems may simply involve working with the hardware such as correctly printing data.

Writing a program takes time. However, a program is never done until it has been tested. Testing helps ensure the program works correctly and reliably. When testing reveals problems, the programmers must fix them whether they're minor (such as displaying the wrong icon on the screen) or major (the program crashes). That's why testing is a crucial part of any software project.

Common Types of Programming Errors

Ultimately, there are a nearly infinite number of ways a program can fail. The simplest problems involve typing a command wrong, forgetting a comma, or adding too many parentheses or curly brackets. These types of problems, called *syntax errors*, occur when you don't type in commands exactly the way the compiler expects.

Syntax errors are the easiest problems to fix because the editor will often catch these problems and highlight them. To minimize the chances of typing anything wrong, many editors include code snippets that act like templates for common programming commands, such as creating an if-then statement or a loop, as shown in Figure 11-1.

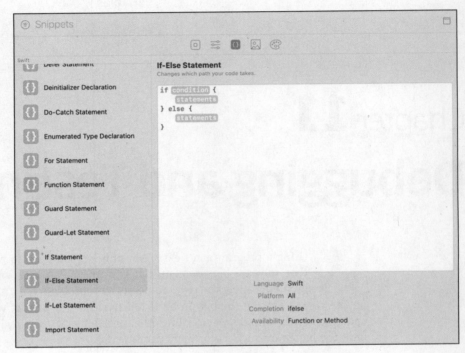

FIGURE 11-1:
Code snippets
can provide
templates for
writing common
statements.

Because programming languages offer so many commands, most programmers will never remember how to spell every command from memory. That's why many editors offer a code completion feature that detects what you're typing so it can display a pop-up menu of options it thinks you want to type.

Now instead of typing an entire command, you can type part of the command, wait for the editor to display a pop-up menu, and then choose the option you want from that pop-up menu as shown in Figure 11-2. As soon as you choose an option, the editor automatically types your chosen command correctly so there's no risk of mistyping anything.

By using code snippets and code completion, you can minimize your chances of mistyping commands to avoid common syntax errors. Syntax problems are fairly easy for the editor to spot, but logic errors are much harder to spot.

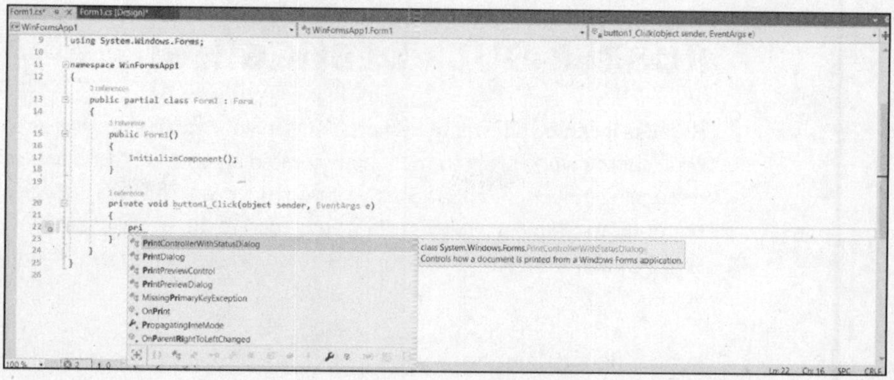

FIGURE 11-2:
Code completion displays several commands so you can choose the one you want.

A logic error occurs when you (the programmer) write commands that you think are correct, but when you run the program, it doesn't work. Because you already thought you did everything correctly, the problem lies in identifying your faulty logic.

Suppose you need to write a simple function that converts temperatures in Fahrenheit into Celsius. You might write a formula like this:

```
tempC = tempF - 32 * 5/9
```

This formula is correct, but it neglects mathematical precedence, which defines the order that the computer calculates operations. In this case, multiplication and division have higher precedence than addition and subtraction. That means the formula actually multiples 32 by 5 (to get 160) and then divides 160 by 9 (to get 17.78). Finally, it subtracts 17.78 from the temperature measured in Fahrenheit.

So, if the temperature were 212 degrees Fahrenheit, the formula would calculate the equivalent Celsius temperature as 194.22. Although the formula is correct, the mathematical precedence of computers makes this formula fail. The real formula should be this:

```
tempC = (tempF - 32) * 5/9
```

The parentheses force the formula to subtract 32 from the temperature in Fahrenheit first. Just this subtle difference makes the formula work. Yet the incorrect version of this formula looked like it should've worked as well. Because logic errors require you to fix code you already think should work, it can be hard to find your mistake.

RUBBER-DUCK DEBUGGING

Because it can be difficult to find problems in your code when you already think your code should work, programmers have created an unusual technique called rubber-duck debugging (https://rubberduckdebugging.com). The idea is that you talk to a rubber duck and explain what you want your code to do. By talking out loud and explaining, step-by-step, what you want your code to do, you can often spot flaws in your logic and your code.

Rubber-duck debugging may seem silly, but just speaking your thoughts out loud can often clarify your thinking and identify flaws in your logic. Because talking to a rubber duck is far less threatening and intimidating than talking to a live person, rubber-duck debugging is actually considered a valid way to find and fix problems in a program.

If talking to a rubber duck feels silly, feel free to talk to any inanimate object, such as a plant or a chair, or talk to a pet, such as your dog or cat. Ultimately, it doesn't matter how silly you look to others as long as the technique helps you create better and more reliable software.

Debugging with Comments and Print Statements

To find a *bug* (problem) in a program, you need to identify what the problem is and where it's occurring. When you know where to find the problem, you can fix the code that's causing the problem.

That means debugging is mostly like hunting for a needle in a haystack. The smaller the program, the less code you'll need to examine to find the bug. The larger the program, the more code you'll need to examine.

Therefore, the first goal of debugging is to narrow your search by eliminating chunks of code that cannot possibly be causing the problem. If a program is poorly organized, you may need to examine the entire program from beginning to end. However, if a program is properly organized into separate files, subprograms, and objects, then you can often narrow down your search to the most likely areas where the bug could be occurring.

Perhaps the most primitive, yet effective way to search for bugs is to rely on

>> Comments

>> The print statement

Comments are usually reserved for documenting your code. However, comments can temporarily remove code without forcing you to delete it entirely. That way you can see how the program reacts without one or more lines of code.

If the program still has the bug despite commenting out one or more lines of code, then you can be certain the bug isn't being caused by the commented-out code. If the bug magically goes away, then you can be nearly certain that the commented code is the culprit.

By commenting out less and less code, you can eventually find the one line that's causing all the problems. When you find that one line, the next step is figuring out why it's causing the problem.

When you find a line of code that's causing problems, there might be two reasons:

>> The line is actually causing the problem.

>> The line is getting bad data from another part of the program.

Suppose you have a line of code that adds two numbers together as follows:

```
age = x + y
```

Yet when you run the program, it appears that the code is actually subtracting two numbers.

If the line of code is at fault, you might have typed a minus sign (–) instead of a plus sign (+). By fixing that line, you can fix the problem.

However, what if the line of code is correctly adding two numbers together. Perhaps the real culprits are the variables this one line of code is trying to add together. Specifically, what if your code expects to add two positive numbers, but somewhere in your program, your code is actually sending negative numbers?

When the line of code adds a negative number to a positive number, it will appear to be subtracting. So, the problem may not be the line of code you're examining, but another line of code spitting out incorrect data.

Now you have to repeat the entire process of guessing where in your program the error may be occurring, commenting out chunks of code, and removing the comments until you find the error.

If multiple lines of code calculate a result, you can insert the print statement throughout your code to print out the values of different variables. Now as your program runs, you can see the results of the print statements and see what part of your code may be storing the wrong data.

Suppose a line of code is adding two numbers wrong. Just inserting two print statements can let us see exactly the values of those two variables before the addition happens like this Swift code shows:

```
print ("The value of x = \(x)")
print ("The value of y = \(y)")
age = x + y
```

In Swift, you can print out any data by enclosing it within the back slash character followed by parentheses like this: \( ). Swift calls this *string interpolation*.

With these two print statements inserted in the code, you can see the exact value of the two variables (x and y). If one of them prints a negative number, the next step would be to find the code creating this negative number.

As you can see, debugging requires lots of detective work digging through your code to find the one line of code that's causing the problem. In many cases, you'll find a bug, but the line you think is causing the problem may really just be receiving invalid data from another part of the program.

Using comments and print statements is a simple, but effective way to debug a program. However, it's clumsy because you must constantly comment out code and then uncomment it back out again. Then you must insert print statements throughout your code and remember to take all those print statements back out again before you actually ship your program. Because comments and print statements can be so tedious to use, programmers have created special debugging tools.

Breakpoints, Stepping, and Watching

When looking for bugs in a program, you may need to run the program over and over again so you can identify which line of code may be causing the problem. If you suspect one part of your program may be causing the bug, you can create a breakpoint, as shown in Figure 11-3.

Breakpoints

```
Var x As Integer, y As Integer
' Clear out the background.
g.DrawingColor = RGB(255, 255, 255)
g.FillRectangle(0, 0, g.Width, g.Height)
g.DrawingColor = RGB(128, 128, 128)
g.DrawRectangle(0, 0, g.Width, g.Height)

' If we have a backdrop picture, draw it.
If Me.Backdrop <> Nil Then
    g.DrawPicture(Self.Backdrop, 0, 0)
End If

' Draw out the block field.
For y = 0 To mBlockField.LastIndex(2)
    For x = 0 To mBlockField.LastIndex(1)
        PaintBlock(x, y, mBlockField(x, y), g)
    Next
Next

' Draw the falling block.
For y = 0 To mCurrentPiece.LastIndex(2)
    For x = 0 To mCurrentPiece.LastIndex(1)
        If mCurrentPiece(x, y) Then
            PaintBlock(x + mCurrentX, y + mCurrentY, mCurrentPieceType, g)
        Else
            ' empty square - don't paint it
        End If
    Next
Next
```

FIGURE 11-3: Breakpoints identify lines of code where you want the program to stop.

A breakpoint essentially tells the computer, "See this line of code? When you reach this line, stop running the program."

When the breakpoint temporarily halts your program, you can then step through your code, line-by-line. Each time you step through a line of code, you can watch how the variables in that code may change or see what happens on the user interface (UI).

This combination of breakpoints (to halt execution of a program), stepping (to examine each line of code one by one), and watching (to see how values in variables may change) can help you find the line of code that's causing an error.

Breakpoints don't physically alter your code, so you can freely place them wherever you want. To make breakpoints even more versatile, you may be able to create conditional breakpoints.

A normal breakpoint halts execution of a program at a specific line of code every time. A conditional breakpoint only halts execution of a program at a specific line if a certain condition is true.

For example, a conditional breakpoint may only halt execution if a variable is greater, less than, or equal to a certain value. That way the breakpoint only stops your program under certain conditions that may be causing problems, as shown in Figure 11-4.

let alert = UIAlert
preferredStyle:

☑ Enable Breakpoint in ViewController.swift:31

Name
    A breakpoint name cannot start with numbers or contain any white space.

Condition > 25

Ignore 0 ⌄ times before stopping

Action [Capture GPU Workload ⌄]   + −

Options ☐ Automatically continue after evaluating actions

REMEMBER

Make sure you clear all breakpoints in your program before you ship it to customers. Otherwise the breakpoints will halt execution of your program and keep it from running properly.

Stepping through code

When a breakpoint has temporarily halted execution of a program, you can step through your code line-by-line to identify which line of code may be causing an error. When stepping through code, you may have several options:

» **Step over:** You go through each line of code, but the moment you come across a subprogram/function call, you treat that subprogram/function name as a single command and you *step over* (ignore) all the code stored in that subprogram/function.

» **Step into:** You go through each line of code, but the moment you come across a subprogram/function call, you start examining all the code inside that subprogram/function, line-by-line.

» **Step out:** When you're inside a subprogram/function and examining its code, line-by-line, you can immediately jump out of the subprogram/function so you don't have to continue stepping through all the code inside that particular subprogram/function.

» **Continue:** You stop stepping altogether and simply run all code to the next breakpoint, if any. Some compilers may include a Continue to Cursor option, which lets you click the mouse or move the cursor using the keyboard to a specific line of code. Then the Continue to Cursor option simply runs to the cursor's location. That way you don't have to add a new breakpoint and run your program from the beginning all over again.

By using these various stepping options, you can choose to examine code inside of subprograms/functions or simply step over them if you realize the error couldn't possibly be inside of those subprograms/functions.

Watching variables

Each time you step through a line of code, the compiler displays a debug window where you can also see the current value of all your variables. Watching lets you see which line of code changes the value of a variable. The moment a line of code changes a variable incorrectly, you can further pinpoint where the error may be occurring.

Because a program may contain multiple variables, you may realize not all of those variables have anything to do with the error you're trying to find. For example, if you're looking for the bug that's causing incorrect mathematical calculations, you would want to watch all variables that hold numbers, but there's no point in watching other variables that may only hold string or Boolean values. So, you may have the option of hiding variables you don't want to watch so you can focus your time watching the variables that may be causing the problem.

TECHNICAL STUFF

Many compilers put special debugging information in a project that can help you find bugs in your program. You may also be able to select different types of debugging information for your particular project, as shown in Figure 11-5. When you're ready to ship your program, you can compile a final release build, which strips away debugging information so it doesn't clutter the file unnecessarily.

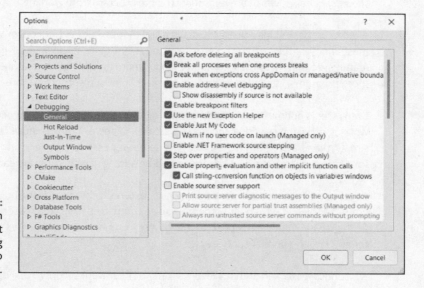

FIGURE 11-5: You can often select different debugging information to use in a project.

Testing Code

Debugging can find many problems, but a final step should be testing. The simplest way to test a program is simply to use it. That means letting potential customers try out the program to make sure it works correctly. Such manual testing is often called *alpha testing* and *beta testing*.

An alpha test is where people (often the programmers themselves and a select group of other people) try using the program and then document any problems they find. During alpha testing, the program's existence may still be kept a secret.

When a program seems mostly stable, that's when it goes into beta testing, which typically means letting the general public test the program. The idea is that the more people who use a program, the more likely someone will find a bug that can be fixed before the program actually ships.

EVERY PROGRAM HAS BUGS

Although alpha and beta testing are meant to find and eliminate bugs, every program still ships with bugs. The main goal of alpha and beta testing is to find and eliminate *showstopper bugs,* which are bugs that stop the program from working.

After a company ships a program, that's when they go back to hunt down and kill the most annoying bugs. Unfortunately, fixing bugs isn't quite as lucrative as adding new features, so that's why most companies focus more on adding new features (to sell more programs) instead of fixing bugs to make an existing program more reliable.

Even rarer is optimizing, or *refactoring,* a program, which involves taking perfectly good, working code and rewriting it to make it smaller, faster, or both. Because refactoring simply makes a program work exactly the same way as it did before, it's far less lucrative for a company to focus on when they could be adding new features instead.

Because the incentive is toward adding new features rather than fixing bugs, most programs will always have bugs in them because companies have little reason to find and fix them. One notable exception to this is when companies offer bounties or rewards for anyone who finds security bugs.

A *security bug* is an error that allows hackers to circumvent security, steal data, or gain unauthorized access. Because security bugs can scare away both potential and current customers, many companies pay large amounts of money (five or six figures) to anyone who can find security bugs and bring it to the attention of the company so they can fix it as soon as possible.

Usually during beta testing, people try using a program in its intended manner. This process can uncover common bugs, but a far more effective technique is to deliberately try to break a program by using it in unintended ways.

For example, if a database expects someone to type a name, what happens if you simply bang on the keyboard instead? How does the program react? If a program expects someone's age, what happens if you type in an extremely large or extremely small number? Will the program still allow someone's age as 902847 or −0.00012?

If a video game lets players control racing cars, what happens if a player tries to go backward or steer off the racetrack completely? What happens if the player simply rams another player's car? What happens if the player tries running the video game on a computer that's connected to four different monitors? By looking for extreme cases, testers can often find bugs that ordinary people would normally overlook.

Letting hordes of people loose on a program through alpha and beta testing is one way to find bugs, but it's a little like giving a roomful of monkeys typewriters and hoping they'll write something coherent. A more systematic approach is to use automated testing where the computer tests your code. Common ways to use automated testing include

>> **Unit tests:** Testing individual blocks of code

>> **Integration tests:** Testing that separate blocks of code work correctly together

>> **User interface tests:** Testing that the UI works

Automated testing lets the computer run multiple tests while changing one part. By running dozens, hundreds, thousands, or even millions of tests, the computer can often find bugs that alpha and beta testers may have overlooked.

Unit tests

Unit tests focus on verifying that a chunk of code, such as a subprogram/function, works exactly as intended. By focusing on small chunks or units of code at a time, you can verify that the code is reliable.

WARNING

Automated testing can verify that your code works as intended, but if the logic behind your code is faulty, unit tests will just verify that your code works but not identify whether it works the way you really need it to work.

Unit testing is meant to verify that a chunk or unit of code is behaving correctly. If code accepts a string and outputs an integer, unit testing can verify that this always works regardless of the size of the text it receives.

Essentially unit testing is about

>> Telling the computer what you expect the code to do

>> Letting the computer run multiple tests to verify the code does what you want it to do

By letting the computer run multiple tests using slightly different data, you can gain more confidence that your code will work in the real world with all possible types of input.

Integration tests

Where unit tests are about verifying that code works, integration testing is about verifying that two or more units of code work together. At the simplest level, integration testing makes sure that one unit of code passes the right data to another unit of code.

On a more sophisticated level, integration testing can identify which unit of code may fail when something goes wrong. Suppose one unit of code requests data over the Internet and then feeds this data into a second unit of code. What happens if there is no Internet connection? What happens if the data received over the Internet is corrupted or simply the wrong type of data? How should these two units of code react to unexpected problems?

It's possible that two units of code may work perfectly well individually but fail when working together. By testing two or more units of code, integration testing can gradually verify all units of code work together, which eventually verifies that the entire program will work correctly. Some different ways to test for integration include

>> **Testing everything at once:** The idea behind testing everything at once is to see how everything works (or doesn't work) and then zero in on the problems. This method can identify problems, but it can also overwhelm developers. It can be like building a 70-story skyscraper and then worrying if the foundation and walls were built correctly.

>> **Testing in increments:** Because testing everything at once can be too late, testing in small increments is often the much better solution. That way as you

go along, you can test different units of code to make sure they work. This gradual testing approach is much easier and simpler to implement and can catch problems early.

>> **Conducting top-down integration tests**: Top-down integration tests the big units of code first and then gradually filters down to smaller units of code.

>> **Conducting bottom-up integration tests**: Bottom-up integration tests begin testing small units of code before building up to larger units of code.

Ultimately the "best" way to test integration is to do a little testing of every type. The more tests you perform, the more likely you'll find different types of bugs. The sooner you can spot problems, the sooner you can fix them.

User interface testing

The whole purpose of a UI is to get out of the way so the user can do what they want. When programmers design UIs, they need to know that every element of the UI works as intended.

If the user clicks or taps a button, that button should respond in the way the user intended — a Print button should start printing, and a Cancel button should cancel a pending task. UI testing can often reveal buttons that don't work or buttons that do work but display the wrong information on the screen.

More important, UI testing can check if a text box can handle if the user types a thousand characters for a name, if the user types a letter instead of a number for a quantity, or if a list scrolls and displays all items whether it displays a dozen items or a thousand.

The main idea behind UI testing is to make sure the UI works as intended and responds to possible problems without crashing.

WARNING

UI testing can verify that a UI works, but it can't identify whether the UI is well designed. Creating intuitive UIs is still an art more than a science. Copying UIs of other programs may make your program easier to learn, but that doesn't necessarily mean the UI is the best design for your particular program.

The ultimate goal of software development is to create a program that solves a problem, works reliably, and is easy to use. That may sound obvious, but you'd be surprised by how many corporations and government agencies forget this time and time again, which is why debugging and testing are so crucial for any project.

3

Data Structures

Contents at a Glance

IN THIS CHAPTER

» Using structures to store and retrieve data

» Creating and working with arrays

» Using resizable arrays

» Running multidimensional arrays

» Combining structures with arrays

» Detailing the drawbacks of arrays

Chapter **1**

Structures and Arrays

All programs need to store data. If a program asks the user to type in their name, the program needs to store that name somewhere so it can find the name again. The most common way programs store data is to dump data in a variable.

Unfortunately, a simple variable can hold only one chunk of data at a time, such as a single number or a single name. If you want to store a person's first *and* last name along with their age, you have to create three separate variables, like this:

```
Dim FirstName As String
Dim LastName As String
Dim Age As Integer
```

Creating separate variables to store related data can be like carrying around three separate wallets — one wallet for your cash, a second wallet for your credit cards, and a third wallet for your driver's license. Just as it's more convenient to store your cash, credit cards, and driver's license in a single wallet, so it's also more convenient to store related data in a single variable. Two ways to store related data in one place are structures and arrays.

REMEMBER

Because structures and arrays are two ways to store data, they're often called *data structures*.

Using Structures

A *structure* (known as a *record* in some programming languages) does nothing more than group separate variables together. So, instead of requiring you to create and keep track of three separate variables, a structure lets you store multiple variables within another variable. If you had three variables — FirstName, LastName, and Age — you could store them all within a structure, like this:

```
Structure Person
    Dim FirstName as String
    Dim LastName as String
    Dim Age as Integer
End Structure
```

A structure is a *user-defined* data type. The different variables grouped together inside of a structure are called *fields*. You can't use a structure until you declare a variable to represent that structure, like this:

```
Dim Employee As Person
```

The preceding code creates an Employee variable that actually contains the FirstName, LastName, and Age fields, as shown in Figure 1-1.

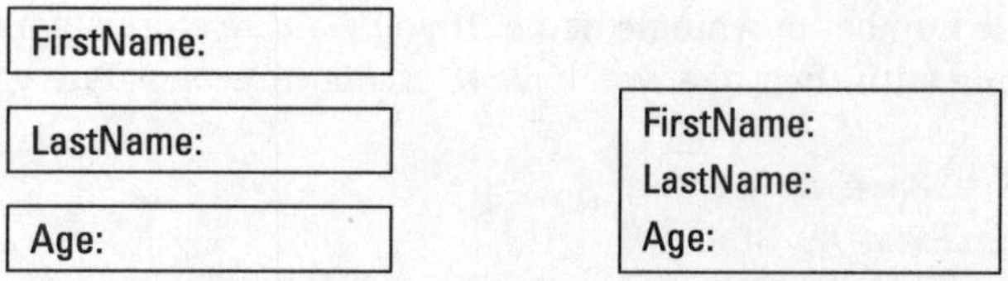

FirstName:

LastName:

Age:

FirstName:
LastName:
Age:

FIGURE 1-1:
A structure
can contain
multiple fields.

Storing data in separate variables means keeping track of each variable

A structure groups separate variables to help you keep related data together.

Storing data

To store data in a structure, you must

1. Identify the variable that represents that structure.

2. Identify the specific field inside the structure to use.

So, if you wanted to store the name J⊃e in the FirstName field inside the Employee variable, you could do the following:

```
Employee.FirstName = "Joe"
```

If you wanted to store the name Smi⊐h in the LastName variable and the number 24 in the Age variable, inside the Emplⴰyee field, you could do the following:

```
Employee.FirstName = "Joe"
Employee.LastName = "Smith"
Employee.Age = "24"
```

Retrieving data

After you store data in a structure, you can always retrieve it again. Just identify

» The variable that represents that structure

» The actual variable name that holds the data

Suppose you defined a structure, as follows:

```
Structure Worker
    Dim Name as String
    Dim ID as Integer
    Dim Salary as Single
End Structure
```

To retrieve data from this structure, identify the variable name that represents that structure and the field that holds the data, like this:

```
Print Employee.FirstName
```

This would retrieve the data in the FirstName variable, stored in the Employee variable structure. If you stored the string "Joe" in the FirstName property, this command would print Joe onscreen.

REMEMBER

Structures are just a way to cram multiple fields into a single variable. A structure can hold only one group of related data. To make structures more useful, programmers typically use structures with another data structure such as an array.

Using an Array

The problem with a single variable is that it can hold only a single chunk of data. So, if you wanted to store a name, you could create a variable, like this:

```
Dim Name as String
```

If you wanted to store a second name, you'd have to create a second variable, like this:

```
Dim Name as String
Dim Name2 as String
```

The more names you wanted to store, the more separate variables you'd need to create. Because creating separate variables to store similar types of information can get tedious, computer scientists have created a "super" variable, called an *array.* Unlike an ordinary variable that can hold only one chunk of data, an array can hold multiple chunks of data.

REMEMBER

To create an array, you need to define these three items:

» A variable name

» The number of items you want to store (the *array size*)

» The type of data to store (such as *integers* or *strings*)

If you wanted to store four names in a variable, you could create a name array, like this:

```
Dim NameArray(4) as String
```

The preceding code tells the computer to create a NameArray array, which can hold up to 4 strings, as shown in Figure 1-2.

FIGURE 1-2:
An array can hold multiple chunks of data.

John Doe	Gary Wilkins	Holly Creamer	Bobby Jones

TECHNICAL STUFF

Many languages just let you define a variable name for an array and the data type it can hold but don't require you to define the array size. This means your array can grow and shrink as needed while your program runs. By defining arrays that can change size, you never have to worry about defining an array too large (and waste memory) or too small (and not be able to hold any more data).

Defining the size

An array acts like a bunch of buckets (dubbed *elements*) that can hold exactly one item. When you create an array, you must first define the size of the array, which defines how many elements that the array can hold.

Bounds

The size of an array is defined by two numbers:

>> The **lower bound** defines the *index number* (often referred to as just the *index*) of the *first* array element.

>> The **upper bound** defines the index number of the *last* array element.

DEFAULT BOUNDS

The default value of the lower bound depends on the programming language:

>> Many programming languages, including the curly-bracket language family of C and Java, always define the lower bound of an array starting with the number 0 (known as *zero-based arrays*).

>> Other programming languages always define the lower bound of an array starting with the number 1 (known as *one-based arrays*).

The following BASIC code actually creates a zero-based array that can hold six elements, numbered 0 through 5, as shown in Figure 1-3:

```
Dim LotteryNumbers(5) as Integer
```

If the programming language created a one-based array, the array would hold only five elements.

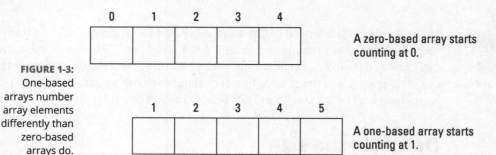

FIGURE 1-3:
One-based arrays number array elements differently than zero-based arrays do.

A zero-based array starts counting at 0.

A one-based array starts counting at 1.

REMEMBER

Zero-based arrays were made popular in the C language. As a result, any language derived from the C language, such as C++, C#, Java, Python, and Objective-C, will also use zero-based arrays. Because many programmers are familiar with zero-based arrays, many other programming languages also use zero-based arrays, such as Visual Basic and Xojo. One-based arrays are less common, but they're found in some versions of BASIC along with less popular languages like Pascal and Smalltalk.

REMEMBER

When defining arrays, always make sure you know whether your programming language creates zero-based or one-based arrays. Otherwise, you may try to store data in nonexistent array elements.

DEFINABLE BOUNDS

To avoid confusion, some programming languages (such as Pascal) let you *define* both the lower and upper bound arrays.

If you wanted to create an array to hold five integers, you could use the following code:

```
Var
   LotteryNumbers[1..5] of Integer;
```

This would number the LotteryNumbers array from 1 to 5. However, you could choose *any* number range of five like this:

```
Var
   LotteryNumbers[33..37] of Integer;
```

This would create an array of five elements, numbered from 33 to 37, as shown in Figure 1-4.

FIGURE 1-4:
Some
programming
languages let
you define the
numbering
of an array.

Var
LotteryNumbers[33..37] of Integer;

33	34	35	36	37

TIP

One advantage of defining the numbering of an array is that you can use meaningful numbers. For example, if you wanted to store the names of employees in an array, you could number the array so each array element is identified by an employee number. So, if Jan Howards has employee ID number 102, Mike Edwards has employee ID number 103, and John Perkins has employee ID number 104, you could create a three-element array, as shown in Figure 1-5, like this:

```
Var
   EmployeeList[102..104] of String;
```

Var
EmployeeList[102..104] of String;

102	103	104
Jan Howards	Mike Edwards	John Perkins

FIGURE 1-5:
By defining your
own numbering
for an array, you
can make those
numbers useful
and meaningful.

Employee ID	Employee
102	Jan Howards
103	Mike Edwards
104	John Perkins

Initializing

When you define an array, you can create either an empty array or an array filled with initial values such as

>> **Zeroes** for storing *numbers* in an array

>> **Empty strings** for storing *strings* in an array

LOOPS

To initialize an array, most programmers use a *loop*. This code uses a `For-Next` loop to initialize an array with zeroes:

```
Dim LotteryNumbers(5) as Integer
For I = 1 to 5
  LotteryNumbers(I) = 0
Next I
```

DECLARATIONS

Some programming languages let you initialize an array without a loop. Instead, you *declare* an array and its initial data on the same line. This C++ code declares an array that can hold five integers and stores 0 in each array element:

```
int lotterynumbers[] = {0, 0, 0, 0, 0};
```

Storing data

To store data in an array, you need to define two items:

» The array name

» The array element where you want to store the data

If you wanted to store data in the first element of a zero-based array, you could do this:

```
int myarray[5];
myarray[0] = 357;
```

If you wanted to store data in the first element of a one-based array, you could do this:

```
Dim myarray(5) as Integer
myarray(1) = 357
```

You can store data in array elements in any order you want — for example, storing the number 47 in the first array element, the number 91 in the fourth array element, and the number 6 in the second array element, like this:

```
int myarray[5];
myarray[0] = 47;
```

```
myarray[3] = 91;
myarray[1] = 6;
```

Retrieving data

To retrieve data from an array, you need to identify

>> The array name

>> The array element number that contains the data you want to retrieve

Suppose you had the following BASIC code that creates an array that stores three names:

```
Dim Names(3) as String
Names(1) = "Nancy Titan"
Names(2) = "Johnny Orlander"
Names(3) = "Doug Slanders"
```

If you wanted to retrieve and print the data stored in the second element of the Names array, you could use the following:

```
Print Names(2)
```

This would print Johnny Orlander onscreen.

Working with Resizable Arrays

One problem with arrays is that you must define their size before you can use them. If you define an array too large, you waste memory. If you define an array too small, your program can't store all the data it needs to keep.

To get around these problems, some programming languages let you create *dynamic* or *resizable arrays*. A resizable array lets you change the array's size while your program is running.

Here are pros and cons of using resizable arrays:

>> **Pros:** You can make the array expand or shrink as needed so you don't waste memory creating an array too large or limit your program by creating an array too small.

>> **Cons:** Constantly having to define the size of an array is a nuisance, as is the possibility that some programming languages won't let you preserve the contents of a resizable array each time the array expands or shrinks.

To create a resizable array, every programming language requires different steps. The following sections provide a couple of examples.

BASIC

In BASIC, you can declare an array like this:

```
Dim BigArray(5) as String
```

Then to change the size of that array, you have to use the ReDim command and define a new upper bound for the array like this (see Figure 1-6):

```
ReDim BigArray(2)
```

Dim BigArray(5) as String

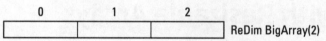

0	1	2	3	4	5
Jan Howards	Mike Edwards	John Perkins	Tiffany Allens	Zack Lilly	Bobby Canter

0	1	2
Jan Howards	Mike Edwards	John Perkins

ReDim Preserve BigArray(2)

0	1	2

ReDim BigArray(2)

FIGURE 1-6: Resizing an array lets you expand or shrink an array.

WARNING

Resizing an array erases everything currently stored in that array.

If you want to resize an array and save the data in the array, you can use the Preserve command, like this:

```
ReDim Preserve BigArray(2)
```

REMEMBER

Not every programming language lets you resize an array and preserve its contents.

C#

To create an array in C#, you have to go through slightly different steps.

First, you must define an array like this:

```
int[] arr = {3, 6, 9, 12, 15, 18, 21};
```

This creates an array that can hold integers. If you wanted to resize the array to hold only three elements (numbered 0 through 2), you could use the following:

```
int[] arr = {3, 6, 9, 12, 15, 18, 21};
Array.Resize(ref arr, 3);
```

After resizing, the array now only contains three elements (3, 6, and 9).

Swift

Defining an array size and then resizing it (and preserving its contents) can be tedious. That's why modern languages, such as Swift, make every array resizable. You can define an array by specifying the data type it can hold, like this:

```
var numberArray = [Int]()
```

This creates an empty array that can hold only integer (Int) values. Then you can add new items to expand the size of the array or delete items to shrink the size of the array. You never have to specify a new size for the array or worry about losing the contents of an array when you expand or shrink it.

TECHNICAL STUFF

Because resizing arrays automatically can be so convenient, many other programming languages offer similar features. Some languages use a similar data structure called a *list*.

Working with Multidimensional Arrays

Most arrays are one-dimensional because you define only the array's length. However, you can create multidimensional arrays by defining multiple array sizes.

The most common multidimensional array is a two-dimensional array, which looks like a grid, as shown in Figure 1-7.

Dim BigArray (4,2) as String

BigArray(1,1)	BigArray(1,2)
BigArray(2,1)	BigArray(2,2)
BigArray(3,1)	BigArray(3,2)
BigArray(4,1)	BigArray(4,2)

FIGURE 1-7:
A two-dimensional array lets you store data in a grid.

TECHNICAL STUFF

You can create 3-, 4-, or even 19-dimensional arrays. However, after you get past a three-dimensional array, understanding how that array works can be too confusing, so most programmers stick to two-dimensional or three-dimensional arrays.

Creating a multidimensional array

To create a multidimensional array, you have to define the upper bound for each dimension of the array. So, if you wanted to create a 4-x-2 two-dimensional array, you could use the following BASIC code:

```
Dim BigArray(4,2) as String
```

To create the same two-dimensional array in C++, you could use the following code:

```
string bigarray[4][2];
```

To create three or more dimensional arrays, keep adding on additional bounds, like this:

```
Dim BigArray(2,4,3,8) as String
```

The equivalent multidimensional array in C++ would look like this:

```
string bigarray[2][4][3][8];
```

Storing and retrieving data

To store data in a multidimensional array, you need to specify the specific array location. If you had a two-dimensional array, you'd have to specify each of the two dimensions, like this:

```
Dim BigArray(4,2) as String
BigArray(4,1) = "Ollie Bird"
```

After you store data in a multidimensional array, you can retrieve that data again by specifying the array name and the specific array element that contains the data you want. If you had previously stored the string "Ollie Bird" in a two-dimensional array, you could retrieve the data stored in the 4,1 array element, like this:

```
Print BigArray(4,1)
```

This command would print the string "Ollie Bird".

WARNING

The more dimensions you add to your array, the more space you create in your array, and the more memory your program needs. Don't be afraid to use a multi-dimensional array; just don't create one unless you really need one.

TIP

Two-dimensional arrays can be useful for modeling real-life items, such as checkerboards or tic-tac-toe games, which already look like two-dimensional arrays (grids) anyway.

Using Structures with Arrays

All arrays can hold only one specific data type, such as integers or strings. So, if you create an array that contains five elements, all the elements must contain the same data type, such as all integers.

Instead of defining an array to contain a simple data type, like strings or integers, you can also define an array to contain a structure. A structure lets you cram multiple variables into a single variable, but a single structure by itself is fairly useless. After you store data in a single structure, you don't have any room left to store anything else, as shown in Figure 1-8.

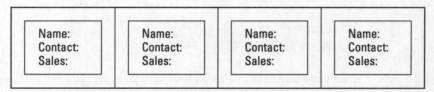

FIGURE 1-8:
A structure can hold only one group of related data, but an array of structures can hold multiple groups of related data.

To use a structure with an array, you must first define a structure and the fields you want to store inside that structure. If you wanted to store a company name, contact person, and total sales made to the company, you could define a structure like this:

```
Structure Company
   Dim Name as String
   Dim Contact as String
   Dim Sales as Single
End Structure
```

Next, you can define your array, but instead of making your array hold a simple data type, like strings or integers, you can make your array hold your structure like this:

```
Dim Customers(3) as Company
```

This code creates an array, with elements numbered from 0 to 3, which holds the Company structure that you defined, as shown in Figure 1-9.

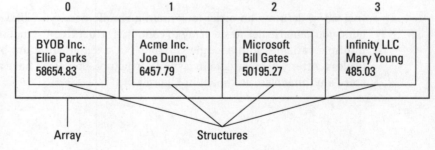

FIGURE 1-9:
An array of structures acts like a simple database.

To store data in an array of structures, you need to identify the array element (in this example numbered 0 to 3) and the specific variable inside the structure to store your data. So, if you wanted to store data in array element number 2, you could do the following:

```
Customers(2).Name = "Microsoft"
Customers(2).Contact = "Bill Gates"
Customers(2).Sales = 50195.27
```

Retrieving data from an array of structures means you must identify

>> The array name

>> The array element

>> The field name stored in that structure

If you wanted to print the name stored in the Contact variable of array element number 2, you could do the following:

```
Print Customers(2).Contact
```

This code would print Bill Gates onscreen. Storing and retrieving data from an array of structures means identifying the following items:

>> The array name (such as Customers)

>> The array element number (such as 2)

>> The field inside the structure (such as Contact)

Drawbacks of Arrays

Arrays can be handy for storing lists of related data in a single location. However, arrays have several drawbacks:

>> Large arrays can take up memory unnecessarily if most of the array is empty.

>> Arrays can hold only one data type at a time.

>> Searching and sorting arrays is difficult.

>> The specific location of any data stored in an array can constantly change.

>> Inserting and removing data from arrays is clumsy.

I cover these issues in more detail in the following sections.

Data types

One major limitation of arrays is that they can hold only one data type at a time. If you want to store a list of names and numbers, you have to create two separate arrays:

>> One array to store the names

>> Another array to store the numbers

TECHNICAL STUFF

Some programming languages allow you to create a data type called a *variant*. A variant data type can hold any type of data, so if you create an array of variant data types, you can create an array that can hold both strings and numbers. However, if your program expects to retrieve an integer from an array but winds up retrieving a string instead, that program might crash unless you write extra code to check and verify that it's retrieving the right data type at any given time.

Searching and sorting

Another problem with arrays is searching and sorting an array. If you create an array to hold 10,000 names, how can you find the name `Bill Gates` stored in that array? To search for data stored in an array, you have to search through the entire array from start to finish. For a small array, this can be acceptable, but searching through an array that contains thousands of names or numbers can get tedious and slow, especially if you need to search through an array on a regular basis.

If an array contains 10,000 names and the name you want is the last element in that array, you have to search through 10,000 array elements just to find the name you want.

More cumbersome than searching an array is sorting an array. If you store 10,000 names in an array and suddenly decide you want to sort those names in alphabetical order, you have to move and sort the entire list one array element at a time. Doing this once may be acceptable, but doing it on a regular basis can be cumbersome and slow.

Adding and deleting

Instead of dumping all your data in an array and trying to sort it out later, you might want to sort data while you store it. Adding data to an empty array is easy: Dump the data in any array element. The problem comes when you want to add data in between two array elements.

Suppose you have the names "Charles Green" and "Mary Hall" in an array, as shown in Figure 1-10. If you wanted to insert the name "Johnny Grey" in between "Charles Green" and "Mary Hall", you'd have to copy all array elements starting with "Mary Hall" and move them to the next array element.

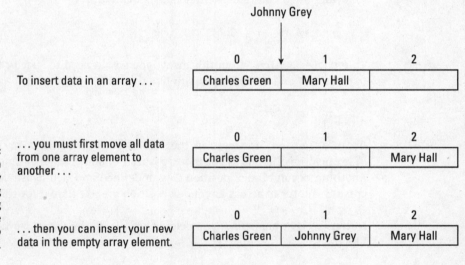

FIGURE 1-10: Inserting data into an array means copying and moving data from one array element to another.

To insert data in an array . . .

. . . you must first move all data from one array element to another . . .

. . . then you can insert your new data in the empty array element.

For a small array, this isn't a problem, but for a large array of 10,000 names, copying and moving several thousand names consistently is cumbersome and slow.

Even worse, what if you want to delete an array element? It's easy to delete an array element by just setting that array element to a blank value, such as zero or an empty string. However, the more items you delete from an array, the more empty spaces you have, wasting space.

TIP

The time to use arrays depends on both the amount of data you need to store and whether you need to manipulate that data later:

>> **Perfect:** Store a small, fixed-size list of one data type.

>> **Not so good:** Store large amounts of data that can change in quantity, needs to be sorted or searched, or data that contains different types of information, such as numbers and text. In this case, arrays can be too restrictive. You may want to look at other data structures, such as *collections* (see Book 3, Chapter 3).

Identifying the location of data in an array

The location of any data within an array is defined by its index position. The following Swift code stores three names in an array:

```
var nameArray = ["Bob", "Janice", "Pat"]
```

To retrieve "Janice" from this array, you would need to specify the array name (nameArray) and its index position like this:

```
print (nameArray[1])
```

Because "Janice" is stored in the second position of the array, it's located at index position 1 ("Bob" is at index position 0, and "Pat" is at index position 2). Anything beyond index position 2 is undefined and will cause your program to crash if you try to access any index position greater than 2 for this array.

However, what happens if you delete "Bob" from the array? Now the array looks like this:

```
["Janice", "Pat"]
```

"Janice" is now at index position 0, and "Pat" is at index position 1. If you insert two names in the beginning, the index position of "Janice" would now change once more:

```
["Walter", "Mary", "Tammy", "Oliver", "Janice", "Pat"]
```

Now the index position of "Janice" is 4. Because the same data in an array can change its index position as an array shrinks or grows, it can be hard to predict exactly where data may be stored.

REMEMBER

The data structure you choose for your program can determine the speed and efficiency of your program:

>> Choose the right data structure, and writing your program is easy.

>> Choose the wrong data structure, and you may waste time writing code to overcome the limitations of your chosen data structure, such as writing code to sort an array that contains 10,000 names.

Chapter **2**

Sets and Linked Lists

An array can be handy for storing data that consists of the same type of information, such as integers. However, arrays can often be too restrictive. You must define the size of an array ahead of time, and you can only store one data type. In addition, searching, rearranging, or deleting data from an array can be cumbersome.

To solve the problems of arrays, programming languages have come up with a variety of solutions. The obvious solution involves modifying the way arrays work, such as letting you create *dynamic* (resizable) arrays that can store a special Variant data type. Unlike an Integer data type (which can hold only whole numbers) or a String data type (which can hold only text), a Variant data type can hold both numbers and text. (Not all programming languages offer dynamic arrays or Variant data types.)

Instead of modifying the way arrays work, many programming languages allow you to create other types of data structures. Two popular alternatives to arrays are sets and lists. This chapter shows you how to use sets and lists when arrays are too restrictive and cumbersome.

Using Sets

If someone showed you the days of the week (Monday, Tuesday, Wednesday, Thursday, Friday, Saturday, and Sunday), you'd know that those days are related as a group that defines a week, but how do you tell a computer that? Here's one way:

1. **Create an array to hold seven separate variables, like this:**

```
Dim Day(6) as String
```

2. **Assign each variable a different name, like this:**

```
Day(0) = "Monday"
Day(1) = "Tuesday"
Day(2) = "Wednesday"
Day(3) = "Thursday"
Day(4) = "Friday"
Day(5) = "Saturday"
Day(6) = "Sunday"
```

This would store all the days of the week inside a single array variable.

However, there's a simpler way to lump related data together: Use a data structure called a *set*. Like an array, a set groups data in a single variable name, but a set has several advantages:

» You don't have to define a fixed size ahead of time.

» You don't have to identify each chunk of data with an index number.

Defining a set *lists* all the data you want to store, as shown in this Python programming language example:

```
days = {'Monday', 'Tuesday', 'Wednesday', 'Thursday', 'Friday',
    'Saturday', 'Sunday'}
```

In this Python language example, the variable days contains the entire set or group of the days. To print the contents of this set, you can use a print command followed by the name of the set like this:

```
print (days)
```

This command may print the following:

```
{'Monday', 'Sunday', 'Thursday', 'Friday', 'Wednesday',
  'Saturday', 'Tuesday'}
```

Sets don't store data in any particular order. If you print out the contents of a set, the items in that set could come out in a different order than the way you may have stored those items in the set.

Adding and deleting data in a set

To add data to or delete data from a set, use the add and delete commands. In Python, the add command is add, and the delete command is remove.

Every programming language uses slightly different names for the same command, so don't worry about the particular command names. You just need to understand the basic principles.

To add more data to a set in Python, you have to identify the set name followed by the add command and the data you want to add. So, if you had a set called clubmembers, you could use the following commands:

```
clubmembers = {'Bill Evans', 'John Doe', 'Mary Jacobs'}
```

You could add a new name to that set by using the following command:

```
clubmembers.add('Donna Volks')
```

To remove a name from a set, you have to identify the set name, use the remove command, and specify which data you want to remove, like this:

```
clubmembers.remove('Bill Evans')
```

Figure 2-1 shows how add and remove commands change the contents of a set:

>> When you delete data from a set, the set is just one item smaller.

>> When you delete data from an array, you're left with an empty space in the array.

To remove all data in a set, most programming languages include a command that clears out an entire set. In Python, the command is clear:

```
clubmembers.clear()
```

| Bill Evans | John Doe | Mary Jacobs | | Original set |

| Bill Evans | John Doe | Mary Jacobs | Donna Volks | Adding an item to a set just makes the set bigger. |

| John Doe | Mary Jacobs | Donna Volks | Removing an item from a set just makes the set smaller. |

0	1	2	
Bill Evans	John Doe	Mary Jacobs	Donna Volks

If an array isn't big enough, you can't add any more data to it.

FIGURE 2-1: Adding and removing data in a set is easier than adding and removing data in an array.

0	1	2
	John Doe	Mary Jacobs

Deleting data from an array leaves an empty space in that array.

Checking for membership

If you store a bunch of names in an array, how could you verify whether a specific name is in that array? Older programming languages often had to examine each element in the array and compare it with the name you're looking for until you either found a match or reached the end of the array.

Sets avoid this problem by making it easy to check whether a chunk of data is stored in a set. If you had a list of country club members stored in a set, it might look like this in Python:

```
clubmembers = {'Bill Evans', 'John Doe', 'Mary Jacobs'}
```

To check whether a name is in a set (that is, a *member* of that set), use a simple in command like this:

```
'John Doe' in clubmembers
```

If this command finds the name John Doe in the set defined by the clubmembers set, this would return a True value. If this command can't find the name John Doe in the clubmembers set, the command would return a False value.

Another way to check for membership is to use the not command with the in command like this:

```
'Hugh Lake' not in clubmembers
```

This command asks the computer whether the name Hugh Lake is not in the clubmembers set. In this case, the name Hugh Lake is not in the clubmembers set, so the preceding command would return a True value.

If you used the following command to check whether the name John Doe is not in the clubmembers set, the following command would return a False value because the name John Doe is in the clubmembers set:

```
'John Doe' not in clubmembers
```

Avoiding duplicate data

One huge advantage of sets is that they won't store duplicate data. With an array, it's possible to store duplicate data multiple times, like this:

```
var nameArray = ["Bob", "Sally", "Bob", "Peter", "Bob",
    "Hannah"]
```

In this array, "Bob" gets stored three times. However, sets automatically exclude duplicate data. That way you can be sure that all data in a set is unique. Let's create a set in Swift and print it, like this:

```
var nameSet: Set = ["Bob", "Sally", "Bob", "Peter", "Bob", "Hannah"]
print(nameSet)
```

The first line creates a set and fills it with strings. Notice that "Bob" appears three times. The second line prints the set but because the set strips out duplicate data, it prints the following:

```
["Bob", "Sally", "Peter", "Hannah"]
```

Manipulating two sets

A set by itself can be handy for grouping related data together, but if you have two or more sets of data, you can manipulate the data in both sets. For example, suppose you have a set of country club members and a second set of people applying for membership.

You can combine both sets together to create a third set (a *union*), find the common data in both sets (an *intersection*), or take away the common data in both sets (the *difference*).

Combining two sets into a third set with the union command

A union simply takes data from two sets and smashes them together to create a third set that includes all data from the first two sets, as shown in Figure 2-2.

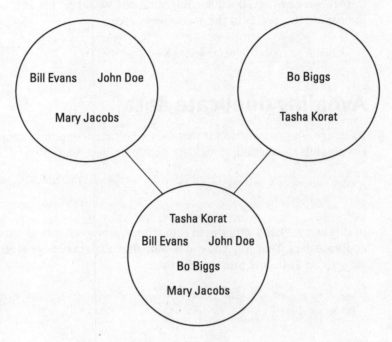

FIGURE 2-2:
The union command combines data from two sets to create a third set.

To use the union command in Python, you need to identify the two set names with the union command. Suppose you had one set called club-members and another set called applicants, as follows:

```
club_members = {'Bill Evans', 'John Doe', 'Mary Jacobs'}
applicants = {'Bo Biggs', 'Tasha Korat'}
```

Now if you wanted to combine the data in both sets and store it in a third set called every_member, you could use the union command as follows:

```
every_member = club_members.union(applicants)
```

This creates a third set called every_member and stores the data from both sets into the every_member set. The data in the other sets isn't modified in any way.

REMEMBER

The order in which you define the two sets is irrelevant:

» You can put the `club_members` set name first, like this:

    every_member = club_members.union(applicants)

» You could switch the two set names around, like this:

    every_member = applicants.union(club_members)

The end result is identical to creating a third set and dumping data from both sets into this third set. If you combine two sets that happen to contain one or more identical chunks of data, the *union* (combination of the two sets) is smart enough not to store duplicate data twice.

Combining the common elements of two sets into a third set with the intersection command

Whereas the `union` command combines two sets into one, the `intersection` command creates a third set that only includes data stored in both sets, as shown in Figure 2-3.

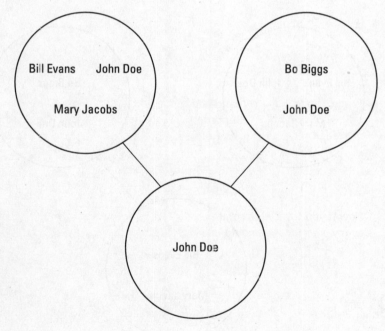

FIGURE 2-3: The intersection command takes only data common in both sets and stores that data in a third set.

To use the intersection command in Python, you need to identify the two set names with the intersection command. Suppose you had one set called club_members and another set called politicians, as follows:

```
club_members = {'Bill Evans', 'John Doe', 'Mary Jacobs'}
politicians = {'Bo Biggs', 'John Doe'}
```

Now if you wanted to find only that data stored in both sets, you could use the intersection command to store this data in a third set, as follows:

```
new_set = club_members.intersection(politicians)
```

This creates a third set — new_set — which contains the name John Doe. The other names are omitted because they aren't in *both* original sets.

Combining the different elements of two sets into a third set with the difference command

If you have two sets, you may want to identify all the data stored in one set that isn't stored in a second set. To do this, you'd use the difference command, as shown in Figure 2-4.

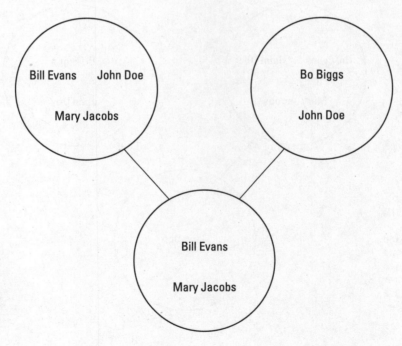

FIGURE 2-4:
The difference command strips out data in common with a second set.

To use the difference command in Python, you need to identify the two set names with the difference command. Suppose you had one set called club_members and another set called politicians, as follows:

```
club_members = {'Bill Evans', 'John Doe', 'Mary Jacobs'}
politicians = {'Bo Biggs', 'John Doe'}
```

Now if you wanted to store data from the first set that is not in the second set, you could use the difference command to store this data in a third set, as follows:

```
newset = club_members.difference(politicians)
```

This creates a third set — newset — which contains the names Bill Evans and Mary Jacobs.

WARNING

The third set does not contain the name Bo Biggs. That's because the order in which you list the sets determines how the difference command works. If you list the sets in this order:

```
newset = club_members.difference(politicians)
```

You're telling the computer to take all the data from the first set (club_members), find all the data common in both the club_members and politicians sets, and remove that common data from the first set. Now take what's left and dump this data into the newset (refer to Figure 2-4).

If you switched the commands around, like this, you'd get an entirely different result:

```
newset = politicians.difference(club_members)
```

This tells the computer to take the data stored in the politicians set, find all the data common in both the politicians and club_members sets, and remove this common data from the politicians set. Now store what's left in the newset, as shown in Figure 2-5.

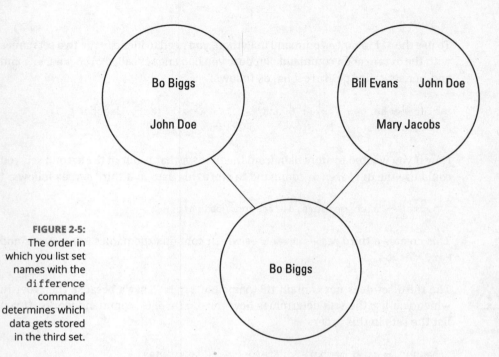

FIGURE 2-5:
The order in
which you list set
names with the
di fference
command
determines which
data gets stored
in the third set.

Using Linked Lists

Sets are handy for lumping related data in a group. However, sets aren't organized. So, if you want to group related data together and keep this data sorted, you
can use another data structure: a *linked list.*

Whereas an array creates a fixed location for storing data (think of an egg carton),
a linked list more closely resembles beads tied together by a string. It's impossible
to rearrange an array (just as you can't rip an egg carton apart and put it back
together again in a different way). However, you can rearrange a linked list easily
just as you can rearrange beads on a string.

The basic element of a linked list is a *node,* which is just a *structure* (see Book 3,
Chapter 1) that contains two parts:

>> A pointer

>> A variable for storing data

Figure 2-6 shows how the parts of a linked list work.

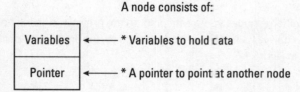

A node consists of:

FIGURE 2-6:
A node consists
of a pointer
and one or
more variables
to store data.

| Variables | ← | * Variables to hold data |
| Pointer | ← | * A pointer to point at another node |

TECHNICAL STUFF

Pointers are often used to access specific locations in the computer's memory. If you've stored data in memory and you need to share that data, you could make duplicate copies of that data, which would take up space. Or you could use a pointer, which allows different parts of a program to access that same data without creating duplicate copies of that data and wasting space.

WARNING

Accessing the computer's memory is like probing your brain with a sharp needle. If you know what you're doing, pointers can give you complete control over a computer, but if you make a mistake, pointers can mess up the computer's memory, causing the entire operating system to crash.

Creating a linked list

A linked list consists of one or more identical nodes that can hold the same number and types of data, such as a `string` and an `integer`. Each time you create a node, you have to define the following:

» The data to store in the node

» The node to point at

REMEMBER

Nodes in a linked list must all contain the same data types, much like an array.

A node can store either

» A single data type (such as a string)

» Another data structure (such as a structure or an array)

Each time you create a node, the node is empty. To make the node useful, you must store data in that node and define which node to point at:

» The first node you create simply points at *nothing*.

TECHNICAL STUFF

The term `nil` or `null` is commonly used in programming languages to represent the absence of data.

>> Any additional nodes you create point to the previous existing nodes, so you create a daisy-chain effect of nodes linked to one another by pointers, as shown in Figure 2-7.

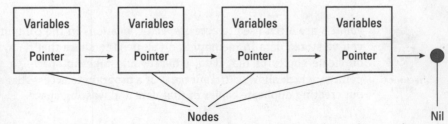

FIGURE 2-7:
A linked list stores data in each node that points to another node.

Modifying a linked list

After you create a linked list and store data in it, you can easily modify that linked list by rearranging the pointers, as shown in Figure 2-8.

This linked list organizes names in this order: Abby, Bob, Charlie, and Danny.

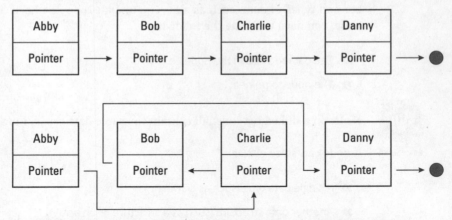

FIGURE 2-8:
Rearranging the order of a linked list is as simple as rearranging pointers.

Just by rearranging pointers, you can rearrange the order of data. This linked list now organizes names in this order: Abby, Charlie, Bob, and Danny.

To add data to a linked list, you can just rearrange pointers to include the new data in any position within the linked list, as shown in Figure 2-9.

To delete data from a linked list, you can delete an entire node. Then you must change the pointers to keep your linked list together, as shown in Figure 2-10. Unlike arrays, linked lists give you the flexibility to rearrange data without physically moving and copying it to a new location.

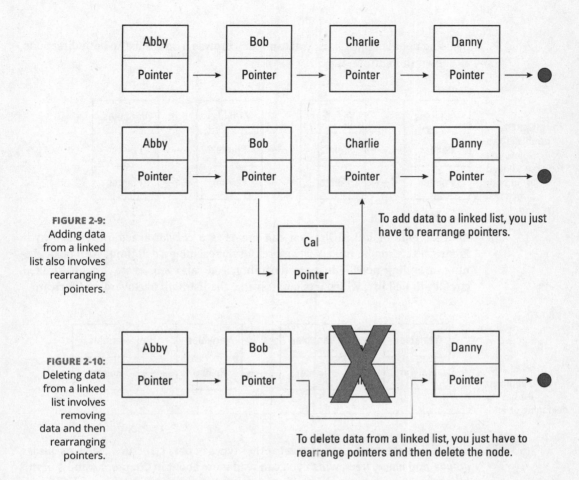

FIGURE 2-9: Adding data from a linked list also involves rearranging pointers.

To add data to a linked list, you just have to rearrange pointers.

FIGURE 2-10: Deleting data from a linked list involves removing data and then rearranging pointers.

To delete data from a linked list, you just have to rearrange pointers and then delete the node.

Linked lists also let you add data anywhere just by rearranging the pointers (refer to Figure 2-9 and Figure 2-10). By using linked lists, you can add, delete, and rearrange data quickly and easily.

Creating a double linked list

An ordinary linked list contains pointers that point in one direction only. That means if you start at the beginning of a linked list, you can always browse the data in the rest of the linked list. However, if you start in the middle of a linked list, you can never browse the previous nodes.

To fix this problem, you can also create *a double linked list,* which essentially creates nodes that contain two pointers:

» One pointer points to the *previous* node in the list.

» The other pointer points to the *next* node in the list.

By using double linked lists, you can easily browse a linked list in both directions, as shown in Figure 2-11.

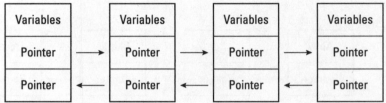

FIGURE 2-11:
A double linked list lets you traverse a linked list in both directions.

Another type of linked list you can create is a *circular linked list,* as shown in Figure 2-12. Circular linked lists more closely resemble a doughnut with no beginning or ending node. For more flexibility, you can even create a double linked, circular linked list, which lets you traverse the list both backward and forward.

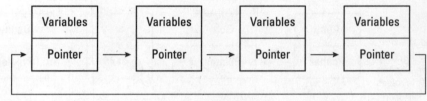

FIGURE 2-12:
A circular linked list has no beginning or end.

TECHNICAL STUFF

Linked lists are often used to create other types of data structures, such as *queues, graphs,* and *binary trees,* which you can read more about in Chapters 4 and 5 of this minibook.

Drawbacks of Sets and Linked Lists

Sets make it easy to group and manipulate related data, but unlike arrays, there isn't always an easy way to access and retrieve individual items in a set. Sets are best used for treating data as a group rather than as separate chunks of data.

Linked lists are much more flexible than arrays for adding, deleting, and rearranging data. However, the two biggest drawbacks of linked lists are the complexity needed to create them and the potentially dangerous use of pointers.

Problems with pointers

The most common problem with linked lists occurs when pointers fail to point to either nil or a valid node of a linked list. If you delete a node from a linked list but forget to rearrange the pointers, you essentially cut your linked list in two, as shown in Figure 2-13.

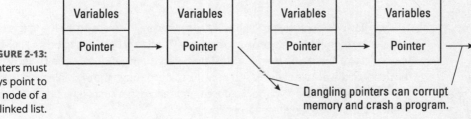

Dangling pointers can corrupt memory and crash a program.

Even worse, you could create a *dangling pointer* (the pointer no longer points to a valid node). Dangling pointers can wind up pointing to any part of the computer's memory, usually with catastrophic consequences that crash the entire computer.

TECHNICAL STUFF

Dangling pointers are a common cause of problems using languages like C or C++. Other languages (such as C#, Java, Python, and Swift) prevent dangling pointers.

Problems with accessing data

Accessing data in an array is easy. You can access data by its index number or by starting at the beginning of the array and browsing through each element until you reach the end of the array.

If you want to access data stored in a linked list, you have to start at the beginning. If you start in the middle, you can never go backward to the front of the linked list (unless you're using a double linked list). Arrays let you jump straight to specific data by using an index number. Linked lists don't offer that same feature.

REMEMBER

For ease in *storing, adding,* and *removing* data, linked lists are more flexible than arrays. For *retrieving* data, arrays are much simpler and faster.

COMPLEXITY OF CREATING LINKED LISTS AND POINTERS

Creating and managing a linked list with all its pointers is easy in theory, but writing the code to create and manage a linked list can get complicated in a hurry. The more confusing and complicated the code, the more likely errors will creep in and cause your linked list to not work at all or to work in unexpected ways.

To show you how confusing pointers and nodes can be to create, study the following Pascal programming language examples. Pascal is actually designed to be an easy-to-read language, but even creating linked lists in Pascal can get clumsy. (Don't worry too much about the details of the Pascal code. Just skim through the examples and follow along the best you can. If you get confused, you can see how implementing linked lists in any programming language can get messy.)

To create a linked list, you must first create a node, which is a *structure*. (In Pascal, structures are called *records*.) To define a structure in Pascal, you could do this:

```
Type
  NodePtr = ^Node;
  Node = RECORD
    Data : String;
    Next : NodePtr;
  END;
```

This Pascal code creates a NodePtr variable, which represents a pointer to the Node structure (record). The caret symbol (^) defines a pointer, whereas the Node name defines what structure the pointer can point at.

The Node structure declares two variables: Data and Next. The Data variable holds a string (although you can change this to Integer or any other data type). The Next variable represents a pointer to the Node record. Every node absolutely must have a pointer because pointers are how the nodes can point, or *link*, together to form a linked list.

If this were a double linked list, you'd have two variables (such as Previous and Next) declared as node pointers like this:

```
Type
  NodePtr = ^Node;
  Node = RECORD
    Data : String;
```

```
        Previous, Next : NodePtr
    END;
```

After you define a node as a structure, you can't use that node until you declare a variable to represent that node, like this:

```
Var
    MyNode : NodePtr;
```

After you declare a variable to represent a pointer to a node (structure), you must create a new node, stuff data into it, and then set its pointer to point at something, such as NIL or another node:

```
Begin
    New (MyNode);          (* Creates a new node *)
    With MyNode^ do        (* Stores data in the node *)
        Begin
            Data := 'Joe Hall';
            Next := NIL;
        End;
End.
```

To create a linked list in a language like Pascal, you must

1. Define a node structure.

2. Declare a pointer to that node (structure).

3. Declare a variable to represent that pointer.

Now you can use your node to store data and link with other nodes.

If you mess up on any one of those steps, your linked list won't work, and because linked lists use pointers, your pointers could point anywhere in memory, causing all sorts of random problems. The bottom line: Linked lists are a powerful and flexible data structure, but they come at a price of added complexity for the programmer. Accidentally create one dangling pointer, and you can bring your entire program crashing to a halt.

Chapter **3**

Collections and Dictionaries

An array can be handy when you need to store the same type of information, such as a group of integers. However, if you need to store different information, such as both integers and strings, and you aren't sure how many items you need to store, you probably can't use an array. Instead, you can use a collection or a dictionary.

A *collection* (also called a *list* in some languages) acts like a resizable array that can hold different data types at the same time while identifying each chunk of data with a number. A *dictionary* acts like a collection that identifies each chunk of data with a unique key.

The purpose of both collections and dictionaries is to make it easier to store different types of data and retrieve them again with the size and single data type restrictions of an array.

Using a Collection

A collection acts like a super array that can grow and expand without requiring any special commands. In addition, a collection can store different data types (such as integers or strings) or even other data structures, such as an array.

TECHNICAL STUFF

Not all programming languages offer the collection data structure:

>> In some programming languages (like Python and Smalltalk), collections are a built-in feature of the language.

>> In other languages (like C or Pascal), you have to use more primitive data structures (like arrays) to mimic the features of a collection.

>> In many newer languages (like C# and Visual Basic), someone else has already created a collection out of more primitive data structures, so you can use them without knowing how they were created.

Because a collection is nothing more than a data structure, like an array, the first step to creating a collection is to declare a variable as a collection, such as the following Visual Basic example shows:

```
Dim MyStuff As New Collection
```

This command simply identifies a MyStuff variable as a collection data structure. The New command tells the computer to create a new collection.

Adding data to a collection

When you first create a collection, it contains zero items. Each time you add a new chunk of data to a collection, it expands automatically so you never have to specify a size beforehand (like an array) or deliberately resize it later (like a dynamic array).

To add data to a collection in Visual Basic, you must use an Add command like this:

```
Dim MyStuff As New Collection
MyStuff.Add("Dirty socks")
```

Each time you add another element to a collection, the computer tacks that new data at the end of the collection. So, if you added the string "Dirty socks", the number 7348, and the number 4.39, the collection would look like Figure 3-1.

1
Dirty socks

Each time you add an item to a collection . . .

1	2
Dirty socks	7348

. . . the collection grows automatically.

1	2	3
Dirty socks	7348	4.39

```
Dim MyStuff As New Collection
MyStuff.Add("Dirty socks")
MyStuff.Add(7348)
MyStuff.Add(4.39)
```

Every element in a collection gets numbered with the first element given an index number of 1, the second given an index number of 2, and so on, similar to a one-based array.

REMEMBER

Although some programming languages number the first element of an array as 0, they often number the first item in a collection as 1.

For greater flexibility in adding data to a collection, you may be able to insert data before or after existing data, depending on the programming language. (In Visual Basic, you can add data before or after existing data in a collection, but in Xojo, you can't.)

Suppose you had the following Visual Basic code to create a collection:

```
Dim HitList As New Collection
HitList.Add("Billy Joe")
HitList.Add(99)
HitList.Add("Johnny McGruffin")
```

If you wanted to add the name Hal Perkins to the end of the collection, you could use this command:

```
HitList.Add("Hal Perkins")
```

Instead of always adding data to the end of a collection, you can also specify that you want to store new data before or after a specific location in the array. The location is specified by the collection's *index number*.

So, if you wanted to add the number 3.14 before the second element in a collection, you could use the following:

```
HitList.Add(3.14,,2)
```

The preceding command inserts the number 3.14 before the second element of the collection, as shown in Figure 3-2.

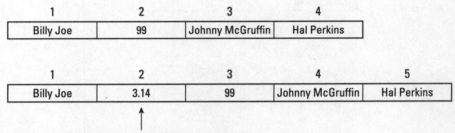

FIGURE 3-2:
You can insert data before a specific location in an array.

Adding new data in the middle of a collection automatically renumbers the rest of the collection.

If you wanted to add the name Gini Belkins after the third element in the collection, you could use the following command:

```
HitList.Add("Gini Belkins",,,3)
```

This command would insert the name Gini Belkins after the third element in the collection, as shown in Figure 3-3.

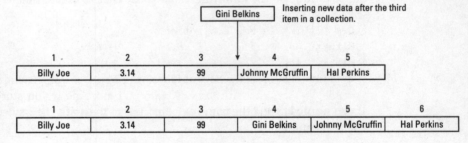

FIGURE 3-3:
You can insert new data after an existing location in a collection.

Deleting data from a collection

After you store data in a collection, you can always delete data from that collection. To delete data, you must specify the location of that data by defining an index number. So, if you want to delete the fourth item in a collection, you'd specify deleting data stored at index 4 like this:

```
HitList.Remove(4)
```

When you delete data from an array, that array now contains empty space, but when you delete data from a collection, the collection automatically renumbers the rest of its data so there isn't any empty space, as shown in Figure 3-4.

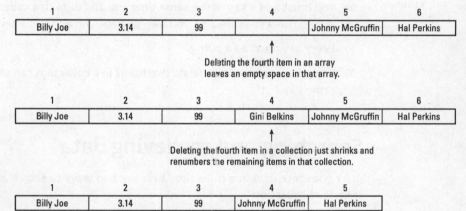

FIGURE 3-4:
When you remove data from a collection, the collection renumbers the rest of its data.

1	2	3	4	5	6
Billy Joe	3.14	99		Johnny McGruffin	Hal Perkins

↑
Deleting the fourth item in an array
leaves an empty space in that array.

1	2	3	4	5	6
Billy Joe	3.14	99	Gini Belkins	Johnny McGruffin	Hal Perkins

↑
Deleting the fourth item in a collection just shrinks and
renumbers the remaining items in that collection.

1	2	3	4	5
Billy Joe	3.14	99	Johnny McGruffin	Hal Perkins

Identifying data with keys

One problem with collections implemented in some languages is that they identify data by their position in the collection. If you don't know the location of specific data in a collection, you have to search the entire collection, item by item, to find specific data. Another option is to identify data with any descriptive string, called a *key*.

For example, if you stored the name of your boss in a collection, you could identify it with the key boss. If you stored the name of your friend in a collection, you could identify it with the key best friend. And if you stored the name of your ex-boss in a collection, you could identify it with the key moron, as shown in Figure 3-5.

FIGURE 3-5:
Identify data by its location or by a key.

1	2	3
Key: boss	Key: best friend	Key: moron
Fred Jones	Tasha Korat	Mike Ross

Collections give you the choice to find data based on location . . .

. . . or by descriptive keys.

When you add data to a collection, you can optionally also assign a key to that data, which you can later use to search and retrieve that data again. So, if you wanted to add the data Mike Ross along with the key moron, you could use the following command:

```
HitList.Add("Mike Ross", "moron")
```

When adding a key to data in a collection, your key must meet these criteria:

>> **You must add a key at the same time you add data to a collection.** After you add data to a collection, you can't go back later and add a key to that data.

>> **Every key must be a string.**

>> **Every key must be unique; no two items in a collection can share the same key.**

Searching and retrieving data

After you store data in a collection, here are two ways to search and retrieve data from that collection:

>> Use the index number of that data.

>> Use the key of that data.

If you don't store a key with data originally, you can't retrieve that data with a key.

Index numbers

To retrieve data based on its location, you can do something as simple as the following:

```
Dim Junk As New Collection
Junk.Add(3.1415)
Junk.Add(99)
Junk.Add("Bo")
```

If you wanted to retrieve the name *Bo* from the collection, you'd have to know that *Bo* is stored as the third item (index number 3), so the following would store the string "Bo" in the Good variable:

```
Dim Good As String = Junk.Item(3)
```

The problem with relying on index numbers alone is that as you add and delete items from a collection, the index numbers may change, as shown in Figure 3-6.

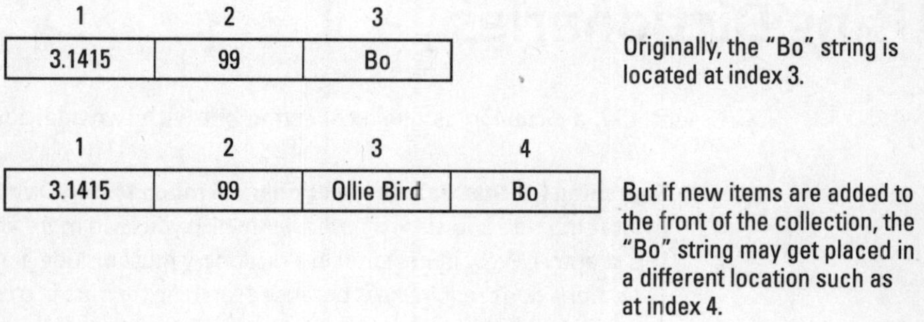

1	2	3
3.1415	99	Bo

Originally, the "Bo" string is located at index 3.

FIGURE 3-6:
Retrieving data by
index numbers
is unreliable
because they
can change.

1	2	3	4
3.1415	99	Ollie Bird	Bo

But if new items are added to the front of the collection, the "Bo" string may get placed in a different location such as at index 4.

Because index numbers don't always stay matched with each item in a collection, a better solution is to assign a key to each item, as described in the following section.

Keys

By assigning a descriptive key to each item, you can use that key to retrieve that item no matter where it may be stored in the collection.

The following code assigns the key "pi" to the first item, the key "secret agent" to the second item, and the key "my cat" to the third item:

```
Dim MoreJunk As New Collection
MoreJunk.Add(3.1415, "pi")
MoreJunk.Add(99, "secret agent")
MoreJunk.Add("Bo", "my cat")
```

To retrieve items from a collection with a key, you have to remember the key associated with each chunk of data. The following code stores the number 3.1415 into the CircleSecret variable:

```
Dim CircleSecret As Single = MoreJunk.Item ("pi")
```

The preceding code tells the computer to find the chunk of data assigned the "pi" key and then store that data in the CircleSecret variable.

The preceding code retrieves the number 3.1415 no matter where its location may be in a collection.

REMEMBER

You can always retrieve data with either its key or its location (index number).

Using Dictionaries

Essentially, a *dictionary* is like a collection but with two additional advantages:

>> **Searching for that data in a dictionary is much faster.** Dictionaries use a data structure known as a *hash table* (which you read more about later in this chapter). Every item stored in a dictionary must include a unique key. Collections don't require keys because searching for data in a collection is *sequential* — the computer must start at the beginning of the collection and examine each item, one by one, to retrieve a specific item. The more items in a collection, the slower the search process.

REMEMBER

If a programming language offers collections, it usually also offers dictionaries. If a programming language doesn't offer collections, it probably doesn't offer dictionaries either.

>> **In a dictionary, the key can be any value, including strings or numbers, which gives you greater flexibility in assigning keys to data.** If a collection uses a key to identify data, that key is usually limited to a specific data type such as a string.

TECHNICAL STUFF

Dictionaries are also called *associative arrays.* When you store data and a key, that's known as a *key-value pair* (refer to Figure 3-5).

Like a collection, a dictionary is a data type, so you must first declare a variable as a dictionary. Then you must create a new dictionary and store data in that dictionary.

To create a dictionary in the Smalltalk programming language, you could use the following:

```
blackbook := Dictionary new.
```

This code declares the blackbook variable as a Dictionary data type. The new command simply creates an empty dictionary.

Adding data to a dictionary

After you declare a variable as a Dictionary data type, you can start adding data to that Dictionary by defining both the data and the key you want to associate with that data. So, if you want to add the name Dick Ross to a dictionary and assign it a moron key, you could use the following:

```
blackbook := Dictionary new.
blackbook at: 'moron'        put:  'Dick Ross'.
```

Every time you add data to a dictionary, you must include a corresponding key.

In Smalltalk, the key appears directly after the at command, and the data appears after the put command, as shown here:

```
blackbook := Dictionary new.
blackbook at: 'moron'        put:  'Dick Ross'.
blackbook at: 'imbecile'     put:  'John Adams'.
blackbook at: 'idiot'        put:  'Sally Parker'.
```

Searching and retrieving data from a dictionary

To access and retrieve data from a dictionary, you need to identify the dictionary variable and the key associated with the data you want to find. So, if you wanted to find the data associated with the key idiot, you could use the following command:

```
blackbook at: 'idiot'
```

This would return:

```
'Sally Parker'
```

Dictionaries are more efficient at searching and retrieving data because the computer doesn't need to search through the entire dictionary sequentially. Instead, the computer searches through data using a hash table. This is like the difference between looking through the phone book, starting from page one, trying to find the phone number of Versatile Plumbing and just skipping straight to the V section of the phone book and looking alphabetically from the beginning of that V section to find the phone number of Versatile Plumbing, as shown in Figure 3-7.

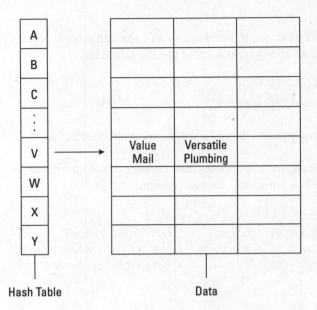

FIGURE 3-7:
Hash tables make searching faster by dividing data into distinct sections.

Hash Table

Data

Understanding Hash Tables

If you stored data without a key in a collection, searching for a specific chunk of data is difficult because the data isn't sorted. So, to ensure you find data in a collection, you must search the entire collection from start to finish. The more data you store, the longer the search takes, just as it takes longer to find a specific playing card in a deck of 52 cards than it does in a deck of only 4 cards.

When you store data with a unique key in a collection, the key is used to help identify and retrieve the data. However, just using a key alone is no better than storing data alone because keys are just another chunk of data. The more data (and keys) you store, the longer it takes the computer to search through its entire list of keys.

Converting keys with a hash function

To speed up searching, dictionaries use hash tables. Basically, a hash table takes the key used to identify data and then converts that key into a *hash value*. This hash value gets stored in a list (known as a *table*), as shown in Figure 3-8.

The exact method used to convert a key into a value is a *hash function*. The converted key, or *hash*, now points directly to the stored data. At this point, the computer actually stores just two chunks of data:

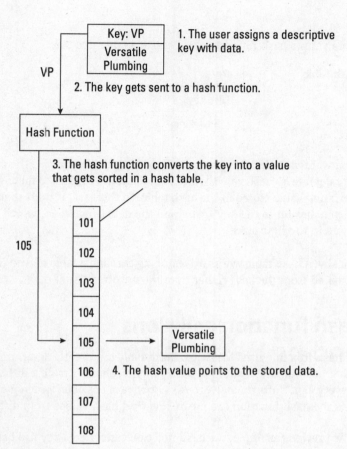

FIGURE 3-8:
Hash tables
convert each
key into a
numeric value.

>> The data itself

>> A hash value calculated from the key

When you want to retrieve data, you give the computer the key associated with the data that you want. The computer takes the key and uses its hash function to convert the key to a value.

Now the computer tries to match this calculated value to its list of values stored in the hash table. When it finds a match, it can then find the data associated with that key.

A simple hash function might just count all the characters in a key and use that total as a value. For example, consider the keys moron and imbecile.

```
blackbook := Dictionary new.
blackbook at: 'moron'      put:  'Dick Ross'.
blackbook at: 'imbecile'   put:  'John Adams'.
```

Such a simple hash function could create a table like this:

Hash Table	Data
5	Dick Ross
8	John Adams

If you wanted to find the data associated with the key moron, the computer would first calculate its hash value, which is 5. Next, it would try to match this value with an existing value stored in the hash table. In this case, it finds that the hash value of 5 matches up to the key moron and the data Dick Ross, which is the data you wanted in the first place.

TECHNICAL STUFF

Basically, a hash table works by searching through a table of data (the hash values calculated from the key) rather than the unsorted list of data.

Hash function collisions

The hash function used to create a hash table can greatly determine the efficiency of that hash table. Ideally, the hash function should create a different hash value for every key. Unfortunately, that's not always possible, which means that sometimes the hash function can create identical hash values from different keys.

In the previous example, the hash function converted a key to a hash value just by counting the number of characters used in the key. So, if two different keys have the same number of characters, the hash function will create the same hash value like this:

```
blackbook := Dictionary new.
blackbook at: 'moron'      put: 'Dick Ross'.
blackbook at: 'imbecile'   put: 'John Adams'.
Blackbook at: 'idiot'      put: 'Sally Evans'.
```

Using the simple hash function to count the number of characters in each key would create a table like this:

Hash Table	Data
5	Dick Ross
8	John Adams
5	Sally Evans

Hash tables can't have duplicate values because every hash value must match with a single chunk of data. A *collision* occurs when a hash function creates duplicate values from different keys. Here are two ways to prevent collisions:

>> **Develop a better hash function.** Unfortunately, no matter how many different hash functions you create, the more data stored, the greater the chance that any hash function will eventually calculate a duplicate value from two different keys.

>> **Find a way to deal with hash value collisions.** The following sections provide solutions.

Solving collisions by chaining

The simplest way to deal with collisions (duplicate hash values) is *chaining*.

Normally, each hash value points to a single chunk of data. The idea behind chaining is that each hash value can actually point to a list of data, as shown in Figure 3-9.

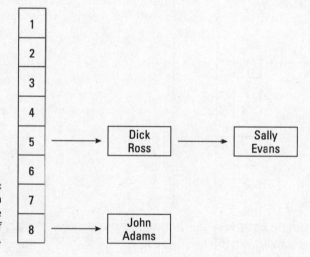

FIGURE 3-9: Chaining lets a single hash value point to a list of multiple items.

Now if you search for data using a key, the computer

1. Calculates the hash value of that key, which points to a list of data

2. Searches through this list sequentially, one by one

Chaining works because searching a *shorter list* sequentially is faster than searching the *whole list* sequentially. (It's like finding Versatile Plumbing in the phone book by starting with the V section instead of the first page of the phone book.)

Avoiding collisions with double hashing

Another way to avoid collisions is to use *double hashing*:

1. The hash function calculates a hash value for each key.

2. If a collision occurs, the computer calculates a second hash value.

Essentially, you wind up with a much shorter list of items within the hash table, as shown in Figure 3-10.

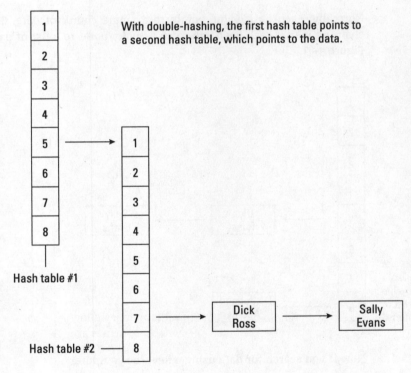

With double-hashing, the first hash table points to a second hash table, which points to the data.

FIGURE 3-10:
Double hashing creates miniature hash tables within a larger hash table.

Double hashing can reduce the number of collisions, but here are a couple of drawbacks:

> » **A collision can still occur even after the double hashing.**

> » **Double hashing is a more complicated solution than chaining.** And the more complex a program, the greater the chances of something going wrong.

In general, the simpler the data structure (such as arrays), the easier they are to implement and the lower the odds that something will go wrong. Of course, the simpler the data structure, the more restrictive the data structure.

Both collections and dictionaries (using hash tables) give you added flexibility but at the cost of added complexity:

> » In many programming languages, such as C, you have to create dictionaries and hash tables from scratch.

> » In other programming languages, such as C# or Python, collections and dictionaries are built-in features of that language, which makes these data structures easy to use and implement.

Sometimes you may find collections or dictionaries easier to use, and other times you may find arrays or sets easier to use. By understanding the different types of available data structures and the pros and cons of each, you're more likely to choose the one that will make it easy to solve your particular problem.

Chapter 4

Stacks, Queues, and Deques

Collections and dictionaries are best suited for storing and organizing data, but they aren't as useful for retrieving data in an orderly fashion. Trying to keep track of data stored by index numbers or by keys can get cumbersome. As a simpler alternative, computer scientists have created three other data structures: stacks, queues, and deques. Unlike collections or dictionaries, these three data structures are designed for storing and removing data in a predictable order.

A list or an array is much simpler to use but much less flexible than a queue or a stack. Unfortunately, stacks, queues, and deques add greater complexity to your program in exchange for their added flexibility.

TIP

If you need to store and remove data that's often stored and removed within short periods of time, stacks, queues, and deques are better suited than arrays, collections, or dictionaries. A queue might be useful for an online reservation system that handles the oldest request first.

Different data structures can be useful for different purposes. Choose the right data structure, and a program can suddenly be easier to write. Choose the wrong data structure, and your program can suddenly be much more difficult to write.

Using Stacks

The stack data structure gets its name because it resembles a stack of clean dishes, typically found in a cafeteria. When you put the first plate on the counter, that plate appears at the bottom of the stack. Each time you add a new plate to the stack, the first plate gets buried farther underneath. Add another plate to the stack, and the newest plate appears on top. To remove a plate, you have to take the top plate off.

That's the same way the stack data structure works, as shown in Figure 4-1. With a stack, you don't keep track of the data's location. Instead, you can keep adding new data to store, and the stack expands automatically.

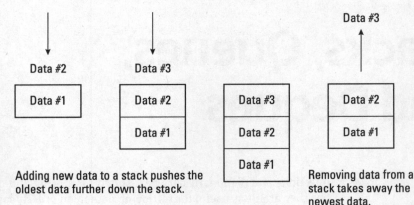

FIGURE 4-1: Stacks store the oldest data on the bottom and the newest data on top.

Adding new data to a stack pushes the oldest data further down the stack.

Removing data from a stack takes away the newest data.

The only way to remove data from a stack is from the top. Each time you remove data, the stack shrinks automatically. Because a stack only lets you remove the last item stored on the stack, it's often called a *last in, first out* (LIFO).

TECHNICAL STUFF

Few programming languages offer the stack data structure as a built-in feature. Instead, you have to create a stack using other data structures, such as an array or a linked list. When you create another data structure out of a built-in data structure, the new data structure created is an *abstract data structure*. To save you the time and trouble of creating a stack data structure, many programming language compilers come with libraries (or *classes* in object-oriented languages) of subprograms that have created the stack data structure for you.

Because a stack is just a data structure, you can declare a variable to represent a stack in Visual Basic by doing the following:

```
Dim BlowMyStack As New Stack
```

This command simply identifies a BlowMyStack variable as a stack data structure. The New command tells the computer to create a new stack.

Adding data to a stack

When you first create a stack, it contains zero items. Each time you add a new chunk of data to a stack, it expands automatically. Unlike other data structures, such as collections, you can only add new data to the top of the stack; you can never add data in a specific location in a stack.

REMEMBER

Like a collection or a dictionary, a stack can typically hold different data, such as both numbers and strings.

The only way you can store or remove data from a stack is through the top of the stack. To add data to a stack, you *push* that data on the stack. In Visual Basic, you specify the Push command along with the stack name like this:

```
Dim BlowMyStack As New Stack
BlowMyStack.Push("My cat")
```

This command stores the string "My cat" on top of the stack. Each time you add another chunk of data to a stack, you have to put that data on the top, which pushes any existing data farther down the stack.

If you added the string "My cat", the number 108.75, and the string "Fat dog", the stack would look like Figure 4-2.

```
Dim BlowMyStack As New Stack
BlowMyStack.Push("My cat")
BlowMyStack.Push(108.75)
BlowMyStack.Push("Fat dog")
```

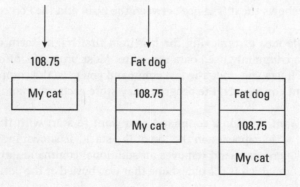

FIGURE 4-2: When you add data to a stack, the oldest data keeps getting pushed farther down the stack.

Removing data from a stack

When you store data in a stack, the only way you can remove data from that stack is by removing the top item. Removing data from a stack is known as *popping* the data off the stack. If you just want to retrieve the data from a stack without removing it, you may be able to use the Peek command, which lets you retrieve the top item from a stack.

To use the Peek command, you have to assign the value of the Peek command to a variable, like this:

```
Dim BlowMyStack As New Stack
Dim X As Object
BlowMyStack.Push("My cat")
BlowMyStack.Push(108.75)
BlowMyStack.Push("Fat dog")
X = BlowMyStack.Peek
```

The preceding code assigns the value "Fat dog" to the X variable, which is declared as an Object data type. (In Visual Basic, an Object data type can hold any type of data, including integers, strings, and decimal numbers, such as 108.75.)

The Peek command retrieves the data but leaves it on top of the stack.

REMEMBER

If you want to remove data, you use the Pop command, which retrieves *and* removes data, as shown in the following Visual Basic example:

```
Dim BlowMyStack As New Stack
Dim X As Object
BlowMyStack.Push("My cat")
BlowMyStack.Push(108.75)
BlowMyStack.Push("Fat dog")
X = BlowMyStack.Pop
```

Figure 4-3 shows the difference between the Peek and the Pop commands.

Although the idea of removing the last item first might seem counterintuitive, stacks are a commonly used data structure. Most programs offer an Undo command, which lets you undo the last command you gave the computer. If you give five different commands, the program may store each command in a stack.

When you want to undo a command, you want to start with the last command you gave it, which appears on the top of the stack, as shown in Figure 4-4. Each succeeding Undo command removes an additional command until you get to the last command, which is the oldest one that was buried at the bottom of the stack.

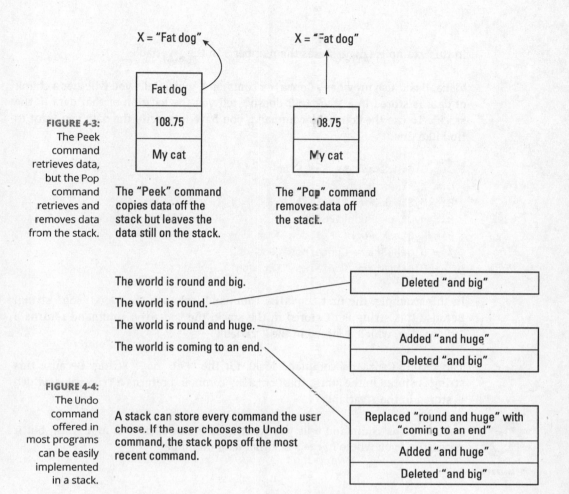

X = "Fat dog"

X = "Fat dog"

Fat dog
108.75
My cat

108.75
My cat

The "Peek" command copies data off the stack but leaves the data still on the stack.

The "Pop" command removes data off the stack.

The world is round and big.

The world is round.

The world is round and huge.

The world is coming to an end.

Deleted "and big"

Added "and huge"
Deleted "and big"

Replaced "round and huge" with "coming to an end"
Added "and huge"
Deleted "and big"

A stack can store every command the user chose. If the user chooses the Undo command, the stack pops off the most recent command.

Counting and searching a stack

Because stacks can expand and shrink depending on the amount of data you push on them, many programming languages give you commands to count the total number of items currently stored in a stack.

In Visual Basic, you can count the number of items currently stored in a stack by using the Count property. Here's an example:

```
Dim BlowMyStack As New Stack
Dim X As Integer
BlowMyStack.Push("My cat")
BlowMyStack.Push(108.75)
BlowMyStack.Push("Fat dog")
X = BlowMyStack.Count
```

In this example, `Count` stores the number 3 in the `X` variable.

Visual Basic also provides a `Contains` command, which tells you whether a chunk of data is stored in a stack (but doesn't tell you the location of that data in the stack). To use the `Contains` command, you have to specify the data you want to find like this:

```
Dim BlowMyStack As New Stack
Dim X, Y As Boolean
BlowMyStack.Push("My cat")
BlowMyStack.Push(108.75)
BlowMyStack.Push("Fat dog")
X = BlowMyStack.Contains("Good dog")
Y = BlowMyStack.Contains("Fat dog")
```

In this example, the first `Contains` command looks for the "Good dog" string. Because this string isn't stored in the stack, the `Contains` command returns a `False` value, which it stored in the `X` variable.

The second `Contains` command looks for the "Fat dog" string. Because this string is stored in the stack, this `Contains` command returns a `True` value, which is stored in the `Y` variable.

REMEMBER

The `Contains` command tells you whether a chunk of data is in a stack, but it doesn't tell you where in the stack that data might be.

Using Queues

Similar to a stack is another data structure: a *queue.*

TIP

A queue gets its name because the data structure resembles a line of waiting people, such as a line at a bank teller. The first person in the *queue* (line) is also the first person who gets to leave the queue. As a result, a queue is often called a *first in, first out* (FIFO) data structure, as shown in Figure 4-5.

Like a stack, a queue can expand and shrink automatically, depending on the amount of data you store in it. Unlike a stack that only lets you store and retrieve data from the top, a queue lets you store data on one end but remove that data from the opposite end.

New data gets added to the end of the queue.

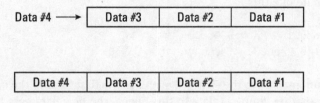

Data #4 ⟶ | Data #3 | Data #2 | Data #1 |

| Data #4 | Data #3 | Data #2 | Data #1 |

FIGURE 4-5:
The queue data
structure mimics
a line of people.

| Data #4 | Data #3 | Data #2 | ⟶ Data #1 |

Old data gets removed from the front of the queue.

**TECHNICAL
STUFF**

Most programming languages don't offer the queue data structure as a built-in feature. Instead, you have to create a queue with other data structures, such as an array or a linked list, to create an *abstract data structure.* Fortunately, many programming language compilers come with libraries (called *classes* in object-oriented languages) of subprograms that have created the queue data structure for you.

Because a queue is just a data structure, you can declare a variable to represent a queue in Visual Basic by using the following command:

```
Dim LongLine As New Queue
```

This command simply identifies a LongLine variable as a queue data structure. The New command tells the computer to create a new queue.

Adding data to a queue

New data always gets stored at the end of the queue:

>> When you first create a queue, it contains zero items.

>> Each time you add a new chunk of data to a queue, the queue expands automatically.

>> The front of the queue always contains the first or oldest data.

REMEMBER

Like a collection or a dictionary, a queue can hold different data, such as both numbers and strings.

To add data to a queue, Visual Basic uses the Enqueue command along with the queue name like this:

```
Dim LongLine As New Queue
LongLine.Enqueue("Tasha")
```

This command stores the string "Tasha" as the first item in the queue. Each time you add another chunk of data to this queue, the new data gets tacked on to the end. That means the oldest data always remains at the front of the queue.

If you added the string "Tasha", the number 7.25, and the string "Gray", the stack would look like Figure 4-6.

```
Dim LongLine As New Queue
LongLine.Enqueue("Tasha")
LongLine.Enqueue(7.25)
LongLine.Enqueue("Gray")
```

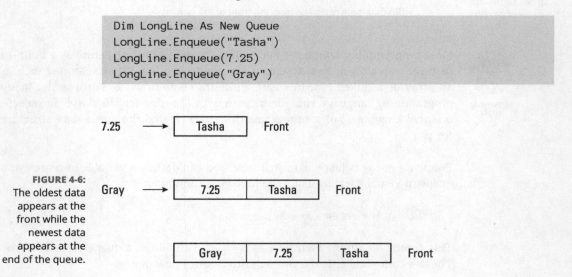

FIGURE 4-6: The oldest data appears at the front while the newest data appears at the end of the queue.

Removing data from a queue

You always remove data from a queue by taking that data off the front of the queue. The front of the queue always contains the data that's been stored in the queue the longest.

In Visual Basic, you can remove and retrieve data off a queue by using the Dequeue command, as shown in the following Visual Basic example:

```
Dim LongLine As New Queue
Dim X As Object
LongLine.Enqueue("My cat")
LongLine.Enqueue(108.75)
LongLine.Enqueue("Fat dog")
X = LongLine.Dequeue
```

As an alternative to removing data from a queue, you can retrieve data by using the Peek command. To use the Peek command, you have to assign the value of the Peek command to a variable like this:

```
Dim LongLine As New Queue
Dim X As Object
LongLine.Enqueue("Tasha Korat")
LongLine.Enqueue(7.25)
LongLine.Enqueue("Gray")
X = LongLine.Peek
```

The preceding code assigns the value "Tasha Korat" to the X variable, which is declared as an Object data type.

REMEMBER

The Peek command only retrieves the data but leaves it at the front of the queue. Figure 4-7 shows the difference between the Peek and the Dequeue commands.

The "Peek" command retrieves data from a queue without removing data from the queue.

| Gray | 7.25 | Tasha | X = "Tasha"

| Gray | 7.25 | → Tasha X = "Tasha"

The "Dequeue" command removes data from the queue while retrieving that data.

FIGURE 4-7: The Peek command retrieves data, but the Dequeue command retrieves and removes data.

Counting and searching a queue

Because a queue expands each time you add more data to it, most programming languages provide a way to count the total number of items currently stored in the queue.

In Visual Basic, you can count the number of items currently stored in a queue by using the Count property. Here's an example:

```
Dim LongLine As New Queue
Dim X As Object
LongLine.Enqueue("Tasha")
LongLine.Enqueue(7.25)
```

```
LongLine.Enqueue("Gray")
X = LongLine.Count
```

In this example, Count stores the number 3 in the X variable.

Visual Basic also provides a Contains command, which tells you whether a chunk of data is stored in a queue (but doesn't tell you the location of that data in the queue). To use the Contains command, you have to specify the data you want to find, like this:

```
Dim LongLine As New Queue
Dim X, Y As Boolean
LongLine.Enqueue("Tasha")
LongLine.Enqueue(7.25)
LongLine.Enqueue("Gray")
X = LongLine.Contains("Gray")
Y = LongLine.Contains("Orange juice")
```

In this example, the first Contains command looks for the "Gray" string. Because this string is stored in the queue, the Contains command returns a True value, which it stored in the X variable.

The second Contains command looks for the "Orange juice" string. Because this string isn't stored in the stack, this Contains command returns a False value, which is stored in the Y variable.

The Contains command just tells you whether a chunk of data is in a queue, but it doesn't tell you where in the queue that data might be.

Using Deques

A queue only lets you add data on one end of the data structure and remove data from the opposite end. A deque (pronounced *deck*) acts like a queue that lets you add or remove data from either end, as shown in Figure 4-8.

Most programming languages don't deque the deque data structure as a built-in feature. Instead, you have to create a queue with other data structures, such as a linked list, and then write code to manage the storage and removal of data from both ends of the deque.

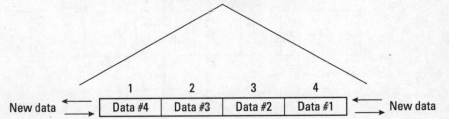

A deque allows you to add or remove data from both ends of the data structure.

FIGURE 4-8:
A deque acts like a two-way queue.

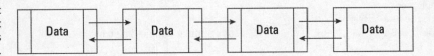

	1	2	3	4	
New data ←	Data #4	Data #3	Data #2	Data #1	← New data

A deque is similar to a linked list of nodes that contain data and two pointers:

>> One pointer points to the previous node.

>> The second pointer points to the next node, as shown in Figure 4-9.

A double-linked list consists of nodes that hold data and two pointers that point to the next and previous node.

Data	Data	Data	Data

Initially, a deque consists of a single node with both pointers pointing to nothing, which is often defined in most programming languages as a NIL value. When you add (or remove) data, you must specify on which end of the deque to put that data, either the front or the back.

Deques can either be implemented as a double-linked list, as shown in Figure 4-10. That means you need to keep track of which node represents the front and which represents the end.

Typical command names used for adding or removing data from a deque include

>> push_front: Adds data to the front of the deque

>> push_back: Adds data to the end of the deque

>> pop_front: Removes data from the front of the deque

>> pop_back: Removes data from the end of the deque

A double-linked list can either be a straight line . . .

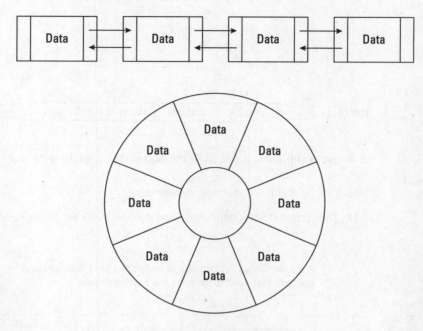

FIGURE 4-10:
Two ways to
implement a
deque as a
linked list.

. . . or a circular double-linked list.

Because you can add data to both ends of a deque, a deque can grow in both directions, as shown in Figure 4-11.

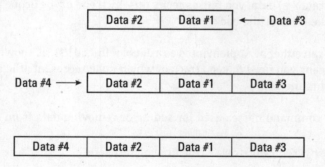

FIGURE 4-11:
A deque can grow
in two different
directions.

Unlike a stack that always removes the newest data or a queue that always removes the oldest data, a deque can never predictably remove either the oldest or newest data. When you add data to both ends of the deque, the oldest data tends to get sandwiched and buried in between the newest data on both ends.

TIP

Like stacks and queues, deques only allow you to remove data from a specific part of the data structure. Every data structure has pros and cons depending on what your program may need.

A deque might be useful for an antivirus program that needs to examine messages being sent out and coming in to a particular computer. When messages come in, the antivirus program stores each message in the deque. Messages scanned as virus-free are sent through the other end of the deque, whereas messages caught carrying a virus are rejected from the same end of the deque, as shown in Figure 4-12.

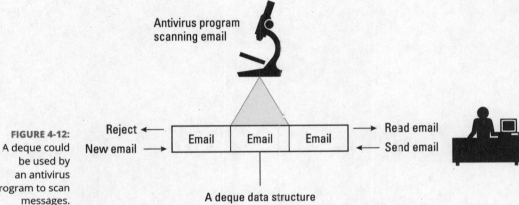

FIGURE 4-12: A deque could be used by an antivirus program to scan messages.

Antivirus program scanning email

Reject ← New email →

Email | Email | Email

→ Read email ← Send email

A deque data structure

Chapter **5**

Graphs and Trees

M ost data structures (such as arrays, dictionaries, and queues) store data in a linear format with one chunk of data neatly sandwiched in between exactly two other chunks of data. Linear data structures can be fine for just storing data, but what if you want a data structure that can model a real-life problem?

Picking the right data structure to model a real-life problem can greatly simplify programming. One advantage of a queue is that it closely mimics a line of people (or orders on a website) that need to be handled one at a time, starting with the oldest item. Using a queue data structure to handle incoming orders from a website makes logical sense, but using a dictionary or even an array makes less sense because dictionaries require keys assigned to each item (which isn't needed) and arrays need to be resized constantly.

So, if you have a problem that doesn't mimic a linear data structure, using a linear data structure can just make programming harder, much like trying to use a screwdriver to pound in a nail when you really need a hammer.

For example, suppose you're creating a chess game. You could use a collection data structure to represent each space on the chessboard, but a more intuitive data structure would just be a two-dimensional array.

Modeling a chessboard with a two-dimensional array works because both a two-dimensional array and a chessboard are uniformly shaped grids. Now, what if you need to model a real-life problem that doesn't neatly match a uniformly shaped grid?

Suppose you need to keep track of trucks traveling to different cities so you can route them to the shortest distance between two cities, as shown in Figure 5-1.

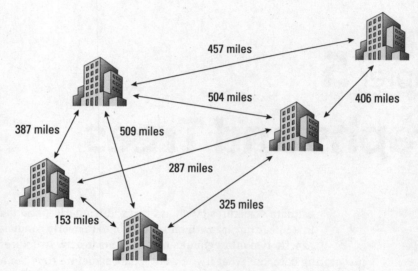

FIGURE 5-1:
Modeling
a map of
different cities.

You could model this problem as a two-dimensional array like this:

	Los Angeles	San Diego	Las Vegas	San Francisco	Salt Lake City
Los Angeles	0	153	287	387	X
San Diego	153	0	325	509	X
Las Vegas	287	325	0	504	406
San Francisco	387	X	504	0	457
Salt Lake City	X	X	406	457	0

Although this two-dimensional array accurately models the map of different city distances, it's not easy to understand what this data represents. A better data structure would be a graph.

Understanding Graphs

A graph is typically created by using a linked list that can point to multiple nodes. As a result, a graph doesn't follow a linear structure but has a more haphazard appearance, which makes it perfect for modeling nonlinear data, such as the map of different cities and distances, as shown in Figure 5-2.

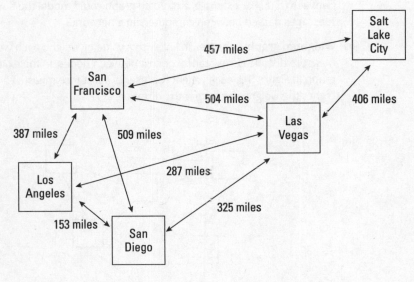

FIGURE 5-2: A graph data structure can model the mapping problem better than an array.

The two parts of every graph are

» **Nodes (or *vertices*):** Contain data.

» **Connections (or *edges*):** Represent some relationship between two or more nodes.

In the map example, nodes represent cities, and connections represent distances.

TECHNICAL STUFF

An entire branch of mathematics, called *graph theory*, is dedicated to studying graphs.

Graph data structures are used less for storing and retrieving data and more for understanding the relationship between data.

Graphs and Trees

Types of graphs

Three types of graphs are shown in Figure 5-3:

» **Undirected graph:** Connects data in different ways to show a relationship, such as modeling all the links connecting the pages of a website.

» **Directed graph:** Adds arrows to show you the direction of a relationship between data. For example, a directed graph could model the flow of messages passed between computers in a network.

» **Weighted graph:** Labels each link with a value or weight; each weight might measure distances, resistance, or cost between nodes. In the example of the graph in Figure 5-3, each weight represents a distance measured in miles. The higher the weight, the farther the distance.

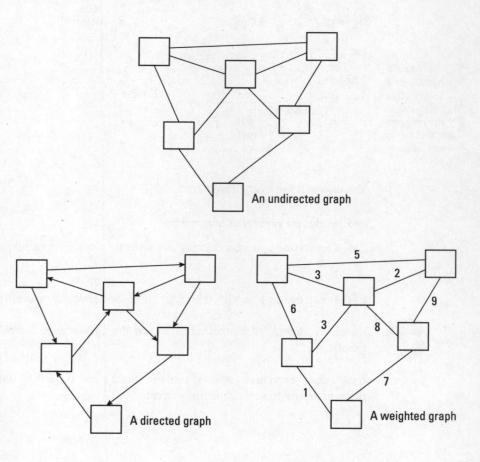

An undirected graph

A directed graph

A weighted graph

FIGURE 5-3:
The three types
of graphs.

384   BOOK 3 **Data Structures**

REMEMBER

You can also combine weights with direction and create a *directed, weighted* graph.

Uses for graphs

Graphs are used to model a variety of real-world problems, such as finding the most efficient way to route email through a computer network or finding the shortest way for airplanes to travel to different cities. Molecular biologists even use graphs to model the structure of molecules.

Designing a single path with the Seven Bridges of Königsberg

One of the first uses for graphs appeared in 1736 in a problem known as the Seven Bridges of Königsberg. The question was whether it was possible to walk across all seven bridges of Königsberg exactly once, as shown in Figure 5-4.

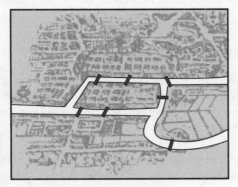

The Seven Bridges of Königsberg

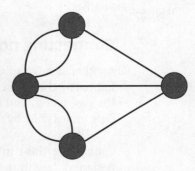

The Seven Bridges of Königsberg represented as a graph

FIGURE 5-4:
The Seven Bridges of Königsberg represented as a graph.

A mathematician named Leonhard Euler used a graph to prove that this was impossible. In the Seven Bridges problem, one node has five bridges leading to it (5 degrees), while each of the other three nodes only have three bridges leading to it (3 degrees). Euler proved that the only way you could cross every bridge exactly once was if a graph had, at the most, two nodes with an odd number of bridges (degrees), and each odd-numbered degree node had to be the starting and ending point.

Although solving a problem of walking across a bridge exactly once might seem trivial, knowing how to solve this problem can help design truck or airplane routes as efficiently as possible.

Finding the shortest path through a graph

After using Euler's proof to design a graph that can be traversed in a single path, graph theory can now help you find the shortest path through that graph.

A problem, dubbed the Traveling Salesman problem, tries to find the shortest round-trip route through a graph where the same node is both the starting and ending point. In this case, the shortest route through a graph may not necessarily be the shortest round-trip route to return to the same starting point.

The Traveling Salesman problem can get more complicated with a weighted or directed graph. A directed graph may restrict movement in one direction, such as traveling through one-way streets in a city, whereas a weighted graph can make one route longer than two shorter routes combined. Adding in directed and weighted graphs can alter the best solution.

TECHNICAL STUFF

If you ever looked up directions on a mapping website or app, such as Google Maps, you've used a graph to find the most efficient way from one location to another.

Connecting nodes in a graph

Another use for graphs involves *topological graph theory.* This problem is highlighted by the Three Cottages problem, in which three cottages need to connect to the gas, water, and electricity companies, but their lines can't cross each other. (It's impossible, by the way.)

Connecting lines in a graph without crossing is a problem that circuit board designers face in the placement of chips. Another example of eliminating intersections involves transportation designs, such as the design of highways or railroad tracks.

Creating Trees

Graphs typically represent a chaotic arrangement of data with little or no structure. To give graphs some form of organization, computer scientists have created special graphs dubbed *trees.* Like a graph, a tree consists of nodes and edges, but unlike a graph, a tree organizes data in a hierarchy, as shown in Figure 5-5.

A tree arranges a graph in a hierarchy with a single node (called the *root node*) appearing at the top and additional nodes appearing connected underneath. If a node has no additional nodes connected underneath, those nodes are *leaf nodes,* as shown in Figure 5-6.

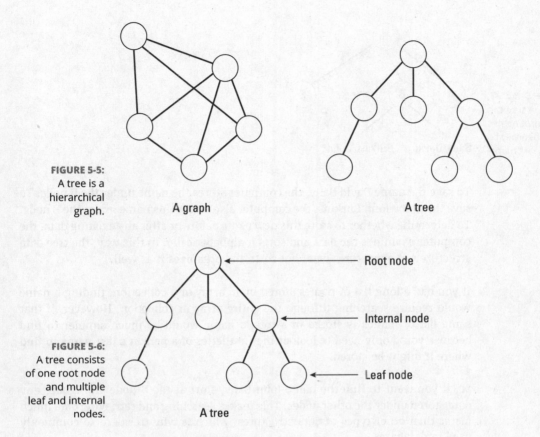

FIGURE 5-5:
A tree is a hierarchical graph.

A graph

A tree

Root node

Internal node

Leaf node

FIGURE 5-6:
A tree consists of one root node and multiple leaf and internal nodes.

A tree

Ordered trees

When a tree stores information at random in its different nodes, it's dubbed an *unordered tree.* However, the tree is already in the form of a hierarchy, so it may make sense to take advantage of this built-in structure and create an *ordered tree.*

An ordered tree provides a distinct beginning node (the root node) with additional nodes organized in a hierarchy, such as organizing nodes alphabetically from left to right. Such a hierarchy can store and show relationships of a corporate management team or the spread of a flu epidemic through different cities. As a result, ordered trees are a common data structure used to both model and organize data.

TIP

One common use for ordered trees involves storing data. Under each root node, you can have 26 internal nodes, each of which represents a single letter of the alphabet from A to Z. Under each of these letter nodes, you can have multiple nodes that contain the actual data, as shown in Figure 5-7.

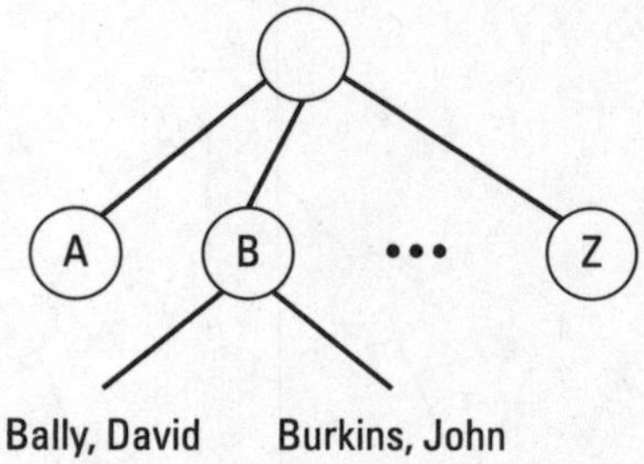

FIGURE 5-7:
A tree can
organize names
alphabetically by
last name.

To save the name David Bally, the computer stores the name under the B node. To save the name John Burkins, the computer also stores this name under the B node. To determine whether to store this new name before or after any existing data, the computer examines the data and sorts it alphabetically. In this way, the tree data structure not only stores data, but sorts and organizes it as well.

If you had a long list of names stored in an array or a collection, finding a name would require searching through the entire array or collection. However, if that same list of names is stored in a tree, a name would be much simpler to find because you'd only need to look at the first letter of a person's last name to find where it might be stored.

So, if you want to find the name John Bally, start at the B node and ignore any data stored under the other nodes. This makes searching and retrieving data much faster than other types of data structures, which is why trees are so commonly used in databases.

Binary trees

A *binary tree* is a variation of an ordered tree. Unlike an ordinary tree, every node in a binary tree has, at most, two nodes connected underneath. To sort data, the left node contains values less than its parent node whereas the right node contains values greater than its parent node, as shown in Figure 5-8. By limiting each node to a maximum of two connected nodes, binary trees make searching and sorting data fast and efficient.

For example, an ordinary tree allows each node to have multiple nodes underneath. As a result, the more data an ordinary tree stores, the more nodes that can appear directly underneath a single node, as shown in Figure 5-9.

To find the number 11 in an ordered binary tree is simple. Start with the root (top) node and compare the number 11 to the root node value (10). Because the number you want to find is greater than the root node, you'd branch to the right. At this next node (12), the computer repeats the process and determines that 11 is less than 12, so it branches to the left node, which is where it finds the number 11.

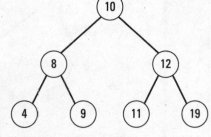

FIGURE 5-8:
An ordered binary tree stores and sorts data by value.

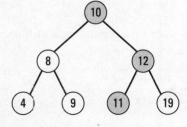

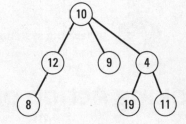

FIGURE 5-9:
An ordinary tree is more difficult to search than an ordered binary tree.

To find the number 11 in a sorted binary tree, you have to search three nodes.

To find the number 11 in an unordered, non-binary tree means having to search every node.

Searching through a sorted binary tree is simple, especially when compared to searching through an unordered tree. Because an unordered tree can scatter data anywhere, searching an unordered tree means methodically searching each node, one by one, until you find the data you want. In a large unordered tree, this search time can be slow and inefficient.

B-trees

Another variation of a tree is a *B-tree*. Here are the two main features of a B-tree:

» All nodes can store multiple nodes underneath it, such as three nodes.

» All leaf nodes remain at the same level as or depth of the tree, as shown in Figure 5-10.

When you add or subtract data, the B-tree constantly adjusts to keep all leaf nodes at the same level. Keeping all leaf nodes at the same level ensures that searching for some data (stored farther down a tree) won't take a long time compared to searching for other data (stored closer to the root node of the tree).

A variation of a B-tree is a B+ tree. A B+ tree stores data only in its leaf nodes. Because all leaf nodes are the same distance from the root node, this makes searching for any type of data equal.

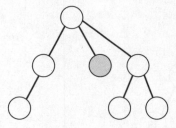

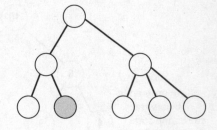

FIGURE 5-10:
In a B-tree, all leaf
nodes appear at
the same level.

In an ordinary tree, leaf nodes can appear on different levels.

In a B-tree, all leaf nodes appear on the same level.

TECHNICAL STUFF

Operating systems often use B+ trees for keeping track of files on a disk.

Taking Action on Trees

Trees are flexible data structures because they organize data and allow fast retrieval of that data. Some of the different actions you can perform on trees include

>> Searching for a specific item

>> Adding a new node or a sub-tree

>> Deleting data or a sub-tree

Traversing a tree to search for data

When you store data in an array or a collection, that data is stored in a line so you can search the entire data structure by starting at one end and examining each data chunk, one by one, until you get to the end. However, trees are different because they offer multiple branches.

To search a tree, the computer must examine multiple nodes exactly once, which is known as *traversing a tree*. There are four popular ways to search a tree, as shown in Figure 5-11:

>> Preorder traversal

>> In-order traversal

>> Postorder traversal

>> Level-order traversal

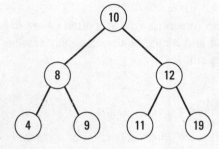

FIGURE 5-11:
The four different ways to traverse a tree.

Preorder: 10, 8, 4, 9, 12, 11, 19

In-order: 4, 8, 9, 10, 11, 12, 19

Postorder: 4, 9, 8, 11, 19, 12, 10

Level-order: 10, 8, 12, 4, 9, 11, 19

Preorder traversal

Preorder traversal starts at the top of a tree (the root node) and then traverses the left nodes. When it reaches a leaf node, it backtracks and goes down the right nodes, as follows:

1. Visit the root node.

2. Traverse the left sub-tree in preorder.

3. Traverse the right sub-tree in preorder.

In-order traversal

When traversing an ordered binary tree, the in-order traversal retrieves data in order by following these steps:

1. Traverse the left sub-tree using in-order.

2. Visit the root node.

3. Traverse the right sub-tree by using in-order.

Postorder traversal

Postorder traversal traverses the left and right sub-trees first and then visits the root node, as follows:

1. Traverse the left sub-tree in postorder.

2. Traverse the right sub-tree in postorder.

3. Visit the root node.

Level-order traversal

Level-order traversal starts at the top level of a tree and traverses the row of nodes on the same level, from left to right. Then it drops to the next lower level and repeats the process all over again.

REMEMBER

When writing actual code to traverse a tree, it's often easier to write a recursive subprogram that calls itself and traverses a successively smaller part of the tree (or sub-tree) until it finally stops.

Adding new data

Adding data to a linear structure, like a collection or a stack, is straightforward because the data structure simply gets bigger. Adding data to a tree is slightly more complicated because you can add new data at the end of a tree (on one of its leaf nodes) or anywhere in the middle of the tree.

In an unordered tree, you can insert data anywhere, but in an ordered binary tree, inserting new data means sorting the data at the same time, as shown in Figure 5-12.

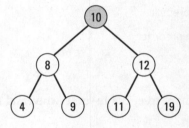

(7) Start at the root node. Since 7 is less than 10, traverse the left sub-tree.

Compare 7 with the first node on the left sub-tree. Since 7 is less than 8, traverse the left sub-tree.

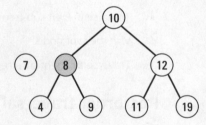

Compare 7 with the next node on the left sub-tree. Since 7 is greater than 4, add the 7 node to the right of the 4 node.

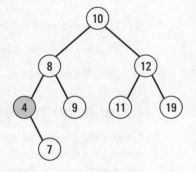

FIGURE 5-12: Inserting new data in an ordered binary tree.

REMEMBER

The order in which you store data determines the position of that data in a tree because newly added data gets added based on the existing data's values.

Deleting data

Deleting data from a tree can cause special problems because after deleting data, you may need to rearrange any nodes that were underneath the deleted data, as shown in Figure 5-13.

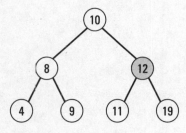

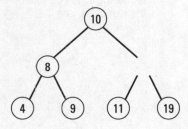

FIGURE 5-13:
After deleting data from a tree, you may need to rearrange the remaining data to keep the tree sorted.

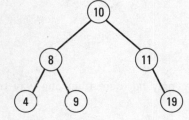

REMEMBER

If you delete data and immediately add it back to the tree again, the tree looks different because reinserting the data sorts and organizes it based on the existing data. So, if you delete the 12 node and immediately add it back again, it now appears as a left node under the 19 node.

Pruning and grafting sub-trees

A *sub-tree* is a smaller tree, such as part of an existing tree. Instead of deleting a single node, you can delete an entire sub-tree, which is known as *pruning a tree*, as shown in Figure 5-14.

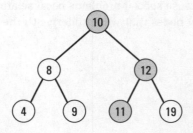

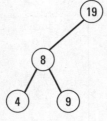

Removing a sub-tree can leave remaining nodes disconnected from the rest of the tree.

FIGURE 5-14:
Pruning a
tree removes
two or more
nodes from
a tree.

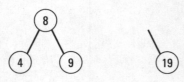

or

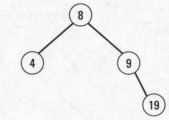

REMEMBER

After pruning a sub-tree, there may be more than one way to rearrange the remaining nodes.

Adding or grafting a sub-tree to an existing tree can cause problems if the sub-tree data contains different values than the original tree. In that case, you can't just graft the sub-tree to the existing tree; you have to rearrange the data in both the tree and the grafted sub-tree to sort data once more, as shown in Figure 5-15.

Tree data structures are most useful for storing and sorting data, such as for databases. However, tree data structures are also handy for creating artificial intelligence in games, such as chess.

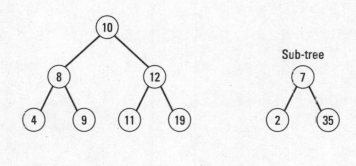

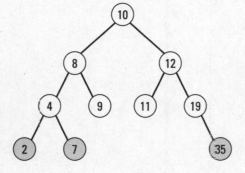

FIGURE 5-15:
Grafting a
sub-tree
can require
rearranging
the entire
modified tree.

Grafting a sub-tree can
require rearranging nodes.

The computer might use a tree data structure to represent all possible moves when the root node represents one possible move. Then each alternating level in the tree represents the possible human responses and the best possible computer responses, as shown in Figure 5-16.

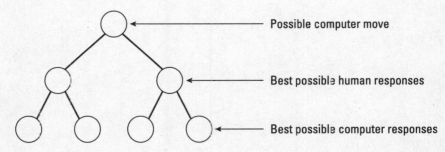

FIGURE 5-16:
A tree can help a
computer plan its
next move.

By organizing possible moves in a tree, a computer can determine the best possible move to make that will give its human opponent the worst possible moves later. This strategy is *minimax* — the computer *minimizes* the human's best possible moves and *maximizes* its own best moves.

Despite having to create trees out of other data structures (such as linked lists) and being more complicated to create and manage than other data structures, trees are one of the most useful and flexible data structures available.

Algorithms

Contents at a Glance

Chapter **1**

Sorting Algorithms

E very program handles data (numeric or text). Besides saving data, most programs also need to organize that data in some way, which involves sorting that data in a specific order, such as alphabetically or numerically. A database needs to sort names alphabetically by last name or by sales region, whereas a video game needs to sort the top-ten highest scores.

Despite the simple idea behind sorting a list of names or numbers, sorting is practically a field of computer science in itself. Computer scientists constantly study different ways to sort through data to find the fastest, most efficient method possible. Each of these different sorting methods is a *sorting algorithm. Algorithm* is a fancy term for a method of doing something, so a sorting algorithm is a specific method for telling the computer how to sort data. The reason computer scientists keep creating and studying sorting algorithms is because no single sorting algorithm is best for all purposes.

Some sorting algorithms are easy to create but work slowly. Other sorting algorithms are much harder to create but work much faster. Ironically, some sorting algorithms work horribly when sorting a small number of items, such as a dozen numbers, but work quickly when sorting thousands of items.

Four factors for considering sorting algorithms include

>> **Ease of implementation:** Defines how complicated the sorting algorithm is to implement in any programming language. Some sorting algorithms are easy to write but slow in actual use. Other sorting algorithms are much harder to write but perform much faster.

>> **Speed:** Measures how fast the algorithm can sort data of different sizes. Some sorting algorithms work quickly with small lists but slow down dramatically when dealing with larger lists. Other sorting algorithms work quickly when a list is mostly sorted but slow to a crawl when working with completely unsorted lists.

>> **Memory requirements:** Define how much memory the sorting algorithm needs to run. Some sorting algorithms can accept and sort data while they receive the data, which is an *online algorithm*. (An *offline algorithm* has to wait to receive the complete set of data before it can even start the sorting process.) Sorting algorithms that use recursion (see Book 2, Chapter 6) may be easy to implement and fast but can require lots of memory to sort large amounts of data.

TECHNICAL STUFF

Another factor that determines a sorting algorithm's memory requirements is whether the algorithm is an *in-place algorithm.* An in-place algorithm can sort data by using the existing data structure that holds the data. For example, if you have an array of numbers, an in-place algorithm can sort the data in that array without needing a separate data structure to hold the data temporarily.

>> **Stability:** Refers to whether a sorting algorithm preserves the order of identical data. Suppose you had a list of first and last names, such as John Smith and Mary Smith, and John Smith appears at the beginning of a list and Mary Smith appears at the end. A stable sorting algorithm sorts both names and keeps John Smith ahead of Mary Smith, but an unstable algorithm might move Mary Smith ahead of John Smith. (Out of all the sorting algorithms presented in this chapter, heap sort and selection sort are unstable algorithms.)

REMEMBER

Ultimately, there's no perfect sorting algorithm. However, a trade-off in size, speed, ease of implementation, and stability finds the best sorting algorithm for your specific needs.

Using Bubble Sort

The simplest way to sort any amount of data is to start at the beginning and compare the first two adjacent items. So, if you need to sort a list of numbers, you compare the first number with the second number. If the first number is bigger, you swap its place with the second number. If the second number is bigger, you don't do anything at all.

After comparing the first two items, you move down to comparing the second and third items, and so on. Repetitively comparing two adjacent items is the basic idea behind the bubble sort algorithm, as shown in Figure 1-1. The bubble sort algorithm gets its name because small values tend to *bubble up* to the top.

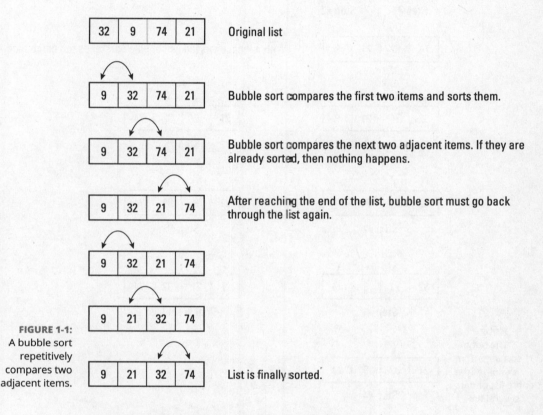

| 32 | 9 | 74 | 21 | Original list

| 9 | 32 | 74 | 21 | Bubble sort compares the first two items and sorts them.

| 9 | 32 | 74 | 21 | Bubble sort compares the next two adjacent items. If they are already sorted, then nothing happens.

| 9 | 32 | 21 | 74 | After reaching the end of the list, bubble sort must go back through the list again.

| 9 | 32 | 21 | 74 |

| 9 | 21 | 32 | 74 |

| 9 | 21 | 32 | 74 | List is finally sorted.

FIGURE 1-1:
A bubble sort repetitively compares two adjacent items.

Basically the bubble sort algorithm works like this:

1. Compare two adjacent items.

2. Swap the two items if necessary.

3. Repeat Steps 1 and 2 with each pair of adjacent items.

4. Repeat Steps 1–3 to examine the entire list again until no swapping occurs and then the list is sorted.

Although the bubble sort algorithm is easy to implement, it's also the slowest and most inefficient algorithm because it must examine an entire list multiple times.

For sorting a small list of mostly sorted data, the bubble sort algorithm works efficiently. For sorting large lists of unsorted data, any other sorting algorithm is much faster than the bubble sort algorithm, as shown in Figure 1-2.

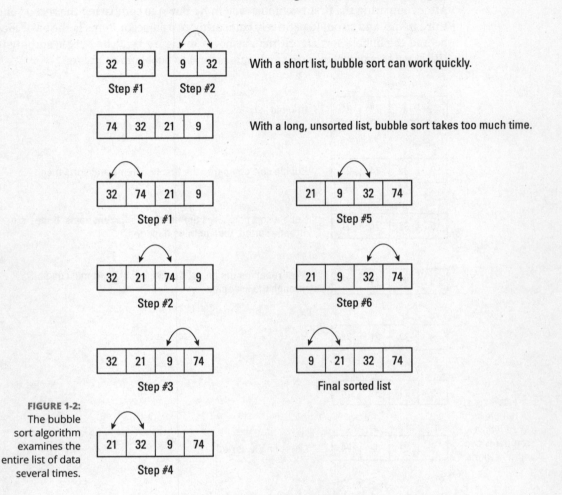

With a short list, bubble sort can work quickly.

With a long, unsorted list, bubble sort takes too much time.

FIGURE 1-2: The bubble sort algorithm examines the entire list of data several times.

Using Selection Sort

Another simple way to sort a list is to search the entire list until you find the smallest value. Then swap that value to the front of the list. Now repeat the process all over again, skipping the first item. By repetitively searching for the smallest item and moving it to the front of the list, the selection sort algorithm can eventually sort an entire list, as shown in Figure 1-3.

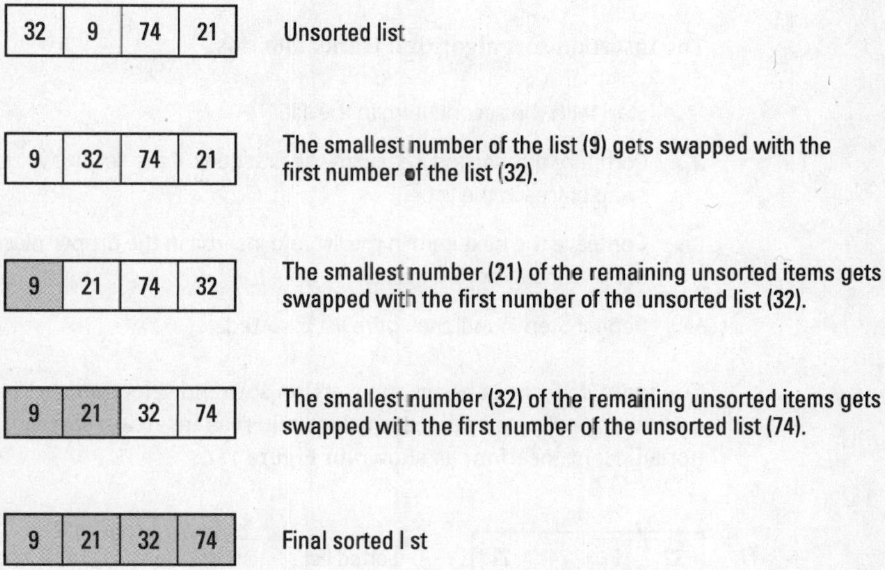

| 32 | 9 | 74 | 21 | Unsorted list

| 9 | 32 | 74 | 21 | The smallest number of the list (9) gets swapped with the first number of the list (32).

| 9 | 21 | 74 | 32 | The smallest number (21) of the remaining unsorted items gets swapped with the first number of the unsorted list (32).

| 9 | 21 | 32 | 74 | The smallest number (32) of the remaining unsorted items gets swapped with the first number of the unsorted list (74).

| 9 | 21 | 32 | 74 | Final sorted list

FIGURE 1-3: Selection sort repetitively moves the smallest value to the front of the list.

The selection sort algorithm works like this:

1. Find the smallest item in a list.

2. Swap this value with the value currently at the front of the list.

3. Repeat Steps 1 and 2 with the current size of the list minus one (list size = list size – 1).

For sorting small lists, selection sort can actually be faster than other sorting algorithms, but for sorting large lists, selection sort needs too much time progressively examining smaller sections of a list. Despite this drawback with sorting large lists, selection sort is popular because it's simple to implement.

Using Insertion Sort

The insertion sort algorithm acts like a cross between the bubble sort and the selection sort algorithm. Like bubble sort, insertion sort examines two adjacent values. Like selection sort, insertion sort moves smaller values from their current location to an earlier position near the front of the list.

The insertion sort algorithm works like this:

1. Start with the second item in the list.

2. Compare this second item with the first item. If the second value is smaller, swap places in the list.

3. Compare the next item in the list and insert it in the proper place in relation to the previously sorted items.

4. Repeat Step 3 until the entire list is sorted.

The main difference between insertion sort and selection sort is that the selection sort swaps only two adjacent values whereas insertion sort can move a value to a nonadjacent location, as shown in Figure 1-4.

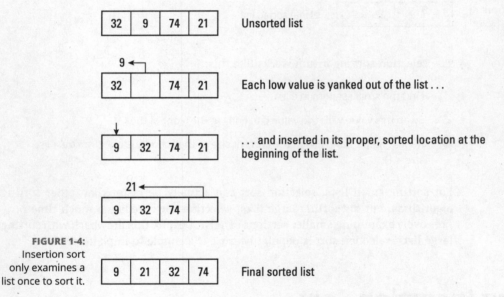

Unsorted list

Each low value is yanked out of the list . . .

. . . and inserted in its proper, sorted location at the beginning of the list.

Final sorted list

FIGURE 1-4:
Insertion sort only examines a list once to sort it.

TIP

One major advantage of the insertion sort algorithm is that it only needs to examine an entire unsorted list once to sort it. In comparison, bubble sort must repetitively examine the entire list multiple times, and selection sort must repetitively examine progressively smaller lists multiple times. As a result, the insertion sort algorithm is much faster while being easy to implement as well.

Using Shell Sort

To speed up the performance of the insertion sort algorithm, Donald Shell, a computer scientist, created a variation of the insertion sort algorithm dubbed *shell sort.*

One problem with insertion sort is that it must examine one value at a time. In a long list, this can take a long time. Shell sort works by dividing a long list into several smaller ones and then performing an insertion sort on each smaller list. After each smaller list gets sorted, the shell sort algorithm uses an ordinary insertion sort to sort the entire list one last time. By this time, the longer list is nearly sorted, so this final insertion sort occurs quickly, as shown in Figure 1-5.

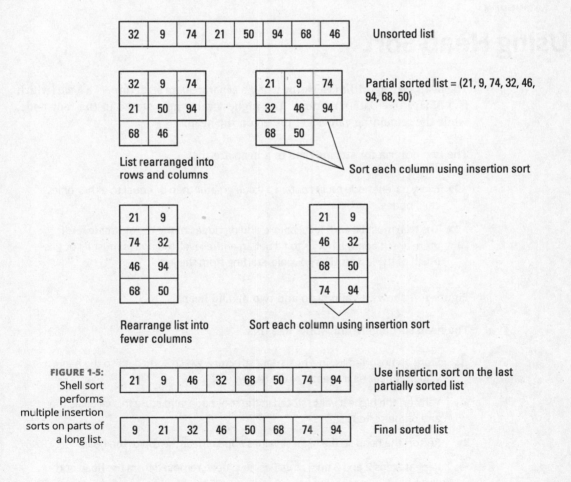

FIGURE 1-5: Shell sort performs multiple insertion sorts on parts of a long list.

Basically, shell sort works like this:

1. Divide a long list into multiple smaller lists.

2. Arrange each list in a grid or table consisting of rows and columns. Each row represents the original, unsorted list. Each column holds one item in the list.

3. Use an insertion sort to sort the columns.

4. Repeat Steps 1–3 with progressively smaller lists until only a single list is left to be sorted with the insertion sort algorithm.

REMEMBER

The shell sort algorithm isn't necessarily a different sorting algorithm. Instead, shell sort is a way to use the insertion sort algorithm more efficiently.

Using Heap Sort

The heap sort algorithm works by using a separate data structure — a *heap* (which is a binary tree data structure). The highest value gets stored in the root node, while the remaining values get tossed on the heap.

The two criteria for storing data in a heap are that

» Every parent node must contain a value greater than or equal to either of its child nodes.

» The tree must fill each level before adding nodes to the next lower level. If there aren't enough nodes to fill out an entire level, the nodes must fill out as much of the last level as possible, starting from the left.

Figure 1-6 shows a valid heap and two invalid heaps.

The heap sort algorithm works like this:

1. Store an unsorted list in a heap data structure, which sorts data so the highest values appear near the top of the heap.

2. Yank off the highest value stored in the root node, and store this value as the end of the sorted list.

3. Re-sort the heap so the highest values appear near the top of the heap.

4. Repeat Steps 2 and 3 until all values have been removed from the heap and sorted.

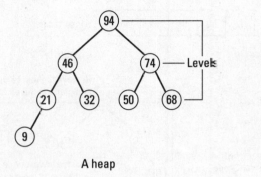

A heap

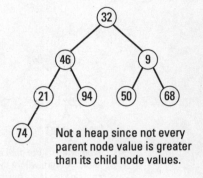

Not a heap since not every parent node value is greater than its child node values.

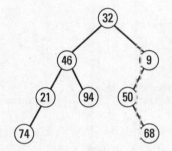

Not a heap since earlier levels are not full.

FIGURE 1-6:
Valid and invalid heap binary trees.

Heap sort dumps an unsorted list of data into the heap, always making sure the highest value appears in the root node. Then this highest value in the root node gets stored at the end of the list. Now the heap rearranges its values again, putting the highest remaining value in the root node and repeating the process all over again, as shown in Figure 1-7.

Initially, the heap sort algorithm may seem complicated because you need to create a heap data structure, copy and sort values among nodes, and delete nodes while you remove values and store them back in a sorted list. Although you can create a heap data structure by using a linked list, a much simpler method is to create a heap data structure by using an array, as shown in Figure 1-8.

The first array element represents the root node, the next two elements represent the child nodes of the root, and so on. Instead of manipulating a linked list as a heap, it's much simpler to rearrange values stored in an array, as shown in Figure 1-9. Because arrays are easy to implement in any programming language, the heap sort algorithm is also easy to implement. Although slightly more complicated than bubble sort or selection sort, the heap sort algorithm offers faster performance.

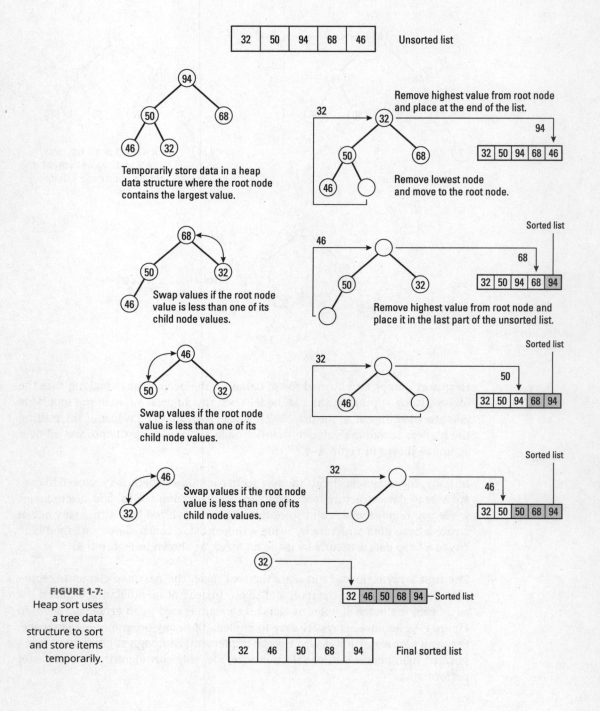

FIGURE 1-7: Heap sort uses a tree data structure to sort and store items temporarily.

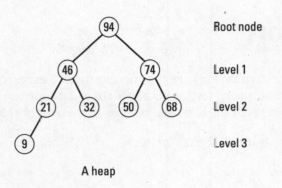

Root node — 94

Level 1 — 46, 74

Level 2 — 21, 32, 50, 68

Level 3 — 9

A heap

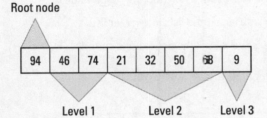

Root node

| 94 | 46 | 74 | 21 | 32 | 50 | 68 | 9 |

Level 1   Level 2   Level 3

FIGURE 1-8: An array can mimic a heap data structure.

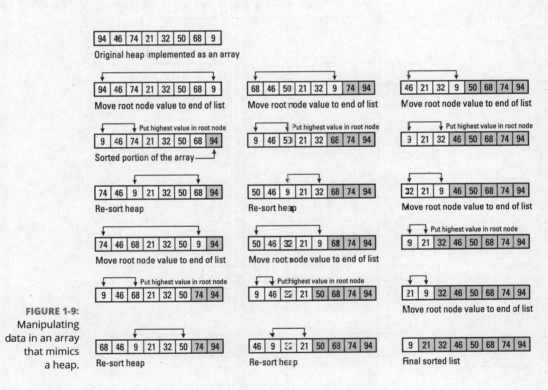

| 94 | 46 | 74 | 21 | 32 | 50 | 68 | 9 |

Original heap implemented as an array

| 94 | 46 | 74 | 21 | 32 | 50 | 68 | 9 |

Move root node value to end of list

| 9 | 46 | 74 | 21 | 32 | 50 | 68 | 94 |

Put highest value in root node

Sorted portion of the array

| 74 | 46 | 9 | 21 | 32 | 50 | 68 | 94 |

Re-sort heap

| 74 | 46 | 68 | 21 | 32 | 50 | 9 | 94 |

Move root node value to end of list

| 9 | 46 | 68 | 21 | 32 | 50 | 74 | 94 |

Put highest value in root node

| 68 | 46 | 9 | 21 | 32 | 50 | 74 | 94 |

Re-sort heap

| 68 | 46 | 50 | 21 | 32 | 9 | 74 | 94 |

Move root node value to end of list

| 9 | 46 | 50 | 21 | 32 | 68 | 74 | 94 |

Put highest value in root node

| 50 | 46 | 9 | 21 | 32 | 68 | 74 | 94 |

Re-sort heap

| 50 | 46 | 32 | 21 | 9 | 68 | 74 | 94 |

Move root node value to end of list

| 9 | 46 | 32 | 21 | 50 | 68 | 74 | 94 |

Put highest value in root node

| 46 | 9 | 32 | 21 | 50 | 68 | 74 | 94 |

Re-sort heap

| 46 | 21 | 32 | 9 | 50 | 68 | 74 | 94 |

Move root node value to end of list

| 9 | 21 | 32 | 46 | 50 | 68 | 74 | 94 |

Put highest value in root node

| 32 | 21 | 9 | 46 | 50 | 68 | 74 | 94 |

Move root node value to end of list

| 9 | 21 | 32 | 46 | 50 | 68 | 74 | 94 |

Put highest value in root node

| 21 | 9 | 32 | 46 | 50 | 68 | 74 | 94 |

Move root node value to end of list

| 9 | 21 | 32 | 46 | 50 | 68 | 74 | 94 |

Final sorted list

FIGURE 1-9: Manipulating data in an array that mimics a heap.

Using Merge Sort

The merge sort algorithm works on the principle that it's easier to sort a small list than a large list. So, merge sort breaks a large list of data into two or more smaller lists. Then it sorts each small list and smashes or merges them together.

The merge sort algorithm works like this:

1. Divide a large list in half.

2. Divide each smaller list in half until each small list consists only of one value.

3. Sort this single value with a neighboring single value list.

4. Merge these smaller, sorted lists into larger lists.

5. Repeat Steps 3 and 4 until the entire list is sorted.

Figure 1-10 shows how merge sort works.

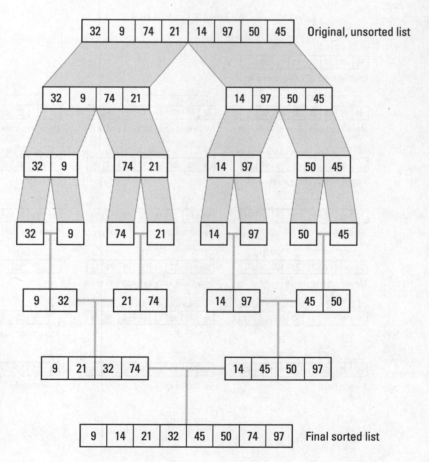

FIGURE 1-10: Merge sort breaks a long list into several smaller lists and then merges these lists back into a longer list.

Because the merge sort algorithm successively divides a list in half, merge sort often creates temporary data structures (such as arrays) to store data while it divides and merges values. When sorting a small list, creating a temporary data structure is simple, but when sorting a large list, creating a temporary large data structure can gobble up memory.

Using Quick Sort

The quick sort algorithm gets its name because it's generally the fastest sorting algorithm in most cases. Like the merge sort algorithm, the quick sort algorithm works on the principle that it's easier and faster to sort a small list than a large list, so quick sort divides a large list into two parts.

To divide a list into two parts, quick sort picks a *pivot* (value) from the list:

>> Any value less than the pivot goes into one list.

>> Any value greater than the pivot goes into the second list.

Quick sort repetitively divides each list into two parts until it creates multiple lists that contain only one value each. By then, the entire list will be sorted, as shown in Figure 1-11.

The quick sort algorithm uses a pivot value to presort values into two different lists. Sorting values by this pivot value alone makes quick sort generally faster than merge sort.

Basically, the quick sort algorithm works like this:

1. Pick a pivot value from the list.

2. Divide the list in two, placing values less than the pivot value in the first list and values greater than the pivot value in the second list.

3. Repeat Steps 1 and 2 until the lists contain only one item.

The key to speeding up the quick sort algorithm is to choose the proper pivot for dividing each list. Ideally the pivot value will be a middle value in a list. Notice that the merge sort algorithm (refer to Figure 1-10) still sorts values through every step, whereas pivot values make the quick sort algorithm (refer to Figure 1-11) sort the entire list in fewer steps.

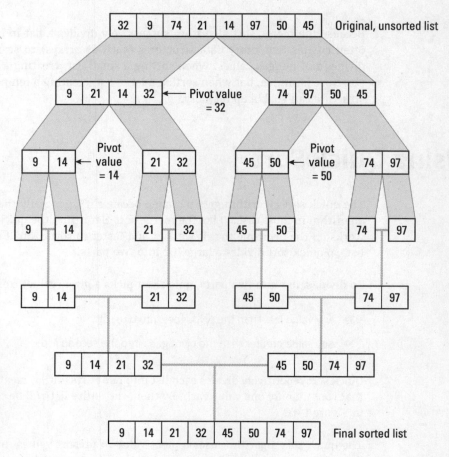

FIGURE 1-11:
Quick sort repetitively divides a large list into two smaller lists, sorting items based on a pivot value.

Comparing Sorting Algorithms

To compare the speed of sorting algorithms, computer scientists consider the following scenarios:

>> **Best-case scenario:** Measures the speed of different algorithms sorting a list of values that are already completely sorted

>> **Worst-case scenario:** Measures the speed of different algorithms sorting a list that's completely unsorted

>> **Average-case scenario:** Measures the speed of different algorithms sorting random values in a list

To measure the speed and efficiency of an algorithm, computer scientists measure how much time an algorithm needs to run based on different sizes of input, which is designated by the letter *n*. A small value of *n* means the input is short whereas a large value of *n* means the input is large.

Thus, an algorithm's *efficiency* (how fast it runs) is based on its input size *n*. In mathematical terms, this is referred to as an order of *n*. If an algorithm runs at the same speed no matter how much data it receives, it's said to run at constant time, which can be written in Big O notation as $O(1)$.

If an algorithm's speed depends directly on the number of items it receives, it's said to run at a linear time, written as $O(n)$. Some common Big O notations for different algorithms include

>> **$O(\log n)$:** Logarithmic time

>> **$O(n^c)$:** Polynomial

>> **$O(c^n)$:** Exponential

>> **$O(n!)$:** Factorial

REMEMBER

Describing algorithm efficiency as its order is known as Big O notation because the letter O is always capitalized.

Computer scientists have already calculated the Big O values of different sorting algorithms. Table 1-1 gives different Big O values for different sorting algorithms for the best-case, worst-case, and average-case scenarios.

TABLE 1-1

Comparison of Different Sorting Algorithms

Algorithm	Average	Best	Worst
Bubble sort	$O(n^2)$	$O(n)$	$O(n^2)$
Selection sort	$O(n^2)$	$O(n^2)$	$O(n^2)$
Insertion sort	$O(n^2)$	$O(n)$	$O(n^2)$
Heap sort	$O(n[\log n])$	$O(n[\log n])$	$O(n[\log n])$
Merge sort	$O(n[\log n])$	$O(n[\log n])$	$O(n[\log n])$
Quick sort	$O(n[\log n])$	$O(n[\log n])$	$O(n^2)$

To compare the efficiency of different algorithms, plug in different values for *n*.

For example, the Big O notation for the bubble sort algorithm is $O(n^2)$. To sort one item, the bubble sort algorithm's efficiency is $O(1^2)$ or $O(1)$. To sort five items, the bubble sort's efficiency is $O(5^2)$ or $O(25)$. The higher the Big O value, the slower and less efficient the algorithm is, which means that the more items the bubble sort algorithm needs to sort, the slower it runs.

The quick sort algorithm has a Big O notation of $O(n[\log n])$. To see how quick sort compares to bubble sort when sorting five items, plug in a value of 5 for n, such as $O(5[\log 5])$, $O(5[0.70])$, or $O(3.5)$.

With the bubble sort algorithm, the more items needed to sort n, the higher its Big O value. To sort five items, the bubble sort algorithm's Big O notation is $O(25)$, which is much larger than the quick sort algorithm's similar Big O notation of $O(3.5)$. The difference in these two values can give you a rough idea how much slower bubble sort works compared to quick sort when sorting the same number of items.

TIP

Table 1-1 shows that some algorithms, such as bubble sort, may be superior to other sorting algorithms depending on whether the data is mostly sorted.

The insertion sort algorithm is unique in that it runs the fastest in a best-case (already-sorted) scenario. Although the quick sort algorithm is considered the fastest, notice that in a worst-case scenario, it's actually one of the slowest algorithms. If your data will be completely unsorted, avoid using the quick sort algorithm.

TIP

The best sorting algorithm is the one that's the fastest for sorting your type of data. If you need to write a program that regularly needs to sort random data (average-case scenario), you might choose one sorting algorithm, whereas if you need to sort completely unsorted data (worst-case scenario), you'd probably choose a different algorithm. The fastest sorting algorithm always depends partially on the sorted (or unsorted) data that the algorithm needs to manipulate.

REMEMBER

The three fastest sorting algorithms are heap sort, merge sort, and quick sort. Although quick sort is considered the fastest of the three algorithms, merge sort is faster in worst-case scenarios.

Chapter **2**

Searching Algorithms

O
ne of the most common functions of a computer program is searching. A database needs to search through names and addresses, a word processor needs to search through text, and even a computer chess game needs to search through a library of moves to find the best one.

Because searching is such an important part of computer programming, computer scientists have developed a variety of algorithms to search for data. When searching for data, the main limitation is time. Given enough time, any search algorithm can find what you want, but there's a big difference between finding data in five seconds and finding it in five hours.

The time a search algorithm takes is always related to the amount of data to search, which is the *search space*. The larger the search space, the longer the search algorithm takes. If you only need to search a small search space, even a simple and slow search algorithm can be fast enough.

The two main categories of search algorithms are

» ***Uninformed* (brute-force):** Uninformed, or brute-force, search algorithms work by simply examining the entire search space, which is like losing your car keys in your apartment and searching every apartment in the entire building. Eventually, you find your keys, but it may take a long time to do it.

>> *Informed* (heuristic): Informed, or heuristic, search algorithms work by selectively examining the most likely parts of the search space. This is like losing your car keys in your apartment but only examining the bedroom where you last saw your car keys. By using knowledge of the search space, informed search algorithms can speed up a search algorithm by eliminating obvious parts of the search space that don't contain the data you want to find.

Uninformed search algorithms are much simpler and faster to write in any programming language, but the price you pay may be slower searching speed. Informed search algorithms always take more time to write, but the speed advantage may be worth it especially if your program needs to search data on a regular basis. One problem with informed search algorithms is that they often require that the data be sorted first or stored in a data structure that requires more complicated traversing through all items, such as a tree data structure.

REMEMBER The perfect search algorithm is easy for you to implement in your favorite programming language while also being fast enough for your program.

Sequential Search

A *sequential search* is an example of an uninformed search algorithm because it searches data one item at a time, starting from the beginning and searching through to the end. In the best-case scenario, a sequential search finds data stored as the first element in a data structure. In the worst-case scenario, a sequential search has to search an entire data structure to find the last item stored, as shown in Figure 2-1.

FIGURE 2-1:
The speed of sequential search depends directly on the size of the data to be searched.

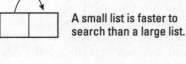

A small list is faster to search than a large list.

To speed up sequential searching, you can add simple heuristics. Some popular ways to speed up sequential searching include

>> Backward or forward searching

>> Block searching

>> Binary searching

>> Interpolation searching

Backward or forward searching

If the data is sorted, you can make the sequential search start looking through a data structure from either the beginning or the end. So, if you need to search an array that contains numbers organized in ascending order from 1 to 100, searching for the number 89 will probably be faster if you start at the end of the array, as shown in Figure 2-2.

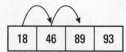

| 18 | 46 | 89 | 93 |

Searching from the front can take two jumps.

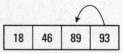

| 18 | 46 | 89 | 93 |

Searching from the end can be faster is the data is near the end of the list.

FIGURE 2-2: Sequential search can be made faster by searching from either the front or end of a data structure.

The backward or forward searching algorithm works like this:

1. In a sorted data structure, compare the value to find with the average of the first and last item.

2. If the data to find is in the first half of the data structure, start at the front of the data structure; otherwise, start at the end.

3. Search sequentially until the data is found or confirmed not to exist in the data structure.

TIP

Searching either backward or forward also has an advantage when searching through data structures that organize data by age. If data is stored in a queue, the oldest data appears at the front, and the newest data appears at the end. So, if you can identify the age of the data you want to find, you could speed up the search for knowing whether to start at the beginning of the queue or the end.

Block searching

Another technique to speed up sequential searching on sorted data is *block searching* (also known as *jump searching*). Instead of searching one item at a time, this method jumps over a fixed number of items (such as five) and then examines the last item:

» If the last item is *greater* than the value the algorithm is trying to find, the algorithm starts searching backward.

» If the last item is *less* than the value the algorithm is trying to find, the algorithm jumps another block forward, as shown in Figure 2-3.

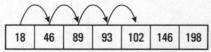

Searching for the number 102 takes four jumps in a normal sequential search.

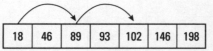

FIGURE 2-3:
Block searching can speed up a sequential search on sorted data.

Searching for the number 102 can only take two jumps in a block search.

The block searching algorithm works like this:

1. Jump ahead a fixed number of items (a *block*).

2. Compare the last value of the block.

   If this value is less than the data to find, search sequentially within the block; otherwise, jump to the end of a new block and repeat Step 2.

The basic idea behind block searching is to skip ahead through a sorted list of data and then slow down when it gets closer to that data. This is like looking through a phone book for the name Winston Smith by skipping every ten pages until you reach the S section and then searching sequentially until you find the name *Smith* and finally the name *Winston Smith*.

Block searching can work only with sorted data. If data isn't sorted, block searching can't work at all.

Binary searching

A variation of block searching is *binary searching*, which essentially uses a block half the size of the list. After dividing a list in half, the algorithm compares the last value of the first half of the list. If this value is smaller than the value it's trying to find, the algorithm knows to search the second half of the list instead. Otherwise, it searches the first half of the list.

The algorithm repeatedly divides the list in half and searches only the half of the list that contains the range of values it's trying to find. Eventually, the binary search finds the data, as shown in Figure 2-4.

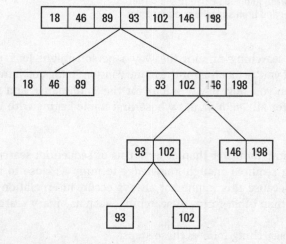

FIGURE 2-4:
Binary searching divides a list in half until it eventually finds its data.

Binary searching keeps dividing a list in half until it eventually finds the data, such as finding the number 102.

The binary search algorithm works like this:

1. Divide a sorted list in half.

2. Compare the last value of the first half of the list.

   If this last value is greater than the desired value, search this half of the list; otherwise, search the other half of the list.

3. Repeat Steps 1 and 2 until the desired value is found or confirmed not to exist.

Interpolation searching

Instead of jumping a fixed number of items (like block searching) or dividing a list in half (like binary searching), *interpolation searching* tries to guess the approximate location of data in a sorted list. After it jumps to the approximate location, the algorithm performs a normal sequential search, as shown in Figure 2-5.

FIGURE 2-5: Interpolation searching tries to jump straight to the approximate location of the target data.

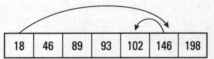

| 18 | 46 | 89 | 93 | 102 | 146 | 198 |

Interpolation search jumps as close to the target data as possible, and then searches sequentially.

Interpolation searching mimics the way a person might look up a name in a phone book. If you're looking for the name *Winston Smith*, you jump straight to the *S* section. Then you slow down to look for the *Smith* name, and slow down even more to look for all *Smith* names whose first name begins with *W* until you find *Winston Smith*.

WARNING

Although potentially faster than other forms of sequential searching, interpolation searching requires enough knowledge to jump as close to the desired data as possible. Because this might not always occur, interpolation searching isn't always faster than other forms of searching, such as binary searching.

Interpolation searching follows these steps:

1. Jump to the approximate location of the target data in a sorted list.

2. Start searching sequentially until the desired data is found or confirmed not to exist.

The key to interpolation searching relies on the computer accurately jumping to the position where the data is likely to be stored. One way of guessing the location of data is to use Fibonacci numbers, creating the *Fibonacci searching* technique.

TECHNICAL STUFF

Fibonacci numbers are a series of numbers that are calculated by adding the last two numbers in a series to determine the next number in the series. The first Fibonacci number is 0, the second is 1, the third is 1 (0 + 1), the fourth is 2 (1 + 1), the fifth is 3 (1 + 2), the sixth is 5 (2 + 3), and so on like this:

0, 1, 1, 2, 3, 5, 8, 13, 21, 34, 55 . . .

Fibonacci numbers tend to occur in nature, such as measuring the branching of trees or the curves of waves. Instead of dividing a list in half, like binary searching, Fibonacci searching divides a sorted list into progressively smaller lists, based on Fibonacci numbers, until it finally finds the data or confirms that the data doesn't exist.

Fibonacci searching works like this, as shown in Figure 2-6:

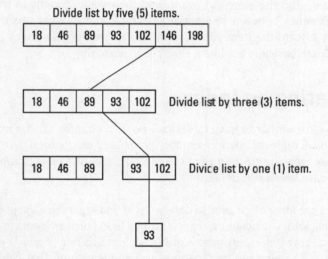

Divide list by five (5) items.

| 18 | 46 | 89 | 93 | 102 | 146 | 198 |

| 18 | 46 | 89 | 93 | 102 | Divide list by three (3) items.

| 18 | 46 | 89 | | 93 | 102 | Divide list by one (1) item.

| 93 |

FIGURE 2-6:
Fibonacci numbers divide and search a list more efficiently than a binary search.

Fibonacci searching divides a list into parts that correspond to Fibonacci numbers starting with 5, 3, and finally 1.

1. Determine the size of the sorted list (dubbed *n*).

2. Find the largest Fibonacci number that's less than the size of the sorted list (dubbed *p*).

3. Examine the value stored at the *p*th location of the sorted list.

If this value is the one you want to find, stop.

4. If the value at this *p*th location is less than the data you're searching for, search the list to the right of the *p*th location. If the value at this *p*th location is greater than the data you're searching for, search the list to the left of the *p*th location.

5. Repeat Steps 1–4.

Using Indexes

Imagine yourself trying to find a certain store in a large shopping mall. You could wander up and down the corridors and examine each store, one by one, which is like a sequential search. Even if you use the various sequential search tactics, like block searching, sequential searching can still take a long time.

Instead of searching each store sequentially, here's a faster way: Look at the mall directory, find the store you want, and then walk straight to that store. That's the difference between sequential searching and indexes. An index points you directly toward the item you want to find no matter how many items there may be. Indexes basically act like a shortcut to searching.

Creating an index

Indexes are similar to hash tables (see Book 3, Chapter 3). The main difference is that a hash table calculates a unique value based on the total data stored, whereas an index typically stores part of the data in a separate table that points to the rest of the data, as shown in Figure 2-7.

Indexes are most often used in databases. If you organize a list of data in rows and columns, with each column representing a field (such as Name or Phone Number) and each row representing a record (that contains one person's name and phone number), an index can be as simple as a single column that consists of the data you're most likely to use for searching.

For example, if you have a database of names, addresses, and phone numbers, you probably spend more time looking up someone's phone number by looking up their last name. So, you could use the Last Name field as an index. At the simplest level, an *index* is nothing more than an organized list of existing data, such as a list of last names organized alphabetically (see Figure 2-7).

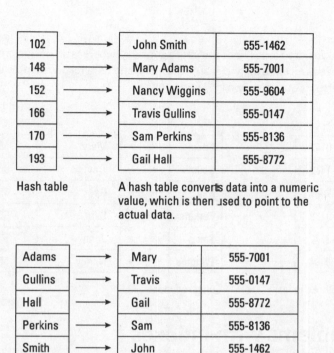

102	⟶	John Smith	555-1462
148	⟶	Mary Adams	555-7001
152	⟶	Nancy Wiggins	555-9604
166	⟶	Travis Gullins	555-0147
170	⟶	Sam Perkins	555-8136
193	⟶	Gail Hall	555-8772

Hash table

A hash table converts data into a numeric value, which is then used to point to the actual data.

Adams	⟶	Mary	555-7001
Gullins	⟶	Travis	555-0147
Hall	⟶	Gail	555-8772
Perkins	⟶	Sam	555-8136
Smith	⟶	John	555-1462
Wiggins	⟶	Nancy	555-9604

FIGURE 2-7:
Comparison
of hash tables
and indexes.

Index

An index uses part of the data to organize the rest of the data

If you create an index based on last names and you need to search by last name, an index can find your data easily. However, what if you want to search by phone number or city, but your index consists only of last names? In that case, you can create multiple indexes, one for each type of data.

Clustered and unclustered indexes

There are two types of indexes:

>> **Clustered:** A clustered index sorts the actual data. If you have a list of names and addresses, a clustered index could sort the data by last name, which physically rearranges the data in order. Because a clustered index physically rearranges data, you can have only one clustered index per file. Sorting data by a single field, such as last name, is an example of a clustered index.

>> **Unclustered:** An unclustered index doesn't physically rearrange data but creates pointers to that data. Because unclustered indexes don't rearrange the data, you can have as many unclustered indexes as you need. The drawback of unclustered indexes is that they're slower than clustered indexes.

A clustered index finds the data right away, whereas an unclustered index needs an extra step to search the index and then follow the pointer to the actual data, as shown in Figure 2-8.

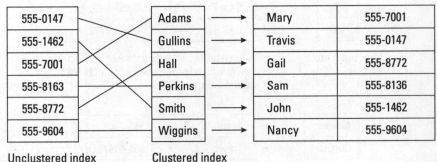

FIGURE 2-8: Clustered indexes physically rearrange data, whereas unclustered indexes point to data.

Unclustered index   Clustered index

Problems with indexes

A single clustered index makes sense because it rearranges data in a specific way. Multiple, unclustered indexes can help search data in different ways. Although indexes make searching faster, they make inserting and deleting slower because every time you add or delete data, you must update and organize the index at the same time.

If you've created multiple indexes, adding or deleting data means having to update every multiple index. If you have a small amount of data, creating and using an index may be more trouble than it's worth. Only when you have large amounts of data is an index (or multiple indexes) worth using.

Also consider how often you may need to search on that index. You may need to search a customer database using a name or ID number fairly often, but you probably won't often need to search for a customer based on their gender or marital status, so these would be poor choices for an index.

Adversarial Search

One of the most popular uses for searching is an *adversarial search.* This type of search is often used to create artificial intelligence in video games.

Essentially, the computer analyzes the current game situation, such as a tic-tac-toe game, and calculates its list of possible moves. For each possible move, the computer creates a tree where the root node represents one of the computer's possible moves and each alternating level represents the human opponent's possible counter-moves, as shown in Figure 2-9.

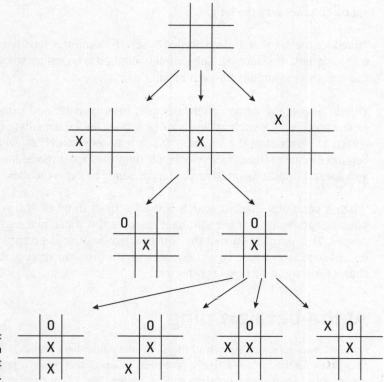

FIGURE 2-9:
A tree can analyze the best possible move.

Each possible move is given a specific value:

» A positive value signifies a good move.

» A negative value signifies a bad move.

Assuming the human opponent chooses one possible counter-move, the next level of the tree displays the computer's possible responses and so on. The more levels (or *plys*) the computer can analyze, the more it can anticipate and plan ahead and the smarter the computer can appear.

Depth versus time

Given enough time, the computer can examine every possible move and all possible counter-moves until it finds the best move to make that will lead to its inevitable victory. In simple games, like tic-tac-toe, where the number of choices is relatively small, this brute-force approach of searching all possible moves works. When applied to more complicated games, like chess or Go, such a brute-force approach takes way too long.

To reduce the amount of time needed to search, computer scientists have come up with a variety of solutions. The simplest method is to reduce the number of plys the computer examines for each move.

This is how many games offer beginner, intermediate, and expert modes. The expert mode may search 24 levels in each tree, the intermediate mode may only search 12 levels, and the beginner mode may only search 4 levels. Because the beginner mode searches far fewer levels than the expert mode does, it runs faster and doesn't appear as *smart* as the intermediate or expert modes.

TECHNICAL STUFF

When a computer doesn't search beyond a fixed number of levels, it can miss potential problems that it might have discovered if it had just searched a little bit deeper. This event is dubbed the *horizon effect* because the computer doesn't see the consequences beyond a certain move, so the problem appears to lie outside the computer's sight, or *beyond the horizon.*

Alpha-beta pruning

Another way to speed up searching is to use *alpha-beta pruning.* The idea behind this tactic is that it's relatively pointless to keep searching a tree if a potential move would represent a horrible choice. For example, in a chess game, two possible moves might be moving the king into a position where it'll get checkmated in two moves or moving a pawn to protect the king.

If a computer always searches every possible move down to 12 levels, it wastes time evaluating the bad move that results in the king getting checkmated in two moves. To save time, alpha-beta pruning immediately stops searching a tree the moment it detects a terrible move and makes the computer focus on studying good moves instead. As a result, the computer's time can be spent more profitably examining potentially good moves.

For example, consider the tree in Figure 2-10; the boxes represent possible moves for the computer, and the circles represent possible counter-moves by a human opponent. The higher the value in each box or circle, the better the move. So, the human opponent will most likely choose moves with high values. In response, the computer must look at the best possible counter-moves based on what the human opponent is likely to choose.

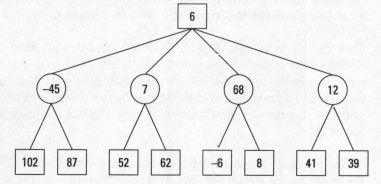

FIGURE 2-10: Assigning values to possible moves helps the computer evaluate the best possible move.

So, if the computer considers a move with a value of 6 (the root node), the human opponent might have 4 possible moves with values ranging from –45 to 68. Assuming the human chooses the best move (68), the computer may have a choice of only 2 possible moves (–6 and 8). The goal is to choose the best possible move *(max)* for the computer that leaves the human opponent with a choice of nothing but the worst possible moves *(min)*, so arranging moves on a tree and assigning values is known as a *minimax tree.*

The goal is to minimize the best choices your opponent can choose while maximizing the best choices you can choose. Assuming the computer chooses this original move (6) and the human opponent responds with the best possible move of 68, the computer now has a choice of evaluating the –6 or 8 move. Because evaluating the –6 move appears to be a losing option, alpha-beta pruning would stop the computer from further evaluating this move and just focus on the 8 move instead.

Looking up a library of good moves

Alpha-beta pruning relies on examining every tree of possible moves and immediately cutting off the least promising ones. Obviously, some moves aren't worth considering, but the computer has no way of knowing that until it evaluates every move.

However, at the beginning of every game, there's always a list of good and bad moves, so many games include a library of these good moves. Now at the start of the game, the computer doesn't have to waste time searching every move but can just pick from its library of best possible moves and examine those moves in depth.

A way to use this technique in the middle of a game is to analyze all possible moves in two steps. In the first step, the computer only examines every possible move through a small number of levels, such as two. The idea is that most bad moves can be identified immediately, like moving a queen in a chess game so it can be captured by the opponent's pawn in the next move.

After the computer examines all possible moves in such shallow depth, it can eliminate the obviously bad moves and then for the second step, examine the remaining moves in more detail. Although this technique takes slightly more time to examine all possible moves through a shallow depth, it ultimately saves time by preventing the computer from examining both bad and good moves at a much deeper level.

Ultimately, searching always involves examining every item in a list, which means the larger the list, the longer the search time. The only way to speed up searching algorithms is to use different techniques to maximize the chances of finding data as soon as possible.

The simplest way to speed up any search algorithm is to sort the data beforehand. After a list has been sorted, the computer can use various techniques, such as block jumping or Fibonacci searching, to speed up the search.

If data isn't sorted, it may be possible to use an index. An index works most effectively when it organizes part of the stored data, such as indexing the last names of a customer list that contains names, addresses, and phone numbers. Although indexes can speed up searching, their need for constant updating makes adding and deleting data slower.

Instead of searching through stored data, strategy games such as chess must search through continuously changing data based on the position of the game pieces. To search through this ever-changing data, strategy games must rely on techniques to quickly eliminate bad moves so the computer can spend its time focusing only on evaluating the best moves.

Chapter **3**

String Searching

S earching for data is one of the most common functions in writing a computer program. Most searching algorithms focus on searching a list of values, such as numbers or names. However, there's another specialized type of searching, which involves searching text.

Searching text poses unique problems. Although you can treat text as one long list of characters, you aren't necessarily searching for a discrete value, like the number *21* or the last name *Smith.* Instead, you may need to search a long list of text for a specific word or phrase, such as *ant* or *cat food.* Not only do you need to find a specific word or phrase, but you also may need to find that same word or phrase multiple times. Because of these differences, computer scientists have created a variety of searching algorithms specifically tailored for searching text.

REMEMBER

Computers only recognize and manipulate numbers, so every computer represents characters as a universally recognized numeric code. Two common numeric codes include the American Standard Code for Information Interchange (ASCII) and Unicode. ASCII contains 256 codes that represent mostly Western characters whereas Unicode contains thousands of codes that represent languages as diverse as Arabic, Chinese, and Cyrillic. When searching for text, computers actually search for numeric codes that represent specific text, so text searching is ultimately about number searching.

TECHNICAL STUFF

One of the most popular uses for text searching algorithms involves a field called *bioinformatics*, which combines molecular biology with computer programming. The basic idea is to use long text strings, such as *gcacgtaag*, to represent a DNA structure and then search for a specific string within that DNA structure (such as *cgt*) to look for matches that could indicate how a particular drug could interact with the DNA of a virus to neutralize it.

Sequential Text Search

The simplest text-searching algorithm is the brute-force sequential search, which simply examines every character. To look for the string *GAG* in text, the brute-force sequential search examines the text character by character. The moment it finds the letter *G*, it checks to see whether the next letter is *A* and so on. To find anything, this search algorithm must exhaustively examine every character, as shown in Figure 3-1.

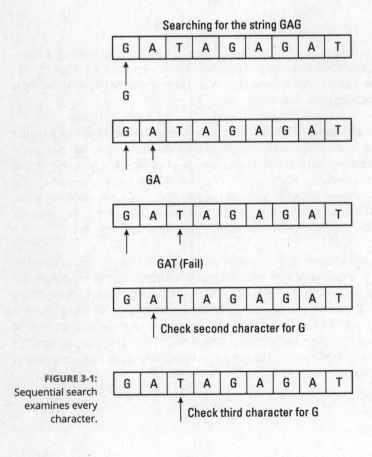

FIGURE 3-1:
Sequential search examines every character.

In searching for the string *GAG*, a brute-force search starts with the first character and finds a matching *G* character. Next, it checks whether the next two characters are an *A* and a *G*.

In this example, the third character *(T)* doesn't match, so the brute-force algorithm starts all over again by examining the second character, even though it had previously examined that character. Because the brute-force method examines every character individually, this method is the slowest and least efficient method for finding text.

Although the brute-force method works, it can take too much time, especially when searching through large amounts of text. To make text searching faster and more efficient, computer scientists have developed a variety of alternative algorithms.

The Boyer-Moore algorithm

To speed up text searching, the computer should skip any previously examined text and jump straight to unexamined text. That's the basis for a text-searching algorithm developed by two computer scientists, Bob Boyer and J. Strother Moore, called the Boyer–Moore algorithm.

Like the brute-force algorithm, the Boyer–Moore algorithm examines text character by character. After the Boyer–Moore algorithm finds a partial match, it's smart enough to skip over any previously examined characters that couldn't possibly be the beginning of the text string to find. By skipping previously examined characters that can't match the search criteria, the Boyer–Moore algorithm speeds up the entire search process, as shown in Figure 3-2.

The Rabin–Karp algorithm

Although much faster than a brute-force search, the Boyer–Moore algorithm still searches one character at a time. If you're searching for a text string, you can speed up the search by examining blocks of text rather than individual characters.

For example, if you're searching for the string *GAG*, you could examine three characters at a time instead of examining a single character three times. To make searching blocks of characters faster, two computer scientists, Michael O. Rabin and Richard M. Karp, created the Rabin–Karp algorithm.

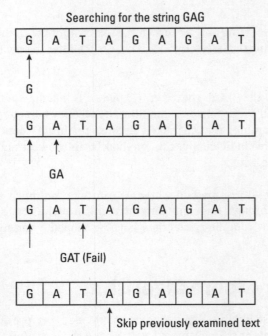

Searching for the string GAG

| G | A | T | A | G | A | G | A | T |

G

| G | A | T | A | G | A | G | A | T |

GA

| G | A | T | A | G | A | G | A | T |

GAT (Fail)

| G | A | T | A | G | A | G | A | T |

Skip previously examined text

FIGURE 3-2: The Boyer–Moore algorithm skips over partially matched characters.

This algorithm uses a hash function to convert a block of characters into a numeric value. Instead of examining individual characters, the Rabin–Karp algorithm uses its hash function to convert the original search string into a numeric value. So, a hash function might convert the three-character string to search *(GAG)* into a numeric value of 3957.

After converting the search string into a numeric value, the Rabin–Karp algorithm repetitively searches for blocks of characters that are the same length of the search string (such as three characters) and uses its hash function to convert those blocks of text into a numeric value. Now instead of searching for matching characters, the Rabin–Karp algorithm searches just for matching hash values, as shown in Figure 3-3.

The key to the Rabin–Karp algorithm is the speed and method of its hash function. If the hash function can create values quickly and ensure that different strings never create the same hash value, this algorithm can run quickly. If the hash function calculates hash values slower than the computer can examine characters individually, this algorithm may run slower than another algorithm, such as the Boyer–Moore algorithm. Also, if the hash function calculates identical hash values for two different strings, this algorithm won't be accurate enough because it finds the wrong data.

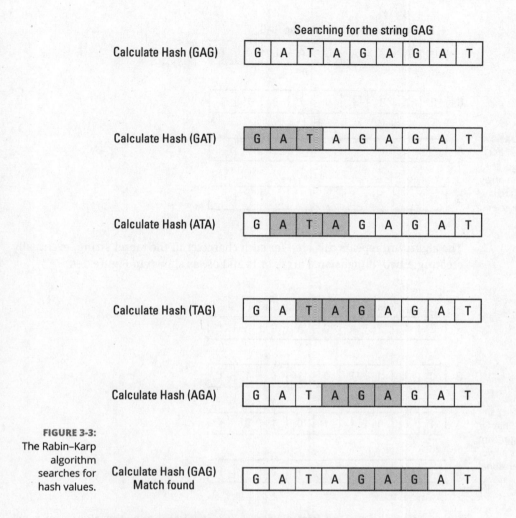

Searching for the string GAG

Calculate Hash (GAG)

Calculate Hash (GAT)

Calculate Hash (ATA)

Calculate Hash (TAG)

Calculate Hash (AGA)

FIGURE 3-3:
The Rabin–Karp
algorithm
searches for
hash values.

Calculate Hash (GAG)
Match found

The Shift Or algorithm

The Shift Or algorithm takes advantage of the fact that computers are much faster at manipulating 1s and 0s than they are at manipulating and comparing characters. First, the algorithm creates an empty array the same length as the text that you want to search. Then it compares the first character of the *target string* (what you're trying to find) with each character in the search string. Every time it finds a match, it stores a 0 in the array element. Every time it doesn't find a match, it stores a 1 in the array element, as shown in Figure 3-4.

After creating an array by comparing the first character with each character in the search string, the algorithm next looks only for a 0, which identifies where the first character of the target string was found. Now it compares the character to the right. If a match is found, it stores a 0 in a second array that represents matching the first and second characters of the target string. If a match isn't found, it stores a 1 in this second array.

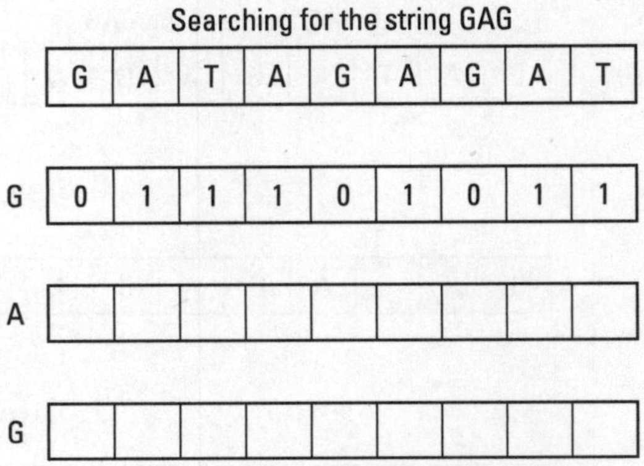

Searching for the string GAG

G	A	T	A	G	A	G	A	T

G | 0 | 1 | 1 | 1 | 0 | 1 | 0 | 1 | 1 |

A | | | | | | | | | |

G | | | | | | | | | |

FIGURE 3-4: The Shift Or algorithm creates an array of matching characters.

The algorithm repeats this step for each character in the target string, eventually creating a two-dimensional array of 1s and 0s, as shown in Figure 3-5.

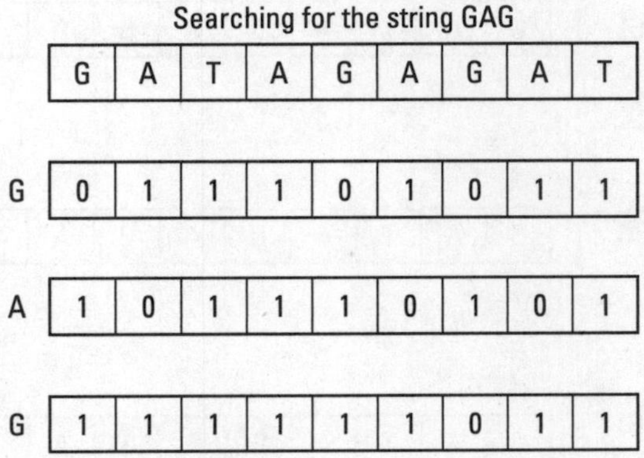

Searching for the string GAG

G	A	T	A	G	A	G	A	T

G | 0 | 1 | 1 | 1 | 0 | 1 | 0 | 1 | 1 |

A | 1 | 0 | 1 | 1 | 1 | 0 | 1 | 0 | 1 |

G | 1 | 1 | 1 | 1 | 1 | 1 | 0 | 1 | 1 |

FIGURE 3-5: The Shift Or algorithm creates a two-dimensional array.

When searching for the first character (G), in Figure 3-5, the algorithm must check every character in the entire string. However, when searching for the second character (A), the algorithm only has to look for the 0s in the previous row of the two-dimensional array, which identifies where the G character appears. In Figure 3-5, this means only searching three characters out of the entire string to look for a possible match of the GA string.

When searching for the third character (G), the algorithm now only checks for 0s in the second row of the two-dimensional array, which means it only checks three characters out of the entire string.

As soon as the algorithm finds three 0s that form a diagonal line in the two-dimensional array, it can identify the exact location of the GAG string in the much larger string. The Shift Or algorithm gets its name because the matching string patterns look like binary numbers where the 0 constantly gets shifted one place to the right, like this:

$$G \rightarrow 011$$

$$A \rightarrow 101$$

$$G \rightarrow 110$$

Although the Shift Or algorithm takes more steps than a simple brute-force search, it's another way to search that could be faster, depending on the data. Sometimes the simplest algorithms aren't always the best.

The finite automaton algorithm

In the finite automaton algorithm, first, the algorithm creates a finite state machine, which is a directed graph (see Book 3, Chapter 5). Each node represents a state such as finding a single character in the target string, and each link represents finding a specific character. So, if you wanted to find the string *GAG*, this algorithm creates a finite state machine where the first node represents a starting state where no characters of the string have been found yet.

The second node represents finding the first letter, *G*; the third node represents finding the second letter, *A (GA)*; and the fourth node represents finding the final letter, *G (GAG)*, as shown in Figure 3-6.

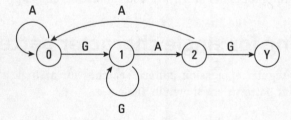

Searching for the string GAG

| G | A | A | G | G | A | G | A | A |

FIGURE 3-6:
A finite state machine consists of nodes and arrows.

After this algorithm creates a finite state machine for the target string, it examines each character in the search string. In this example, the search string is *GAAGGAGAA*.

Initially, the algorithm starts at node 0. The first character it finds is the letter *G*, so it moves to node 1. The second character it finds is the letter *A*, so it moves to node 2. However, the third character it finds is the letter *A*, so it starts back at node 0 again. (The algorithm would jump back to the starting state for any character that does not represent the third character it's looking for, such as *G*.)

The fourth character it finds is the letter *G*, so it moves back to node 1. The fifth character it finds is also the letter *G*, so it stays at node 1. The sixth character that it finds is the letter *A*, so now it moves to node 2. The seventh character that it finds is the letter *G*, so it moves to the last node, which signals a match has been found.

TECHNICAL STUFF

This algorithm is commonly used in Internet search engines, such as Google and Yahoo!

Searching with Regular Expressions

The finite automaton algorithm is the basis for a special text-searching technique known as *regular expressions* (sometimes abbreviated as *RegEx*). Instead of writing your own code to implement a finite automaton search algorithm, you can use regular expressions that are built in to many languages (such as Perl and PHP) or added as libraries (such as Java and .NET languages like C# and Visual Basic).

The basic idea behind regular expressions is to search not just for specific strings but also for patterns. This provides greater flexibility because you may not always know exactly what you want to find. For example, a normal search algorithm doesn't find a string unless you know the entire string you want to find, such as the last name of *Smith*. If you only know some of the characters of a last name (such as searching for *Smith* or *Smyth*), you can use regular expressions instead.

Searching for single character patterns

The simplest regular expression pattern searches for a single character. Some single character patterns are shown in Table 3-1.

Suppose you want to search for a string that begins with the letters *c* or *f*. To specify specific characters, you can define your own set, like this:

```
[cf]at
```

TABLE 3-1

Single Pattern Regular Expressions

Pattern Character	What It Finds	Example	Find
. (period)	Any single character	s.m	sum sam
\w	Any letter or number	\wats	cats 8cats
\W	Any character except a letter or number	213\W	213- 213@
\d	Any digit from 0 to 9	\d\d\d-1234	597-1234 409-1234
\D	Any character except a digit from 0 to 9	W\D9-1234	WP9-1234 W$9-1234

This regular expression finds strings, such as *cat* and *fat* but not *rat*. Sometimes it may be easier to define which characters you *don't* want rather than the ones you do want. In that case, you can use the ^ character in a set to define which characters you don't want, like this:

    [^rht]oss

This finds any four-character strings that end with *oss* except for *ross*, *hoss*, and *toss*. The ^rht expression tells the computer to match any characters except for *r*, *h*, and *t*.

TECHNICAL STUFF

In addition to matching individual characters, regular expressions can match ranges of characters, such as all lowercase letters from *c* to *z* (like this: [a-z]) or all uppercase letters from *C* to *G* (like this: [C-G]).

Searching for multiple character patterns

If you want to search for multiple characters, you could use a single character pattern several times. For example, to find a three-number string, you could use this regular expression pattern:

    \d\d\d

However, if you want to find a string consisting of 100 numbers, typing **\d** 100 times is impractical. If you need to search for a string multiple times and the specific number of patterns isn't important, you can specify multiple patterns with either the * or + symbol.

Both symbols appear directly after a single-character pattern, such as \d* or \d+. The * symbol looks for zero or more instances of the pattern, whereas the + symbol looks for one or more instances of the pattern. So, \d*123 finds the strings *9123*, *899123*, and *123*, but \d+123 finds only the *9123* and *899123* strings.

The * and + symbols can also work with single character sets, like this:

```
[rht]*oss
```

This searches for any string that ends with *oss* and contains zero or more of the *r, h,* or *t* characters, such as *oss, thtrtoss,* and *tthrrhhhhhtoss.*

Searching for alternate patterns

If you want to find the names *John Smith* and *Mary Smith,* you could search twice. However, a simple solution is to search for both patterns at the same time with the alternation operator (|), like this:

```
John Smith|Mary Smith
```

This regular expression tells the computer to find either the string *John Smith* or the string *Mary Smith.* You can combine the alternation operator with any pattern, like this:

```
[rht]*oss|\d+-1234
```

This regular expression finds strings, such as *rthrross* and *5-1234.*

TECHNICAL
STUFF

Every programming language implements regular expressions slightly differently, so the examples shown here may not work in your favorite programming language without modification.

Searching Phonetically

Regular expressions can make it easy to find strings when you know only part of the characters to find. However, sometimes you may know the pronunciation of a string you want to find, but you aren't sure of the exact spelling. Trying to find the word *elephant* with a regular expression of `elefa\w*` doesn't work if you don't realize that the letters *ph* in elephant makes an *f* sound. To search strings phonetically, use a phonetic algorithm, such as the Soundex algorithm.

TECHNICAL
STUFF

The Soundex algorithm was actually patented in 1918 by Margaret O'Dell and Robert C. Russell. This algorithm is based on dividing spoken speech into six phonetic classifications based on where you put your lips and tongue to make sounds.

Basically, the Soundex algorithm converts each string into an alphanumeric code that begins with the first letter of the string. So, if you had the name *Harry*, the Soundex algorithm might convert that name into the alphanumeric code H600 by following these steps:

1. Capitalize all letters in the string.

2. Retain the first letter of the word.

3. Change all occurrences of the following letters to *0* (zero): A, E, I, O, U, H, W, Y.

4. Replace any letters with the following numbers:

   - 1 = B, F, P, V

   - 2 = C, G, J, K, Q, S, X, Z

   - 3 = D, T

   - 4 = L

   - 5 = M, N

   - 6 = R

5. Replace all pairs of identical digits with a single digit, such as replacing *66* with just *6*.

6. Remove all zeros from the string.

7. Pad the string with trailing zeros so the entire Soundex code consists of the following format:

```
<uppercase letter> <digit> <digit> <digit>
```

Table 3-2 shows how the Soundex algorithm calculates identical Soundex codes for the strings *Harry* and *Hairy*.

If you had the string *Harry* stored in a file, the Soundex algorithm would convert that string into the H600 code. Now if you searched for the string *Hairy* with the Soundex algorithm, the computer would convert *Hairy* into the Soundex code H600 and then find the same H600 code stored at the string *Harry*, thus finding a matching string phonetically.

TECHNICAL STUFF

Phonetic algorithms are used in spellcheckers. The algorithm calculates a code for each misspelled word and then matches that code to correctly spelled words that have the same phonetic code. There are also specialized algorithms to handle other languages such as the Daitch–Mokotoff Soundex algorithm, which better matches surnames of Slavic and Germanic origin.

TABLE 3-2

Calculating a Soundex Code

Soundex Algorithm Step	String #1 (Harry)	String #2 (Hairy)
1	HARRY	HAIRY
2	H	H
3	H0RR0	H00R0
4	H0660	H0060
5	H060	H060
6	H6	H6
7	H600	H600

String-searching algorithms must examine every character, so the only way to speed up an algorithm is to simplify how it examines a string of text. Paradoxically, string-searching algorithms often run faster by organizing text in a specific way and then searching that method of organization rather than the actual text itself, which is how the Shift Or and Soundex algorithms work. As a general rule, the faster the string-searching algorithm, the harder and more complicated it is to implement.

Chapter **4**

Data Compression Algorithms

The main idea behind data compression is to shrink information. Not only does compressed data take up less storage space, but it also takes less time to transfer.

There are two types of data compression algorithms: lossless and lossy.

With *lossless compression*, the algorithm can compress the data without losing any information, which is used for archiving and compressing multiple files into a single file, such as a ZIP archive. Think of lossless compression as a way to pack existing data more efficiently, like refolding clothes to make them fit in a suitcase.

With *lossy compression*, the algorithm actually loses some information to compress data. Typically, this lost information isn't noticed anyway. The most common examples of lossy compression involve MP3 audio files and video files. When compressing audio, the MP3 standard throws out the audio parts that the human ear can't distinguish. When compressing video, compression algorithms toss out colors that the human eye doesn't notice. By throwing out information, lossy compression algorithms can save space, much like throwing away clothes to make packing the remaining clothes in a suitcase easier.

Because lossy compression throws out data, it can compress the same data much smaller than lossless compression. However, lossy compression has only limited use. You wouldn't want to use lossy compression when storing documents because you can't afford to lose any data, for example. If you absolutely must preserve data, use lossless compression. If you can afford to lose some data in exchange for tighter compression, use lossy compression.

Lossless Data Compression Algorithms

The basic idea behind lossless data compression is to find a way to pack data in a smaller space more efficiently without losing any of the data in the process. To do this, lossless data compression algorithms are typically optimized for specific data, such as text, audio, or video, although the general principles remain the same no matter what type of data the algorithm is compressing.

Run-length encoding

The simplest lossless data compression algorithm is *run-length encoding* (RLE). Basically, this method looks for redundancy and replaces any redundant data with a much shorter code instead. Suppose you had the following 17-character string:

WWWBBWWWWBBBBWWWW

RLE looks for redundant data and condenses it into a 10-character string, like this:

3W2B4W4B4W

The number in front of each letter identifies how many characters the code replaced, so in this example, the first two characters, 3W represents WWW, 2B represents BB, 4W represents WWWW, and so on.

TECHNICAL STUFF

RLE is used by fax machines because most images consist of mainly white space with occasional black areas that represent letters or drawings.

The Burrows–Wheeler transform algorithm

One problem with RLE is that it works best when repetitive characters appear grouped together. With a string, like WBWBWB#, RLE can't compress anything because no groups of W and B characters are bunched together. (However, a smart version of the RLE algorithm notices the two-character repetitive string WB and encodes the string as 3(WB)#, which would tell the computer to repeat the two-character pattern of WB three times.)

When redundant characters appear scattered, RLE can be made more efficient by first transforming the data to group identical characters together and then use RLE to compress the data. That's the idea behind the Burrows–Wheeler transform (BWT) algorithm, developed by Michael Burrows and David Wheeler.

The BWT algorithm must use a character that marks the end of the data, such as the # symbol. Then the BWT algorithm works in three steps:

1. It rotates text through all possible combinations, as shown in the Rotate column of Table 4-1.

In Table 4-1, the last character repetitively moves to the front of the string.

2. It sorts each line alphabetically, as shown in the Sort column of Table 4-1.

3. It outputs the final column of the sorted list, which takes the last character and copies it into the Output column of Table 4-1.

TABLE 4-1

Rotating and Sorting Data

Rotate	Sort	Output
ABACAB#	ABACAB#	#
#ABACAB	AB#ABAC	C
B#ABACA	ACAB#AB	B
AB#ABAC	BACAB#A	A
CAB#ABA	B#ABACA	A
ACAB#AB	CAB#ABA	A
BACAB#A	#ABACAB	B

In this example, the BWT algorithm transforms the string ABACAB# into #CBAAAB.

At this point, the BWT algorithm hasn't compressed any data but merely rearranged the data to group identical characters together; the BWT algorithm has rearranged the data to make the RLE algorithm more efficient. RLE can now convert the #CBAAAB string into #CB3AB, thus compressing the overall data (the three As).

After compressing data, you'll eventually need to uncompress that same data. Uncompressing this data (#CB3AB) creates the original BWT output of #CBAAAB, which contains all the characters of the original, uncompressed data but not in the right order. To retrieve the original order of the uncompressed data, the BWT algorithm repetitively goes through two steps, as shown in Figure 4-1.

Add (#1)	Sort (#1)	Add (#2)	Sort (#2)
#	A	#A	AB
C	A	CA	AB
C	A	BA	AC
A	B	AB	BA
A	B	AB	B#
A	C	AC	CA
B	#	#	#A

Add (#3)	Sort (#3)	Add (#4)	Sort (#4)
#AB	ABA	#ABA	ABAC
CAB	AB#	CAB#	AB#A
BAC	ACA	BACA	ACAB
ABA	BAC	ABAC	BACA
AB#	B#A	AB#A	B#AB
ACA	CAB	ACAB	CAB#
B#A	#AB	B#AB	#ABA

Add (#5)	Sort (#5)	Add (#6)	Sort (#6)
#ABAC	ABACA	#ABACA	ABACAB
CAB#A	AB#AB	CAB#AB	AB#ABA
BACAB	ACAB#	BACAB#	ACABAC
ABACA	BACAB	ABACAB	BACAB#
AB#AB	B#ABA	AB#ABA	B#ABAC
ACAB#	CABAC	ACABAC	CAB#AB
B#ABA	#ABAC	B#ABAC	#ABACA

Add (#7)	Sort (#7)		
#ABACAB	ABACAB#	ABACAB#	ABACAB#
CAB#ABA	AB#ABAC	AB#ABAC	
BACABAC	ACAB#AB	ACAB#AB	
ABACAB#	BACABAC	BACABAC	
AB#ABAC	B#ABACA	B#ABACA	
ACAB#AB	CAB#ABA	CAB#ABA	
B#ABACA	#ABACAB	#ABACAB	

| | | Find the line with the end of the data character at the end | Original data retrieved |

FIGURE 4-1: Reconstructing the original data from the BWT transformation.

The BWT algorithm works in reverse by adding the original BWT output (#CBAAAB) and then sorting the lines repetitively a number of times equal to the length of the string. So, retrieving the original data from a 7-character string takes seven adding and sorting steps.

The algorithm starts with the initial output string (#CBAAAB) and sorts it in alphabetical order. Each successive add operation simply places the same output string (#CBAAAB) at the front of the sorted list.

After the final add-and-sort step, the BWT algorithm looks for the only line that has the end-of-data character (#) as the last character, which identifies the original, uncompressed data. The BWT algorithm is simple to understand and implement, which makes it easy to use for speeding up ordinary RLE.

Dictionary encoding

RLE is a simple algorithm that works well with redundant characters grouped together but doesn't work as well with redundant data scattered throughout. An alternative to RLE is dictionary coding. The basic idea behind *dictionary coding* is to replace large data chunks with much smaller data chunks. Suppose you had the following text:

See Dick. See Jane.

You could replace the redundant text *See* with a simple code, such as 1, and create a new string:

1 Dick. 1 Jane.

Now you could replace *Dick* with one code and *Jane* with another code, such as 2 and 3 respectively, to create a compressed version, like this:

1 2. 1 3.

Uncompressing this data means replacing the codes with the actual data, using a dictionary. Each code refers to the actual data, so looking up 1 retrieves the *See* string, 2 retrieves *Dick*, and 3 retrieves *Jane*, as shown in Figure 4-2.

If you know the data you want to compress ahead of time, such as condensing the entire contents of an encyclopedia on a DVD, you can optimize the dictionary to create the smallest codes, which represent the most common data chunks, such as the word *the*. In most cases, you don't know the data to compress ahead of time, so you need an algorithm that can analyze data, create a dictionary on the fly, and then compress data using that dictionary. Three popular dictionary encoding algorithms include LZ77, LZ78, and LZW.

FIGURE 4-2:
Uncompressing
data requires
using a dictionary
to replace codes
with actual data.

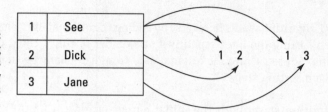

The LZ77 algorithm

The LZ77 algorithm was created by two computer scientists — Abraham Lempel and Jakob Ziv — who first published their algorithm in 1977 (hence, the name LZ77). The LZ77 algorithm works by looking for repetitive data. Instead of storing this repetitive data in a separate dictionary, the LZ77 remembers the location of this data in the original file.

When the algorithm finds this same data stored somewhere else, it removes the data (compressing the overall information) and substitutes a pointer to the previously recognized data, as shown in Figure 4-3.

FIGURE 4-3:
The LZ77
algorithm
replaces
redundant data
with pointers.

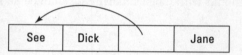

Because pointers take up less space than the actual data, the LZ77 algorithm compresses information. The more redundant the data, the more efficient the compression.

The LZ78 algorithm

The LZ77 algorithm stores redundant data directly in the compressed data itself. To improve compression, the same computer scientists developed a variation of the LZ77 algorithm — the LZ78 algorithm.

The LZ78 algorithm removes all redundant data and stores it in a separate dictionary. Then the algorithm substitutes the redundant data with much smaller codes stored in the dictionary. By removing this data, the LZ78 algorithm can compress data even further than the LZ77 algorithm.

To uncompress this data, the computer follows each code to the dictionary to retrieve the appropriate data chunk.

The LZW algorithm

The LZW algorithm gets its name from Terry Welch, who created his own variation of the LZ78 algorithm, dubbed the LZW algorithm. The LZW algorithm works by creating a dictionary, just like the LZ78 algorithm. But whereas the LZ78 algorithm creates a dictionary of codes that consist of the same size, the LZW algorithm creates a dictionary of codes of different sizes.

When compressing text, the LZW algorithm starts out by creating a dictionary of individual letters. Assuming all uppercase letters, A would be represented by 1, B by 2, and so on. However, substituting a number for a single character isn't likely to save much space, so the LZW algorithm continues examining the text for repetitive multiple-character strings to store as a number, such as AB, ABC, ABCD, and so on.

Like most compression algorithms, the LZW algorithm works best on data that contains redundant information, like this:

IAMSAMSAMIAM#

First, the LZW algorithm creates a dictionary of single characters represented by numbers. *I* gets stored as 9, *A* as 1, *M* as 13, and *S* as 19.

When the LZW algorithm finds the second letter *A*, it doesn't encode the letter *A* all over again because it has done that once already. Instead, the algorithm encodes the next two characters, which happen to be *AM*, and assigns this two-character combination to the next available number, which is 27. (Numbers 1 through 26 are assigned to the individual letters of the alphabet.)

When the algorithm sees the letter *S* again, it encodes the next two-character string, *SA*, as the number 28. Then it finds the letter *M* again, so it encodes the next two-character string, *MI*, as the number 29. Finally, it sees the letter *A* again, so it checks the next two-character string, which is *AM*. Because the algorithms already encoded *AM* before (as the number 27), the algorithm expands to encode the three-character string, *AM#*, as the number 30, as shown in Figure 4-4.

At the beginning of data, the LZW algorithm isn't very efficient because it's slowly creating its dictionary. When the algorithm's dictionary grows with larger amounts of redundant data, it can replace these large chunks of redundant data with small number codes.

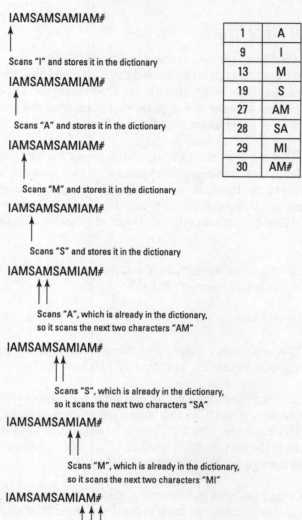

1	A
9	I
13	M
19	S
27	AM
28	SA
29	MI
30	AM#

IAMSAMSAMIAM#

Scans "I" and stores it in the dictionary

IAMSAMSAMIAM#

Scans "A" and stores it in the dictionary

IAMSAMSAMIAM#

Scans "M" and stores it in the dictionary

IAMSAMSAMIAM#

Scans "S" and stores it in the dictionary

IAMSAMSAMIAM#

Scans "A", which is already in the dictionary,
so it scans the next two characters "AM"

IAMSAMSAMIAM#

Scans "S", which is already in the dictionary,
so it scans the next two characters "SA"

IAMSAMSAMIAM#

Scans "M", which is already in the dictionary,
so it scans the next two characters "MI"

IAMSAMSAMIAM#

Scans "A" and "AM", which is already in the dictionary,
so it scans the next three characters "AM#"

FIGURE 4-4:
The LZW algorithm stores increasingly larger strings as numbers.

TECHNICAL
STUFF

The LZW algorithm is used to compress graphic images stored in the Graphics Interchange Format (GIF). Originally, this algorithm was patented in 1985 and the patent holder, Unisys, demanded royalties from software companies that sold programs that could create GIF files. This patent problem caused computer scientists to create and promote an alternate graphics format — Portable Network Graphics (PNG). Although the PNG format has largely replaced the GIF file format, the GIF format is still used mostly for storing animation. Use of the GIF format is now legal because the LZW patent expired on June 20, 2003.

Lossy Data Compression

Lossy data compression shrinks data through a combination of packing data more efficiently (like lossless compression) and throwing out chunks of data that aren't considered crucial. As a result, lossy compression is used less often for text (where losing data is unacceptable because a single missing word or number can alter the entire meaning of the text) and more often for audio, graphics, and video.

Basically, lossy data compression reduces the size of data much more than lossless compression because lossy data compression can pack data more efficiently, like lossless compression, while also saving additional space by throwing out small chunks of data that aren't missed anyway.

REMEMBER

Most lossy compression methods use lossless compression algorithms in addition to throwing out unnecessary data.

For example, the human eye and ear can only distinguish a fixed range of colors and sounds. So, lossy compression simply removes colors and audio that most people don't notice. When done selectively, compressed audio, graphic, or video can be indistinguishable from the original, but at a certain point, lossy compression eventually degrades the original to an unacceptable level, as shown in Figure 4-5.

FIGURE 4-5: Comparison of compressed graphic images.

TECHNICAL STUFF

A specific method for compressing audio or video files is a *codec*, short for compressor/decompressor. Some popular audio codecs include MP3, AAC (Advanced Audio Coding), and WMA (Windows Media Audio). Some popular video codecs include AV1, WMV (Windows Media Video), and MPEG-4.

The trick behind lossy compression is knowing which data can be removed without degrading quality too far. In an audio file, such as an MP3 file, lossy compression throws out the audio portion that's beyond the human hearing range. In graphics, an image may consist of three shades of blue that are so close as to be nearly indistinguishable. That's when the algorithm strips out the two least-used shades of blue and replaces them with the most frequently used shade of blue. This saves space because repetition of identical data makes it easier for compression algorithms to reduce the space needed to store this information in a file.

Video basically saves successive still images, so lossy compression can save space by looking for identical backgrounds between video frames. Instead of storing the same background multiple times, lossy compression stores the background only once and uses that identical image multiple times. Because the same background may appear in several video frames, this technique can shrink the size of a video considerably.

Another way to compress data is to alter the bit depth. *Bit depth* defines how many bits are used to store data, such as 96-bit or 160-bit. The more bits used, the greater the quality but the larger the file size. The fewer bits used, the less storage space required and the less data saved, reducing the file size. That's why a 96-bit MP3 file is smaller than the same file saved as a 160-bit MP3 file. The 96-bit file can't store as much data as the 160-bit file, which means lower audio quality than the 160-bit file.

When compressing a file, lossy compression may use constant bit rate (CBR) or variable bit rate (VBR) compression. CBR reduces the bit rate uniformly throughout the entire file and makes compression faster. Unfortunately, this also means that quieter portions of an audio file get compressed at the same rate as noisier parts of the audio file, resulting in less-than-optimum compression.

VBR alters the bit rate, depending on the complexity of the data. This improves quality but at the cost of a slower compression time. For even higher quality, some compression algorithms offer two-pass VBR, which means the program analyzes the file twice to get the maximum quality and the smallest file size possible, but at the expense of much slower compression speed.

All types of compression are always a trade-off. With lossless compression, the trade-off is between size and speed. The smaller you want to compress the file, the longer it takes. With lossy compression, the trade-off is mostly between size and quality. The smaller the file size, the lower the overall quality. Both lossless and lossy compression algorithms are necessary, depending on which type better suits your needs.

Chapter **5**

Encryption Algorithms

E ncryption involves scrambling information, or *plaintext*, and converting it into another format — *ciphertext* — essentially, turning ordered data into seemingly random gibberish. By encrypting information, you can keep data information out of the hands of other people, which can be useful for sending coded messages for military use, sending credit card information over the Internet to online shopping websites, or just hiding your personal documents from the prying eyes of family members, coworkers, or strangers.

How Encryption Works

The simplest form of encryption is a *substitution cipher,* which basically replaces each letter with a specific symbol, such as another letter. A simple algorithm, called the *Caesar cipher,* is a substitution cipher that replaces one letter with another letter from the alphabet a fixed distance away, such as replacing the letter *A* with the letter *Z,* the letter *B* with the letter *A,* the letter *C* with the letter *B,* and so on.

TECHNICAL STUFF

In the 1950s and 1960s, Sicilian Mafia boss Bernardo Provenzano wrote notes to his henchmen using a modified form of the Caesar Cipher. The Caesar Cipher was easily cracked by the police, so they were able to read his messages and arrest many of his collaborators.

In this case, each letter gets replaced by the previous letter in the alphabet, like this:

I AM HOT

Replacing the letter I with the letter H, the letter A with the letter Z, and so on creates the following ciphertext:

H ZL GNS

This information may be scrambled, but after someone discovers that each letter in the ciphertext actually represents the next letter in the alphabet, this simple substitution cipher can be cracked easily. When an encryption method can be broken easily, it's *weak* encryption. If an encryption method can't be broken easily, it's *strong* encryption.

The key to deciphering the substitution cipher is recognizing both the method it's using (replacing one letter with another) and the specific way it implements that method (replacing each letter with the previous letter in the alphabet). A slightly more-complicated substitution cipher might replace each letter with the third letter from the current letter. So, the letter *A* would be replaced by the letter *D*, the letter *B* by the letter *E*, and so on. In this case, the method is the same, but the implementation is slightly different while being only marginally harder to decipher.

Although substitution ciphers are easy to implement, they're also easy to break. After you know to replace a letter in the ciphertext by another letter that's shifted by a specific distance in the alphabet (such as the third letter), you can easily break the code. One way to avoid this problem is to use a *one-time pad*, which consists of a series of random numbers that tell how far to shift the next letter in a message. So, a one-time pad might contain three random numbers, like this:

2 7 3

The first number, 2, tells the algorithm to shift the first letter of the text by two letters. So, if the first three letters of the message are SAM, the first letter, *S*, would get replaced by the second letter from *S* in the alphabet, which is *U*.

The second number, 7, tells the algorithm to shift the second letter by seven letters. So, the letter *A* gets replaced by the seventh letter down, which is *H*. Finally, the third number, 3, tells the algorithm to shift the third letter by the third letter down, so the letter *M* gets replaced by the letter *P*. Now the entire message, SAM, gets encrypted as the ciphertext UHP.

The one-time pad gets its name because the random series of numbers are used only once. Now it's virtually impossible for anyone to discover how the letters are substituted because the replacement letters don't follow a recognizable pattern. The only way to decipher this ciphertext is to get a copy of the one-time pad.

Of course, the one-time pad has its drawbacks. To work, both parties need a copy of the same one-time pad. If you could transfer a copy of the one-time pad securely, you might as well transfer the message you're delivering instead. Also, one-time pads can be used only once. If they're used more than once, someone can eventually guess the random pattern of letters.

Even worse is that a one-time pad must specify how far to shift each letter in a message. If you're encrypting a message consisting of 1,000 letters, you need a one-time pad to specify how to shift all 1,000 letters. If you're encrypting a message consisting of 10,000 letters, you need a one-time pad that specifies how to shift all 10,000 letters.

Given these problems, one-time pads are generally impractical for normal use. A slight variation of the one-time pad is the use of a password. A *password* acts like a one-time pad; instead of defining how to alter each individual character in a message, the password determines how to scramble data. Even if you know how data is being scrambled, you won't know how to read the scrambled data without knowing the right password. Passwords are simply smaller and more convenient versions of one-time pads.

The Basics of Encryption

Encryption involves three parts:

>> The encryption algorithm

>> The implementation of the encryption algorithm

>> The length of the encryption key

The encryption algorithm defines the specific method for scrambling data. Some people try to invent their own, obscure encryption algorithms under the theory that if no one knows how the algorithm works, they won't know how to break the encryption. This theory is *security through obscurity,* and it usually fails because a single flaw can leave the encryption vulnerable, much like how locking a bank is useless if a single door is left unlocked. Because it's nearly impossible for a single person to spot all possible flaws in an encryption algorithm, most encryption algorithms are published for anyone to see.

The idea behind publishing an encryption algorithm is to let as many people as possible examine an encryption algorithm for flaws. The more people examining an encryption algorithm, the more likely any flaws will be discovered and patched before people start using the algorithm to encrypt critical information.

Two common ways to encrypt data involve substitution and permutation. *Substitution* involves replacing data with another chunk of data. The group of algorithms that substitutes data is typically called a *substitution box* or *S-box*. *Permutation* involves rearranging bits of data, usually represented as a binary number. The group of algorithms that performs this permutation is typically called a *permutation box* or *P-box*. Most encryption algorithms use a combination of S-boxes and P-boxes to scramble data.

After an encryption algorithm is deemed mathematically sound and secure, the second step is correctly implementing that algorithm in a particular programming language. Because there are virtually millions of different ways to accomplish the same task in any programming language, the encryption algorithm may be secure, but the implementation of the encryption algorithm may not be secure.

After you have a valid encryption algorithm that's been implemented properly in a particular programming language, the final step to creating a secure encryption algorithm is the key length used to scramble the data.

In a simple substitution cipher, the key length could be considered the value 1 because it offers only one way of replacing letters with another letter, such as shifting each letter by a fixed position in the alphabet. To encrypt a 1,000-character message, a one-time pad would need 1,000 different random numbers for shifting each letter in the message, so the key length could be considered 1,000.

The key length is crucial because the details of an encryption algorithm are often published for anyone to examine. As a result, the security of most encryption algorithms rests solely on the key length used for the password. You don't need to create a long password of 1,000 or more characters; the encryption algorithm needs to use more bits of data to store any password whether the password consists of 1 character or 100.

REMEMBER

The length of the password simply makes it harder for other people to guess. A one-letter password means someone needs only 26 guesses. A 100-letter password forces someone to try all possible combinations of letters, making guessing much more difficult. The key length simply defines the amount of space used to store the password but doesn't specify the physical length of the password. That means someone can still use a weak one-letter password no matter how big the algorithm specifies the key length could be.

As a simple analogy, think of encryption key lengths like the physical key to your front door. A physical key pushes up rods that drop down to prevent a doorknob from turning. The more rods used, the harder it is to pick the lock. The fewer rods used, the easier it is to pick the lock.

In the same way, encryption keys are used to hold passwords. The shorter the key length (measured in bits), the fewer possibilities exist and the weaker the encryption, making it more vulnerable to being broken. The longer the encryption key length, the less likely the encryption will break.

No encryption is considered unbreakable, but the goal of every encryption algorithm is to make unscrambling data *so difficult* that the time needed to read the encrypted message takes too long. Typically an encrypted message might take the world's fastest computer a million years to break, which effectively makes the encryption "unbreakable."

TECHNICAL STUFF

At one time, a 56-bit key was considered unbreakable, but with today's computers, the smallest secure key length is 128 bits, although many people prefer using 256-bit or 512-bit keys for added security.

Encryption algorithms generally fall into two categories — stream and block ciphers. A *stream cipher* encrypts data one item at a time, such as individual characters in a message. A *block cipher* encrypts data in fixed chunks or blocks. So, instead of encrypting individual characters, a block cipher might encrypt text in ten-character blocks.

THE 56-BIT KEY OF THE DES ALGORITHM

In the late 1960s, IBM created an encryption algorithm dubbed LUCIFER, which used a 128-bit key. When IBM decided to release LUCIFER as a commercial product, the National Security Agency (NSA) asked IBM to reduce the key length from 128 bits to 56 bits. Then the U.S. government declared IBM's LUCIFER encryption algorithm as the new government standard encryption algorithm, dubbed the Data Encryption Standard (DES).

Mathematicians suspect that the NSA reduced the key length to make DES encryption easier to crack. To prove the security of DES encryption, a company called RSA Security offered a contest challenging anyone to crack DES encryption. In 1997, a group of computers, connected over the Internet, finally managed to crack a DES encrypted message, proving once and for all that DES encryption was no longer secure.

Generally, stream ciphers are used when encrypting data of unknown length, such as voice messages, whereas block ciphers are used to encrypt data of fixed lengths, such as a file.

Stream ciphers

A stream cipher borrows the features of the one-time pad. Whereas a one-time pad must be as long as the message being encrypted, a stream cipher uses smaller keys of fixed lengths, such as 128 bits. Another major difference is that a one-time pad consists of truly random numbers, whereas a stream cipher generates a list of random numbers based on a *key* (password). Computers can't generate truly random numbers, so computer-generated random numbers are often called *pseudorandom numbers.*

TECHNICAL STUFF

A computer uses an algorithm to generate random numbers, but these aren't true random numbers because the algorithm generates the same list of random numbers over and over again. To alter the way computers generate random numbers, computers use a starting value, or *seed.* The computer uses this seed to generate a list of numbers; so by giving the computer different values for its seed, a computer can generate a different list of random numbers. Because this list always changes based on the seed value, any computer-generated random numbers are pseudorandom numbers.

HACKING A SLOT MACHINE

The fact that computers can't generate truly random numbers allowed computer hackers to hack the newest computerized slot machines used in many casinos. The slot machine would seed its random number generator with a value and then use this list of pseudorandom numbers to determine payoffs.

Hackers soon discovered that certain slot machines used the same seed value every time, so the generated list of pseudorandom numbers could be predicted. Then they used a handheld computer that generated that same list of pseudorandom numbers as the slot machine. By knowing which pseudorandom number the slot machine would use next, the hackers could determine when the slot machine would hit a jackpot.

So, all the hackers did was watch a certain slot machine and wait for someone else to churn through all the losing pseudorandom numbers and leave. When the slot machine was close to a winning pseudorandom number, the hackers would only have to put a few coins into the slot machine before they'd hit a jackpot. Then they'd leave and wait for someone else to churn through the next batch of losing pseudorandom numbers before playing that same slot machine and hitting another jackpot.

A stream cipher uses a key to generate a list of pseudorandom numbers. Then it uses this generated list of pseudorandom numbers to encrypt each character by replacing it with a different character based on this pseudorandom number, as shown in Figure 5-1.

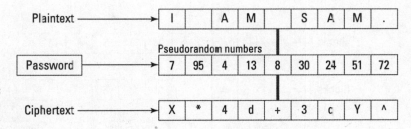

FIGURE 5-1:
How a stream cipher works.

Stream ciphers use two different methods to generate a list of pseudorandom numbers:

» A **synchronous stream cipher** generates pseudorandom numbers independent of the plaintext data.

» A **self-synchronizing stream cipher** generates pseudorandom numbers based on part of the plaintext.

Stream ciphers are often fast and simple to implement. Stream ciphers encrypt data in a continuous stream instead of waiting to receive a block of data. That's why stream ciphers can be convenient for real-time communication such as encryption for wireless communication.

TECHNICAL
STUFF

The most popular stream cipher is RC4, named after its creator, Ron Rivest. RC4 is used in the two wireless encryption standards — Wired Equivalent Privacy (WEP) and Wi-Fi Protected Access (WPA), both of which are commonly used to protect wireless Internet connections.

Block ciphers

Block ciphers encrypt data in chunks, although you can think of a stream cipher as a block cipher with each character representing a single data chunk. A typical block size is 64 or 128 bits. Because most data doesn't fit into neat 64- or 128-bit blocks, a block cipher must pad the last chunk of data with information, such as zeroes.

Electronic codebook (ECB)

After a block cipher divides plaintext into blocks, it has several different ways to encrypt that data. The simplest way to encrypt data is to encrypt each block of data separately with the same key, which is the *electronic codebook method,* as shown in Figure 5-2.

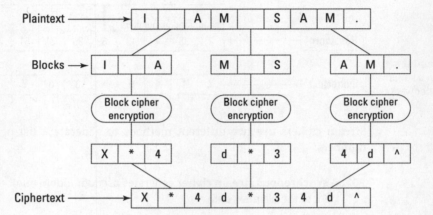

FIGURE 5-2:
The electronic codebook encrypts blocks of data separately with the same key.

Encrypting with the electronic codebook method is simple and fast, but because it uses the same key to encrypt data, it tends to encrypt redundant data in identical chunks. So, the message I am Sam. Sam I am might create two blocks of encrypted data that would look nearly identical, such as X*4d*34d^ and 34d*X*4d^. A cursory examination of these two encrypted blocks can reveal that X represents the letter *I,* * represents a space, 4d represents *am,* 3 represents *S,* and ^ represents a *period.* The same input generates the same output, which makes cracking the encryption much easier.

Cipher-block chaining (CBC)

The ideal encryption algorithm takes identical data and scrambles it in two different ways to avoid revealing any redundant data. The idea behind the cipher-block chaining (CBC) method is to use the encrypted output from one block as input to encrypt a second block. Because the output from one encrypted block directly affects the encryption of another block, identical plaintext data gets converted into completely different ciphertext, as shown in Figure 5-3.

HASH FUNCTIONS

One type of algorithm commonly associated with encryption is a *hash function*. A hash function takes data as input and, based on the size and content of that data, calculates a unique mathematical value. This value isn't used as part of the encryption but as a way to authenticate that certain data hasn't been altered.

Hash functions are often used when downloading files. A website might offer a file for download and display its hash value. Now if you download that file and run that file through the hash function, you should get the same hash value. If you get a different value, the file you downloaded has been modified and is missing some information or has new information added. In encryption, hash functions can verify that an encrypted message hasn't been altered. If a file has been altered, it could mean the file simply got corrupted, or that someone tried to insert or remove data from the encrypted message, which means you shouldn't trust the validity of that message.

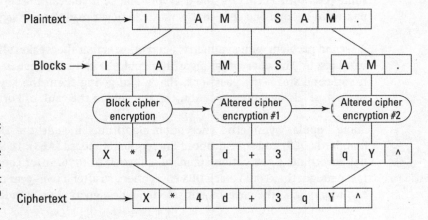

FIGURE 5-3: Cipher-block chaining uses the output from one block as the input for encrypting a second block.

Symmetric/Asymmetric Encryption Algorithms

The most common type of encryption algorithm is a *symmetric algorithm*, which uses the same password to encrypt and decrypt data. Basically, this means that the password that scrambles the data can also reverse the process and unscramble the data, as shown in Figure 5-4.

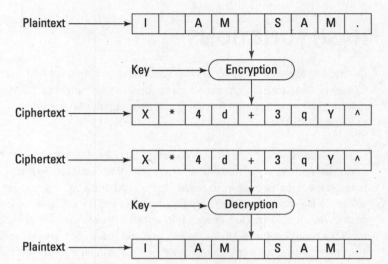

Plaintext ⟶ | I | | A | M | | S | A | M | . |

Key ⟶ (Encryption)

Ciphertext ⟶ | X | * | 4 | d | + | 3 | q | Y | ^ |

Ciphertext ⟶ | X | * | 4 | d | + | 3 | q | Y | ^ |

Key ⟶ (Decryption)

Plaintext ⟶ | I | | A | M | | S | A | M | . |

FIGURE 5-4:
A single password can encrypt and decrypt a message.

The biggest problem with symmetric encryption is that both parties need the same password to encrypt and decrypt data, so if you can't securely transfer the password to someone else, that person can never read the message.

A second problem with symmetric encryption is that the weakest link is the password itself. The encryption algorithm could be the strongest in the world, but if someone steals the password, that's like giving them the key to unlock the 10-foot-thick steel doors guarding all the gold in the vault of Fort Knox.

TECHNICAL STUFF

Some popular symmetric encryption algorithms include the Data Encryption Standard (DES) and the Advanced Encryption Standard (AES). DES was the original government encryption standard approved in 1976. After computers became fast enough, they could crack DES encryption, so after a five-year contest between cryptographers, the government selected a new encryption standard, AES.

Symmetric encryption is often called *private-key encryption* because both the sender and the receiver need an identical copy of the key to encrypt and decrypt a message. Another type of encryption algorithm is the *asymmetric* or *public-key encryption*. Unlike symmetric encryption, asymmetric encryption requires one key for the sender and another key for the receiver.

These two keys are the *public key* and the *private key*. You can make a million copies of your public key and give them out, but you want only one copy of your private key. If someone wants to send you a message, they need to encrypt a message with your public key. After someone encrypts a message with your public key, the only way to decrypt that message is to use your private key, as shown in Figure 5-5.

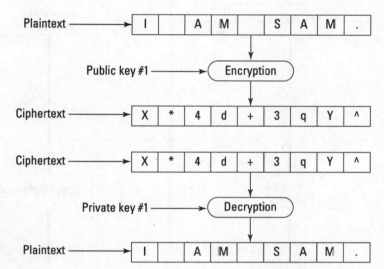

FIGURE 5-5: Public keys encrypt data, and private keys decrypt data.

In addition to encrypting with a public key and then decrypting with a private key, you can encrypt with a private key and decrypt with a public key. When you encrypt a message with your private key, that message can be decrypted only with your public key. Because you're the only person with a copy of your private key, the only possible way a message can be decrypted with your public key is if it was originally encrypted with your private key. (Unless, of course, someone steals your private key. In that case, they can mimic you online.)

Public-key and private-key encryption are commonly used together in programs, such as Pretty Good Privacy (PGP), that are designed for sending encrypted messages. You exchange a password using private-key encryption and send a message encrypted using this password. The receiver unlocks this password using their private key and then unlocks the actual message using the password, as shown in Figure 5-6.

The reason for using both private-key (symmetric) and public-key (asymmetric) encryption is that public-key encryption tends to run much slower than private-key encryption. That's because with public-key encryption, you need to encrypt data using the combination of the sender's private key with the receiver's public-key. With private-key encryption, you need only one key to encrypt data.

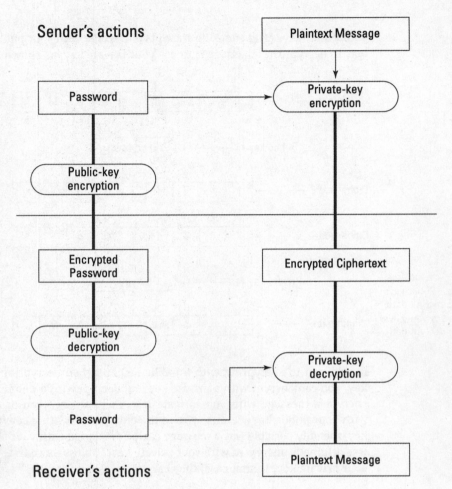

Sender's actions

Plaintext Message

Password → Private-key encryption

Public-key encryption

Encrypted Password

Encrypted Ciphertext

Public-key decryption

Private-key decryption

Password →

Plaintext Message

FIGURE 5-6:
Public-key and private-key encryption can work together.

Receiver's actions

TECHNICAL STUFF

Public-key encryption is used in Secure Sockets Layer (SSL) and its more secure replacement, Transport Layer Security (TLS), which is how you can connect to a secure shopping website and safely transfer your credit card numbers over the Internet. The shopping website basically gives your computer its public key to exchange a unique key known only by the website and your computer.

Using this unique key, you can encrypt any sensitive information (such as your credit card number) and send it securely over the Internet. Now the only one who can decrypt your credit card number is the shopping website holding the unique key.

HIDING IN PLAIN SIGHT WITH STEGANOGRAPHY

One unusual form of encryption involves hiding data within another chunk of data, such as hiding a text message inside an audio or graphic image. Hiding data within another form of data is *steganography*. The idea is that no one can read your messages if they can't find them in the first place.

Steganography works on the principle that data in audio, video, and graphic files can be removed without noticeably affecting the quality of the original file. After removing chunks of information from such a file, which leaves gaps in the original file, the next step is to insert the plaintext or ciphertext into these open gaps.

If you insert plaintext into an audio, video, or graphic file, anyone can read your message if they know how to find it. If you encrypt your message and then insert the ciphertext into a file, someone would need to know where to find your message and then know the password to decrypt that message. Steganography isn't necessarily a form of encryption so much as it's a way to keep anyone from knowing you're sending secret messages at all.

Cracking Encryption

Encryption works by scrambling data, but anything scrambled can always be unscrambled. What makes the difference between strong and weak encryption is how many possible ways exist to unscramble the encrypted data.

If only ten possible ways exist to scramble data, that's much easier to crack than a message that offers ten million different ways to scramble data. To unscramble data that offers ten possible ways of scrambling a message, you can just use a brute-force attack.

Brute-force attacks

Basically, a *brute-force attack* tries every possible combination of ways a message can be scrambled. Think of a combination lock that opens only if you align the right number. If the combination lock offers 36 numbers, you can use a brute-force attack and exhaustively try all 36 numbers until you find the one that opens the lock.

Now consider a more complicated combination lock that not only displays 36 numbers but forces you to choose three different numbers in the correct order. You can still exhaustively try every possible number combination, but the time needed to do this is likely more than most people are willing to take, which effectively makes the lock secure.

That's the same idea behind encryption. Every form of encryption can eventually be cracked with a brute-force attack, but the time needed to exhaustively try every possibility is too long. It's possible to crack even the toughest encryption algorithm with a brute-force attack, but you might need a room full of million-dollar supercomputers running 24 hours a day for the next million years to eventually crack the encryption. By making the costs in resources and time too high, encryption algorithms are essentially unbreakable through a brute-force attack alone.

A variation of the brute-force attack is the *Chinese lottery.* The idea is that if you gave each person in China (with its population of more than a billion people) a computer and assigned each computer a different range of brute-force attacks on the same encrypted data, eventually one of them would crack the encryption and, hence, "win" the lottery.

Instead of performing a brute-force attack sequentially, the Chinese lottery attack performs the same brute-force attack in parallel, drastically cutting down the time needed to crack the encryption.

A second improvement of the Chinese lottery attack involves reducing the cost of resources necessary to conduct the brute-force attack. A typical brute-force attack requires a fast computer to exhaustively search all possible combinations. The Chinese lottery attack requires a vast network of much slower and less expensive computers because each computer needs only to exhaustively brute-force attack a much smaller range of possibilities.

Although the Chinese lottery attack is mostly theoretical, it's possible for someone to write a computer worm that can spread and infect computers all over the world and conduct a brute-force attack on a problem. The worm that finally cracks the problem can then send its *winning ticket* (the cracked message) to the original programmer of the worm.

Dictionary attacks

A brute-force attack is the simplest encryption cracking method, but it's never the fastest. Because the strength of any encryption algorithm relies solely on the password used, it's often much simpler just to guess the password instead.

THE CHINESE LOTTERY AND BLOCKCHAINS

Cryptocurrencies, such as Bitcoin, rely on a blockchain, which consists of a series of records linked together in blocks. Each block uses a hash function to validate the contents of that block and link to the previous block. If someone tries to modify a block, it will create a different hash value, alerting others that the block has been altered. The link to the previous block prevents someone from inserting a new block of data into the blockchain. At any given time, there can be multiple copies of a blockchain but hash functions ensure that every copy contains the exact same information.

Maintaining the blockchain and creating new blocks takes time and effort, so Bitcoin dangles an incentive to people by offering them Bitcoins. To earn new Bitcoins, computers (called *miners*) must calculate a mathematical puzzle. The first computer that solves this mathematical puzzle gets rewarded with Bitcoins and that process extends the blockchain to hold more data.

Because earning (or mining) Bitcoins can be so lucrative, many people set up dedicated computers to solve the next mathematical puzzle. With millions of computers trying to solve the same mathematical puzzle, it's only a matter of time before one computer will solve it and get its Bitcoin reward.

To increase the chances of mining Bitcoins, many people join a pool of computers. Now if one computer in that pool solves the mathematical puzzle and earns Bitcoins, every computer in that same pool gets an equal share. By working together in computer pools, Bitcoin miners are using a variation of the Chinese lottery.

Most people use simple passwords that they can remember, such as *password*, *sex*, *love*, *123*, or names (such as the names of their pets or favorite movie stars). Because passwords can vary in length, a simple brute-force attack is impractical because not only do you need to exhaustively check all five-character passwords, but also all six-, seven-, eight-, nine-, and ten-character passwords.

A dictionary attack is a type of brute-force attack, but rather than try all possible character combinations, it tries the most common passwords. Besides trying the previously mentioned common passwords, like *love* and *123*, a dictionary attack tries common words from *Star Trek*, Shakespeare, sports, and popular culture.

Because many people use a common password along with an additional character, such as *password5*, a dictionary attack combines its dictionary with a brute-force attack by picking a common word and trying different variations of that word, such as adding a different character at the beginning or end of the password or spelling the password backward.

Think of a dictionary attack as a smarter and faster version of a brute-force attack. The odds of someone choosing a password, like *s&$k#*, is much less than someone choosing a password of *sonja*, which is why dictionary attacks are so often successful.

Plaintext and ciphertext attacks

The easiest way to defeat any form of encryption is to steal the original plaintext message. Although this lets you read a single message, it doesn't help you read any additional messages encrypted with the same password. However, after you have the plaintext version of a message along with the encrypted version of that same message, you may be able to deduce the password used to encrypt that message.

Comparing the plaintext version of a message with its encrypted version is a *plaintext attack.* Because it's rarely possible to retrieve the plaintext of an entire message, a more common code-breaking technique is to examine the ciphertext for patterns with *frequency analysis.*

The idea behind frequency analysis is that certain letters (such as *e*) or words (such as *and*) are more likely to appear in a message. A poor encryption algorithm encrypts the letter *e* and the word *and* with identical characters in different parts of the encrypted message. From this simple clue, it's possible to gradually deduce the encrypted symbols that represent the second-most-frequently used letters and words.

Although no form of encryption is unbreakable, the goal of every encryption algorithm is to resist all known forms of attack so as to make cracking the encryption unfeasible due to the lack of time or resources. As computers get faster and more powerful, today's encryption algorithms will only get weaker and easier to crack. By the time that occurs, mathematicians and computer scientists will have created newer and better encryption algorithms until those age and become easily broken all over again.

One serious threat to encryption is quantum computing, which can solve integer factorization much faster than traditional computers. Because factorization of prime numbers forms the basis of many encryption algorithms, finding a fast way to solve factorization means quantum computers could theoretically crack encryption faster and easier than ever before.

CODE CRACKING IN THE BATTLE OF MIDWAY

Cracking a code is pointless if you can't understand the message inside. During World War II, American code breakers broke the Japanese encryption, so they could read every message the Japanese military sent. Based on these cracked messages, the United States knew that the Japanese were planning a large-scale attack sometime around June 1942, but the big question was where?

According to the Japanese messages, the next target was *AF*. Some military analysts thought that AF represented Hawaii, while others feared that AF actually meant the Japanese were going to attack and invade the West Coast itself. However, military analysts soon suspected that AF really referred to a tiny island in the Pacific called Midway.

To verify their suspicions, the American commanders ordered the military base on Midway to send a plain, unencrypted message claiming that their water station had broken down. Soon afterward, the American code breakers intercepted a Japanese encrypted message stating that "AF was out of water." The Japanese never knew their encryption had been broken, and the Americans managed to trick them into revealing their intentions. Based on the knowledge that AF meant Midway, the American Navy was able to surprise and ambush the Japanese task force, effectively turning the tide in the Pacific.

5

Web Programming

Contents at a Glance

Chapter **1**

HyperText Markup Language

The language used to create every web page in the world is HyperText Markup Language (HTML). Although you can create web pages with specialized web page editing programs, such as Adobe Dreamweaver, it's still nice to know how HTML works so you can modify web pages manually or create unique effects that may be difficult or impossible to accomplish with a web page editing program.

Similar to the way a traditional programming language relies on keywords, HTML relies on *tags* (keywords) that follow a rigidly defined syntax. Instead of creating a working program like a traditional programming language, HTML creates web pages that browsers can view.

In a traditional programming language, an error or bug can keep the entire program from running or make it calculate incorrectly. In HTML, an error can keep a web page from appearing or just make the web page display incorrectly. If you're interested in understanding the heart of web page design, you need to understand the basics of using HTML.

The Structure of an HTML Document

The basic HTML tag defines the entire HTML document like this:

```
<html>

</html>
```

Anything between the `<html>` and `</html>` tags will appear on the web page.

The last tag uses a forward slash (/) to identify the end of the tag.

Generally, HTML tags work in pairs — the first tag defines something, and the second tag (the one beginning with a forward slash) marks the end of that definition. If you omit one of the `<html>` or `</html>` tags, your HTML web page won't appear.

HTML tags aren't case-sensitive, so you can define the tags as `<HTML>` and `</HTML>` if you prefer.

Creating a title

Most web pages have a title, which appears in the title bar of a window. To display text in a window's title bar, type text in between the `<title>` and `</title>` tags inside the `<head>` and `</head>` tags like this:

```
<html>
   <head>
      <title>This text appears in the title bar.</title>
   </head>
</html>
```

Creating the body text

The bulk of a web page falls within the `<body>` and `</body>` tags. To display text, you need to use the paragraph tags, `<p>` and `</p>`, like this:

```
<html>
   <head>
      <title>This text appears in the title bar.</title>
   </head>
```

```
<body>
    <p>This text appears on the web page.</p>
</body>
</html>
```

The trailing `</p>` is optional but can be helpful to make it clear where a specific paragraph ends.

If you want to make sure a line of text breaks at a certain point, you can use the `<br>` tag, such as

```
<html>
    <head>
        <title>This text appears in the title bar.</title>
    </head>

    <body>
        <p>This text appears on the web page.<br>This appears on
        a separate line.</p>
    </body>
</html>
```

The preceding HTML code displays two lines of text like this:

```
This text appears on the web page.
This appears on a separate line.
```

With lots of text appearing on a web page, you may want to separate text with headings. HTML offers six types of headings that use tags, such as `<h1>` and `</h1>`. The following code produces the results shown in Figure 1-1:

```
<html>
    <head>
        <title>This text appears in the title bar.</title>
    </head>

    <body>
        <h1>Heading 1</h1>
        <h2>Heading 2</h2>
        <h3>Heading 3</h3>
        <h4>Heading 4</h4>
        <h5>Heading 5</h5>
        <h6>Heading 6</h6>
```

```
         <p>This text appears on the web page.</p>
      </body>
   </html>
```

Heading 1

Heading 2

Heading 3

Heading 4

Heading 5

Heading 6

This text appears on the web page.

```
<html>
  <head>
    <title>This text appears in the title bar.</title>
  </head>

  <body>
    <h1>Heading 1</h1>
    <h2>Heading 2</h2>
    <h3>Heading 3</h3>
    <h4>Heading 4</h4>
    <h5>Heading 5</h5>
    <h6>Heading 6</h6>
    <p>This text appears on the web page.</p>
  </body>
</html>
```

FakeWebPage.html

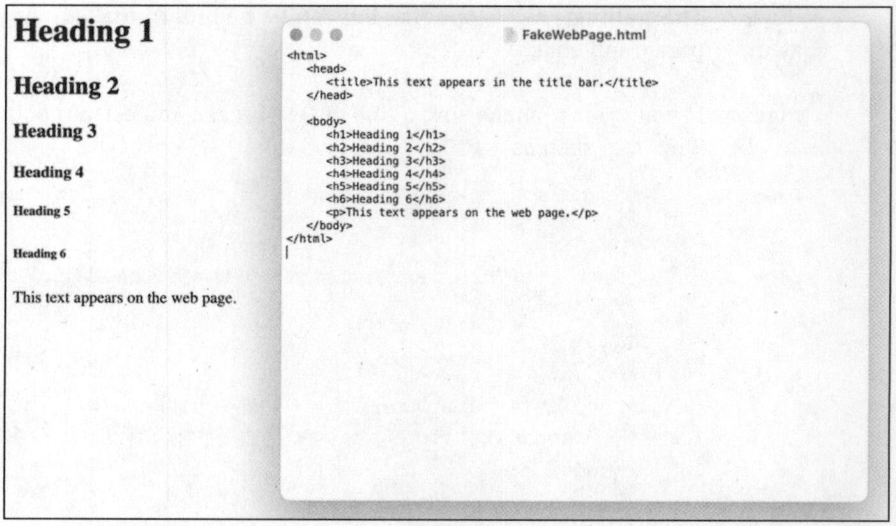

FIGURE 1-1:
HTML can create
six different
headings.

Aligning text

Text normally appears left-aligned, but you can right-align or center-align text as well. To align text, you need to insert the following inside the first part of the paragraph or heading tag. The following code produces the results shown in Figure 1-2:

```
<html>
   <head>
      <title>This text appears in the title bar.</title>
   </head>

   <body>
      <h1 align = "center">Heading 1</h1>
      <p align = "right">This text appears on the web page.</p>
   </body>
</html>
```

FIGURE 1-2:
You can specify
text to appear
center- or
right-aligned.

Emphasizing text

To make text stand out, you can emphasize it as bold, italicized, or underlined by using the following tags:

» `<b>` and `</b>` to display text in bold

» `<i>` and `</i>` to display text in italics

» `<u>` and `</u>` to display text as underlined

Just place these tags around the text you want to emphasize, like this:

```html
<html>
   <head>
      <title>This text appears in the title bar.</title>
   </head>

   <body>
      <p>This text appears <b>bold</b>.</p>
      <p>This text appears <i>italicized</i>.</p>
      <p>This text appears <u>underlined</u>.</p>
   </body>
</html>
```

TECHNICAL STUFF

Another way to emphasize text is to use the `<strong>` and `</strong>` tags. Depending on the browser, the `<strong>` tag often displays text in bold:

```
<strong>Often displays text in bold</strong>
```

Adding color

Color can further emphasize the appearance of text. To color text, surround it with the `<font color = #xxyyzz>` and `</font>` tags where #xxyyzz represents a color code, as shown in Table 1-1.

TABLE 1-1

HTML Color Codes

Color	Color Code
Red	#FF0000
Turquoise	#00FFFF
Light blue	#0000FF
Dark blue	#0000A0
Light purple	#FF0080
Dark purple	#800080
Yellow	#FFFF00
Pastel green	#00FF00
Pink	#FF00FF
White	#FFFFFF
Light gray	#FFFFCC
Black	#000000
Orange	#FF8040
Brown	#804000
Burgundy	#800000
Forest green	#808000
Grass green	#408080

Colors are defined in shades of red, blue, and green, represented as hexadecimal values. The xx portion defines the amount of red, the yy defines the amount of blue, and the zz defines the amount of green. The absence of a color is 00 whereas the maximum amount of a color is FF. By varying the shades of red, blue, and green as hexadecimal values, you can define your own colors. If you prefer, you can choose from a list of standard colors such as "red", "gold", or "lavender" (see www.w3schools.com/tags/ref_colornames.asp).

The following HTML code displays text in red (#FF0000):

```
<html>
    <head>
        <title>This text appears in the title bar.</title>
    </head>

    <body>
        <p>This text appears in <font color = #FF0000>red</font>
        on the web page.</p>
    </body>
</html>
```

Changing the font size

You can also make text appear larger or smaller by defining a size from 1 (smallest) to 7 (largest). The following HTML code makes the text appear large:

```
<html>
    <head>
        <title>This text appears in the title bar.</title>
    </head>

    <body>
        <p>This text appears <font size = "7">large</font> on the
        web page.</p>
    </body>
</html>
```

Instead of specifying a value from 1 to 7, you can increase or decrease the font size relative to the current font size by adding a number (+3) or subtracting a number (−2) like this:

```
<html>
   <head>
      <title>This text appears in the title bar.</title>
   </head>

   <body>
      <p>This text appears <font size = "+3">large</font> on
      the web page.</p>
   </body>
</html>
```

Adding comments

Because pages filled with HTML code can often be confusing to understand, you can sprinkle comments anywhere on your web page. Comments always begin with <!-- and end with -->, so anything you place within those two comment tags are ignored by the computer, like this:

```
<html>
   <head>
      <title>This text appears in the title bar.</title>
   </head>

   <!-- This is a comment in a web page. -->

   <body>
      <p>This text appears <font size = "7">large</font> on
      the web page.</p>
   </body>
</html>
```

Adding Graphics

Three common types of graphic files you can add on a web page are JPEG (Joint Photographic Experts Group), GIF (Graphics Interchange Format), and PNG (Portable Network Graphics) files.

To add graphics on a web page, you need to specify the graphic filename that you want to appear. So, if you had a graphic image named duck.jpg stored in the same location as the HTML file, you could add it to a web page like this:

```
<html>
    <head>
        <title>This text appears in the title bar.</title>
    </head>

    <body>
        <img src = "duck.jpg">
    </body>
</html>
```

Defining the Background

By default, web pages can look pretty boring with a plain white background. To spice up the appearance of a web page, you can modify the background to display a color or a graphic image. To define a background color, you have to define either a color name (such as "black") or a RGB hexadecimal value like this:

```
<body bgcolor = #xxyyzz>
```

To define a background graphic, you need to specify the graphic filename like this:

```
<body background = "filename.ext">
```

You can define both a background color and a background image by combining both HTML commands on a single line like this:

```
<body bgcolor = #xxyyzz background = "filename.ext">
```

REMEMBER

If you're displaying both a background color and a background image, make sure the background image contains transparent parts so the background color can appear.

Creating Hyperlinks

Web pages typically contain text and graphics, but the heart of web pages are *hyperlinks* that connect a web page to another web page or a different part of the currently displayed web page. The HTML code to create a hyperlink looks like this:

```
<a href = "address">hyperlink text</a>
```

The "address" can be a website URL (short for *Uniform Resource Locator*), such as www.whitehouse.gov or www.dummies.com, or a filename that links to a web page, an image, a PDF file, or any other resource, such as index.html. The *hyperlink text* is the word or phrase that appears as a link. So, if you wanted to turn the term *White House* into a link, you could use the following HTML code:

```
<a href = "www.whitehouse.gov">White House</a>
```

When you click a link to a web page, the link takes you to the top of that web page. If you want a link to jump to a specific part of a web page, such as a paragraph in the middle of the web page, you have to go through two steps:

1. **Define an anchor that represents the specific part of the web page that you want people to see when they click a link.**

2. **Define a link to take users to that specific part of the web page.**

Defining an anchor point

When you define an anchor point, you need to create a name for your anchor point and then define the actual text that will act as the anchor point, like this:

```
<a name = "anchorname">
```

The anchor point can be any descriptive name. After you place an anchor point within a web page, the next step is to create a link to the anchor point. This link can be on the same web page as the anchor point or on a different web page.

Linking to an anchor point

After you've created an anchor point, you must create a hyperlink that points to that anchor point. If the hyperlink appears on the same web page as the anchor point, you can just specify the anchor point name, like this:

```
<a href = "#anchorname">Jump to anchor point</a>
```

The # symbol identifies the anchor point. The text after the anchor name link (Jump to anchor point, in this example) appears as a hyperlink that the user can select. The </a> tag marks the end of the hyperlink.

If the anchor point appears on another web page, you must specify the web page filename followed by the anchor point name, such as

```
<a href = "webpage.html#anchorname">Jump to anchor point</a>
```

Making Tables

Tables help align text and graphics in rows and columns. For greater flexibility, you can choose to make the table borders appear visible or invisible or give the table a background color or image. When table borders appear invisible, any items stored in the table appear aligned but without the distraction of borders.

When creating a table, you need to define the table appearance, the table headings, and the actual data that appears inside the table.

Defining a table

When you create a table, you have the option to define one or more of the following:

>> **Alignment:** Defines the alignment of the table

>> **Border:** Defines the thickness of the lines that define the table

>> **Cell padding:** Defines the spacing between data and the cell borders

>> **Cell spacing:** Defines the spacing between adjacent cells

>> **Width:** Defines the size of the table in pixels or as a percentage of the window's width

To define the alignment of the table, you can choose between center, left, or right, like this:

```
<table align = "center"> </table>
```

To define the border of a table, specify a border value like this:

```
<table border = "2"> </table>
```

If you set the table border to "0", you can make the border invisible.

To define the cell padding and cell spacing, specify a value like this:

```
<table cellpadding = "2" cellspacing = "3"> </table>
```

To define the width of the table, define a percentage like this:

```
<table width = "75"> </table>
```

If you want to define multiple options, it's probably easier to store them on separate lines like this:

```
<table
  align = "center"
  border = "2"
  cellpadding = "2"
  cellspacing = "3"
  width = "75%">
</table>
```

When defining the width of a table, you can choose either a percentage ("75%") of the window width or a specific pixel size ("75px").

Defining a table heading

You may want to define headings for a table with the ‹th› and ‹/th› tags. The following code produces the results shown in Figure 1-3:

```
<html>
  <head>
    <title>This text appears in the title bar.</title>
  </head>

  <table border = "1">
    <th>Column 1</th>
    <th>Column 2</th>
  </table>
</html>
```

Each time you use the ‹th› and ‹/th› tags, you create another column in your table.

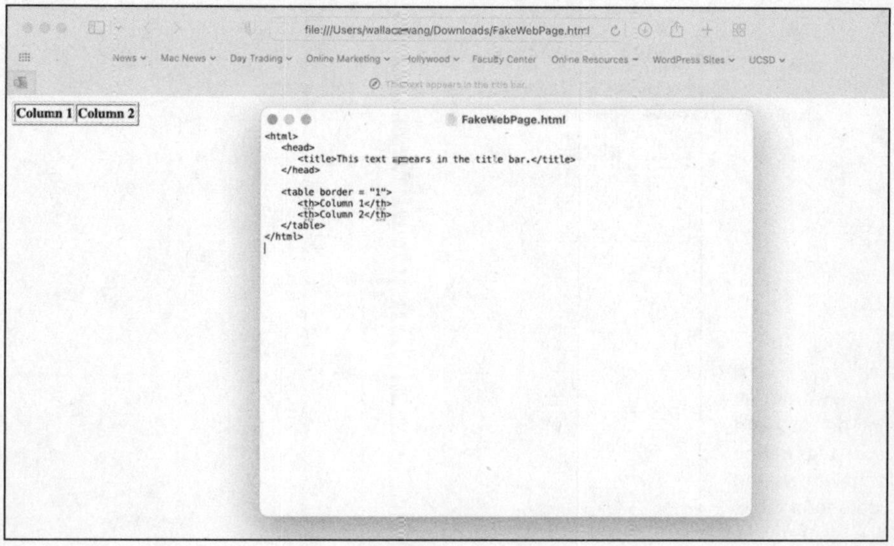

FIGURE 1-3:
The ‹th› and
‹/th› tags define
the headings for
the table.

Creating table rows and data

To fill a table with data, you need to use the ‹tr› and ‹/tr› tags to define a row and then fill in that row with the ‹td› and ‹/td› tags, which define the data. The following code produces the results shown in Figure 1-4:

```
<html>
    <head>
        <title>This text appears in the title bar.</title>
    </head>

    <table border = "1">
        <th>Column 1</th>
        <th>Column 2</th>
        <tr>
          <td>Stuff here</td>
          <td>Useful data</td>
        </tr>
        <tr>
          <td>Second row</td>
          <td>More data</td>
        </tr>
    </table>
</html>
```

FIGURE 1-4:
The <tr> and
<td> tags define
new rows and
data for a table,
respectively.

You can define the width and alignment of each cell individually like this:

```
<td align = "center"; width = "100px">Stuff here</td>
```

Displaying a table caption, header, and footer

If you want to create a caption to appear above your table, you can use the <caption> and </caption> tags. Captions can be useful to name or describe the data stored inside the table.

Tables can also store a header and footer. The header typically appears as the first row of the table, whereas the footer typically appears as the last row of the table. To define a table header and footer, you need to use the <thead> and <tfoot> tags, respectively. The following code produces the results shown in Figure 1-5:

```
<html>
   <head>
      <title>This text appears in the title bar.</title>
   </head>

   <table border = "1">
      <caption>This is a table caption.</caption>
      <thead>
         <tr>
```

```
            <td>This is a table header</td>
        </tr>
    </thead>
    <th>Column 1</th>
    <th>Column 2</th>
    <tr>
        <td>Stuff here</td>
        <td>Useful data</td>
    </tr>
    <tr>
        <td>Second row</td>
        <td>More data</td>
    </tr>
    <tfoot>
        <tr>
            <td>This is a table footer</td>
        </tr>
    </tfoot>
    </table>
</html>
```

Notice that the header and footer in Figure 1-5 appears in a single cell, but it may look better if it can span across multiple cells. To do that, you can use colspan or rowspan tags to define how many columns or rows to span.

FIGURE 1-5:
The <caption>
and </caption>
tags define text
to appear over
a table.

In this example, I just want the header and footer text to span across two columns, so I can adjust the header like this:

```
<td colspan = "2">This is a table header</td>
```

Then I can do the same for the footer, like this:

```
<td colspan = "2">This is a table footer</td>
```

This would allow both the header and the footer text to span across two columns, as shown in Figure 1-6.

FIGURE 1-6:
The colspan attribute lets text expand across multiple columns.

Chapter **2**

CSS

Designing web pages with HyperText Markup Language (HTML) lets you create and display text that can be read through a browser on a variety of devices such as personal computers, mobile phones, and game consoles. However, changing the content on a web page often means changing the HTML code as well. Ideally, you want to leave the HTML code untouched and just change the content, much like pouring different liquids (such as coffee, juice, or milk) into a bottle so each type of liquid always appears in the shape of that bottle.

That's the idea behind cascading stylesheets (CSS). First, you store different styles in a separate file or in a separate area in the same file, which contain instructions for formatting text. Second, you apply that stylesheet to a text file or text in that same file. The combination of the stylesheet file and the text creates the display of the web page inside a browser.

Cascading stylesheets get their name because you can apply multiple stylesheets to the same text file. The end result is a combination of styles defined by two or more stylesheets. If one stylesheet defines a certain font but a second stylesheet defines a different font, the text appears with the font defined by the last stylesheet.

By using stylesheets, you can make formatting text on your web pages easy, fast, and simple.

The Structure of a Stylesheet

Like ordinary HTML, stylesheets use tags to define how to format text. To define a style, you use the <style> and </style> tags and then define the type of text you want to format such as heading 1 text (defined by the <h1> and </h1> tags), like this:

```
<style>
<!--
  textstylename {
    attribute: value;
  }
-->
</style>
```

In this example, the style appears inside the comment characters: <!-- and -->. So, if you wanted to display the color red for all heading 1 text, your style would look like this:

```
<html>
   <head>
      <title>This text appears in the title bar.</title>
   </head>

   <style>
   <!--
     h1 {
       color : #FF0000;
     }
   -->
   </style>

   </head>
   <body>
      <h1>This heading is defined by the style.</h1>
   </body>
</html>
```

You can define multiple styles that define additional attributes, including

>> border

>> font-family

>> text-align

The following stylesheet defines text in both the ‹h1› heading and the ‹p› paragraph text:

```
<html>
   <head>
      <title>This text appears in the title bar.</title>
   </head>

<style>
<!--
   h1 {
      color : #FF0000;
   }
   p {
      color : #00FF00;
      background-color: #FF0000;
      text-align : center;
   }
-->
</style>

</head>
<body>
   <h1>This heading is defined by the h1 heading style.</h1>
   <p>This text is modified by the paragraph style.</p>
</body>
</html>
```

REMEMBER

Instead of defining colors using cryptic codes, you can also use more descriptive names, such as red or pink.

Creating Style Classes

Styles can define the formatting for a particular type of text, such as text displayed as a ‹h2› heading or ‹p› paragraph. Every time you display text in those ‹h2› or ‹p› tags, your style formats that text the same way.

If you want the flexibility to choose different styles to use for text stored within identical tags, you can define style classes. A *style class* lets you define formatting; then you can apply this style class to any type of text stored within different types of tags. For example, the following style defines formatting for the `<p>` paragraph text:

```
<html>
   <head>
      <title>This text appears in the title bar.</title>
   </head>

   <style>
   <!--
     h1 {
       color : #FF0000;
     }
     p {
       color : #00FF00;
       background-color: #FF0000;
       text-align : center;
     }
   -->
   </style>

   </head>
   <body>
      <h1>This heading is defined by the h1 heading style.</h1>
      <p>This text is modified by the paragraph style.</p>
      <p>This text also is modified by the paragraph style.</p>
   </body>
</html>
```

In this example, a single style formats text stored in both `<p>` tags. To create a style class, define a class name and its formatting attributes like this:

```
<style>
<!--
  .classname {
    attribute: value;
  }
-->
</style>
```

To use a style class, include the class name within a tag, like this:

```
<tag class = "classname">Text to be formatted</tag>
```

Style classes let you apply different styles to text stored within identical tags, like this:

```html
<html>
   <head>
      <title>This text appears in the title bar.</title>
   </head>

<style>
<!--
   .firstclass {
     color : #FF0000;
   }
   .secondclass {
     color : #00FF00;
     text-align : center;
   }
-->
</style>

</head>
<body>
   <h1 class = "firstclass">This heading is defined by the
   firstclass style.</h1>
   <p class = "firstclass">This text is modified by the
   firstclass style.</p>
   <p class = "secondclass">This text is modified by the
   secondclass style.</p>
</body>
</html>
```

Separating Styles in Files

You can embed styles directly into an HTML page. However, if you want to reuse those styles in another HTML page, you have to copy the styles and store them a second time. To separate styles completely from the HTML web page they're modifying, store stylesheets in separate files.

When stored as a separate file, the stylesheet simply contains the tag or class names along with the attributes you want to modify, like this:

```
h1 {
   color : #FF0000;
   }

.myclass {
   color : #00FF00;
   text-align : center;
   }
```

After you store one or more styles in a separate file saved with the .css file extension, you need to include that stylesheet file in your HTML web page by adding the <link> tag:

```
<link rel = "stylesheet" jref = "stylesheet.css" type = "text/
   css" media = "screen">
```

The media portion of the <link> tag defines how the web page will be viewed. Besides "screen", some other media types include

>> "braille": For tactile braille readers

>> "aural": For speech synthesis software

>> "handheld": For handheld devices such as mobile phones

For example, suppose you stored the following styles in a styleme.css file:

```
.firstclass {
    color : #FF0000;
  }
  .secondclass {
   color : #00FF00;
   text-align : center;
  }
```

Now you can include this stylesheet in any HTML web page by using the <link> tag like this:

```
<html>
  <link rel = "stylesheet" href = "./styleme.css" type =
  "text/css" media = "screen">
   <head>
```

```
        <title>This text appears in the title bar.</title>
    </head>

    <body>
      <h1 class = "firstclass">This heading is defined by the
      firstclass style.</h1>
      <p class = "firstclass">This text is modified by the
      firstclass style.</p>
      <p class = "secondclass">This text is modified by the
      secondclass style.</p>
    </body>
</html>
```

TECHNICAL STUFF

The ./ characters tell the computer to look within the current directory.

Storing stylesheets in separate files makes it easy to modify formatting without having to modify any of your actual HTML web pages.

Cascading Stylesheets

You can store stylesheets as external files or embedded as part of the HTML code that defines a web page. If one stylesheet defines how to format text stored inside the <h1> and </h1> tags and a second stylesheet defines how to format text stored inside the <p> and </p> tags, both stylesheets *cascade* (act as one) to define the text on a single web page. By applying the formatting of different stylesheets, you get more flexibility in formatting your web pages.

If two stylesheets try to format text stored within the same tags, the *internal stylesheet* (the one embedded in the HTML code of the web page) takes precedence over the *external stylesheet* (the one stored in a separate file).

TIP

In this way, you can use external stylesheets to provide the bulk of the formatting for a web page and then use smaller internal stylesheets within your HTML code to define a particular tag, such as text within the <h3> and </h3> tags.

If you have two external stylesheets that format the same text, define the order to apply the external stylesheets by using multiple <link> tags like this:

```
<html>
  <link rel = "stylesheet" href = "./file1.css" type =
  "text/css"
 media = "screen">
```

```
   <link rel = "stylesheet" href = "./file2.css" type =
   "text/css"
   media = "screen">
   <body>
   </body>
</html>
```

In the preceding example, the styles stored in the file2.css stylesheet take precedence over the styles stored in the file1.css. Any styles stored in the HTML code of your web page takes precedence over any styles stored in either the file2.css or file1.css external files.

The general rule is that text will be formatted according to the stylesheet closest to the text. So, an internal stylesheet is closer to text than an external stylesheet, which is why styles stored in an internal stylesheet take precedence over an external stylesheet.

If you want to create a web page with a unified appearance, you might define the formatting for every tag inside a single external stylesheet. Then modify one or two styles (stored in additional external stylesheets or embedded in the HTML code of a specific web page) in case you want to format some text differently.

N THIS CHAPTER

» **Understanding the JavaScript structure**

» **Creating comments and declaring variables**

» **Using operators**

» **Working with branching and looping statements**

» **Creating functions**

» **Working with arrays**

» **Making your user interface look good**

Chapter **3**

JavaScript

The problem with most web pages is that they're static, much like staring at a page from a book except displayed on a computer screen. Although nothing's wrong with static web pages for displaying information, you may want to create interactive web pages that can respond to the user's actions. To create interactive or dynamic web pages, computer scientists developed various programming languages dubbed *scripting languages.* Although you can choose several languages for creating dynamic web pages, the most popular scripting language is JavaScript.

JavaScript programs are stored either as part of a web page file or in a separate file altogether. When you visit a website, the computer storing the web pages (the *server*) sends its web pages and JavaScript files to your computer (the *client*). Your computer now runs an interpreter to run the JavaScript programs.

Instead of creating stand-alone applications like a system programming language (such as C++ or Swift) can do, JavaScript programs are often much shorter and designed to create simpler programs. For example, a JavaScript program may display a text box for you to type a password. Whatever you type, the JavaScript program can verify whether the password is valid and then decide whether to let you into the website.

Because JavaScript works with most browsers and computers, JavaScript is a simple way to create dynamic web pages without relying on browser plug-ins that users may not have or want. However, one major disadvantage is that JavaScript programs may run slowly. Even worse, some people turn off JavaScript support to speed up their browser. So, if your web pages rely on JavaScript, anyone who turned off JavaScript won't see your fancy web pages.

Despite its name, JavaScript is a completely different programming language from Java, although both languages borrow heavily from the C++ syntax that includes the use of curly brackets and semicolons ending each statement.

The Structure of a JavaScript Program

At the simplest level, a JavaScript program can consist of one or more commands, like this:

```
<html>
  <script language="javascript">
    document.writeln("This is a simple JavaScript program.");
  </script>
  <body>
  </body>
</html>
```

The `<script>` and `</script>` tags define the beginning and ending of a JavaScript program. The first `<script>` tag identifies the scripting language used, which in this case is always JavaScript. Sandwiched in between the two `<script>` tags are the actual JavaScript commands.

However, it's more common to divide a JavaScript program into functions with each function acting like a separate building block. For example, a simple JavaScript program might look like this:

```
<html>
  <script language="javascript">
    function hello() {
      alert("This is also a simple JavaScript program.");
```

```
    }
  </script>
  <body onLoad = "hello()">
  </body>
</html>
```

The onLoad command tells your computer when to run a particular function.

As an alternative to storing JavaScript code directly in the HTML code of a web page, you can store JavaScript programs in a separate file with the .js file extension. This .js JavaScript file then contains all the code within the <script> and </script> tags, but not the <script> or </script> tags themselves. Then you need to define the name of that JavaScript file to load and run it within your web page, like this:

```
<html>
  <script language=javascript src="filename.js"></script>
  <body onLoad = "hello()">
  </body>
</html>
```

Creating Comments

To write a comment in JavaScript, use double forward slashes so anything that appears to the right is a comment, like this:

```
<html>

  <script language=javascript src="filename.js">
  // The JavaScript code is stored in a file that has the .js file extension.
  </script>
  <body>
  </body>
</html>
```

Double forward slashes are handy for adding a comment to a single line. If you want to write a comment over multiple lines, you can use the /* and */ characters, like this:

```
<html>
  <script language=javascript src="filename.js">
  /* The JavaScript code is stored in a file that
```

```
    has the .js file extension. */
  </script>
  <body>
  </body>
</html>
```

Declaring Variables

JavaScript variables can hold any type of data, such as numeric (integers and decimals), strings ("like this"), Boolean values (true or false), or nothing at all (defined as null). JavaScript variables act like temporary containers that can hold any data. One moment it might hold an integer, the next a decimal value, and then a string.

To declare a variable in JavaScript, you must use the var keyword followed by the variable name, like this:

```
var variableName;
```

The name variableName can be any descriptive name. Because JavaScript is a case-sensitive language, it treats My2008Tax as a completely different variable than my2008tax. Some programmers use uppercase letters to make variable names easier to find whereas others use all lowercase. To declare multiple variables, just cram them all on a single line, separated by a comma, like this:

```
var variableName1, variableName2, variableName3;
```

Using Operators

The three types of operators used are mathematical, relational, and logical. Mathematical operators calculate numeric results such as adding, multiplying, or dividing numbers, as shown in Table 3-1.

TABLE 3-1

Mathematical Operators

Mathematical Operator	Purpose	Example
+	Addition	5 + 3.4
−	Subtraction	203.9 − 9.12
*	Multiplication	39 * 146.7
/	Division	45 / 8.41
%	Modulo (returns the remainder)	35 % 9 = 8

REMEMBER

The + operator can also concatenate two strings together, such as "Hi there," + "good looking". This would create one string that contains "Hi there, good looking".

Relational operators compare two values and return a true or false value. The six comparison operators available are shown in Table 3-2.

TABLE 3-2

Relational Operators

Relational Operator	Purpose
==	Equal
!=	Not equal
<	Less than
<=	Less than or equal to
>	Greater than
>=	Greater than or equal to

WARNING

The relational operator in JavaScript is two equal signs (==), whereas the relational operator in some other programming languages is just a single equal sign (=). If you use only a single equal sign to compare two values in JavaScript, your program will work but not the way it's supposed to.

Logical operators compare two Boolean values (true or false) and return a single true or false value, as shown in Table 3-3.

JavaScript

TABLE 3-3

Logical Operators

Logical Operator	Truth Table
&& (And)	true && true = true
	true && false = false
	false && true = false
	false && false = false
|| (Or)	true || true = true
	true || false = true
	false || true = true
	false || false = false
! (Not)	!true = false
	!false = true

Increment and decrement operators

Like C/C++, JavaScript has special increment (++) and decrement (−−) operators, which simply add or subtract 1 to a variable. Typically, adding 1 to a variable looks like this:

```
j = 5;
i = j + 1;
```

The increment operator replaces the + 1 portion with ++, like this:

```
j = 5;
i = ++j;
```

In this example, the value of i is j + 1 or 6, and the value of j is also 6.

REMEMBER

If you place the increment operator after the variable, like this:

```
j = 5;
i = j++;
```

Now the value of i is 5, but the value of j is 6.

The decrement operator works the same way except that it subtracts 1 from a variable, like this:

```
j = 5;
i = --j;
```

In this example, the value of i is j – 1 or 4, and the value of j is also 4.

REMEMBER

If you place the decrement operator after the variable, like this:

```
j = 5;
i = j--;
```

Now the value of i is 5, but the value of j is 4.

Assignment operators

Most programming languages use the equal sign to assign values to variables, like this:

```
i = 59;
```

However, JavaScript also includes combination assignment and mathematical operators, as shown in Table 3-4.

TABLE 3-4

Assignment Operators

Assignment Operator	Purpose	Example
+=	Addition assignment	i += 7 (equivalent to i = i + 7)
-=	Subtraction assignment	i -= 4 (equivalent to i = i - 4)
*=	Multiplication assignment	i *= y (equivalent to i = i * y)
/=	Division assignment	i /= 3.5 (equivalent to i = i / 3.5)
%=	Modulo assignment	i %= 2.8 (equivalent to i = i % 2.8)

JavaScript

Branching Statements

The simplest branching statement is an if statement that only runs one or more commands if a Boolean condition is true, like this:

```
if (condition) {
  Command;
}
```

To make the computer choose between two mutually exclusive sets of commands, you can use an if–else statement, like this:

```
if (condition) {
  Command1;
} else {
  Command2;
}
```

As an alternative to the if–else statement, you can also use the switch statement to offer two or more choices, like this:

```
switch (expression) {
  case value1:
    Command1;
    break;
  case value2:
    Command2;
    break;
  default:
    Command3;
}
```

REMEMBER

The switch statement often includes the break command to tell the computer when to exit out of the switch statement.

The above switch statement is equivalent to the following if–else statement:

```
if (expression == value1) {
  Command1;
} else if (expression == value2) {
  Command2;
} else {
  Command3;
}
```

To check if a variable matches multiple values, you can stack multiple case statements, like this:

```
switch (expression) {
  case value1:
  case value2:
    Command1;
    break;
  case value3:
  case value4:
    Command2;
    break;
  default:
    Command;
}
```

This switch statement is equivalent to the following if-else statement:

```
if ((expression = value1) || (expression = value2)) {
  Command;
} else if ((expression == value3) || (expression == value4)) {
  Command;
} else {
  Command;
}
```

Looping Statements

A *looping statement* repeats one or more commands a fixed number of times or until a certain Boolean condition becomes false. To create a loop that repeats a fixed number of times, use the for loop, which looks like this:

```
for (startvalue; endvalue; increment) {
  Command;
  }
```

If you wanted the for loop to run four times, you could set the start value to 1 and the end value to 4, like this:

```
for (i = 1; i <= 4; i++) {
  Command;
  }
```

If you don't know how many times you need to repeat commands, use a while loop, which looks like this:

```
while (condition) {
   Command;
}
```

If the condition is true, the loop runs at least once. If this condition is false, the loop doesn't run.

A variation of the while loop is the do—while loop, which looks like this:

```
do {
   Command;
} while (condition);
```

The main difference between the two loops is that the while loop may run zero or more times, but the do—while loop will always run at least once.

WARNING

Somewhere inside a while and do—while loop, you must have a command that can change the condition from true to false; otherwise, the loop will never end, and your program will appear to hang or freeze.

Creating Functions

In JavaScript, every subprogram is a function that can return a value. (A function that returns a null value simply acts like a procedure in other programming languages.) The format of a typical function looks like this:

```
function functionname (Parameter list) {
   Commands;
   return value;
}
```

Here are the two parts of a JavaScript function:

>> Parameter list: Defines any data and their data types that the function needs to work. If the function doesn't need to accept any values, the parameter list can be empty.

>> return: Defines a value to return.

If a function doesn't return a value or accept any parameters, it might look like this:

```
function myfunction (){
  Command;
}
```

Using Arrays

JavaScript offers two ways to create an array. First, you can define an array and the elements inside that array by using square brackets, like this:

```
var myArray = [data1, data2. data3];
```

JavaScript arrays can store any type of data, such as integers, decimal values, strings, or Boolean values like this:

```
var myArray = [93.42, "Hi there", 3];
```

Another way to create a JavaScript array is to define the array size and then store data in that array like this:

```
var myArray = new Array(x);
```

Here, x is the size of the array, such as 4 or 9. After defining an array, you can store items in that array like this:

```
myArray[2] = "This works";
```

REMEMBER

JavaScript arrays are zero-based, which means if you define an array like this:

```
var myArray = new Array(2);
```

The array elements are numbered myarray[0], myarray[1], and myarray[2].

Designing User Interfaces

JavaScript can retrieve data from the user by creating different types of user interface (UI) elements, such as dialog boxes and windows. Such UI items can display information to the user, creating an interactive web page.

Creating dialog boxes

The three types of dialog boxes JavaScript can create are

>> **Alert:** Displays a message on the screen and gives the user the option of closing the dialog box

>> **Confirmation:** Displays a message and offers the user two or more choices

>> **Prompt:** Gives users a chance to type in data

Alert dialog boxes

To create an alert dialog box, you need to define the text you want displayed, like this:

```
alert("Message here");
```

An alert dialog box displays an OK button. As soon as the user clicks the OK button, the alert dialog box goes away.

Confirmation dialog boxes

A confirmation dialog box gives users a choice of OK and Cancel buttons. To create a confirmation dialog box, you must display text and include commands that do something when the user clicks either OK or Cancel:

```
if (confirm("Text message")) {
  command;
} else {
  command;
}
```

The following JavaScript code creates a confirmation dialog box:

```
<html>
  <script language="javascript">
    if (confirm("Do you want to retaliate with nuclear weapons?")) {
      document.write("Now starting World War III.");
    } else {
      document.write ("Let's give peace a chance.");
}
  </script>
  <body>
  </body>
</html>
```

Prompt dialog boxes

To create a prompt dialog box, you need to display text to appear in the dialog box and then optional text to appear as a default value, like this:

```
var result = prompt("Text to display", optionalvalue);
```

If you wanted to display the text "How many politicians are disappointing?" and display a default value of "All of them", you'd use this JavaScript code:

```
<html>
  <script language=javascript>
    var result = prompt ("How many politicians are disappointing?", "All of
    them");
  </script>
  <body>
  </body>
</html>
```

Creating windows

JavaScript can open windows, which can display additional web pages inside. (Many browsers may include a feature to block pop-up windows. This feature blocks JavaScript from opening a window because many pop-up ads rely on JavaScript to display annoying ads on your screen.)

To create a window, you need to use the following:

```
variablename = open ("address");
```

So, if you wanted to open the Dummies website, you could use the following code:

```
myWindow = open ("http://www.dummies.com");
```

IN THIS CHAPTER

» **Understanding the structure of a PHP program**

» **Creating comments and declaring variables**

» **Using operators**

» **Working with branching and looping statements**

» **Using functions**

» **Working with arrays**

» **Using objects**

Chapter **4**

PHP

I n the old days, web pages were used to display information, such as text and graphics. Nowadays, web pages are dynamic, so they not only need to respond to the user but often need to retrieve information off a web page and store it in a database, such as when you type your credit card number to buy something off a website.

HTML can create simple user interfaces, but when you need to transfer data from a web page to another program, such as a database, you need to use a programming language. Although programmers have used C, Perl, and Java to link web pages to other programs like databases, one of the most popular programming languages for this task is PHP, which is a recursive name that stands for PHP Hypertext Processor (www.php.net).

Although languages such as C and Perl can be used to create stand-alone applications, PHP programs are unique in that they can run only on web pages. Not only is PHP designed for creating programs within web pages, but PHP is also free and capable of running under many different operating systems. If you're already familiar with C and Perl, you'll find that PHP mimics much of the syntax from both languages. Although you can create dynamic websites with other programming languages, you may find PHP easier and simpler to use.

Examining the Structure of a PHP Program

At the simplest level, a PHP program can consist of one or more commands embedded in a web page's HTML code, like this:

```
<html>
   <body>
      <?php
         echo "<h1>Greetings from PHP.</h1>";
      ?>
   </body>
</html>
```

The `<?php` and `?>` tags define the beginning and ending of a PHP program. PHP *scripts* (programs) are usually stored in a file that ends with the `.php` filename extension.

TECHNICAL STUFF

If the PHP code in this book doesn't work quite right, chances are, it's because your server hasn't been configured to run PHP embedded within HTML files.

Creating Comments

To write a comment in PHP, you have three choices: `//`, `#`, or `/*` and `*/`. Both the double forward slash (`//`) and the number sign (`#`) are used to create comments on a single line, like this:

```
<html>
   <body>

   // This is the beginning of the PHP program.

      <?php
```

```
      echo "<h1>PHP is a unique web-specific language</h1>";
   ?>


  # This is the end of the PHP program.


  </body>
</html>
```

If you want to write a comment over multiple lines, use the /* and the */ characters, like this:

```
<html>
  <body>

  /* This is the beginning of the PHP program.
     If a comment extends over multiple lines,
     It's easier to use these types of comment
     symbols instead. */

    <?php
      echo "<h1>PHP can be fun and profitable</h1>";
    ?>
  </body>
</html>
```

Declaring Variables

PHP variables can hold any type of data, so a variable might hold a string one moment and a number the next. To declare a variable in PHP, you must begin every variable name with the dollar symbol ($), like this:

```
$variableName = value;
```

You can choose variableName to be any descriptive name, but PHP is a case-sensitive language, so $myAge is considered a completely different variable from $myage. Some programmers use uppercase letters to make variable names easier to find, and others use all lowercase letters.

One unique feature of PHP is its ability to reference the same value. For example, consider the following code:

```
$myAge = 35;
$yourAge = $myAge;
$myAge = 109;
```

In this example, the $myAge variable is initially set to 35 and the $yourAge variable is set to the $myAge variable, which means the $yourAge variable also contains the value of 35. The third line stores the value 109 into the $myAge variable, but the $yourAge variable still holds the value of 35.

By referencing variables with the ampersand symbol (&), PHP allows a variable to contain identical data without specifically assigning those values. For example:

```
$myAge = 35;
$yourAge = &$myAge;
$myAge = 109;
```

The second line in the preceding PHP code tells the computer that the $yourAge variable references the $myAge variable, so whatever value the $myAge variable contains from now on will automatically be stored in the $yourAge variable.

After the third line, the $myAge variable now contains the value of 109, so the $yourAge variable contains 109, too.

Using Operators

The three types of operators used in PHP are mathematical, relational, and logical operators.

Mathematical operators calculate numeric results, such as adding, multiplying, or dividing numbers, as shown in Table 4-1.

Relational operators compare two values and return a true or false value. The seven comparison operators available are shown in Table 4-2.

TABLE 4-1

Mathematical Operators

Mathematical Operator	Purpose	Example
+	Addition	5 + 3.4
–	Subtraction	203.9 – 9.12
*	Multiplication	39 * 146.7
/	Division	45 / 8.41
%	Modulo (returns the remainder)	35 % 9 = 8

TABLE 4-2

Relational Operators

Relational Operator	Purpose
==	Equal
===	Identical
!= or <>	Not equal
<	Less than
<=	Less than or equal to
>	Greater than
>=	Greater than or equal to

REMEMBER

PHP uses three equal signs (===) to compare two values and determine whether they're of the same data type. For example, PHP treats 14.0 and 14 as equal because both are numbers, but 14.0 and "14.0" wouldn't be considered identical because one is a number and the other is a different data type (a *string*).

Logical operators compare two Boolean values (true or false) and return a single true or false value, as shown in Table 4-3.

Increment and decrement operators

PHP has a special increment (++) and a decrement (--) operator, which simply adds or subtracts 1 to a variable. Typically, adding 1 to a variable looks like this:

```
j = 5;
i = j + 1;
```

TABLE 4-3

Logical operators

Logical Operator	Truth Table
&& (AND)	true && true = true
	true && false = false
	false && true = false
	false && false = false
|| (OR)	true || true = true
	true || false = true
	false || true = true
	false || false = false
XOR (Exclusive OR)	true XOR true = false
	true XOR false = true
	false XOR true = true
	false XOR false = false
! (NOT)	!true = false
	!false = true

The increment operator replaces the + 1 portion with ++, like this:

```
j = 5;
i = ++j;
```

In the preceding example, the value of i is j + 1 or 6, and the value of j is also 6.

REMEMBER

If you place the increment operator after the variable, like this:

```
j = 5;
I = j++;
```

Now the value of i is 5, but the value of j is 6.

The decrement operator works the same way, except it subtracts 1 from a variable, like this:

```
j = 5;
i = --j;
```

In the preceding example, the value of i is j − 1 or 4, and the value of j is also 4.

REMEMBER

If you place the decrement operator after the variable, like this:

```
j = 5;
i = j--;
```

Now the value of i is 5, but the value of j is 4.

Assignment operators

Most programming languages use the equal sign (=) to assign values to variables, like this:

```
i = 59;
```

However, PHP also includes combination assignment and mathematical operators, as shown in Table 4-4.

TABLE 4-4

Assignment Operators

Assignment Operator	Purpose	Example
+=	Addition assignment	i += 7 (equivalent to i = i + 7)
-=	Subtraction assignment	i -= 4 (equivalent to i = i - 4)
*=	Multiplication assignment	i *= y (equivalent to i = i * y)
/=	Division assignment	i /= 3.5 (equivalent to i = i / 3.5)
%=	Modulo assignment	i %= 2.8 (equivalent to i = i % 2.8)

Branching Statements

The simplest branching statement is an if statement that runs only one or more commands if a Boolean condition is true, like this:

```
if (condition) {
  Command;
}
```

To make the computer choose between two mutually exclusive sets of commands, you can use an if-else statement, like this:

```
if (condition) {
  Command1;
} else {
  Command2;
}
```

Although the if-else statement can only give the computer a choice of two groups of commands to run, the if-elseif statement can offer the computer multiple groups of commands to run, like this:

```
if (condition1) {
  Command;
} elseif (condition2) {
  Command;
} elseif (condition3) {
  Command;
}
```

As an alternative to the if-elseif statement, you can also use the switch statement to offer two or more choices, like this:

```
switch (expression) {
  case value1:
    Command1;
    break;
  case value2:
    Command2;
    break;
  default:
    Command3;
}
```

REMEMBER

The switch statement often includes the break command to tell the computer when to exit out of the switch statement.

The preceding switch statement is equivalent to the following if-else statement:

```
if (expression == value1) {
  Command;
} elseif (expression == value2) {
```

```
   Command;
} else {
   Command;
}
```

To check whether a variable matches multiple values, you can stack multiple case statements, like this:

```
switch (expression) {
  case value1:
  case value2:
    Command1;
    break;
  case value3:
  case value4;
    Command2;
    break;
  default:
    Command3;
}
```

The preceding switch statement is equivalent to the following if-else statement:

```
if ((expression == value1) || (expression == value2)) {
  Command1;
} else if ((expression == value3) || (expression == value4)) {
  Command2;
} else {
  Command3;
}
```

Looping Statements

A looping statement repeats one or more commands a fixed number of times or until a certain Boolean condition becomes false. To create a loop that repeats a fixed number of times, use the for loop, which looks like this:

```
for (startvalue; endvalue; increment) {
  Command;
  }
```

If you wanted the for loop to run four times, you could set the start value to 1 and the end value to 4, like this:

```
for ($i = 1; $i <= 4; $i++) {
  Command;
  }
```

If you don't know how many times you need to repeat commands, use a while loop, like this:

```
while (condition) {
  Command;
}
```

If the condition is true, the loop runs at least once. If this condition is false, the loop doesn't run.

WARNING

Somewhere inside a while loop, you must have a command that can change the condition from true to false; otherwise, the loop will never end, and your program will appear to hang or freeze.

Creating Functions

To break up programming problems, you can create subprograms that solve a specific task. Such subprograms are called *functions.* The format of a typical function looks like this:

```
function functionname (Parameter list) {
  Commands;
  return $value;
}
```

The two parts of a PHP function are

>> Parameter list: Defines any data that the function needs to work. If the function doesn't need to accept any values, the parameter list can be empty.

>> return: Defines a value to return.

If a function doesn't return a value or accept any parameters, it might look like this:

```
function myfunction () {
  Command;
}
```

Using Arrays

PHP creates arrays that can hold any type of data and grow as large as you need them without having to define a size ahead of time. To create an array, define an array name, the data you want to store, and the index number where you want to store that item in the array like this:

```
$arrayname[index] = data;
```

So, if you wanted to store the string "Hello" and the number 4.23 in the first and second elements of an array, you could do the following:

```
$myarray[0] = "Hello";
$myarray[1] = 4.23;
```

For greater flexibility in retrieving data, PHP lets you create associative arrays, which let you identify data by a unique string (called a *key*) rather than an arbitrary index number. Instead of assigning data to a specific index number, you assign data to a unique string, like this:

```
$arrayname["key"] = data;
```

If you wanted to assign the number 3.14 to the "pi" key, you'd do this:

```
$myarray["pi"] = 3.14;
```

To retrieve data from an associative array, use the key value, like this:

```
$variable = $arrayname["key"];
```

So, if you wanted to retrieve data stored under the key "pi", you could do the following:

```
$myarray["pi"] = 3.14;
$number2use = $myarray["pi"];
```

The first line stores the value 3.14 into the array and assigns it to the key "pi". The second line yanks out the data, associated with the key "pi", and stores that data into the $number2use variable.

TECHNICAL STUFF

PHP includes a library of built-in array functions for manipulating arrays such as array_pop (which removes the last element from an array), array_push (which adds an element to the end of an array, and sort (which sorts arrays in ascending order).

Creating Objects

PHP supports object-oriented programming. To create an object, you must define a class, which specifies the properties and methods, like this:

```
class classname {
  public $propertyname;

  public function methodname() {
    commands;
  }
}
```

To create an object, you must use the following syntax:

```
$objectname = new classname();
```

To assign a value to an object's property, specify the object name and the property you want to use, like this:

```
$objectname->propertyname = value;
```

When assigning a value to an object's property, notice that the dollar sign ($) isn't used to designate the property name.

To tell an object to run a method, specify the object name followed by the method name, like this:

```
$objectname->methodname();
```

PHP allows *single inheritance* (where an object can inherit from one class), in contrast to *multiple inheritance* (which allows an object to inherit from two or more classes). To inherit from a class, use the extends keyword followed by the class name you want to inherit from, like this:

```
class classname1 {
  public $propertyname;

  public function methodname() {
    commands;
  }
}

class classname2 extends classname1 {
  public $propertyname;

  public function methodname() {
    commands;
  }
}
```

N THIS CHAPTER

» **Understanding the structure of a Ruby program**

» **Creating comments and declaring variables**

» **Using operators**

» **Working with branching statements and looping statements**

» **Creating functions**

» **Working with data structures**

» **Making objects**

Chapter **5**

Ruby

The Ruby programming language was created by Yukihiro "Matz" Matsumoto, a Japanese programmer who named the language after a gemstone in reference to the Perl (pearl) programming language. Although most languages focus on wringing out extra performance from computer hardware, Ruby focuses on a clean language syntax that's easy for programmers to understand and use. Instead of trying to increase machine efficiency, Ruby tries to increase programmer efficiency. The overriding principle of Ruby is to create a language of *least surprise*, meaning that after you're familiar with Ruby, you aren't suddenly surprised that its features can be used in an entirely different way, which often occurs with languages such as C++.

Ruby is an interpreted, object-oriented language for creating interactive web pages. Although Ruby is similar to Perl and Python, Ruby abandons the C syntax of Perl and more closely resembles the syntax of programming languages like Smalltalk or Ada. Instead of enclosing blocks of commands in curly brackets like C or Perl, Ruby encloses blocks of commands with keywords like Ada or more modern versions of BASIC.

A programming framework, dubbed *Ruby on Rails*, makes it easy to manipulate databases through web pages and has attracted the attention of many former Java programmers. Like Ruby itself, Ruby on Rails is free, which has further fueled its growth. Although still a relatively young language (created in 1995), Ruby has attracted a worldwide following and will likely play a major role in future applications developed for the web.

REMEMBER

To get a copy of the free Ruby interpreter for different operating systems, visit the official Ruby website (www.ruby-lang.org).

The Structure of a Ruby Program

A Ruby program can consist of one or more commands:

```
print('What is your name? ')
my_name = gets()
puts( "Welcome to Ruby, #{my_name}")
```

Unlike other programming languages, Ruby programs don't need to define a *main* program, don't enclose blocks of commands with curly brackets, and don't end statements with a semicolon. Type a command, and Ruby obeys without its syntax interfering with your thinking.

The preceding Ruby program simply asks the user to type a name. Whatever name the user types gets stored in the my_name variable. Then the last line prints the string "Welcome to Ruby", followed by the contents of the my_name variable.

Creating Comments

To write a comment in Ruby, use the # symbol. Anything that appears to the right of the # symbol is considered a comment, which the computer ignores:

```
# This is a comment
print('What is your name? ')
my_name = gets()  # This is also a comment
puts( "Welcome to Ruby, #{my_name}")
```

If you want to write a comment over multiple lines, define the start and end of a comment block with =begin and =end, like this:

```
=begin This is a block of comments
       that make it easy to comment
       out multiple lines. However,
       Ruby's block commenting is kind
       of ugly so it's rarely used.
=end
print('What is your name? ')
my_name = gets()
puts( "Welcome to Ruby, #{my_name}")
```

Defining comments with the =begin and =end lines is often cumbersome, so it's more common for programmers to use multiple # symbols in front of each line instead, like this:

```
# This program was written by John Doe
# on January 24, 2009. It took him a
# long time to write so maybe he deserves
# a big fat raise or at least some extra
# sick days so he can look for a better job.
print('What is your name? ')
my_name = gets()
puts( "Welcome to Ruby, #{my_name}")
```

Declaring Variables

Ruby uses symbols to identify different types of variables:

>> **Local:** Begins with a lowercase letter, such as myage

>> **Instance:** Begins with an at sign (@), such as @house

>> **Class:** Begins with two at signs (@@), such as @@mathclass

>> **Global:** Begins with a dollar sign ($), such as $mymoney

REMEMBER

In Ruby, constants are identified with an initial uppercase letter like Pi or Taxrate. To avoid confusing constants with local variables, it's best to use all uppercase letters to name constants like PI or TAX_RATE.

TECHNICAL STUFF

Both class and instance variables are used inside classes that define objects.

To store data into a variable, define the variable name and set it equal to a value:

```
Variable_name = value
```

The name of your variable can be anything, but Ruby is a case-sensitive language so my_Age is considered a completely different variable than my_age.

Using Operators

The three types of operators used in Ruby are mathematical, relational, and logical operators. *Mathematical operators* calculate numeric results such as adding, multiplying, or dividing numbers, as shown in Table 5-1.

TABLE 5-1

Mathematical Operators

Mathematical Operator	Purpose	Example
+	Addition	5 + 3.4
−	Subtraction	203.9 − 9.12
*	Multiplication	39 * 146.7
/	Division	45 / 8.41
%	Modulo (returns the remainder)	35 % 9 = 8
**	Exponentiation	2 ** 3 = 8

REMEMBER

If you divide two integers with the / operator, the answer will be rounded to the nearest integer. If you want to return a decimal value, at least one of the numbers must be written as a decimal value, such as 2.0 / 3 or 2 / 3.0. If you just type **2 / 3**, the answer will be 0.

Relational operators compare two values and return a true or a false value. The seven comparison operators available are shown in Table 5-2.

REMEMBER

Ruby uses three equal signs (===) to compare two values and determine whether they're the same data. For example, Ruby treats 1.0 and 1 as identical because both are numbers, but 1.0 and "1.0" wouldn't be considered equal because one is a number and the other is a different data type (a *string*).

TABLE 5-2

Relational Operators

Relational Operator	Purpose
==	Equal to
===	Identical to (such as 1 === 1.0)
!=	Not equal to
<	Less than
<=	Less than or equal to
>	Greater than
>=	Greater than or equal to

Logical operators compare two Boolean values (true or false) and return a single true or false value, as shown in Table 5-3.

TABLE 5-3

Logical Operators

Logical Operator	Truth Table
&& (AND)	true && true = true
	true && false = false
	false && true = false
	false && false = false
|| (OR)	true || true = true
	true || false = true
	false || true = true
	false || false = false
^ (XOR)	true ^ true = false
	true ^ false = true
	false ^ true = true
	false ^ false = false
! (NOT)	!true = false !false = true

Most programming languages use the equal sign (=) to assign values to variables, like this:

```
i = 59
```

However, Ruby also includes combination assignment and mathematical operators, as shown in Table 5-4.

Assignment Operators

Assignment Operator	Purpose	Example
+=	Addition assignment	i += 7 (equivalent to i = i + 7)
-=	Subtraction assignment	i -= 4 (equivalent to i = i - 4)
*=	Multiplication assignment	i *= y (equivalent to i = i * y)
/=	Division assignment	i /= 3.5 (equivalent to i = i / 3.5)
%=	Modulo assignment	i %= 2.8 (equivalent to i = i % 2.8)

REMEMBER

Because Ruby lacks an increment and decrement operator like C++, you must increment variables with the assignment operator. So, although C++ lets you use an increment operator like this:

```
++i;
```

The equivalent increment operator in Ruby might look like this:

```
i += 1
```

Branching Statements

The simplest branching statement is an if statement that runs only one or more commands if a Boolean condition is true, like this:

```
if condition
   Command
end
```

If you write the entire if statement on a single line, you must make sure you include the then keyword:

```
if condition then Command end
```

Ruby also includes a negated form of the if statement called the unless statement, which looks like this:

```
unless condition
   Command
end
```

The unless statement runs only if the condition is false.

```
a = 5
unless a < 1
   puts "This will print out.'
end
```

Because the condition a < 1 is false, the preceding unless statement runs the command sandwiched between the unless keyword and the end keyword.

Both the if and unless statements can make the computer choose between two mutually exclusive sets of commands by including an else keyword, like this:

```
if condition
   Command1
else
   Command2
end
```

Although the if-else statement can only give the computer a choice of two groups of commands to run, the if-elsif statement can offer the computer multiple groups of commands to run:

```
if condition1
   Command
elsif condition2
   Command
elsif condition3
```

```
    Command
end
```

As an alternative to the `if-elsif` statement, you can also use the `case` statement to offer two or more choices, like this:

```
case variable
  when value1
     Command1
  when value2
     Command2
  else
     Command3;
end
```

Instead of checking whether a variable equals a specific value, the `case` statement can also check whether a variable falls within a range of values by using the `..` characters, like this:

```
case variable
  when value1..value4
     Command1
  when value5
     Command2
  else
     Command3
end
```

Looping Statements

A looping statement repeats one or more commands a fixed number of times or until a certain Boolean condition becomes `true`. To create a loop that repeats a fixed number of times, use the `for` loop, which looks like this:

```
for variable in startvalue..endvalue
  Command
end
```

If you wanted the for loop to run four times, you could set the start value to 1 and the end value to 4, like this:

```
for i = 1..4
   Command
end
```

If you don't know how many times you need to repeat commands, use a while loop, which looks like this:

```
while condition
   Command
end
```

If the condition is true, the loop runs at least once. If this condition is false, then the loop doesn't run.

Ruby also offers a negated form of the while loop called an until loop, which looks like this:

```
until condition
   Command
end
```

The until loop keeps running until a condition becomes true.

WARNING

Somewhere inside a while or an until loop, you must have a command that can change the condition from true to false; otherwise, the loop will never end and your program will appear to hang or freeze.

Creating Functions

To break up programming problems, you can create subprograms that solve a specific task. Such subprograms are *functions* or *methods*. The format of a typical function looks like this:

```
def functionname (Parameter list)
   Commands
   return value
end
```

The two parts of a Ruby function are

>> `Parameter list`: Defines any data that the function needs to work. If the function doesn't need to accept any values, omit the parentheses altogether.

>> `return`: Defines a value to return.

If a function doesn't return a value or accept any parameters, it might look like this:

```
def myfunction
  Command
end
```

Using Data Structures

Ruby offers two built-in data structures: arrays and hashes (also known as *associative arrays*):

>> An **array** can hold any number of items of different data types, such as strings and numbers. Each item is identified by an index number, starting with 0.

>> A **hash** stores a unique key value with every item. To retrieve a value from a hash, you need to know its key.

To create an empty array, use the `new` class method like this:

```
Array_name = Array.new
```

To create an array and list the items to store in that array, use the `Array` keyword followed by the data to store in the array inside square brackets like this:

```
array_name = Array[data1, data2, data3]
```

So, if you wanted to store the string `"Ruby is cool"` and the number `84.3` in the first and second elements of an array, you could do the following:

```
my_stuff = Array["Ruby is cool", 84.3]
```

To retrieve data from an array, specify the array name and index number. So, if you wanted to retrieve the first item in an array, you could do this:

```
puts (my_stuff[0])
```

One problem with arrays is that to retrieve specific data, you need to know its exact location in the array. For greater flexibility, Ruby offers hashes so you can assign a unique value (a *key*) to each item. To create a hash and store data along with a key, do this:

```
hashname = {key => value, key => value}
```

Ruby defines a collection with square brackets but defines a hash with curly brackets.

If you wanted to assign the number 3.14 to the "pi" key, you could do this:

```
myhash = {"pi" => 3.14}
```

If you need to store multiple keys and values in a hash, you might prefer this alternate way of storing keys and data in a hash:

```
hashname = Hash.new
hashname[key] = value
hashname[key] = value
```

When defining a hash with multiple lines, use square brackets.

To retrieve data from a hash, identify the hash name and a key value, like this:

```
puts (hashname["key"])
```

So, if you wanted to retrieve data stored under the key "pi", you could do the following:

```
hashname = Hash.new
hashname["pi"] = 3.14
puts (hashname["pi"])
```

The first line creates a hash data structure. The second line stores the value 3.14 into the hash using the key "pi". The third line prints out the value identified by the "pi" key in the hash data structure.

Creating Objects

Ruby supports object-oriented programming. To create an object, you must define a class with a name like this:

```
class Box

end
```

The next step is to create an initializer, which defines properties such as width and height, like this:

```
class Box
   def initialize(w,h)
      @width, @height = w, h
   end
end
```

This initializer lets you create an object from the class and define two values — a width (w) and a height (h) — which get stored in the @width and @height properties, respectively.

Next, you can create a method to manipulate properties stored in the class like this:

```
class Box
   # constructor method
   def initialize(w,h)
      @width, @height = w, h
   end
   # instance method
   def calculateArea
      @width * @height
   end
end
```

To create an object from a class, you must use the following syntax:

```
objectname = Classname.new
```

So, to create an object from the Box class defined earlier, you need to define the class (Box), use the new keyword, and pass in two values for the width and height, respectively, like this:

```
room = Box.new(15, 17)
```

To call a method inside of a class, you need to specify the object name (such as room) along with the method name to run, like this:

```
area = room.calculateArea()
puts ("Area of the box is : #{area}")
```

This creates a variable called area, which stores the value calculated by the calculateArea method. Then it prints this value: Area of the box is : 255.

To assign a value to an object's property, you need to specify the object name and the property you want to use, like this:

```
objectname.propertyname = value
```

To tell an object to run a method, you need to specify the object name followed by the method name, like this:

```
objectname.methodname(parameters)
```

Ruby allows *single inheritance,* where an object can inherit from one class (in contrast to *multiple inheritance,* which allows an object to inherit from two or more classes). To inherit from a class, use the < symbol followed by the class name you want to inherit from, like this:

```
class Classname1
  def propertyname
    @propertyname
  end
  def propertyname=(propertyname)
    @propertyname = propertyname
  end

  def methodname(parameter list)
    commands
  end
end

class Classname2 < Classname1
  # property and method definitions go here
end
```

6

Programming Language Syntax

Contents at a Glance

Chapter **1**

C and C++

The C language focuses on simplicity (for the computer, not for human programmers). Whereas other programming languages include a large number of keywords, the C language consists of a much smaller number of keywords. As a result, creating C compilers is relatively easy compared to creating compilers for other programming languages, which means that C compilers are easy to write for every operating system. This makes it easier to *port* (transfer) C programs from one computer to another.

Because the C language consists of relatively few keywords, it lacks features commonly found in other programming languages, such as offering a string data type. To compensate for its relative sparseness of features, most C compilers include a variety of library files that contain prewritten C code that adds these useful features to the C language. The main problem with C compilers is that every C compiler tends to offer different library files, so a C program designed to run on Windows may not run correctly with a different C compiler on Linux.

The C++ language builds on the C language by adding object-oriented features while retaining the C language's hardware access, speed, and portability. Most large and complicated programs, such as operating systems, are written in C++.

WARNING Because C/C++ gives complete access to all parts of the computer, a mistake in a C/C++ program can wipe data off a hard disk or crash the entire operating system of the computer. Writing C/C++ programs may be straightforward, but understanding and fixing C/C++ programs can be difficult.

Despite these problems, C/C++ is heavily used throughout the computer industry. To understand programming, you must become familiar with the C/C++ programming language.

Looking at the Structure of a C/C++ Program

A C program is divided into multiple functions where each function acts like a separate building block. To identify the starting point of a C program, one function is always designated as the main function. A simple C program looks like this:

```c
int main()
{
  printf("This is a simple C program.\n");
  return 0;
}
```

Large C programs consist of multiple functions where each additional function appears defined separate from the main function. In the following example, the separate function is printme:

```c
void printme()
{
  printf("This is a simple C program.\n");
}

int main()
{
  printme();
  return 0;
}
```

TECHNICAL STUFF

In many programming languages, you can define a function inside another function. However in C/C++, you can't do this.

Often, a C program needs to use a feature defined in a separate library, so you may see programs that define a library to add, like this:

```c
#include <stdio.h>
int main()
{
  printf("This is a simple C program.\n");
  return 0;
}
```

The structure of a typical C++ program looks similar. The following C++ example includes a C++ library called iostream and uses elements defined in a standard C++ library called std:

```cpp
#include <iostream>
using namespace std;

int main ()
{
  cout << "This is a simple C++ program.";
  return 0;
}
```

Despite minor differences, C and C++ programs basically consist of a single main function and zero or more additional functions.

Creating Comments

To write a comment in C/C++, you have two choices. First, you can use double forward slashes so anything that appears to the right is a comment, like this:

```cpp
#include <iostream>
using namespace std;

// This is a comment at the beginning of the program
int main ()
{
  cout << "This is a simple C++ program.";
  return 0;
}
```

The double forward slashes are handy for adding a comment to a single line. If you want to write a comment over multiple lines, you can use the /* and */ characters:

```
/* This C program was written as a simple example
   to show people how easy C can be to learn. */

#include <stdio.h>
int main()
{
  printf("This is a simple C program.\n");
  return 0;
}
```

Declaring Variables

When declaring variables in C/C++, first you declare the data type and then you declare the variable name:

```
datatype variable_name;
```

You can make `variable_name` any descriptive name. Because C/C++ is a case-sensitive language, it treats `SalesTax` as a completely different variable than `salestax`. Some programmers use uppercase letters to make variable names easier to find; other programmers use all lowercase. To declare multiple variables of the same data type, cram them all on a single line, separated by a comma, like this:

```
datatype VariableName1, VariableName2, VariableName3;
```

Declaring string data types

Unlike other programming languages, C/C++ doesn't support a string data type. Instead, C/C++ offers two alternatives: a character data type and a library.

First, C/C++ offers a character data type, which can hold a single character. Instead of using a string data type, you can use an array of character data types, which is clumsier, but workable. To declare a character data type, use the `char` keyword followed by your variable name:

```
char variable_name;
```

To mimic a string data type, declare an array of characters:

```
char arrayname[arraylength];
```

So, if you wanted to create an array that can hold 20 characters, you could do this:

```
char firstname[20];
```

An alternative is to include a library (string) that implements a string data type in C++, like this:

```
#include <string>
using namespace std;
string stringvariable;
```

Declaring integer data types

Whole numbers represent integers such as –59, 692, or 7. A whole number can be positive or negative. The most common type of integer data type is `int` and is used as follows:

```
int variablename;
```

If you need to restrict a variable to a smaller range of values, you can declare a `short int` or a `short` variable as follows:

```
short int smallvariable;
short smallvariable;
```

REMEMBER

The `long` integer data type in some implementations can be identical to the regular `int` data type.

All integer types (`int`, `short`, and `long`) can also be signed or unsigned. *Signed* data types can represent positive or negative numbers whereas *unsigned* data types can represent only positive numbers.

To define positive values for an integer variable, you could do this:

```
unsigned int variablename;
```

REMEMBER

The `signed` declaration isn't necessary because

```
signed long variablename;
```

is identical to

```
long variablename;
```

Table 1-1 shows the range of values that common integer data types in C/C++ can hold.

TABLE 1-1

Typical Storage and Range Limitations of C/C++ Integer Data Types

Data Type	Number of Bytes	Range
short	2	Signed: –32,768 to 32,767
		Unsigned: 0 to 65,535
int	4	Signed: –2,147,483,648 to 2,147,483,647
		Unsigned: 0 to 4,294,967,295
long	4 or 8	Signed: –2,147,483,648 to 2,147,483,647
		Unsigned: 0 to 4,294,967,295

REMEMBER

The exact number of bytes and range of all integer data types depends on the compiler used and the operating system, such as whether you're using a 32-bit or a 64-bit operating system. With many compilers, the range of values is identical between int and long data types.

Declaring floating-point data types

Floating-point values represent decimal values, such as 3.158 or –9.4106. Just as you can limit the range of integer values a variable can hold, so you can limit the range of floating-point values a variable can hold.

The three types of floating data types are float, double, and long double, as shown in Table 1-2.

REMEMBER

Real numbers (float, double, and long double) are always signed data types (positive or negative). With many compilers, the range of values is identical between double and long double data types.

TABLE 1-2

Typical Floating-Point Data Types

Data Type	Number of Bytes	Range
float	4	–1.4023 E–45 to 3.4028 E38
double	8	–4.9406 E–324 to 1.7977 E308
long double	8 or 16	–4.9406 E–324 to 1.7977 E308

Declaring Boolean values

In the C language, there are no Boolean data types. Any nonzero value is considered to represent True, and zero represents False. To mimic a Boolean data type, many C programmers define numeric values for TRUE and FALSE, like this:

```
#define FALSE 0
#define TRUE 1
int flag = FALSE;
```

Although this is workable, such an approach forces you to create an integer variable to represent a Boolean value. To avoid this problem, C++ offers a special bool data type (a Boolean value like most programming languages):

```
bool variablename;
```

A C++ bool data type can hold a value of 0 (False) or 1 (True).

Using Operators

The three types of operators used are mathematical, relational, and logical. *Mathematical operators* calculate numeric results such as adding, multiplying, or dividing numbers, as shown in Table 1-3.

Relational operators compare two values and return a 1 (true) or 0 (false) value. The six comparison operators available are shown in Table 1-4.

WARNING

The relational operator in C/C++ is two equal signs (==), whereas the relational operator in non-curly-bracket programming languages is often a single equal sign (=). If you use only a single equal sign to compare two values in C/C++, your program will work but not the way it's supposed to.

TABLE 1-3

Mathematical Operators

Mathematical Operator	Purpose	Example
+	Addition	5 + 3.4
−	Subtraction	203.9 − 9.12
*	Multiplication	39 * 146.7
/	Division	45 / 8.41
%	Modulo (returns the remainder)	35 % 9 = 8

TABLE 1-4

Relational Operators

Relational Operator	Purpose
==	Equal to
!=	Not equal to
<	Less than
<=	Less than or equal to
>	Greater than
>=	Greater than or equal to

Logical operators compare two Boolean values (1/true or 0/false) and return a single true or false value, as shown in Table 1-5.

Increment and decrement operators

Both C/C++ have a special increment operator (++) and a decrement operator (−−), which simply adds 1 to a variable or subtracts 1 from a variable, respectively. Typically, adding 1 to a variable looks like this:

```
j = 5;
i = j + 1;
```

The increment operator replaces the + 1 portion with ++:

```
j = 5;
i = ++j;
```

TABLE 1-5   **Logical Operators**

Logical Operator	Truth Table
&&	True && True = True
	True && False = False
	False && True = False
	False && False = False
||	True || True = True
	True || False = True
	False || True = True
	False || False = False
!	!True = False
	!False = True

In the preceding example, the value of i is j + 1 or 6, and the value of j is also 6.

REMEMBER

If you place the increment operator after the variable, like this:

```
j = 5;
i = j++;
```

Now the value of i is 5, but the value of j is 6.

The decrement operator works the same way except that it subtracts 1 from a variable, like this:

```
j = 5;
i = --j;
```

In the preceding example, the value of i is j − 1 or 4, and the value of j is also 4.

REMEMBER

If you place the decrement operator after the variable, like this:

```
j = 5;
i = j--;
```

Now the value of i is 5, but the value of j is 4.

C and C++

Assignment operators

Most programming languages use the equal sign (=) to assign values to variables:

```
i = 59;
```

However, C/C++ also includes combination assignment and mathematical operators, as shown in Table 1-6.

TABLE 1-6 **Assignment Operators**

Assignment Operator	Purpose	Example
+=	Addition assignment	i += 7 (equivalent to i = i + 7)
-=	Subtraction assignment	i -= 4 (equivalent to i = i - 4)
*=	Multiplication assignment	i *= y (equivalent to i = i * y)
/=	Division assignment	i /= 3.5 (equivalent to i = i / 3.5)
%=	Modulo assignment	i %= 2 (equivalent to i = i % 2)

Branching Statements

The simplest branching statement is an if statement that only runs one or more commands if a Boolean condition is true, such as

```
if (condition) {
   Command;
}
```

To make the computer choose between two mutually exclusive sets of commands, you can use an if-else statement:

```
if (condition) {
   Command;
} else {
   Command;
}
```

To allow more than two possible sets of commands to run, you can also use the if-elseif statement. This uses two or more Boolean conditions to choose which of two or more groups of commands to run:

```
if (condition1) {
  Command;
} else if (condition2) {
  Command;
}
```

Although the if-else statement can only give the computer a choice of two groups of commands to run, the if-elseif statement can offer the computer multiple groups of commands to run:

```
if (condition1) {
  Command;
} else if (condition2) {
  Command;
} else if (condition3) {
  Command;
}
```

As an alternative to the if-elseif statement, you can also use the switch statement, like this:

```
switch (expression) {
  case value1:
    Command1;
    break;
  case value2:
    Command2;
    break;
  default:
    Command3;
}
```

REMEMBER

The switch statement often includes the break command to tell the computer when to exit the switch statement.

The preceding switch statement is equivalent to the following if-elseif statement:

```
if (expression == value1) {
  Command1;
```

C and C++

```
  } else if (expression == value2) {
    Command2;
  } else {
    Command3;
  }
```

To check whether a variable matches multiple values, you can stack multiple case statements:

```
switch (expression) {
  case value1:
  case value2:
    Command1;
    break;
  case value3:
  case value4;
    Command2;
    break;
  default:
    Command3;
}
```

The preceding `switch` statement is equivalent to the following `if-elseif` statement in C++:

```
if ((expression == value1) || (expression == value2)) {
  Command1;
} else if ((expression == value3) || (expression == value4)) {
  Command2;
} else {
  Command3;
}
```

Looping Statements

A *looping statement* repeats one or more commands a fixed number of times or until a certain Boolean condition becomes `false`. To create a loop that repeats a fixed number of times, use the `for` loop, which looks like this:

```
for (startvalue; endvalue; increment) {
  Command;
}
```

If you wanted the for loop to run five times, you could set the start value to 1 and the end value to 5, like this:

```
for (int i = 1; i <= 5; i++) {
  Command;
}
```

If you don't know how many times you need to repeat commands, you'll have to use a while loop, which looks like this:

```
while (condition) {
  Command;
}
```

If the condition is true, the loop runs at least once. If this condition is false, the loop does not run.

A variation of the while loop is the do-while loop, which looks like this:

```
do {
  Command;
} while (condition);
```

The main difference between the two loops is that the while loop may run zero or more times, but the do-while loop always runs at least once.

WARNING

Somewhere inside a while and a do-while loop, you must have a command that can change the condition from true to false; otherwise, the loop will never end, and your program will appear to hang or freeze.

Creating Functions

In C/C++, every subprogram is a function that can return a value. The format of a typical function looks like this:

```
Datatype functionname (Parameter list){
  Commands;
  return value;
}
```

The three parts of a C/C++ function are

>> Datatype: Defines the type of value the function returns, such as an integer (int) or a floating-point number (float). If you don't want a function to return a value, declare its data type as void.

>> Parameter list: Defines any data and their data types that the function needs to work.

>> return: Defines a value to return. This value must be the same data type specified right before the function name.

If a function doesn't return a value or require any data, it might look like this:

```
void myfunction (){
   Command;
}
```

If the function needs to return an integer value, it might look like this:

```
int myfunction()
   {
   Command;
   return value;
   }
```

In the preceding example, value represents any integer value.

To accept data, a function needs a parameter list, which simply lists a variable to hold data along with their specific data type, such as an integer or character. To create a function that accepts an integer and a character, you could do something like this:

```
int myfunction (int mynumber, char myletter){
   Command;
   return value;
}
```

The preceding function accepts two parameters by value, so the function can change the values of variables in its parameter list, but those changed values won't appear outside that function.

If you want a function to change the values of its parameters, you need to define a parameter list by identifying which variables accept values by reference. To identify values passed by reference, use the ampersand symbol (&), like this:

```
int myfunction (int& mynumber, char myletter) {
  Command;
  return value;
}
```

Data Structures

Many C/C++ compilers include libraries that offer data structures, such as stacks or collections. However, three built-in data structures of C/C++ are structures, enumerations, and arrays.

Creating a structure

A *structure* is a variable that typically holds two or more variables. To create a structure, use the struct keyword as follows:

```
struct name {
  datatype variable;
};
```

The name of a structure can be any descriptive name, such as BaseballTeam or MyGrades. Inside a structure, you must declare one or more variables. A typical structure might look like this:

```
struct MyGrades {
  char grade;
  int class_number;
};
```

After defining a structure, you can declare a variable to represent that structure, like this:

```
struct MyGrades chemistry;
```

As a shortcut, you can define a structure and declare a variable to represent that structure, as follows:

```
struct MyGrades {
  char grade;
  int class_number;
} chemistry;
```

Creating enumerations

Enumerations act like a list that lets you name a group of items, such as the days of the week, names of people in a group, and so on. A typical enumeration list might look like this:

```
enum name {item1, item2, item3};
```

So, if you wanted to define the names of the days in a workweek, you could do the following:

```
enum weekend {saturday, sunday};
```

Now you can declare a variable as a weekend data type, such as:

```
enum weekend timeoff;
```

As an alternative, you can define an enumeration and declare a variable of that type at the same time, such as

```
enum {saturday, sunday} timeoff;
```

Creating an array

Arrays in C/C++ are zero-based arrays, which means that the first element of the array is located at index number 0, the second element of the array is located at index number 1, and so on.

To create an array, declare its data type and size:

```
datatype arrayname[size];
```

The array name can be any descriptive name. The array size defines how many items the array can hold. To create an array that can hold ten integers, you could define an array like this:

```
int mynumbers[10];
```

You can create an array and store values in it at the same time by doing the following:

```
int mynumbers[4] = {23, 8, 94, 102};
```

This is equivalent to:

```
int mynumbers[4];
mynumbers[0] = 23;
mynumbers[1] = 8;
mynumbers[2] = 94;
mynumbers[3] = 102;
```

Using Objects

Before C++, object-oriented programming was more of an academic exercise that required special programming languages. After C++ appeared, ordinary programmers could use their knowledge of C to use object-oriented programming for practical purposes.

To create an object, you must create a separate class that looks like this:

```
class ClassName{
  public:
    datatype propertyname;

    void methodname();
};
```

The class lists one or more properties and the type of data that property can hold, such as an integer or floating-point number. A class also lists one or more method names, which contains code for manipulating an object in some way. The class defines the method name and its parameter list, but the actual code for that method appears outside the class definition, like this:

```
class ClassName{
  public:
    datatype propertyname;

    void methodname();
};

void className::methodname(){
  Commands;
}
```

TECHNICAL STUFF

You can also define the method inside the class instead of defining it outside the class.

After you define a class, you can create an object from that class by declaring a variable as a new class type:

```
className objectname;
```

So, if you created an `animal` class, you could create an object (`things_at_the_zoo`) from that class as follows:

```
animal things_at_the_zoo;
```

The C++ language allows both single and multiple inheritance. With single inheritance, you can declare a class name and state the class to inherit from with a colon, like this:

```
class className : public classtoinheritfrom{
  // Code goes here
};
```

To inherit from multiple classes, name each class as follows:

```
class className : public class1, public class2{
  // Code goes here
};
```

REMEMBER

Understanding inheritance can be confusing enough, but trying to understand multiple inheritance can be even more complicated. As a result, many C++ programmers never use multiple inheritance, so don't feel like you're missing out on anything if you ignore multiple inheritance.

Chapter **2**

Java and C#

The Java language was meant to build upon the success of C++, but with added safety features and true cross-platform capabilities. Unlike C++, which gives programmers access to every part of the computer (along with the equal capability of screwing up every part of the computer), Java restricts access to the computer hardware. Although this limits Java's flexibility, it provides greater stability and reliability of Java programs.

The most appealing feature of Java is its cross-platform capabilities. Although porting a C++ program to run on other operating systems is possible, it's rarely easy or painless. Theoretically, Java lets you write a program once and then run it on multiple operating systems, a feature often described as *write once, run everywhere* (or more whimsically, *write once, test everywhere*).

Sun Microsystems developed Java; in response to Java's popularity, Microsoft developed C#, a similar language with equivalent goals. Like Java, C# is meant to build upon the C++ language while providing safety features to make it harder to write programs that could crash an entire computer.

To make programming easier, C# relies on the .NET framework. The idea behind .NET is to shield the programmer from the complexities of the operating system. That way any programs created using the .NET framework can be ported to other operating systems, so C# can run on any operating system that can run the .NET framework.

Although C/C++ remains popular, both Java and C# represent the programming languages of the future. Java is popular because it's platform independent, so Mac and Linux users can take advantage of Java. C# is most popular among Windows programmers because Microsoft has positioned C# as the future programming language for Windows.

Looking at the Structure of a Java/C# Program

Java forces object-oriented programming on you whether you like it or not. Every Java program consists of a class:

```
public class programname
{
  public static void main(String args[])
  {
     System.out.println("This is a simple Java program.");
  }
}
```

Because Java relies on object-oriented programming, a Java program looks more complicated than it should. Basically, the main program is considered a class that has a single main function. To print something, the preceding program uses a `println` command, which is accessed through the `System` class.

The equivalent Java program might look like the following C# program:

```
using System;
class MyClass
{
  static void Main()
  {
    Console.WriteLine("This is a simple C# program.");
  }
}
```

Creating Comments

To write a comment in Java/C#, you have two choices. First, you can use double forward slashes so that anything that appears to the right of the slashes is a comment:

```
using System;
class MyClass  // This is a C# comment
{
  static void Main()
  {
    Console.WriteLine("This is a simple C# program.");
  }
}
```

Double forward slashes are handy for adding a comment to a single line. If you want to write a comment over multiple lines, you can use the /* and */ characters, like this:

```
/* This is a multiline comment to show people how
   easy Java can be to learn. */

public class programname
{
  public static void main(String args[])
  {
    System.out.println("This is a simple Java program.");
  }
}
```

Declaring Variables

Because Java and C# are closely derived from C/C++, they both declare variable data types the same way: by first listing the data type and then listing the variable name, like this:

```
datatype variableName;
```

The `variableName` can be any descriptive name. Both Java and C# are case-sensitive, so the variable `TeamMembers` is a completely different variable than `Teammembers`. Some programmers use uppercase letters to make variable names easier to find; other programmers use all lowercase. To declare multiple variables of the same data type, cram them all on a single line, separated by a comma, like this:

```
datatype variableName1, variableName2, variableName3;
```

Declaring string data types

Both Java and C# offer a string data type (which isn't found in C/C++), which you can declare as this:

```
String variablename; // Java's String data type has a capital S
string variablename; // C#'s String data type has a lowercase s
```

Like most programming languages, both Java and C# allow you to declare and initialize a variable at the same time, like this:

```
String variablename = "text"; // Java's String data type has a capital S
string variablename = "text"; // C#'s String data type has a lowercase s
```

REMEMBER

Java defines a String data type with an uppercase *S* while C# defines a string data type with a lowercase *s*.

Declaring integer data types

Whole numbers represent integers, such as −9, 62, or 10. A whole number can be positive or negative. The most common integer data type is int, and it's used as follows:

```
int variablename;
```

Besides integer values, Java also offers a variety of other integer data types that can hold a different range of values, as shown in Table 2-1.

C# also offers a variety of different integer data types, which can be signed (positive and negative values) or unsigned (only positive values), as shown in Table 2-2. To declare an unsigned variable, add the letter u in front of the data type, like this:

```
int profit;
uint pets_owned;
```

```
short taxes;
ushort age;
```

TABLE 2-1

Typical Storage and Range Limitations of Java Integer Data Types

Data Type	Number of Bytes	Range
byte	1	–128 to 127
short	2	–32,768 to 32,767
int	4	–2,147,483,648 to 2,147,483,647
long	8	–9,223,372,036,854,775,808 to 9,223,372,036,854,775,807

TABLE 2-2

Typical Storage and Range Limitations of C# Integer Data Types

Data Type	Number of Bytes	Range
byte	1	Signed: –128 to 127
		Unsigned: 0 to 255
short	2	Signed: –32,768 to 32,767
		Unsigned: 0 to 65,535
int	4	Signed: –2,147,483,648 to 2,147,483,647
		Unsigned: 0 to 4,294,967,295
long	8	Signed: –9,223,372,036,854,775,808 to 9,223,372,036,854,775,807
		Unsigned: 0 to 18,446,744,073,709,551,615

Declaring floating-point data types

Floating-point values represent decimal values, such as 78.52 or –5.629. Just as you can limit the range of integer values a variable can hold, so can you limit the range of floating-point values a variable can hold.

The three types of floating data types are float, double, and decimal (C# only), as shown in Table 2-3.

TABLE 2-3

Typical Floating Point-Data Types

Data Type	Number of Bytes	Range
float	4	−1.4023 E−45 to 3.4028 E38
double	8	−4.9406 E−324 to 1.7977 E308
decimal (C# only)	16	−1.0 E−28 to 1.0 E28

REMEMBER

The ranges of the different data types listed in Table 2-3 are approximate values.

Declaring Boolean variables

To remedy the deficiency of C/C++, both Java and C# offer a Boolean data type. In Java, you can declare a Boolean variable like this:

```
boolean variablename;
```

In C#, you can declare a Boolean variable like this:

```
bool variablename;
```

Using Operators

The three types of operators used are mathematical, comparison, and logical. *Mathematical operators* calculate numeric results, such as adding, multiplying, or dividing numbers, as shown in Table 2-4.

TABLE 2-4

Mathematical Operators

Mathematical Operator	Purpose	Example
+	Addition	5 + 3.4
−	Subtraction	203.9 − 9.12
*	Multiplication	39 * 146.7
/	Division	45 / 8.41
%	Modulo (returns the remainder)	35 % 9 = 8

Relational operators compare two values and return a true or false value. The six relational operators available are shown in Table 2-5.

TABLE 2-5

Relational Operators

Relational Operator	Purpose
==	Equal to
!=	Not equal to
<	Less than
<=	Less than or equal to
>	Greater than
>=	Greater than or equal to

WARNING

The equality operator in Java/C# is two equal signs (==). If you only use a single equal sign to compare two values in Java/C#, your program will work but not the way it's supposed to.

Logical operators compare two Boolean values (true or false) and return a single true or false value, as shown in Table 2-6.

TABLE 2-6

Logical Operators

Logical Operator	Truth Table
&&	true && true = true
	true && false = false
	false && true = false
	false && false = false
||	true || true = true
	true || false = true
	false || true = true
	false || false = false
!	!true = false
	!false = true

Java and C#

Increment and decrement operators

Both Java and C# have a special increment (++) and a decrement (--) operator, which simply adds or subtracts 1 to a variable. Typically, adding 1 to a variable looks like this:

```
j = 5;
i = j + 1;
```

The increment operator replaces the + 1 portion with ++, like this:

```
j = 5;
i = ++j;
```

In the preceding example, the value of i is j + 1 or 6, and the value of j is also 6.

REMEMBER

If you place the increment operator after the variable, like this:

```
j = 5;
i = j++;
```

Now the value of i is 5, but the value of j is 6.

The decrement operator works the same way except that it subtracts 1 from a variable:

```
j = 5;
i = --j;
```

In the preceding example, the value of i is j - 1 or 4, and the value of j is also 4.

REMEMBER

If you place the decrement operator after the variable, like this:

```
j = 5;
I = j--;
```

Now the value of i is 5, but the value of j is 4.

Assignment operators

Most programming languages use the equal sign (=) to assign values to variables:

```
i = 59;
```

However, Java/C# also includes combination assignment and mathematical operators, as shown in Table 2-7.

TABLE 2-7

Assignment Operators

Assignment Operator	Purpose	Example
+=	Addition assignment	i += 7 (equivalent to i = i + 7)
-=	Subtraction assignment	i -= 4 (equivalent to i = i - 4)
*=	Multiplication assignment	i *= y (equivalent to i = i * y)
/=	Division assignment	i /= 3.5 (equivalent to i = i / 3.5)
%=	Modulo assignment	i %= 2.8 (equivalent to i = i % 2.8)

Branching Statements

The simplest branching statement is an `if` statement that only runs one or more commands if a Boolean condition is true:

```
if (condition) {
  Command;
}
```

To make the computer choose between two mutually exclusive sets of commands, you can use an `if-else` statement like this:

```
if (condition) {
  Command1;
} else {
  Command2;
}
```

Java and C# also offer an `if-elseif` statement, which uses two or more Boolean conditions to choose which of two or more groups of commands to run:

```
if (condition1) {
  Command1;
```

```
} else if (condition2) {
   Command2;
}
```

Although the if–else statement can only give the computer a choice of two groups of commands to run, the if–elseif statement can offer the computer multiple groups of commands to run:

```
if (condition1) {
   Command1;
} else if (condition2) {
   Command2;
} else if (condition3) {
   Command3;
}
```

As an alternative to the if–elseif statement, you can also use the switch statement:

```
switch (expression) {
   case value1:
      Command1;
      break;
   case value2:
      Command2;
      break;
   default:
      Command3;
      break;
}
```

REMEMBER

The switch statement often includes the break command to tell the computer when to exit the switch statement.

The preceding switch statement is equivalent to the following if–elseif statement:

```
if (expression == value1) {
   Command;
} else if (expression == value2) {
   Command;
} else {
   Command;
}
```

To check whether a variable matches multiple values, you can stack multiple case statements, like this:

```
switch (expression) {
  case value1:
  case value2:
    Command1;
    break;
  case value3:
  case value4:
    Command2;
    break;
  default:
    Command3;
    break;
}
```

The preceding switch statement is equivalent to the following if-elseif statement in C++:

```
if ((expression == value1) || (expression == value2)) {
  Command1;
} else if ((expression == value3) || (expression == value4)) {
  Command2;
} else {
  Command3;
}
```

REMEMBER

One main difference between C# and Java is the way each language handles *fall-through*, where multiple case statements can run if a break command isn't inserted into each one. Consider the following switch statement in Java, which allows fall-through:

```
switch (age) {
  case 17:
  case 18:
  case 19:
  case 20:
    System.out.println("You're too young to drink.");
  case 21:
    System.out.println("You're old enough to drink.");
}
```

In this example, the switch statement will print the following if the value of age is 17, 18, 19, or 20:

```
You're too young to drink.
You're old enough to drink.
```

Because no break command is right above the case 21: statement, the Java program falls through to the next case statement. In C#, you must explicitly define the fall-through (if this is what you want), like this:

```
switch (age) {
  case 17:
  case 18:
  case 19:
  case 20:
    Console.WriteLine("You're too young to drink.");
    goto case 21;
  case 21:
    Console.WriteLine("You're old enough to drink.");
    break;
}
```

This C# switch statement explicitly tells the computer to fall through to the case 21: statement. If you omit the goto case 21 statement, the preceding C# switch statement won't work. By forcing you to explicitly define the fall-through in a switch statement, C# helps prevent mistakes in writing a switch statement incorrectly.

Looping Statements

A *looping* statement repeats one or more commands for a fixed number of times or until a certain Boolean condition becomes true. To create a loop that repeats a fixed number of times, use the for loop, which looks like this:

```
for (startvalue; endvalue; increment) {
  Command;
}
```

If you wanted the for loop to run five times, you could set the start value to 1 and the end value to 5, like this:

```
for (i = 1; i <= 5; i++) {
   Command;
}
```

If you don't know how many times you need to repeat commands, use a while loop, which looks like this:

```
while (condition) {
   Command;
}
```

If the condition is true, the loop runs at least once. If this condition is false, the loop doesn't run.

A variation of the while loop is the do-while loop, which looks like this:

```
do {
   Command;
} while (condition);
```

The main difference between the two loops is that the while loop may run zero or more times, but the do-while loop will always run at least once.

WARNING

Somewhere inside a while and do-while loop, you must have a command that can change the condition from true to false; otherwise, the loop will never end, and your program will appear to hang or freeze.

Creating Functions

In Java/C#, every subprogram is a function that can return a value. The format of a typical Java function looks like this:

```
AccessSpecifier Modifier Datatype functionname (Parameter list)
  {
    Commands;
    return value;
  }
```

The four parts of a Java function are

>> AccessSpecifier (optional): Defines the scope of the function such as Public, which means the function can be called from anywhere. Protected means the function can only be called within the class and its subclasses. Private means the function can only be called within the class.

>> Modifier: Defines whether a function is static. A static function is independent of any instances created for a class.

>> Datatype: Defines the type of value the function returns, such as an integer (int) or floating-point number (float). If you define the data type as void, then the function doesn't return a value.

>> Parameter list: Defines any data and their data types that the function needs to work.

>> return: Defines a value to return. This value must be the same data type specified right before the function name.

If a function doesn't return a value or require any data, it might look like this:

```
public static void myfunction()
{
  Command;
}
```

If the function needs to return an integer value, it might look like this:

```
private static int myfunction()
{
  Command;
  return value;
}
```

In the preceding example, value represents any integer value.

To accept data, a function needs a *parameter list*, which simply lists a variable to hold data along with its specific data type, such as an integer or character. To create a function that accepts an integer and a character, you could do something like this:

```
private static int myfunction(int mynumber, char myletter)
{
  Command;
  return value;
}
```

The preceding function accepts two parameters by value, so the function can change the values of its parameter, but those changed values won't appear outside that function.

If you want a function to change the values of its parameters, define a parameter list by identifying which variables accept values by reference. To identify values passed by reference in C#, use the ref keyword, such as

```
int myfunction (ref int mynumber, char myletter)
{
  Command;
  return value;
}
```

REMEMBER

Java doesn't let functions change the values of parameters (called *pass by reference*). Java only lets you pass a copy of data as a parameter (called *pass by value*).

Data Structures

Through built-in libraries, Java and C# offer a variety of data structures beyond most programming languages. In Java, the most common data structures are arrays and linked lists. In C#, the .NET framework provides a variety of data structures including structures, arrays, collections, dictionaries, queues, and stacks.

Creating a C# structure

Unlike Java, C# offers a structure, which can hold two or more variables. To create a structure, use the struct keyword as follows:

```
struct name {
  public datatype variable;
};
```

The name of a structure can be any descriptive name, such as people2get or my_relatives. Inside a structure, you must declare one or more variables. A typical structure might look like this:

```
struct MyGrades {
  public char grade;
  public int class_number;
};
```

After defining a structure, you can declare a variable to represent that structure:

```
MyGrades geology = new MyGrades();
```

After declaring a variable as a structure, you can store data in the individual fields of a structure like this:

```
MyGrades geology = new MyGrades();
geology.grade = 'A';
geology.class_number = 302;
```

Creating an array

Arrays in Java/C# identify the first element of the array at index number 0, the second element of the array at index number 1, and so on.

To create an array in Java, declare its data type and size, like this:

```
datatype[] arrayname = new datatype[arraysize];
```

The array name can be any descriptive name. The array size defines how many items the array can hold. To create an array that can hold ten integers, you could define an array like this:

```
int[] mynumbers = new int[10];
```

In C# (but not Java), you can create an array and store values in it at the same time by doing the following:

```
int[] mynumbers = {25, 81, 4, 712};
```

This is equivalent to declaring an array and then adding items to the array separately, like this:

```
int[] mynumbers = new int[4];
mynumbers[0] = 25;
mynumbers[1] = 81;
mynumbers[2] = 4;
mynumbers[3] = 712;
```

Creating a Java linked list

Java offers a linked list class, which simplifies managing a linked list. By using a linked list, you can create other data structures, such as stacks and queues. To create a linked list, import the following Java library:

```
import java.util.*;
```

Then define a variable:

```
LinkedList listname = new LinkedList();
```

To add an item to a linked list, use the add, addFirst, or addLast method with the name of the linked list:

```
LinkedList shopping_list = new LinkedList();
shopping_list.add("Eggs");
shopping_list.addFirst("Milk");
shopping_list.addLast("Bacon");
```

The first item stored in the linked list would be "Milk", followed by "Eggs", and "Bacon".

To retrieve data from a linked list, you can use the getFirst, remove, removeFirst, or removeLast method. The getFirst method only retrieves data from the linked list, whereas the remove, removeFirst, and removeLast methods physically yank that data out of that linked list:

```
LinkedList shopping_list = new LinkedList();
shopping_list.add("Eggs");
shopping_list.addFirst("Milk");
System.out.println("First = " + shopping_list.removeFirst());
System.out.println("First = " + shopping_list.getFirst());
```

The preceding Java code would print the following:

```
First = Milk
First = Eggs
```

Creating C# data structures

C# includes queues, stacks, and dictionaries, which you can create by using the same syntax, like this:

```
Queue<int> queuename = new Queue<int>();
Stack<string> stackname = new Stack<string>();
Dictionary<string, int> tablename = new Dictionary(<string, int>);
```

Each type of data structure uses different methods for adding and removing data. A queue uses the Enqueue and Dequeue methods to add and remove data. A stack uses the Push and Pop methods to add and remove data. A dictionary uses the Add and Remove methods to add and remove data.

Using Objects

Both Java and C# emphasize object-oriented programming where you can create and use objects. To create an object, you must define a class where a typical class definition looks like this:

```
class ClassName
   {
   datatype propertyname;

   void methodname()
     {
      Commands;
     }
   }
```

A class can define zero or more properties and the type of data those properties can hold, such as an integer or a floating-point number. A class can also define methods, which contain code for manipulating an object in some way.

After you define a class, you can create an object from that class by declaring a variable as a new class type:

```
ClassName objectname = new ClassName();
```

So, if you created a `Furniture` class, you could create a `table` object from that class, as follows:

```
Furniture table = new Furniture();
```

To use inheritance in Java, use the `extends` keyword, like this:

```
class ClassName extends ClassToinheritFrom
{
    // Code goes here
}
```

To use inheritance in C#, use the colon to identify the class to inherit from:

```
class ClassName : ClassToinheritFrom
{
    // Code goes here
}
```

Chapter **3**

Perl and Python

P erl and Python are scripting languages meant to help programmers create something easily. The main difference between Perl and Python over traditional programming languages is their intended use.

Systems languages (such as C/C++) are meant to create stand-alone applications, such as operating systems or word processors, which is why systems languages are almost always compiled.

Scripting languages are meant more for linking different programs together, such as transferring data that someone types into a web page and storing it in a database. As a result, scripting languages are almost always interpreted, which makes them more portable across different operating systems.

Systems languages are often known as *type-safe* because they force you to declare a specific data type (such as integer or string) for each variable. In contrast, scripting languages often allow a variable to hold anything it wants. One moment it may hold a string, the next an integer, and after that a decimal number. Such typeless scripting languages give you greater flexibility at the possible expense of causing errors by variables containing unexpected data.

Perl's philosophy is that there's always more than one way to do it, so Perl often offers multiple commands that accomplish the exact same thing. The goal is to let you choose the way you like best.

Python takes the opposite approach and emphasizes a small and simple language that relies less on symbols (like C/C++) and more on readable commands to make programs easier to understand. Although Perl retains much of the syntax familiar to C/C++ programmers, Python abandons curly brackets and semicolons for a cleaner language that's simpler to read and write.

Both Perl and Python are used in web applications, as well as for more specialized uses, such as text manipulation. Perl is particularly popular in the field of bioinformatics and finance, whereas Python has been adapted as a scripting language for many graphics and animation programs and artificial intelligence (AI) research.

Although system programming languages like C/C++ were designed to maximize the efficiency of computer equipment, languages like Perl and Python are designed to maximize the efficiency of programmers, who are now more expensive than computer equipment. When programmers need to write something in a hurry that doesn't involve manipulating the hardware of a computer, they often turn to Perl and Python.

Python is often associated with the British comedy troupe Monty Python's Flying Circus. It's considered good form among Python programmers to slip *Monty Python* references into their programs whenever possible. ("It's just a flesh wound. . . .")

Reviewing the Structure of a Perl or Python Program

Because Perl and Python are interpreted languages, you can often type commands one line at a time or type and save commands in a file. A simple Perl program might look like this:

```
print "This is a simple Perl program.\n";
```

A Python program is even simpler:

```
print ('This is a simple Python program.')
```

TECHNICAL STUFF

When using strings in Python, you can use either single or double quotation marks. Whatever style you choose, be consistent.

Perl adapts the syntax of the C language, including the use of semicolons at the end of each statement and the use of curly brackets to identify a block of commands. Python omits semicolons; also, instead of using curly brackets to identify a block of commands, Python uses indentation. To identify a block of commands in Perl, use curly brackets like this:

```
if ($x > 5)
{
  command1;
  command2;
}
```

In Python, the same program might look like this:

```
if x > 5:
  command1
  command2
```

REMEMBER

You can write both Perl and Python programs from a command-line prompt (meaning you type commands one at a time) or saved as a file and then loaded into the interpreter. For testing short programs, typing them in one line at a time is probably faster, but for creating large programs, saving commands in a text file is easier.

Creating Comments

To write a comment in Perl, use the hash symbol (#). Anything that appears to the right of the # is treated as a comment:

```
# This is a comment.
print "This is a simple Perl program.\n";
exit;   # This is another comment.
```

In Python, you can also use the # symbol to create comments on a single line. If you want to create a comment covering multiple lines, use triple quotes to define the start and end of a comment, like this:

```
""" This is a multiple-line comment.
    The triple quotes highlight the beginning
```

```
    and the end of the multiple lines. """
print ('This is a simple Python program.')
```

Defining Variables

Both Perl and Python allow variables to hold any data types. In Perl, variable names begin with a dollar sign ($), such as $myVar. Perl and Python are case-sensitive languages, so the Perl variable $myVar is completely different from $MYVar, while the Python variable DueDate is completely different from the variable duedate.

WARNING

If you misspell a variable in Perl or Python, both languages will treat the misspelled variable as a completely new and valid variable.

Using Operators

The three types of operators used are mathematical, relational, and logical. *Mathematical operators* calculate numeric results such as adding, multiplying, or dividing numbers, as shown in Table 3-1.

TABLE 3-1

Mathematical Operators

Mathematical Operator	Purpose	Example
+	Addition	5 + 3.4
−	Subtraction	203.9 − 9.12
*	Multiplication	39 * 146.7
/	Division	45 / 8.41
%	Modulo (returns the remainder)	35 % 9 = 8
**	Exponentiation	5 ** 2 = 25
divmod(x,y) (Python only)	Returns both x / y and x % y	divmod(12,8) = (1,4)

WARNING

When Python uses the division operator (/) to divide two integers, the result will be a floating-point value, like this:

9 / 4 = 2.25

If at least one number is a floating-point value, the result will also be a floating-point value:

9.0 / 4 = 2.25

Or

9 / 4.0 = 2.25

Relational operators compare two values and return a True or False value. The six relational operators available are shown in Table 3-2.

TABLE 3-2

Relational Operators

Relational Operator	Purpose
==	Equal to
!=	Not equal to
<	Less than
<=	Less than or equal to
>	Greater than
>=	Greater than or equal to
< = > (Perl only)	Comparison with signed result

WARNING

The equality operator in Perl and Python is two equal signs (==). A single equal sign (=) usually assigns a value to a variable.

Perl offers a unique *comparison with signed result operator* (<=>), which compares two values and returns 0 (if the two values are equal), 1 (if the first value is greater than the second), or –1 (if the first value is less than the second), as shown in Table 3-3.

Logical operators compare two Boolean values (True [1] or False [0]) and return a single True or False value, as shown in Table 3-4.

CHAPTER 3 **Perl and Python** 581

TABLE 3-3

Using Perl's Comparison with Signed Result Operator

Example	Result
5 <=> 5	0
7 <=> 5	1
2 <=> 5	−1

TABLE 3-4

Logical Operators

Logical Operator	Truth Table
&& (Perl)	1 and 1 = 1
and (Python)	1 and 0 = 0
	0 and 1 = 0
	0 and 0 = 0
|| (Perl)	1 or 1 = 1
or (Python)	1 or 0 = 1
	0 or 1 = 1
	0 or 0 = 0
! (Perl)	!1 = False (0)
not (Python)	!0 = True (1)

REMEMBER

In Python, Boolean values are True or False, but in Perl, Boolean values are typically represented as true by 1 or false by 0.

Increment and decrement operators

Perl (but not Python) has an increment operator (++), which adds 1 to a variable, and a decrement operator (−−), which subtracts 1 from a variable. Typically, adding 1 to a variable looks like this:

```
j = 5;
i = j + 1;
```

The increment operator replaces the + 1 portion with ++:

```
j = 5;
i = ++j;
```

In the preceding example, the value of i is j + 1 or 6, and the value of j is also 6.

REMEMBER

If you place the increment operator after the variable, like this:

```
j = 5;
i = j++;
```

Now the value of i is 5, but the value of j is 6.

The decrement operator works the same way except that it subtracts 1 from a variable:

```
j = 5;
i = --j;
```

In the preceding example, the value of i is j – 1 or 4, and the value of j is also 4.

REMEMBER

If you place the decrement operator after the variable, like this:

```
j = 5;
i = j--;
```

Now the value of i is 5, but the value of j is 4.

Assignment operators

Most programming languages use the equal sign (=) to assign values to variables:

```
i = 59;
```

However, Perl and Python also include combination assignment and mathematical operators, as shown in Table 3-5.

TABLE 3-5

Assignment Operators

Assignment Operator	Purpose	Example
+=	Addition assignment	i += 7 (equivalent to i = i + 7)
-=	Subtraction assignment	i -= 4 (equivalent to i = i - 4)
*=	Multiplication assignment	i *= y (equivalent to i = i * y)
/=	Division assignment	i /= 3.5 (equivalent to i = i / 3.5)
%=	Modulo assignment	i %= 2.8 (equivalent to i = i % 2.8)

Branching Statements

The simplest branching statement is an if statement that only runs one or more commands if a Boolean condition is true. In Perl, the IF statement uses curly brackets to enclose one or more commands:

```
if (condition) {
  Command1;
  Command2;
}
```

In Python, the if statement uses indentation to enclose one or more commands:

```
if (condition):
  Command1
  Command2
```

To make the computer choose between two mutually exclusive sets of commands, you can use an if-else statement in Perl, like this:

```
if (condition) {
  Command;
  Command;
}
else {
  Command;
  Command;
}
```

In Python, the `if-else` statement looks like this:

```
if (condition):
  Command
  Command
else:
  Command
  Command
```

The `if-else` statement offers only two choices. If you want to offer multiple choices, you can use the `if-elseif` statement, which uses two or more Boolean conditions to choose which of two or more groups of commands to run. In Perl, use the `elsif` keyword:

```
if (condition1) {
  Command;
  Command;
}
elsif (condition2) {
  Command;
  Command;
}
elsif (condition3) {
  Command;
  Command;
}
```

In Python, use the `elif` keyword:

```
if (condition1):
  Command
  Command
elif (condition2):
  Command
  Command
elif (condition3):
  Command
  Command
```

REMEMBER

Unlike other programming languages, neither Perl nor Python provides a `switch` statement. In Perl, you can use a `switch` statement by installing and including a Switch module, like this:

```
use Switch;
```

Looping Statements

A *looping* statement repeats one or more commands a fixed number of times or until a certain Boolean condition becomes `false`. To create a loop that repeats a fixed number of times, use the `for` loop, which looks like this:

```
for (startvalue; endvalue; increment) {
  Command;
}
```

If you wanted the `for` loop to run five times, you could set the startvalue to 1 and the endvalue to 5, like this:

```
for ($i = 1; $i <= 5; $i++) {
  Command;
}
```

In Python, the `for` loop looks dramatically different:

```
for variable in (list):
  Command
  Command
```

To make a Python `for` loop repeat five times, you could do this:

```
for x in (1,2,3,4,5):
  print (x)
```

The preceding Python `for` loop would print the following:

```
1
2
3
4
5
```

If you want a `for` loop to repeat many times (such as 100 times), it can be tedious to list 100 separate numbers. So, Python offers a `range()` function that eliminates listing multiple numbers. To use the `range()` function to loop five times, you could do this:

```
for x in range(5):
  print (x)
```

Because the range() function starts with 0, the preceding Python for loop would print the following:

```
0
1
2
3
4
```

Another way to use the range() function is to define a lower and upper range, like this:

```
for x in range(25, 30):
  print (x)
```

This for loop would print the numbers 25, 26, 27, 28, and 29. Rather than increment by one, you can also use the range() function to define your own increment, which can be positive or negative:

```
for x in range(25, 30, 2):
  print (x)
```

This for loop would print 25, 27, and 29.

If you don't know how many times you need to repeat commands, use a while loop, which looks like this:

```
while (condition) {
  Command;
  Command;
}
```

If the condition is true, the loop runs at least once. If this condition is false, the loop doesn't run. In Python, the while loop looks like this:

```
while condition:
  Command
  Command
```

WARNING

Somewhere inside a while loop, you must have a command that can change the condition from true to false; otherwise, the loop will never end, and your program will appear to hang or freeze.

Creating Functions

In Perl and Python, every subprogram is a function that can return a value. The format of a typical Perl function looks like this:

```
sub functionname {
   Commands;
   return $value;
}
```

When you pass parameters to a Perl function, that function can access them with the foreach keyword and the @_ array, like this:

```
sub functionname {
   foreach $variablename (@_) {
     Commands;
   }
   return $value;
}
```

The foreach command plucks each item from the @_ array and temporarily stores it in $variablename.

A typical Python function looks like this:

```
def functionname (parameter_list):
   Commands
   return value
```

If you don't want a function to return a value, omit the return line.

Making Data Structures

Storing data in single variables can work, but when you need to store groups of related data together, it's too cumbersome to create multiple variables, especially if you don't know how many you're going to need ahead of time.

Instead of creating multiple, separate variables, use a data structure. Data structures group related data together so you can easily store and retrieve that data later.

Perl data structures

Two common types of data structures available in Perl include

>> **Arrays:** An *array* stores multiple items, identified by an index number.

>> **Hashes:** A *hash* stores multiple items, identified by a key, which can be a number or a string.

Creating a Perl array

Like C/C++, Perl arrays are zero-based, so the first element of an array is considered 0, the second is 1, and so on. When you create a Perl array, you must name that array with the at sign (@). You can also define the elements of an array at the time you create the array, like this:

```
@arrayname = (element1, element2, element3);
```

If you want to create an array that contains a range of numbers, you can list each number individually like this:

```
@numberarray = (1, 2, 3, 4, 5);
```

You can also use the range operator (..) to define the lower and upper bounds of a range:

```
@numberarray = (1..5);
```

To access the individual elements stored in an array, use the dollar sign ($) in front of the array name:

```
@numberarray = (1..10);
$thisone = $numberarray[0];
```

The value stored in the $thisone variable is the first element of the @numberarray, which is 1.

One unique feature of Perl arrays is that you can use arrays to mimic a stack data structure with Perl's push and pop commands. To push a new item onto an array, you can use the push command:

```
push(@arrayname, $item2add);
```

To pop an item off the array, use the pop command, like this:

```
$variablename = pop(@arrayname);
```

Creating a Perl hash

A hash stores an item along with a key. Perl offers two ways to store values and keys. The first is like this:

```
%hasharray = (
   key1 => value1,
   key2 => value2,
   key3 => value3,
);
```

Notice that hash arrays are identified by the percent sign (%).

A second way to define a hash array is like this:

```
%hasharray = ("key1", value1, "key2", value2, "key3", value3);
```

To retrieve data from a hash array, you need to know the key associated with that value and identify the hash array name by using the dollar sign ($), like this:

```
$variable = $hasharray {"key1"};
```

The preceding command would store the value associated with "key1" into the $variable.

Python data structures

Python offers tuples, lists, and dictionary data structures. Both tuples and lists contain a series of items, such as numbers and strings. The main difference is that items in a tuple can't be changed, whereas items in a list can be. A dictionary stores values with keys, allowing you to retrieve a value using its distinct key.

Creating a Python tuple

A *tuple* can contain different data, such as numbers and strings. To create a tuple, list all the items in parentheses like this:

```
tuplename = (item1, item2, item3)
```

To retrieve a value from a tuple, you must identify it by its index number, where the first item in the tuple is assigned a 0 index number, the second item is assigned a 1 index number, and so on. To retrieve the second item (index number 1) in a tuple, you could use this:

```
variablename = tuplename[1]
```

Creating a Python list

Unlike a tuple, a Python *list* lets you change, add, or delete items. To create a list, identify all items in the list by using square brackets, like this:

```
listname = [item1, item2, item3]
```

To retrieve a value from a list, you must identify it by its index number, where the first item in the list is assigned a 0 index number, the second item is assigned a 1 index number, and so on. To retrieve the first item (index number 0) in a list, you could use this:

```
variablename = listname[0]
```

To add new items to a list, use the append command:

```
listname.append(newitem)
```

The append command always adds a new item at the end of a list. If you want to insert an item in a specific location in the list using its index number, use the insert command, like this:

```
listname.insert(index, newitem)
```

To remove the first instance of an item in a list, use the remove command:

```
listname.remove(existingitem)
```

REMEMBER

If a list contains identical items (such as 23), the remove command deletes the item with the lowest index number.

Creating a Python dictionary

A dictionary contains values and keys assigned to each value. To create a dictionary, use curly brackets, like this:

```
Dictionary_name = {key1:value1, key2:value2, key3:value3}
```

To retrieve a value using its key, use the get command like this:

```
Variable = dictionary_name.get(key)
```

Using Objects

Both Perl and Python are object-oriented programming languages where you can create and use objects in your programs. To create an object, you must define a class. In Perl, a typical class definition looks like this:

```
package classname;
sub new {
  my $objectname = {
    Data;
    Data;
  };
  bless $objectname, $classname;
  return $objectname;
}
sub methodname{
  Commands;
  Commands;
};
```

In Python, a class looks like this:

```
class ClassName:
  Data
  Data
  def methodname (self):
    Commands
    Commands
    Commands
```

A class lists *properties* (data) along with one or more methods, which contain code for manipulating an object in some way.

After you define a class, you can create an object from that class by declaring a variable as a new class type. In Perl, you create an object by creating a constructor method, commonly called new:

```
my $variablename = classname->new();
```

In Python, create an object like this:

```
objectname = new classname()
```

To use inheritance in Perl, use the @ISA variable inside a new class:

```
package newobject;
use class2inheritfrom;
@ISA = qw(class2inheritfrom);
```

To use inheritance in Python, identify the class to inherit from when you create a new class:

```
class ClassName(class2inheritfrom):
  Data
  Data
  def methodname(self):
    Commands
    Commands
    Commands
```

To inherit from multiple classes in Python, define additional classes, separated by a comma:

```
class ClassName(class2inheritfrom, anotherclass):
  Data
  Data
  def methodname(self):
    Commands
    Commands
    Commands
```

IN THIS CHAPTER

» **Understanding the structure of Kotlin programs**

» **Making comments**

» **Declaring variables and constants**

» **Using mathematical operators**

» **Working with branching and looping statements**

» **Creating functions, data structures, and objects**

Chapter **4**

Kotlin

When the world of mobile computing (smartphones and tablets) swept over the world, programmers wanted to create apps for these new devices. When the iPhone redefined the smartphone market, Google quickly released a similar operating system called Android.

Initially, Google endorsed Java as the favored language for creating Android apps. However, after various lawsuits involving Oracle (the owner of Java), Google looked for other ways to create Android apps. That's when a company called JetBrains developed Kotlin (https://kotlinlang.org), a language similar to Java. Now Google has officially endorsed Kotlin as the preferred language for creating Android apps.

Although Kotlin is mostly used to create Android apps, you can use the language to create iPhone apps as well. If you want to create mobile apps, you need to understand Kotlin for the still-growing mobile computing market on both Android and iOS.

Looking at the Structure of a Kotlin Program

Although Kotlin is a completely new programming language, it's meant to work with Java. Kotlin's libraries depend on the Java Class library and Kotlin programs compile to the Java virtual machine (JVM). Programmers can either use Kotlin together with Java or as a completely independent language. Think of Kotlin as an improved, cleaner version of Java.

The typical structure of a Kotlin program begins with a main function like this:

```
fun main() {
  println("This is a typical Kotlin program")
}
```

REMEMBER

Unlike Java and other curly-bracket languages like C++, Kotlin commands don't end with a semicolon.

The fun keyword declares a function as a block of code while main() is the main function that every Kotlin program needs.

Like Java and C++, Kotlin encloses blocks of commands within curly brackets. The println command simply prints data.

Creating Comments

Because Kotlin is based on curly-bracket languages (C/C++), it uses the same symbols for creating comments. To define a single-line comment, just use the double forward slash (//), where anything to the right of the // is ignored by the compiler, like this:

```
// This is a single-line comment in Kotlin.
```

To create multiline comments, use the /* and */ symbols to enclose multiple lines, like this:

```
/* This is a multiline comment.
   Notice that anything trapped between these
   two symbols will get completely ignored
   by the compiler.
*/
```

Declaring Variables

In most programming languages, you declare a variable and the data type it can hold. With Kotlin, you can simply assign a value to a variable and Kotlin can infer the data type of that value. For example, if you wanted a variable to store an integer, you could just store an integer into that variable, like this:

```
var myNumber = 84
```

Because 84 is an integer, Kotlin assumes that the variable can hold integer (Int) data types. Just to make it clear, you can add the data type of a variable like this:

```
var myNumber: Int = 84
```

You can also just declare a variable and its data type without assigning it a value initially. Then assign a value to that variable later, like this:

```
var myNumber: Int
myNumber = 84
```

Declaring string data types

Kotlin can store a single character ('A') in the Char data type, or several words ("This is a string of text") in the String data type. To declare a string variable, use the String keyword:

```
var variableName1: String
```

In Kotlin, strings are enclosed in double quotation marks. After you declare a variable to hold a string, you can assign a string to that variable, like this:

```
variableName1 = "This string gets stored in the variable."
```

If you only want to store a single character, you can use the Char keyword:

```
var variableName2: Char
```

Then you can assign a single character to this variable, like this:

```
variableName2 = 'B'
```

Kotlin

TECHNICAL STUFF

When assigning text to a String data type, enclose the text in double quotation marks. When assigning a single character to a Char data type, enclose the single character in single quotation marks.

Kotlin treats strings as arrays of characters. That means you can access individual characters in a string by specifying the string variable plus an index value where an index value of 0 represents the first letter of the string, an index value of 1 represents the second letter of the string, and so on. The following two println statements would print the first letter of the string (index value 0) and the sixth letter of the string (index value 5):

```
var message = "The cat is on the shelf."
println(message[0]) // Returns 'T'
println(message[5]) // Returns 'a'
```

Declaring integer data types

Whole numbers represent integers such as 349, –152, or 41. A whole number can be positive or negative. The most common type of integer data type is Int and is used as follows:

```
var intValue: Int
```

To accept different ranges of integer values, Kotlin offers several integer data types. For example, if a variable needs only to hold a small range of values from –128 to 127, you can declare it as a Byte data type, like this:

```
var byteValue: Byte
```

Different integer data types limit the range of integer values. The greater the range of values you need to store, the more memory needed. The smaller the range of values, the less memory required. Table 4-1 shows different integer data types and the range of values they can hold.

TABLE 4-1

Kotlin Integer Data Types

Data Type	Range
Byte	–128 to 127
Short	–32,768 to 32,767
Int	–2,147,483,648 to 2,147,483,647
Long	–9,223,372,036,854,775,808 to 9,223,372,036,854,775,807

TECHNICAL STUFF

When assigning an integer to a Long data type, you can add an L to the end of the number to make it clear the number is a Long data type, like this

```
var Variablename1: Long
Variablename1 = 678L
```

Declaring floating-point data types

Floating-point values are numbers such as 1.88 or –91.4. Just as you can limit the range of integer values a variable can hold, so you can limit the range of decimal values a variable can hold. In Kotlin, the two floating-point data types are Float and Double, as shown in Table 4-2.

TABLE 4-2

Kotlin Floating-Point Data Types

Data Type	Range
Float	3.4 E–38 to 3.4 E38
Double	1.7 E–308 to 1.7 E308

REMEMBER

If you assign a floating-point number to a variable, Kotlin assumes the data type is Double unless you specifically declare the variable as a Float data type.

TECHNICAL STUFF

When assigning decimal numbers as a Float data type, you can add an F at the end of the floating-point number to make it clear it's a Float data type, like this

```
var Variablename1: Float
Variablename1 = 67.257F
```

Declaring Boolean values

Besides storing text and numbers, variables can also hold a Boolean value — true or false. To declare a variable to hold a Boolean value, use the Boolean keyword, as follows:

```
var Variablename1: Boolean
Variablename1 = true
```

Declaring Constants

Constants always represent a fixed value. In Kotlin, you can declare a constant and its specific value as follows:

```
const val CONSTANT_NAME = value
```

So, if you wanted to assign 3.14 to a PI constant, you could do this:

```
const val PI = 3.1415
```

REMEMBER

You can only assign a value to a constant once. When a constant holds a value, you can never change that value later in your program.

WARNING

Declaring a constant in Kotlin requires the const val keywords, but declaring a variable uses the var keyword. Because these two keywords look so similar, it's easy to declare a constant by mistake and then wonder why you can't change its value like a variable (or vice versa).

Using Operators

The three types of operators used are mathematical, relational, and logical. *Mathematical* operators calculate numeric results such as adding, multiplying, or dividing numbers. Table 4-3 lists the mathematical operators used in Kotlin.

TABLE 4-3

Mathematical Operators

Mathematical Operator	Purpose	Example
+	Addition	5 + 3.4
−	Subtraction	203.9 − 9.12
*	Multiplication	39 * 146.7
/	Division	45 / 8.41
%	Modulo (returns the remainder)	35 % 9 = 8

Relational operators compare two values and return a true or false value. The six relational operators available in Kotlin are shown in Table 4-4.

TABLE 4-4

Relational Operators

Relational Operator	Purpose
==	Equal to
!=	Not equal to
<	Less than
<=	Less than or equal to
>	Greater than
>=	Greater than or equal to

Logical operators, as shown in Table 4-5, compare two Boolean values (true or false) and return a single true or false value.

TABLE 4-5

Logical Operators

Logical Operator	Truth Table
&&	true && true = true
	true && false = false
	false && true = false
	false && false = false
||	true || true = true
	true || false = true
	false || true = true
	false || false = false
!	!true = false
	!false = true

Branching Statements

The simplest branching statement is an if-then statement that only runs one or more commands if a Boolean condition is true, such as

```
if (condition) {
    // Commands
}
```

To make the computer choose between two mutually exclusive sets of commands, you can use an if–else statement:

```
if (condition) {
    // Commands
} else {
    // Other commands
}
```

If a Boolean condition is true, the if–else statement runs the first group of commands; if the Boolean condition is false, the if–else statement runs the second group of commands. No matter what, an if–else statement will always run one set of commands or the other.

Kotlin offers a variation of the if–else statement that lets you assign values to a variable, like this:

```
val age = 21
var message = if (age < 21) "You are still a minor" else "You are legally an
    adult"
println(message)
```

The preceding code works by checking the (age < 21) condition. Because the value of age is 21, 21 < 21 evaluates to false. That means the else portion assigns "You are legally an adult" into the message variable. If the value of age were 12, then the (age < 21) condition would be true and the code would assign "You are still a minor" into the message variable.

One problem with the if–else statement is that it only gives you two possible choices. One way to offer multiple choices is through the if–else if statement, like this:

```
if (condition1) {
    // Commands
} else if (condition2) {
    // Other commands
}
```

If condition1 is true, then the first set of commands runs. However, if condition1 is false, then it checks whether condition2 is true. If so, then it runs the second set of commands.

If both condition1 and condition2 are false, then no commands will run at all. That's why if-else if statements often include an else portion at the end, like this:

```
if (condition1) {
    // Commands
} else if (condition2) {
    // Other commands
} else {
    // Default commands to run
}
```

Now if both condition1 and condition2 are false, then the commands stored under the else portion will run by default. The else portion ensures that one set of commands will always run.

The problem with the if-else if statement is that when you start checking for multiple conditions, the entire if-else if statement can look cluttered and hard to read:

```
if (condition1) {
    // Commands
} else if (condition1) {
    // Other commands
} else if (condition2) {
    // Other commands
} else if (condition3) {
    // Other commands
} else if (condition4) {
    // Other commands
} else {
    // Default commands to run
}
```

To provide multiple options in a much cleaner form, Kotlin offers a when statement that looks like this:

```
var day = 3
var result = when (day) {
    0 -> "Sunday"
    1 -> "Monday"
    2 -> "Tuesday"
    3 -> "Wednesday"
    4 -> "Thursday"
```

```
  5 -> "Friday"
  6 -> "Saturday"
  else -> "No such day."
}
println(result)
```

The preceding when statement is equivalent to the following if-else if statement:

```
var day = 3
if (day == 0) {
    result = "Sunday"
} else if (day == 1) {
    result = "Monday"
} else if (day == 2) {
    result = "Tuesday"
} else if (day == 3) {
    result = "Wednesday"
} else if (day == 4) {
    result = "Thursday"
} else if (day == 5) {
    result = "Friday"
} else if (day == 6) {
    result = "Saturday"
} else {
  result = "No such day"
}
println(result)
```

To check whether a variable matches multiple values, you can separate multiple values with commas or you can match a range of values, like this:

```
var number = 6
var result = when (number) {
  1, 2, 3 -> "1, 2, or 3"
  in 4..6 -> "4, 5, or 6"
  else -> "Not within the range of 1 - 6"
}
println(result)
```

The preceding when statement is equivalent to the following if-else if statement:

```
var number = 6
var result: String
```

```
if (number == 1 || number == 2 || number == 3) {
  result = "1, 2, or 3"
} else if (number >= 4 && number <= 6) {
  result = "4, 5, or 6"
} else {
  result = "Not within the range of 1 - 6"
}
println(result)
```

Looping Statements

A *looping* statement repeats one or more commands a fixed number of times or until a certain Boolean condition becomes true. To create a loop that repeats a fixed number of times, use the for loop, which looks like this:

```
for (variable in start..end) {
    // Commands
}
```

If you want the for loop to run five times, set the start value to 1 and the end value to 5, like this:

```
for (x in 1..5) {
    println(x)
}
```

Normally, the for loop counts up, but you can use the downTo keyword to make the for loop count backward, as shown in this example:

```
for (x in 5 downTo 1) {
    println(x)
}
```

If you don't know how many times you need to repeat commands, use a while or a do-while loop.

The while loop repeats while a condition remains true and looks like this:

```
while (condition) {
    // Commands
}
```

If the condition is `false` right from the start, this loop won't even run once. Here's an example of a `while` loop:

```
var x = 0
while (x < 5) {
  println(x)
  x += 1
}
```

WARNING

When using a `while` or a `do-while` loop, make sure the loop eventually changes the condition so it becomes `false`. If you fail to do this, you risk creating an endless loop that will freeze your program.

If you want a loop that runs at least once, use the `do-while` loop, which looks like this:

```
do {
  // Commands
} while (condition)
```

This loop runs at least once before checking a condition. If the condition is `false`, the loop stops. An example of a `do-while` loop looks like this:

```
var x = 0
do {
  println(x)
  x += 1
} while (x < 5)
```

Creating Functions

Functions let you define mini-programs that can contain code that might be useful multiple times throughout your program. Instead of writing the same code in multiple locations, it's better to write the code once, store it in a function, and then *call* (run) that function whenever another part of your program needs to run that code.

To create a function, use the `fun` keyword:

```
fun myFunction() {
  // Commands
}
```

To run or call that function, just use the function name. Functions without any parameters will do the same thing over and over again, so most functions need to accept one or more parameters that define a variable name and its data type:

```kotlin
fun myFunction(firstName: String) {
  println("Hello, " + firstName + ". Glad you re here!")
}
```

This function accepts a string and then prints out "Hello, " followed by the string that was passed into the function, and concluding with ". Glad you're here!" Here's how to call the preceding function:

```kotlin
fun main() {
  myFunction("Betty")
  myFunction("Joe")
  myFunction("Florence")
}

fun myFunction(firstName: String) {
  println("Hello, " + firstName + ". Glad you're here!")
}
```

Here's another alternative to concatenating strings together:

```kotlin
fun myFunction(firstName: String) {
  println("Hello, $firstName. Glad you're here!")
}
```

When defining a parameter in a function, you must define the parameter name (such as firstName) and its data type (such as String). When you call the function, you just need to pass it the type of data it expects, such as myFunction("Florence").

Sometimes you may want a function to return a value. To do that, you must specify the data type that the function name represents:

```kotlin
fun multiplyMe(x: Int, y: Int): Int {
  return x * y
}
```

This function accepts two integers (x: Int, y: Int) and returns an integer value (: Int). Then it multiplies x by y and returns the result.

When calling this function, treat the function name like a value and assign it to a variable, like this:

```
fun main() {
  var answer: Int

  answer = multiplyMe(4, 8)
  println(answer)
}
```

This main function declares an answer variable to hold integer (Int) data types. Then it calls the multiplyMe function by passing it two numbers (4, 8). The multiplyMe function multiplies x by y and returns the value (32).

This value (32) then gets stored in the answer variable, which finally gets printed.

Creating functions that return a value involves a three-step process:

1. **Define the data type that the function needs to return (such as Int or String).**

2. **Make sure the function uses the return keyword followed by the proper data type (such as Int or String).**

3. **Call the function and treat the function name as a single value.**

Creating Data Structures

Data structures are ways to organize related variables together. Three common data structures used in Kotlin are

>> **Lists:** Store multiple variables inside a single variable

>> **Arrays:** Store multiple items that consist of the same data type

>> **Sets:** Store an arbitrary collection of items

Creating a list

A *list* lets you store one or more variables in a single variable. Lists can contain multiple variables of the same data type or completely different data types. If you want to create a read-only list, you can do this:

```
var pets = listOf("Oscar", 7, true)
```

Lists are ordered, which means you can retrieve them by referencing the list name followed by an index value where the first item in a list has an index value of 0, the second item has an index value of 1, and so on. The following retrieves the second item in a list:

```
var pets = listOf("Oscar", 7, true)
println(pets[1])
```

When you create a list, you need to store all the data in it that you want. Otherwise, you can't add or remove items later. However, if you want to add and remove items from a list, you'll need to create a mutable list:

```
var pets = mutableListOf("Oscar", 7, true)
```

With a mutable list, you can use the add and remove commands to modify a list such as:

```
var pets = mutableListOf("Oscar", 7, true)
pets.add("fish")
pets.remove("Oscar")
println(pets)
```

This code creates a mutable list and fills it with a string ("Oscar"), an integer (7), and a Boolean (true). Then it adds another string ("fish") to the end of the list. Finally, it removes an item ("Oscar") and prints it out.

REMEMBER

Kotlin is a case-sensitive language, which means if you try to remove "oscar" instead of "Oscar", Kotlin won't find "oscar" in the list so the remove command won't do anything.

You can also add or remove data from a specific location by identifying the index value. So, if you want to remove the second item in a list, you can do this:

```
var pets = mutableListOf("Oscar", 7, true)
pets.removeAt(1)
```

This would remove the item at index position 1, which is the second item (7). To add data at a specific index position in a list, you could do this:

```
var pets = mutableListOf("Oscar", 7, true)
pets.add(2, 9.37)
```

The preceding add command puts the number 9.37 in index position 2, which makes the number 9.37 appear in the third position in the list.

Creating an array

To create an array in Kotlin, you must use the arrayOf command, like this:

```
var pets = arrayOf("Oscar", 7, true)
```

If you want to retrieve a single item from the array, you need to specify the array name plus the index value of the data you want to retrieve, like this:

```
println(pets[1])
```

This command would print the second item (at index position 1) from the pets array, which would be 7.

To replace an item in an array with a new value, just specify the array name and the index position where you want to put the data, like this:

```
var pets = arrayOf("Oscar", 7, true)
pets[1] = "Frank"
```

This code replaces 7 with "Frank".

Creating a set

Kotlin includes a data structure known as a *set.* A set lets you define a group of unique items with no duplicate data. You can create a set that you can't modify later using the setOf command, like this:

```
var fixedSet = setOf("cat", "fish", 12, 8.3)
print(fixedSet)
```

If you want to add and delete items from a set, you can create a mutable set using the `mutableSetOf` command, like this:

```
var mutableSet = mutableSetOf("cat", "fish", 12, 8.3)
print(mutableSet)
```

After you define a mutable set, you can use the `add` or `remove` commands to add items to a set or remove specific items from a set, like this:

```
var mutableSet = mutableSetOf("cat", "fish", 12, 8.3)
println(mutableSet)
mutableSet.add("treehouse")
println(mutableSet)
mutableSet.remove("fish")
println(mutableSet)
```

This code first creates a mutable set filled with two strings ("cat" and "fish"), one integer (12), and one floating-point number (8.3).

Then it adds a string ("treehouse") to the set. Finally, it removes "fish" from the set. If "fish" is not found in the set, the `remove` command won't do anything at all.

Creating Objects

Kotlin lets you create class files that define the *properties* (variables) and *methods* (functions) that work together. Then you can create one or more objects from a single class file. To define a class, create one or more properties and assign them initial values, like this:

```
class Animal {
  var name = ""
  var age = 0
  var weight = 0.0
}
```

After defining a class, you can create an object from that class:

```
var cat = Animal()
```

In this example, the object cat is defined by the Animal class. After you've created an object, you can assign data to the object's various properties like this:

```
cat.name = "Fluffy"
cat.age = 3
cat.weight = 12.48
println(cat.name)
println(cat.age)
println(cat.weight)
```

In this example, I created a class file with multiple properties that have an initial value. It's possible to define a class with properties that are undefined like this:

```
class Animal(var name: String, var age: Int, var weight: Double)
```

When you create an object from this class, you need to specify data for each property like this:

```
var cat = Animal("Fluffy", 3, 12.48)
```

Now you can access the object's properties:

```
println(cat.name)
println(cat.age)
println(cat.weight)
```

Finally, a class can also contain methods that can accept parameters and calculate results:

```
class Animal(var name: String, var age: Int, var weight: Double) {
  fun greeting(animalNoise: String) {
    println("$name makes this sound: " + animalNoise)
  }
}
```

Now you can call this method by creating an object and specifying the object name and the method name to run, like this:

```
fun main() {
  var cat = Animal("Fluffy", 3, 12.48)
  cat.greeting("meow")
}
```

This would print out "Fluffy makes this sound: meow".

IN THIS CHAPTER

» **Understanding the structure of Swift programs**

» **Making comments**

» **Declaring variables and constants**

» **Using mathematical operators**

» **Working with branching and looping statements**

» **Creating functions, data structures, and objects**

Chapter **5**

Swift and SwiftUI

When the iPhone first came out, you couldn't create apps for it. Developers pressured Apple into letting them create apps, and Apple finally relented and adopted Objective-C as the official language for creating iPhone apps.

Unfortunately, Objective-C can be just as difficult to learn as C++. That's why in 2014, Apple introduced a much simpler, yet still powerful language called Swift. The main idea behind Swift is to offer a language that's faster, safer, and easier than Objective-C. Because Swift is Apple's official programming language, you should learn Swift if you plan to write apps for any of Apple's various products (Mac, iPhone, iPad, Apple Watch, or Apple TV).

REMEMBER

Although Swift is open source and has been partially ported to Linux and Windows, it's still largely an Apple-only programming language.

Considering the Structure of a Swift Program

Because Swift is a relatively new language, it embraces the best features of languages like C++, Java, and Python, while focusing on clarity and safety. Clarity means the code is easy to read and understand because most programs are rewritten and modified over time. Safety means that Swift avoids the worst features of C++ and makes it difficult to write code that can cause problems such as memory leaks, which is when a program gobbles up memory until there's no more left for any other program.

The most common way to use Swift is through Xcode, which is Apple's free compiler. When using Xcode, you have a choice of creating apps that use two types of user interfaces (UIs):

>> Storyboards

>> SwiftUI

Storyboards get their name from filmmaking where artists sketch out scenes so the director can decide the best way to film it. Storyboards in Xcode work in a similar visual manner by letting you drag and drop UI items on the screen, as shown in Figure 5-1.

The problem with storyboards is that you have to place UI items in precise locations on the screen, which works until your app needs to run on a different-size screen found in many of the different iPhone and iPad models.

Because getting storyboards to adapt to different screen sizes and orientations can be so troublesome, Apple created a second way to design UIs called SwiftUI. Where storyboards let you define exact values for size, distance, and location for UI items, SwiftUI lets you design UIs by placing items on the UI in the center of the screen. Then SwiftUI takes care of adapting the UI automatically between different screen sizes and orientations.

REMEMBER

You can combine storyboards and SwiftUI in the same project. That way, you can use the best features of each UI design method.

Understanding SwiftUI

SwiftUI is a unique framework for creating UIs similar to Google's Flutter (see Book 6, Chapter 6). Where Flutter was designed to let you write one program that could run on both Android and iOS, SwiftUI was designed by Apple to let you write one program that could run on all of Apple's operating systems for the Mac, iPhone, iPad, Apple TV, and Apple Watch.

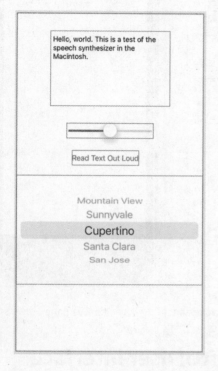

FIGURE 5-1:
A storyboard lets you visually design a user interface.

A program written in SwiftUI for the Mac can adapt to the UI of an Apple Watch with minor changes. By using SwiftUI, you can write programs for all of Apple's operating systems.

Every SwiftUI program consists of several parts, as shown in Figure 5-2:

>> An import line to use the SwiftUI framework

>> One or more structures to define the UI

>> A preview structure to display the UI in a Canvas pane

>> A Canvas pane to let you see your UI

To create a user interface in SwiftUI, you add Views such as a Text view to display text on the screen or an Image view to display a graphic image on the screen. To align Views together, you place them in stacks, which organize Views horizontally, vertically, or overlapping. Stacks act like containers to hold UI Views.

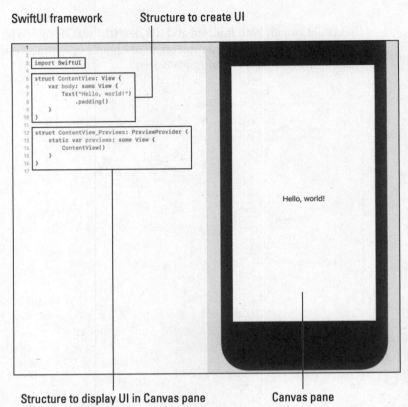

FIGURE 5-2:
The parts of a
SwiftUI program.

Creating a SwiftUI user interface

The basic element of a SwiftUI program is a View. Some Views display UI items on the screen, such as a TextField or a Button. Other Views simply define how other Views appear on the screen and aren't visible at all.

To create a UI, you simply add a View to your UI and then add modifiers. These modifiers can affect the View's appearance (such as color or size) or its position on the screen (such as its *x* and *y* position). A View can contain zero or more modifiers, as shown in Figure 5-3.

Understanding SwiftUI state variables

To make a SwiftUI user interface respond to the user, you need to create special variables called *State variables*. The main idea is that some Views can change a State variable, while other Views might just display that State variable.

A Text view without any modifiers to define its appearance.

```
struct ContentView: View {
    var body: some View {
        Text("Hello, world!")
    }
}
```

Hello, world!

A Text view with modifiers that change its appearance.

```
struct ContentView: View {
    var body: some View {
        Text("Hello, world!")
            .font(.title)
            .fontWeight(.bold)
            .padding()
            .background(Color.yellow)
            .offset(x: 25, y: 40)
    }
}
```

Hello, world!

FIGURE 5-3:
Modifiers affect a
View displayed in
the Canvas pane.

For example, a Text view just displays text, but a TextField view lets the user enter data, which gets stored in the State variable. Each time the user types something in a TextField view, that changes the State variable.

As soon as a State variable changes, it automatically sends the changed data to any view that uses that State variable, as shown in Figure 5-4.

#1: Typing in the TextField
changes the State variable.

#2: As soon as the State variable changes, it sends the new data to any view that uses that State variable.

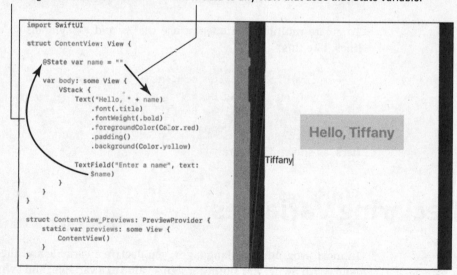

```
import SwiftUI

struct ContentView: View {

    @State var name = ""

    var body: some View {
        VStack {
            Text("Hello, " + name)
                .font(.title)
                .fontWeight(.bold)
                .foregroundColor(Color.red)
                .padding()
                .background(Color.yellow)

            TextField("Enter a name", text:
                $name)
        }
    }
}

struct ContentView_Previews: PreviewProvider {
    static var previews: some View {
        ContentView()
    }
}
```

Hello, Tiffany

Tiffany

FIGURE 5-4:
State variables
let changed
data appear in
multiple locations
automatically.

Here are the basic steps to the way State variables work in a project:

1. The user manipulates a View (such as a TextField) that changes a State variable.

   In SwiftUI, views that can change a State variable display the dollar sign [$] in front of the State variable name.

2. The State variable, defined with @State in front of the var keyword, contains the new or modified data.

3. The State variable sends any new data or changes to any View that uses that State variable.

With storyboards, you have to write code to send changed data to other parts of the UI. With State variables, this process happens automatically, which helps simplify creating programs using Swift and SwiftUI.

Creating Comments

Because Swift is based on curly-bracket languages (C/C++), it uses the same symbols for creating comments. To define a single-line comment, just use the double forward slashes (//)where anything to the right of the // is ignored by the compiler, like this:

```
// This is a single-line comment in Swift.
```

To create multiline comments, use the /* and */ symbols to enclose multiple lines, like this:

```
/* This is a multiline comment.
   Anything trapped between these
   two symbols will be completely
   ignored by the compiler.
*/
```

Declaring Variables

In most programming languages, you declare a variable and the data type it can hold. With Swift, you simply assign a value to a variable, and Swift infers the data type of that value. For example, if you want a variable to store an integer, you can just store an integer into that variable, like this:

```
var myNumber = 102
```

Because 102 is an integer, Swift assumes that the variable can hold integer (`Int`) data types. Just to make it clear, you can add the data type of a variable, like this:

```
var myNumber: Int = 102
```

You can also just declare a variable and its data type without assigning it a value initially. Then assign a value to that variable later, like this:

```
var myNumber: Int
myNumber = 102
```

Swift has the unique ability to use foreign-language characters and emojis (Unicode characters) as part or all of a variable name, as shown in Figure 5-5.

FIGURE 5-5:
Swift allows
Unicode
characters
to be used in
variable names.

```
var 你好 = "Hello (in Chinese)"
var مرحبا = "Hello (in Arabic)"
var 😊 = "Smiling face"
```

Declaring string data types

To declare a string variable, use the `String` keyword:

```
var variableName1: String
```

In Swift, strings are enclosed in double quotation marks. After you declare a variable to hold a string, you can assign a string to that variable, like this:

```
variableName1 = "This string gets stored in the variable."
```

As a shortcut, it's far more common in Swift to declare variables and assign them an initial value:

```
var variableName1 = "This string gets stored in the variable."
```

Because you're storing a string in the variable, Swift infers that the data type must be `String`.

Declaring integer data types

Whole numbers represent integers such as 349, –152, or 41. A whole number can be positive or negative. The most common type of integer data type is Int, and it's used as follows:

```
var intValue: Int
```

Because Swift programmers commonly assign data immediately after declaring a variable, you can do this:

```
var intValue: Int = 38
```

Or to make it shorter, omit the data type declaration altogether, like this:

```
var intValue = 38
```

Swift offers different integer data types that hold different ranges of integer values. The greater the range of values you need to store, the more memory needed. The smaller the range of values, the less memory required. Table 5-1 shows some of the different integer data types and the range of values they can hold.

TABLE 5-1

Swift Integer Data Types

Data Type	Range
Int8	– 127 to 127
UInt8	0 to 255
Int32	–2,147,483,648 to 2,147,483,647
UInt32	0 to 4,294,967,295
Int64	–9,223,372,036,854,775,808 to 9,223,372,036,854,775,807
UInt64	0 to 18,446,744,073,709,551,615

TECHNICAL STUFF

On 32-bit platforms, Int is the same as Int32. On 64-bit platforms, Int is the same as Int64.

Declaring decimal data types

Decimal values are numbers such as 1.88 or –91.4. Just as you can limit the range of integer values a variable can hold, so you can limit the range of decimal values a variable can hold. In Swift, the two types of decimal data types are Float and Double, as shown in Table 5-2.

TABLE 5-2

Swift Decimal Data Types

Data Type	Range
Float	1.2 E–38 to 3.4 E38
Double	12.3 E–308 to 1.7 E308

REMEMBER

If you assign a decimal number to a variable, Swift assumes the data type is Double unless you specifically declare the variable as a Float data type. For clarity, it's usually best to specify the data type for decimal number variables, like this:

```
var weight: Double = 145.37
var distance: Float = 102.3904
```

TECHNICAL STUFF

When working with graphics, Swift uses a third data type for holding decimal numbers called CGFloat (CG stands for Core Graphics).

You can use the underscore character to make large numbers easier to read:

TIP

```
var bigNumber = 784_135_000.84   // 784135000.84
```

Declaring Boolean values

Besides storing text and numbers, variables can also hold a Boolean value — true or false. To declare a variable to hold a Boolean value, use the Bool keyword, as follows:

```
var boolValue: Bool
boolValue = true
```

Declaring Constants

Constants always represent a fixed value. In Swift, you can declare a constant and its specific value as follows:

```
let constantName1 = value
```

So, if you want to assign 3.14 to a pi constant, you could do this:

```
let pi = 3.1415
```

REMEMBER

You can only assign a value to a constant once. When a constant holds a value, you can never change that value later in your program.

Using Operators

The three types of operators used are mathematical, relational, and logical. *Mathematical operators* calculate numeric results such as adding, multiplying, or dividing numbers. Table 5-3 lists the mathematical operators used in Swift.

TABLE 5-3

Mathematical Operators

Mathematical Operator	Purpose	Example
+	Addition	5 + 3.4
−	Subtraction	203.9 − 9.12
*	Multiplication	39 * 146.7
/	Division	45 / 8.41
%	Modulo (returns the remainder)	35 % 9 = 8

Relational operators compare two values and return a true or false value. The six relational operators available in Swift are shown in Table 5-4.

TABLE 5-4

Relational Operators

Relational Operator	Purpose
==	Equal to
!=	Not equal to
<	Less than
<=	Less than or equal to
>	Greater than
>=	Greater than or equal to

Logical operators, as shown in Table 5-5, compare two Boolean values (true or false) and return a single true or false value.

TABLE 5-5 ## Logical Operators

Logical Operator	Truth Table
&&	true && true = true
	true && false = false
	false && true = false
	false && false = false
||	true || true = true
	true || false = true
	false || true = true
	false || false = false
!	!true = false
	!false = true

Branching Statements

The simplest branching statement is an if-then statement that only runs one or more commands if a Boolean condition is true, like this:

```
if condition {
    // Commands
}
```

To make the computer choose between two mutually exclusive sets of commands, you can use an if-else statement, like this:

```
if condition {
    // Commands
} else {
    // Other commands
}
```

If a Boolean condition is true, the if-else statement runs the first group of commands; if the Boolean condition is false, the if-else statement runs the second group of commands. No matter what, an if-else statement will always run one set of commands or the other.

Swift offers a shortcut of the if-else statement that looks like this:

```
var age = 21
var message: String

message = age >= 21 ? "You are an adult" : "You are a minor"
print(message)
```

The preceding code works by checking the (age = 21) condition. Because the value of age is 21, 21 >= 21 evaluates to true. That means "You are an adult" gets stored in the message variable. If the value of age were 12, then the (age >= 21) condition would be false and the code would assign "You are a minor" to the message variable.

One problem with the if-else statement is that it only gives you two possible choices. One way to offer multiple choices is through the if-else if statement:

```
if condition1 {
    // Commands
} else if condition2 {
    // Other commands
}
```

If condition1 is true, then the first set of commands runs. However, if condition1 is false, then it checks whether condition2 is true. If condition2 is true, then it runs the second set of commands.

If both condition1 and condition2 are false, then no commands will run at all. That's why if-else if statements often include an else portion at the end, like this:

```
if condition1 {
    // Commands
} else if condition2 {
    // Other commands
} else {
    // Default commands to run
}
```

If both condition1 and condition2 are false, the commands stored under the else portion will run by default. The else portion ensures that one set of commands will always run.

The problem with the if-else if statement is that when you start checking for multiple conditions, the entire if-else if statement can look cluttered and hard to read, like this:

```
if condition1 {
    // Commands
} else if condition2 {
    // Other commands
} else if condition2 {
    // Other commands
} else if condition3 {
    // Other commands
} else if condition4 {
    // Other commands
} else {
    // Default commands to run
}
```

To provide multiple options in a much cleaner form, Swift offers a switch statement that looks like this:

```
var day = 3
var result: String
switch day {
    case 0: result = "Sunday"
    case 1: result = "Monday"
    case 2: result = "Tuesday"
    case 3: result = "Wednesday"
    case 4: result = "Thursday"
    case 5: result = "Friday"
    case 6: result = "Saturday"
    default: result = "No such day"
}
print(result)
```

The preceding switch statement is equivalent to the following if-else if statement:

```
var day = 3
var result: String
```

```
if (day == 0) {
    result = "Sunday"
} else if (day == 1) {
    result = "Monday"
} else if (day == 2) {
    result = "Tuesday"
} else if (day == 3) {
    result = "Wednesday"
} else if (day == 4) {
    result = "Thursday"
} else if (day == 5) {
    result = "Friday"
} else if (day == 6) {
    result = "Saturday"
} else {
  result = "No such day"
}
print(result)
```

To check whether a variable matches multiple values, you can separate multiple values with commas or you can match a range of values, like this:

```
var number = 4
var result: String
switch number {
    case 1, 2, 3: result = "1, 2, or 3"
    case 4...6: result = "4, 5, or 6"
    default: result = "Not within the range of 1 - 6"
}
print(result)
```

TECHNICAL STUFF

When checking a range of values, Swift offers two options. Using three dots is called a *closed range* because Swift counts from the lower number up to and including the upper number. In the preceding example, 4...6 tells Swift to include 4, 5, and 6. Instead of using three dots, you can use two dots and a less-than symbol (<), which is called a *half-open range* and looks like this: 4..<7. This tells Swift to include 4, 5, and 6, but *not* 7.

The preceding switch statement is equivalent to the following if-else if statement:

```
if (number == 1 || number == 2 || number == 3) {
  result = "1, 2, or 3"
} else if (number >= 4 && number <= 6) {
```

```
    result = "4, 5, or 6"
} else {
    result = "Not within the range of 1 - 6"
}
print(result)
```

Looping Statements

A *looping* statement repeats one or more commands a fixed number of times or until a certain Boolean condition becomes true. To create a loop that repeats a fixed number of times, use the for loop, which looks like this:

```
for (variable in Start...End) {
    // Commands
}
```

If you want the for loop to run five times, set the start value to 1 and the end value to 5, like this:

```
for x in 1...5 {
    print(x)
}
```

Normally the for loop counts up, but you can use the stride keyword to define three parameters — the starting value, the ending value, and the increment value, which is –1 in this example:

```
for x in stride(from: 5, through: 1, by: -1) {
    print(x)
}
```

If you don't know how many times you need to repeat commands, use a while or a do-while loop.

The while loop repeats while a condition remains true; it looks like this:

```
while condition {
    // Commands
}
```

If the condition is `false` right from the start, this loop won't even run at least once. Here's an example of a `while` loop:

```
var x = 0
while (x < 5) {
  print(x)
  x += 1
}
```

If you want a loop that runs at least once, use the `repeat-while` loop, which looks like this:

```
repeat {
  // Commands
} while (condition)
```

WARNING

When using a `while` or a `repeat-while` loop, make sure the loop eventually changes the condition so it becomes `false`. If you fail to do this, you risk creating an endless loop that will freeze your program.

This loop runs at least once before checking a condition. If the condition is `false`, the loop stops. An example of a `repeat-while` loop looks like this:

```
var x = 0
repeat {
  print(x)
  x += 1
} while (x < 5)
```

Creating Functions

Functions let you define mini-programs that can contain code that may be useful multiple times throughout your program. Instead of writing the same code in multiple locations, it's better to write the code once, store it in a function, and then *call* (run) that function whenever another part of your program needs to run that code.

To create a function, use the `func` keyword:

```
func myFunction() {
  // Commands
}
```

To run or call that function, just use the function name. Functions without any parameters will do the same thing over and over again, so most functions need to accept one or more parameters that define a variable name and its data type, like this:

```swift
func myFunction(firstName: String) {
  print("Hello, " + firstName + ". Glad you're here!")
}
```

This function accepts a string and then prints out "Hello, " followed by the string that was passed into the function, and concluding with ". Glad you're here!" The following shows how to call the preceding function:

```swift
myFunction(firstName: "Betty")
myFunction(firstName: "Joe")
myFunction(firstName: "Florence")

func myFunction(firstName: String) {
  print("Hello, " + firstName + ". Glad you're here!")
}
```

REMEMBER

When defining a parameter in a function, you must define the parameter name (such as firstName) and its data type (such as String). When you call the function, you must pass it the type of data it expects and use the parameter name, such as myFunction(firstName: "Florence").

Sometimes you may want a function to return a value. To do that, you must specify the data type that the function name represents, like this:

```swift
func multiplyMe(x: Int, y: Int) -> Int {
  return (x * y)
}
```

This function accepts two integers (x: Int, y: Int) and returns an integer value (-> Int). Then it multiplies x by y and returns the result.

When calling this function, treat it like a value and assign it to a variable, like this:

```swift
var answer: Int

answer = multiplyMe(x: 4, y: 8)
print(answer)
```

This main function declares an answer variable to hold integer (Int) data types. Then it calls the multiplyMe function by passing it two numbers (x: 4, y: 8). The multiplyMe function multiplies x by y and returns the value (32) in the multiplyMe function name.

This value (32) then gets stored in the answer variable, which finally gets printed.

Creating functions that return a value involves a three-step process:

1. **Define the data type that the function needs to return (such as** -> Int **or** -> String**).**

2. **Make sure the last line in the function uses the** return **keyword followed by the proper data type (such as** Int **or** String**) that the function should return (as defined in Step 1).**

3. **Call the function and treat the function name as a single value.**

Data Structures

Data structures are ways to organize related variables together. Three common data structures used in Swift are

» **Arrays:** Store a list of items that consist of the same data type

» **Dictionaries:** Store a list of items using a key paired with data

» **Sets:** Store an arbitrary list of items

Creating an array

Arrays in Swift usually contain the same data type, such as Int or String. The simplest way to create an array is to simply define a list in square brackets to a variable name, like this:

```
var pets = ["cat", "dog", "fish", "bird"]
```

If you want to specify the data type, you can do this:

```
var pets: [String] = ["cat", "dog", "fish", "bird"]
```

If you just want to create an empty array, specify the data type followed by empty parentheses, like this:

```
var pets = [String]()
```

If you want to retrieve a single item from the array, you need to specify the array name plus the index value of the data you want to retrieve, like this:

```
print(pets[1])
```

The preceding command would print the second item (at index position 1) from the pets array, which would be "dog".

To replace an item in an array with a new value, just specify the array name and the index position where you want to put the data, like this:

```
var pets = ["cat", "dog", "fish", "bird"]
pets[1] = "lizard"
```

The preceding code replaces "dog" with "lizard".

To add data to the end of the array, use the append command, like this:

```
var pets: [String] = ["cat", "dog", "fish", "bird"]
pets.append("lizard")
```

If you want to insert data in a specific location, use the insert command to specify the data to insert into the array followed by the index position to place it:

```
var pets: [String] = ["cat", "dog", "fish", "bird"]
pets.insert("lizard", at: 1)
```

This places "lizard" as the second item in the array and pushes the rest of the items to the right, like this:

```
["cat", "lizard", "dog", "fish", "bird"]
```

You can also remove items from an array by specifying the index position of the item you want to remove. So, if you wanted to remove the third item from an array, you could use the remove command, like this:

```
var pets: [String] = ["cat", "dog", "fish", "bird"]
pets.remove(at: 3)
```

This would remove "bird" so the entire array would look like ["cat", "dog", "fish"].

Creating a dictionary

The biggest problem with an array is that you have to find items using the index position. You can always add or remove items, which can change the index position of an item, so keeping track of index positions can be troublesome. That's why Swift offers another data structure called a *dictionary.*

The idea behind a dictionary is to store data with a key linked to data. This key-data pair then gets stored in the dictionary. To retrieve data, you just need to know the key linked to the data you want to retrieve.

Both the key and the data can be of any data type, but every key in a dictionary must be of the same data type, such as Int or String, and all stored data must be of the same data type, such as Double or String. To create a dictionary, specify the data type of the key and data pair, and then store data in that dictionary, like this:

```
var myDictionary: [Int: String] = [
    10: "cat",
    20: "dog",
    30: "fish",
    40: "bird"
]
```

If you want to retrieve a single item from the dictionary, you need to specify the dictionary name plus the key linked to the data you want to retrieve, like this:

```
print (myDictionary[20]!)
```

The preceding command would print the data linked to the 20 key, which would be "dog".

TECHNICAL STUFF

The exclamation point (!) at the end of myDictionary[20] exists because there's a chance there is no key number 20. If you omit the exclamation point, Swift would print Optional("dog"), so the exclamation point exists to eliminate the Optional part of the returned data. If you try to retrieve data and there is no key 20, the code will crash.

To add data to a dictionary, just specify a new key and assign it data, like this:

```swift
var myDictionary: [Int: String] = [
    10: "cat",
    20: "dog",
    30: "fish",
    40: "bird"
]
myDictionary[20] = "tarantula"
print (myDictionary)
```

The preceding code replaces "dog" with "tarantula" for key 20. If key 20 didn't previously exist, then the preceding code would add a new key (20) and data ("tarantula") to the dictionary.

REMEMBER

Unlike arrays, dictionaries don't order their data. That means the order in which you store data in a dictionary is not the order that the dictionary actually arranges the data.

Creating a set

An array and a dictionary can potentially contain duplicate data. That's why Swift offers a *set*, which can never hold duplicate data. To define a set, list items within square brackets and specify a variable as a set, like this:

```swift
var mySet: Set = ["cat", "dog", "fish", "bird']
```

If you want to add items to a set, use the insert command and specify the data to add, like this:

```swift
mySet.insert("lizard")
```

To remove an item from a set, use the remove command and identify the data to remove, like this:

```swift
mySet.remove("dog")
```

This command removes "dog" from the set. If "dog" doesn't exist in the set, then the remove command does nothing.

Creating Objects

Swift lets you create class files that define *properties* (variables) and *methods* (functions) that work together. Then you can create one or more objects from a single class file. To define a class, create one or more properties and assign them initial values, like this:

```
class Animal {
  var name = ""
  var age = 0
  var weight = 0.0
}
```

After defining a class, you can create an object from that class, like this:

```
var cat = Animal()
```

In this example, the object `cat` is defined by the `Animal` class. After you've created an object, you can assign data to the object's various properties, like this:

```
cat.name = "Fluffy"
cat.age = 3
cat.weight = 12.48
print (cat.name)
print (cat.age)
print (cat.weight)
```

In this example, I created a class file with multiple properties that have an initial value. You can define a class with properties that are undefined, but if you create properties that are undefined, you must create an initializer, like this:

```
class Animal {
    var name: String
    var age: Int
    var weight: Double
    init(name: String, age: Int, weight: Double) {
        self.name = name
        self.age = age
        self.weight = weight
    }
}
```

When you create an object from this class, you need to specify data for each property when you create the object, like this:

```
var cat = Animal(name: "Fluffy", age: 3, weight: 12.48)
```

Now you can access the object's properties, like this:

```
print (cat.name)
print (cat.age)
print (cat.weight)
```

Finally, a class can also contain methods that can accept parameters and calculate results, like this:

```
class Animal {
    var name: String
    var age: Int
    var weight: Double
    init(name: String, age: Int, weight: Double) {
        self.name = name
        self.age = age
        self.weight = weight
    }
    func greeting(animalNoise: String) {
        print ("This animal makes this sound: " + animalNoise)
    }
}
```

Now you can call this method by creating an object and specifying the object name and the method name to run, like this:

```
var cat = Animal(name: "Fluffy", age: 3, weight: 12.48)

cat.greeting(animalNoise: "meow")
```

This would print out "This animal makes this sound: meow".

Chapter **6**

Flutter and Dart

When the mobile computing market arrived, developers rushed to create apps for iPhone and Android devices. Initially, Google endorsed Java as the official programming language for Android, but it shifted its support to Kotlin instead.

Unfortunately, writing apps in Java or Kotlin meant you had to rewrite the entire app all over again in Objective-C or Swift to create an iPhone app. Forcing programmers to learn and write apps in two completely different languages wasn't practical. That's why Google released Flutter in 2017.

The idea behind Flutter is to create a universal user interface (UI) framework that would allow developers to design an app that would run on Android and iOS with little or no modifications.

After you create a UI using Flutter, the next step is to make it actually work by using a programming language called Dart. Where Flutter focuses on the UI, the Dart programming language focuses on the actual code (algorithms) that you write to calculate results and create useful information of some kind.

TECHNICAL
STUFF

Initially, Flutter was designed to let you write one program that could run on both Android and iOS. Now Flutter has expanded its list of target platforms to include Linux, macOS, and Windows.

Working with Flutter

The main idea behind Flutter is to create a program out of smaller components called *widgets*, where each widget represents a UI element such as a button or text. By arranging widgets on the screen, you can create your app's UI.

Depending on the operating system a Flutter app runs on, it will automatically adapt to the native appearance and behavior of that particular operating system. In this way, Flutter apps look and behave like apps specifically designed for that operating system.

One unique feature of Flutter is called *hot reload*. This allows developers to change the source code and see the results of that change instantly on the UI. Hot reload lets you experiment faster with different designs until you find the one you like best.

Understanding the structure of a Flutter program

Flutter programs tend to resemble C code because the Dart programming language (covered later in this chapter) is inspired by curly-bracket languages like C:

```
import 'package:flutter/material.dart';

void main() {
  runApp(
    const Center(
      child: Text(
        'Flutter here!',
        textDirection: TextDirection.ltr,
      ),
    ),
  );
}
```

REMEMBER

Indentation is optional in Dart, but it can make your code easier to understand.

In this Flutter program, the Center widget aligns the Text widget in the center of the screen. Then the Text widget displays text on the screen and also defines the direction in which text should appear (ltr stands for *left to right*):

```
const Center(
    child: Text(
```

```
      'Flutter here!',
      textDirection: TextDirection.ltr,
    ),
  ),
```

Working with widgets in Flutter

To design a UI in Flutter, you use various widgets that work together. Widgets often contain other widgets. Some widgets deal with input and output and are visible (for example Text, Button, and TextField widgets). Other widgets are invisible because they're designed to contain other widgets and organize them on the screen.

Every Flutter program starts running a main() program so you can define the first widget you want to load initially, like this:

```
void main() {
  runApp(
      // Insert Dart code here
  );
}
```

Although you could type different widgets directly into the main() function, it's better to organize code in separate widgets. That means you need to create a widget, which means defining whether the widget is stateful or stateless:

>> **Stateful:** A stateful widget is one that can change its appearance based on the state of a value, such as a Boolean variable. If the state of a Boolean variable is true, the widget may appear in one color if it's false and in a different color if it's true.

>> **Stateless:** A stateless widget is one that's static and doesn't need to change, such as displaying a new text or a new image on the screen. To create a stateless widget, you need to define a class with an arbitrary name, such as MyWidget, like this:

```
class MyWidget extends StatelessWidget {

  const MyWidget({Key? key}) : super(key: key);
  @override
  Widget build(BuildContext context) {
    return const MaterialApp();
  }
}
```

The `MyWidget` class returns a `MaterialApp` widget that provides additional UI widgets. Within this `MaterialApp` widget, you can define a home widget, which will be the first widget that will appear on the screen. You can define this widget using the `Scaffold` widget, which can display additional UI widgets:

```
class MyWidget extends StatelessWidget {
  const MyWidget({Key? key}) : super(key: key);
  @override
  Widget build(BuildContext context) {
    return const MaterialApp(
      home: Scaffold(

      ),
    );
  }
}
```

Within the `Scaffold` widget, you can define the body of the widget. I want to center text inside the `Scaffold` widget, so I can define a `Center` widget like this:

```
class MyWidget extends StatelessWidget {
  const MyWidget({Key? key}) : super(key: key);
  @override
  Widget build(BuildContext context) {
    return const MaterialApp(
      home: Scaffold(
        body: Center(

        ),
      ),
    );
  }
}
```

Finally, within the `Center` widget, you can display text through the `Text` widget, like this:

```
class MyWidget extends StatelessWidget {
  const MyWidget({Key? key}) : super(key: key);
  @override
  Widget build(BuildContext context) {
    return const MaterialApp(
      home: Scaffold(
        body: Center(
```

```
          child: Text("Flutter here!"),
        ),
      ),
    );
  }
}
```

The Text widget displays text on the screen, but you may want to change its appearance in different ways, such as changing the font style, font size, font weight, font color, or background color. You can change these properties like this:

```
Text("Flutter here!",
        style: TextStyle(fontWeight: FontWeight.bold,
                         fontStyle: FontStyle.italic,
                         color: Colors.red,
                         backgroundColor: Colors.yellow,
                         fontSize: 24),
    )
```

A complete program using the Text widget with multiple properties might look like this:

```
import 'package:flutter/material.dart';

void main() {
  runApp(const MyWidget());
}

class MyWidget extends StatelessWidget {
  const MyWidget({Key? key}) : super(key: key);
  @override
  Widget build(BuildContext context) {
    return const MaterialApp(
      home: Scaffold(
        body: Center(
          child: Text(
            "Flutter here!",
            style: TextStyle(fontWeight: FontWeight.bold,
                             fontStyle: FontStyle.italic,
                             color: Colors.red,
                             backgroundColor: Colors.yellow,
                             fontSize: 24),
          ),
        ),
```

```
        ),
    );
  }
}
```

Figure 6-1 shows how properties can modify the appearance of text that appears on the screen through the Text widget.

Flutter here!

FIGURE 6-1:
Adding properties
can change the
appearance of
the Text widget.

Aligning widgets in rows and columns

The key to designing UIs in Flutter lies in organizing widgets inside of other widgets. From there, you can choose different properties to modify a widget's appearance in the UI. Two commonly used widgets to align widgets on the screen are Row and Column.

The Row widget organizes widgets horizontally. The Column widget organizes widgets vertically. Both the Row and Column widgets let you define one or more children widgets, defined within square brackets, like this:

```
Row(
  children: [

  ],
```

One useful widget to use within rows or column is the Expanded widget, which spaces items apart within a row or a column so they don't appear smashed against each other:

```
Row(
  children: [
    Expanded(
      child: Text(
        "Cross-platform"
      ),
    ),
    Expanded(
      child: Text(
        "Flutter here"
      ),
    )
  ]
]
```

The following code displays two Text widgets horizontally, as shown in Figure 6-2:

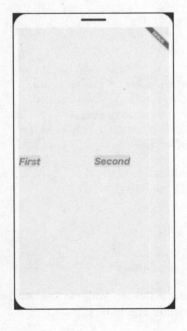

FIGURE 6-2:
The Expanded widget inside the Row widget can space items apart.

```dart
import 'package:flutter/material.dart';

void main() {
  runApp(const MyWidget());
}

class MyWidget extends StatelessWidget {
  const MyWidget({Key? key}) : super(key: key);
  @override
  Widget build(BuildContext context) {
    return const MaterialApp(
      home: Scaffold(
        body: Center(
          child: Row(
        children: [
          Expanded(
            child: Text(
              "First",
              style: TextStyle(fontWeight: FontWeight.bold,
                              fontStyle: FontStyle.italic,
                              color: Colors.red,
                              backgroundColor: Colors.yellow,
                              fontSize: 24),
            ),
          ),
          Expanded(
            child: Text(
              "Second",
              style: TextStyle(fontWeight: FontWeight.bold,
                              fontStyle: FontStyle.italic,
                              color: Colors.red,
                              backgroundColor: Colors.yellow,
                              fontSize: 24),
            ),
          ),
        ],
      )),
      ),
    );
  }
}
```

If you change the Row widget to the Column widget, the two Text widgets will appear stacked vertically, as shown in Figure 6-3.

FIGURE 6-3:
The Column widget arranges widgets vertically.

Understanding the Dart Language

Flutter relies on a programming language called Dart. When you create a Flutter project, you need to design the UI using widgets and then use the Dart programming language to make that UI respond to the user.

REMEMBER

Like C++ and Java, Dart requires every line to end with a semicolon.

Creating comments

To write a comment in Dart, use double forward slashes (//). Anything that appears to the right of the // is ignored by the compiler, like this:

```
// This is a comment.
```

If you want to create a comment covering multiple lines, use the /* and */ symbols to define the start and end of a comment, like this:

```
/* This is a multiple-line comment.
   You just need to define the beginning
   and the end of the multiple lines. */
```

Declaring variables

Four common data types defined by Dart include

» `int`: Integer or whole numbers (such as 8, –23, or 910)

» `double`: Decimal numbers (such as 3.1415, –0.892, or 194.5)

» `String`: Text strings (such as `"Hello"`, `"Goodbye"`, or `"Flutter is fun"`)

» `bool`: Boolean values (such as `true` or `false`)

You can explicitly define a data type when declaring variables like this:

```
int x = 10;
double weight = 12.74;
```

Another option is to use the `var` keyword to declare a variable and let Dart infer the data type, like this:

```
var x = 10;  // int data type
var weight = 12.74;  // double data type
```

When using the `var` keyword to declare a variable, you must assign an initial value to that variable.

To create a constant that can accept a value once and never change after, use the `const` keyword, like this:

```
const flag = 34;
```

Using operators

The three types of operators used are mathematical, relational, and logical. *Mathematical* operators calculate numeric results such as adding, multiplying, or dividing numbers, as shown in Table 6-1.

Relational operators compare two values and return a `true` or `false` value. The six relational operators available are shown in Table 6-2.

WARNING

The relational operator in Dart is two equal signs (==), whereas the relational operator in other programming languages is just a single equal sign (=). If you only use a single equal sign to compare two values in Dart, your program will work but not the way it's supposed to.

TABLE 6-1

Mathematical Operators

Mathematical Operator	Purpose	Example
+	Addition	5 + 3.4
–	Subtraction	203.9 – 9.12
*	Multiplication	39 * 146.7
/	Division	45 / 8.41
~/	Division (returns integer)	45 / 7 = 6
%	Modulo (returns the remainder)	35 % 9 = 8

TABLE 6-2

Relational Operators

Relational Operator	Purpose
==	Equal to
!=	Not equal to
<	Less than
<=	Less than or equal to
>	Greater than
>=	Greater than or equal to

Logical operators compare two Boolean values (true or false) and return a single true or false value, as shown in Table 6-3.

Increment and decrement operators

Dart has an increment operator (++), which adds 1 to a variable, and a decrement operator (−−), which subtracts 1 from a variable. You can place an increment or decrement operator before (prefix) or after (postfix) a variable.

TABLE 6-3 ## Logical Operators

Logical Operator	Truth Table
&&	true && true = true
	true && false = false
	false && true = false
	false && false = false
||	true || true = true
	true || false = true
	false || true = true
	false || false = false
!	!true = false
	!false = true

TIP

Prefix means the increment or decrement operator changes the value of a variable first. *Postfix* means the increment or decrement operator changes the value of a variable last. The following code demonstrates the difference between prefix and postfix:

```
var x = 7;
print(x++); // prints 7

var y = 7;
print(++y); // prints 8

var a = 7;
print(a--); // prints 7

var b = 7;
print(--b); // prints 6
```

Assignment operators

Dart uses the equal sign (=) to assign values to variables, but it also includes combination assignment and mathematical operators, as shown in Table 6-4.

TABLE 6-4

Assignment Operators

Assignment Operator	Purpose	Example
+=	Addition assignment	i += 7 (equivalent to i = i + 7)
-=	Subtraction assignment	i -= 4 (equivalent to i = i - 4)
*=	Multiplication assignment	i *= y (equivalent to i = i * y)
/=	Division assignment	i /= 3.5 (equivalent to i = i / 3.5)

Using branching statements

The simplest branching statement is an if statement that only runs one or more commands if a Boolean condition is true. In Dart, the if statement uses curly brackets to enclose one or more commands:

```
if (condition) {
   Command1;
   Command2;
}
```

To make the computer choose between two mutually exclusive sets of commands, you can use an if-else statement in Dart, like this:

```
if (condition) {
   Command;
   Command;
}
else {
   Command;
   Command;
}
```

The if-else statement offers only two choices. If you want to offer more than two choices, you can use the if-elseif statement, which uses two or more Boolean conditions to choose which of two or more groups of commands to run, like this:

```
if (condition1) {
   Command;
   Command;
```

```
}
else if (condition2) {
  Command;
  Command;
}
else if (condition3) {
  Command;
  Command;
}
```

Instead of using multiple if-else if statements, you can use a switch statement, like this:

```
var x = 4;

switch (x) {
    case 2: {
        print("2");
        break;
    }
    case 3: {
        print("3");
        break;
    }
    case 4: {
        print("4");
        break;
    }
    default: {
        print("Unknown");
    }
}
```

REMEMBER

At the end of each case, include a break statement to ensure that when a case statement finds a match, it doesn't "fall through" to the next case statement below.

Using looping statements

A looping statement repeats one or more commands a fixed number of times or until a certain Boolean condition becomes true. To create a loop that repeats a fixed number of times, use the for loop, which looks like this:

```
for (startvalue; endcondition; increment) {
    Command;
}
```

If you wanted the for loop to run five times, you can declare a start value as an integer and set its initial value to 1 (such as int i = 1). Then define the end condition (such as i <= 5), like this:

```
for (int i = 1; i <= 5; i++) {
    print(i);
}
```

This for loop would print the following:

```
1
2
3
4
5
```

If you don't know how many times you need to repeat commands, use a while loop, which looks like this:

```
while (condition) {
    Command;
    Command;
}
```

If the condition is true, the loop runs at least once. If the condition is false, the loop doesn't run. The following while loop runs five times:

```
int i = 1;
while (i <= 5)
{
    print(i);
    ++i;
}
```

REMEMBER

Somewhere inside a WHILE loop, you must have a command that can change the condition from true to false; otherwise, the loop will never end, and your program will appear to hang or freeze.

Flutter and Dart

An alternative to the while loop is the do-while loop, which always runs the loop once before checking whether a condition is true or false. The following do-while loop runs five times:

```
int i = 1;
do {
    print(i);
    ++i;
}
while (i <= 5);
```

Creating functions

A function lets you write a mini program that performs a specific task. Dart lets you create a function in two ways. First, you can define the function by using the void keyword, an arbitrary name, and a parameter list, like this:

```
void functionname() {
  Commands;
}
```

Optionally, you can omit the void keyword altogether and just specify the function name and its parameter list, like this:

```
functionname() {
  Commands;
}
```

To call this function, just use the function name like a command:

```
void greeting() {
    print ("Hello!");
}

greeting();
```

For a function to receive data, just declare the data type to receive followed by a variable name that will be used within the function, like this:

```
void greeting(String name) {
    print ("Hello, " + name);
}
```

To call this function, you must use the function name followed by any data to pass into the parameter list. The data must be of the right data type, like this:

```
greeting("Frank");
```

This function sends the string "Frank" to the function called greeting, which accepts "Frank" and prints "Hello, Frank".

Sometimes a function can represent a value. To declare a function that returns a value, you must identify the data type the function returns right before the function name, like this:

```
String greeting(String name) {

}
```

Make sure that any function that returns a value includes the return keyword followed by the data that matches the data type, like this:

```
String greeting(String name) {
    return ("Hello, " + name);
}
```

When you call this function and pass it data, you can treat the function call as a single value, like this:

```
print(greeting("Frank"));
```

This function call passes "Frank" to the greeting function, which returns "Hello, Frank" back to the print statement.

Creating data structures

Dart offers lists, queues, and map data structures. A list is like an array in other languages that can hold one or more items. A queue creates a data structure where you can remove items from the beginning or end of the queue. A map stores values with keys, allowing you to retrieve values using its distinct key.

REMEMBER

A list in Dart acts like an array in other languages. Likewise, a map in Dart is like a dictionary in other languages.

Creating a list

A Dart list lets you change, add, or delete items. To create a list, identify a variable name as a list and use the new keyword to create that list, like this:

```
List pets = new List();
```

To add items to this list, use the add command followed by the data to store in the list, like this:

```
pets.add("cat");
```

You can use the length property to retrieve the total number of items in the list. To retrieve a specific item from the list, identify the list name followed by an index number, where 0 represents the first item in the list, 1 represents the second item, and so on.

The following code creates a list; adds "cat", "dog", "fish", and "bird" to the list; and prints out the length (4) and the item stored in index position 1 (the second item, which is "dog"). Then it removes "fish" from the list and retrieves the length again (3):

```
List pets = new List();
pets.add("cat");
pets.add("dog");
pets.add("fish");
pets.add("bird");

print (pets.length);
print(pets[1]);

pets.remove("fish");
print (pets.length);
```

Creating a queue

A queue stores multiple items but gives you the option of adding or removing items from the front or back of the queue. To create a queue, you must define its data type to hold, like this:

```
import "dart:collection";
```

REMEMBER

You must import the dart:collection library to use queues like this.

The following program creates a queue and adds four items in this order: "cat", "dog", "fish", and "bird". Then it removes the first item ("cat") and the last item ("bird"):

```
import "dart:collection";
void main(){

    Queue<String> pets = new Queue<String>();
    pets.add("cat");
    pets.add("dog");
    pets.add("fish");
    pets.add("bird");

    print(pets);

    print(pets.length);

    pets.removeFirst();
    pets.removeLast();
    print(pets);
}
```

Creating a map

A map contains values and keys assigned to each value. To create a map, declare a map variable name and then store key-value pairs inside curly brackets, like this:

```
var mapname = {key1:value1, key2:value2, key3:value3}
```

The following code creates a map with three key-value pairs and then prints out the value associated with the 15 key:

```
var pets = {10:"cat", 15:"dog", 20:"fish"};
print(pets[15]);
```

REMEMBER

The keys and values in a map can be any data type. If the key is an integer, all keys must be integers. If the value is a string, all values must be strings.

Another way to create a map is to create a new Map() and then assign values to the keys like this:

```
var pets = new Map();
pets[10] = "cat";
pets[15] = "dog";
```

```
pets[20] = "fish";
print(pets[15]);
```

Using objects

To create an object in Dart, you must define a class, which looks like this:

```
class className {
  // properties

  dataType methodname() {
    Commands;
    Commands;
  }
}
```

A class lists *properties* (data) along with one or more methods, which contain code for manipulating an object in some way.

The following class defines a single property and a method:

```
class Car {
    // field
    String engine = "6-cylinder";

    // function
    void disp() {
       print(engine);
    }
}
```

After declaring the class, you can then create an object, print a property, and run a method:

```
void main(){

  var vroom = new Car();
  print (vroom.engine);
  vroom.disp();
}
```

The preceding code prints vroom.engine, which is "6-cylinder". Then it runs the disp method, which also prints the engine property ("6-cylinder").

7 Applications

Contents at a Glance

Chapter **1**

Database Management

D atabase management is all about storing organized information and knowing how to retrieve it again. Although the idea of storing and retrieving data is simple in theory, managing databases can get complicated in a hurry. Not only can data be critical, such as bank records, but data retrieval may be time-sensitive as well. After all, retrieving a person's medical history in a hospital emergency room is useless if that information doesn't arrive fast enough to tell doctors that the patient has an allergic reaction to a specific antibiotic.

Because storing and retrieving information is so important, one of the most common and lucrative fields of computer programming is database management. Database management involves designing and programming ways to store and retrieve data. Because nearly every type of business — from agriculture to banking to engineering — requires storing and retrieving information, database management is used throughout the world.

Understanding the Basics of Databases

A database acts like a big bucket where you can dump information. The two most important parts of any database are storing information and yanking it back out again. Ideally, storing information should be just as easy as retrieving it, no matter how much data you may need to store or retrieve.

To store and retrieve data, computer scientists have created several types of database designs:

>> Free-form

>> Flat-file

>> Relational

Free-form databases

Free-form databases are designed to make it easy to store and retrieve information. A free-form database acts like a scratch pad of paper where you can scribble any type of data, such as names and addresses, recipes, directions to your favorite restaurant, pictures, or a list of items that you want to do the next day. A free-form database gets its name because it gives you the freedom to store dissimilar information in one place, as shown in Figure 1-1.

Database File

FIGURE 1-1:
A free-form
database can
store randomly
structured
information.

Being able to store anything in a database can be convenient, but that convenience is like the freedom to throw anything you want in a closet, such as pants, books, written reports, and photographs. With such a wide variety of stuff dumped in one place, finding what you need can be much more difficult.

To retrieve data from a free-form database, you need to know at least part of the data you want to find. So, if you stored a name and phone number in a free-form database, you could find it again by typing part of the name you want to find (such as typing **Rob** to find the name *Robert*). If you stored a recipe in a free-form database, you could find it by typing one of the ingredients of that recipe, such as **milk**, **shrimp**, or **carrots**.

WARNING

Free-form databases have two big disadvantages:

>> **They're clumsy for retrieving information.** For example, suppose you stored the name *Robert Jones* and his phone number *555-9378*. The only way to retrieve this information is by typing part of this data, such as **Rob**, **555**, or **nes**. If you type **Bob**, the free-form database doesn't find *Robert*. So, it's possible to store information in a free-form database and never be able to find it again, much like storing a cherished photo in an attic and forgetting exactly where it might be.

>> **They can't sort or filter information.** If you want to see the phone numbers of every person stored in a free-form database, you can't. If you want to see only information in the free-form database that you stored in the past week, you can't do that either.

TIP

Because free-form databases are so limited in retrieving information, they're best used for simple tasks, such as jotting down notes or ideas, but not for storing massive amounts of critical information. To store data with the ability to sort, search, and filter data to view only specific types of information, you need a flat-file database.

Flat-file databases

The biggest difference between a free-form database and a flat-file database is that a flat-file database imposes structure. Whereas a free-form database lets you type random information in any order, flat-file databases force you to add information by first defining the structure of your data and then adding the data itself.

Before you can store data, you must design the structure of the database. This means defining what type of data to store and how much room to allocate for storing it. So, you might decide to store someone's first name and last name and allocate up to 20 characters for each name.

Each chunk of data that you want to record, such as a first name, is a *field*. A group of related fields is a *record*. If you want to store names and addresses, each name and address is a field, and each name and its accompanying address make up a single record, as shown in Figure 1-2.

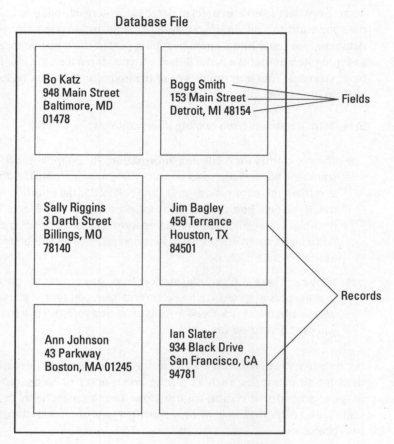

FIGURE 1-2:
A flat-file
database stores
data in fields
and records.

Flat-file databases impose a structure on the type of information you can store to make retrieving information much easier later. However, you need to design the structure of your database carefully. If you define the database to store only first and last names, you can't store any information other than first and last names.

Designing the size and types of fields can be crucial in using the database later. If you create a Name field but allocate only ten characters to hold that data, the name *Bob Jones* will fit, but another name, such as *Daniel Jonathan Perkins,* will be cut off.

Another problem is how you define your fields. You could store names in one big field or separate them into three separate fields for holding first, middle, and last names. Using a single field to store a name might initially look simpler, but separating names into different fields is actually more useful because it allows the database to search and sort by first, middle, or last name.

Although such a rigid structure might seem to make flat-file databases harder to use, it makes them easier to search and sort information. Unlike free-form databases that may contain anything, every record in a flat-file database contains the exact same type of information, such as a name, address, and phone number. This makes it possible to search and sort data.

If you want to find Robert Jones's telephone number, you could tell the flat-file database to show you all the records that contain a first name beginning with the letter R. If you want to sort your entire database alphabetically by last name, you can do that, too.

A flat-file database gets its name because it can work only with one file at a time. This makes a flat-file database easy to manage but also limits its usefulness. If you have one flat-file database containing names and addresses and a second flat-file database containing names and telephone numbers, you might have identical names stored in the two separate files. If you change the name in one flat-file database, you need to change that same name in the second flat-file database.

Relational databases

For storing simple, structured information, such as names, addresses, and phone numbers, flat-file databases are adequate. However, if you need to store large amounts of data, you're better off using a relational database, which is what the majority of database programs offer.

Like a flat-file database, you can't store anything in a relational database until you define the number and size of your fields to specify exactly what type of information (such as names, phone numbers, and email addresses) you want to save.

Unlike flat-file databases, relational databases can further organize data into *tables* (groups). Whereas a free-form database stores everything in a file and a flat-file database stores everything in a file but organizes it into fields, a relational database stores everything in a file that's divided into tables, which are further divided into fields, as shown in Figure 1-3.

REMEMBER

Think of database tables as miniature flat-file databases that can connect with each other.

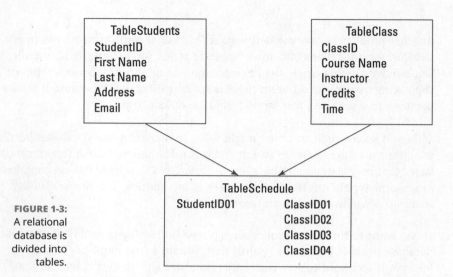

FIGURE 1-3:
A relational database is divided into tables.

Just as storing a name in separate First Name and Last Name fields gives you more flexibility in manipulating your data, grouping data in separate tables gives you more flexibility in manipulating and sharing information.

Suppose you have a list of employees that includes names, addresses, and telephone numbers. Now you may want to organize employees according to the department where they work. With a flat-file database, you'd have to create a separate file and store duplicate names in these separate databases, as shown in Figure 1-4.

Every time you added a new employee, you'd have to update both the employee database and the specific department database that defines where they work. If an employee left, you'd have to delete their name from two separate databases as well. With identical information scattered between two or more databases, keeping information updated and accurate is difficult.

Relational databases solve this problem by dividing data into tables with a table grouping the minimum amount of data possible. So, one table might contain employee names and ID numbers, whereas a second table might contain only employee names and department names, as shown in Figure 1-5.

TECHNICAL STUFF

A column in a table represents a single field, often called an *attribute.* A row in a table represents a single record, often called a *tuple.*

What makes tables useful is that you can link them together. So, whereas one table may contain names and addresses, while a second table may contain names and departments, the two tables are actually sharing information. Instead of having to type a name twice in both tables, you need to type the name only once, and the link between the separate tables automatically keeps that information updated and accurate in all other linked tables.

Employees

Media Department

FIGURE 1-4:
Flat-file databases must store duplicate data in separate files.

Table

Name	Employee ID
Bill Adams	4Y78
Sally Tarkin	8U90
Johnny Brown	4T33
Doug Hall	4A24
Yolanda Lee	9Z49
Sam Collins	1Q55
Randy May	2E03
Al Neander	4M79
Kal Baker	2B27

Table

Name	Department
Bill Adams	Public relations
Sally Tarkin	Human resources
Johnny Brown	Engineering
Doug Hall	Engineering
Yolanda Lee	Human resources
Sam Collins	Engineering
Randy May	Public relations
Al Neander	Public relations
Kal Baker	Human resources

FIGURE 1-5:
Tables separate data into pieces.

By linking or relating tables together, you can combine data in different ways. If you have a list of customers stored in one table and a list of sales in another table, you can relate these two tables to show which customers are buying which products, or which products are most popular in specific sales regions. Basically, relating tables together allows you to create *virtual* databases by sharing and combining data from separate database tables. By combining data from separate tables, you can uncover hidden information behind your data, as shown in Figure 1-6.

Table

Name	Employee ID
Bill Adams	4Y78
Sally Tarkin	8U90
Johnny Brown	4T33
Doug Hall	4A24
Yolanda Lee	9Z49
Sam Collins	1Q55
Randy May	2E03
Al Neander	4M79
Kal Baker	2B27

Table

Name	Department
Bill Adams	Public relations
Sally Tarkin	Human resources
Johnny Brown	Engineering
Doug Hall	Engineering
Yolanda Lee	Human resources
Sam Collins	Engineering
Randy May	Public relations
Al Neander	Public relations
Kal Baker	Human resources

Name	Employee ID	Department
Bill Adams	4Y78	Public relations
Sally Tarkin	8U90	Human resources
Johnny Brown	4T33	Engineering
Doug Hall	4A24	Engineering
Yolanda Lee	9Z49	Human resources
Sam Collins	1Q55	Engineering
Randy May	2E03	Public relations
Al Neander	4M79	Public relations
Kal Baker	2B27	Human resources

FIGURE 1-6:
Relational databases let you combine data from different tables.

Uncovering hidden relationships between data is called *data mining.* Data mining can be especially useful for statistics and machine learning.

Tables divide data into groups, but taken on a larger scale, it's possible to divide an entire database into multiple databases that are physically separate. Such databases are called *distributed databases.*

A company might use a distributed database to keep track of all its employees. A branch office in Asia might have a database of employees in Singapore, another branch in Europe might have a database of employees in England, and a third branch in the United States might have a database of employees in California. Combining these separate databases would create a single database of all the company's employees.

Manipulating Data

After you define the structure of a database by organizing information in tables and fields, the next step is to write commands for modifying and manipulating that information. This can be as simple as adding data to a specific table or as complicated as retrieving data from three different tables, reorganizing this information alphabetically by last name, and displaying this list on the screen with mathematical calculations showing sales results for each person and a total amount for an entire department and company.

The three basic commands for using data are *Select, Project,* and *Join.* The Select command retrieves a single row or tuple from a table. So, if you want to retrieve someone's name to find their email address, you could use the Select command, as shown in Figure 1-7.

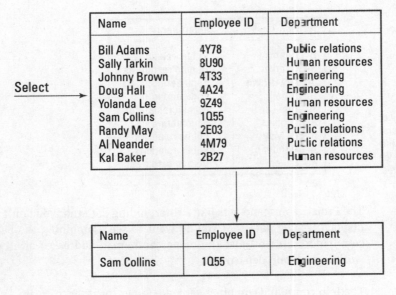

Name	Employee ID	Department
Bill Adams	4Y78	Public relations
Sally Tarkin	8U90	Human resources
Johnny Brown	4T33	Engineering
Doug Hall	4A24	Engineering
Yolanda Lee	9Z49	Human resources
Sam Collins	1Q55	Engineering
Randy May	2E03	Public relations
Al Neander	4M79	Public relations
Kal Baker	2B27	Human resources

Select →

Name	Employee ID	Department
Sam Collins	1Q55	Engineering

FIGURE 1-7: The Select command retrieves a single record or tuple.

Besides retrieving a single record or tuple, the Select command can retrieve multiple tuples, such as a list of all employees who work in a certain department.

The Project command retrieves one or more entire columns or attributes from a database table. This can be useful when you just want to view certain information, such as the names of employees along with the department where they work, as shown in Figure 1-8.

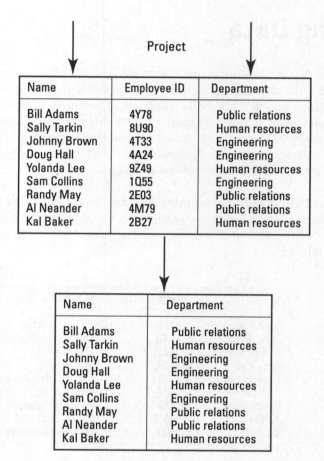

FIGURE 1-8:
The Project
command
retrieves selected
columns or
attributes.

The Project command acts like a filter, hiding data that you don't want to see and displaying only data that you do want to see. Combining the Select and Project commands can find just the names and email addresses of all employees who work in a certain department.

The Join command combines separate tables together to create a virtual table that can show new information. For example, a Join command might combine a table of products, and a table of customers with a table of salespeople to show which salesperson is best at selling certain products and which products are most popular with customers, as shown in Figure 1-9.

Table

Name	Employee ID
Bill Adams	4Y78
Sally Tarkin	8U90
Johnny Brown	4T33
Doug Hall	4A24
Yolanda Lee	9Z49
Sam Collins	1Q55
Randy May	2E03
Al Neander	4M79
Kal Baker	2B27

Table

Name	Department
Bill Adams	Public relations
Sally Tarkin	Human resources
Johnny Brown	Engineering
Doug Hall	Engineering
Yolanda Lee	Human resources
Sam Collins	Engineering
Randy May	Public relations
Al Neander	Public relations
Kal Baker	Human resources

Join

Name	Employee ID	Department
Bill Adams	4Y78	Public relations
Sally Tarkin	8U90	Human resources
Johnny Brown	4T33	Engineering
Doug Hall	4A24	Engineering
Yolanda Lee	9Z49	Human resources
Sam Collins	1Q55	Engineering
Randy May	2E03	Public relations
Al Neander	4M79	Public relations
Kal Baker	2B27	Human resources

FIGURE 1-9: The Join command matches two or more tables together.

WARNING

The Select, Project, and Join commands are generic terms. Every database uses its own terms for performing these exact same actions, so be aware of these terminology differences.

Writing database commands

Many relational database programs include a proprietary programming language for creating custom applications. Microsoft Access uses a programming language called VBA (short for *Visual Basic for Applications*), whereas FileMaker uses a language called FileMaker Script. Most databases actually consist of separate files, with one file containing the actual data and a second file containing programs for manipulating that data.

The main difference between a general-purpose language, like C++, and a database language is that the database language only needs to define what data to use and how to manipulate it, but the database program (or the *database engine*) takes care of the actual details.

The SQL language

Although every relational database engine comes with its own language, the most popular language for manipulating large amounts of data is SQL (short for *Structured Query Language*). SQL is used by many different database programs, such as those sold by IBM, Microsoft, and Oracle. If you're going to work with databases as a programmer, you have to understand SQL.

SQL commands, like all database programming languages, essentially hide the details of programming so you can focus on the task of manipulating data. To retrieve names from a database table named Employees, you could use this SQL command:

```
SELECT FirstName, LastName FROM Employees
```

To selectively search for certain names, you could use this variation:

```
SELECT FirstName, LastName FROM Employees
WHERE FirstName = 'Richard'
```

To add new information to a table, you could use the following command:

```
INSERT INTO Employees
VALUES ('John', 'Smith', '555-1948')
```

To delete information from a table, you could use the following command:

```
DELETE FROM Employees
WHERE LastName = 'Johnson'
```

To modify a phone number, you could use the following command:

```
UPDATE Employees
SET PhoneNumber = '555-1897'
WHERE LastName = 'Smith'
```

An ordinary user can type simple database commands to retrieve information from a database, but because most users don't want to type a series of commands, it's usually easier for someone else to write commonly used database commands and then store these commands as miniature programs. Then instead of being forced to type commands, the user can just choose an option, and the database will run its program associated with that option, such as sorting or searching for information.

Data integrity

With small databases, only one person may use the database at a time. However with large databases, it's possible for multiple people to access the database at the same time. The biggest problem with multiuser databases is maintaining data integrity.

Data integrity ensures that data is accurate and updated. You may run into a problem with data integrity when multiple users are modifying the same data. An airline reservation system might let multiple travel agents book seats on the same airplane, but the database must make sure that two travel agents don't book the same seat at the same time.

To prevent two users from modifying the same data, most database programs protect data by letting only the first user modify the data and locking others out. While the first user is modifying the data, no one else can modify that same data.

Locking can prevent two users from changing data at the same time, but sometimes, changing data may require multiple steps. To change seats in an airline reservation system, you may need to give up one seat (such as seat 14F) and take another one (such as seat 23C). But in the process of giving up one seat, it's possible that another user could take the second seat (23C) before the first user can, which would leave the first user with no seats at all.

To prevent this problem, database programs can lock all data that a user plans to modify, such as preventing anyone from accessing seats 14F and 23C. Another solution to this problem is a *rollback*. If a second user takes seat 23C before the first user can get to it, the database program can roll back its changes and give the first user the original seat, 14F.

Multiuser databases have algorithms for dealing with such problems, but if you're creating a database from scratch, these are some of the many problems you need to solve, which explains why most people find it easier just to use an existing database program instead of writing their own database programs.

Data mining

Data mining simply looks at separate databases to find information that's not obvious in either database. For example, one database might contain tax information, such as names, addresses, and Social Security numbers. A second database might contain airline passenger information, such as names, addresses, and flight numbers. A third database might contain telephone calling records that contain names, addresses, and phone numbers called.

By themselves, these separate databases may seem to have no connection, but link the tax database with an airline passenger database, and you can tell which passengers traveled to certain countries and reported an income less than $25,000. Just by combining these two databases, you can flag any suspicious travel arrangements. If someone reports income under $25,000, but has made ten different trips to Saudi Arabia, Venezuela, and the Philippines, that could be a signal that something isn't quite right.

Now toss in the telephone calling database and you can find everyone who reported less than $25,000 in income, made ten or more overseas trips to other countries, and made long-distance phone calls to those same countries. Retrieving this type of information from multiple databases is what data mining is all about.

Data mining finds hidden information stored in seemingly innocuous databases. As a result, data mining can be used to track criminals (or anti-government activists) and identify people most likely to have a genetic disposition to certain diseases (which can be used for preventive treatment or to deny them health insurance). With so many different uses, data mining can be used for both helpful and harmful purposes.

Database Programming

At the simplest level, a database lets you store data and retrieve it again. For storing a list of people you need to contact regularly, a flat-file database can be created and used with no programming. However, if you want to store large amounts of data and manipulate that information in different ways, you may need to write a program.

The three parts of a database program include the *user interface* (UI), the *database management system* (DBMS; which contains commands for manipulating data), and the actual *information* stored in a database, as shown in Figure 1-10.

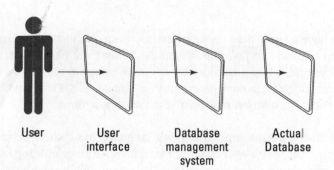

FIGURE 1-10:
The three parts
of a database
program.

User User
interface Database
management
system Actual
Database

The UI lets people use the data without having to know how the data is stored or how to write commands to manipulate the data. The database stores the actual information, such as dividing data into tables and fields. The commands for manipulating that data may include printing, searching, or sorting through that data, such as searching for the names of all customers who recently ordered more than $10,000 worth of products in the past month.

There are three ways to write a database program:

>> **Use an ordinary programming language, such as C++ or Java.** The problem with using a programming language like C++ is that you have to create all three parts of a database from scratch. Although this gives you complete control over the design of the database, it also takes time.

As a simpler alternative, many programmers buy a database toolkit, written in their favorite programming language, such as C++. This toolkit takes care of storing and manipulating data, so all you need to do is design the database structure (tables and fields) and create the UI.

>> **Start with an existing relational database program and use its built-in programming language to create a UI and the commands for manipulating the data.** The advantage of this approach is that you don't have to create an entire database management system from scratch, but the disadvantage is that you have to learn the proprietary language of that particular database, such as Microsoft Access or FileMaker.

>> **Use a combination of existing database programs and general-purpose programming languages, like C++.** First, use a database program to design the structure of the data. Then you use the database's programming language to write commands for manipulating that data. Finally, use your favorite programming language, such as C++ or Java, to create a UI for that database.

This approach takes advantage of the database program's strengths (designing database structures and manipulating data) while avoiding its weakness in designing UIs. General-purpose languages, like C++ or Java, are much better for designing UIs, which can make your database program much easier to use.

If you have a lot of time on your hands, you could create an entire database from scratch with C++ or Java. But if you don't want the hassle of creating an entire DBMS yourself, buy a commercial database program and customize it using the database program's own programming language. This second approach is the most common solution for creating database programs.

If you find a database programming language too clumsy or too restrictive for designing UIs, write your own UI in your favorite programming language and slap it on an existing database program. This may involve the hassle of integrating your UI (written in C++) with the database file and data manipulating commands created by a database program (such as MySQL).

Ultimately, database programming involves making data easy to access and retrieve, no matter which method you choose. Because storing information is so crucial in any industry, database programming will always be in demand. If you understand how to design and program databases, you'll always have plenty of work for as long as you want it.

Chapter **2**

Bioinformatics

B*ioinformatics,* also known as *computational biology,* combines computer science with molecular biology to solve biological problems on a molecular level. This basically means using computers to study proteins and genes to predict protein structures, drug interactions, and gene splicing.

Because bioinformatics embraces both computer science and molecular biology, there are two common paths to working in bioinformatics. The first involves studying computers and then learning about molecular biology so you'll know what your programs are supposed to do. The second involves studying molecular biology and then learning computer programming so you can write programs to aid in your research.

Each way depends on your main interest. Not all computer scientists want to know or study molecular biology and not all molecular biologists want to go through the hassle of learning computer programming. As a result, bioinformatics is a rare combination of diverse skills that will be in high demand in the near future. If the idea of using a computer to study cloning, genetic engineering, and cures for diseases appeals to you, bioinformatics may be the perfect outlet for your talent.

TECHNICAL STUFF

The terms bioinformatics and computational biology are often used interchangeably. Technically, bioinformatics focuses more on creating algorithms and writing programs, whereas computational biology focuses more on using computers as tools for biological research.

The Basics of Bioinformatics

To understand bioinformatics, you must first understand its purpose. Before computers, biologists had two ways to study any problem:

» They could perform an experiment in a laboratory under controlled conditions, which is known as *in vitro* (in glass).

» They could perform an experiment on a living organism, such as a guinea pig or a human volunteer. Because this type of experiment occurs on a living creature, it's called *in vivo* (in life).

Both in vitro and in vivo experiments are expensive and time-consuming. Performing in vitro experiments requires laboratory equipment, whereas performing in vivo experiments requires both laboratory equipment and live subjects.

Bioinformatics offers biologists a third way to conduct experiments: *in silico* (in silicon). Instead of using expensive laboratory equipment and living creatures, bioinformatics lets biologists conduct simulated experiments with a computer.

What makes in silico experiments just as valid as in vitro or in vivo experiments is that they all work with molecules. An in vitro experiment studies molecules in a test tube, an in vivo experiment studies molecules in a live animal, and an in silico experiment studies molecules as nothing more than data inside the computer. Specifically, in silico experiments (bioinformatics) represent molecules as strings that the computer manipulates.

By using knowledge of how different molecules interact, bioinformatics can simulate molecular interactions, such as how a certain drug might interact with cancer cells. This makes experiments not only faster, but easier and less expensive to conduct as well. After a bioinformatics experiment confirms a certain result, biologists can go to the next step — testing actual drugs and living cells in test tubes *(in vitro)* or on living creatures *(in vivo)*.

Representing molecules

Bioinformatics manipulates molecules. Of course, biologists don't care about every molecule in existence — just the ones involved in life, such as proteins. Four important molecules that biologists study are the ones that make up the structure of deoxyribonucleic acid (DNA). These four molecules are identified by a single letter: *A* (for *adenine*), *C* (for *cytosine*), *G* (for *guanine*), or *T* (for *thymine*).

When these molecules form a DNA strand, they link together in a sequence, like this:

    ACTGTTG

In a computer, such sequences of molecules can be represented as a string, like this:

```
$DNA = 'ACTGTTG';
```

Of course, these aren't the only four molecules that biologists study, but the idea is to use computers to represent molecules and structures as just another type of data.

Unfortunately, most molecular structures consist of long strings of redundant one-letter codes. Trying to read these long molecular structures, let alone manipulate them by hand, is nearly impossible. That's where computers and bioinformatics come in.

Computers simplify and automate the tedious process of examining and manipulating molecular structures. Biologists simply have to type the molecular structure correctly and then tell the computer how to manipulate that structure as a series of strings.

Manipulating molecules in a computer

The type of programming language used to manipulate strings of molecules is irrelevant. What's more important is how to manipulate molecular structures. The simplest form of string manipulation is *concatenation,* which joins multiple strings into one.

In the world of biology, concatenation is similar to gene splicing — biologists can experiment with tearing a molecular structure apart and putting it back together again to see what they can create. In Perl, concatenation can be as simple as the following example:

```
$DNA1 = 'ACTGTTG';
$DNA2 = 'TGTACCT';
$DNA3 = "$DNA1$DNA2";
print $DNA3;
```

This simple Perl program would print the following:

```
ACTGTTGTGTACCT
```

Another way to manipulate strings (molecular structures) is by replacing individual molecules with other ones, which can simulate mutation. A mutation simulation program could pick a molecule at random and replace it with another molecule. So, the initial structure might look like this:

```
CCCCCCCCCCC
```

Then each mutation could progressively scramble the structure by a single molecule, like this:

```
CCCCCCCCCCC
CCCCCCCTCCC
CCCCACCTCCC
CCCCACCTCCG
CACCACCTCCG
```

Mutation and concatenation are just two ways to manipulate molecular structures within a computer. If you created half a DNA sequence, you still need to determine the other half. Because DNA consists of two strands bound together in a double-helix form, it's easy to determine the second sequence of DNA after you know the first one. That's because each adenine (A) links up with thymine (T) and each cytosine (C) links up with guanine (G).

The two strands of DNA are *complementary sequences.* To calculate a complementary sequence by knowing only one of the sequences, you can use a simple program that replaces every *A* with a *T*, every *C* with a *G*, every *T* with an *A*, and every *G* with a *C*. A Perl program to do this might look like this:

```
$DNA = 'ACTGTTG';
$compDNA = $DNA;
$compDNA =~ tr/ACGT/TGCA/;
```

The tr command simply tells Perl to translate or swap one character for another. So, the preceding tr/ACGT/TGCA/; command tells Perl to translate every *A* into a *T*, every *C* into a *G*, every *G* into a *C*, and every *T* into an *A* all at once.

The second step in determining a complementary sequence is to reverse the order of that sequence. That's because sequences are always written a specific way, starting with the end of the sequence known as 5′ phosphoryl (also known as 5 prime or 5′) and ending with 3′ hydroxyl (known as 3 prime or 3′). So, to display the complementary sequence correctly, you have to reverse it using this Perl command:

```
$DNA = 'ACTGTTG';
$compDNA = $DNA;
$compDNA =~ tr/ACGT/TGCA/;
$revDNA = reverse $compDNA;
```

TIP

It's important to know both sequences that make up a DNA strand so you can use both DNA sequences to search for information. When faced with an unknown structure, there's a good chance someone else has already discovered this identical molecular structure. So, all you have to do is match your molecular structure with a database of known structures to determine what you have.

Database Searches

After biologists discover a specific molecular structure, they store information about that sequence in a database. That way other biologists can study that sequence so everyone benefits from this slowly growing body of knowledge.

Unfortunately, there isn't just one database, but several databases that specialize in storing different types of information:

» **GenBank** stores nucleotide sequences.

» **Swiss-Prot** stores protein sequences.

» **Online Mendelian Inheritance in Man (OMIM)** stores human genes and genetic disorders data.

After you find a particular sequence, you can look up articles about particular sequences in PubMed (https://pubmed.ncbi.nlm.nih.gov), a database of articles published in biomedical and life-science journals.

Although it's possible to search these databases manually, it's usually much faster and easier to write a program that can send a list of sequences to a database, search that database for known sequences that match the ones sent, and then retrieve a list of those known sequences for further study.

Because searching databases is such a common task, biologists have created a variety of tools to standardize and simplify this procedure. One of the more popular tools is Basic Local Alignment and Search Tool (BLAST). BLAST can look for exact matches or just sequences that are similar to yours within specified limits, such as a sequence that's no more than 10 percent different. This process of matching up sequences is called *sequence alignment* or just *alignment*.

By finding an exact match of your sequence in a database, you can identify what you have. By comparing your sequence with similar ones, you can better understand the possible characteristics of your sequence. For example, a cat is more similar to a dog than a rattlesnake, so a cat would likely behave more like a dog than a rattlesnake.

TECHNICAL STUFF

The BLAST algorithm and computer program was written by the U.S. National Center for Biotechnology Information (NCBI) at Pennsylvania State University (`https://blast.ncbi.nlm.nih.gov/Blast.cgi`).

The basic idea behind BLAST is to compare one sequence (called a *query sequence*) with a database to find exact matches of a certain number of characters, such as four. For example, suppose you had a sequence like this:

ATCACCACCTCCG

With BLAST, you could specify that you only want to find matches of four characters or more, such as:

AT<u>CACC</u>TGGTATC

Although you could type molecular sequences by hand, it's far easier to let the computer do it for you, especially if you want to compare a large number of sequences with BLAST. After BLAST gets through comparing your sequences, it returns a list of matching sequences.

TECHNICAL STUFF

Using BLAST to compare sequences to a database of known sequences is an example of data mining. (See Chapter 1 of this minibook for more information about data mining.)

You could scan through this list of matching yourself, but again, that's likely to be tedious, slow, and error-prone. Writing a program that can parse reports generated by BLAST to look for certain characteristics is much simpler. Essentially, you can use the computer to automate sending data to BLAST and then have the computer filter through the results so you see only the sequences that you care about, as shown in Figure 2-1.

Now you could write another program to skim or parse the database results to filter out only the results you're looking for. Because every database stores information in slightly different formats, you may need to write another program that converts file formats from one database into another one.

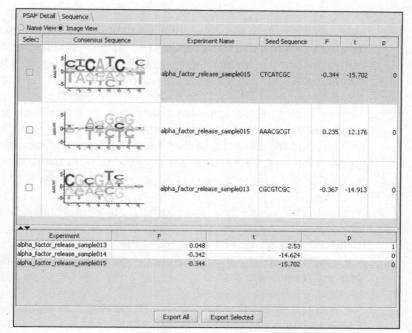

FIGURE 2-1:
A bioinformatics program can help you search through large amounts of raw data.

Because every biologist is using different information to look for different results, there's no single bioinformatics program standard. As a result, bioinformatics involves writing a lot of little custom programs to work with an ever-growing library of standard programs that biologists need and use every day.

Some biologists can learn programming and do much of this work themselves, but it's far more common for biologists to give their data to an army of bioinformatics technicians who take care of the programming details. That way the biologists can focus on what they do best (studying biology) while the programmers can focus on what they do best (writing custom programs). The only way these two groups can communicate is if biologists understand how programming can help them and the programmers understand what type of data and results the biologists need.

Bioinformatics Programming

Because biologists use a wide variety of computers (Linux, Mac, Unix, and Windows), they need a programming language that's portable across all platforms. In addition, biologists need to work with existing programs, such as online databases. Finally, because most biologists aren't trained as programmers, they need a simple language that gets the job done quickly.

Although a language like C/C++ runs on multiple platforms, porting a program from Windows to Linux often requires rewriting to optimize the program for each particular operating system. Figuring out C/C++ isn't necessarily hard, but it's not easy either.

A more appropriate programming language is a *scripting language.* Scripting languages, such as Perl, run on almost every operating system, are easy to learn and use, and include built-in commands for manipulating strings. Best of all, scripting languages are specifically designed to work with existing programs by feeding data to another program and retrieving the results back again.

Although Perl has become the unofficial standard programming language for bioinformatics, biologists also rely on other programming languages because many people feel that Perl is too confusing. Perl's motto is "There's more than one way to do it" — you can perform the exact same action in Perl with entirely different commands.

For example, to concatenate two strings, Perl offers two different methods. The first is to smash two strings together, like this:

```
$DNA3 = "$DNA1$DNA2";
```

The second way to concatenate the same two strings uses the dot operator, like this:

```
$DNA3 = $DNA1 . $DNA2;
```

The second most popular language used in bioinformatics is Python. Python offers features similar to those offered by Perl, but many people feel that Python is a simpler language to understand and use because its motto is, "There should be one — and preferably only one — obvious way to do it." To concatenate strings in Python, you can use this command:

```
dna3 = dna1 + dna2
```

Another popular bioinformatics programming language is Java. Not only are more programmers familiar with Java, but Java's cross-platform capability allows it to create compiled programs for each operating system. In comparison, both Perl and Python are *interpreted languages* — you must load the source code of a Perl or Python program and run it through an interpreter first. Java gives you the convenience of copying and running a compiled program without the nuisance of running source code through an interpreter.

If you're going to work in bioinformatics, make sure you learn Java, Perl, or Python. The more languages you know, the easier it will be to work with other people's programs and data.

TIP

Biologists have written subprograms in various programming languages to make writing bioinformatics programs easier:

>> **C++:** BioC++ (http://biocpp.sourceforge.net)

>> **Java:** BioJava (https://biojava.org)

>> **JavaScript:** BioJavaScript (http://biojs.net)

>> **Perl:** BioPerl (https://bioperl.org)

>> **PHP:** BioPHP (http://biophp.org)

>> **Python:** BioPython (https://biopython.org)

>> **Ruby:** BioRuby (http://bioruby.org)

Because bioinformatics involves performing the same type of tasks, these libraries of bioinformatics subprograms offer code for

>> Accessing databases

>> Transforming database information from one file format to another

>> Manipulating sequences

>> Searching and comparing sequences

>> Displaying results as graphs or 3D structures

The field of bioinformatics is still growing and changing — the tools and techniques used today may become obsolete tomorrow. (If you've spent any time in the computer industry, you probably already know that applies to every aspect of computers by now.)

In most other fields of computer science, programmers spend more time maintaining and updating existing programs than writing new ones. In bioinformatics, every biologist has different needs, so you could actually spend more time writing custom programs and less time getting stuck patching up someone else's program.

With its curious mix of computer science and biology, bioinformatics is a unique field that's wide open for anyone interested in life science and computer science. If the idea of working in the growing field of biotechnology appeals to you, bioinformatics might be for you.

Chapter 3

Computer Security

Computer security is the equivalent of playing cops and robbers with a computer. On one side are the bad guys, trying to destroy, modify, or steal data. On the other side are the good guys, trying to protect that data. (Then again, sometimes the good guys are trying to destroy, modify, or steal data from the bad guys.)

In the early days of computers, the biggest threat to data was losing it through an accident. Then malicious computer hackers emerged. Unlike the original band of computer hackers, responsible for creating operating systems and language compilers, malicious hackers use their programming skills to break into computers and hurt others.

Initially, these computer break-ins were more of a nuisance than a danger. Computer hackers might have tied up resources, but they rarely wrecked anything except by sheer accident. In fact, many computer administrators grudgingly allowed hackers to stay on their computers as long as they didn't disturb anything, and many hackers returned the favor by warning computer system administrators of flaws in their programs that could allow less honorable hackers to sneak in and destroy files.

As more people picked up hacking skills, inevitably a small percentage of these hackers began using their skills for destructive purposes. At first, there was only the joy of crashing a computer or wrecking data for bragging rights to other hackers, but hackers soon had a new motive for breaking into computers. As more people began shopping online and more computers began storing credit card numbers and other personal information, such as Social Security numbers, hackers were now motivated by money.

Malicious hackers are bad enough, but what makes them an even greater threat is when they have the financial support and legal protection of corporations and nation-states. Corporations have borrowed hacker tricks for financial purposes ranging from spying and stealing corporate secrets to flooding computers with unwanted advertising.

Nation-states regularly spy on friends and foes alike to gain an advantage for their own self-interest or for their national corporations. Sometimes nation-states hack into the computer systems to steal military secrets, but far more often, nation-states are more interested in exploiting computer systems in other countries for political and financial gain.

Although nation-state hackers may target major corporations or governments, other hackers target individuals. This can involve stealing identities by collecting as much personal information about a person to mimic them online, or by getting money directly from victims, often through ransomware, which are programs that encrypt files on a computer and hold them for ransom. The only way the victim can get access to their data is by paying off the hacker to get the decryption key.

That means the bad guys are no longer stereotypical computer nerds staying up late at night. Today's threats are well-financed organizations intent on breaking into computers for their financial goals.

With so much at stake, it's no surprise that one of the hottest fields of computer science is *computer security*. Computer security is more than just locking doors and guarding computer rooms. Today, computer security is stopping threats, repairing damage, and hunting the criminals by using nothing more than programming skills.

Stopping Malware

One of the earliest and most prominent threats to computers is malicious software, often called *malware*. Malware is any program designed specifically to damage another computer, such as by erasing all its files. What makes malware particularly dangerous is that it's so common and capable of spreading without the intervention of the original programmer. Some common types of malware threats include

Viruses

Computer *viruses* are nothing more than programs that attach themselves to another file, such as a program or a word-processing document. The virus spreads when you run an infected file on another computer.

Besides spreading, most viruses also carry a *payload*. This payload can range from the harmless (such as displaying a humorous message onscreen) to the malicious (such as erasing every file stored on a hard disk). The most effective way to stop viruses is to capture one and dissect it to see how it works.

To dissect a virus (or any program), you need to use a *disassembler,* which essentially converts, or reverse-engineers, a program into assembly language source code. By studying the assembly language code of a virus, you can understand how it works and, more important, how to identify the virus, essentially capturing that virus's digital fingerprint.

Capturing the digital fingerprint of a virus is crucial because that's how most antivirus programs work. Antivirus programs scan files for known signs of specific viruses. Because new variations of viruses appear every day, the database of an antivirus program must be updated constantly.

Worms

Similar to viruses are *worms.* Unlike a virus, a worm doesn't need to infect a file to propagate itself. Instead, a worm can duplicate and spread to other computers all by itself. In the early days of computers, when computers were isolated from one another, the only way files could spread from one computer to another was by physically copying a file to a floppy disk and inserting that floppy disk into another computer. That's why viruses were so popular in the early days of computers.

Nowadays, most computers are connected to the Internet, so there's no need to infect any files to spread. Instead, worms can spread on their own by looking for connections to another computer and then copying themselves over that connection, such as through a group of networked computers.

There are two ways to protect a computer against a worm:

>> **Capture a worm and dissect it like a virus to see how the worm works.** After they capture a worm's digital fingerprint, they can store this information in an antivirus program's database so it knows how to recognize and remove that particular worm.

>> **Block the worm's access to other computers over a network.** The way computers connect to one another is through *ports* (virtual openings). Worms simply look for unsecured open ports on an infected computer so they can travel out and infect another computer.

The simplest way to block ports on a computer is to use a special program called a *firewall*. Firewalls can defeat worms in two ways:

>> A firewall can block or restrict a computer's ports to keep a worm from infecting the computer in the first place.

>> If the worm has already infected the computer, a firewall can also block the computer's ports that could allow the worm to sneak out and infect another computer.

Although you could write your own firewall in your favorite programming language, it's much easier just to use an existing firewall program and configure it properly. *Configuring* a firewall means defining exactly what the firewall allows and what the firewall blocks.

On the simplest level, you can tell a firewall to allow certain programs to connect over the Internet, as shown in Figure 3-1. On a more complicated level, you can configure a firewall to allow only certain types of data to pass in and out. Allowing certain data to pass through a firewall, instead of just allowing certain programs, can defeat both Trojan horses and spyware.

Trojan horses

Trojan horses are programs that masquerade as something else to entice you to copy and run them. The moment you run it, the Trojan horse unleashes its payload, which can range from attacking your hard disk to installing another program, such as a virus, on your computer. The main reason to sneak a virus or worm onto a computer through a Trojan horse is to get the virus or worm past the computer's defenses.

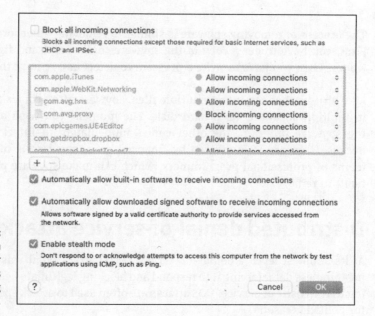

FIGURE 3-1:
Firewalls can
block ports or
certain programs
from accessing
a network.

If a firewall allows a browser to access the Internet, that browser can be used to download a Trojan horse, which the firewall will allow. However, if you configure the firewall to allow only certain data (such as web pages) but block any other data (such as an executable file that might contain a Trojan horse), the firewall can protect a computer from Trojan horses.

One common version of a Trojan horse is a *remote access Trojan* (RAT). A RAT sneaks onto a computer and then allows a hacker to control that computer remotely over a network connection. RATs are often used to steal passwords, read emails, and even delete files.

Common defenses against a Trojan horse are a *firewall* and an *antivirus program*. A firewall can block a Trojan horse from getting into a computer and also keep it from communicating with another computer. An antivirus program can search for the digital fingerprints of a Trojan horse and remove it.

Spyware

Spyware is a special program that installs itself on a computer and connects to an outside computer over the Internet. Instead of allowing a hacker to remotely control an infected computer, spyware may send advertisements on to the infected computer or steal passwords or credit card numbers.

The process of removing spyware is similar to removing other forms of malware: First, you have to get a copy of the spyware to dissect it and figure out how it works. Then you have to write a program to detect and remove that spyware.

Like viruses that can infect multiple files, spyware often copies and hides itself in multiple locations on a hard disk. The moment you wipe out one copy of the spyware program, the other copies immediately re-infect the computer. Because spyware is motivated by financial gain, spyware is often written by teams of professional programmers, which can make spyware particularly difficult to remove.

Distributed denial-of-service attacks

At its simplest level, a denial-of-service (DOS) attack bombards a website with meaningless data, forcing it to respond and blocking legitimate users from accessing that website or service. DOS attacks are often used to attack specific computers for political reasons.

If just a single computer kept bombarding a website with useless data, that website could just refuse to accept data from that one computer. That's why most DOS attacks come from multiple computers.

ATTACKING NUCLEAR REACTORS IN IRAN WITH STUXNET

If you wanted to wreck a nuclear reactor without anyone knowing you did it, how would you do it? That's the question Israel faced as it watched Iran get closer to developing a nuclear weapon. The solution was a special worm dubbed Stuxnet.

Stuxnet's programmers designed Stuxnet to spread easily among computers in the Middle East. By letting Stuxnet loose, its creators wanted the worm to find its way into the Iranian computers that controlled centrifuges monitored by Windows PCs and Siemens SIMATIC S7 software that were part of Iran's nuclear research program.

Stuxnet spun the centrifuges too fast while reporting to the technicians that everything was actually okay. This resulted in Stuxnet tearing apart one-fifth of Iran's gas centrifuges, significantly delaying its nuclear ambitions. Although security officials suspect Stuxnet was a joint project between Israel and the United States, nobody can definitively prove this, which made Stuxnet one of the first known cyberweapons designed by one nation-state specifically to harm another nation-state.

That way there are so many different computers attacking that the target computer can't block them all. Because it's impractical for an individual to manually send data to a single computer over and over again, hackers create automatic programs to do this for them, called *bots*.

Hackers simply infect thousands or millions of computers and install a bot on those computers. This collection of infected computers is known as a *botnet*, and a single hacker can control this entire botnet to blast out data on command.

Hackers often establish botnets and then rent them out for sending out spam from multiple computers. Now if an email server blocks one bot-infected computer, the hacker can simply direct a different bot-infected computer to send spam to that same email server.

The challenge with botnets is taking down the entire botnet rather than exhaustively taking down individual bot-infected computers. Because a botnet can control computers all over the world and the hacker running the botnet can be located anywhere in the world, finding and destroying botnets is a difficult and ongoing problem.

Stopping Hackers

Malware is a constant threat to computers that can strike at any time. Besides worrying about malware infection, computer security professionals have to also worry about the source of malware: The hackers who create malware in the first place.

Unlike malware, which can behave predictably, every hacker is different and can attack a computer network from inside or outside that network. As a result, stopping computer hackers involves programming skills and detective work at the same time.

Users represent the first line of defense against hackers, but they're also the weakest link as well. The more users on a network, the more likely some of those users will choose weak passwords or practice sloppy computer practices such as downloading files from suspicious email messages or websites. Because users can't be expected to be vigilant against hackers all the time, the next line of defense rests on technical solutions.

The basic defense against a hacker is a firewall. Hackers can sneak in only through an open port on a computer, so a firewall shuts the hacker out as effectively as locking the front door. Unfortunately, although firewalls can stop worms from sneaking in, firewalls aren't as effective against hackers. That's because a hacker can always find another way into a computer network that can circumvent any firewalls.

The simplest way to circumvent a firewall is to use a computer that's already located beyond the protective firewall. This is the way insiders can break into a computer network because, as employees of a company, they're already authorized to use that computer network anyway. To detect intruders on a computer network, computer security professionals have to rely on special programs known as *intrusion detection systems* (IDSs).

Intrusion detection systems

An IDS acts like a burglar alarm. The moment the program detects suspicious activity, such as someone on the network at 2 a.m., the IDS sounds the alarm to alert a human system administrator. At this point, the system administrator's job is to study the activity on the computer network to determine whether the threat is valid.

STOPPING CHEATERS IN VIDEO GAMES

The video-game industry dwarfs the movie and music industries combined. With so many people playing video games and so many people buying and selling virtual goods within video games, it's no surprise that the video-game industry has been hit by hackers as well.

Some hackers simply cheat at the game to give themselves more power or invincibility so they can beat other players and destroy other players' sense of fun. This can drive players away from a particular video game if too many cheaters flood the game and make it unappealing for non-cheaters to play. For the video-game publisher, this means the potential of losing millions of dollars from paying customers.

Another way hackers cheat in video games is by stealing virtual goods from other players within a video game. This allows the cheaters to profit while upsetting players following the rules. The end result is the same in that non-cheating players risk leaving the game, costing the video-game publisher millions of dollars in lost revenue.

Because millions of dollars are at stake, video-game companies hire people specifically to stop and find cheaters who could ruin their games. If you like the idea of playing video games and hacking, working as a security professional in the video-game industry might be a dream job for you.

The problem is that seemingly false threats could actually turn out to be real. Seeing an authorized user on a computer network at 2 a.m. may look suspicious, but if that authorized user regularly accesses the computer at that time of night, a system administrator may simply ignore that alert. However, a hacker could have hijacked an authorized user's ID and password to masquerade as an authorized user.

At this point, a system administrator might study the authorized user's actions to determine whether anything looks out of place, such as deleting files or accessing files in other parts of the computer that the authorized user should have no business peeking at (such as an engineer poking around the accounting department's files).

To help identify potential hackers, many system administrators rely on a special program called a *honeypot,* which acts like a trap to snare hackers. A honeypot creates an entirely phony part of a computer network and loads it with tempting, but fake data, such as blueprints for a new weapon, a list of Social Security numbers, or usernames and passwords of nonexistent employees.

No authorized users would ever need to browse through the fake files of a honeypot because authorized users won't know the honeypot even exists. The moment anyone accesses the phony honeypot files, the IDS can positively identify that user as an intruder.

A honeypot isolates an intruder into a fictional part of the computer network where they can't cause any damage. However, after a hacker has accessed a computer network, system administrators have two problems:

>> They have to find a way to keep the intruder out.

>> They need to make sure the intruder can never get back in.

Rootkit detectors

After breaking into a computer network, the hacker's first goal is to plant a rootkit. A *rootkit* provides tools for covering the hacker's tracks to avoid detection along with providing tools for punching holes in the computer defenses from the inside. By installing a rootkit on a computer, hackers ensure that if one way into the computer gets discovered, they still have half a dozen other ways to get right back into that same computer all over again.

Even if a honeypot distracts a hacker from accessing sensitive areas of a network, the mere presence of a hacker means that some part of the network's defenses has been breached. To ensure that hackers can't get back into a computer, system administrators need to rely on rootkit removal programs.

Rootkit removal programs simply automate the process a computer expert would follow to look for and remove a rootkit from a network. Unfortunately, hackers develop new rootkits all the time, and one rootkit might hide in a different way than another rootkit. Instead of creating a single rootkit removal program, system administrators often have to create custom rootkit removal programs.

An IDS can find a hacker, and a rootkit removal program can detect and wipe out a rootkit from a network. For many companies, those two tasks alone are enough to keep an army of programmers busy. But if a company wants to take legal action against a hacker, it needs to provide evidence of the hacker's activities, and that evidence falls under the category of forensics.

Forensics

If you've ever accidentally deleted a file and then recovered it again, you've practiced a simple form of forensics. Basically, *forensics* is about finding what happened to deleted data. When hackers break into a computer network, the network often keeps track of all activity on the computer in a special file, called a *log.* To cover their tracks, hackers often modify this log to erase all traces of the hacker's activities on the computer network.

Of course, anything deleted on a computer can usually be recovered again, so computer forensics captures and restores this information. Such forensics computer evidence can pinpoint exactly what day and time a hacker entered a computer network, what the hacker did while on the network, and which computer the hacker used to access the network. This pile of evidence can pinpoint the hacker's physical location, which the police can use to find and arrest the hacker.

Computer forensics has another use in supporting criminal cases unrelated to computer hacking. Many Internet predators store emails and photographs of their contact with their victims, but if they suspect the police might be watching them, they'll erase this incriminating evidence off their hard disk. To recover this evidence, the police can turn to computer forensics to retrieve these missing emails and photographs.

Finally, computer forensics can come in handy if a hacker or malware wipes out an entire hard disk loaded with valuable files. Forensics may be able to recover these files as if they were never wiped out at all.

The art of computer forensics involves low-level access to computer hardware, which means forensic practitioners are often skilled in assembly language and C programming. If the idea of combining detective work with mysteries and computer programming sounds appealing, computer forensics and computer security might be a field for you.

Secure Computing

Most computer security revolves around preventing intrusions and fixing any problems that occur because of the intrusion. Such an approach is fine, but for a proactive approach that stops malware and hackers from attacking at all, programmers are learning a new field: *secure computing*.

The idea behind secure computing is to design computer programs with security in mind right from the start. This might seem logical until you realize that nearly all software has been developed without thinking of security at all. If anything, security has always been considered a distant afterthought.

That's one of the reasons why Microsoft Windows XP (and earlier incarnations of Windows) has proven so vulnerable to malware and hackers. Windows was designed under the assumption that only one person would use the computer and no programs (or people) would deliberately try to wreck the computer.

Then along came the first wave of computer viruses, followed by a second wave of computer worms, Trojan horses, and spyware that has cluttered and clogged most Windows computers as effectively as throwing sand and metal shavings inside a Formula One race car engine.

Now the assumption is that malware will try to take down computers and hackers will try to break into them. That's why secure computing tries to build security into a program as part of the design process. So, not only must programmers learn the basics of object-oriented programming and algorithm analysis, but they must also learn the practices of secure computing as well.

Patching as an afterthought

Because so many programs were originally designed without security in mind, it's no surprise that much computer security work involves analyzing the security flaws of an existing program and then writing a patch that fixes those problems.

Every program has flaws, so every program needs patching. Armies of programmers love probing programs — especially the major ones, like Android, iOS, Linux, macOS, and Windows — so they can be the first one to report a possible flaw in a program. Programmers devote their time to uncovering the flaws in other programs to enhance their own reputation (which can translate into better job opportunities), but also for the sheer challenge of looking for weaknesses in other people's programs.

After someone discovers a flaw in a program, other programmers typically verify that the flaw does exist, examine how the flaw could be exploited as a security risk, and then write a software patch that fixes that problem (and hopefully doesn't introduce any new problems).

Security in coding

Instead of waiting for flaws to appear and then wasting time patching these flaws that shouldn't have been in the program in the first place, another form of computer security involves making programs secure from the start. The idea is that if programmers focus on security when designing a program, they won't have to waste time patching up their programs later.

The first type of security involves examining the code of a program to remove any flaws. The most common type of flaw involves code that works but can be manipulated to cause an unexpected result. A common example of this type of problem is a *buffer overflow.*

A buffer overflow occurs when a program expects data that fits a certain size, such as accepting up to ten characters for a password. If you feed the computer data that's larger than expected, such as a 12-character password, the program should just ignore these extra 2 characters. However, a computer might accidentally store these extra two characters in its memory.

Normally such excess data would be harmless, but sometimes this excess data gets stored in a part of memory that contains other data that the computer uses, such as a list of tasks the computer will follow next. By flooding the computer with excess data, a hacker can literally change the computer's behavior.

One way to exploit this flaw is to shove excessive data to flood the computer's memory and then tack on an extra set of commands for the computer to follow. This tacked-on command then gets buried in the computer's memory, which causes the computer to follow those instructions. Oftentimes, those instructions tell the computer to weaken its defenses, such as opening a hole in the firewall to let the hacker into the computer.

To prevent problems, such as buffer overflows, programmers need to sift through their code and make sure that their code handles unexpected data correctly instead of just dumping it anywhere in memory. Examining code can be tedious, so programmers often use special testing tools that can spot such problems automatically.

TECHNICAL STUFF

Buffer overflow problems are especially common in programs written in C and C++. That's why more programmers are flocking to newer languages, like C# and Java, because these languages (mostly) prevent buffer overflows, which can result in more secure and reliable software.

Security by design

Most security patches close common flaws in programs, but just removing these flaws is like locking a screen door to keep out intruders. A more proactive solution is to design security into a program from the beginning, which is like getting rid of a screen door and replacing it with a solid metal door instead.

The idea behind designing security into a program from the start is to anticipate possible flaws and then design the program so those types of flaws can never even appear. This is like designing banks with only one entrance to limit the number of escape routes, and designing the lobby so anyone in the bank can be seen at all times.

Because operating systems are the most common target for an attack, many operating systems include a variety of defensive mechanisms. The most common defense is to divide access to a computer into separate accounts. This is like limiting bank tellers to just handling a certain amount of money while only the bank president and a few other trusted people have actual access to the bank's vaults.

Such access control limits what people can do from within their specific accounts on the computer. This reduces the chance of a catastrophic accident wiping out data used by other people while also reducing the threat from hackers at the same time. If a hacker breaks into an ordinary user account, the hacker can't cause too much damage, which is like a burglar breaking into a garage but not being able to access the rest of the house.

Another common defense mechanism is *data execution protection* (DEP), which protects against buffer overflow attacks. Trying to wipe out all possible buffer overflow exploits may be impossible, so DEP simply tells the computer never to run any commands found in its memory buffer. Now hackers can flood the computer with all the malicious commands they want, but the computer simply refuses to run any of those commands.

One way that hackers exploit programs is that they know programs behave predictably by storing data in the same areas. So, another defense mechanism is *address space layout randomization* (ASLR). The idea behind ASLR is to keep changing the address of its memory. If hackers or malware can't reliably predict where a program is storing specific data, they can't insert their own commands or programs into the computer to trick the computer into running those commands instead.

Computer security is actually less about protecting the physical parts of a computer and more about protecting the data stored on those computers. As individual hackers have given way to organized criminals, untrustworthy government agencies, and self-serving corporations, the field of computer security is constantly growing and changing. If there's one certainty in society, it's that crime will never go away, which means guaranteed opportunities for anyone interested in protecting computers from the prying eyes of others.

Chapter **4**

Artificial Intelligence

C omputers have always been so quick at calculating mathematical problems that people inevitably looked at computers as nothing more than electronic brains. As computers grew in power, a lot of people naturally assumed it'd only be a matter of time before computers could become just as smart as human beings. To study how to make computers smart, computer scientists have created a special field: *artificial intelligence* (AI).

One mathematician, Alan Turing, even proposed a test for measuring when a computer's calculating ability could be considered a form of intelligence. This test, known as the *Turing test*, consisted of hiding a computer and a human being in a locked room. A second human being, acting as the interrogator, could type questions to both the computer and the human without knowing which was which. If the computer could consistently respond in a way that the human interrogator couldn't tell whether they were chatting with a computer or a human, the Turing test claimed the computer could be considered intelligent. (No one suggested the Turing test might really prove that the human interrogator could just be a moron.)

The main goal of AI is to give computers greater reasoning and calculating abilities because most interesting problems don't have a single, correct solution. Calculating mathematical formulas is an easy problem for computers because there's only one right answer. Calculating the best way to translate one foreign language into another language is a hard problem because there are multiple solutions that depend on the context, which is difficult to teach computers to understand.

STRONG VERSUS WEAK ARTIFICIAL INTELLIGENCE

The idea that computers can think has divided computer scientists into two camps — *strong AI* and *weak AI*. The strong AI camp claims that not only can computers eventually learn to think, but they can become conscious of their thinking as well. The weak AI camp claims that computers can never think in the same sense as humans because their thinking process is nothing more than clever algorithms written by a human programmer in the first place.

Strong AI proponents claim that the human brain is nothing more than a set of algorithms, known as *instinct,* that's already embedded in our brains, so putting algorithms in a computer is no different. Weak AI proponents claim that consciousness is something that only living creatures can have, so it's impossible for a computer to ever become aware of itself as a sentient being.

Neither side will likely persuade the other, but this endless debate does prove that just because someone has earned a PhD in computer science from a prestigious university doesn't mean that they can't waste time arguing about a question that no one can ever answer anyway.

Basically, AI boils down to two topics:

» **Problem solving:** When faced with a situation with missing information, the computer can calculate an answer anyway.

» **Machine learning:** The computer can gradually learn from its mistakes so it won't repeat them again (which is something even humans have a hard time mastering).

Problem Solving

Computers are great at solving simple problems that have a clearly defined path to a solution. That's why a computer can calculate the optimum trajectory for launching a rocket to the moon because this problem involves nothing more than solving a lot of math problems one at a time.

Although the idea of calculating the trajectory of a moon rocket may seem daunt–ing, it's a problem that a human programmer can define how to solve ahead of time. Computers don't need to be smart to solve this type of problem. Computers just need to be fast at following directions.

Unfortunately, human programmers can't write algorithms for solving all types of problems, so in many cases, the computer is left with trying to solve a problem without any distinct instructions for what to do next. To teach computers how to solve these types of problems, computer scientists have to create algorithms that teach computers how to gather information and solve indistinct problems by themselves.

Game-playing

Because teaching a computer how to solve a variety of problems is hard, computer scientists decided to limit the scope of the problems a computer might face. By limiting the types of problems a computer might need to solve, computer scientists hoped to figure out the best ways to teach computers how to learn.

Solving any problem involves reaching for a goal, so the first test of AI revolved around teaching computers how to play games. Some games, such as tic-tac-toe, have a small set of possible solutions that can be identified in advance. Because there's only a small number of possible solutions to the problem of playing tic-tac-toe, it's easy to write algorithms that specifically tell the computer what to do in any given situation.

The game of chess is an example of a hard problem because the possible number of valid moves is far greater than any human programmer can write into a program. Instead, human programmers have to give the computer guidelines for solving a problem. These guidelines are *heuristics*.

A heuristic is nothing more than a general set of rules to follow when faced with similar problems. Telling a child to look both ways before crossing the street is an example of a heuristic. Telling a child to look left and then look right before crossing the corner of Fifth Street and Broadway is an example of a specific direction, which is absolutely useless for solving any problem except that one.

To teach a computer to play chess, programmers typically use a tree data structure (see Book 3, Chapter 5) that the computer creates before making a move. The tree represents all possible moves, so the human programmer simply writes algorithms for telling the computer how to solve each problem by gathering information about that problem. Because games have distinct rules, teaching a computer to play a game also taught computer scientists the best way to teach a computer to solve any type of problem.

Of course, the problem with this theory is that teaching a computer to play chess created a great computer that can only play chess. Game playing taught computer scientists how to make computers play better games but not be able to solve problems outside a fixed set of rules.

Not surprisingly, the one area that has benefited from game-playing research has been using AI techniques to create better computer opponents in video games. The next time you play your favorite video game and the computer seems particularly clever, you can thank all the research in AI for making smarter video games.

TECHNICAL STUFF

The ultimate goal of chess-playing computers is to beat a human chess grandmaster. In 2005, a computer specially built for playing chess, dubbed Hydra, defeated grandmaster Michael Adams. In 2006, another dedicated chess-playing computer called Deep Fritz defeated Vladimir Kramnik. Computers have now proven they're capable of defeating chess grandmasters, so this goal of AI has finally been achieved, although the lessons learned by beating chess grandmasters aren't easily transferred to solving other types of problems.

Natural language processing

In science-fiction movies, artificially intelligent computers are always able to understand human language, which is known as *natural language processing* (NLP). The goal of NLP is to make computers even easier to use. By accepting spoken or written commands to the computer, NLP frees users from having to learn the arcane and cryptic syntax of ordinary computer commands.

The first problem with understanding any human language is to understand the meaning of each specific word. This problem is rather trivial because it involves nothing more than identifying a word and then looking up its meaning in a dictionary data structure that links the word to its definition.

If human language were logical, this would be all that NLP would have to do. Unfortunately, the meaning of words often depends on their context, which is difficult to program into a computer. For example, the phrases *fat chance* and *slim chance* actually mean the same thing even though the adjectives *fat* and *slim* are antonyms.

Humans can understand this difference by virtue of their exposure to different uses of words and phrases, but computers need this information programmed into them. With so many words and alternate meanings, programming the context of every possible word is nearly impossible, so computer scientists have to rely more on rules for deducing the meaning of words rather than providing actual definitions for every word.

More confusing than understanding the context of words is understanding misspellings of words. When faced with a misspelled word, a computer must guess at its meaning, based on the meaning of surrounding words.

If you've ever used Google Translate or any other translation program, you've used an NLP program. Although the translations from one language to another may be accurate with individual words or short phrases, these translation programs often stumble when faced with complete sentences or idioms, but they can still get the main idea across.

One of the most successful NLP programs was written by Joseph Weizenbaum, PhD, and dubbed ELIZA after Eliza Doolittle, a working-class character who is taught to speak properly in George Bernard Shaw's play *Pygmalion*.

You can experiment with an online version of ELIZA by visiting `https://web.njit.edu/~ronkowit/eliza.html`.

The ELIZA program mimicked a Rogerian therapist by asking questions and parroting back replies based on the user's answers. A typical conversation with ELIZA might look like this:

ELIZA: How are you?

PATIENT: I'm feeling sad.

ELIZA: Why are you feeling sad?

PATIENT: My sister is mad at me.

ELIZA: Do you have problems with your family?

PATIENT: They say I spend too much time with my computer.

ELIZA: Do computers frighten you?

ELIZA doesn't actually understand the meaning of words. Instead, ELIZA just knows how to arrange words in their proper position to mimic an intelligent conversation. When ELIZA spots a word, such as *sister*, *brother*, or *father*, it immediately searches its database for a list of canned replies related to asking the user questions about their family.

By combining both canned phrases and parroted replies, ELIZA succeeded in mimicking an ordinary conversation. Although Joseph Weizenbaum originally created ELIZA to research NLP, he was astounded at how readily people accepted ELIZA and treated it as an intelligent computer even though they knew how it was programmed. When Weizenbaum found his secretary typing her problems into ELIZA and requested that he leave so she could have privacy, he became an advocate against AI.

One common application of NLP can be seen in the help system of many programs. If you type **How do I print a document**, the help system for your word processor might display a list of topics for printing files. The computer didn't actually understand the sentence. Instead, the computer, like ELIZA, just scanned the sentence, looking for keywords that it could recognize and then responded based on the keywords that it found.

TECHNICAL STUFF

To poke fun at ELIZA, Kenneth Colby, a psychiatrist at Stanford University, wrote a similar program dubbed PARRY. Whereas ELIZA mimicked a therapist, PARRY mimicked a paranoid schizophrenic patient. Computer scientists often connect ELIZA with PARRY to see what amusing conversation these two programs could create with each other. You can experiment with PARRY by visiting www.botlibre.com/browse?id=857177.

Speech recognition

Similar to NLP is speech recognition. Like NLP, speech recognition must identify a word and deduce its meaning. But unlike NLP, speech recognition has the added burden of trying to do all this in real time. The moment someone says a word, the speech recognition computer must quickly understand that word because the speaker won't likely pause for long before saying the next word.

The simplest form of speech recognition involves choosing from a limited selection of distinctly different-sounding words. Many voicemail systems offer this feature by asking a question such as, "Do you want to leave a message?" At this point, the speech recognition computer listens for any sound that resembles either Yes or No. Because the speech recognition computer has such a limited selection to choose from, its accuracy rate can be almost perfect.

Apple's Siri first introduced the world to an intelligent voice assistant in 2011. Since then, Amazon Alexa and Google Assistant have appeared, both of which can also recognize spoken commands and respond to them. Even more amazing is that each voice assistant can recognize spoken commands in accents along with multiple languages, such as Arabic, Italian, Japanese, and Thai.

While companies improve the already impressive accuracy of speech recognition software, the next step is to understand the context of spoken commands better than before. The ultimate goal of speech recognition software is to respond intelligently like the computers you see in science-fiction movies. When computer scientists get computers to respond intelligently to any type of questions, they may be considered smarter and more capable than many human politicians.

Image recognition

Another form of pattern recognition involves recognizing images, such as faces in a picture or handwritten letters on a piece of paper. Recognizing written characters is known as *optical character recognition* (OCR) and is commonly used in computer scanners.

OCR software studies an image of a character, and based on its knowledge of letters, the OCR program tries to match the written character with its database of known characters. After OCR finds a match, it can decipher the contents of a written phrase letter by letter.

OCR programs have trouble identifying nearly identical characters, such as the lowercase letter *l* and the number *1*, or the letter *O* and the number *o*. That's why OCR scanning programs often insert incorrect characters in the middle of scanned text.

Image recognition is a much harder problem but one that's commonly used in security systems, such as in casinos. Every casino contains a photographic database of known cheaters. If a casino suspects one of these known cheaters has entered its premises, security guards can zoom in on the suspect and use image recognition software to determine whether that person is actually a known cheater in the database.

Such image recognition software examines the shape of a person's face along with the physical position of the nose in relation to the eyebrows, lips, and chin. No matter how many disguises cheaters may wear, they can't hide or change the physical dimensions of their faces, which is how such image recognition programs can spot them.

REMEMBER

Image recognition software can only work as well as the data it's trained on. That's why many image recognition programs have trouble recognizing people of different ethnic backgrounds — the software was trained using faces of people from a narrow range of ethnicities.

In the field of robotics, image processing is crucial because it gives robots the ability to sense their environment and avoid or move toward certain objects. Teaching a robot to avoid objects in its path might seem easy until the robot looks through a plate-glass window and mistakes the window for an opening that it can roll through to get to the other side.

Although image recognition might help a robot identify the edges of walls or the end of a road, image recognition must also teach a computer to recognize shadows or reflections that can distort images. Primitive image recognition might simply distinguish between patches of light and dark, but more sophisticated image recognition could not only recognize an object in its path but also identify what that object might be, which involves a related category of AI known as *image processing*.

In a limited domain of objects, seeing and understanding images can be determined in advance, but in the real world, the number of images a computer might see and need to recognize is nearly infinite. To solve the problem of not only recognizing an image but also understanding what that image might be, computers need to be independent of their human programmers.

Machine Learning

The preceding examples of problem-solving AI programs only mimic intelligence, but the computer's intelligence must be programmed by humans ahead of time. When faced with different situations, these problem-solving programs behave the same way no matter what the circumstances might be.

That's why the second and more important focus of AI involves teaching computers to learn, otherwise known as *machine learning.* Machine learning can involve training by humans, but it's more commonly associated with self-learning in an unsupervised environment.

One way to mimic machine learning is to insert problem-solving knowledge into a program and then allow the program to modify its database of knowledge. That's the idea behind two popular programming languages — LISP and Prolog — which are specially designed for AI.

With LISP, every command is also considered data that can be manipulated. So, a LISP program can literally rewrite its own commands and data while it runs. Prolog works in a similar way; basically, a Prolog program consists of rules and data, so Prolog programs can modify both the rules that they follow and their data.

Both languages make self-modifying programs possible for mimicking machine learning, but using an AI language alone doesn't make your program any smarter. Instead, programmers also need specific methods for mimicking intelligence in a computer.

THE DANGER OF MACHINE LEARNING

Computer scientists use the acronym GIGO, which stands for *garbage in, garbage out.* That means if you give a computer meaningless data, it can only spit back more meaningless data. One problem of machine learning is that it's only as smart as the data it's given to learn from.

Back in 2016, Microsoft created Tay, a machine learning bot that people could chat with just like a human. The idea was that Tay would learn from the text that people typed so it would gradually become more fluent in responding to any human.

The problem was that people thought it would be funny to bombard Tay with racist, sexist, violent questions and comments. Not knowing any better, Tay's machine learning algorithms assumed that a steady stream of racist, sexist, and violent comments was normal speech, so it gradually learned to respond to any comment with equally racist, sexist, and violent language. In less than 24 hours, people on the Internet had trained Tay to become a racist, sexist, violent bot, and Microsoft had to pull the plug on Tay for good.

Bayesian probability

One simple example of machine learning is based on *Bayes' theorem*, after Thomas Bayes. This theorem deals with probabilities. Put into practical application, many spam filters use Bayesian filtering, which basically examines junk email and compares it to valid email.

Based on this comparison, a spam filter based on Bayes' theorem can gradually assign probabilities that new messages are either junk or valid messages. The more junk and valid email the Bayesian filter can examine, the "smarter" it gets in recognizing and sorting email into their proper categories. Essentially an anti-spam filter's "intelligence" is stored in its growing database of characteristics that identify spam.

Neural networks

One problem with machine learning is organizing information so that the computer can modify its own data. Although languages — like LISP and Prolog — allow self-modifying programs, computer scientists have created a way to model the human brain using ordinary data structures, such as graphs with each node mimicking a neuron in a brain. This entire connection of interlocking nodes, or mimicking neurons, is a *neural network*, as shown in Figure 4-1.

Neurons

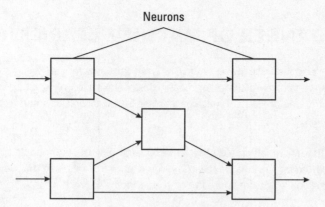

A neural network models itself on the human brain, which is divided into a net-work of interlocking neurons. Each neuron acts like a primitive computer that can receive input and produce output, which gets fed into another neuron as input.

Although a single neuron may not be capable of doing much, a network of inter-connected neurons acts like a group of tiny computers that can tackle different parts of a problem simultaneously, which is known in computer science as *parallel processing.* Ordinary computers represent a single, fast machine that can tackle a problem in sequential steps. The strength of a computer is that it can perform these multiple steps much faster than a human can, which is what makes com-puters so powerful.

Human brains can't calculate as fast as a computer, but they can process multiple data simultaneously. That makes human brains better at solving seemingly sim-ple problems, like recognizing a face from a crowd. On the other hand, computers have trouble recognizing faces because computers try to follow a sequential series of steps. As a result, computers are slow at recognizing faces while a human's ability to recognize faces is nearly instantaneous.

In a neural network, each neuron can accept data. The data is weighted by a spe-cific value. This total value is then compared to the neuron's threshold. If this value is less than the threshold, the neuron produces an output of 0. If this value is greater than the threshold, the neuron produces an output of 1, as shown in Figure 4-2.

Threshold

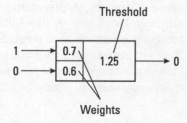

Weights

The neuron in Figure 4-2 receives an input of 1 and 0. The 1 value is weighted by 0.7 while the 0 value is weighted by 0.6, like this:

(1)(0.7) + (0)(0.6) = 0.7

Because this value is less than the threshold value of 1.25, the neuron outputs a value of 0.

A single neuron accepts data and produces a response, much like an ordinary if-then statement used in a regular program. To train a neural network, you can feed it specific data with known results and examine the output of the neural network. Then you can adjust the weights of different neurons to more closely modify the output to a specific result.

ROBOTICS AND ARTIFICIAL INTELLIGENCE

Throughout the years, AI has always aimed at a moving target. Initially, opponents boasted that computers could never beat a chess grandmaster, but when a computer finally did it, AI critics claimed that chess computers were nothing more than fast search algorithms that had little to do with actual reasoning. Although NLP programs, like ELIZA, can already claim to have passed the Turing test, AI critics claim that parroting back phrases to trick a human still doesn't qualify as true intelligence.

Robotics may be the final test of AI because the stereotypical robot combines multiple aspects of AI: speech recognition, image recognition, and machine learning. AI critics will have a hard time dismissing an intelligent robot that can talk, understand spoken commands, and learn while it walks up and down a flight of stairs.

Before robotics can ever achieve this ultimate dream of creating a robot that mimics a human being, robotic engineers must literally first learn to crawl before they can walk. Like early AI research, most robots are designed to excel within an extremely narrow domain. Assembly-line robots know how to weld car frames together but can't answer a simple question. Military-drone robots may know how to recognize targets on the ground but can't understand spoken commands about French literature.

Despite these limitations, robotics has a growing future. Essentially, robots are nothing more than computers capable of moving or manipulating their environment. Maybe one day we'll finally have true AI at the same time we finally have a true robot that meets the criteria set by science-fiction authors so long ago. Until then, however, robotics is likely to remain a fledging offshoot of computer science and AI. Don't expect a robot servant capable of understanding spoken commands and able to reason and learn any time soon, but don't be surprised when someone finally invents one either.

Artificial Intelligence

Such training can be time-consuming, so another approach is to let the neural network train itself. Based on its output, a neural network can use its own output as input to change the overall neural network's result. Such self-training neural networks effectively mimic the learning process.

Applications of Artificial Intelligence

Initially, AI had grand plans that bordered on science fiction. Computer scientists had visions of intelligent computers that could carry on spoken conversations while being fully conscious of their own thoughts. The reality proved much less dramatic. Instead of intelligent computers, we just have faster ones that are no closer to consciousness.

Although AI never lived up to its initial dreams, its applications have seeped into ordinary use. Spam filters are one simple way that machine learning has been put to use along with game-playing techniques for making smarter computer-generated opponents in video games.

Intrusion detection systems use a primitive form of AI to determine whether a computer hacker has penetrated a computer network, whereas many financial traders on Wall Street use neural networks to track the movement of stocks and commodities to predict future stock prices. Perhaps the ultimate goal of AI is to create thinking robots that can not only move on their own but also reason for themselves.

Whether computer scientists can ever create an actual thinking machine is beside the point. The real use for AI isn't in re-creating human brains in electronic form, but in finding ways to make computers help us solve numerous tasks on their own. The more problems computers can solve without human supervision, the more time people can spend working on more difficult problems that computers can't solve — at least not yet.

Chapter **5**

Mobile and Wearable Computing

Computers have shrunk in size from mainframes that took up entire rooms to personal computers that anyone could put on their desk. Laptop computers made computing even easier on the go, but carrying around a computer can still be cumbersome.

That's why mobile and wearable computers have become popular. Rather than replace traditional computers that rely on keyboards and a mouse or trackpad, mobile and wearable computers offer unique features that traditional computers can't.

Desktop computers could look up maps and travel directions, but only a mobile computer can give you real-time directions that change as you travel. Desktop computers may be able to store your health data, but only a wearable computer can conveniently monitor your health for you to review at your convenience.

Essentially, mobile and wearable computers aren't meant to replace desktop computers; instead, they provide features that desktop computers can't do well or can't do at all.

Understanding the Different Generations of Computing

Study each generation of computers, and you'll see how they change the way people interact with them. In the early days, mainframe and minicomputers forced people to spend long periods of time writing a program and then submitting it to the computer to run. Hours, sometimes even days later, the computer would print out the results.

Waiting hours or days to get a result was clearly clumsy, which is why personal computers proved so popular — they gave people immediate results. The world's first spreadsheet, VisiCalc, let accountants, engineers, and scientists create mathematical models and see the results instantly. If they wanted to test out different values to see how that might affect the results, spreadsheets could respond right away.

That meant people tended to spend hours using a personal computer (desktop or laptop) using a spreadsheet, a database manager, or a word processor. Even though laptops were portable, you had to find a place to sit down if you wanted to use them.

Then the world of mobile computing arrived with the introduction of the iPhone. Unlike personal computers, which you needed a flat surface to use, smartphones could be used anywhere, any time. It's common for people to use a smartphone while walking, riding a bus, or waiting in line at a restaurant.

Because smartphones gave people mobile computing, their interaction time with the computer shrank dramatically. Where someone might spend hours sitting in front of a personal computer, they might only spend a few minutes at a time using a smartphone throughout the day.

Even more dramatic was the way people interacted with these two different types of computers. Not only did personal computers allow people to use them for hours at a time, but they also forced people to interact with personal computers through keyboards and a mouse or trackpad.

On the other hand, smartphones lack physical keyboards, a large screen, and a mouse or trackpad. Instead, smartphones rely entirely on touch-screen interfaces with limited voice control. Personal computers are often used for creating large amounts of data, such as writing a novel. Smartphones are more often used for creating short bits of information, such writing text messages.

Smartphones and their related cousins, tablets, helped define the world of mobile computing that allows people to use a computer almost anywhere. Just as people started to get used to communicating through smartphones and tablets, the next generation of computing has arrived in the form of wearable computers.

Wearable computers, such as smart watches and smart glasses, offer even more limited user interfaces (UIs) than personal computers or mobile computers. Wearable computers lack a large screen, so they can only be used for brief seconds at a time. With their limited size, wearable computers rely more on *haptics* (touch) and voice to communicate with the user.

You can see the trend: As computers get smaller, people interact with them more often, but for smaller periods of time. That means the world of programming is no longer confined to personal computers but extends to mobile and wearable computing as well.

By understanding these differences in computers, you can better understand the types of apps needed for each type of device. Table 5-1 shows the major differences between each generation of computers.

TABLE 5-1

Understanding the Different Generations of Computing

Computer Type	User Interface	Typical Time Per Interaction	Typical Uses
Mainframe and minicomputers	Punch-card readers, teletype printers, terminals	Days	Calculating mathematical results
Personal computers (desktop and laptop)	Keyboard, mouse, monitor	Hours	Word processing, spreadsheets, databases, video games, web browsing, email
Mobile computers (smartphones and tablets)	Touch screen, microphone, and speaker	Minutes	Phone calls, text messages, web browsing, email, video games
Wearable computers (smart watches and smart glasses)	Touch screen, microphone, speaker, haptics	Seconds	Phone calls, text messages, receiving notifications and alerts

Giving Data to the User

Personal computers could always rely on showing data to the user through a computer screen. That meant programmers just needed to create UIs that filled an entire screen or gave the user options to resize windows on the screen to let them view data from one or more programs at the same time. No matter how big or how small the user's monitor might be, programs for personal computers would treat all monitors as if they were the same size by shrinking or expanding accordingly.

When smartphones and tablets appeared, smartphones displayed smaller screens, while tablets displayed much larger screens. Even more confusing, users could rotate the orientation of smartphone and tablet screens from landscape mode to portrait mode.

Because users can change the orientation of smartphones and tablets at any time, apps must adapt to different screen sizes and orientations, which is something personal computer programs never had to worry about.

When creating smartphone or tablet apps, you must not only write a program that solves a useful problem, but also create an adaptive UI. One early and clumsy solution to creating adaptive UIs involved defining constraints on UI items, such as buttons, text fields, and images. These constraints defined the distance between each UI item and/or the distance between the sides of the screen, as shown in Figure 5-1.

Because every screen size is different, constraints must adapt to both smaller and larger screens. Instead of defining a constraint to represent a fixed distance, you must define a constraint to represent a range of possible values, such as never shrinking below 25 points or never growing larger than 80 points. Because a single UI item needs multiple constraints, getting all constraints to work on a single UI requires testing on different screen sizes.

Instead of forcing programmers to define constraints on every item on the UI, the latest trend is to create UI items that always appear centered in the middle of the screen. You no longer define fixed values to represent distances between UI items; now you simply add spacers that act like springs that automatically push UI items apart to remain usable on any size screen.

TECHNICAL STUFF

This adaptable method for defining the relative distances between UI items is the basis for SwiftUI, Apple's newest way to design UIs using the Swift language.

Smartphones and tablets typically have a much smaller screen to display information than personal computers. However, smart watches have an even smaller screen than the smallest smartphone screen. That makes smart-watch screens suitable for displaying a limited amount of information at any given time.

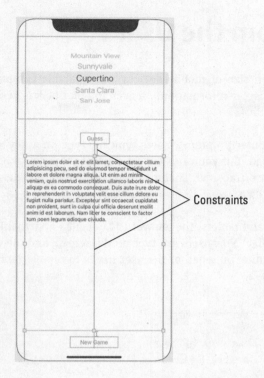

Constraints

Where UIs for personal computers, smartphones, and tablets can display differ-ent information on the screen, smart watches must focus on displaying only the most important information the user needs at that moment, whether it's to see the time, the weather, a text message, or the amount of calories expended during the day.

When someone uses a smart watch, they want to see important information at a glance. When someone uses smart glasses, they may want to see certain informa-tion, such as traveling directions, but they don't want that information to block their view of their surroundings. So, both smart watches and smart glasses can only show small chunks of information at a time.

To get around the problem of a tiny screen, smart watches offer another way to give information to the user through haptics. To alert users which way to turn when following travel directions, smart watches can vibrate in distinct ways to let the user know when to turn left or right without needing to glance at the screen at all.

When creating apps for smart watches or smart glasses, programmers need to rethink their ideas for a UI. Slapping a UI from a personal computer program on to a smartphone or tablet app won't work, and neither will porting a smart-phone or tablet app UI to a smart watch or smart glasses app. Each type of com-puter needs a UI designed for the particular way users interact with that device.

Getting Data from the User

The smaller screen size of mobile devices and wearable computers challenges programmers to display information. An even tougher task is designing a UI that lets users input data.

For personal computer programs, users typically type on a keyboard or click on a mouse or trackpad. But you can't expect a smartphone or tablet user to have a keyboard or a mouse/trackpad. That means mobile computers need their own way for users to input data.

For smartphones and tablets, the answer is to display a virtual keyboard on the touch-screen display. Now users can type on the screen, and the virtual keyboard can change depending on whether the user needs to type letters or numbers, as shown in Figure 5-2.

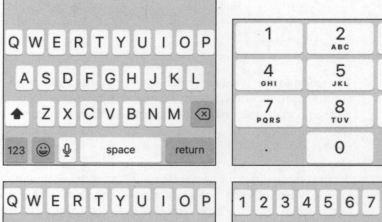

FIGURE 5-2: Virtual keyboards can adapt to the user's needs.

Virtual keyboards are fine for inputting text such as letters, punctuation, and numbers, but another way to accept input from the user is through touch gestures. The touch screen can recognize common gestures such as swipes, pinches, and rotation along with simple taps. By letting users manipulate objects onscreen directly (such as selecting, resizing, and rotating a picture), touch screens provide a more intuitive way to accept input.

Because smart watches and smart glasses have much smaller screens, users are forced to rely on simple swipe and tap gestures. However, because smart-watch and smart-glasses users often don't want to interact with a tiny touch screen, voice control is another option.

Such hands-free control lets users give voice commands to their smart watch or smart glasses. Then the smart watch or smart glasses can give aural feedback to the user. Although voice control is possible for personal computers, smartphones, and tablets, it can be crucial for smart-watch and smart-glasses users.

Tracking Motion and Location

Desktop computers aren't meant to be moved, whereas laptops are meant to be moved frequently but not used away from a flat surface or a place where you can sit down. Because mobile and wearable computers are meant to be used while moving, they often track the user's movements and location.

The ability to track the user's movements and location opens up a whole new world of apps that were never possible with personal computers. Ride-sharing services rely on riders using a smartphone that identifies their location. While waiting for their ride to show up, users can track the location of their driver so they know approximately when the car will arrive.

While you're driving, smartphone apps can detect the movement of other drivers so you can view the most recently updated map that can highlight traffic jams so you can avoid them. By collecting movement and location data from multiple smartphone users at once, mapping apps can create accurate traffic maps within seconds.

Tracking the user's movement is especially useful for wearable computers because they can constantly monitor a user's movements throughout the day. Smart watches can determine whether the user is moving enough times during the day and, if not, the smart watch can provide prompts to keep the user exercising.

Smart glasses can display traveling directions and identify landmarks to overlay additional information about stores or transit schedules without requiring the user to look at a computer screen.

Just as personal computers provided individuals with the power to manipulate words, calculate numbers in a spreadsheet, or search a database that they couldn't do with mainframe or minicomputers, so do mobile and wearable computers offer new ways to track information that you couldn't previously get using a personal computer.

Tracking Real-Time Health Data

Perhaps the greatest advantage of wearable computers is the ability to provide real-time health monitoring that personal computers and smartphones could never do. One of the simplest, yet most effective sensors on smart watches is the ability to detect the user's arm movement.

During ordinary circumstances, a person's arm will move in predictable ways. However if the user suddenly falls and remains still, the smart watch can deduce that the user may have fallen and alert authorities to the user's location and condition.

The ability to provide constant, real-time health monitoring has allowed smart watches to save countless lives. With heart-rate sensors, smart watches have alerted users to potential heart problems so they can see a doctor before suffering a catastrophic event.

With noninvasive glucose monitoring, smart watches can help diabetics monitor their blood sugar levels. Now if their blood sugar level spikes or drops, they can take immediate action and avoid more serious health problems later.

Personal computers may be useful to create data and mobile computers may be useful to consume data, but wearable computers are vital to keeping people healthy and alive. If you plan to develop apps for smart watches or smart glasses, think of how your UI must rely on body sensors and voice control to provide information and accept data from the user.

Today's wearable computers require you to put them on and take them off. Tomorrow's wearable computers will let you keep them on constantly. Besides smart watches that wrap around your wrist and smart glasses that appear on your face, ear buds may also gain smart capabilities to provide audio feedback directly into a user's ears while measuring body conditions through the ear canal. Wearable computers are here to stay, and they'll continue providing crucial uses that personal computers and mobile computers could never do.

Looking to the Future of Augmented Reality and Wearable Computers

One of the most popular mobile games in 2016 was Pokémon Go, which let people look for and capture cartoon monsters through the camera of their smartphone or tablet. Using augmented reality (AR), Pokémon Go let people see the real world through their camera but find cartoon monsters in specific coordinates.

Holding up a smartphone or tablet is a simple way to use AR, but constantly viewing AR through a mobile device can get tiring. That's why AR is much better suited for smart glasses instead.

One common use for smart glasses is to recognize certain landmarks and display accompanying text or graphics, such as the name of a business or directions to help you reach a specific destination.

Ordinary eyeglasses already represent a simple form of AR by improving a person's eyesight. However computational AR will likely prove even more useful by giving travelers turn-by-turn directions in unfamiliar areas or helping locate lost items in a house by showing you a cartoon image of the missing item through a solid wall.

Each generation of computers finds its own unique applications. Fast calculations made mainframe computers and minicomputers useful, while spreadsheets, databases, and word processors made personal computers indispensable.

Mobile devices like smartphones took advantage of location tracking to spur the development of ride-sharing services, and wearable computers like smart glasses will take full advantage of AR.

If you want to get involved in the next generation of computer programming, look for applications that new computers can offer that previous computer types could not, and that's where you'll likely find a lucrative future.

Chapter **6**

Game Engines

I n the early days, lone programmers created entire video games. Back then, video games were still fairly simple, but as they got more sophisticated, they became harder to make. Because games tended to offer similar features, game programmers realized they didn't need to create an entire game from scratch every time. Instead, they could reuse common parts of a game and customize it for their particular needs.

These common game development components, dubbed *game engines,* made it easy to create new games. Although many companies have created their own proprietary game engines, other companies have developed game engines that anyone can use. These game-engine companies then make money by taking a percentage of the profits from any game made using their game engines.

Although game engines are mostly used for creating video games, they've also been used to create virtual worlds for other industries outside the video-game industry, such as architecture, product design, advertising, and filmmaking. If you like video games and programming, you can combine both skills to pursue a career in game-engine programming.

Understanding Game Engines

Game engines are designed to make creating games easy by providing common game components, such as:

>> Input

>> Graphics

>> Physics

>> Sound

>> Networking

>> Graphical user interfaces (GUIs)

Every game needs to receive input from the player through a variety of devices such as a keyboard, mouse/trackpad, touch screen, joystick, steering wheel, or motion detector. Writing a program to detect mouse movements or touch-screen gestures can be tedious and cumbersome, so a game engine does this task for you. That way, you can focus on making your game instead of writing code to detect different types of user input.

Graphics form the heart of any game, so game engines make it easy to place, move, and manipulate graphics items without worrying about the details in displaying a 2D or 3D image on the screen. When combined with the input component, the graphics component makes it easy for programmers to control objects on the screen, such as a knight on horseback, a jet fighter, or a dragon flying through the air.

Instead of bogging you down in the mathematics and nuances of moving objects in two or three dimensions, a game engine lets you focus simply on telling where the object should go. The game engine calculates the mathematical equations to make that movement happen.

When the player or game moves objects on the screen, the potential for collisions always exists. Just as game engines make movement easy, so do they also make dealing with collisions between objects simple by calculating the physics of collisions. Instead of writing complex mathematical equations to deal with gravity and collisions between a cartoon car and a cartoon goat, the game engine takes care of the details so you just have to specify how you want the car and the goat to react when they collide in the game.

Games are almost never silent but include sound to provide feedback to the user, sound effects to create greater realism, and background music to set the mood of the game. So, the sound component of a game engine lets you specify what you want to play and how you want that audio to sound instead of wrestling with the details of playing sound.

In a single-player game, dealing with sound might be easy, but in a massive multiplayer game where multiple players may be playing at once, trying to play sound for each player at the appropriate time would be extremely troublesome if you tried to program it yourself. That's why the sound component of a game engine relieves you of this burden.

Getting a game to work on a single computer may be fairly easy compared to getting a game to work simultaneously on multiple computers over a network. The code alone to coordinate multiple players would be extremely difficult to write, but a game engine's networking component takes care of those details.

Finally, games rarely use the same user interfaces (UIs) as common programs like word processors or spreadsheets. That's why game engines provide common GUIs that you can customize for your particular game.

The main goal of a game engine is to abstract the details of making a game so you can focus on the fun part: making a unique game that relies on common game components that the game engine provides.

Picking a Game Engine

There are three types of game engines:

>> **Proprietary:** Proprietary game engines are created by game companies solely for their own programmers to create additional games. Companies create their own game engines so they can customize them to do exactly what they need, create unique features unavailable in other game engines (and, hence, unavailable to their rivals), and avoid paying royalties to potential rival game companies that also sell game engines.

>> **Open source:** Open-source game engines are developed by volunteers. Not only are they free for anyone to use, but they include the source code so you can examine how the game engine works and possibly even modify it yourself. Some popular open-source game engines include Armory (https://armory3d.org), Defold (https://defold.com), Godot (https://godotengine.org), and Open 3D Engine (www.o3de.org). Even though open-source game engines are run by volunteers, support, features, and documentation can rival commercial game engines.

>> **Commercial:** Commercial game engines are proprietary, but anyone can use them for a price. The two most popular commercial game engines are Unity (https://unity.com) and Unreal (www.unrealengine.com), along with a relative newcomer called the Flax Engine (https://flaxengine.com). Flax, Unity, and Unreal are free to use, but when your sales pass a certain threshold, you're obligated to pay a fee or royalties based on your sales. Because Flax, Unity, Unreal have financial incentives for their publishers, they tend to offer the latest features needed to develop 2D and 3D games while making advanced game development as easy as possible. The drawback is that you must pay these game-engine companies a portion of your profits, which is why many game companies prefer creating and using their own proprietary game engines or open-source game engines instead.

Some proprietary game engines, such as GameMaker Studio (www.yoyogames.com), offer a free version so you can experiment with making games. If you want to use more advanced features, you'll have to pay additional fees. Still other game engines, such as AppGameKit (www.appgamekit.com), charge an upfront free. The advantage of paying for a game engine upfront is that any profits you make using that game engine are royalty-free, which means you don't need to share any profits with the game-engine maker.

Every game engine offers different features. One game engine might be better for creating mobile apps on smartphones and tablets, another game engine might be easier to learn and use, and yet another game engine might offer superior 3D graphics for game consoles. The best game engine depends entirely on the type of game you want to create and the platform you want to publish the game on (game console, PC, smartphones, websites, and so on).

Programming a Game Engine

Most game engines are designed to work on multiple operating systems (Linux, macOS, or Windows), so they tend to be written in C/C++. That means you can use a game engine to create a game on a Mac and publish the game to run on Windows (or vice versa).

To create a game using a game engine, you must use a programming language. The three most common game-engine programming options are

>> **Popular programming languages:** To encourage as many programmers as possible to use their game engines, most game-engine makers let you use a popular programming language such as C# (Unity) or C++ (Unreal).

Because C++ and C# can still intimidate nonprogrammers, many game engines are adopting the much simpler Lua scripting language (www.lua.org). By learning Lua, you'll be able to program different game engines.

» **Proprietary scripting languages:** Some game engines use their own proprietary scripting language similar to JavaScript or Python. These scripting languages are often much easier to learn and use, which makes them perfect for programmers and nonprogrammers alike.

» **Visual scripting languages:** Because many game developers may not know any programming language at all, many game-engine makers also offer visual scripting. Instead of requiring you to type code to control a game engine, visual scripting lets you drag-and-drop nodes and connect them with lines that show how data flows from one node to another, as shown in Figure 6-1.

Visual scripting can be used by programmers and nonprogrammers alike. For nonprogrammers, visual scripting gives them a way to create a game without learning a programming language. For programmers, visual scripting can be a fast way to prototype ideas and allow nonprogrammers to collaborate.

Each node lets you control a single part of the game such as an individual character, a barrier in the game, or an abstract item like a timer. To control the different parts of a game, you create a graph with that object's node, and then connect it with other nodes to visually design the behavior of an object in a game.

REMEMBER

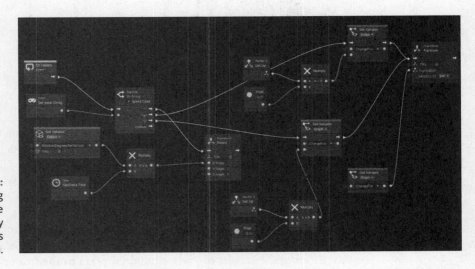

FIGURE 6-1:
Visual scripting lets you create a program by connecting nodes in a graph.

Some game engines offer all three programming options, while others may offer only one option.

REMEMBER

You can create a game using all three methods. The bulk of your game might be programmed using C++, another part of that same game could be programmed using the game engine's scripting language, and a third part of that game could be programmed using the game engine's visual scripting language.

Because the video-game industry is so huge and lucrative, game studios always need programmers to help them develop their next video games. Game-engine programming is fast becoming a new programming specialty.

REMEMBER

The more knowledgeable you are about using a particular programming language to control a specific game engine, the greater the chances you could get a job working in the video-game industry.

Exploring the Future Uses of Game Engines

Game engines were originally designed to create video games. However, video games are designed to depict realistic images that can move and interact with other objects in the scene. That means video games are now being used outside the video-game industry. Some common uses for game engines outside of video-game development include

>> Filmmaking

>> Architecture and engineering

>> Marketing

Filmmaking

Making movies is expensive, and one of the biggest expenses is sending a film crew and actors out to a location. If that location doesn't exist (such as a futuristic space ship exterior or the exterior of the Eiffel Tower after it's fallen apart after decades of neglect), filmmakers must design or modify a set, which takes time and money.

Filming on the streets of Paris might be cumbersome, but filming on the streets of Paris back in the 1920s will require building a set of 1920s-era buildings and streets. Filming the streets of Paris a hundred years in the future after a nuclear war where the Eiffel Tower is barely standing will require an even *more* expensive set.

Instead of wasting money building expensive sets of exotic locations, filmmakers are using game engines to create any setting they want. Just as video-game designers can set a game in any historical, imaginary, or contemporary setting just by creating the right graphical images, so can filmmakers use game engines to create virtual sets at far less cost and time than they would spend building a set.

Instead of paying traveling costs for an entire film crew and actors, studios can film entire scenes inside a single building that displays a screen large enough to display the virtual setting created by a game engine. Best of all, changing the appearance of virtual settings can be done quickly and easily, just by modifying the graphical images or the game engine.

Unlike green-screen technology that forces actors to respond to a blank screen that filmmakers use to superimpose real images on later, game engines can display the *actual* images on the screen around the actors. That way actors can see the scene location that they're performing in and react to real images.

TECHNICAL STUFF

The TV shows *The Mandalorian* and *Westworld* were filmed using the Unreal game engine to create many of the shows' settings.

Instead of using a game engine to help make a movie, some filmmakers are using game engines to create entire animated films. After all, a game engine can already create realistic or cartoonish worlds. By using a game engine, filmmakers can let the game engine animate characters within a unique setting and eliminate the need for expensive computer animation software.

Architecture and engineering simulations

When architects design a building, they often make models that let them see what a building might look like so they can determine whether they need to change anything. Likewise, when engineers design new products such as cars or airplanes, they also make clay, wooden, or plastic models so they can see their designs before they actually build anything.

Needless to say, creating physical models takes time. If you need to change the design of a building or car, then you need to change your model, or create an entirely new model, both of which take more time.

But if you design a building or machine using a game engine, you can make changes quickly and easily. Then you can go one step further and apply different materials to the surface, such as changing a building from brick to steel or a car from red to green. By letting you experiment endlessly at no cost beyond a little time, game engines help architects and engineers visualize their creations faster than before.

By using a game engine as part of virtual reality, users can walk through imaginary buildings. This can give people a better sense of what a building might look like before spending any money creating a physical model.

One unique use for game-engine simulations involves creating military exercises. By creating different environments and weapons within the virtual world of a game engine, military commanders can experiment with various scenarios without the physical expense of moving soldiers and equipment around.

Soldiers can conduct training within the safety of a virtual world with no danger of accidents. When they feel comfortable in certain situations, they can advance to live training in the field with actual weapons and equipment.

Marketing and advertising

When companies need to sell and promote their products, they often make commercials, websites, and promotional videos. That's essentially filmmaking, so many advertising agencies are using game engines to create images and videos virtually. That saves time and money and allows the advertising agency to experiment with changing a product's color or size through the game engine.

In the past, advertising agencies might film a commercial that fits within their budget, but by creating an entire commercial in a game engine, they have more freedom to create multiple versions of a commercial.

Game engines lower costs, save time, and allow for fast and easy experimentation. With more variations to choose from, advertising agencies can now test the different varieties with test markets, which would be impossible to do producing only a single commercial the traditional way.

One candy company filmed a commercial using live actors, promoting a specific candy bar. When it wanted to promote a different candy bar, it could've filmed the commercial again, but that would've taken time and cost more money. Instead, it used a game engine to substitute a different candy bar in the existing commercial. By doing this multiple times, the company could promote several different candy bars using the same commercial with minimal additional cost, thanks to the game engine.

With so many different ways to use game engines outside the video-game industry, knowing how to program a game engine can be a crucial skill that can separate you from the hordes of programmers who just know how to write programs. Ultimately, the more skills you have that are valuable to an employer, the more opportunities you'll have in the future.

By learning both programming in general and game-engine programming in particular, you can take advantage of more opportunities in practically any industry you want to pursue.

Chapter **7**

The Future of Computer Programming

The computer industry is changing all the time, which means that the programming tools and techniques of today will likely become obsolete by tomorrow. Just trying to keep up with the computer industry is a full-time occupation, and even computer experts can never agree on what the future may bring.

Although it's impossible to predict the future, it is possible to identify trends in the computer industry and, based on these trends, predict what *might* occur in the future. In the world of computer programming, the most important lesson is to learn the logic of programming without getting bogged down by the specific syntax of any particular programming language. That's because programming languages rise and fall out of favor. If you learn to program in only one particular language, your programming ability will be restricted by the limitations of that particular language.

REMEMBER

Programming is nothing more than problem solving, and problem solving is invaluable no matter which programming language, computer, or operating system may be popular at any given time. If you can solve problems, you'll always have a job.

Picking a Programming Language

Computer scientists eternally debate the merits of one programming language over another, but no matter which programming language may be popular today, the real issue boils down to efficiency and complexity.

Throughout history, the most popular language has always been the one that offers the greatest amount of efficiency for solving the most complicated problems. Initially, programmers used machine language to write entire programs because that was all that was available. However, as soon as assembly language appeared, few people wrote entirely in machine language. Instead, they switched to assembly language because it allows programmers to write more complicated programs. (Turn to Book 1, Chapter 1 for more on machine language and assembly language.)

In the early days of personal computers, nearly every programmer used assembly language. One of the first popular word processors, WordStar, even ran on two different processors — the Zilog Z80 and the Intel 8088. To run on these two different processors, the company had to write WordStar in two completely different assembly languages.

When programs were fairly simple, that could be possible, but as programs grew in complexity, writing programs entirely in assembly language proved too cumbersome. That's when programmers switched to C.

Most operating systems today are written entirely in C for maximum efficiency, but as programs have grown in complexity, C has quickly fallen out of favor, just as assembly language and machine language have done before. To maintain maximum efficiency to deal with growing complexity, programmers have moved from C to C++ and other object-oriented programming languages.

Although C++ adds object-oriented features to C, it still retains all the drawbacks of C. That's why computer scientists have been developing safer, more specialized languages based on C and C++, such as C#, Dart, Go, Java, Python, Rust, Scala, and Swift. If you learn a curly-bracket language (based on C), you'll be able to adapt to any language inspired by C.

Besides learning a curly-bracket language based on C, consider learning a specialized programming language that can make certain tasks easier. For manipulating data, learn SQL. For data mining, consider F or R. The more familiar you are with different programming languages, the easier it will be to work on nearly any project.

Just as being fluent in multiple human languages can open up more opportunities for you, so can knowledge of different programming languages increase your future opportunities whatever you choose to do with your programming skills.

REMEMBER

The popularity of programming languages changes all the time, so the only sure bet is to keep learning. Master the languages you already know but don't be afraid to learn something different. Programming is a combination of problem-solving skills and knowing the syntax and nuances of a particular language. Keep improving both your problem-solving skills and your knowledge of different languages, and you'll always be able to keep up with the latest trends, no matter what type of computer and operating system become popular next.

Picking an Operating System

In the early days of computers, every computer had its own operating system, which made writing programs difficult. Not only did you have to learn a specific programming language, but you also had to learn how to write programs for a specific operating system.

To avoid this problem, computer companies standardized around the most popular operating systems. An early popular operating system was CP/M-80, which later gave way to MS-DOS and finally to Microsoft Windows. Later, Linux grew in popularity, while macOS attracted people who wanted an easier user interface (UI).

By focusing on a single operating system, you can optimize your program for that one operating system. Knowing which operating system to support can define the success (or failure) of an entire software company.

Back in the early days of personal computers, two companies developed a program that everyone called a *killer application* (or *killer app* for short). Both of these programs were greatly improved spreadsheet programs used by businesses, but each company took a different approach. One company wrote its spreadsheet program entirely in assembly language and optimized it to run quickly on a single operating system (MS-DOS). The second company developed its spreadsheet to run on multiple operating systems, but to achieve this feat, the company wrote its program in the UCSD Pascal programming language, which ran slowly on multiple operating systems.

Although both programs offered similar features, there was no comparison from the user's point of view. The program written in assembly language and optimized for the MS-DOS operating system became Lotus 1-2-3, one of the most popular programs ever. The second program, Context MBA, ran so slowly on every operating system that nobody had the patience to use it. Context MBA went out of business, and Lotus 1-2-3 dominated the spreadsheet market — until the standard operating system changed from underneath it.

Lotus 1-2-3 had originally been written in assembly language, but as the program grew in complexity, major portions of the program were rewritten in C. When personal computers switched from MS-DOS to Microsoft Windows, Lotus 1-2-3 wasn't ready. That's when Microsoft Excel, written in C, took over, and it has dominated the spreadsheet market ever since.

As Microsoft Excel grows in complexity, major portions of the program are now being rewritten in C++. Eventually, it's likely that maintaining Microsoft Excel in C++ will become too difficult, and a new spreadsheet program will emerge, written in an entirely different programming language.

That's because the days of a single operating system standard seem to be fading. Instead of Microsoft Windows being the dominant operating system, rivals — such as Linux and macOS — have grown in popularity to challenge the popularity of Microsoft Windows on desktop computers.

With the introduction of mobile computing, iOS became the dominant operating system for Apple's iPhone and iPad, while Android dominated the mobile computing market for any device not made by Apple.

Unlike the early days, when you could write a program for the dominant operating system and capture 90 percent of the market, today if you write a program for a single operating system, you'll capture an ever-shrinking chunk of the market.

No matter what operating system you prefer, become familiar with another one. That way, if your favorite operating system falls out of favor, you'll be able to switch to a different one and still be able to use your favorite programming languages. By becoming familiar with Linux, macOS, and Windows, you'll be able to write programs for nearly any computer.

REMEMBER

You might use one operating system for your programming computer but develop programs for a completely different operating system. For example, many game developers write programs using Windows but develop programs for the Sony PlayStation or Android.

Doing Cross-Platform Programming

In the old days, writing programs to run on multiple operating systems was a waste of time because most people used the same operating system. WordPerfect, a once-popular word processor, wasted millions of dollars and several years devoting its resources to creating a version of WordPerfect that ran on Atari ST, Commodore Amiga, Macintosh, and MS-DOS computers. Although WordPerfect focused on making its word processor run on multiple operating systems (known *as cross-platform capabilities*), Microsoft focused on making its Microsoft Word program run efficiently on a single operating system (Microsoft Windows) and nearly wiped WordPerfect off the face of the Earth.

The problem wasn't that WordPerfect spent time writing a cross-platform version of its word processor. The problem was that it wasted time supporting operating systems that hardly anybody used. The number of people who used Atari ST and Commodore Amiga computers was miniscule compared to the number of people who used Macintosh computers, and the number of people who used Macintosh computers was just as tiny compared to the number of people who used MS-DOS and Microsoft Windows.

Cross-platform capabilities make sense only when supporting operating systems of nearly equal popularity, such as Android and iOS. The most straightforward way to write a cross-platform program is to write identical programs with two completely different languages. That approach is possible for simple programs, but for more complicated programs, it takes too much time.

The portability of C

One reason why the C language has proven so popular is because of its portability. The C language is relatively simple, which makes it easy to create C compilers for different operating systems. That also makes compiling C programs to run on different operating systems with minimal changes easy.

Writing programs in C is how companies like Adobe and Microsoft can develop and sell programs that run on both macOS and Windows, such as Adobe Photoshop and Microsoft Word. The bulk of their programs run identically on both operating systems, so all they need to do is write a small portion of the program to customize it to run on each particular operating system.

Unfortunately, as programs grow more complicated, writing programs in C is getting more difficult. Although most programmers have now switched to C++, even C++ is becoming too hard to use. That's why Sun Microsystems developed Java (now owned by Oracle), Microsoft developed C#, and Apple developed Swift. All these languages are meant to improve on C++ while being easier to learn and safer to use.

Cross-platform languages

As operating systems grow more complicated, programmers are finding they're spending more time customizing their C/C++ programs for each specific operating system and less time actually updating their programs. So, another way to write cross-platform programs is to use a *cross-platform compiler.* The idea behind a cross-platform compiler is that you can write a program in a specific programming language, and the compiler takes care of creating identically working programs for different operating systems.

One popular cross-platform development tool is React Native, which was created by Facebook to let programmers write one program that can run on multiple operating systems, such as Android, iOS, macOS, and Windows. Google created its own cross-platform tool called Flutter, which lets programmers write software for Android, iOS, Linux, macOS, Windows, and Google's new operating system, Fuchsia.

Because many Windows programmers know and use C#, Microsoft acquired Xamarian, a development tool that lets you write programs in C# that you can compile to Android and iOS. That way, you can write apps for Android and iOS using the C# language rather than learn Java or Kotlin (for Android) or Objective-C or Swift (for iOS).

One problem with cross-platform compilers is that they're never perfect. Ideally, you want to write a single program, compile it for multiple operating systems, and have all versions of your program run identically under each different operating system. In reality, every operating system has its quirks, so you often have to write specific code for each operating system. The amount of operating-system-specific code is much less than is required when rewriting your entire program from scratch for a different operating system, but this process isn't trivial.

Create a program that can run on three different operating systems, and now you have to worry about maintaining and fixing problems with your program on three different operating systems. It's possible for your program to work perfectly under Linux, but crash under macOS and Windows. The more operating systems your program supports, the greater the complexity in getting your program to work right under all these different operating systems.

Virtual machines

The main advantage of cross-platform compilers is that they compile programs directly into machine language for each specific operating system, which makes your programs run as fast as possible. With today's faster computers, speed is rarely as important as in the old days when slow programs could literally take hours to perform a single task.

Because speed isn't as crucial as in the past, computer scientists have created another way to create cross-platform programs known as *virtual machines* (VMs). Rather than compile a program for a specific processor, VM programming languages compile programs to a generic format (called *bytecode, pseudocode,* or *p-code*) that can run on a VM. This VM, running on different operating systems, essentially tricks the program into thinking it's running on a single computer, as shown in Figure 7-1.

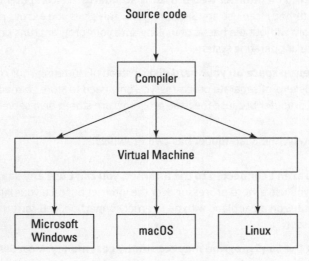

FIGURE 7-1:
A virtual machine lets a program run on multiple operating systems.

The biggest problem with VM programming languages, can be their lack of speed. Because VM languages aren't compiled, they run slower than true compiled programs. That's why many languages, such as Java, use just-in-time (JIT) compilers that produce machine code as needed. This helps speed up programs while still letting them maintain portability across multiple platforms.

Even worse, VM languages can run only on operating systems that have VMs written for them. To maintain this ability to run on multiple operating systems, Oracle (the owner of Java) must constantly update each VM for different operating systems. This added complexity earned Java its initial reputation as a "write once, debug everywhere" language — you had to fix your program on multiple operating systems.

Software as a service

The latest trend is toward selling software as a service (SaaS). The idea is that instead of having a copy of a program stored on your computer, you use the Internet to access a program stored on a server. SaaS offers several advantages:

>> **It's consistent.** With programs written in C, cross-platform compilers, or VM languages (like Java), the end result is always a program stored on each person's computer. So, one person could be using version 1.0 of a program, another could be using version 1.4, and a third person could be using version 1.57, which makes supporting all these different versions difficult. With SaaS, all users can access the same version of the software through the Internet. If you've ever used Google Docs to write and share a document, you know that Google's word processor is always available to you over the Internet but never gets stored anywhere on your computer.

>> **It's based on Internet web-browsing standards.** If a computer can access the Internet, it can use any SaaS program. This gives you a cross-platform program without the hassle of making sure your program runs on each particular operating system.

>> **It frees up space on your hard disk.** Instead of cluttering your computer with dozens of separate programs, you only need to store your actual files on your computer because the SaaS programs are stored on a server.

Unfortunately, the SaaS model has two drawbacks:

>> **If you aren't connected to the Internet, you can't use any SaaS program.** So, if you use a word processor over the Internet but take your laptop computer on an airplane with no Internet connection, you can't use that word processor.

>> **Using the SaaS program may constantly cost money.** Most SaaS programs charge a monthly fee, which gives you the right to use the program for that month. Although this monthly fee is nominal (such as $5 a month), the cost can add up. Buying a simple word-processing program might cost you $50. Using a SaaS word-processing programming might cost you $5 a month, so after ten months, you could've just bought the program instead.

For each succeeding month, the cost continues, so you'll wind up paying several hundred dollars just to use a single program. For large corporations, the SaaS model may make sense. For individuals, the SaaS model can sometimes be too expensive.

To eliminate monthly fees, SaaS companies are offering their programs for free but earning profits by selling advertising. Seeing advertisements may be a minor annoyance, but it makes SaaS available to everyone (although there's still the problem of not being able to use a program without a constant and reliable Internet connection).

Data science

With computers, mobile phones, and the Internet gathering information on people every second of the day, there's a tremendous need to analyze all this information. This combination of computer science, statistics, machine learning, and data mining falls under the category of *data science.* It's nearly impossible for humans to sift through massive amounts of data, but it's relatively easy for computers to sort and sift through data to find patterns.

Every time you visit an e-commerce site to shop online, that site can analyze what you look at, what you buy, and what other products people bought in addition to that particular product. When you visit a social media network, that network's algorithms analyze what type of information you liked in the past and tries to guess what you might like to see right now.

Java and Python have been popular for data science, but they're also general languages. To make analyzing data easier, computer scientists have created specialized languages like MATLAB (www.mathworks.com) and R (www.r-project.org).

One field related to data science is *algorithmic trading.* That's where people write programs to track financial markets (stocks, commodities, cryptocurrencies, and so on) and automatically buy and sell assets far faster than human traders could ever do. By defining specific trading strategies using programming languages like Java, Perl, and Python, traders can automate their trading process and let their computer find trading opportunities that they might have otherwise overlooked.

Algorithmic trading, also known as *black box trading,* is heavily used by special programmers called *quantitative analysts* (*quants* for short). Quants typically work for hedge funds and investment bankers in a field known as *financial engineering.* By combining statistics, finance, and computer programming, quants use their programming knowledge to make money in every major financial market around the world.

The world generates tons of new data every second of the day, and this never-ending flow of new data won't stop any time soon. If anything, it's just going to increase from a variety of sources. That means there's always going to be plenty of work for anyone fascinated by statistics and digging through massive amounts of data looking to uncover hidden nuggets of useful information.

Website programming

In the early days of the Internet, programmers wrote HTML code to create websites. As people demanded faster changes and more interactivity from web pages, programmers started creating websites using content management systems (CMSs) like Drupal, Joomla, and WordPress.

In addition to programming and designing websites, another lucrative programming field involves the back-end servers controlling the websites. After all, when somebody orders a product online, the server needs to process that data, and that requires the services of even more programmers using scripting languages like JavaScript, PHP, or Ruby.

There's even an entire field of people who do nothing but analyze and optimize websites for maximum efficiency. Search engine optimization (SEO) involves designing websites to maximize the chances that search engines will find it. The field of analytics analyzes how people react to web pages and how to modify web pages to keep people looking at them longer and taking action, such as ordering a product.

Programing websites and back-end servers is a field that won't go away any time soon. The technology may change, but the purpose will remain the same, which means plenty of opportunities for the future.

Macro programming

Many people think programming is about creating new programs or modifying existing ones. But far too many people overlook *macro programming*. Macros essentially let you write mini programs that run within an existing program.

Perhaps the most popular macro programming language is Visual Basic for Applications (VBA), which lets you write macros to control the Microsoft Office suite of products, including Access, Excel, PowerPoint, and Word. By writing macros, you can create useful programs that can take advantage of existing features.

Instead of writing a mathematical or financial calculating program from scratch using C++ or Java, it's far simpler to use the mathematical and financial calculating features of Excel and just write a macro that guides users into entering data. Then the macro can use Excel's built-in functions to calculate a useful result. By writing macros within an existing program, you can create custom applications for others.

Macros let you write mini programs that can automate complicated tasks. Operating systems typically offer scripting or macro languages for automating a computer. Windows offers PowerShell, while Apple's macOS offers AppleScript and Shortcuts, which provides a drag-and-drop interface to reduce the need for writing any code at all.

There are even separate macro-recording programs that you can run to automate multiple programs that may not have been designed to work together. Every program in the Microsoft Office suite can share data, but you may need to create a macro to link Excel to a hospital management program or link a web page to a specialized stock-trading program.

Macros let you automate tasks within a single program or between different programs. By learning to write macros to automate or simplify complex tasks, you can help individuals and organizations save time and money.

Robotics programming

If programming a computer sounds like fun, programming a walking, flying, or rolling robot may be even more exciting! Programming a robot is essentially like programming a computer that can move and manipulate its environment.

Programming a robot from scratch can be tedious, so much of robotics programming revolves around developing and using special robotics-programming frameworks. The framework provides basic commands for controlling the robot, such as making it move. Such a robotics framework isolates programmers from the tedium of how to make a robot work and just tells the robot what to do. A typical robotic program might look like this:

```
Move arm 34 degrees
Close gripper
Move arm 180 degrees
Open gripper
```

Just as high-level languages like BASIC or Fortran isolate you from manipulating the details of a computer, robotics-programming frameworks can isolate you from manipulating the specific details of a robot's parts.

Robotics programmers have used programming languages like C++, Java, and even Python to control a robot, so if you master a popular computer programming language, there's a good chance you'll be able to transfer your skills to program a robot as well.

TIP

For a playful introduction to robotics, buy a LEGO Mindstorms NXT robotics kit, which lets you create a robot out of LEGO building blocks and use the LEGO visual programming language to make your robot move.

Robotics combines mechanical engineering with computer science and artificial intelligence (AI). You can program a robot to learn, recognize spoken commands, navigate around obstacles, and make decisions on its own, given incomplete information. Although AI often remains an academic exercise, robotics lets you put AI in a moving robot so you can see how well your programs actually work. (A well-designed robot program might know enough to avoid trying to roll down a staircase. A poorly designed robot program might make the robot cheerfully roll off the top of a staircase and crash at the bottom of the steps below.)

Robotics is a growing field with no clear-cut robotics language standard yet to emerge. Who knows? With a little bit of creativity, you might be responsible for creating the next standard in robotics programming.

Blockchain programming

The world of cryptocurrency changed with the introduction of Bitcoin in 2008. Although the idea of money stored as encrypted data challenges the traditional idea of money backed by tangible assets like gold, the real excitement around cryptocurrency centers around its underlying blockchain technology.

Programmers need to create the underlying blockchains themselves that involves cryptography, security, optimization, and resource management, which usually involves a variety of languages like C++, Dart, Go, Java, JavaScript, Python, or Rust.

Then there's programming on top of a blockchain to create programs such as smart contracts that are a major feature of the Ethereum cryptocurrency. Smart contracts not only store data to verify their existence and initial date, but can also respond to outside data (such as the date and amount of payments sent or received). Because smart contracts are part of a blockchain that can be examined but never modified, they offer a transparent way to record important data (such as real-estate property ownership or the date a screenwriter first submitted a story idea).

Whether you want to use your programming skills to create a new blockchain, maintain an existing one, or write programs on top of a blockchain to create smart contracts, there will be plenty of opportunities for all types of programming in the growing world of blockchains and cryptocurrencies.

Defining Your Future in Programming

Although there will always be dominant programming languages, there will never be a single perfect programming language because everyone's needs and preferences are different. Some people prefer C for its raw power and control, whereas others prefer Java and other high-level languages for making programming easier by hiding the technical details of manipulating the computer. If you're planning to learn programming, the only certainty is that the language you learn today will likely not be the language you'll be using tomorrow.

Teaching yourself other languages

With so many programming languages available, most schools focus on teaching the most popular languages, such as C++ or Java. However, learning a popular programming language is just a start. If you never learn any programming language beyond the popular ones taught in schools, you'll have far few opportunities than someone who learns more specialized programming languages not normally taught in most schools.

You may not always have time to take formal classes, so it's important to get in the habit of keeping up with trends and learning new programming languages on your own. New programming languages appear all the time, and many companies use a variety of programming languages for different purposes. Your ability to learn and master new programming languages is crucial for long-term success.

That means getting comfortable using different operating systems, different programming languages, and different programming tools like editors and compilers. The more adaptable you can be programming different computers, from supercomputers to *embedded systems* (computers hidden inside larger items, such as refrigerators, cars, or water pumps), the more opportunities you can choose.

The computing industry changes rapidly. One day, the world is clamoring for people who can write programs for Blackberry smartphones and Palm Pilots, and the next day those markets disappear. Google once encouraged everyone to write Android apps in Java; then it encouraged programmers to write Android apps using Kotlin instead. Apple used to encourage programmers to write apps using Objective-C; then it started encouraging programmers to write apps using Swift.

TIP

To learn new programming languages, start by playing around with an online compiler, which you can find by searching the web for "Kotlin online" or "Java online compiler." By practicing with an online compiler that you can access through a web browser, you can learn the basics of a new programming language without downloading and installing any additional software.

The only certainty is that computers and programming languages will change, so if you can get comfortable learning something new all the time, you'll be in a far better position than someone who never bothers learning anything new at all.

Combining other interests besides programming

The common idea is that if you want to learn programming, you need to learn math. Math can help, but it's not necessary to become a programmer. Many people from diverse backgrounds can become programmers — programming is nothing more than a skill that anyone can learn.

Many music majors become programmers because programming and music both involve logic, self-expression, and collaborating with others. Many philosophy majors also excel at programming because philosophy teaches you to think carefully, analyze situations, and build a complete understanding of a problem before drawing any conclusions. Math is just a minor part of programming, but if you don't know how to think clearly, all the math in the world won't help you.

REMEMBER

Just knowing a programming language will never be enough. Make sure you develop skills in other fields as well. For example, programmers with accounting experience would be far more likely to work on an accounting program than someone who knows nothing about accounting at all. Music majors would likely excel at writing software for audio engineers, while someone experienced in running a restaurant would be more knowledgeable about creating restaurant management software.

Combine your knowledge of programming with medicine, and you could create programs specifically for controlling medical equipment or targeting hospitals, which programmers lacking medical knowledge and experience would have a much harder time trying to do. The more you know beyond programming, the better your chances of finding unique and interesting opportunities in your field of interest.

Getting experience and knowledge

Many people believe that you need a college degree to become a programmer, but that's not true at all. Given a choice between someone with lots of programming experience and knowledge and someone who just has a college degree, guess which person most companies will value more?

Whether you have a college degree or not, you need experience writing programs professionally. Students can often rely on a college degree to justify that they have basic competency in programming, but they may not have any experience programming in the real world. So, if you have no experience in programming and companies won't hire you until you do have experience, what can you do?

The best way to get experience in any field is to do it for free. Volunteer on an open-source project to gain experience and network with more experienced programmers. By working on an open-source project, you can demonstrate your knowledge of a specific programming language or on a particular type of program, such as an operating system. Whether you write code, write documentation, search for bugs, design part of the UI, or help keep the whole project on track, you can demonstrate skills that will make you far more valuable than someone who just has a college degree.

If you can't find an open-source project that you like, just volunteer your programming skills to help your local library, animal shelter, church, food bank, school, or any other organization that would be open to accepting free help. Although many charitable organizations may not be able to pay you, they can let you gain valuable experience solving real problems. If you do a great job, others might hear about you. That can open up more opportunities for you in the future that you might never have known about if you had never volunteered to work for free in the first place.

Another option is to write programs and publish them on the many app stores available for different types of computers. By demonstrating that you created an entire app yourself, got it approved on an app store, and maintained your code while dealing with customers, you can demonstrate far more skills than just your programming ability. Having a working program that others can see, use, and evaluate will demonstrate your abilities far more than any grade in a programming class can ever do.

Finally, if there's a particular industry or specific company you want to work for, do your homework and find out what they need and what software and computers they use. For example, if you want to work for a specific video-game company, find out what game engine they use, what programming language they prefer, and what programming tools (editor and compiler) they use. By familiarizing yourself with the tools a specific company already uses, you'll be in a better position to fit in if they have an opening.

With every industry using computers, there's no shortage of opportunities waiting for you and your programming skills. Instead of taking the first opportunity given to you, take time to plan where you want to go and what you want to do. That way, you can steer all your efforts toward creating the career of your dreams.

REMEMBER

The programming language you use is less important than your ability to solve problems and create useful programs. What you do with your programming skills will always transcend the specific knowledge of a particular programming language. Ultimately, the most important part of programming is you!

Index

M

machine language
  debuggers, 92
  defined, 11
  overview, 11–12
machine learning
  Bayesian probability, 707
  danger of, 707
  defined, 700
  neural networks, 707–710
macOS, 20, 733
macro languages. *See* scripting languages
macro programming, 740–741
malware
  defined, 686
  distributed denial-of-service attacks, 690–691
  spyware, 689–690
  Trojan horses, 688–689
  viruses, 687
  worms, 687–688
manipulating data. *See* data manipulation
maps, Dart, 655–656
mathematical operators
  built-in math functions, 146–147
  C language, 545–546
  C#, 562
  C++, 545–546
  Dart, 647
  Java, 562
  JavaScript, 499
  Kotlin, 600
  operator precedence, 144–145
  overview, 143–144
  Perl, 580–581
  PHP, 513
  Python, 580–581
  Ruby, 526
  Swift, 622
MATLAB, 739
Matsumoto, Yukihiro "Matz," 523
memento design pattern, 230

memory leaks, 18
memory requirements, sorting algorithms, 400
menus
  Edit menu, 280
  File menu, 280
  overview, 278–279
  pull-down menus, 279–280
merge sort algorithm, 410–411
method overloading, 239–242
methods, 109, 218–219. *See also* subprograms
Microsoft, 54–55, 84. *See also* C# language; Visual Basic
Microsoft Access, 75, 669
Microsoft Excel, 734, 740–741
Microsoft Visual Studio compiler, 84
Microsoft Windows, 20, 733–734
Microsoft Word, 735
Mindstorms language (LEGO), 57, 58
minimax strategy, trees, 395
mnemonic commands, assembly language, 12
mobile and wearable computing
  augmented reality, 718–719
  constraints, 714–715
  future of, 718–719
  generations of computing, 712–713
  getting data from users, 716–717
  giving data to users, 714–715
  overview, 711
  tracking motion and location, 717
  tracking real-time health data, 718
modeling, OOP, 45
module variables, 137–138
modulo operator, 143–144
Moore, J. Strother, 431
motion tracking, 717
MS-DOS, 733–734
multidimensional arrays
  creating, 324
  overview, 323–324
  retrieving data, 325
  storing data, 325

About the Author

Wallace Wang started off as a writer and wound up becoming a computer programmer. Then he wound up circling around again to become a writer about computers. He has spent most of his life writing about and programming a variety of personal computers, ranging from an ancient PC running MS-DOS 1.25 to Windows to the latest Macintosh computer running macOS to write apps for the iPhone and iPad. His only preference for any computer is that it works.

Wallace first learned about programming from his high school's ancient teletype terminal that connected to a mainframe computer through a 300 baud acoustic modem that often disconnected in the middle of his BASIC programming sessions. At the time, he didn't know much about programming. He taught himself BASIC from a book and illegally gained access to the teletype terminal by using somebody else's password. Later in the year, he actually signed up for a computer class and finally gained legitimate access to the teletype terminal to do everything he had been doing illegally long before.

The first time Wallace wrote a BASIC program on his own, it was a game that simulated flying a nuclear-armed bomber through a variety of anti-aircraft defenses including surface-to-air missiles and jet fighters trying to shoot you down. When this program worked for the first time, he felt like Dr. Frankenstein watching his creation twitch and come to life. To this day, he still experiences that same feeling of exhilaration in creating something from an idea and turning it into an actual working program. Only other programmers can understand the strange sense of power and elation that comes from a working program, and it's this same sense of wonder and exploration that Wallace hopes you'll experience as you use this book to explore the world of programming on your own computer.

Wallace may be considered a computer veteran after all these years, but that doesn't mean that he can't still experience that same feeling of satisfaction in typing that final command and watching an entire program work exactly as he wanted. Although he has written plenty of other books both on computers (*Microsoft Office For Dummies*) and far away from computers altogether (*Breaking Into Acting For Dummies*), programming still fascinates him to this day.

As an author, Wallace hopes to help you discover your own path to learning programming, and as a programmer, he hopes to provide an overview of computer programming in general. You may not become an expert programmer after reading this book, but if you come away with a greater appreciation for programming, he will have fulfilled his duty as both an author and a programmer.

Dedication

This book is dedicated to anyone who wants to learn how to program a computer. Computer programming can be one of the most creative ways to express your ideas, so if you have your heart set on writing programs for fun or profit, you've just joined a select group of fellow renegades, entrepreneurs, and hobbyists who find programming an enjoyable intellectual exercise. When lost in the world of programming, you can often elevate your spirit to lofty heights of pleasure and wind up crashing right back down to Earth again when a single syntax error causes your program to crash an entire computer. Welcome to the wonderful world of programming. You deserve to achieve whatever your mind can envision and your programming skills can create.

Author's Acknowledgments

This is the part of the book that most people skip over because it usually lists a bunch of names that most people have never heard before, so before you skip over this page, I'd like to thank you for buying (or at least reading) this book. If you're interested in learning to program a computer, you've already separated yourself from the masses who are ecstatic when they can just get their computers to work in the first place. As a programmer, you have the power to control how people may use computers in the future. This power can give you the chance to help others or to make someone completely helpless in their agony when trying to use a computer, so use your programming skills wisely.

On another note, this book owes part of its existence to Bill Gladstone and Margot Hutchison at Waterside Productions and another part of its existence to Elizabeth Kuball for turning this project into reality. Some other people who helped shape this project include Kelsey Baird at Wiley and Rod Stephens.

I also want to acknowledge all the stand-up comedians I've worked with over the years, including Darrell Joyce, Leo "the Man, the Myth, the Legend" Fontaine, Chris Clobber, and Dobie "The Uranus King" Maxwell. Another round of thanks goes to Steve Schirripa (who appeared in HBO's hit show *The Sopranos*) for giving me my break in performing at the Riviera Hotel and Casino in Las Vegas, until they blew up that casino to make way for yet another luxury hotel and casino targeting rich people who want to lose their money faster.

Additional acknowledgements also go to my fellow video game and e-sports enthusiasts who have discovered the joy of playing video games along with the excitement of using video games as an educational tool to get students interested in programming, math, science, history, psychology, marketing, and practically any other field you can think of. Thanks go to my fellow e-sports instructors at both

San Diego State University and IFERS (http://ifers.org): Dane Henderson, Dr. Newton Lee, Sam Diamond, Christopher Davis, Katherine Amoukhteh, and six-time Grammy Award–winning recording engineer Bonzai Caruso (www.bonzaicaruso.com).

To all the people I've met through various screenwriting groups, thank you. I keep collecting my thoughts and sharing ideas about screenwriting on my screenwriting blog called The 15-Minute Movie Method (http://15minutemoviemethod.com). More thanks go to the cat lovers around the Internet who enjoy my Cat Daily News site (http://catdailynews.com), where I share the latest stories about cats taking over the world.

I'd also like to acknowledge Cassandra (my wife) and Jordan (my son) for putting up with my long hours and my cluttered office containing a graveyard of old PCs, Macs, iPhones, and iPads. Final thanks go to Oscar and Mayer, my Norwegian Forest cats, who like to walk all over the keyboard, stand in front of the monitors, and constantly shed wherever they can.

Publisher's Acknowledgments

Associate Acquisitions Editor: Kelsey Baird
Project Editor: Elizabeth Kuball
Copy Editor: Elizabeth Kuball
Technical Editor: Rod Stephens

Production Editor: Tamilmani Varadharaj
Cover Image: © SuperOhMo/Shutterstock

PERSONAL ENRICHMENT

Staying Sharp
9781119187790
USA $26.00
CAN $31.99
UK £19.99

Facebook
Carolyn Abram
9781119179030
USA $21.99
CAN $25.99
UK £16.99

Guitar
Mark Phillips
Jon Chappell
9781119293354
USA $24.99
CAN $29.99
UK £17.99

Investing
Eric Tyson, MBA
9781119293347
USA $22.99
CAN $27.99
UK £16.99

Beekeeping
Howland Blackiston
9781119310068
USA $22.99
CAN $27.99
UK £16.99

Digital Photography
Julie Adair King
9781119235606
USA $24.99
CAN $29.99
UK £17.99

Meditation
Stephan Bodian
9781119251163
USA $24.99
CAN $29.99
UK £17.99

Pregnancy ALL-IN-ONE
9781119235491
USA $26.99
CAN $31.99
UK £19.99

Samsung Galaxy S7
Bill Hughes
9781119279952
USA $24.99
CAN $29.99
UK £17.99

iPhone
Edward C. Baig
Bob "Dr. Mac" LeVitus
9781119283133
USA $24.99
CAN $29.99
UK £17.99

Crocheting
Karen Manthey
Susan Brittain
9781119287117
USA $24.99
CAN $29.99
UK £16.99

Nutrition
Carol Ann Rinzler
9781119130246
USA $22.99
CAN $27.99
UK £16.99

PROFESSIONAL DEVELOPMENT

Windows 10
Andy Rathbone
9781119311041
USA $24.99
CAN $29.99
UK £17.99

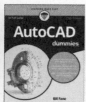
AutoCAD
Bill Fane
9781119255796
USA $39.99
CAN $47.99
UK £27.99

Excel 2016
Greg Harvey, PhD
9781119293439
USA $26.99
CAN $31.99
UK £19.99

QuickBooks 2017
Stephen L. Nelson, MBA, CPA, MS in Taxation
9781119281467
USA $26.99
CAN $31.99
UK £19.99

macOS Sierra
Bob "Dr. Mac" LeVitus
9781119280651
USA $29.99
CAN $35.99
UK £21.99

LinkedIn
Joel Elad, MBAs
9781119251132
USA $24.99
CAN $29.99
UK £17.99

Windows 10 ALL-IN-ONE
Woody Leonhard
9781119310563
USA $34.00
CAN $41.99
UK £24.99

SharePoint 2016
Rosemarie Withee
Ken Withee
9781119181705
USA $29.99
CAN $35.99
UK £21.99

Fundamental Analysis
Matt Krantz
9781119263593
USA $26.99
CAN $31.99
UK £19.99

Networking
Doug Lowe
9781119257769
USA $29.99
CAN $35.99
UK £21.99

Office 2016
Wallace Wang
9781119293477
USA $26.99
CAN $31.99
UK £19.99

Office 365
Rosemarie Withee
Ken Withee
Jennifer Reed
9781119265313
USA $24.99
CAN $29.99
UK £17.99

Salesforce.com
Liz Kao
Jon Paz
9781119239314
USA $29.99
CAN $35.99
UK £21.99

Coding
Nikhil Abraham
9781119293323
USA $29.99
CAN $35.99
UK £21.99

dummies.com

dummies
A Wiley Brand